J.W. McCONNELL

J.W. McCONNELL

FINANCIER, PHILANTHROPIST, PATRIOT

William Fong

McGill-Queen's University Press

Montreal & Kingston · London · Ithaca

© McGill-Queen's University Press 2008
ISBN 978-0-7735-3270-0

Legal deposit fourth quarter 2008
Bibliothèque nationale du Québec

Printed in Canada on acid-free paper that is 100% ancient forest free
(100% post-consumer recycled), processed chlorine free

McGill-Queen's University Press acknowledges the support of the Canada Council
for the Arts for our publishing program. We also acknowledge the financial support
of the Government of Canada through the Book Publishing Industry
Development Program (BPIDP) for our publishing activities.

LIBRARY AND ARCHIVES CANADA CATALOGUING IN PUBLICATION

Fong, William Jesse, 1948–
J.W. McConnell : financier, philanthropist, patriot / William Fong.

Includes bibliographical references and index.
ISBN 978-0-7735-3270-0

1. McConnell, John W. (John Wilson), 1877–1963.   2. Philanthropists – Canada – Biography.
3. Businessmen – Canada – Biography.   4. Capitalists and financiers – Canada –
Biography.   5. Directors of corporations – Canada – Biography.   6. Montréal
(Québec) – Biography.   I. Title.

HV28.M32F66 2008   971.06092   C2008-903262-4

Set in 11/14 Bulmer with Grotesque Condensed
Book design & typesetting by Garet Markvoort, zijn digital

For
Mrs Peter M. Laing

Contents

Preface and Acknowledgments

In his time, 1877 to 1963, John Wilson McConnell was one of the few Canadians, and certainly one of the few Canadian businessmen, of international renown. Yet, while McConnell aggressively sought and attained success, he did not always enjoy the publicity that came with it, which is perhaps what Prime Minister Lester Pearson had in mind when he paid tribute to McConnell's quintessential Canadianism. Now he and his sort of Canadianism are almost forgotten, however, both in Toronto, where he began his career, and in Montreal, where he spent most of his life. They are forgotten as well in New York and London, where both his philanthropy and his business acumen won him deep respect. For most of his life, he was probably the richest of all Canadians and yet also among the most generous men, of whom there is a record anywhere.

There was more to McConnell than his businesses and his benefactions. He was also a presence. Handsome and dignified, nearly always immaculately and occasionally flamboyantly dressed, he could display, when he chose, irresistible Irish charm. And his admirers were many. Royalty gratefully accepted his hospitality. Aristocrats gravitated to him. Imperial proconsuls and foreign diplomats sought his advice, as did politicians. The poor, the sick, the dispossessed, the young, the old, and the hopeless – all turned to him for help, and nearly always did they receive it. So did probably thousands of others who had never asked for it, and had hardly heard of him. His philanthropy was almost compulsive, and he may have exerted more effort in giving away his fortune than he had in making it.

Among his colleagues and competitors, McConnell inspired reverence mixed with fear, while many of his friends and their children found him mischievous, fun, and wholly lacking in self-importance. But he could be hard, and in others his success inspired envy and malice. His relations with his own sons were distant, since it seemed impossible for them to emulate his success. Even his contemporaries speculated on the propriety of his acquisition of such great wealth, and on the motivation for his munificent giving to others. Since his death, he has received almost uniformly unflattering notice. On the rare occasions on which he has been recalled, at least in print, he has been reviled as the symbol of the English oppression of French Canada, an anti-Semite, an unbending big business Tory, an exploiter of the working class, an enemy of academic and press freedom, and, in short, a sinister manipulator with incalculable political and economic influence and power. Ignorance of the facts of his career has led to the belief that there is a mystery at the root of his success, something that he did not want the public to know.

McConnell's later years are within the memory of many alive in the early years of the twenty-first century. He died only three weeks before President John F. Kennedy and three months before the first arrival of the Beatles in the United States. From this perspective, he seems almost contemporary. Yet he was born in a log cabin, without electricity or running water, when Canada was only a decade old, and he had become an extremely successful man even before the First World War. Though scarcely half a century has passed since McConnell's death, historians and others have much to learn about the world that he occupied. The present work can offer, therefore, merely a first look at this long life, in the hope of encouraging others, general readers as well as professional researchers, to go deeper.

Although this volume is long, it is less than a quarter of the length of the original text out of which it has been radically condensed and simplified. My interpretation in the original text contains far more detail, nuance, analysis, documentation, cross-referencing, and context. I hope to publish it electronically so that it can be read by those wanting to follow up on the subjects covered here and to learn about related topics. There is also much material in the McConnell Papers now deposited in the McGill University Archives as MG 4240, and elsewhere, never used by any researcher before me.

Because McConnell's life was so multifaceted, even the abbreviated story in this book is somewhat unconventional in its structure. While most biographies follow a strictly chronological approach, this one mixes chronology with themes. Broadly speaking, however, the presentation is chronological and divided into four main sections: chapters 1 through 4 cover McConnell's early years to 1914; chapters 5 through 13 the period from the First World War to the Second (though chapter 5, on St Lawrence Sugar, extends beyond 1945); chapters 14 through 17 the Second World War and afterwards (with all but the first of these chapters also reaching back to the pre-war period). Finally, chapters 18 and 19 examine respectively the McConnell Foundation and McConnell's last years. Within this only roughly chronological framework, there is some overlap, which is both unavoidable and fitting. McConnell was a man of many parts, none of which can be neatly separated from the others.

A life such as McConnell's may be of inherent interest to a variety of readers, who will doubtless reach their own conclusions. This book does not seek to rehabilitate or to exaggerate his importance, much less to defend him. The very paradoxes of his legacy and his reputation insist that we try to see him in the round. It is probably impossible to cover exhaustively all the issues that this life raises, even in a much larger book than this. In any case, it may be premature to try until more work is done on his contemporaries. Studies especially of certain industries and of political and economic trends, relevant to McConnell, are beginning to appear. It therefore seems that a responsible evaluation of him must remain a work in progress, so that no interpretation, whether this book or the much more elaborate work on which it is based, can be taken as definitive.

It is especially premature and imprudent, perhaps, to pass sweeping judgment on, say, the ethics of either McConnell's era or him personally. For many professional historians, in any case, lightly summoning figures from the past to the bar of history for moral judgment is now old-fashioned, reckless, and pointless. It is much more interesting, for me at any rate, to try to understand people in their own terms, and to deepen our understanding by learning more about their context, than, say, to find them wanting in our terms, which will date as fast as theirs have.

It is clear, moreover, that much of the business practice and ethics of the present day would have horrified McConnell and his generation. As this book goes to press, the world is said to be facing the worst economic crisis since the Great Depression. In particular it is suffering from a contraction of credit as a result of disastrous lending practices. There is little new about the businesses abuses of today; and McConnell would be dismayed by how the lessons of the Depression, in which he himself lost so much, must be relearned yet again. *Plus ça change, plus c'est la même chose.*

What distinguishes the present is not moral superiority but the virtual repudiation of the strong character, reputation, and conscience that were so revered by McConnell and many of his colleagues. The extent to which they succeeded in maintaining these may be debated. But it would be hazardous to discount the religion of McConnell, in particular, as hypocrisy or a ruse, or to underestimate how much it influenced his political and social attitudes.

To write on the basis of *autres temps, autres moeurs* is not to admit that moral judgment or revisionism is impossible. It is perfectly natural and arguably proper for people to condemn elements of the past. But it seems to me more pressing, in this first look at him, to explain why some of McConnell's contemporaries and successors have taken such a dim view of him, and to evaluate the validity of this view on the basis of evidence rather than of hindsight. In rigorous context, the lives of everyone in his world can gain in richness and texture. History has been called argument without end, and there will probably be others who can argue about McConnell better and with more information. This is but a start to a fresh evaluation of him.

Before he died, J.W. McConnell asked his secretary, Mary Clarke, to destroy all his files. This she did to the best of her ability, so that there is almost no correspond-

ence extant relating to his business and other activities. McConnell's wish was neither unusual nor necessarily sinister. Almost no businessmen leave extensive, much
less comprehensive, records of their activities. Among his contemporaries, only Lord
Beaverbrook left a large archive for public consultation, and even this has been culled.

Fortunately for us, a huge amount of McConnell material survived outside his files.
These include stray letters, notebooks, ledgers, photographs, books, and much else.
Thirty-five years after his death, the attic of his house on Pine Avenue in Montreal
was full of everything from portraits of royalty to household bills. Much of his wife's
correspondence has survived, as have engagements and address books and irregularly
kept diaries. The vaults of the McConnell Foundation and Commercial Trust vaults
yielded the minute books of the boards of St Lawrence Sugar and the *Montreal Star*.
A rusty box at the former St Lawrence refinery contained valuable ledgers. Kit Laing,
McConnell's daughter, had bundles of letters between her parents, as well as vital
scrapbooks, now unfortunately but unavoidably disassembled, full of press cuttings
and other memorabilia. Other members of the family and their friends were very generous in lending or giving photographs and other material, and it all became almost
overwhelming in both its bulk and its richness. Most notably, the material found
included a vast amount of financial data that were highly confidential in McConnell's
lifetime. From the point of view of historians, these data are a resource almost unique
for someone so successful as an investor as well as a businessman. The search for
McConnelliana went on for years and it is a saga in itself.

Since this book is a very condensed account intended for a general audience, and a
pioneering effort, the documentation here is, like the text itself, very restrained. The
manuscript material discovered raises many questions only hinted at in this text, if
touched upon at all here, although some of them receive detailed treatment in the
long version. Some of these questions are highly technical ones, relating to accounting and the law relating to competition, tax, corporations, and securities. Others may
be of interest only to academic historians and touch upon broader themes of imperial,
Canadian, and American history, economics, and politics. I have been acutely aware
of many of these and of the inadequacy of my treatment of them even in the long version, but I tried to provide some guidance in my long version for future researchers.
Whether others write more on McConnell's life or simply on its context, I both found
and left enough raw research material to occupy them for some time to come.

After the text had been written, the bulk of the manuscript material on which it was
based was deposited at the McGill University Archives, and the McConnell Fonds
there is the largest relating to an individual person, apart from that of Sir William
Dawson. The minute books and ledgers of the *Montreal Star*, St Lawrence Sugar and
Commercial Trust are among the McConnell Papers at McGill. Most unreferenced
citations in this book are to material at McGill, where a copy of the longer version of
my biography of McConnell may also be consulted. The other citations come from

interviews with several people. Many of the family photographs are now deposited in the archives of the McCord Museum of Canadian History, and material on McConnell's houses is now in the Blackader Library at McGill and in the library of the Canadian Centre for Architecture. Artefacts and portraits of the McConnells have been given to the McCord Museum, the Montreal Museum of Fine Arts, and the National Gallery of Canada, in addition to some material to the Canadian War Museum. There remains at present a vast amount of research material, in the form of notes, pictures, photocopies, and analyses of financial data in my hands, the future of which remains uncertain.

The Bibliography here consists chiefly of sources referred to in the endnotes, with added entries discussed in the longer version. It is not a guide to more than a small number of primary and secondary sources potentially relevant to McConnell's life and times. Those interested in further bibliographical guidance, especially on manuscripts, are referred to the endnotes in the long version, which also contain much on genealogical, social, and business connections and other historical background, in an attempt to depict a more authoritative and nuanced portrait.

My debts incurred to others during the writing of this book are numerous. Some who have helped have asked to remain anonymous and many are dead. There are others whose aid is unrecognized especially in this much-condensed text, and still others whose names I have inadvertently omitted or never really known. To these last I offer my apologies for failing to mention them here, as to those that I mention only generically. To those who have helped me in any way I am deeply grateful. History is a bond between the living and the dead, and if I make no distinction between them in listing these names, it is because the benefit of their assistance is ongoing.

Without asking me to do more than tell the truth, members, in-laws, and former members of the McConnell family have been helpful throughout, especially McConnell's daughter Kit (Mrs Peter M. Laing) and his four daughters-in-law – Marjorie (Mrs Wilson McConnell), Elspeth (Mrs John G. McConnell), Peggy (Mrs John Kirwin-Taylor, formerly Mrs John G. McConnell), and Cynthia (Mrs Bert Hyndman, formerly Mrs David McConnell). Of the next generation, Peter McConnell, Jill Price (and Derek Price), Christopher McConnell, Anette McConnell, Murdoch Laing, David Laing, and Gloria McConnell (Mrs J.R. McConnell) have been similarly kind. Nicolas McConnell, a great-grandson, almost deserves recognition as my co-author, since he helped with nearly all the research and introduced me to his family and their friends. He is the author of the appendix to this book that summarizes a vast amount of financial data. In California, Mary Anna and Mark Kienholz, Terence McConnell, William McConnell, and Shirley McConnell were exceptionally helpful. Bruce McNiven, who has been my friend for over thirty years, introduced me to Nicolas McConnell and later to countless others vital to my work at every stage of this project.

He has sustained his interest in the project, dislodging obstacles and developing and improving the final product. His devotion to the heritage of Montreal has inspired me and many others.

Members of the staff of the family, of Commercial Trust and of Starlaw Investments, and especially of the J.W. McConnell Family Foundation assisted in countless ways. To Tim Brodhead, Joan McCammon, Claude David, Sandra Sinclair, Joyce Molnar, Johanne Moehring, the trustees, and everyone else at the Foundation I owe special thanks. Among my friends who did research or read drafts and gave moral support were David Hilliard, Portia Leggat, Michael Danby-Smith, Martin Lynch, Christopher McCreery, Allan Megill, Mark Meredith, and John Parsons.

In England, I wish to thank the Earl of Airlie, Earl Alexander of Tunis, James Ashley Cooper, Mary Countess of Bessborough, Lady Moyra Browne, Lord Charteris, Lady Hermione Cobbold, Sir Edward Ford, Lady Forwood, John Grigg, Lord Nicholas Gordon Lennox, Mrs David Hankinson, Duff Hart-Davis, the Earl of Harewood, Lord Hartwell, the second and third Lords Iliffe, Renée Lady Iliffe, Countess Lanza, Mrs Mary Redmond, the Duke of Richmond, Sir David Steel, Lord Somerleyton, and Lord Strathcona.

In Canada, I express my gratitude to Susan Alain, Fred Angus, Christopher Armstrong, Cathy Auld, Michael Ballantyne, Sébastien Barangé, W. John Bennett, Paul Berry, Diane Bertozzi, G. Drummond Birks, Michael Bliss, Art Bond, Col. and Mrs John Bourne, Raymonde Bowen, Mrs Edward Brodhead, Peter Bronfman, Tina Carozza, Mrs T.R. Carsley, Mme Claude Casgrain, Martine Chabot, Lord Chatfield, Warren Chippindale, Gerald Clark, Derrick Clements, Mrs Toby Cleveland, Freeman Clowery, John Cowans, David Culver, Victoria Dickenson, Arthur Drache, Pierre Dubois, Mrs Pam Dunn, Jamie Dunton, Nancy Dunton, Jacques Dussault, Jay Eberts, Greg Fauquier, Dr William Feindel, David Ferguson, Timothy Findley, Maurice Forget, Michel Gauthier, Charles Goodfellow, Mr and Mrs Allan Gordon, Stefan Grossman-Hensel, Michael Gundy, Hugh Hallward, Mr and Mrs John Hallward, Patricia Hardy, Mrs Conrad Harrington, Mrs Eric Harrington, Eiren Harris, Bruce Henry, F.C. Henshaw, E. Peter Hersey, David Y. Hodgson, Alan Hustak, the Reverend Charles Johnston, Bruce Kippen, Tracy Kit, Col. James Knox, Warren Laing, Mrs Celia Z. Lafleur, Henri Philip Lafleur, Jo LaPierre, Bertrand Laverdure, Mr and Mrs William Leggat, Stephen Lyons, George and Joan McCammon, Hartland M. MacDougall, David McEntyre, Barbara A. McGibbon, Mrs Allan Mackay, Mrs David Mackenzie, Mrs Anson McKim, Eric McLean, Wilson McLean, Joanne MacPhail, Pam Main, Nancy Marelli, David Marler, Dr Eric Marler, Gloria Menard, Pamela Miller, R.E. Miller, Senator Hartland de M. Molson, Mrs Bartlett Morgan, Elizabeth Morgan, Graham Nesbitt, Michael Ogilvie, Mme Berthe O'Neill, Jean Ostiguy, Carl Otto, Alex Paterson, Robert Cowans Paterson, the Rt Hon. Jack Pickersgill, Senator Michael Pitfield, Mr and Mrs A. Blaikie Purvis, Mr and Mrs Walter Ratcliffe, Alexander Reford, Nikola Reford-Delplace, T.L. Regehr, Susan Riddle, Janice Rosen, Marcel Roy, Cynthia Smith, Robert Sparrow, Heward Stikeman, Judge and Mrs D.C. Thomas, Tom Thompson, Rosanne Todd, Yolande Toussaint, Vincent M. Tovell, Judge François Tremblay, Scott Turnbull, Dr David Wanklyn, Jeanne Warwick, Eric Webster, Lorne Webster, Philip Webster, Mrs Stuart Webster, Galen Weston, Edward Whittaker, Mr and the Hon. Mrs. John Worsley, Willa Worsley, and Janice Zubalik.

In the United States, my thanks go to the JM Foundation, Mrs J.R. Crawford, Mark and Florence Farrell, Dan Fox, Eric Hake, Dora Kerr, Mary Anna and Mark Kienholz, Jeremiah Milbank II, Rupert Murdoch, Chris K. Olander, and Tom Rosenbaum; in Thailand, Anuspasna Suwanmongkol; in Japan, Princess Takamatsu; and in the Netherlands, Mike Moll.

Archivists and librarians in three countries were indispensable, and I owe much to the staff of each. In England, the Royal Archives at Windsor, the British Library, the Public Record Office (now the British National Archives), the House of Lords Record Office, and the libraries of the universities of Oxford, Cambridge, Durham, and Birmingham were the chief repositories that I consulted. In the United States, they were the Rockefeller Center, the Houghton and Baker libraries at Harvard University, the business library at Columbia University, and the New York Public Library. In Canada they were Library and Archives Canada, the Archives of Ontario, the Archives of Nova Scotia, the Metropolitan Toronto (now City of Toronto) Archives, the YMCA Archives in Toronto and Montreal, the United Church Archives, the Archives nationales du Québec, the Bank of Montreal Archives, the CPR Archives, the Séminaire de Trois-Rivières Archives, the Inco Archives, the University of New Brunswick Archives, the Centre d'Archives de l'Hydro-Québec, the Loblaw Companies Archives, the Holt Renfrew Archives, the Scotiabank Archives, the CIBC Archives, the Royal Bank Archives, the Bank of Canada (National Currency Collection), the Sherwin-Williams Archives in Cleveland, and various libraries and archives of McGill, Queen's, York, and Concordia universities and the University of Toronto. I owe the McGill University Archives and the McCord Museum of Canadian History a special debt, especially Gordon Burr, Shannon Hodge, Nora Hague, and Heather McNabb.

Several lent their technical expertise to me or Nicolas McConnell, especially Art Bond, Jene-Réné Bouchard, Patricia Desjardins, Sylvain Gaudet, Nora Hague, Pam Main, Roxanne Raby, John Salib, and Newton Siao. Gerald Wareham spent many months going through ledgers and summarizing financial data. I thank all the staff of the McGill-Queen's University Press for seeing this book through to publication, and Curtis Fahey, my editor.

Nicolas McConnell is grateful to Conrad Black for encouraging him, many years ago, to initiate the research leading to this book.

Finally, although I never met J.W. McConnell or any of his family, except Nicolas McConnell, before beginning this work, I had met a few of his close friends such as Malcolm MacDonald. I had come to know fairly well two of them in particular,

Margot Viscountess Hardinge and Sir Shuldham Redfern. Although unfortunately I never thought to ask them about McConnell, my happy memories of them have helped me to summon up the world that they shared with him.

William Fong
Montreal, 2008

J.W.McCONNELL

CHAPTER ONE

A Boyhood in Muskoka: Blood, Religion, Sentiment, and Community, 1877–91

I was brought up … in maybe the wildest kind of backwoods in the whole of Ontario. I cannot say positively but it took me a long time to get tame after moving to the City.

J.W. McConnell, c.1904

Jack McConnell, as he was known as a child and to his close friends in later life, was born on 1 July 1877 in Monck Township in Muskoka, a rural district about one hundred miles north of Toronto.[1] His father was Scots Irish and his mother probably English, but little else is known about his family background. One legend relates that Jack's paternal grandfather had been a mill-owner in Belfast and died intestate. The ensuing confusion left Jack's father, John McConnell, personally bankrupt, and he fled Ireland for Canada in 1863, thus escaping his creditors but still so poor that he and Jack's mother were obliged to work on the ship to earn their passage. Another legend holds that Jack's father had been in the Irish constabulary and had studied the law.

Conflicting documents record that Jack's father was born on 27 June 1834, in County Armagh or in 1838 in Belfast, the son of John or James McConnell and Mary McConnell. They give the name of Jack's mother as Mary Ann Wilson or Margaret Anna Wilson, but she signed "Margaret Anna McConnell" on at least one legal instrument. She was born apparently on 11 July 1834 or on 11 June 1838, in Manchester, and is said to have moved to Belfast as a child. Their wedding took place on 21 September 1862 at St Anne's, an Anglican church in Belfast; John McConnell, aged twenty-seven, is described in the church register as a "Labourer" and the son of James McConnell, "Steward." Mary Anne Wilson, aged twenty-five, is described as a "Weaver" and the daughter of Alexander Wilson, "Labourer." Both parties wrote "X" in the register in place of their names, as did their witnesses, John Taggart and Anne Macartney.

Although it appears from the document selling their farm in 1893 that Mr and Mrs John McConnell could manage confident signatures by then, their previous illiteracy suggests strong cultural and material limitations. Whatever these may have been, the

New World was to propel some of the next generation of McConnells into relative respectability at a speed inconceivable in Ireland. It seems that a brother of Jack's mother became a doctor in California. Of Jack's own siblings, one sister married a doctor and one brother became a highly decorated lieutenant-colonel.

Family tradition is correct in claiming that the McConnells emigrated to Canada East (after 1867, Ontario) in 1863; and for almost eight years they lived somewhere in York Township, which encompassed the city of Toronto.[2] Their first child, James, was born there. Conceived on the boat, in later life he would often rock himself constantly and silently. In 1871 the McConnells abandoned their relatively urban life for newly created Monck Township in Muskoka. The province of Ontario, only four years old, was offering free land to settlers willing to move north. Boats and tugs, supplemented by stagecoaches, were then making Muskoka much more accessible than it had been in the past, when the sole mode of transport had been oxcarts.

A land of swamps and lakes and teeming with wild animals, early European travellers described Muskoka as "one vast forest of pine, hemlock, spruce and hardwood of every species."[3] From 1815, it was logged intensively in order to provide timber for the building of ships for the Royal Navy; but when this market declined in the 1860s, the lumber industry began scouring it anew in search of smaller pieces of wood for the building of houses and other structures and the making of furniture. The demand continued to be so relentless that, by 1881, the *Canadian Lumberman* was noting that the forests of Muskoka were being "thinned out."[4] This second lumber boom lasted until about 1920.

Within three years following the Free Grants and Homestead Act of 1868, the district was divided into 319 town and village lots. In Monck Township alone there were 89 registered landholders. These settlers, a few farming land comparable to that of the best agricultural areas in the province, cultivated a variety of grains and vegetables, and they hunted animals for fur.[5] Above all, Monck produced children. As one local chronicler was to recall, "next to the Province of Quebec, Monck had, I think, the highest birthrate; our people were very prolific. The primitive rigours of pioneer life and the remoteness from medical aid did not in the least deter the stork."[6] To the McConnells, the stork delivered seven children, the last three in Muskoka: James Alexander (Jim) (1863–1937), Margaret Anna (Annie) (1865–1927), Elizabeth Agnes (Lizzie or Beth) (1867–1922), Ada Eleanor (Ada) (1870–1951), Walter Adam (Walter) (1873–1955), Susan Mary (Sue) (1875–1902), and finally John Wilson (Jack) (1877–1963).

By 1871, the year of the relocation of the McConnells, Ontario had already sold the most profitable parts of Muskoka to lumbermen. The Free Grants legislation preserved still potentially profitable pine lands from settlement, and these fell into the hands of settlers only after the trees were harvested. As there was no policy of reforestation, settlement was the only remaining use for them. The McConnells were

Stony farmland in Muskoka with tree stumps, 1890s.
Archives of Ontario. F 1132-2-1-1/St 1171

among the first to apply for land under the 1868 act. Jack's parents took possession of their land probably in September 1871, in time to build a shanty in which to pass the winter. They spent the following five years clearing, building, and planting.

On paper, the act contained numerous provisions to give the new settlers a reasonable start.[7] A married man was eligible for two hundred acres, which is what John McConnell received. In principle, the lots granted were free of rocks, lakes, and swamps. The law stipulated however that it was for the prospective settlers themselves to ascertain whether the lots that they wished to acquire were in fact in this condition. In practice many found their land too overgrown with thick bush to determine how rocky and swampy it was. Often they found themselves obliged to burn the stumps left by the lumbermen, in an effort to clear the necessary acres for planting. Most of the grantees had also been misled by talk about the high productivity of the land. In fact, much of the soil of Muskoka was unsuitable for cultivation – acidic and thin and lying over bedrock. It eroded easily, and heavy rains flushed it into the lakes.[8] Contrary to their hopes, there were no surplus crops to export, and the markets of the populous towns of southern Ontario were in any case remote and difficult of access.

The fertility of farms in Monck Township in particular, though never spectacular, varied considerably. The McConnell farm was about half covered by the grandly named Canadian Shield, the mass of rock that renders much of Canada uninhabitable or at least uncultivable. The other half of their property was not much better. Only twenty acres of it (one tenth of their grant) were even with difficulty arable, and even then suitable only for hay and grain. For the McConnells, the rocky land, small broken fields, steep hills, swampy gullies, and short growing season all reduced life to grim, unremitting toil with little hope of improvement. What farming beyond subsistence that did develop in Muskoka was in response "to a local demand created by the logging boom."[9]

Like many pioneers, Jack was born in a split-log cabin, where he also spent all his childhood. His birth occurred on 1 July 1877, exactly ten years after the formation of the Dominion of Canada but ten years before 1 July became known as Dominion Day. In the 1870s, gangs of itinerant workers were building cabins such as Jack's all over Muskoka, supplemented by neighbours working in "bees." Cabins usually consisted of only one room, with two windows and a door. Jack's brother Walter would recall their entire family of nine sleeping in the loft. The McConnell property included a pond and a barn built of pine boards.

The Riley family occupied the lots immediately to the west and the south. Their cabin, which they occupied from 1876 to 1916, was probably identical to the McConnells'. A stove stood in the middle of the room, and pots,pans and kettles hung from the walls. The stove was the only source of heat in winter, and it usually took one person an entire day to chop enough wood to keep it going for twenty-four hours. Cords of firewood stood piled inside. The cabin itself was highly flammable, especially in summer. Residents had to scramble up ladders stored on their roofs, to brush off sparks that had fallen from the chimneys onto the cedar shingles. Their food typically consisted of "hard salt pork, potatoes, oatmeal, molasses, rice and flour for bread."[10] There was little fresh meat, and the beavers and muskrats that they trapped were used chiefly for their skins.

For his first fourteen years, Jack probably never wore shoes or clothes that were not homemade. There is a legend that the congregation of a chapel that he attended took up a collection to buy him shoes. For all such austerities, he did develop an enormous sense of fun. He learned to swim, fish, shoot, and ride bareback, to delight in the variety of the trees all around him, and to revel in the simplicity and the warmth of his neighbours. He also acquired a life-long love of dogs, probably because of an early brush with death. One day he was at home alone with one of his sisters while the

Charles William Riley at his cabin across from the Butter and Egg Road and
the McConnell cabin in Muskoka (which was probably almost identical in
appearance), c.1889. Private collection, courtesy of Walker and Kapya Riley.

rest of the family was digging up tree stumps, and only the barking of the family dog
alerted them to a fire in the cabin.

Even by the 1880s, the farm was singularly bleak. The McConnells, if not others
before them, had felled most of its trees. In place of the majestic old growth of before,
there remained only stumps of white pine, blackened by fire, and young cedar sap-
lings. The farm probably supported a pair of horses, a milk cow, a pig or two, and a
few chickens, but not all its animals were so domestic. To his children, Jack would
recall shooting a bear in the cabbage patch. At the age of fifty-nine, hunting with the
Maharaja of Gwalior in India, he would still be able to fell a tiger with two shots.

Outside of farming, life in Muskoka seemed monotonous, busy, and predictable,
but it could also be shattered at any moment. Hurricanes could lay waste to half an
acre, leaving "windfalls" or narrow belts of uprooted trees extending for miles. Acci-
dents were common, caused by axes or animals, and there was almost no medical
care available, few doctors and no hospitals. The precariousness of life, impressed
itself deeply on Jack. Neighbours decades later would recall his extraordinarily acute
sensitivity to suffering, and his offering water to "nurse" a baby.

When he later left for Toronto, he spared himself many years of back-breaking farm labour, but he did not forget how a farming community worked. In Muskoka, every task "counted" in the struggle to survive, and for the biggest tasks the community as a whole pulled together in various "bees." All took for granted that they had constantly to pull their weight; and when some were weak or infirm, the others came to their aid. Everyone was also flexible about how to earn a living. To supplement their pitiful farm income, it was customary for settlers to find temporary work in commercial logging.

Fortunately, lumbering was not the only non-agricultural source of employment for many Muskokans. By the 1870s, there was also an emerging tourist industry. As late as 1862, only birch-bark canoes had been plying the Muskoka lakes. Soon, however, a wooden rowboat joined them, followed by a sailboat and finally by a steam-powered sidewheeler in 1866.[11] As early as 1858, the Muskoka Colonization Road, made of logs, had also reached North Falls, later called Bracebridge; but it was desperately uncomfortable to travel on and often made impassable by mud. The construction of a railway from Toronto began in 1869, but it did not reach Bracebridge until 1885, when at last mass tourism in Muskoka became possible.[12]

Muskoka's early tourists stopped first at Toronto. Their route was then by train to Barrie, followed by a steamer on Lakes Simcoe and Couchiching, onto a "rotten" or dirt road between Washago and Gravenhurst (McCabe's Bay), and finally to three lakes – called Muskoka, Joseph, and Rosseau – joined by locks. Despite the depletion of the wildlife by commercial fur trappers, the district remained a paradise for recreational hunters and fishermen – with its bear, deer, trout (locally called "salmon"), pickerel, mink, beaver, rabbits, ruffed grouse ("partridge"), and much else.[13]

Bracebridge was a lumber town, but about ten miles from it was the summer resort of Beaumaris. It consisted of a village called Milford Bay, on the shore of Lake Muskoka, and of Tondern Island and some smaller islands facing it. During McConnell's childhood, its summer cottages and hotels were full. The village sponsered regattas – with sailing, rowing, paddling, and swimming races – and fishing camps near by. From the smoky, industrial towns to the south, came hayfever sufferers in particular, drawn by the fabled clean air of Muskoka. So many rich Pennsylvanians, such as the Mellons came each year that Beaumaris acquired the nickname of "Little Pittsburgh."

With its visitors, general store, and post office, Beaumaris connected the McConnells to a much richer, more sophisticated world beyond their farm. In 1873 the Prowse family began to build the Beaumaris Hotel on Tondern Island, with a tower nearly 70 feet high, the main building surrounded by 220 feet of verandah, and the interior endowed with pianos, a bowling alley, and a dance hall. Lodgers gathered "at the wharf, either to meet or to part with friends, or to gratify curiosity by seeing 'who's who' on the boat; while numerous urchins, in every conceivable boating-costume disport[ed] themselves in all manner of craft."[14] Beaumaris was fast becoming one of the most highly fashionable places on the continent in which to spend a vacation. To this day, Muskoka conjures up memories of massive wooden structures with stone fireplaces and mounted animal heads, billiard tables, and chintz-covered furniture, where ladies in long gowns took afternoon tea.[15] Ease and wealth were within easy sight, but not within easy reach, of the McConnell homestead.

The physical isolation of Muskoka made summer visitors a captive market for local farmers, who happily supplied them with foodstuffs. Through the forest, the farmers blazed "butter and egg" routes, named after their two most basic provisions, to serve the summer vistors, and for transporting, in other seasons, such products as maple syrup and ice.[16] Paul Dane, who in 1868 had bought Tondern Island, built one of these routes. A footbridge connected his island to the village of Milford Bay, and then a road stretched for about three miles to a hamlet called Bardsville. Locals called this dirt track rutted with potholes simply Butter and Egg Road. About halfway between Milford Bay and Bardsville stood the McConnell farm.

Jack's father served as the reeve, or president of the council, of Monck Township in 1874–76. Then he served for about sixteen years as the assessor and collector of taxes for Monck. When he retired in 1893, he was praised as "a good neighbour and an efficient officer" by the council, in a letter kept by Jack all his life.[17] It seems, however, that he may not have been the best husband and father. When a friend asked McConnell, many years after he had left Muskoka, why he did not serve alcohol in his house, he responded that if she had seen what his father had done to his mother, she would not have alcohol in her house either. He added that he had promised his mother on her deathbed that he would never drink wine.[18] Jack seems to have been much closer to his mother, who was also his first teacher and, according to family tradition, instilled in him a deep love of the Bible. Later in life, he kept a Bible on his desk, and he frequently laced his letters and newspaper editorials with citations from Scripture.

Taking the pledge to abstain from alcohol, as Jack did, entailed a commitment to a way of life that most Ontario men considered abnormal. Especially in rural areas, drinking binges were badges of manliness. Jack however joined a local temperance group known as the Blue Ribbon Boys, formed by Charles Bard, the builder of the first Methodist chapel in Monck and the superintendent of its Sunday school, as well as the postmaster of Bardsville. Jack found in Bard his first mentor and probably a surrogate father, and he supported him for decades to come, presenting him with $500 on his hundredth birthday in 1937.

The Blue Ribbon Boys' movement had started in New England in association with the Woman's Christian Temperance Movement, distinguished by their own white ribbons, and the Boys were also related to temperance groups for children that had originated in England in 1847 as Bands of Hope, which became particularly asso-

Mr and Mrs Charles Bard of Bardsville, Muskoka, on their golden wedding anniversary. Private collection, courtesy of Mary Anna and Mark Kienholz.

ciated with Methodism. The Boys pledged themselves to abstain from tobacco and bad language as well as alcohol, and to strengthen their resolve they read Scripture, sang hymns, and listened to lectures on purity.[19] Jack's group probably consisted of no more than him and four of Bard's children, including one girl, but it gave him an experience of sober family life. For years after leaving Muskoka, Jack would return to stay with Bard's daughter Nellie Mears, who ran a boardinghouse there.

Jack's commitment to temperance was no passing fancy. Not only did he remain a teetotaller all his life, he also offered his own daughters-in-law and other young people cash if they would pledge not to drink before they were twenty-one. One who accepted his challenge as late as the 1950s was Cynthia Thomas. He dubbed Cynthia an honorary Blue Ribbon Boy of Bardsville. Cynthia's grandmother Elizabeth Killen, known as Bessie, had been Jack's only teacher. Only five years older than Jack, at her home in neighbouring Ziska and with her five sisters, she would join Jack around an organ, singing such hymns as "Sweet By and By." The Killens were recent immigrants from Ireland. Over cups of tea, they would croon with Jack such lyrics as "Oh, how I'm longing for my ain folk, though they may be but lowly, plain and pure folk, though it's far beyond the sea, it's ever there I'll be with my old folk."

Bessie's one-room schoolhouse in Bardsville probably ran along lines typical of the era. A school board of three unpaid trustees and a paid secretary-treasurer levied taxes, hired the teacher, and bought firewood. Pupils supplied their own books, though the teacher would try to arrange for the loan of books for poorer children. Many parents could not afford notebooks, pens, and ink either, and so their children had to take their homework home on an old cracked slate. As one Muskokan was to recall of the neighbouring Chaffey Township in the years before 1918: "Our school was only one room with classes from primer to Senior 4th. It was about 30 feet long by 24 feet wide with four rows of double seats. The two centre rows were shorter in order to make room for a large pot-bellied stove that sat near the one and only door. There was a porch entrance. In this porch was kept our drinking water in a pail, and beside the pail was a communal granite drinking cup ... What we called a library consisted of an old scuffed and scarred bookcase with the doors broken off the hinges, containing about two dozen torn and dog-eared books, some with their pages either missing or misplaced."[20]

From 1846 and for almost a century, the school curriculum in Canada East and Ontario was centrally controlled and standardized. It derived from the curriculum of the British administration in Ireland. By 1884, its Irish National Readers were being replaced by Ontario Readers. Jack is likely to have used one series of readers or the other or perhaps both, along with *Elementary Arithmetic* by Smith and McMurchy or Kirkland and Scott.[21] He may have read *First Lessons in Christian Morals*, written by the first superintendent of education for Ontario and a Methodist minister, Egerton Ryerson, which was an authorized text between 1871 and 1875. For Ryerson, "Happiness consisted not in riches, or in the pleasures of exalted rank and station, but in moderation in expectations ... good habits ... and the consciousness of His favour."[22]

One commentator summarized the effect of the Irish National Readers as: "Two contrary impressions of their content stand out: the factual material and information is eclectic and surprisingly contemporary, while aesthetic or literary values are largely ignored. In the initial section of prose and poetry the selections were chosen for their didactic qualities rather than their stylistic merit ... clearly the object was to cultivate the reader's moral, not aesthetic sensibilities." They also introduced liberal economic theory and were "an apology for the class relations and the political alignments of the emerging industrial capitalist economy."[23]

The chief proponent of the Irish series had been Richard Whately, a Protestant archbishop of Dublin. His *Easy Lessons on Money Matters for the Use of Young People*, originally published in 1833, was included in it. It praised the virtues of hard work, perseverance, and thrift, and it foresaw backsliding or lack of will as dooming one to poverty or worse. As for the rich man, Whately wrote "though he appears to have so much larger a share allotted to him, [he] does not really consume it but is only the channel through which it flows to others. And it is by this means much better distributed than it would have been otherwise."[24]

Jack may have taken such aphorisms to heart, for in the 1880s teachers and reading material were so scarce that textbooks were sometimes committed to memory. And in the newer Ontario Readers, every page was permeated by "an omnipotent and omniscient God ... the creator of the universe and of human life, meting out both earthly and heavenly rewards and punishments." They admonished children to treat the poor kindly and to be persistent, obedient, truthful, brave, gentle, generous, and wise.[25]

For its times, Ontario's educational system was unusually good. At the Paris Exhibition of 1878, the Ontario Department of Education won awards in six classes, more than Britain and the rest of the empire together, and at the World's Columbian Exhibition in Chicago in 1893, one British judge pronounced Ontario's "the finest practical system of education ... that the world affords today."[26] In later years, it was clear that McConnell had learned his lessons, especially in mathematics, well. He himself wrote to one of Bessie Killen's daughters, Dora McKay Kerr: "I owe a good deal to your mother. She understood mathematics. I knew my math. When two or three parties were talking over a deal, I could already figure out percentages before they had finished."[27]

Jack left school at the age of thirteen or fourteen, with as much schooling as most Canadians of his generation. In Ontario elementary schools, only 42 per cent of children of school age attended school in 1872 and 50 per cent in 1887; in rural areas in 1887 it was only 47 per cent. In 1871, only 5 per cent went on to high school; by 1901, it was 10 per cent. University was largely deemed the preserve of clergymen, scholars, and sometimes engineers and lawyers, and in Ontario it was uncommon for even lawyers to attend university until the 1950s. Certainly, business was not part of the university curriculum, and few businessmen of any kind had attended university, also until the 1950s.

It is not easy to determine exactly how much of each year Jack spent in school. In Muskoka, farm work competed with school, and the attendance of pupils was irregular. As late as 1872, 61 per cent in rural Ontario schools attended class for fewer than one hundred days a year.[28] Jack, as the youngest of three sons, may have spent more time in school, spared some of the heavier duties that naturally fell to his brothers. At any rate by 1891, seven-eighths of Ontario students were reaching the 4th class, roughly grade 7 or 8 in modern terms, which is probably where Jack finished.[29]

In Muskoka, McConnell's sense of identity began to take shape. At its core was a deep well of British patriotism that would remain throughout his life. For him, the British Empire, which was reaching its apogee in his first twenty years, was the embodiment of civilization and a force for progress; and Canada, as a part of it, enjoyed both the privileges and the responsibilities of this magnificent enterprise.

Although his mother was probably English, McConnell always thought of himself as Irish in origin, with considerable affinity to Scotland. He seems to have visited Ireland only once, in 1904, when he stopped in Belfast, then the shipbuilding capital of the world. The hardworking enterprise and self-sufficiency of the Protestant north of Ireland were in his bones. Splendid as it was to be Canadian and British, to be Irish in addition implied a distinct temperament. Moreover, to be from Ulster, was even better as as it incorporated much stirring Scottish history. Although no scholar, Jack would typically probe into the ancestry and other connections of everyone he dealt with. His life, like that of most of his generation, was suffused with historical consciousness. Every life was to him precious and to be judged in the light of eternity.

Late in his life, McConnell was not surprised to learn that his son John, on his first visit to Ireland in the early 1960s, had been often mistaken for a native Irishman there. He was also delighted when John presented him with a typical Irish workingman's cap as a souvenir. After McConnell's death, John would erect an imposing Celtic cross over his father's grave, based on an Irish design. McConnell made provision for all his children, their spouses, and their own children to be buried at the foot of this cross in the Mount Royal Cemetery in Montreal. The McConnell plot was a little corner of Quebec that was to be forever Ireland.

Jack McConnell would often hold forth on the extraordinary success of Ulstermen and Scotsmen, seemingly so disproportionate to their numbers. He understood the alleged peculiar strengths of the Celts, with their "hard brains and soft hearts." Among the governors general whom he came to know, he seemed to warm more to the Scotsman Lord Tweedsmuir and the Ulsterman Lord Alexander than to the essentially English – with an Irish earldom – Lord Bessborough, or the Germanic prince with another Irish earldom, Lord Athlone. Among his business friends, he particularly valued such Scotsmen as Arthur Purvis, Sir Patrick Ashley Cooper, and Lord McGowan. Like McConnell himself, they were not exclusive. One of his closest social friends was John Bassett of the Montreal *Gazette*, a fiercely proud native of Protestant Ulster and yet a noted friend of Catholics.

Nothing, however, moulded McConnell more than Muskoka. It is only a slight exaggeration to say that he was always to see the world generally as Muskoka writ large. Part of what he had acquired in Muskoka was a supremely practical cast of mind. All his life, despite his well-cut clothes and urbanity, McConnell retained the whiff of the homespun about him and could not understand how anyone could disdain plain speaking and plain living. His preferred food was roast chicken and roast potatoes; and although he travelled a good deal, he hated being away from home. Three weeks in India in 1936 left him often miserable. He bridled at removing his shoes to visit mosques and temples. At lavish banquets hosted by maharajas, he would scrutinize the dishes and ask "What is this stuff?" and then call for ice cream. Perhaps recalling Beaumaris, he wanted the comforts of a luxury hotel at home and the comforts of home at a luxury hotel.

At the same time, he was no smug provincial. What drove him was a desire to project what he had learned in his youth into a wider arena. Much of what he built derived from the community solidarity that he had seen in Monck. The very limitations of Muskoka, which were obvious to him, were seeds for his causes. One was limited access to education. He was never ashamed of being an autodidact, and he freely quoted *Reader's Digest*. Yet his favourite cause for over thirty years was McGill University, and he was a decisive voice in its affairs for most of this time.

Another problem in Muskoka had been the lack of medical care. There was no hospital in the district until 1928, when one opened for veterans in the former Bracebridge home of McConnell's friend, James Fenn, a hardware merchant.[30] McConnell would recall the bad teeth of the Muskokans of his youth to the end of his life. Thus he generously supported and raised funds for almost every hospital in Montreal and he was a founder of the Montreal Neurological Institute. In the Blue Ribbon Boys of Bardsville, too, can be seen the origins of the boys' clubs that he would later found in Quebec and his tireless dedication to the Young Men's Christian Association (YMCA). Above all, the poverty of his Muskoka days doubtless led to his legendary generosity to individuals, from the very young to the very old. For those dedicated to others, especially nurses and ministers, he set up pensions, and for students of all kinds he set up scholarships.

Even more than poverty, the idea of dispossession took hold in McConnell's mind once his family had lost its Monck Township farm. In June 1877, six months after his parents obtained confirmation of their land grant, and on the very day before Jack was born, they took out a $200 mortgage from the North British Investment Company for five years, which was later extended for another five years. Just before the expiry of this extension, on 2 May 1887, they assigned their interests to John William Beresford Topp, a dentist. Topp immediately resold the property to Jack's mother, the consideration for each of these transactions being one dollar. Five years later, on 1 May 1893, Jack's mother sold the property to Joseph Scriven (husband of the community midwife). This sale was subject to the terms of the original grant as amended by the patent of freehold and, rather paradoxically, "to the sale of Prime Timber" (by licensed lumbermen, who might still log white pine if there was any left) to Judge William Mahaffy.

Why Jack's father had surrendered his interest to his wife in 1887 is unclear, but it may have been to avoid seizure of the house by his creditors. At any rate, the final sale price of $500, less the mortgage of $200, yielded a profit of only $300, after twenty-two years of toil. This $300 was the apparent net worth of the family in 1893. The family left immediately with their money for Toronto, having surrendered more than their property. Under the Free Grants and Homestead Act, on attaining the age of eighteen, the children of settlers, women as well as men, might each claim a further grant of one hundred acres. By leaving Muskoka, all of the McConnell children including Jack waived this right.

Jack must have been traumatized by the financial uncertainty that his family had battled in Muskoka. In any case, he became obsessed with leaving his children secure. As early as 1898, he took out life insurance on himself, and he bought insurance policies long after he had become a millionaire. When his eldest son was about marry, McConnell set up a trust that in effect prohibited two generations of McConnells from disposing of shares in his newspaper, sugar, and flour companies. Instead, they were to live off dividends. McConnell also revised his will often and set up a web of holding companies and trusts to avert encroachment on capital. At his death, he left at least seventy copies of his last will and testament.

Happier memories of Muskoka were also never far from his mind. Recalling its natural landscape, as well as its destruction by both lumbermen and settlers, McConnell always retained a deep love of trees and was to plant hundreds of them. He also prized the tranquillity of the countryside. Even his imposing mansion on Pine Avenue in Montreal was set in a secluded estate, from which he would ride in the evenings. His country houses at Dorval and in the Laurentian Mountains stood in acres of woods, fronted by large lakes. He built an enormous log cabin in the Laurentians, suitable for the entertainment of royalty and yet reminiscent of the Beaumaris Hotel with its tower. Even more isolated and rustic was his fishing camp on the Restigouche in the Gaspé, where he would spend part of many summers and entertain close friends. In all his houses, there were both wholesome fun and lavish hospitality. Descendants of his siblings were astonished to find him in his seventies trying to tip their canoe in a duel with paddles. One neighbour, in her best dress, found him pouring water over her from his perch on the neo-classical portico of his house at Dorval. "It's good for you, honey," he assured her. With his closest friends, bun fights raged.

McConnell returned often to Muskoka following his departure for Toronto in 1891. Always he would visit the Killens as well as the Bards, and he remained in touch with his old teacher Bessie and her daughter Dora. In January 1957, his eightieth year, McConnell approached Bessie's other daughter, Margaret (Arla), to ask for her help in setting up the John McConnell and Margaret Ann Wilson McConnell Foundation for the needy in Bracebridge. He originally endowed this foundation with $500,000 in securities, which he hoped would yield 5 per cent a year in income, enabling it to distribute $25,000 annually.[31] He confined it to charitable and educational purposes in Muskoka alone. The Children's Aid Society, the Bracebridge Memorial Hospital, bursaries and scholarships, were to be typical beneficiaries of its aid. With typical efficiency, through the assistance of Premier Leslie Frost of Ontario, McConnell had

McConnell talking from his home in Montreal to Reeve Jack Johnston of
Monck Township, Muskoka, who had made the first long-distance call to
him from the Milford Bay exchange, 19 May 1960. LAC, PA 132014.

the foundation established within weeks, while, from Premier Maurice Duplessis of
Quebec, he obtained a declaration that income from the foundation was to be exempt
from Quebec taxes. He also arranged with the chairman and president of the Royal
Bank of Canada for the Royal Bank manager in Bracebridge to be the foundation's
treasurer. Judge Douglas Thomas, Arla's husband, long administered it.

Towards the very end of his life, sitting in his Montreal house surrounded by furnishings from the Italian Renaissance and by portraits of royalty and nobility, Jack
received the first long-distance telephone call ever made from Muskoka. It was from a
reeve, and Jack recalled the work of another reeve, his own father. As one of the most
successful men ever born in the district, Jack was almost an ambassador from it to the
world generally. He had moved from Muskoka seventy years earlier, but, in some very
fundamental sense, he never left it at all.

CHAPTER TWO

Onward, Ever Onward, Jack: Toronto and the Making of a Man, 1892–99

> He does well who does his best.
> J.W. McConnell, notes for a Sunday school class, c.1900

From 1892 to 1899, Jack McConnell came of age in Toronto. It was here that he acquired a practical education in life, equipping him to be supremely functional in an urban environment that was reshaping both itself and the rural culture, beyond it, into which he had been born.

In the 1890s, Toronto was rapidly expanding in its wealth and its dreams, and well on its way to becoming the metropolis of a new industrial economy. In their origins, most of its people were even more homogeneous than those of Muskoka, but they were also much more densely housed. By 1901, they numbered 156,098 (including the suburbs), over 91 per cent of Anglo-Saxon or Celtic ancestry. They were also almost all Christian, including 8,095 Anglicans, 6,040 Methodists, 5,270 Presbyterians, 4,701 Roman Catholics, and 1,256 Baptists.[1] The rivalry among the Protestant denominations in particular was generally friendly, and McConnell's Methodism, combined with his Irish and English ancestry, inclined him from the start to become almost a typical Torontonian.

Huddled near Toronto harbour, church spires, tentative business "skyscrapers," and smokestacks were projecting convergent spiritual and material aspirations. Business leaders were practising a vigorous, distinctly worldly Christianity, notably embodied in their seven-storied steel Board of Trade Building, which recalled the chapterhouse of a Gothic cathedral and yet foreshadowed the emergence of more blatantly secular "cathedrals of commerce," such as the Woolworth Building in New York City (1913) or the head office of the Canadian Bank of Commerce in Toronto itself (1927).

Crossing the principal thoroughfare, Yonge Street, King and Queen streets were largely dedicated to retailing, and Wellington and Front streets to wholesaling. Stores and offices shared this compact commercial district with houses of worship. At King

McConnell in Toronto, c.1893. Private collection.

and Church streets, St James Church, later the Anglican cathedral, towered near the headquarters of William Mackenzie's growing railway empire that was spreading in Spain and Brazil as well as Canada. On Queen Street, the Methodist "cathedral," Metropolitan Church, stood beside its affiliated Fred Victor Mission to the poor. A short walk west led to Eaton's and Simpson's department stores, which were starting to transform Canadian society from one of agricultural self-sufficiency into one of mass consumption. Wellington Street was full of warehouses supplying them and their mail-order customers beyond. East from Yonge Street along Front Street, buildings stretched in a riot of styles, such as the heavily ornamented Bank of Montreal at Bay Street, the slender triangle-shaped, "Flat Iron" or Gooderham office building at Church Street, and the imposingly industrial Christie Brown biscuit factory at Duke Street. These buildings, businesses, and institutions were more than a backdrop to McConnell's life. Almost without exception, they were about to shape its course.

From Muskoka, the McConnell family moved to the city in stages, with Jack's sister Annie leading the way and Jack himself following in 1891 or 1892, just before the sale of the family farm. Thanks to city directories, we can trace exactly where all the members of his family worked and lived. The first sign of them in Toronto appears in the 1893 directory, compiled in 1892. From this we learn that Jack lived with Jim, Ada, and Annie at 358 Yonge Street, near Elm Street, just north of where the Eaton Centre would be standing a century later. They occupied rooms above a shop called the Fleming Estate, owned by the James Fleming, which sold flowers. By 1893, Annie was a clerk at Fleming's and Jack an apprentice, which meant a delivery boy. Jim and Ada seem to have been packers. By the following year, their farm in Muskoka sold, Jack's parents and remaining siblings had arrived, and the family moved a little north to 42 Gerrard Street West, just off Yonge Street and steps from Elm Street. John McConnell opened a confectionery shop a little to the north, at the southwest corner of Yonge and College streets (the site of the future Eaton's, College Street, later College Park), and Jack was his assistant there.

The first Toronto house occupied by all the McConnells was in St John's Ward, a foetid district bounded by Yonge Street, University Avenue, Queen Street, and College Street. They lived a minute east of the Toronto poorhouse, the House of Industry at Elm and Chestnut streets. Unlike English poorhouses, this provided outdoor relief, and it assisted 2,000 families between December 1893 and February 1894 alone, 250 more than in the previous winter.[2]

By 1893–94, the Ward had a significant number of Yiddish-speaking Jewish immigrants from central Europe who worked in the *schmatte* or clothing trade. Crowded, smelly, and noisy, the neighbourhood resembled the ghettos or *shtetls* to which they had been confined in Europe. The Jews of Toronto grew from 534 in 1881 to 1,425 in 1891 and 3,044 in 1901, when they represented just 2 per cent of the total population.

St John's Ward, Toronto, 1905.
Archives of Ontario, F1075-9-0-7/ S 8953.

Nearly all of them inhabited this new *shtetl*, however, and they accounted for 15 per cent of the city's garment workers. It was probably through seeing them that McConnell first developed his lifelong respect for the self-reliance and community spirit of the Jews. These traits were reminiscent of the Muskoka pioneers, but the Jews were all the hardier because of discrimination against them by the larger community.

Apart from its Jewish character, the Ward reeked of decay. Like central Toronto generally, it was full of hawkers, scavengers, and horse-dealers. For almost a decade, Jack's daily experience of going to work entailed wending his way among rag-pickers, bottle-collectors, used-furniture dealers, and pedlars, as well as factory hands. The Ward in particular housed three times as many widows as widowers, evidence of the perilous lives led by male workers amid dangerous machinery and lethal fumes. Its narrow streets were full of little "frame cottages, junk wagons, pit privies, lean-tos in back lanes, open drains, the smell of rotting plaster and manure, sweatshops, malnourished children, families crowded together."[3] Most of the houses were shacks, constructed of wood, with sometimes a thin shell of plaster, leaving their residents vulnerable to wind, cold, heat, and humidity. They drew their water from wells and cisterns at the risk of typhoid. Cash was always short, and credit from shops was essential to their survival, as it had probably been in Muskoka for the McConnells. Most work was seasonal at best, and such necessities as sewing machines for female home pieceworkers were typically beyond their meagre savings.

Nevertheless, in the last two decades of the nineteenth century, Toronto was enjoy-ing spectacular economic growth. From 1881 to 1891, the total number of businesses in the city more than tripled, the workforce doubled in size, and the capital invested increased by roughly 250 per cent. Toronto had established itself as a leading centre of printing and publishing and chemical and secondary wood production.[4] Meat-packing, steelware manufacture, and food processing were among other major indus-tries of the city, and there was much demand for manual as well as skilled labour. For the ambitious, it was therefore not difficult to find at least temporary employment.

In the period from 1894 to 1901, McConnell's brothers were remarkably versatile. Jim in the 1890s worked as a machinist, a packer, a labourer, and a fireman, while Walter worked as a clerk, a machinist, a driver, a laundryman, and a manager. Ada and Annie worked as clerks for at least two years while Agnes and Lizzie were dress-makers from 1895 onwards.

The 1891 census had revealed clothing manufacture as the dominant industry in Toronto for Gentiles as well as for Jews.[5] It employed 26 per cent of the total work-force, making the city the garment centre of the entire country.[6] Females comprised 97.3 per cent of the makers of women's wear. Every day they were to be seen "strug-gling up Bay Street with great bundles of clothing, some of them barely able to walk," and often using baby carriages to transport their bundles.[7] The garment industry promised earnings directly related to individual effort, and from it "experience and capital would be acquired solely by personal conscientiousness."[8]

Toronto was also the centre of Canadian retailing, which was largely an offshoot of clothing manufacture. The department-store owner Timothy Eaton had introduced a mail-order service in 1884 to take advantage – with the imminent completion of the Canadian Pacific Railway (CPR) – of the growing market in the west. He was both cre-ating and catering to a new demand for ready-made clothing – a novelty to most Cana-dians, accustomed as they had been to making their own. In 1893 Eaton completed a four-storey factory to make clothes between James and Yonge streets, just south from where the McConnells were then living. A national market for imported goods and custom-made clothing, and a vast retail network, based in Toronto, was also taking root. In the following year, 1894, across Queen Street from Eaton's department store, Robert Simpson opened his rival department store, the two establishments being the nuclei of nationally competing chains. In 1895 Jack himself began working for the firm of a wholesale milliner on Bay Street, just south of Eaton's, and thus he joined Agnes and Lizzie in the clothing industry.

The fact that Agnes and Lizzie worked as dressmakers raises the question of the economic condition of the McConnell family in the last five years of the century. In some cases, the term "dressmaker" was a euphemism for someone who did piece-work at home, hired by middlemen for one of the large garment manufacturers of the city. Some female garment workers in Toronto, not described in the city guide as dressmakers, earned as little as 75 cents a week, although the usual wage was between $3 and $4.50, with $3 being considered "fair." In 1897 Mackenzie King, who twenty-four years later was to become prime minister of Canada and, much later still, a close friend of McConnell's, wrote a series of articles on immigrants and sweat labour in Toronto for the *Mail and Empire* newspaper. King interviewed one girl, sixteen years of age, "thin and sickly in appearance," who had worked for eight years for a large wholesale garment-working house for $2 a week. One of her sisters made $2 a week in a large shop for making buttonholes in coats. The sisters had also been making knick-erbockers at five cents a pair, men's pants at from 12½ cents a pair, and all the while they were supplying the thread themselves.[9]

We do not know how much Ada and Lizzie made in wages. Their identification of the family home as their place of work suggests that they were doing piecework, though not necessarily the worst-paid that King was to observe. The family portrait of the McConnells taken in 1895, with one healthy looking sister sporting a handsome lace bib, suggests that their lives were modest but not miserable. At any rate, later in 1895, Annie and Ada both married and so in theory at least had found husbands to spare them the poverty of single female garment workers.

Whatever their jobs, unemployment, at least from time to time, was inevitable for such families as the McConnells. Jim was apparently unemployed in 1896, and all the sisters probably were at best sporadically employed in their work as dressmakers or clerks. The same was true of their father, following the failure of his candy shop and his grocery. With unemployment or underemployment for such families as the McConnells, there was always the threat of hunger if not utter destitution.

The economic insecurity that he and his family experienced, both in Muskoka and in Toronto, was to have a profound and long-lasting impact on McConnell. Although he would always remain fundamentally opposed to trade unions and socialism, he never shared the middle-class Victorian view that the unemployed had only their own moral failings to blame for their condition. His family's situation made it clear to him that unemployment, and the hunger that it threatened, was generally the result not of flawed character – laziness, drunkenness, and the like – but of economic forces beyond the control of individuals. It was also a problem that, while inevitable, needed to be addressed by those more fortunate. Philanthropy, for him, would not be an issue of mere pity or charity but a way of enabling people to "get on" in life; he was sure that

The McConnells, Toronto, 1895. Back row: Margaret, Elizabeth, James, Walter.
Front row: Jack, Father, Mother, Susan, and Ada (private collection).

others could emulate him if given the right tools. Alone among his business colleagues
in the years to come, he had known both rural and urban poverty at first hand, and he
never forgot it. Even at the end of his life, in the 1950s, he kept in the lavatory attached
to his office an old and worn brown tweed jacket. It had been his first, and he showed
it shyly to Maureen Forrester, a young and highly promising singer of modest background to whom he gave over $25,000 for her education, declaring that it was there to
remind him of where he had come from.[10]

In 1895–96 the McConnells settled into a new house and new work. From Gerrard Street, they moved several miles to the west, to 15 Arthur Street, roughly
where Dundas Street met Bloor Street. John McConnell opened a grocery store at
155 Markham Street. Ada, Annie, and Walter were all clerks, possibly in this shop
although this is unclear, and Lizzie was still a dressmaker. There is no record in these
years of Susie or of their mother, or indeed of Jim, although he appears as a packer
again in 1896. The confectionery shop abandoned, Jack was working that year as a
baker and a packer at Christie, Brown, which was the major biscuit maker in the city,
at its plant at Duke and Front streets. His made $3 a week there, of which habitually he
gave 30 cents to religious or charitable causes.

From 1895 to 1899, McConnell worked at G. Goulding and Sons, which occupied
a building at 55 Bay Street, just south of Wellington Street and north of Front Street.[11]

George Goulding's staff, c.1895, McConnell in the front row,
fourth from left. McCord Museum M2003.8.6.36.

The Goulding's building was near the customs house, in a district then full of ware-houses and of wholesalers of stationery, dry goods, and millinery. George Goulding was a major wholesale importer of "millinery and fancy dry goods," and his business reflected a shift away from reliance in Toronto on Montreal dry-goods importers in favour of local ones.

From a picture dated 1895, we can see that Goulding's staff consisted of at least nineteen young men, at least some of whom were George's sons. The conditions of the office were not unusually harsh, and that its atmosphere resembled that of an extended family, with a sense of brotherhood and equality of opportunity among the young men, was confirmed by Jack's own rapid advance in the firm. He began as an entry clerk in the basement, but he took charge of the books of the firm within a year, at the age of twenty, and his salary rose to $12 a week. At Goulding's, Jack seems to have had the first happy job of his career, and he kept up with colleagues whom he had met there for years afterwards. So grateful was he to the Goulding family for giving him work and caring for him that he continued to send cash gifts at Christmas to at least one Goulding descendant to the end of his life.[12] By 1899, McConnell was described in the city directory as a Goulding's salesman. He spent only about a year with Goulding's in this capacity, but it was but the start for him of a lifetime of sell-ing – an activity that prized equally the ability to persuade and the ability to be liked. McConnell excelled at both.

Salesmen traditionally had specialized in certain products, and they were not easily differentiated from the producers of their wares. They tended also to work in cities, so that, even in McConnell's childhood, a farm family typically made whatever it required because it never encountered salesmen. What was new in the late nineteenth century was the emergence of the generic salesman of any and all products, whose talents equipped him to peddle life insurance and soap with equal flair. He was not confined to one city, or even to cities, for by train and ship he could now traverse whole countries and even continents. Thus there emerged the salesman who could sell almost anything to anyone anywhere. The department store was but an extension of this technologically based expansion of sales, and much more than a big building in the centre of a city. Through its mail-order catalogues, particularly those of Eaton's and Simpson's, it could reach all but the most remote consumers with a range of enticements not offered by the most tireless individual salesman.

Towards the end of the nineteenth century, various guides to selling were published, and, on his death, McConnell owned at least three copies of a salesman's manual called *Ginger Talks* by Worthington C. Holman. Holman had worked for the National Cash Register Company, commonly known as the Cash, in which McConnell himself was to own substantial shares. Holman dedicated his book to the president of the Cash, John Henry Patterson (1844–1922), a legendary figure credited with turning "the dynamics and art form of salesmanship into a partially disciplined vocation, if not quite a bona fide profession."[13] Patterson's most famous disciple was Thomas J. Watson (1874–1956), who developed International Business Machines (IBM) into not merely the biggest computer-manufacturer in the world but also perhaps the most successful corporate educator of salesmen in the twentieth century, such that large Japanese corporations were to adopt its teaching methods for their salesmen.

The qualities of an effective salesman, as taught in *Ginger Talks*, have not changed much – hard work, enthusiasm, belief in the product, earnestness, and warmth of personality. Important, too, are knowledge of the product, an armoury of unanswerable arguments, effective time management, cheerfulness, courtesy, tact, fortitude, exuberance, and intelligence. Intensity, constant study, knowledge of human nature, perseverance, honesty with the self, an interest in others, flexibility, and initiative are also addressed by Holman.

Comradely as it may have been, Goulding's breathed an atmosphere that was athletic and competitive – two adjectives that sum up much in McConnell's career more generally. A photograph of this period shows McConnell as the lithe young man who had won first prize in the Five Mile Handicap bicycle race, an annual event held by the Goulding's staff. To the end of his life, McConnell kept a handsome engraved silver coffee-pot commemorating this victory.

Goulding's seems to have been a hothouse for the ambitious. One mentor there was J.D.D. Lloyd, later a journalist, who wrote to McConnell in 1904 to congratulate

George Goulding and Sons, annual staff bicycle race
in 1897; first prize, five-mile handicap, won from
scratch by J.W. McConnell. Private collection.

him on his rapid rise in the company. Comparing a letter from McConnell to a "waft from the ocean" or "the smell of a dinner of steak and onions to a hungry man,"[14] Lloyd reflected on "the brotherly and friendly instinct that has stirred my heart for you ever since I saw you as a raw youth from school in that basement at 55 Bay St." He attributed McConnell's success to "the Great Father of All," and he counselled, as the only way to live, "hewing straight to the line [and] let[ting] the chips fall where they may." Lloyd concluded with remarks that might well have been McConnell's own: "My great trouble is that I have always been cramped. I love big things, big people, big business because it all is educative. It makes us big. We none of us know of the extent of our possibilities, but we frequently lack the opportunity."

Goulding's as well as Holman taught McConnell to be ingratiating and charming as well as aggressive, and to project the image of a successful, highly respectable

McConnell probably when he was a bookkeeper at
Goulding's, c.1895. Private collection.

white-collar worker in order to engender confidence. Other photographs apparently
taken during his years at Goulding's show an extremely dapper young man with a big
gold watch on a chain. His interest in clothes was never to diminish, so that several
years later he could write with both experience and confidence of ribbons and fab-
rics to his extremely fashion-conscious fiancée, and for fifteen years he was to run a
whole department store devoted to fashion, largely by himself. Yet he mixed disdain
for dressing up and fussing generally with extreme fastidiousness about his appearance, with the consequence that he even in later years he could wear immaculately
clean and pressed but still distinctly worn clothes without any self-consciousness.
Even after he had become a very rich man, on hot days at his office on St James Street
in Montreal, he would hang his shirt outside a window to dry. He would always do
his best to meet public expectations, immaculately turned out and conscious of his
good looks.

It was at this early stage, at Goulding's, that McConnell developed the daily habits of austerity and discipline that would mark his life to the end. Even in old age and long after he had retired from sales, every morning he would rise to "battle my cold bath," as he described it, as though readying himself for his first "cold call" of the day. He would brush his hair, first one way and then the other, presumably to rid it of dandruff, and scrupulously follow other toilet rituals to ensure that there was nothing to offend a prospective client. He would, of course, touch no alcohol, and he displayed restraint in what he ate. While others would devour soufflés and other elaborate desserts, he would confine himself to fresh fruit. He preferred reading to conversation, and even with guests present he would retire at ten in the evening.

This was the heyday of the cult of the self-made man, epitomized by the stories of Horatio Alger. For McConnell, being self-made involved hard work but not heroism. There was no Herculean struggle in his self-creation through work, but there was method. Strength, fortitude, and determination were not enough. Also needed were initiative, prudence, and, most important, education. Knowledge, in the form of skills rather than of scholarship, was power. For one of McConnell's early partners, Hudson Allison, shorthand was the key. For McConnell himself, it was bookkeeping; indeed, from his first employment at Goulding's in the 1890s, he was known essentially as a bookkeeper. Keeping track of income and expenditure, valuing assets – it was all like breathing to him. In this he was not unusual. Bookkeeping was then the widely perceived route to business success, wherever it was studied. In 1867, 23 per cent of Ontario secondary-school students were studying it, while by 1897, 48 per cent were doing so, the same percentage as were studying stenography and typing.[15] These studies were purely practical in purpose, and they formed part of systematic "self-help" programs that the students devised for themselves to advance in their careers. In McConnell's case, he would always feel more comfortable with accountants than with lawyers; and numbers rather than words were his tools of choice.

During his years at Goulding's, McConnell also began his life-long association with the Young Men's Christian Association which had opened its first branch in North America in Montreal in 1852. The new Toronto "Y" building of 1888, replacing one on Queen Street and not to be confused by the even newer "Y" opened in 1913 on College Street near Elizabeth Street, was at Yonge and McGill streets. It was minutes from the McConnells' lodgings on Yonge Street and then on Gerrard Street and (in 1894) from their confectioner's shop on the southwest corner of Yonge and College streets.[16] At least one of the Goulding brothers was active in this branch. The "Y" was an overwhelmingly Protestant but non-denominational society with particularly strong Methodist and Presbyterian as well as Congregational and Baptist connections. As an educational as well as a recreational centre, it ran a business school, one of the few places where young men might study such new disciplines as advertising. It is possible that McConnell learned how to be a bookkeeper there.

Toronto YMCA Building with the British American Business College
attached. City of Toronto Archives, SC 497–27

As the nineteenth century was drawing to a close, even apart from its business
school, the Toronto YMCA was starting to offer exactly the sort of support that
McConnell needed, and indeed it seemed designed with men like him in mind. As
early as the late 1880s, there had been growing dissatisfaction in the YMCA movement
with the "rescue work" that it had been conducting among "sinners," presumably
chiefly female prostitutes. This dissatisfaction led to a new emphasis: the "prevention" of loss among "young men newly arrived in the city from rural areas."[17] The
focus was now on respectable, "normal" men, perhaps somewhat sceptical, and especially on young clerks in banks and stores. For them, the Toronto "Y" devised a program to provide for "social, intellectual and spiritual development," as distinct from
the more traditional emphasis on evangelism, jail visitation, tract distribution, and
Bible study.

The practical business and administrative background of the YMCA directors
in Toronto gave real authority to its educational programs. They saw the "Y" "as a
means of drawing young men away from ... 'evil' towards 'approved recreations' ...
[of] instilling solid virtues which provided their own lives with direction and satisfaction and which formed, they believed, the moral structure upon which social progress was based."[18] Through their understanding of the Gospel, these leaders loudly
opposed what they saw as capitalism without charity, in the broadest sense of the

word. As the prominent lawyer and politician Samuel Blake had declared to YMCA members in Ontario and Quebec in 1875: "Fix this therefore in your minds … there are few things more contemptible than a rich man who stands upon his riches … Have money by all means, as you must as to enable you to pay your tailor's bills; but never set your heart on what they call making a fortune."[19]

Not only were selfishness and materialism evils: honesty, compassion, charity, and fairness in human relations were virtues. So were cleanliness and "clean living" generally. In the "Y" ethos there was no place for alcohol consumption, gambling, sexual vice, and desecration of the Sabbath. The YMCA thus reinforced the same ethos that Charles Bard had instilled in McConnell in Muskoka. It inculcated an ethos of intelligent but not intellectual men. There was nothing in it to favour the philosophically speculative or the theologically abstruse. Some of McConnell's surviving letters contain passages taken almost verbatim from YMCA tracts, complete with the ejaculatory preface "Poor fools!"

The "Y" also committed itself to developing its members' physical fitness to complement their mental and spiritual fitness. In 1890 the Toronto YMCA began noting that the gymnasium, in its new building, was attracting "more young men than any other department of our Association."[20] The education of the physique was in the service of the *whole* man – body, mind, and soul. It was possibly here that McConnell developed his lifelong interest in athletics for young people, at least in part as a way to keep them from unhealthy temptations. He himself was to remain physically active for nearly all his life. He rode and played golf whenever he could; he swam in summer and cross-country skied in winter. As late as 1936, while on a world cruise at the age of fifty-nine, he was still playing tennis two or three times a day. Of all the many later causes that he supported, probably none was dearer to his heart than boys' clubs, with their athletic facilities for boys and later girls of poor families.

While many in the 1890s were railing against the evils of capitalism, the YMCA was preaching the creation of moral and intellectual capital through investment. The Toronto branch sponsored "practical talks" on history and business. A.E. Ames, who had founded his own increasingly successful stockbrokerage in 1889, when he was only twenty-three, was one of its lecturers. As the announcement of these talks concluded, the best investment of all is "of oneself in the service of God … the only investment which always brings lasting and satisfactory returns." The branch also published, in 1897, a booklet entitled *A Talk with Young Men about Investments*. Disclaiming any reference to the gold rushes in the "Klondyke and the Yukon," this cited a saying by Benjamin Franklin: "The best investment a young man can make of his money is to put it into his head." A little money, it continued, "accompanied with time and grit, goes a long way when invested in self-improvement." The "capital investments" that it described included courses on business arithmetic, penmanship, and composition, so that acquiring practical knowledge was itself an investment.

In addition to its practical talks, the Toronto "Y" offered eight Bible classes a week. Through them, as well as through its bicycle and chess clubs and social reunions, it claimed that "a hearty SOCIAL SPIRIT permeates our Building. Each evening a committee of members is on hand to greet strangers and 'show the opportunities for investment.'" It is unclear to what extent McConnell was able to take advantage of the YMCA's social facilities. But any contact with the "Y" at all was bound to introduce him to leading businessmen of the city.

These men included the founders of some of the principal businesses of Canada in the twentieth century. In 1896–97 Samuel Blake was the Toronto branch's president and Harris Henry Fudger its first vice-president. Blake's law firm, and in particular his partner Z.A. Lash, was closely connected with the railway builder and financier William Mackenzie. Fudger owned a wholesale-goods company and was a founder of Sherbourne Street Methodist Church. In 1897 Fudger joined two of his fellow Sunday school teachers from this church in a new business venture. One was Ames, who was a son-in-law of the banker Senator George Augustus Cox. The other was a meat-packer and a trustee of the Toronto "Y," Joseph Flavelle. Fudger, Ames, and Flavelle took over the Robert Simpson Company on the death of its founder in 1898. McConnell came to know Fudger's assistant, and later (in 1929) successor to both Fudger and Flavelle as the president of Simpson's, Charles Luther Burton. Burton's book, *A Sense of Urgency: Memoirs of a Canadian Merchant*, published in 1952, McConnell was to describe as a source of wisdom for any young man. With Ames and Flavelle, McConnell was to do a wide variety of business for years, and from all of these men he absorbed sufficient interest in department stores, in particular, to open his own in Montreal only a little more than a decade later, in 1910.

Beyond the moral precepts of the Y, how did such men see the function of "capital?" To a bookkeeper such as McConnell, capital was not a vague or an abstract concept, and he was not to become a distinguished capitalist without a clear understanding of how to exploit it. This same understanding formed the basis of his philanthropy and established this philanthropy as a very modern phenomenon, distinct from traditional charity. In a strictly business, as opposed to Y, context, capital played an organizational function and had to be understood in terms of keeping books. The dynamic concept of "capital" differs from the static concept of "wealth" as displayed in treasure, art and architecture, or mercantilist ideas. It was a resource, an *asset*, of a corporation *intended for continuing, productive use*.[21] The capitalist's money produced more money by circulating from one investment to another: the money "therefore is not spent, it is merely advanced."[22] The system is dynamic: money under capitalism cannot sit back contentedly but must always be in search of new opportunities for increasing itself.[23]

As a bookkeeper McConnell had to constantly keep track of his assets and liabilities. An asset account told the story of the results of his capital expenditure and revealed the result of the administration of properties. A liability account told the story of his methods of *financing* and of *obligations entered into to obtain capital.* As a capitalist, McConnell's duty was to keep the money flowing, and not to hoard it or to let it stagnate. It was to capitalize whatever he touched, whether it was an isolated business venture, a new corporation, a church, or society as a whole.

Capital for McConnell was never about apparent wealth. It was crucially important not to fantasize about prospects. Capital resources, such as shares owned in other companies, had to be valued in the books at their original cost. If they were tangible property, bookkeepers had to make an allowance for depreciation.

These concepts were at the core of McConnell's mind and his integrity. Although he left several notebooks with occasional musings on the venality of others, there is no hint that he ever doubted his own integrity. His Methodism inculcated in him the necessity for constant, probably daily, self-examination, and so he had plenty of opportunity to question his own conscience. As one modern historian has observed, double-entry bookkeeping had effects that exceeded transcription and calculation. One of its *social* effects was to proclaim the honesty of merchants as a group. One of its *epistemological* effects was to make the formal effect of the double-entry system, which drew on the rule-bound system of arithmetic, *seem* to guarantee the accuracy of the details that it recorded.[24] These two kinds of effects reinforced each other.

All of McConnell's closest office colleagues were primarily bookkeepers. Although he jealously guarded the secrets of his ledgers from the public, these ledgers served as testimony to his honesty among those who had access.

Beyond its private use, with the codification of its rules bookkeeping became a public system of accounting. It produced public knowledge, for example in declaring that a firm's profit was legitimate, a public declaration of credibility. Bookkeeping not only recorded but also reworked data according to rules, thus seeming to make rule-governed writing a guarantee of the accuracy and the transparency of the information there recorded.[25] This appearance was reinforced by the interchangeability of bookkeepers. For Protestant capitalists bookkeeping had long been a mirror of conscience. In the statement of assets and liabilities, "the balance conjured up both the scales of justice and the symmetry of God's world. It was profoundly egalitarian both numerically and even politically. Because the numbers added to make the balance often referred to no outside reality, double-entry bookkeeping could be a system of self-actualizing *fictions* and not a system of total disclosure. This is reflected in the difference that McConnell and other businessmen typically kept between private and public accounting records. The "memorial," or record of all income and expenditures from day to day, had to be available to his employees. But the inventory and the journal, where initial entries were made, were secret because it was generally accepted that nobody had a right to know a man's estate.

Up to the 1930s Methodists in particular seldom if ever acknowledged even to themselves that their bookkeeping was delusional. Their critics, as in the tramways dispute of 1910–25 described in chapter 7, accused McConnell of furthering this delusion – if not of perpetrating fraud – but these challenges came in the midst of a revolution not merely of how to evaluate corporate assets but also of establishing new accounting norms.

All this was in the future. For the period covered by this chapter, it can be assumed that for McConnell bookkeeping formed the nexus between conscience and business and other activities. As the foremost dry goods merchant in Toronto, Senator John Macdonald, a convert from Presbyterianism to Methodism, preached to his staff, bookkeeping should also protect the public. The two axioms of business were truth and honesty: "Buy the truth and sell it not" and 'A false balance is abomination to the Lord." A false balance was not "the beam merely which is always so adjusted as to placed the customer at a disadvantage, but the selling of a thing for what it is not; taking advantage of the inexperience of the customer to secure one's own profit."[26]

In addition to a dynamic but analytical understanding of capital, in Toronto McConnell learned about leverage, which went well beyond saving cash and investing it to produce more. Largely because they knew one another, the Methodist businessmen, and Cox in particular, relied on "investment credit" – that is, wealth that did not yet exist in tangible form. This has been called the "money of the mind" ("credit" is Latin for "he believes"). Through such institutions as the Canadian Bank of Commerce, they lent money beyond their cash reserves, in the expectation that their borrowers would employ their loans productively, pay interest, and repay the principal.

Although banking and leverage were hardly new, the transformation of business partnerships into corporations offering securities to the public was relatively so. Such pioneers of the investment industry as Ames sold the stocks and bonds of such entrepreneurs as Flavelle, often backed up by nothing but the expectation of a future return on the products of their companies. They were capitalists who made "bets on the future." Their bets were, however, calculated, the antithesis of blind gambles. The use of credit implied credibility, of the business "propositions" being financed as well as of the partners doing the financing. Although business failure was common, reputation in such a small business world counted for much. As the expression went, a man's word was his bond; and ostracism, in the sense of no further business, was the price of betrayal. The Protestantism that nearly all within this world professed did much to inhibit outright fraud, though not necessarily poor judgment or even recklessness leading to bankruptcy.

The practice of this religion was designed to build character, in particular to overcome flaws and destructive temptations. In addition to the "Y," McConnell in these years became associated with the Lord's Day Alliance, a Sabbatarian organization led by Blake, and with the temperance movement, a cause still dear to his heart and led by such prominent Methodists as Hart Massey, the leading manufacturer of farm equipment, and Timothy Eaton, the retailer, as well as Flavelle. Sabbatarians aimed at more than keeping Sunday free of work, business, and frivolity. They wanted it free for the cultivation of Christian fellowship and for attendance at church.

In Muskoka, McConnell had received religious teaching from Bard, a Methodist, but whether the McConnells belonged to a particular religious denomination is uncertain. After arriving in Toronto, however, his denominational affiliation began to take clearer shape. In Toronto, Methodism was flourishing and many if not most of the leading businessmen were Scots Irish in origin like him, as well as Methodists. It was common for them to convert to Methodism usually from Presbyterianism after their arrival in Canada; Timothy Eaton of the department store was the most famous of these converts. What characterized Methodism was not so much theology as cheerfulness combined with personal discipline and productivity, which seemed to many far more suitable to life in a new country than the historic Presbyterianism of the north of Ireland. Both the "Y" and in the temperance movement were strongly Methodist.

McConnell also joined the Epworth League, a burgeoning association of young Methodists. The Christian fellowship that he came to know through them reinforced whatever he had learned about community and cooperation in Muskoka. It remained his sustaining vision for the ideal society for the remainder of his life. Founded in Cleveland in 1889, the League was an offshoot of Christian Endeavour, an interdenominational youth movement set up in Maine in 1881. By 1897, it had 17,500 chapters and 1,600,000 members around the world, including 1,800 chapters and 80,000 members in Canada. In July 1897 Toronto was the scene of the Third International Convention of the League, and its crowded meetings took over Presbyterian and Congregational as well as Methodist churches in the city.[27]

The constitution of the General Epworth League, the umbrella organization, committed it to "promoting intelligent and vital piety among the young people of the Methodist Church; training them in active Christian work; promoting the study of the Bible and Christian literature."[28] An active or full member of the League pledged as follows, with emphasis added:

Taking Christ as my example, and trusting in the help of the Holy Spirit, I promise that I will endeavor to learn and do my Heavenly Father's will; that I will make stated seasons of private prayer and the daily study of the Bible the rule of my life. As an active member of the League, I will, except when excusable to my master, be present at and take part in the meetings in the Christian Endeavor Department, and will be true to all my duties as a member of the

Church. I will abstain from all amusements and habits upon which I cannot ask God's blessing. *I will honor God with my substance as he has prospered me. I will endeavor by kindly words and deeds to cultivate the spirit of Christian friendship and bring my young associates to Christ.*

Members had committees to join. The "lookout committee" was not only to recruit new members but also "affectionately to look after and reclaim any that seem indifferent to their duties, as outlined in the pledge, and to report each month on the spiritual condition of the members of the league to the Superintendent of the Circuit." The temperance and "social purity" committee was dedicated to "the promotion of total abstinence *from*, and the legal prohibition *of*, alcoholic beverages, and also to seek to elevate public opinion regarding the law of personal purity, and the same moral standard for men and women."

Once a month, there was a Consecration Meeting "for religious experience and testimony, at which each active member spoke of "his progress in the Christian life" or renewed his or her vows of consecration. And anyone could "express his feelings by an appropriate verse of Scripture or other quotation." The pledges were also read and the roll called, "and the responses of the members present shall be considered as a renewed expression of allegiance to the pledge." Anyone obliged to be absent had to "send a request to be excused by some one who attends, accompanied, if possible, with at least a verse of Scripture, to be read in response to his name at the roll call."

If a member was absent without excuse, the lookout committee was "in a kind and brotherly spirit [to] ascertain the reason for the absence." Running throughout these provisions for discipline and fellowship was the notion of "affection." There was no hint of the coercive or the punitive. The relationship of the individual soul to God was to be supported and not forced, and charity was to facilitate this relationship, with a view to salvation. The extreme simplicity of the League's piety suggests its openness to all, regardless of denominational affiliation.

The Epworth League, like the YMCA, was designed above all to counter the exodus of young people from the church, a trend that was of increasing concern to many Protestants by 1900. In this work, the League and "Y" were assisted by a modernized Sunday school system, one that specifically aimed at boys from age ten to the mid-teens and that offered weekday as well as Sunday sessions. And, here again, McConnell was involved. In Christmas 1901 McConnell received a book of poetry as an expression of thanks for his work as a teacher in a mission school which, given the date, might have been in either Toronto or Montreal. Toronto seems the more likely, since he moved to Montreal only in 1901. If it was in Toronto, it is almost certain that it was a Sunday school connected with the Fred Victor Mission at Queen and Jarvis streets, the principal Methodist effort in Toronto, which McConnell passed daily on his way to work. This mission, operated by a board with representatives from various downtown Methodist churches, housed in a building constructed by Hart Massey in 1893–94, and operated by volunteers, ministered to the "wretched poor." Besides accommodation and recreational facilities, it offered Bible and Sunday school classes as well as temperance and Junior Epworth League meetings. It also did outreach work in the city's slums. By 1900, the mission's Sunday school had 150 pupils taught by 18 teachers.

It is also possible that McConnell himself was a beneficiary of the work of the Fred Victor Mission, or more probably of its predecessor, the Jarvis Street Mission, in the early 1890s. It was to precisely such children as himself, in St John's Ward where he was living, that this mission devoted so much effort. Indeed, the two essentially Methodist places of worship in the Ward, the Agnes Street Church and the Centre Avenue Mission, were connected to the Fred Victor in 1894, and this arrangement survived until about 1900.

In any case, for over a half-century following his work as a mission teacher, McConnell was to do much to replicate the work of the Fred Victor Mission in Montreal. This was most evident in his fundraising for the YMCA, his building of boys' clubs, and his unwavering support for the work of evangelism of the Methodist (and then the United) Church and for such causes as the Old Brewery Mission. In addition, his generous support and work for nurses probably also dates to his acquaintance with the work of Fred Victor deaconesses, some of whom appear to have attended his sister Sue on her deathbed in 1902.

Napoleon is said to have counselled that in order to understand a man you must know what was happening in his world when he was twenty. In the case of McConnell, this would have been 1897–98. In this year in particular, it was becoming abundantly clear that the dominance of Methodist culture in Toronto was on the wane. The city voted against the legal prohibition of alcohol in a national plebiscite (the country as a whole voted narrowly for it), and Toronto also adopted Sunday streetcar service. McConnell's positions on both issues were revealing.

At this time, campaigners against alcohol were divided into two camps – one favouring temperance and the other favouring outright prohibition. Although McConnell was a teetotaller and associated for decades with such unbending Methodist prohibitionists as S.D. Chown as well as such prohibitionist politicians as G.E. Foster and Sydney Fisher, he himself never was an active supporter of prohibition. Nor did he support even the Dominion Alliance, the umbrella organization for the temperance societies. His teetotallism seems not to have been part of his political agenda. Indeed, he was from 1907 if not before closely associated with Montreal brewers, such as members of the Molson and the Dawes families, and even with a major importer and manufacturer of whisky, Marcelin Wilson. Like his religion, his teetotallism remained essentially a matter for his individual conscience.

Even more telling for McConnell's future career was the apparent equanimity with which in 1897 he may have accepted the running of Toronto streetcars on Sunday. Although his actual position at the time is unknown, he was in the employ of an advocate of Sunday streetcars, Arthur Peuchen. Further, within a few years McConnell himself would be a major promoter of street railways in Montreal, where neither Sabbatarianism nor temperance had ever been a major political cause. The streetcars of Toronto belonged to the Toronto Railway, owned by William Mackenzie since 1892. Sunday service, however, had been banned ever since. The question of whether to let people ride streetcars on Sunday split Toronto down the middle, with fissures running through all the religious denominations.

In favour of Sunday streetcars were Mackenzie and the Citizens' Sunday Car Association, which included eight or nine Anglicans (including Peuchen), two Presbyterians, a Baptist, one Methodist, and one Roman Catholic.[29] They argued that electrification had made the street railway a utility, and that the increase of the population had made easy and cheap transport for townspeople an "important social and moral consideration."[30] Sunday cars would afford relative equality to the poor in gaining access to open-air and public places. They would carry more people to church and healthy recreation, and free the city from the tyranny of a slim Sabbatarian majority. Over 32,000 votes were cast in a referendum on the subject on 15 May 1897, and the supporters of Sunday streetcar service won, attracting 16,273 votes to 16,051 against. On 23 May, Sunday cars ran for the first time in Toronto.

The Masseys, though better known for their farm equipment, were heavily involved at that time in the manufacture of bicycles, the chief competitor of the streetcar. Two other prominent Methodists, G.A. Cox and Joseph Flavelle, had hedged their bets in this controversy, investing not only in the Massey CCM bicycle company but also in William Mackenzie's Toronto Railway and, later, CCM's reincarnation as the Russell Motor Car Company. McConnell did likewise; he, too, held shares in both CCM and the Toronto Railway Company.[31] Apparently, for him as for others, the line between God and Mammon could not be cleanly drawn even by the Sabbatarianism that he had firmly espoused.

McConnell, c.1900.

CHAPTER THREE

Selling Wood Products and Settling Down, 1899–1907

All things come to those who hustle while they wait.

J.W. McConnell to Lily Griffith, 17 January 1904[1]

What happened during this vague period would probably read like Horatio Alger, but neither McConnell nor any of his associates will tell the story. However, one fact is that he started out by selling coal in Toronto and moved there to Montreal, believing probably that colder weather there would mean more chance to sell coal. Shortly after arriving in Montreal, after he'd taken a good look along St. James Street he told a friend, "Within a year I'll own a home, a car and have $5,000 in the bank." He succeeded.

"Sugar Baron," *New Liberty*, March 1949, 23

Out of the deforestation that ravaged the landscape of nineteenth-century Canada there remained enough "waste" to spawn a new pulp and paper industry as well as many other industries with which McConnell was to be associated, beginning with charcoal manufacture. Canadian hardwoods, such as hard maple, yellow birch, and beech, were especially productive in charcoal production. For centuries, people had been engaging in the distillation of hardwood – or heating it in the absence of air – to produce charcoal. The Canadian wood-distillate industry had begun in 1887, when the Rathbun Company, of Deseronto, Ontario, began to convert the vapours from charcoal distillation into saleable products. Ten years later, a rival to Rathbun emerged in the form of the Standard Chemical Company of Toronto.

William Mackenzie set up Standard Chemical as one of his minor ventures in 1897, installing one of his sons as a vice-president.[2] In Eldon Township, two hundred miles north of Toronto, Mackenzie's family had built corduroy (log) roads and manufactured wood shingles and turpentine. In 1874–76 Mackenzie joined James Ross and Ross's land surveyor and office boy, Herbert Holt, in building the Credit Valley Railway. The Canadian Pacific Railway took this over in 1883, and then Ross and Holt became responsible for the completion of the CPR under William Van Horne. They contracted Mackenzie to build bridges in the Rockies, and with Donald Mann and Mackenzie they extended other railways across the west.

In 1891–94 Mackenzie electrified the horse-drawn Winnipeg street railway or transit system. With Ross, Van Horne, G.A. Cox, and Joseph Flavelle, he did the same for the Toronto Railway in 1892–94, and by 1897 he had followed suit with the Montreal system owned by Louis-Joseph Forget. Within a year, Forget and his nephew Rodolphe Forget owned the street railways in both Toronto and Montreal, with R.J. Fleming (a former mayor of Toronto) and Charles Porteous of Quebec as managers of them. The Forgets and Holt were also consolidating control over electrical distribution in Montreal. Mackenzie, the broker Henry Pellatt, Fleming, and others were likewise bidding for control of electrical distribution in Toronto. Thus, in joining Standard Chemical at the age of twenty-two, McConnell was entering into the outer orbit of some of the most ambitious businessmen in Canada. Mackenzie in particular was also making Canadian technology, in the electrification of urban transit, famous abroad, especially in Spain and Brazil.

Mackenzie left the presidency of Standard Chemical to Arthur Godfrey Peuchen, since 1879 a pioneer of the Canadian paint industry. After his marriage in 1893 to the sister of an Orillia lumberman, Peuchen had become acquainted with wood and its by-products, while also supporting Mackenzie and the Citizens' Sunday Car Association in the battle over Sunday streetcar service in 1897. The work of Standard Chemical was to transform hardwood waste through distillation. In addition to charcoal, this distillation yielded pyroligenous acid (wood vinegar), from which derived acetic acid, acetone, and methyl or wood alcohol. Acetone was used in smokeless powder or cordite, a vital ingredient in explosives, and Peuchen would become the first British subject to manufacture it.

In 1899, within two years of its start, Standard Chemical had increased its authorized capital from $80,000 to $450,000 and its sales from $5,084 to $117,971. It was in this year that McConnell began to work as a travelling salesman out of its headquarters in the new Gooderham Building at 49 Wellington Street in Toronto, a few minutes' walk from Goulding's. In joining Standard Chemical, McConnell made a big leap financially, starting on a salary of $100 a month that rapidly rose to $200 and then $300. It was at Standard Chemical that he also began to display his capacity for management and leadership. Within six years, he was both its second vice-president and secretary.

In his first year at Standard Chemical, McConnell accompanied Peuchen on trips through the Ottawa valley in search of sources of hardwood waste, the two of them travelling in luxurious Pullman railway cars. Peuchen seems from the very start to have been grooming McConnell as his successor, and he gave him a taste for high society that McConnell was never to lose. Peuchen was a vice-commodore of the Royal Canadian Yacht Club, a member of the Jockey and Hunt and other clubs, and a captain in the Queen's Own Rifles, which was commanded from 1906 by the broker

Colonel Sir Henry Pellatt and Major Arthur Peuchen,
probably reviewing the Queen's Own Rifles of Canada in
Toronto, c.1910. City of Toronto Archives, SC 244-4026.

Henry Pellatt. With Pellatt, he was a governor of the Grace Hospital, to which he gave
an X-ray department. He led a very fashionable life, with a house on Jarvis Street.
McConnell often went there and also to Woodlands, Peuchen's enormous summer
house on Lake Simcoe, on the tennis courts of which he probably learned one of his
favourite forms of recreation.

McConnell is first mentioned in the minutes of the Standard Chemical board in
November 1900, when he was appointed to run its new office in Montreal. On the
same day, the board considered an arrangement to manufacture acetone for Nobel's
Explosive Company of Glasgow.[3] The two events were not unrelated. By now, with
an arms race between England and Germany well under way, Standard Chemical
had big plans to expand. There was a growing demand for acetone, and Germany
and Austria were the only places in Europe where it was produced. Canada, with its
apparently limitless forests, seemed the ideal source to supply acetone to the empire.

The prospect of an acetone contract with Nobel's would force Standard to search beyond Ontario for hardwood, and its venture in Quebec was its first step in this direction, although McConnell's first duties were to sell its charcoal to Montrealers.

In Montreal, McConnell was responsible for the company's warehouse and charcoal department at 290 St James Street in St Henry Ward[4] as well for its plant on Notre-Dame Street. At the time, American charcoal was cheap and competitive in Canada, and so in October McConnell and Peuchen went to Ottawa to lobby for a duty on American imports. The outlook seemed good, and the company also began negotiations to buy timber limits for a charcoal factory outside Montreal, in Cookshire in the Eastern Townships. By February 1902, McConnell had been placed in charge of this new venture as well.

The move to Montreal was made easier by a personal development. The very first object of McConnell's affections there had been apparently Molly Jones, one of three sisters from Belleville studying nursing at the Royal Victoria Hospital, a cause that would always be especially dear to his heart. With George Goodfellow, his neighbour in a rooming house and later a prominent timber merchant, he came to know all three Jones sisters. One was to marry Goodfellow. Molly herself was to marry Frank Knox, who was to become McConnell's lieutenant as manager of the Montreal Securities Company, founded by McConnell in 1909.

In the summer of 1901, however, at a tea party, McConnell met Lily May Gornall Griffith, who after about 1918 was generally known as Lil. She was a daughter of the Reverend Dr Thomas Griffith, the minister of Douglas Methodist Church, and McConnell caught her attention by throwing a piece of cake into her teacup. For him, evidently, it was love at first sight, but Lily herself – to say nothing of her mother – was not so sure. She rejected his proposal of marriage in September 1902, apparently because she thought his prospects were uncertain. Still, though she had other admirers, such as Stanley McLean, eventually president of Canadian Packers, McConnell eventually won her over, and they became engaged in January 1904.

Apart from his duties in Montreal and Cookshire, McConnell spent much of the first few years of the new century on the road, from Nova Scotia to Ontario and down to Michigan and Minnesota. He often returned to Toronto, where Peuchen was placing increasing responsibilities upon him. Now he stayed at the new and luxurious King Edward Hotel, but he always made time to see his family. In December 1902 his sister Sue died of typhoid, which was a terrible blow to him. The McConnells then moved to Humber Bay, west of the city, and Jack dutifully visited them there, finding Lizzie teaching in a mission Sunday school and his father raising songbirds. In February 1904 McConnell reported to Lily that both his mother and his sister Lizzie had been particularly delighted by their engagement.

With Lily's help, McConnell put down roots as a Montrealer. He had been living in boarding houses, first at 4077 Tupper Street, near Atwater Street and the growing

St James Cathedral and the YMCA Building, Dominion Square, 1890s.
McCord Museum, V–2549.A.

suburb of Westmount, and later at 13 Belmont Street. This was just south of Dorchester Street (later René Lévesque Boulevard), off Beaver Hall Hill, which led to Victoria Square and St James Street, where he was to work for most of his life. McConnell also spent much time at the local YMCA, since 1892 on the northeast corner of Dorchester and Metcalfe streets, facing Dominion Square, the future site of the Sun Life Building. Dominion Square boasted several churches, and McConnell's life was as wrapped up with religion as with business. Across Dominion Square from the YMCA in 1901, at the corner of Dorchester and Windsor (later Peel) streets, was the Dominion Methodist Church. Although his name does not appear in its records, the Dominion was probably a focus of McConnell's social and religious life for his first year in the city. The Roman Catholic Cathedral of St James, the Anglican St George's Church, the American Presbyterian Church, the Emmanuel Church, the Spurgeon Tabernacle, and St Paul's Presbyterian Church were all within a few minutes' walk of Dominion Methodist. The young McConnell was fond of hearing sermons, and he went from church to church in search of good ones.

For a twenty-four-year-old young man from rural Ontario, Montreal was a complex place, full of lingering resentments and grievances, envy and snobbery, dazzling display, and some of the worst social and economic problems on the continent.

McConnell chopping wood, c.1905.
McCord Museum M2003.8.6.5023.78

Though the largest city of Canada, it had fewer than 300,000 people, and its English-speaking businessmen comprised a tiny minority of them. McConnell was joining what was in effect little more than a prosperous village, whose inhabitants not only did business with one other but also intermarried, ultimately fashioning a great network of family and business ties that stretched across Canada to the British Isles and the United States. Reinforcing the social divide between this group and the rest of the city's inhabitants was physical stratification. The city was built on Mount Royal, and generally the higher one lived the higher was one's social status. There was actually an escarpment that marked the boundary between the poor and the middle classes, which extended west from Guy Street to the suburb of Lachine, where the obstacle posed by the rapids in the St Lawrence River blocked entry into the Great Lakes, rendering Montreal the great inland port of Canada. Dorchester Street, at the top of the escarpment, was the divide, and most of the poverty was to be found in what the social reformer and shoe manufacturer Herbert Ames called "the city below the hill," also the title of his exposé of social ills, which was based on his YMCA lectures and published in 1902.

McConnell shooting a rifle, c.1905.
Private collection.

Pine Avenue was the northern boundary of the Square Mile, sometimes called Golden, bounded by Pine Avenue, Côte-des-Neiges Road, Sherbrooke Street, and University Street, where almost all of the most established English-speaking Montrealers lived. It was a small community, smaller than Bracebridge or Beaumaris, and McConnell was to come to know almost everyone in it – from the Ogilvies on Redpath Street to the Anguses and the Drummonds on Drummond Street, the Hosmers on Stanley Street, the Rosses on Peel Street, and the Baumgartens and Josephs on McTavish Street. Its two social centres, the Mount Royal Club and the Ritz-Carlton Hotel, roughly facing each other on Sherbrooke Street, were to be erected in the next decade. The little stretch of Sherbrooke Street extending from there to McGill housed (or was to house) the tobacco magnate Sir William Macdonald, the brokers Louis-Joseph Forget and Isaak Walton Killam, and Sir George Drummond of the Canada Sugar Refinery and the Bank of Montreal. At the very edge of the Square Mile, on University Street, stood the Wesleyan Theological College (of which McConnell was to serve as a governor, with a break in 1918, from 1911 to 1925) and Royal Victoria College, recently established by Lord Strathcona.

Colonel F.C. Henshaw, company director closely connected to the
Forgets and William Mackenzie, and McConnell's first mentor in selling
securities, from Colonel William Wood, *The Storied Province of Quebec*
(Toronto: Dominion Publishing 1931), vol. 3, opposite p. 121.

It was not long before McConnell gained his entrée into this world of wealth, privilege, and power. Soon after his arrival in Montreal, the Standard Chemical board
decided to finance the company's expansion by seeking new capital in Quebec. It
appointed Colonel F.C. Henshaw, with McConnell to accompany him, to solicit
subscriptions to a new issue of company stock.[5] Like Peuchen, Henshaw was a man
of various parts – a commission agent and vice-consul of Uruguay and Argentina in
Montreal, commanding officer of the Victoria Rifles, and a pillar of the Montreal
Amateur Athletic Association. More importantly, he was also a director of Mackenzie's Standard Drain Pipe Company, of the Citizens' Gas Control Company, and of
the Richelieu and Ontario Navigation Company and the Montreal Street Railway, the
last two owned by Senator Louis-Joseph Forget, perhaps the richest man in the city.

Henshaw was at the centre of a network of prominent Quebeckers, nearly all of whom would become well known to McConnell. He was a cousin of Canon F.G. Scott (father of the lawyer Frank Scott and Associate Chief Justice William Scott) and of Frederick Taylor (later Sir Frederick Williams-Taylor, general manager of the Bank of Montreal). He was also a brother-in-law of Forbes Angus, later chairman of Standard Life Assurance, who was a son of R.B. Angus, president of both the Bank of Montreal and the Canadian Pacific Railway. Forbes Angus' sisters were married to Dr W.W. Chipman, the railway engineer F.L. Wanklyn, the broker Charles Meredith, and Dr C.F. Martin.

Henshaw's late wife, Maud, had been the daughter of ironmaster John McDougall, the owner of coalmines and a railway in Nova Scotia, and Mary Cowans. These two families were united again in the following generation when Edgar Mill McDougall joined Percy Cowans in 1901 to form McDougall and Cowans, which was to be McConnell's chief brokerage firm for most of his life.

Together, Henshaw and McConnell easily sold Standard Chemical stock to investors, many of whom were to participate in McConnell's own later promotions shortly afterwards. Among them were five of the richest men of Montreal: Sir Montagu Allan of the Montreal Ocean Steamship company (and the son of Sir Hugh Allan of the original CPR syndicate), Henry Markland Molson (already a director of Standard) of Molsons Bank, Rodolphe Forget (stockbroker), James Carruthers of the Montreal Corn Exchange, and K.W. Blackwell, a civil engineer specializing in street railways. This sale of securities marked McConnell's first effort at raising money, which was to be his principal function for his entire career. In 1901–05, when McConnell was starting to sell securities, the only purchasers were the rich or at least the very established, and thus by in 1901, at the age of twenty-four, McConnell was becoming known to many of the leading business figures of the country

In December 1902 the board of Standard Chemical thanked him for his "energetic and untiring work," expressed its appreciation of "the extra work and attention given by you to the management of the charcoal department," and noted its satisfaction with his "valuable assistance and economical handling of the new factory at Cookshire." It also expressed its appreciation of "the resource and tact evidenced by you in presenting our claim to the government for the renewal of our contract [probably to supply charcoal] with them." Thus in only two years he had established a reputation for himself as a salesman of securities as well as coal and as a factory manager.

In January 1903 McConnell became a director of Standard Chemical and was named its "eastern manager." His success in marketing the new stock in Montreal led in the following May to Standard's decision both to appoint him second vice-president and to send him to England and the continent. There he was "to look into the Foreign Market and dispose of the balance of the unallotted stock … among the better class of English Investors … and if possible the patronage of the English War

Office." To dispatch McConnell on such a mission at the age of twenty-six was testimony to Peuchen's regard for him. Further testimony to the same effect came in the months leading up to McConnell's departure for Europe. Peuchen had McConnell accompany him on a trip to Ottawa in January 1904 to lobby the federal government (through Sir William Mulock, the postmaster general) for tariff protection as well as government contracts, and McConnell was back in Ottawa the following month with the same purpose in mind. Shortly afterwards, when Peuchen went for a holiday to Egypt, he put McConnell in charge of the head office in Toronto.

London in 1904 was both the centre of the greatest empire in history and the principal market for raising capital in the world. On McConnell's arrival in June, the agent general for New Brunswick, Duff Miller, did much to smooth his path, as did the introductions he carried from Peuchen and other leading Montrealers. His first impressions of the city were a mixture of awe and horror. He found it "simply disgusting to see the way the saloons are filled up on every corner, not only with men, but with poor wretched women carrying their babys [sic] in their arms and allowing them to drain the cups that the poor fool mothers have almost emptied. Its [sic] really ten times worse than murder for the poor helpless youngsters."[6] Nevertheless, he was intrigued by Speakers' Corner at Hyde Park, the Strangers' Gallery of the House of Commons, the Olde Cheshire Cheese pub in Fleet Street, and the lions at the Regent's Park Zoo. In the company of Bert (Charles Herbert) McLean, a friend from Douglas Church, who with Frank Knox was to be his right-hand man over the following thirty-five years, McConnell toured Scotland and Ireland for a few days in June. On 1 July, his twenty-seventh birthday, he reported to Lily that he had visited the National Gallery and the Royal Academy.

Accompanied by W.T.R. Preston, the Canadian emigration agent in London (and future hostile biographer of Lord Strathcona), he attended a garden party in honour of Dominion Day given by Strathcona, the high commissioner for Canada and a mentor to young Canadian businessman, at Knebworth, the Elizabethan house that Strathcona was renting. McConnell was extremely impressed with the setting, with Strathcona himself (who, he reported to Lily, was "just a dear old gentleman"), and with the elaborate arrangements for the event. The "stylish folks" in attendance had arrived by special trains "of the very highest class" from London. A band played and pipers walked through the property where the "daintiest kind of refreshments were being served continuously on the lawn in front of the castle" – a spectacle, complete with pipers, that McConnell himself would, within twenty years, carefully replicate at his own house in Dorval near Montreal. Noting that Preston's two daughters had married "wealthy young English men" who had settled £100,000 and £50,000 upon them, he asked Lily, "Don't you think you missed a good chance dearie?"[7]

Also by the end of July, his lobbying of the War Office was reaching a critical stage. As he explained to Lily: "Acetone, you know, is made from hardwood and is a very

Only extant photo of the Douglas Methodist Church, Chomedy
Street, Montreal, n.d. Private collection.

powerful liquid used chiefly for the purpose of dissolving gun cotton and is really
the basis of all manner of explosives. At the present moment the War Office are purchasing their supplies from Germany, Austria and the U.S. We [Standard Chemical]
havent [sic] commenced to make it yet, & before doing so wish to see if it is possible
to get some preference out of the gov'nt for a Canadian concern, over foreign."[8] In due
course, and through McConnell's efforts, Standard Chemical won the contract with
the War Office, a signal achievement apart from the sale of Standard shares.

In London, what is perhaps most striking is how fast he worked. On a typical
day, he could fit five appointments into a morning, and follow all of this with a business lunch. Such a schedule offered no time for idle chatter. Every minute had to be
exploited to extract new information and possibly to clinch a deal. In later years, he
would relate how Lord Overtoun, a Scottish chemical manufacturer, had begun their
conversation with "My boy, I give you three minutes!" McConnell did not hesitate
and convinced Overtoun to buy fifty Standard shares within those three minutes. Mrs
Palmer Howard, the daughter of Lord Strathcona, bought a hundred. Although many
of McConnell's sales calls failed, he did win over some of the most formidable businessmen of the time, such as G.W. Wolff, of Harland & Wolff, the largest shipbuilders in the world; Sir Andrew Noble of Armstrong, Whitworth, the chief competitors
of the arms manufacturer Vickers; and the Glasgow shipbuilder William Beardmore
(later Lord Invernairn). Another purchaser was Lord Brassey, a former governor of

Victoria (in Australia) and the father-in-in law of the future Lord Willingdon, governor general of Canada and viceroy of India, who was to be one of McConnell's closest friends. Like the more sober Strathcona, Brassey, the flashy heir to a railway fortune, seems to have set a model for McConnell of how rich men should live.

All in all, it was a breathtakingly successful sales campaign, legendary on St James Street in Montreal for decades. But McConnell remained, in his own word, a "greenhorn" in the sprawling imperial metropolis. He assured Lily that he still did not play cards or dance, much less go to the theatre, the frivolity of which he disdained. The terrifyingly fast "motres," by which he meant motor cars, attracted his attention, but he could not believe that they would ever replace horses.

Greenhorn though he may have been, McConnell met many people on this visit to England whom he was to admire for the rest of his life, including Sir Hiram Maxim.[9] Maxim was one of the most prolific inventors of his time, devising such things as automatic water sprinklers, hair-curling irons, and vacuum cleaners, pioneering the field of electrical lighting, and developing a fully automatic machine-gun – the item for which he is best known. With an associate, Trevor Dawson, Maxim had also registered several patents designed to eliminate erosion in artillery, and so he was one of the few in England likely to understand the potential of acetone. He and McConnell established a friendship – the first of several that McConnell was to enjoy with inventors – that was to last until Maxim's death in 1916. By now, the Maxim gun was the weapon of choice on the Western Front, sold by Vickers, Son and Maxim chiefly through the mysterious Basil Zaharoff, known popularly as the "merchant of death," whose signed portrait McConnell would keep for decades. Although McConnell was never an arms dealer, he was always to be interested in invention and in investing in the products for peacetime use developed during or in anticipation of war.

In August 1904 McConnell left London for Hamburg, where he had to decline a German order for $36 million of acetone since Standard Chemical was in no position to fulfil it. After a pleasant dinner with some German Jews, he journeyed on to Antwerp, where he felt "very small" beside the multilingual people he met. He raced through Brussels and Paris, where he shopped at the Galeries Lafayette for Lily.

In September, he was back in England, and, apparently with an introduction from the former Canadian prime minister, Sir Charles Tupper, whom he also met on this trip, he called on Joseph Chamberlain, once a nail-manufacturer, now mayor of Birmingham, and a former colonial secretary.[10] He had already met Austen, Watlin, and Arthur Chamberlain, and toured the Kynoch Explosive Works owned by the last two. Chamberlain, perhaps the best-dressed man in England, was almost an idol to young businessmen, the most fervent imperialist of the age and, according to McConnell, a prime minister in waiting. It was, for McConnell, the crowning event of his trip, made all the more memorable by Chamberlain's presentation to him of a signed portrait of himself. After his return to Montreal, McConnell gave a speech, probably to a church group or at the YMCA, in which he called for greater imperial centralization, a scheme dear to Chamberlain's heart and one that McConnell himself would for long espouse.

By the end of August, McConnell was quoting Napoleon to Lily: "What I do is a necessity, I am the child of destiny."[11] He returned to Montreal in September, and the Standard Chemical board formally thanked him for his "placing of 1904 stock; the establishing of a connection with the War Office; negotiations of Inland and Ocean freights and Insurance schedule on factories favorable to this Company; the closing of the sale of Pulpwood at the highest possible price in addition to your enviable reputation as a salesman." As an expression of its gratitude, the board gave him $1,000 in stock or cash, on condition that he remained "in the company's employ," and this would be followed in January 1907 with a further $6,015 as his sales commission.

McConnell's 1904 trip had given him the opportunity to study at first hand a moment of unprecedented growth for the British chemical industry well beyond wood distillation. For the remainder of his life, he would be deeply interested in shipping, mining, metal, and gases in particular. Not all his efforts to sell in Great Britain had succeeded, but meeting Sir John Brunner and Alfred Mond (later Lord Melchett), for example, led to a fascination with chemistry as the basis of new industries. Thus, within little more than twenty years after this trip to England, he would become, with Melchett, a director of International Nickel Company of Canada (INCO), as well as the Canadian Liquid Air Company; he would be closely associated with Lord McGowan, the founder of Imperial Chemical Industries (ICI); he would maintain a life-long friendship with Sir Trevor Dawson of Vickers (Maxim's partner); and, through Dawson and others, he would become involved with Canadian Vickers, Canada Steamship Lines, the Davie Shipyards, Dominion Bridge, and the Steel Company of Canada.

Besides demonstrating McConnell's considerable gifts as a salesman, the 1904 trip made plain that his constant curiosity about new industrial processes would be one of the secrets of his success as an investor. McConnell's mind had already leapt almost effortlessly from wholesale millinery at Goulding's to concentrate on inflammable liquids, effervescing acids, bone black, and gun cotton. He loved every detail, and for the rest of his life he would happily quiz quality surveyors, mechanics, and medical researchers about the most technical aspects of their work. His was a searching intelligence that transcended almost the entire industrial landscape. Even after he had become probably the richest man in Canada, he would describe himself on his passport as a "manufacturer." He was never given to pure financial speculation, for he developed early an increasingly detailed grasp of the world economy as a whole, from raw materials to finished products. And so he understood with some precision how coal was used in the production of steel, and then how a certain grade of steel was necessary in a Maxim gun, and finally how such weapons as the Maxim gun were revolutionizing battle.

Once back from Europe, McConnell assumed heavier responsibilities at Standard Chemical, but he also became increasingly restless. Production of acetone for the War Office in London was proving difficult; the Department of Inland Revenue in Ottawa decided to switch its contract for wood alcohol to the Galt Chemical Company in March 1905; and then he was criticized for placing double liability on his English subscribers for making them sign both the subscription book and transfers for the same shares.

In the meantime, McConnell's commitment to religion did not flag. Thomas Griffith, the minister of Douglas Church and his future father-in-law, was a man for whom he developed special respect. Griffith was a gifted preacher, a bluff and hearty Victorian cleric with a twinkle in his eyes and mutton-chop whiskers, and had been a leading figure among those responsible for unifying various Methodist denominations into the Methodist Church of Canada and Newfoundland in 1875. It was also in that year that Douglas Church had opened, but then it grew so fast that Sir Donald Smith (later Lord Strathcona) laid the foundation stone for a new building in 1889.

William Hanson, a prominent stockbroker, led the financing, and by the time Griffith became its minister in 1901, the church boasted many prominent businessmen in its congregation, such as G.F. Johnston (soon to be McConnell's partner) from New York Life and James Junkin from Sun Life Assurance. In 1911 they were joined by Lorne Webster, a coal merchant from Quebec, who became one of McConnell's closest friends. McConnell formally joined Douglas Church in 1903.

Probably through the Griffiths and J.W. Knox, the superintendent of the Sunday school and the father of Frank, McConnell became closely acquainted with other families – the Lymans, manufacturers of pharmaceuticals with J.W. Knox; the Hollands, wallpaper manufacturers; the McKims, advertisers; and the Birks and the Savages, jewellers. Two families of extraordinary athletes were the Hodgsons and the Rosses. The former were drygoods merchants, manufacturers of iron pipe, and stockbrokers, and the latter mainly accountants. In 1907, the Goodfellows sold their forty acres of lakefront property west of Montreal, called Woodlands, to the Rosses, and it was here that the McConnells spent their happiest days in their first years of marriage, boating, swimming, snowshoeing, picnicking, and singing hymns. Most of their friends were Methodists and some from Dominion Church, but others were Presbyterian or Anglican. Many of them, such as J.W. Ross and Emma Holland, and Phyllis Ross and Gerald Birks, would intermarry; and all would be his friends for life and often partners in both business and charitable fundraising.

On 11 May 1905 Jack and Lily were married by Lily's father at the Douglas.[12] Lily was "gowned in Chantilly lace and carried a shower bouquet of white roses and lilies of the valley." She also wore a simple tiara to hold her wedding veil. This was Jack's present to her and it appears to have cost $400. A reception followed at the parsonage.

The McConnells probably at the time of their wedding,
1905. Private collection.

Jack gave Lily a diamond and emerald ring, and amethyst pendants to the brides-maids.[13] Standard Chemical's wedding present was $500.

The McConnells went immediately on to Quebec to board the *RMS Victorian*, which had already called at Montreal on the 8th, having carried 1,539 passengers on her maiden voyage from England. Now on her return to England, the *Victorian* had been reported as the largest steamship ever to enter Montreal, "like one of the ocean greyhounds running out of New York." In Liverpool, the McConnells joined a large party of the Canadian Manufacturers' Association (CMA) which had been summoned to an audience with King Edward VII at Windsor Castle. As the CMA's "Official Souvenir" recounted, the royal mausoleum at Frogmore, the burial place both of Prince Albert and of Queen Victoria, was "thrown open to the Canadian delegation," and "for half an hour we trod on tiptoe past the tombs of Queen and Consort, or wound our way in and out the archways admiring the architecture, the magnificence of the

McConnell at Windsor, on his honeymoon in 1905.
McCord Museum, M 2003.8.6.5022.91

stained-glass windows, the aptness and beauty of the many quotations from sacred lore painted on walls and ceilings, chiseled in stone and worked in brass." The day was "perfect" and Windsor Castle, "the famous abode of royalty," both "grim and majestic." Moreover, "there was a sort of feeling that we were on sacred ground. It was probably the historical reminiscences that made it so. A home of monarchs for nigh eight hundred years!"

The king eventually appeared in a grey suit and hat, looking "more like a prosperous businessman with a taste for sports than a monarch," and the executive committee were presented by Lord Strathcona. The remainder approached the king and queen in single file, bowing, and then His Majesty addressed the multitude "in the rich, full voice of a cultivated Englishman, with just a slight presence of a German accent, saying simply: 'I thank you very much. I welcome you to England. I welcome you especially to Windsor, and hope you will return to your homes not too much fatigued after your long journey.'"[14] Spontaneously the group "burst into three cheers for their Majesties … and then lustily sang 'God Save the King.'" As Lily reported to her mother: "I tried to steal some gold plate but only got away with a little notepaper. It was lovely to see the castle when everything was uncovered. You see it was very swell as the King is there now. We had great fun coming home in the rain …"[15]

That same afternoon, despite the grease spot on her dress that Lily was sure had been noticed by Queen Alexandra, the McConnells and the manufacturers went on

Jack and Lily McConnell probably on their honeymoon on
the *Victorian*, 1905. McCord Museum, M2003.P.6 5022.7.

to Totteridge, where two former governors general of Canada, the Duke of Argyll
(formerly Lord Lorne) and Lord Minto, gave speeches. It is not clear whether the
McConnells accompanied the CMA party on the rest of its travels in England, but
they do seem to have joined a group of Canadians on a trip to the continent. There is
a photograph, likely dating from the honeymoon, of the McConnells with the Joseph
Flavelles of Toronto, who were connected by marriage to the McLeans, who were
close friends of Lily from the Douglas, and others in St Mark's Square in Venice.

On their return to Montreal, Jack and Lily settled down into their new life as a
married couple. Their first home was at 4074 Tupper Street (which seems to have
been across the street from his old rooming house and renumbered 4089 by 1908).[16]
If, Jack wrote to Lily, he thought she "would not be perfectly contented and happy"
there, "I would a thousand times rather lease it out and look up a more satisfactory
home for ourselves, or even buy another house which would be a good investment for
us." "Whatever," he added, "suits you dear will most decidedly answer my purpose."

The McConnells apparently with Joseph Flavelle (in bowler hat) and
others in St Mark's Square, Venice, c.1905. Private collection.

And so, "if the outside is not particularly attractive, no pains will be spared to make
the inside as cosy as human ingenuity, combined with natural artistic tastes – I don't
mean my own – can make it."[17] This house McConnell bought in October 1905, for
$5,000, to which he added over $800 in improvements.[18] It was very modern, with
electrical fixtures in the drawing room and the dining room. There were Japanese
curtains, lace bedspreads, a leather chair, a white washstand, a chiffonier, two china
cabinets, a tea table for the parlour, a baking cabinet for the kitchen, an umbrella
stand for the vestibule, and bouillon cups and a violet jardinière for the drawing-room
cabinet, among many other items. Pictures on the walls included one of "deers" and
another portraying "the hanging of the crane," and there were as well a trilogy of
"Love and Life" and even a "drinking scene."

A few months after the wedding, Lily's father, now a minister in Ontario, summed
up his view of his daughter's "happy Christian home": "To think of you two running
a house – killing chickens, eating pies homemade, trying to kill yourselves with ice
cream and all the curiosities and cruelties of real old stagers – the thing is too curious
for a circus … I can fancy how nice and snug and beautiful your house will be. The
new doors and glass and mosaic work in the hall must be very nice and give the whole
house an air of cheer and comfort. I am sure your carpets and curtains are beautiful
and with dishes of such brilliant hues and dainty brick-a-brack [sic] you feel yourselves quite well."[19]

Not all McConnell's income went to their house, however. In January 1906, for example, he carefully recorded how he had tithed his income of $3,500 in the previous year. This included $252 to the Douglas ($200 to pay down its debt, $25 for its Sunday school), $10 each to the Welcome Hall and the Brewery Mission, $12 to two poor people, $25 to a general fund for the poor, $10 to the YMCA, and $52 to a special relief fund, the total being more than 10 per cent of his income. In 1906 he gave $694 to charity, including all his 1905 causes and missionaries, educational funds, and five poor women. In 1907 he gave $1,330 to charity. It was such attention to individual needs that was to anchor his life for over fifty years, as he gave thousands and then millions of dollars away.

From the beginning, the marriage of Jack and Lily was an ideal match. Because Lily had been born on 13 September 1880, McConnell described the 13th as his "lucky day" – "and why shouldn't the day that brought into the world the little girl that has brought so much happiness into my life be a lucky day for me?" he asked. "It will," he pledged, "always be my highest ambition dear one to make you truly happy and to bring you as many of the little comforts of life as it shall please our Master to place within my reach. By living all our lives close to Him surely the question of all time happiness is solved and we need have no fear for the morrow."[20] Earlier, when contemplating their imminent wedding, McConnell had written: "We can[not] expect to be perfect, and we may have to meet disappointment at times, but I think by thoughtfulness and consideration we can greatly lessen the numerous little cares & worries and increase our happiness & enjoyment of life. Our chief motives and desires happily run in the same channel and I am sure that neither of us will ever wish to do anything that would be displeasing to the other, therefore we are launching out on pretty sure ground and having the solid foundation established, it should be a comparitively [sic] easy matter to build up happy useful & successful lives that will always be ready to help others when opportunities arise."[21] The future was to bring them their share of sorrow, but this assessment of their marriage prospects was borne out in every respect. Lil (as she was called after 1918) created for Jack the order and the calm necessary for his work, as well providing the social stimulation and the taste and refinement that he appreciated but could hardly have generated alone.

Lil was petite and generally shy but also the most confident of hostesses. Long after she had hired a butler away from Forbes Angus, Raymond Chapman, she would rush to welcome visitors at the door with a big, booming, deep voice. And, even after she had hired Mrs Rendall, her Scottish cook, she would fuss about such details as the need for a kosher chicken from Steinberg's, the grocer, for a Jewish guest. During the Second World War, she would become a surrogate mother, at the age of sixty, to several English children, reporting dutifully to their real mothers about dental emergencies and school uniforms. Like her own mother, she collected clothes for the poor throughout her life, and her munificence – matched if not exceeded by Jack's

Jack with the Griffith family, probably 1905. McCord Museum, M2003.8.6.3.2.

– would only grow over time. They formed a team, ever alert to the needs of others, with most of their gifts made in complete secrecy and to people in no position ever to reciprocate.

Through his marriage, McConnell became part of a much more educated, cultivated family than that of his parents. Yet he and his in-laws were not together for long. Shortly after Jack's marriage in 1905, his father-in-law took up a new appointment as minister of First Methodist Church in St Thomas, Ontario. Over the next several years, virtually every time he was in Ontario, McConnell would visit the parsonage in St Thomas, giving his investment advice, as well as his McConnell relatives.[22] The Griffiths were far more active than McConnell's parents, frequently travelling to Montreal and elsewhere. In contrast, it appears that Jack's parents could not even travel to Montreal in 1907 on the birth of his first child, Wilson Griffith, nicknamed Buster. In 1911 a second son, John Griffith, was born. Granny Griffith, in contrast to Jack's parents, was so much part of Jack and Lil's life that in later years she would occupy the central bedroom of their house in Dorval, outside Montreal, where the McConnells began to establish a country home in 1911. Jack's mother would die in 1909 and his father in 1912, in the same year as Dr Griffith, but Mrs Griffith did not die until 1929. Dr Constantine Griffith, Lil's brother, a general practitioner in the Parkdale district of Toronto, attended both of Jack's parents during their last illnesses and signed their death certificates.

Family portrait with first son, Wilson, c.1909. Private collection.

Jack and Lil remained members of the Douglas until the establishment of the United Church of Canada in 1925, two or three years after which they became members of Dominion-Douglas Church in Westmount, where Lil erected a stained-glass window in memory of her father. The Douglas congregation was very close-knit, and McConnell engaged in fundraising and did business with many of its members.[23] As early as 1904, he had been appointed a church steward; he was a member of the missions committee by 1906; and in 1907 he became church treasurer. He also seems to have taught Sunday school, but not much.

His most important contribution to the church was, not surprisingly, in the area of finance. By the early years of the century, the Douglas was seriously in debt. When it began a campaign to pay it down in 1907, McConnell seems to have been its chief fundraiser; he himself contributed $1,000, Arthur Peuchen gave $100, and William Hanson, the largest donor, $2,500.[24] Within two years the debt was fully cleared.[25]

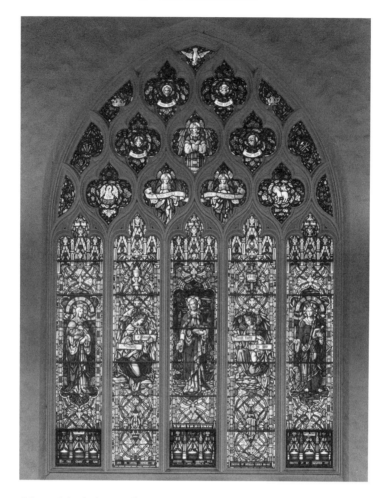

Memorial window to the Reverend Dr Thomas Griffith, erected by
Lily McConnell in 1926 at Dominion-Douglas (now Mountainside)
United Church, Westmount. Private collection.

He also led a whirlwind campaign to raise funds to erect a new Wesleyan Theological
College on University Street, which led to his opening of it in 1914. As late as 1921,
working with Lorne Webster, McConnell and the Douglas raised over $146,000 for
the Methodist Church of Canada and Newfoundland, a sum exceeded by no other
congregation of comparable size.

With his skill as a fundraiser so early established, McConnell found corporate life
cramped. In January 1907 he resigned as Standard's Chemical eastern manager, and
his resignation as secretary and second vice-president was accepted in July. His new
job, as a "financial agent," would now take him from Montreal to a much more turbu-
lent place, Winnipeg.

McConnell's Sunday school class, Douglas Church, c.1908.
McCord Museum, M2003.8.6.3.25.

Wesleyan Theological College, University Street, c.1914.
McCord Museum, V5308.

Next-door neighbours in Dorval and lifelong friends: the McConnells with
C.C. Ballantyne and his family, n.d. Private collection.

The family of Senator Lorne Webster, n.d.
Private collection, courtesy of Philip Webster.

CHAPTER FOUR

Partner, Promoter, and Believer, 1907–14

Sunday evening I dined with my friends, Markelham [Markland] Molson, Mr. and Mrs. Allison [...]. The dinner was an exceptionally good dinner. [...] I had only reached my room and was starting to undress when I felt as though a heavy wave had struck our ship. [...] As I started to go through the grand stairway, I met a friend who said, "Why, we have struck an iceberg."

Major Arthur G. Peuchen, 22 April 1912, testifying to a subcommittee of the United States Senate on the *Titanic*[1]

What's Money, Anyhow?

Money is the loudest sound in the noise of life.
A thing worshipped by all without a single hypocrite.
Something that always gets the glad hand.
Money is the most difficult root to cultivate.
Metal often manufactured from "water" in Wall Street.
The best friend of the masses.
A welcome visitor, but it's always on the run.
The support of the classes,
The aim of the lasses,
And the ruin of the asses.

From clipping from a New York newspaper, c.1910, in J.W. McConnell's possession[2]

Following his sales campaign in England in 1904, McConnell grew increasingly eager to carve out a future for himself outside a company, and this desire led him to join the only partnership of his career. Some time in 1906, three Sunday school teachers, George Franklin Johnston, McConnell, and Hudson Joshua Creighton Allison, the first two from Douglas Church, and the last from Dominion Church, decided to

G.F. Johnston, c.1911. Private collection, courtesy
of the Reverend Charles Johnston.

establish a "financial house" – a term that defies clear definition. They called themselves investment brokers – many of their associates preferred the title of "financial
agent"[3] – and as such they were more than ready to sell insurance, arrange mortgages,
promote new companies, and pursue a wide range of other prospects. Some sources
say that the partnership began in January 1906, but McConnell's letters make it clear
that the correct date is New Year's Day, 1907. They set up a Montreal office in the
Bank of Ottawa Building on St James Street, and their first trip together was to Winnipeg with a view to land speculation.[4]

It was a curious trio. Johnston, with his old-fashioned walrus moustache, was
in striking contrast to the lean, clean-cut, and athletic Edwardian ideal typified by
McConnell. Allison was also clean-cut, but he wore rimless spectacles and was given
to obesity. Appearances apart, the partnership was an alliance of three earnest Methodists as well as of businessmen willing to take risks. They were not merely pious and
ambitious but also possessed of robust confidence in their own selling ability. Com-

J.W. McConnell, c.1911. Private collection.

Hudson Allison, c.1910. McCord Museum 1175079.

mercial success was central to their Methodist world-view, the route for integrating their evangelical beliefs into their lives outside church.

Fifteen years older than McConnell, and nineteen years older than his nephew, Allison, Johnston was clearly the senior partner. On the 1907 trip, he was the one who undertook to pull the other two out of bed in the morning, leading McConnell to complain in a letter to Lily that "not one minute's peace will be given us after he is out until we get up."[5] His grandson was to remember him as "a huge and impressive figure, who spoke in authoritative tones, occasionally punctuated by a gargantuan laugh."[6] Born in Ontario 1861, Johnston had grown up in Chesterville, near Cornwall in Ontario. He was a wild youth before undergoing a conversion experience at the age of seventeen. In 1884 he became a Methodist probationer, serving under superintendents in several circuits and entering the Wesleyan Theological College in Montreal two years later. Then a throat affliction intervened, which forced him to abandon his plans of ordination and instead to become a schoolteacher.

In 1888 Johnston joined the Sun Life Assurance Company, and soon he was sent as an inspector to visit its agents in the West Indies. Afterwards, he became manager of Sun Life in the West Indies, Mexico, and part of South America. In 1889 he married Mary Jane ("Minnie") McFarlane, another devout Methodist and a schoolteacher. In 1898, four children and ten years after joining Sun Life, he became general manager for Canada of the New York Life Insurance Company. In the following year, he was appointed supervisor of New York Life agencies of Canada and New York, New Jersey, Connecticut, and Rhode Island, a post he retained until the end of 1906.

Johnston brought wide experience to the partnership. It was not simply that he had established business connections in Canada, the United States, and Latin America, or that he had supervised insurance salesmen. By then, insurance as an industry had come far from its origins in offering mutual aid, and its assets were a major source of funds for investment by the "professionals" who ran the investment departments of insurance companies. Through selling insurance, Johnston had learned first how to solicit "other people's money," but soon he became interested in how to "manage" this money for greater return than that offered by the bonds that insurance companies had made their typical investments. Thus, Johnston came to combine Methodist high-mindedness with high risk-taking. By 1906, he was displaying little appetite for working his way up as an insurance officer, not when he might make far more money as an independent agent or broker.

Allison, known familiarly to McConnell as "Hud," was a son of Jesse Rose Allison and Phoebe Johnston, the sister of G.F. Johnston. Born in 1881 on a farm just east of Chesterville, Hudson was a clerk in a local shop before studying shorthand in Buffalo, New York. He then went to work for his Uncle Frank in Montreal, selling life insurance there before taking charge of an insurance agency in Winnipeg, where he also sold real estate, possibly with his brothers, George Richey Barber (usually known as G.B.) and William Percival. Although he was a success as an insurance salesman, he came to devote himself exclusively to real estate in the west, which was potentially even more lucrative than insurance. Allison was another devout Methodist and he taught Sunday school at Dominion Church. Shortly after the start of the partnership in 1907, he married Bess Waldo Daniels of Milwaukee. In manner, Allison was more flamboyant than his uncle, as was McConnell, and the two younger men were soon sporting huge gold watches and displaying the swagger that came with fast money.

The partnership of Johnston, McConnell, and Allison was a remarkably loose one. While it was to be of indefinite duration, there was to be an unequal division of profits for the first five years, with more for Johnston. After 1 January 1912, the profits were to be divided equally among the partners, but the alternative was also open for the partners to operate independently of one another, pooling their efforts only when they saw fit. In their independent operations, they did not share their profits, and so there were incentives for them to operate separately as well as together. In law, each was responsible for all the debts of the other two, while in practice and under their partnership agreement they might make deals as individuals, which posed a potential danger for them. Nevertheless, each partner seems to have found highly respectable associates for his own separate deals, while actually benefiting from the sharing of liability for debt with the others.[7]

Their acknowledgment of shared liability as partners enabled them to borrow more money from banks than they could have done as individuals. It appears that McConnell, in the name of the partnership, actually took out loans greater than the other two, for his private ventures. This fact constrained the borrowing of the other two as individuals and of the partnership as a collectivity. Referring to the agreement of 1907, Johnston was to recall to McConnell in January 1912 that the three men had expected that renewing it "would enable us to clean up all our partnership transactions in a satisfactory manner, by going along in the public eye just as we are at the present time, thereby avoiding public suspicion and reduction of credit."[8]

The year 1907 got off to a rollicking start for the three. Writing to Lily "in the Snow & Rockland north of Lake Superior," on 8 January, McConnell reported that "G.F. has just read us a chapter [of the Bible] after which we joined in singing 'Tis the old time religion.'"[9] They had already organized a land deal in Alberta but were awaiting an order-in-council from Ottawa authorizing it, which would delay the McConnells' already-planned next trip to Europe. The centre of their operations was to be Winnipeg, which the three men had earlier visited together in January and August 1906.

In the previous thirty years, with the completion of the Canadian Pacific Railway and the arrival of thousands of immigrants to "open up" the prairies, Winnipeg had shot up from nothing to be the third-largest city in the country, its population growing from 241 in 1871 to 90,153 in 1906. It was the quintessential CPR town, having used subsidies to induce the railway to change its route from the geographically superior location of Selkirk, in order to make Winnipeg a hub. On a visit in August 1906, McConnell had pronounced to Lily that it was "one of the greatest cities in Canada and situated in the centre of the grandest country in the world." He confessed that it had taken him less than ten minutes "to catch the fever of enthusiasm" in this part of the west: "The great prosperity that awaits those with energy, brain and perseverance is more in evidence each time I come out here. And when I walk up and down the magnificent clean, wide and beautifully paved streets, it simply makes one feel mean to compare them with the metropolis where everything *should* be the best."[10]

By 1907, Winnipeg was indeed the boomtown of Canada, and Johnston, McConnell, and Allison were but three of hundreds who had arrived in search of quick profits from one source in particular – real estate. Whether the new partners were among the most infamous land sharks in this group is unclear, but they were certainly not hesitant in adopting the city's "booster" or "hustler" spirit. One commentator has described this attitude as "a broad, general conception that had as its central theme the need for growth; the idea that for the city to become 'better' it had to become bigger."[11] Boosterism went beyond normal social, political, and commercial rivalries, with the boosters seeing themselves as "energetic agents of improvement." Optimistic and aggressive, they constantly measured "their city's progress in quantitative terms – numbers of rail lines, miles of streets, dollars of assessment, size of population, value of manufacturing output or wholesale trade."[12] In the eyes of Johnston, McConnell, and Allison, boosterism was a route to the enrichment of the community as a whole and not a specious justification of fraud and exploitation. Material gain, for them, was perfectly compatible with their duty to privately spread some of their accumulated wealth for the common good.

To understand how the three partners fit into the heady atmosphere of Winnipeg in 1907, it is important to keep certain facts in mind. When Winnpeg was incorporated as a city – of only 1,600 souls – in 1873, it gained the power to borrow 10 per cent of its total tax assessment, whereas villages could borrow only 5 per cent of theirs. Thus, through incorporation, it was designed to grow through leverage. The more it grew, the more it could borrow, and more loans could fuel more growth. During the boom that – despite the brief collapses of 1883 and 1907 – essentially lasted to 1914, local businessmen welcomed land speculators because larger assessment values meant larger tax revenues as well as greater borrowing power.

And the incorporation of new subdivisions led to the extension of urban services, which came from the sale of city bonds and debentures, as well as taxes, leading to business for investment dealers. Between 1874 and 1913, the city grew from 1,920 acres to 14,861, with two major annexations in 1882 and 1906 and minor ones as late as 1913. It was not to expand as significantly again for exactly fifty years.[13] The feeding frenzy built on debt seemed to promise a winning situation for all and to provide a model for Johnston, McConnell, and Allison to emulate.

Prairie towns were overwhelmingly dependent on land taxes. With big profits to be made from selling real estate, the partnership also naturally wanted to flip land deals as rapidly as possible. Speculators often did not expect to hold their land for long, even for over one tax-paying period. If they sold quickly, they were able to shift the burden of taxation onto subsequent purchasers.This was an excellent reason for the partnership to have an office in Winnipeg from which it sold to investors largely in Montreal, where it also maintained an office.

Even before arriving in Winnipeg in January 1907, the three had already bought six acres in the Winnipeg suburb of Headingley. Almost immediately after arriving, they paid $275 for three lots in Calgary, which they sold in March for $950. They then bought four more lots in Calgary for $1,485, which they were able to pay for in full. They concluded a new deal in the wholesale district of Winnipeg for $150,000, with E.B. Greenshields[14] of Montreal and D.W. Harvey as investors.[15] Most of their ventures were linked to the sale and the resale of CPR-owned lands. The CPR itself first benefited from the extension of is lines by selling land, which yielded a total of $16 million between 1900 and 1912, and such speculators as the partners were riding a second wave of profiteering.[16]

For the first few months of 1907, all went beautifully in Winnipeg. The partners were planning to rent offices at Portage and Main, in the very centre of the city. As McConnell reported to Lily, the trains west "are simply packed to overflowing with home seekers and adventurers of every description" – an influx of people that promised "*a vast opportunity* for Real Estate men in the future."[17] He even decided to sell his house in Montreal so that Lily could join him. In April, he made a $3,572 deposit on a Winnipeg house and lots for them at Armstrong's Point.[18] In May, he sold their house on 4074 Tupper Street in Westmount for $7,500, for a profit of $1,500 after the cost of improvements and additions.

In the meantime, he was still attending services as often as twice on a Sunday, at the Grace and Broadway churches. At the house of friends, he participated in a discussion of various Christian denominations and reported to Lily: "I said – well: if I weren't a Methodist do you know what I would be? Someone said 'a Presbyterian?' And another said 'What would you be?' Says I – 'I'd be ashamed of myself.'"[19]

In January 1907, the partners organized the Western Land Improvement Company, with Johnston as president, McConnell as vice-president, and Allison as secretary-treasurer.[20] By the 13th, they had bought land for $40,000; and a day later McConnell was in Calgary, working on the irrigation project for it. In Calgary, he noted that the population had grown from 6,500 to 17,500 in five or six years, with real estate "advancing by leaps and bounds." By the following week, the partners had established relationships with William Molson Macpherson of Molsons Bank in Montreal and with John Somerset Aikins of Aikins and Pepler, prominent real estate agents in Winnipeg.

McConnell was also becoming an investor on his own account. Within a week after the incorporation of Western Land in January 1907 he bought twenty-five shares, of which he sold twenty in October 1908, for a profit of $100.[21] In April 1907, he bought twenty-five shares of another venture, the Canadian Western Development Company (of which he was the secretary), at $1,000 a share. He sold twenty of these in October 1908 for the same price, after collecting a dividend of $500 in September.

Also in April 1907 he paid $1,250 for ten shares of the Sterling Bank, $500 for 2,000 shares of Ruby Silver Mining, and $1,250 for 500 shares of Foster Cobalt. With Arthur Lyman of Montreal, and a firm called Lee and Fox, he incorporated the Perfection Cigar Perforator Company, his 25½ per cent share costing him $750. He bought four shares of the Missisquoi Marble Company in Phillipsburg, Quebec, for $200. What happened to these investments is unclear. One undoubted disaster was Winnipeg Paint and Glass, in which he had invested $1,000 as early as 1905 but whose warehouse and stock were destroyed by fire in 1907.

JOHNSTON McCONNELL & ALLISON 108

REAL ESTATE AND FINANCIAL AGENTS

32 BANK OF OTTAWA BUILDING

INTERIM RECEIPT

Montreal, 28th March 1907.

Received from Mr L. H. Packard of Montreal in the Province of Quebec the sum of Five hundred — Dollars ($500.00) being fifty per cent. of subscription of $1000.00 to the capital stock of a Company being organized with a Capital of $300,000, for the purpose of buying and selling fifty thousand acres of land in Manitoba and Saskatchewan at an average cost of $8.00 per acre.

Note for $500.00 at 3 mos. due 1st Jan

Johnston, McConnell & Allison

Johnston, McConnell, and Allison interim receipt to L.H. Packard for $500, 28 March 1907. Private collection, courtesy of Derek Price

By the beginning of August 1907, eight months after arriving in Winnipeg, McConnell had decided to explore a new opportunity in British Columbia, reporting to Lily that "so far we have been all right and have made handsomely."[22] In another letter to Lily, on 3 August, McConnell admitted that real estate had not really proved to be such a roaring success. But a wood-products enterprise had "opened our eyes to the possibilities along other lines which are really more pleasant & do not carry the second responsibility of retailing lands for our wholesale holders at satisfactory profits which in all cases is not the easiest thing to do in a short time." At the beginning of September, McConnell left for British Columbia to work on this.

Within a few weeks, any prospect of returning to Winnipeg to resume business was brutally cut off., Following a credit crunch caused by the failure of the Knickerbocker Trust in New York in October, financial panic set in all over the world. It spread first from New York to London, the chief source of capital for Canada. Building contractors were unable to arrange mortgages and curtailed construction. Interest rates rose, and by the end of the year the value of construction in Winnipeg totalled only $6.6 million, as opposed to $12.7 million in 1906. Homestead entries declined by a half. Developmental activity, in the form of a Great Northern Railway Terminal,

Share certificate for British Canadian Lumber Corporation, 1911. McCord
Museum, Schulich Collection of Stock Certificates P095-A05/03-119.

a bridge across the Red River, a gas plant, and a hydroelectric power plant, were all
postponed. To such speculators as Johnston, McConnell, and Allison, the banks cut
off credit completely.[23] It would take at least a year for Winnipeg, and the rest of the
world, to recover.

McConnell's Winnipeg adventure was definitively over. Yet his experience there,
despite the brevity of his stay, was to leave a lasting impression on him. Iin Winnipeg
he saw fortunes made from nothing, the houses of the rich stretching along Broadway
into Armstrong's Point, where he had planned to build his own. Nor was he ever to
forget, following the financial turmoil of 1907, that local economic success depended
on global conditions, so that even decades later he was to follow rubber in Malaya as
carefully as aluminum in Canada.

From the bustle of Winnipeg, McConnell now retreated to the mountains of the
West Kootenays, in southeastern British Columbia, to pursue his wood-products
venture. In January 1907, he and a few associates had incorporated the Patrick Lumber Company, with Markland Molson as its president, William C. McIntyre as its
vice-president, McConnell as its secretary-treasurer, and Joseph Patrick, a trustee of
Douglas Church, as its managing director.[24] McConnell's time with Patrick, a Que-
becer of Irish and Methodist origins known as "Joe", was short but eventful. In April
1907 Patrick began to build a sawmill in the Kootenay district, to be followed by a

pool hall, a dance hall, and about twenty houses. His mill was the biggest in the interior, capable of cutting 300,000 board feet a day.[25] With Nelson now the largest city between Vancouver and Winnipeg, Patrick had on his doorstep the forest to meet the growing demand for wooden poles for the new networks of electricity and telephones spreading across the west.[26]

McConnell arrived in Nelson on 5 September 1907, just a few days after Joe's brother Lester (later a famous hockey player like his other brother Frank), who had already found the town "a stunning blend of the bawdy and the beautiful," with its many saloons and brothels overlooking the shimmering lake below the house at 917 Edgehill Avenue, which Joe had just bought from a butcher and where all three men, and Joe's wife, were to live.[27]

At first, McConnell expected to stay only a few weeks, but he was soon captivated by the "entire proposition," which he described as "gilt-edged" and unbeatable anywhere "for fine timber and economical handling."[28] He was "in love" with the venture and wanted to bring Lily for a visit as soon as possible, and even her parents as well, to enjoy the moonlight "thousands of feet above the Kootenay River" and the "splendid" fruit. With plenty of "eggs, bread, butter, potatoes, canned tongue, canned plumbs [sic] and raspberries," he found himself cooking in the bush. Once night, he listened to "Scotch readings" from Patrick. As he reported to Lily, "some of these were good & he had Mrs. Patrick & me weeping gently for awhile, and once or twice he choked up himself."[29] Although one day he nearly drowned in rapids when a boat he was in with Patrick overturned, nothing could dim his enthusiasm.

McConnell was so entranced by the prospects of the timber limits that he began taking options on new properties, with a view to selling them in sixty days, rather as he had been doing in Winnipeg. Despite the grizzly bears, he was greatly enjoying shooting grouse and catching and frying trout, hopping from horse to dugout, and chatting with American "hot-air artists" who were jostling for Patrick's timber rights. By October, he was on his way to Vancouver to see Sir Hibbert Tupper, the brother of his Winnipeg lawyers, about investing in wood products. He had already arranged for investors in St Paul to take over some of Patrick's timber limits and agreed to help them arrange financing.

Even in Nelson, McConnell could not resist applying his fundraising skills, probably first glimpsed in his work at Douglas Church in Montreal, to the building of a new Methodist church that would cost $20,000. Joe Patrick sat on the building committee, which found that it could raise only $7,000 in contributions and a loan of $8,000. After hearing a "rousing sermon," McConnell decided to find a way of guaranteeing the whole $20,000 with subscriptions. He proposed that the subscriptions should total $22,000 in order to allow for shrinkage or defaults. Half would be payable in the first year, and the balance would be in four equal annual amounts. This would pay off the mortgage. The subscriptions were to be binding and to be collected only if

Trinity Methodist Church, Nelson, British Columbia. Kootenay Museum
Association and Historical Society. Neg. 1201/65.29.6B/98.001.02.

the full amount was subscribed. The building company would receive $11,000 in the
summer, and the loan company would be able to advance $9,000 if church members
would guarantee paying off the loan in four years.

This plan went off without a hitch. Patrick put his name down for $500, but
McConnell promised to give $1,000 if Patrick would give $2,000, and within a day
they had raised $18,000. In Montreal, Johnston and Allison found most of the remain-
ing $4,000 necessary. "I felt," he concluded, "rewarded ten times for any little work
that I had given the thing. They made such a fuss about me that I was a bit ashamed
of myself, because the thing that I had done was so simple & was only a great pleasure
to me."[30]

Simple it may have been, but it was encapsulated the secret of much of his success, to the end of his life. Where potential funds for investment seemed inadequate,
he increased them, first by making the terms of the investment – whether purely financial or religious or social – more attractive, and secondly by maximizing the useful-
ness of the capital raised through subscriptions with the precise use of leverage or
borrowing.

Promoting the shares of commercial ventures called for precisely the same skills in
winning subscriptions as financing churches did. For his charitable causes however,
he also issued challenges to others to match his own investment, enticing them by first

giving generously himself and secondly by promising to give even more if they would match his higher contribution. The real pleasure, moreover, that he found in giving he tried to generate in others in order for them to give. Here in Nelson, by so deftly mobilizing the limited resources of the community and beyond, out of nothing he created a church in marble.

Perhaps, however, because of the birth of his first son, Wilson, McConnell suddenly decided to return to Montreal some time in the following year, 1908. Two years later, the partnership bought Patrick Lumber. They discharged its liabilities and sold it in 1911 to British Canadian Lumber, a venture of Johnston and Allison alone, though Patrick Lumber would not be not formally dissolved until 1919.[31]

In March 1908, McConnell bought two Westmount Plateau lots for $1,300, located on what was to become Sunnyside Avenue, high on Mount Royal. These were for his own enormous house, near Johnston's and Allison's,[32] for which he commissioned designs in the French Beaux-Arts style. The house, however, was never built and he gave the land, and a house on it, to his son Wilson as a wedding present in 1937.[33] For more immediate occupancy, the young family secured a property in the village of Dorval, on Lake Saint-Louis, where they lived near their friends the Knoxes, the McLeans, and the Savages. Closer to the office, for $125 a month they rented 400 Elm Avenue, in Westmount, from G.W. Cook, a lumberman, with whose family the McConnells were to be associated over two generations.[34] Comfortably resettled in Montreal, he had no trouble starting a new career as both an investor in and a salesman of corporate securities, all the while remaining a partner of Johnston and Allison.

McConnell's first three full years back in Montreal, from 1909 to 1912, coincided with the greatest boom in industrial consolidation in the history of Canada, which was to lay the foundation for the prosperity of the country for the remainder of the century and beyond. In Winnipeg he had begun to make modest amounts through trading shares. All through 1908, his records show him buying and selling American railroad and copper shares, among other investments. Roughly between 1908 and 1910, in addition to investing in Colonial Novelty, Canadian Light and Power,[35] Mexican Northern Power,[36] and Mexican Light and Power[37] – the two Mexican companies were headquartered in Montreal and Toronto – he held securities in British Canadian Asbestos, Cariboo Limits of B.C., Rivers Inlet Lumber, Red Cedar Lumber of B.C. (of which he was president), Wood Products (of which he was director), and Manitoba Farm Lands.[38] The west evidently retained its allure as a place for investment. McConnell also invested for others, including his mother, two brothers-in-law, a sister-in-law, and his father-in-law.

In 1908, by the age of thirty-one, McConnell in his many lines of work had made and dropped allies often with astonishing swiftness, but he had learned from each of them, and some of them were to prove to be enduring role models. Now, in becoming a fulltime broker, he displayed a new skill, which was his uncanny ability to grasp opportunities in corporate reorganization, often fleeting ones. His sixth sense for what would work, his perspicacity, took time to develop, but not much. By the time he was thirty-five he had extracted what he could from the boom and was embarking on yet another career.

In the language of the day, in his work as a broker from 1908–12 McConnell entertained business "propositions." Some were promising, others were fraudulent, and it was for him to choose which might "fly." Many fell to earth, but others soared, and there were no guarantees. It is probably idle to attempt to trace patterns in his conduct in this crucial period. He extracted what he could out of propositions that he had accepted, big and small, and he attached himself to a great number of other businessmen, many of them much senior to him and richer than he was.

Brokers of the time such as McConnell typically described themselves proudly as "capitalists." Among them were real-estate brokers, bond brokers, stockbrokers, bankers, bond salesmen, and company promoters. These categories often overlapped, as opportunities arose and interests changed. McConnell dabbled in real estate, and he sold bonds and stocks principally to large investors, both individuals and institutions. But, although later a director of the Bank of Montreal, he was never a banker. Nor was he interested in trust and insurance companies except as a director. A.E. Ames, E.R. Wood, J.H. Gundy, I.W. Killam, and F.H. Deacon were better known as salesmen of bonds and stocks than McConnell. He made his name pre-eminently in the promotion of the securities of new or newly merged enterprises, an activity eminently suited to his evangelical "booster" background while disciplined by an extremely precise perception of where opportunities lay and of what tools were necessary to exploit them.

As a well-known contemporary study, published in 1909, explained: "Promotion is based on the recognition of the economic advantage inherent in an industrial situation, and the opportunity for capitalizing this advantage. The promoter is one who, recognizing this advantage, procures or paves the way to the procuring of the capital or equipment necessary to make it available … [he] must from necessity be an enthusiast. Having himself become convinced of extraordinary profits to be derived from the capitalization of the new venture or improved method, it remains for him to convince others. He must be a man of originality and unusual activity. The successful promoter as such recognizes no obstacle that may not be overcome."[39]

A promoter dealt with large issues of stock, which involved appraising the value of companies, preparing prospectuses, and arranging bridge financing until the collection of proceeds from the sale of securities.[40] The expertise of a company promoter lay essentially in lining up capital, in borrowing large pools of money to create assets where there had been none before. This he achieved through the mastery of such tools as debentures, mortgages, bonds, common shares,[41] preference shares,[42] guarantees, and legislation. He frequently took a role in management.

Because most of such work was highly confidential and technical, the promoter became enveloped in what some called the mystery of high finance. But not all excelled at the art; many failed. Why was McConnell not one of them? The answer is complex. One key to borrowing money is the creation of an image of confidence, and all his life McConnell exuded a powerful presence: an ingratiating blend of Methodist rectitude, Irish charm and geniality, and transparent commitment to success. There was nothing pompous or condescending or pretentious about him. Instead there was infectious energy. Throughout his life, despite his occasional losses, he somehow always conveyed that there were new tennis matches to be won, new fortunes to be made, new frontiers to be breached. In creating this persona, McConnell had the advantage of becoming a promoter in a period and a country of almost unbounded optimism. Canada was endowed with more timber, wheat, water, and minerals than it could consume. What it lacked was capital to develop its infrastructure. What McConnell offered was a conduit to lenders in England and later the United States.

From his base in Montreal, the broker and promoter McConnell was to become involved in a number of enterprises over the years. One involved coal and silver mining in Alberta. In 1909 McConnell joined the board of Pacific Pass Coal, formed by E.B. Greenshields and Senator Robert Mackay, both drygoods merchants and his fellow investors in British Canadian Asbestos. With them were Raymond Brutinel, a Frenchman working as a mineralogist in Calgary, William Molson Macpherson, president of the Molsons Bank, and John Theodore Ross, president of the Quebec Bank. McConnell was one of the members of the executive committee. The company held a forty-two-year lease from the federal government, and its capital consisted of $2 million in bonds and $5 million in stock; McConnell seems to have subscribed to $2,500 in bonds. It was a closed corporation, with no public offering of shares, and had an assured market for 75,000 tons of its coal annually.[43] Geological analysis confirmed that the Pacific Pass fields could yield at least eight hundred million tons of coal, four times more than Dominion Coal in Cape Breton. As McConnell explained to the press, Pacific Pass land contained practically "unlimited quantities" of bituminous coal of good quality, the vein being twenty-seven feet thick, lying almost horizontally and almost all above water level.

The Pacific Pass directors also organized ventures called the Lethbridge Coal and the Western Coal and Coke companies. In 1910 McConnell and fellow director H.A. Lovett, a Montreal lawyer, decided to combine all three into a new Canadian Coal and Coke Company. In May 1910 the board of the new company consisted of Mackay, Greenshields, Lovett and his law partner C.H. Cahan, Nathaniel Curry, Rodolphe Forget, and McConnell.

Advertisement for Rodolphe Forget, one of the most successful brokers
on St James Street and nephew of Senator Louis-Joseph Forget,
Montreal *Daily Witness*, 10 December 1910. LAC.

Curry, Cahan, and Forget were to link McConnell to a much wider circle. Curry
was associated with Max Aitken in the Canadian Car and Foundry Company, the
largest rolling-stock firm in the country. Cahan was a former newspaper editor and
politician who, after his call to the bar, became much involved in setting up hydro-
electric utilities in Latin America and the Caribbean (including Mexican Light and
Power in 1902). Canadian Coal and Coke was the start of a long business relationship
among him, Lovett, and McConnell.

Rodolphe Forget, the president of the Montreal Stock Exchange in 1907–09, known
as "the king-pin general of Canadian stock markets" and the "young Napoleon of St.
François-Xavier Street," was one the most daring, even reckless, promoters of his
era. Until 1907 he had worked with his uncle, Senator L.-J. Forget, in the brokerage
house of Forget and Forget. The senator was a director of the CPR and had been the
president of the Montreal Street Railway since 1892. He also owned the Richelieu
and Ontario Navigation Company, the presidency of which he gave to Rodolphe in
1904, and a popular newspaper called *La Presse*. When the conglomerate of Montreal
Light, Heat and Power emerged in 1901, Rodolphe became vice-president and Louis-
Joseph a director.

In addition to Canadian Coal and Coke in 1909, Rodolphe and McConnell worked
together in the financing of the Quebec Railway, Light, Heat and Power Company,
which Forget had established with the lawyer J.N. Greenshields along the lines of

Montreal Power. Forget was also involved with Aitken, Cahan, and Lovett in the formation of Canada Cement, and by 1914 he was the owner of the Toronto Railway Company. He was elected a Conservative MP for Charlevoix in 1904 and for Montmorency in 1911 and represented both constituencies until 1917.

The new holding company of Canadian Coal and Coke also acquired St Albert Collieries near Edmonton. Yet, mainly because of delays in the building of railway branch lines, the venture did not go well. Soon, Canadian Coal and Coke needed $1,500,000, and it implemented a reorganization whereby bondholders in its four constituent companies exchanged their bonds for preference shares in Canadian Coal and Coke. Some, in England at least, were less than content with this development. On 1 October 1913 the London weekly *Truth*, a fiercely independent adviser on British investments all over the world, from Nicaragua and Rhodesia to China and South Africa, published in its "Mammon" column an article on "Broken Canadian Bonds."[44] The problem that *Truth* saw with such companies as Canadian Coal and Coke was that "the tangible assets of a company are practically restricted to the amount of the bonded debt, the [common] share capital being a fancy creation backed by nothing more than goodwill. In such cases the so-called bonds are not so well secured in the ordinary or deferred shares of conservatively managed industrials in the old country."

In May 1912, *Truth* continued, an investor in Paris had been induced to buy a gold bond of Canadian Coal and Coke by the offer of a 50 per cent bonus in common stock. The price was at par and it included accrued interest, and it carried a coupon payable in July. Johnston, McConnell, and Allison had recommended it, supplying a partial list of the bondholders in the four companies controlled by Canadian Coal and Coke. But when the investor presented his coupon for payment by McConnell in July, McConnell wrote to him that the bondholders had "unanimously" voted to exchange their bonds for preferred stock. *Truth* concluded: "Here is a company which first pledges its property on a first mortgage, providing sinking fund provisions, finds like many another borrower even before the days of the 'Merchant of Venice' that a mortgage debt is a bit of a nuisance, and then coolly proposes to get rid of the mortgage, asking its secured creditors to vote themselves unsecured creditors. The natural comment one would be induced to make about such a transaction would be that neither the proposers nor the acceptors of such a plan were the class of people it would be desirable to entrust with money – the former class with other people's, and the latter class with their own."[45]

Canadian Coal and Coke might have survived its refinancing had not the Grand Trunk Pacific (GTP) Railway, effectively its lifeline, gone into insolvency. With the outbreak of war in 1914, the government of Robert Borden had to deal decisively with the overcapacity of the Canadian railways.[46] The total investment in Canadian lines was $2 billion, of which half had come from the taxpayer, and, like the Canadian

Northern Railway of Mackenzie and Mann, the GTP was a chief beneficiary of this public largesse. But then, in 1914, railway construction in Canada ceased, and much painful inquiry followed into the future of the Canadian Northern, the GTP, and the Grand Trunk Railway (responsible for the construction of the GTP).

In 1916 Sir Thomas White, the minister of finance, found that the GTP had been "cooking its books": it was paying dividends to its preferred shareholders while defaulting on its loans from the government. In March 1919 the government ordered the GTP to cease its operations, and in September of the same year the Grand Trunk defaulted on its servicing of GTP bonds. Both were to become part of the new Canadian National Railway, apparently without providing Canadian Coal and Coke with the means to transport its product.[47]

Another, contemporaneous, coal venture was much more successful, and it brought McConnell into association with two well-known Toronto brokers, F.H. Deacon and A.E. Ames. Deacon was one of the earliest Toronto stockbrokers and promoters, while Ames ran an immensely successful stockbrokerage and bond-investment business.[48] In 1910 Ames became vice-president of the Sterling Coal Company, set up to mine coal in Ohio and West Virginia and sell it in Toronto; W.F. Tye, who had been chief engineer of the CPR, was president; Deacon was a Toronto director; and McConnell, Forget, and Curry were Montreal directors. In its first year Sterling produced 204,903 tons, and in 1913 it created the Conger Lehigh Coal Company out of the bankrupt Conger Coal of Toronto to produce and deal in coal, wood, and fuel of all kinds and to explore and develop salt, gas, oil, iron, gold, silver, copper, and other metals and minerals. Sterling appears to have been a successful investment for McConnell, who held on to his shares of it for several years.[49]

In 1909–10 McConnell also became involved in Max Aitken's efforts to consolidate all Canadian primary- and secondary-steel producers into a new firm, the Steel Company of Canada. Aitken was able to negotiate with almost every major steel company, the sole exception being Nova Scotia Steel and Coal. To overcome the opposition of this company's president, R.E. Harris, Aitken, beginning in December 1909, tried surreptitiously to purchase a majority stake in Nova Scotia Steel and Coal, and eventually to have his former ally Harris removed from the board at the next annual meeting.

A proxy fight ensued.[50] There was contemporary comment that this bid for Scotia – as it was familiarly called – was in connection with Aitken's search of cheap steel for the new Canadian Car and Foundry amalgamation, which he had also organized. Lovett admitted that he was standing for a directorship only to keep the seat warm for Curry, the newly appointed president of Canadian Car and Foundry.[51] At any rate, it appears that Aitken enlisted the help of Rodolphe Forget in Montreal and the broker E.B. Osler in Toronto, and he was reported, at the end of March 1910, to have 32,000 of the 70,000 votes possible.[52] How many of the other 38,000 votes were commanded by Harris was to be revealed at the meeting at the New Glasgow YMCA the next day. The press described the fight for control of the Scotia as high drama. Indeed, some of the best-known businessmen of the country were ranged into two opposing camps, but many candidates for the board commanded support from both.

Exactly how the Aitken group, including McConnell, gathered its proxies is hard to trace. But there was much speculation and subsequent comment at the time. For example, on 6 April 1910 the Halifax *Morning Chronicle* published "The Raid upon Scotia," an imaginary description of a meeting at the Windsor Hotel in Montreal just before McConnell set off for New Glasgow with Forget, J.N. Greenshields, and others. Here, Aitken is depicted as referring to the Harris group in the following terms: "I am going to take them and their rotten little proposition and cut their heads off and nail their scalps to the wall of their den." As this comment suggests, it was a dirty fight, and, to the shock of the Aitken group, it ended in a Harris victory.

Later, in an interview with the Montreal *Herald* at the beginning of April 1910, McConnell claimed that proxies, telegraphed to the Harris group at the last minute, had won the day. The Harris group, he said, had borrowed stock overnight from their brokers, at a premium of half a point; that is, the brokers offered to borrow Scotia shares, from existing shareholders, at a nominal price of 86½, promising to return the stock at 86 the following morning – which represented a profit of $50 for every 100 shares thus loaned. At the meeting, Harris as chairman had ruled these telegraphed proxies valid since they had been accompanied by declarations when filed at the telegraph office. He also ruled that telegraphed revocations of proxies originally in his favour were illegal, because no notice of revocation had been given. The same applied to proxies originally made out to him but later transferred to Forget, on the ground that they should have been sent to the office of the company to which the original proxies had been sent.

J.N. Greenshields argued that he and his associates had had a clear majority when they left Montreal, "but overnight fifteen hundred shares were borrowed by brokers just to use against us today, and these shares will be returned in the morning." Harris retorted: "I meet the charge of unfairness Mr. Greenshields makes against me and I hurl it back in his teeth." To Forget's protest that "all that we ask is British fair play," Harris replied: "Is it British fair play to announce in newspapers all over the Dominion that he had secured control of this Company and would turn out its present directorate and President?"

With this battle behind it, Scotia continued to be profitable until its absorption (with the other steel and coal firms of Nova Scotia) into the British Empire Steel Corporation in 1920.[53] Though McConnell had not been deeply involved in the attempted takeover of the company, the defeat was a tremendous blow to the reputation of his close associate Forget. From Forget and Aitken, McConnell must have learned exactly how proxy fights could go wrong; he would do things differently, as will be explained later in connection with his tireless and ultimately successful efforts to wage a proxy fight for control of the Montreal Street Railway. Nor were McConnell's connections with steel in Nova Scotia at a complete end. Years later, to his regret, he would invest in British Empire Steel, which proved a financial disaster.

Another enterprise that did not turn out as well as McConnell had expected was the shoe manufacturer Ames-Holden-McCready. By 1911, McConnell was well acquainted with both Herbert Ames and the Holden family, as well as with the president of their newly formed company, Lorne McGibbon. So it was not surprising that, in 1911, McConnell and his partners floated the initial shares of Ames-Holden-McCready. By 1 March, the *Gazette* was reporting that McConnell had placed $250,000 of the company's bonds locally and $750,000 in London, and that the allotments of the preferred stock were to be made pro rata, since it had been oversubscribed within forty-eight hours. McConnell joined the board as a director. Unfortunately, the future was not as smooth as the financing had been. In 1913 the net profit of Ames-Holden-McCready was $331,390, but with the war this declined to $307,598 in 1914 and $126,829 in 1915,[54] partly, it seems, because of serious deficiencies in the boot that the company was making for the troops

Then there was that new invention of the age, the motor car. Ever alert to the emergence of new trends in technology and consumption, McConnell swiftly grasped the significance of the early Buicks and Packards and Fords that were pushing the horse-drawn carriages off the roads. Over the next half-century, he would own most of the major luxury cars of the time, from a Rolls-Royce to a Cadillac and a Lincoln Continental, while his son Wilson would become an established expert in automobile mechanics and own exotic sports cars. McConnell himself was a good friend for many years of Robert S. McLaughlin of General Motors of Canada and took a special interest in Chrysler as an investment.

His long association with US Rubber, through its Canadian subsidiary, Dominion Rubber, also stimulated in him a keen interest in the production of tires, and in rubber supply. His own venture as a director of a car-manufacturing company, however, was short-lived, like the home-grown Canadian industry generally. In April 1911 the directors of CCM, Joseph Flavelle, the Toronto meatpacker, and Warren Soper, a streetcar pioneer in Ottawa, retired in favour of McConnell and Lloyd Harris, the MP for Brantford and a major shareholder in Massey-Harris. When CCM transformed itself into the Russell Motor Car Company, McConnell was responsible for floating $800,000 of the company's preferred shares and for converting the existing $800,000 of stock into 7 per cent common shares, thus doubling the capitalization.[55]

Wheat was yet another of McConnell's interests. In 1907 Marquis wheat, a new faster-ripening and rust-resistant crop, was spreading across the Canadian prairies. It transformed Canadian agriculture, so that wheat production rose from 55.6 million bushels in 1901 to 230.1 million in 1911, with 90 per cent of the latter total coming from the prairies. Of course, ground wheat becomes flour, and in 1900–10 capital investment in flour milling grew from $14 million to $43 million, and the value of the product from $32 to $82 million. By 1912, Canada was milling four times the flour it could consume and its export trade had doubled from 1909 to 1910 alone.[56] The price of exported wheat flour peaked at $4.85 per bushel in 1910, to be followed however by a decline for several years.

In 1910 McConnell became associated with A.J. Nesbitt, of Investment Trust of Montreal, in the amalgamation of eight small Ontario companies into Canadian Cereal and Milling. Joseph Flavelle, although he had been an organizer of his brother's Maple Leaf Mills, became president of Canadian Cereal, and McConnell was named to the board. The company sold two-thirds of the preferred shares issued, with a total value of $800,000, and half the common stock issued was offered as a 50 per cent bonus to the preferred subscribers.

In April 1911 Canadian Cereal joined International Milling of Minnesota, which operated a mill in Moose Jaw, Saskatchewan, to form the International Milling Company of Canada. This new holding company held 85 per cent of the shares of Canadian Cereal. It issued $1,750,000 of its own bonds, as well as $1,995,400 in preferred shares and $1,279,000 in common shares. Canadian Cereal suddenly sank into deficit in 1911, however, while International Milling of Minnesota was making significant profit. The Americans dissolved the holding company, International Milling of Canada, and renamed their Canadian operation Robin Hood Flour Mills in 1913. By then, a new company, Canadian Cereal and Flour Mills had taken over from Canadian Cereal and Milling, with shareholders of the old company receiving 40 per cent on their holdings.

Perhaps the most significant of McConnell's business activities in these years was his reorganization of the Sherwin-Williams paint company. In 1911 Charles Colquhoun Ballantyne, the managing director of the Canadian operations of Sherwin-Williams of the United States, arranged the merger of his company with its two principal competitors in Canada, Canada Paint and the British firm of Lewis Berger and Sons. The new company – with Ballantyne as vice-president and McConnell as a director – hired the Montreal-London Securities Corporation (formed in 1910 by the corporate lawyers Lovett and Cahan, with McConnell as its principal salesman in Montreal and Henry Joseph as its man in London) to market its shares and bonds. The sales campaign was an extraordinary success, achieving the sale of $3 million in preferred shares in three days.

Later that year, Ballantyne campaigned aggressively against Sir Wilfrid Laurier and his proposed reciprocity treaty with the United States, fearing that the treaty, if implemented, would flood Canada with imported American paint, including paint made by its parent, the original Sherwin-Williams in the United States. The defeat of Laurier's Liberals left Sherwin-Williams as the biggest paint company by far in

Canada, with a total capitalization of $9.5 million, and two years later Ballantyne reported to Aitken that the company's liquid assets were "over five times as great as our current liabilities."[57]

The next year, 1912, marked a turning point for McConnell, both personally and professionally. His mother had already died in March 1909, and now, in January 1912, his father died. The senior John McConnell was buried beside his wife, and their daughter Sue, in Mount Pleasant Cemetery in Toronto. Then, in mid-April 1912, McConnell's father-in-law, Thomas Griffith, died in St Thomas.

McConnell's partnership with Johnston and Allison was also nearing its end. As already noted, the original understanding had been that the profits should be unequal until 1 January 1912, and then equal "if we mutually agreed to join forces on any prop-osition."[58] In the absence of such agreement, the partners were to "operate independ-ently," which they were in fact doing increasingly from the end of 1907 anyhow. Now that the understanding had expired, McConnell wanted to dissolve the partnership. Johnston was not so sure and he wrote to McConnell: "To me it seems utterly foolish for us to dissolve a partnership that has been for five years so extremely pleasant and highly profitable, especially so speaking for myself, as I think there are no other two men in the world quite so clean, straight and honorable as my two partners, and I have as much confidence as any man is capable of developing in them."[59]

Nonetheless, by the end of 1911, Johnston himself, and probably Allison, had ten-tatively agreed with McConnell "that we should operate separately from the 1st of January, or together, just as the mood takes us." But, at the end of January, Johnston was still against making the dissolution of the partnership "known." This would be "business suicide" since there were "so many large transactions incomplete." John-ston had already warned McConnell that he was "going into too many things for the good of your health." Others had told Johnston "that no one man in the world could attend to any one business efficiently and properly so as to divide his attention as you [and McConnell] were compelled to do." One man had told Johnston himself "to put sufficient property in my wife's name that it would ensure my family a livelihood" since McConnell was a "dangerous partner."

Now, contradicting himself, Johnston told McConnell that he wanted the partners to "get out of everything we are in together as soon as possible": "You know that while you have undertaken a great many undertakings individually, under the terms of our partnership, the partnership is responsible and I find it practically impossible for me now, even to make a draft of any size on Hudson in London at the present time, through any of the Banks I know, because you have borrowed from them extensively and they recognize that the firm is responsible, which we are." Johnston marvelled, "What a fellow you are to wear down your health for the sake of increasing your pile, which is already very large and sufficient to keep you and yours the rest of your life."

The mixed messages of the letter did not become any clearer when Johnston expressed his wish that the three partners "continue business in some way whereby I would have an intimate business relation with the men for whom the years of partnership have increased my love and admiration. I am practically lost when I am away from either or both of you for a couple of weeks."

In fact, however, Johnston, McConnell, and Allison seem seldom to have been physically together in the previous five years. They had made a name for themselves as a partnership, particularly with their promotion of Ames-Holden-McCready and Sherwin-Williams of Canada. But increasingly Johnston and Allison had become preoccupied with British Canadian Lumber in British Columbia, which was about to enter into insolvency. Allison retained his interest in real estate and insurance and kept a house in London. McConnell was in Montreal the most, and thus was the partner the most responsible for the success of Ames-Holden-McCready and Sherwin-Williams once these companies had started business in their newly amalgamated form. (Indeed, he alone of the partners was a director of them.) It was the same with the Sterling Coal flotation in 1910, when, under the terms of the partnership agreement, the three shared profits unequally, with Johnston taking the greatest share. To McConnell, it was clear that he could do better without the agreement. In any case, by 1912, Johnston was on the road to financial ruin, his fate being sealed with the collapse of British Canadian Lumber in 1915.

When the end of the partnership actually arrived, it did so with unexpected violence. Having travelled with Johnston to England in February 1911, in search of $20 million for British Canadian Lumber, Allison was again there from late 1911 to the spring of 1912, at least in part on the same business. Late in January 1912, McConnell had gone to England with Lily, but they returned to Canada almost at the same time but separately from Allison, probably via New York on the *Mauretania*, apparently because of the impending death of Thomas Griffith.

The Allisons stayed on to catch the maiden voyage of the pride of the White Star Line, the *Titanic*, which set sail from Southampton on 10 April. It was a fateful mistake, for Hudson, his wife, Bess, their daughter Lorraine, and Lorraine's nurse perished when the *Titanic* sank off the coast of Newfoundland on 14 April. Their son, Trevor, survived, as did the family maid, cook, and chauffeur. Bess Allison was one of the few women in first class to die, and Lorraine was the only child in first or second class to do so. One of Allison's brothers rushed to New York to find Trevor and the servants, who had been rescued by the *Carpathia*.

They were all met in Montreal by Johnston and McConnell. Allison's body was one of the first recovered from the sea; the bodies of his wife and daughter were never found. McConnell contributed generously to the fund set up by the lord mayor of London to assist the relatives of those who had gone down with the ship. McConnell knew other Montrealers who had sailed on the *Titanic*. One was Markland Molson, who had been McConnell's banker in Winnipeg and elsewhere and president of the Molsons Bank as well as Patrick Lumber. Two others were Charles Melville Hays, former president of the Grand Trunk Railway, who was returning to Canada to open the Château Laurier in Ottawa; and Hays's son-in-law, Thornton Davidson, a member of the Montreal Stock Exchange and the son of Charles Peers Davidson, a justice of the Superior Court of Quebec. On the last night that all three of these men were in London, Molson and Davidson had actually dined with McConnell. On the *Titanic*, furthermore, was another former Montrealer – McConnell's old mentor at Standard Chemical Company in Toronto, Arthur Peuchen. Molson, Hays, and Davidson drowned. Peuchen, still Standard Chemical's president, survived, having been pressed into service as a lifeboat oarsman. But, on his return to Canada, he was confronted by accusations of cowardice as he had been one of the few male survivors. He never recovered his reputation and retired from Standard Chemical, ending his days, in 1929, in obscurity.[60]

Allison's death put a legal end to the partnership and triggered the cleaning up of its accounts. For months afterwards, nevertheless, the partnership continued to place advertisements in the financial press and indeed for at least another year or two their office remained open. But Johnston and McConnell were never to work together again. For McConnell's part, he moved into the new Dominion Express Building at 215 St James Street, at the northwest corner with Saint-François Xavier Street. This building was a five-minute walk from the new Montreal Stock Exchange, a two-minute walk from the headquarters of the Bank of Montreal, and steps away from the premises of the Montreal *Star*. It was a distinctive structure from the outside, with its first two floors in granite. Above these stretched seven or eight – depending on how one counted the top – floors of heavily ornamented white glazed ceramic. Provincial coats of arms and colossal caryatids competed for the eye with an almost unbearably weighty fenestration.

Dominion Express occupied the ground floor and part of the basement, which it shared with a restaurant. McConnell's office was on the eighth floor. The only tenant above him was the Montreal Club, one of the principal places to lunch on St James Street, from which he would order lunch on a tray. In an early photograph of McConnell in his Dominion Express office, a telephone is prominent. This was McConnell's chief tool in all his dealings. As the president and chairman of Massey-Ferguson, James S. Duncan, was to recall, McConnell had only "one idiosyncrasy that I knew of": he "could talk more and at greater length on the long distance telephone than any other man I have ever met, either before or since ... and what he had to say was always worth while."[61] Not all McConnell's phone calls were about business; he enjoyed making crank calls – some had him pretending to speak Chinese – to more sombre colleagues. Calls to him generally had to be routed through a switchboard operator,

The Dominion Express Building, St James Street.
McCord Museum V12364 and V12552.

who for almost fifty years was Gladys Davies. McConnell had only one telephone in his office, and if he answered it himself, he would say "Montreal Police Department" in order to screen out unwanted callers.

It was a plain, crowded, and inadequate headquarters for McConnell's increasingly complex web of operations, and almost nothing in it changed over the next half-century. McConnell himself occupied a spacious and austere room, with dark panelling and almost no decoration or pictures. There was a large desk, a sofa to nap on, and a fireplace that was seldom if ever lit. There was no conference room: managers and others simply sat, one or two at a time, with "the chief." Outside the chief's own office, however, was a Dickensian scene out of *David Copperfield*. Since there was not room in the office for more than a few people, including McConnell, those who were also there to see him waited outside until there was an available chair. Mary F. Clarke, McConnell's secretary for decades, sat outside McConnell's office with the others.

For all its limitations, the office in the Dominion Express Building commanded views of much that McConnell helped to build over the first half of the twentieth century. From the time that he moved in, he could, on a clear day, probably have seen the big Sherwin-Williams plant in Verdun to the west, the biggest paint operation in Canada and the headquarters of all of Sherwin-Williams business in the British Empire, from Wellington and Calcutta to Vancouver. He could also look down on the several brokerage firms on Saint-François-Xavier Street – there were more than forty of them in 1912 – including his favoured one, McDougall and Cowans.

After 1912, McConnell was involved in other stock promotions. One was a coffin company: on 6 March 1913 McConnell used his Mount Royal Bond company to amalgamate six casket manufacturers under the umbrella of Dominion Manufacturers.[62] Another, in 1914, was that of Canadian Tube and Steel Products. One of the components of the Steel Company of Canada that Max Aitken formed in 1910 was Mount Royal Rolling Mills. William McMaster, the secretary and effectively the chief executive of Mount Royal, refused to serve under Aitken in the new Stelco, and he advised his son, Ross, to do the same. Though Ross did not heed his father's warning and came eventually to be president of the new company, six former employees of Mount Royal promptly organized Canadian Tube and Iron. In 1914 McConnell merged Canadian Tube and Iron with Colonial Wire Manufacturing and Canadian Rolling Mills, the new entity being known as Canadian Tube and Steel Products. McConnell briefly served as its president.

McConnell was active on other fronts too. Between 1911 and 1914, there was a big real-estate boom in Montreal. The economy generally was flourishing and syndicates rushed to erect skyscrapers and to secure property for future development.[63] Over the course of a single year, 1910–11, the total valuation of Montreal realty rose 14 per cent,[64] almost equal to the increase of the preceding thirty years. By September 1912, W.F. Tye, who had worked with McConnell on Sterling Coal, declared that Montreal was growing faster than the Canadian west.[65] McConnell himself made a good deal of money from this boom. His traceable transactions included two lots on Girouard Avenue, two lots in St Lawrence Ward, a lot extending from St James Street to Fortification Lane, a lot on St Catherine's Street in Westmount, and three lots on St James Street.

Profits accruing from these transactions, combined with his many other business investments, made McConnell a very rich man over the space of just four years, 1910 to 1914. Nothing had prepared either him or Lily for such rapid success. It is said that Lily did not realize she was rich until one day, while shopping for a "dicky," or false shirtfront, she took a fancy to two, and then suddenly realized that she had the money to buy both. Yet the success had not just "happened"; McConnell's hard work and shrewd decisions had brought it about. In his investments, he was widely diversified. He held shares in financial services, public utilities, natural resources, consumer goods, real estate, and industrial products in Canada, Great Britain, and the United States. He was an active participant in the great consolidation of Canadian industry, but also a passive investor in it. And, while he did some active trading, he was extremely conservative in his accounting methods.[66]

There was no magic formula to McConnell's rise. His mastery of bookkeeping and his early connections with such men as Markland Molson and Rodolphe Forget were the crucial elements in his education. But his innate personality traits – charm and competitiveness – were also great assets. So was his luck. As an investor, McConnell was barely affected by the stock-market crash of 1907 and did not try his hand in Montreal, the financial capital of Canada, until 1908, when the greatest economic boom seen up to that time was getting under way. And, as we shall see, by the time of the worldwide recession of 1913, he was a principal owner of perhaps the largest sugar refinery in Canada, part of an oligopoly producing what most consumers then considered an essential product, in bad times as well as good.

He was lucky in other ways too. Between 1870 and 1913, Canada enjoyed the highest growth rate in the world, almost half a per cent more per year than the United States, the second-fastest-growing country.[67] Its real gross national product grew twice as rapidly between 1896 and 1913 as in the decades preceding and following that period – a development that was accompanied by an influx of immigrants into western Canada, the industrialization of central Canada, and an enormous net capital inflow from Britain, such that from 1902 to 1914 Canada received nearly all new British capital flowing to the empire.[68] The new international market in industrial securities forced the growth and linking of organized stock exchanges and the dominance of promoter-financiers in industry. Security issues could create wealth far greater than retained earnings and family savings could otherwise have generated.

McConnell had participated in the industrialization of central Canada at Standard Chemical. He had benefited from the immigration to western Canada in Winnipeg. To the skills of selling securities that he had first honed in London in 1904, he was adding expertise in across almost the whole spectrum of Canadian business. In 1914 he announced his retirement as a broker. But he was by then already a vice-president of the Montreal transit system and the president of one of the largest sugar companies in the Dominion as well as of one of the leading department stores in Montreal. There were more successful promoters such as Max Aitken (later Lord Beaverbrook), better-established brokers such as the Forgets, and more innovative industrialists such as Ross McMaster. But they accepted him as a virtual equal, and McMaster was one of his closest friends for the rest of their lives.

He was unique, moreover, in exceeding them in versatility. Most of his contemporaries were specialized, and only Aitken went on to great success in other fields, namely, newspapers and politics. McConnell himself was to own newspapers although never to enter politics. That his diversity of talents, as well as of his investments, exceeded his luck would be proved by his staying power, as evidenced by his ownership of St Lawrence Sugar Refineries Limited for half a century.

Such was the rapidity of McConnell's rise, however, that many were astonished. They could not believe that he had come by his fortune honestly, especially as so many others, such as Johnston, had failed in similar efforts. One of McConnell's colleagues, Aitken, was to suffer even more and for all his life from rumours about his sharp practice in the amalgamation of Canada Cement. What is beyond doubt in hindsight is that most who invested in their promotions probably did very well over many years. Aitken's Stelco, Canadian Car and Foundry, and many others, including Canada Cement did, it is true, better than McConnell's Ames-Holden-McCready, but Sherwin-Williams of Canada was to prove the most solid of investments. Moreover, neither McConnell nor Aitken sold securities for much more than five years, but both became very rich within those five years. They could not have done so many deals so rapidly and so successfully if many of their contemporaries had not believed in them.

What is also clear is that McConnell, Aitken, and their colleagues played by the rules of the game as they were evolving and understood by sellers of securities and their clients, in the United States as well as in Canada. A gap between changing concepts of share valuation gave rise to the accusations of sharp practice against McConnell, Aitken, and others. The very concept of a corporation with limited liability was fairly new, and most businesses were partnerships, with profits distributed through partners' draws. Bonds with a fixed rate of return were the first securities issued by companies, and then preference shares, which generally paid dividends although these were not as secure as the interest on bonds was. Preference shares were issued at "par value," which could change after issue into "market value," but their market value did not fluctuate much because these shares were seen as pertaining to the "breakup" value of fixed assets, such as plant and equipment, and cash, which could be distributed among the shareholders on the dissolution of the business.

By 1908, rapid technological innovation as well corporate restructuring in the form of mergers were rendering increasingly obsolete the notion of "par." In the place of this fixed view of wealth, there was emerging a market for "common" shares sold at prices that varied with market expectations of future cashflows, and other assets valuable beyond tangible assets and cash. These non-physical assets included patents and "goodwill" – the reputation of a company, or of the people who ran it. Expectations of increased earnings were natural when companies were merged or acquired, the assumption being that the expanded entity should benefit from economies of scale previously unavailable. Common shares were worthless at their time of issue, but they were added to preference shares sold as "sweeteners," and they were paid to the lawyers and the promoters involved in initial public issues of preference shares.

If the future cashflow increased as the promoters expected, a market would develop for these common shares as well; and because they were initially worthless they would increase, from literally nothing, in market value faster than bonds and preference shares. McConnell, like other promoters and the lawyers (such as Lovett and Cahan) associated with him, typically took at least part of his compensation in the form of such shares in addition to a fee in cash or commission. As a securities dealer like Aitken and many others, he also sold common shares to his clients after these shares had acquired a market price. Most of all he bought common shares for himself, once there was a market for them, as the potential for growth lay in them rather than in any other form of security.

If promoters overestimated growth in corporate profits, the common shares would not gain a stable or, even better, a rising market, and they might not be able to sell them for anything. This fact in itself encouraged brutal realism if not outright honesty in the promoters, for they personally had a vested interest in being paid in common shares with real promise, and in not selling common shares without real promise. On the other hand, such was the appetite for shares in this period that frequently a market formed for even the common ones immediately upon their issue. When this happened, the promoters received both their commissions and marketable common shares that might well increase in value and thus become very saleable.

How much money did McConnell make on one of his biggest deals in this period? Although we cannot be sure, we can combine hypothetical numbers with numbers from his ledgers to arrive at an approximation. In the Sherwin-Williams reorganization, $3,000,000 in preference shares was sold in three days. If we assume that Montreal-London Securities Corporation sold half of these shares, and Johnston, McConnell & Allison sold the other half, then the partnership sold $1,500,000 in preference shares at a par value of $100 each. If their commission was, say, 10%, they made from this sale $150,000 in cash. In addition they received common shares as part of their compensation. At the time of the initial public offering in 1911, a common share had the purely nominal value of 20% of a preference share or $20, but from McConnell's records it is clear that this rapidly changed to a market value.

Specifically, from his ledgers, we know that McConnell sold 500 common shares of the new company as early as 1912, at $58 a share, for a total of $29,000. If we assume that the three partners received a total of 15,000 common shares, and that each of these shares was worth $58 in 1912, the total market value of their common shares in that year was $870,000. Divided by three, this total market value of their common shares plus their assumed $150,000 fees in cash yielded each partner at least $350,000 for his work in selling only $1,500,000 in preference shares. If we assume that the Canadian dollar in 1912 was worth as much the dollar in 1914, the first year for which there are Consumer Price Index data, to determine McConnell's compensation in 2008 terms, we have to multiply his assumed $350,000 by 18.77 to yield a value of $6,568,333.

Sherwin-Williams, it is to be remembered, was only one of several promotions that McConnell was engaged in simultaneously. Moreover, the other underwriter of the

Sherwin-Williams issue, Montreal-London Securities, appears to have sold the other $1,500,000 in preference shares in 1911. McConnell was a partner in this firm as well, with Lovett and Cahan as the other two partners. If they divided their profits equally, then McConnell may have made a *further* $6,568,333 in 2008 terms from his work for Sherwin-Williams. This would bring his total compensation to over $13,000,000, in 2008 dollars, for one promotion alone, though only $700,000 in 1912 terms. This compensation moreover was apart from whatever the promoters may have earned from the sale of the $2,450,000 of consolidated sinking-fund gold bonds, which McConnell did not begin until after the summer.

It is clear that McConnell personally received only some of the common shares that were the promoters' fee, and we do not in fact know how many, or when he disposed of them, and at what price. If he had more common shares left to sell in 1912, he might have made even more profit. In 1915, Sherwin-Williams common shares sold for as high as $65 and a low of $55; in 1916, the figures were $60 and $45. The preferred shares in these years sold for even more.

Charges of "stockwatering," that is, the watering down of the value of existing stock through the over-issuing of securities, were made against promoters until the 1930s. These charges recalled the traditional valuation of companies as determined by tangible assets and cash, and they assumed that the market value of common shares, not being tied to tangible assets, was really fictitious or at least dubious, even though traders were willing to pay real money for them. The metaphor of water implied that the common shares were somehow diluting the value of the preference shares and bonds, despite the fact that on the dissolution of the business holders of both bonds and preferred shares would be compensated before those of common shares. McConnell could not accept this view of dilution if he wanted to be a promoter at all, for what he was promoting was the prospect of real growth in value. Eventually investors generally came to agree. The notions of stockwatering and par value were totally abandoned, although not until the middle of the twentieth century, in view of the demonstrated possibility of attaining wealth through common shares, as well as of the wisdom of depreciating tangible assets on the balance sheet.

In any case, McConnell, far from developing a fixed reputation for defrauding investors, became more highly respected with time, for two reasons. First, he demonstrated a sustained ability to create wealth, for others as well as for himself, where there had been none or at least less before, through an accurate appreciation of the value of intangibles. Secondly, he, better than most, could predict accurately future income streams. It was his reputation as a predictor of future earnings that enabled him to raise credit and to sell securities for the same companies, in some cases, more than once. Thus, he became known as a wizard of high finance, an alchemist working to produce the optimal blend of securities instruments and to buy and sell these instruments for maximum profit to the investor.

This wizard, however, was not one for mindless risks. Unlike many of his colleagues and contemporaries, who went bankrupt, faced charges of tax evasion, jumped or were pushed out of companies, and drank or shot themselves to death, McConnell was a steady accumulator of wealth – cautious and systematic – in bad times as well as good. Thousands of pages of his ledgers suggest that he probably knew every day of his life precisely how much money he was making and spending, how much he owed, and how much was owing to him, to the last cent. He seldom borrowed money on his own account, and he always valued his own assets conservatively, writing them down to reflect declining market values.

These ledgers, which almost nobody but he and his closest associates saw in his lifetime, reveal that he was practising what he was preaching, namely, that common shares were the best route to sustained wealth. Nearly all his securities over six decades were in common shares alone, and he held on to many, including those in his own promotions, often for decades. Whether this consistency suggests a fundamental honesty such as to silence the critics of his stock promotions depends on whether it makes sense to associate a now almost universally accepted concept of valuation with honesty or dishonesty. Investors in any case typically care more about profits than about ethics. By about 1912, McConnell was becoming one of the most successful investors of his generation, in addition to all his other roles, and his legendary reputation as an investor would only grow over the next half-century.

Nevertheless, his progress was never to be as easy as it looked. In 1912 he seemed to be unstoppable, but in the following year the stock market declined sharply. Entries from his private records reveal how his conservative accounting for 1913 left him with a loss. His total income for that year was $278,991 but he sternly wrote down his securities by $64,400; and his estimated loss, when all income and expenses were netted out, was $128,223.[69]

CHAPTER FIVE

Bittersweet: St Lawrence Sugar and Regulation, 1912–63

How he cornered the sugar market is no secret. He simply bought up all the opposition that counted. But how he came out of nowhere to gain control of the sugar company is a story which probably only McConnell could tell. Opponents say the deal was the one which made and has kept him publicity-shy.

"Sugar Baron," *New Liberty*, March 1949, 22

Like many rich businessmen, McConnell endured much criticism and was the subject of much speculation in the course of his career. His profits as a broker earned him envy, but they extended only over the few years, from 1908 to 1912, although the money that he invested from his brokerage days yielded him a handsome income for years to come. Most criticisms of rich businessmen are of them as individuals. But from 1912 and for 51 years, McConnell was a leader in an industry that attracted similar opprobrium. With his fellow sugar refiners he was from time to time accused of conspiring against the public interest, which was defined variously as that of the consumer or even the wholesaler. Most of the themes of his critics remained constant over this half century, but they had little effect unless supported by government. How McConnell survived and largely flourished for so long in this environment tells us much about him as an industrialist and also about how big business and government adapted to each other in both war and peace.

The company with which McConnell was longest associated was St Lawrence Sugar.[1] He bought a substantial interest in the firm in 1912 and was effectively its sole owner from 1924 to his death almost forty years later, although he was president only from 1914 to 1951. While he was seldom on the floor of his refinery, McConnell paid close attention to every aspect of its work, from its machinery to the welfare of its workers. During his first fifteen years as its president, St Lawrence was the largest or the second-largest sugar refinery in Canada and not much less important thereafter.[2] It was also the largest employer in Maisonneuve, the industrial heart of Montreal. McConnell often complained about how unprofitable sugar refining was, and

Mr and Mrs Alfred Baumgarten, 1885.
McCord Museum 117431.

the industry lobby always argued the same. But even during the Depression, when his investments generally declined by 40 per cent in value, profits from his company continued to flow. Fortunately, these diminished assets were sufficient so that he did not require these profits for his own use. During the Second World War, he promised Prime Minister Mackenzie King to give all of them to the government for the war effort. These profits also later formed the core of his endowment of the McConnell Foundation.

John Redpath, the builder of the Lachine and Rideau canals, had started the Canadian sugar industry with his Canada Sugar Refinery in 1854. Another refinery later set up by the Molson family closed in 1871, following which the Redpath family faced no competition in Montreal until the opening by Alfred Baumgarten and others of the St Lawrence refinery in 1879. The establishment of this new plant coincided with John A. Macdonald's inauguration of a National Policy of tariff protection for Canadian industry. From this point on, the Canadian sugar industry – otherwise exposed to American competition, wholly dependent on imports of raw sugar, and at the mercy of fluctuating prices set by brokers in London and New York – was highly reliant on tariffs. Even with government protection, however, the industry suffered from ruinous internal competition in the late 1880s and early 1890s. Then, in 1897, St Lawrence, Canada Sugar, and Acadia Sugar came to a secret agreement whereby they were to divide the market into fixed proportions for five years for "the purpose of obviating the inconvenience and loss consequent on overproduction, and also the hardships to our employees, due to broken and intermittent periods of work."[3]

In 1906 the Canadian industry was placed on the defensive when the federal government equalized the tariffs on both raw and refined imported sugar, but there followed a more ominous development in the negotiation by the Laurier government of a reciprocity treaty with the United States in 1911. This treaty would not have abolished tariff protection for the Canadian refiners outright, but it included a provision for reciprocal tariffs on sugar – a prospect that seemed to threaten a fresh flooding of the Canadian market with American refined sugar. Huntly Drummond of Canada Sugar led the refiners' fight against ratification of the treaty in the general elections of that year, which saw Laurier's Liberals go down to defeat at the hands of Robert Borden's Conservatives.

McConnell supported Laurier in that contest; but with the change of government and the abandonment of reciprocity, he saw an opportunity to move into a potentially highly lucrative business, in economic circumstances reminiscent of those that had given birth to it in 1879. He bought a major interest (7,500 shares, for a total of $2.5 million) in St Lawrence Sugar in May 1912, with the aid of a syndicate of British investors acting through Imperial Trust and Montreal Securities, the latter being a private investment house that he had set up for himself. Two years later, on 15 February 1914, Baumgarten and his associates sold at least part of their interests to McConnell and a few others. About six months after this transfer, Baumgarten became the company's honorary president and McConnell the president.

There are various stories about how McConnell secured control of St Lawrence. One is that, after the outbreak of war in August 1914, the controller of enemy property seized St Lawrence from Baumgarten, then deemed a German alien, and sold it at a depressed price to McConnell.[4] The records of the controller at Library and Archives Canada in Ottawa, however, do not mention either Baumgarten or McConnell or St Lawrence Sugar. It has also been said that Baumgarten's house on McTavish Street suffered the same fate at the hands of the controller and McConnell, but, since Mrs Baumgarten sold this house to McGill University, this is likewise a canard. Neither is there any evidence that Baumgarten died poor. He remained, according to various sources, the largest shareholder of the Bank of Montreal. His family kept a huge country house for decades, even after Mrs Baumgarten's death in 1953. In his will, executed in 1919, Baumgarten left $75,000 annually to his family, as well as bequests to three Montreal hospitals.[5]

McConnell, c.1912. Private collection.

However he managed it, McConnell now found himself the head of an immensely profitable business. From May to October 1913, the estimated profit of St Lawrence was $780,249.[6] The industry was now also remarkably stable as a result of the division of the market, in eastern and central Canada, among the three major refineries. From 1900 to 1914, the ranges of market share were between 38.60 and 37.71 per cent for Canada Sugar; between 36.4 and 38.05 per cent for St Lawrence; and between 25.70 and 24.24 per cent for Acadia.

McConnell became president of St Lawrence less than two weeks before the outbreak of the war, and he presided over his first meeting of the board on 7 August, four days after the start of conflict. Eight months later, in May 1915, a German U-Boat sank the *Lusitania* just off the coast of Ireland, killing among others many Canadians, including two of the children of McConnell's friends Sir Montagu and Lady Allan. This was one of the worst atrocities of the war, and anti-German hysteria spread through the British Empire, from London to British Columbia. One of the targets was St Lawrence Sugar, which was roundly attacked for allegedly being still in the hands of enemy Germans.

The truth in all of this is difficult to sort out. Even after the changes in the St Lawrence board on February 1914, most of the shareholders besides Baumgarten and his close associates remained evidently German in origin – Gravenhorst and Company, F.H. Geocker, A. Leuder, E.A. Reinecke, and Gustave Weldner – but there were also James S. Garland, Henry D. Tudor, and Moses Williams. Amid the anti-German hysteria, the directors met on 13 May 1915 and their minutes record their discussion of "the serious menace to the welfare of our business caused by hostile publications in the press against certain parties connected with our Company." The result of their deliberations was a decision that the company's German officers had to go. Baumgarten resigned as director and honorary president. Still the largest shareholder, he had to be bought out.[7] Likewise, O.W. Donner, the vice-president and managing director, and all other shareholders with German-sounding names were bought out. What price McConnell paid for Baumgarten's shares is unknown. Since Baumgarten's sale was forced by anti-German sentiment, he was not in a strong position. But, given that St Lawrence does not appear to have been listed publicly at the time, it is unclear to what extent McConnell may have got a bargain "below market." At any rate, in the following week, St Lawrence published an advertisement proclaiming, "German interests no longer connected with St. Lawrence Sugar Refineries, Limited." It continued:

> With the retirement of Mr. A. Baumgarten and Mr. O.W. Donner, as
> announced last week, the last German of either name or origin has ceased to
> hold any interest as a shareholder and at the present time there is not one single

The St Lawrence Sugar Refinery, 1917. McCord Museum, v17,266.

dollar of German money invested in the Company. On the contrary, the entire Capital is now held by investors of Canadian or British origin.

The present officers and directors of the Company have taken every step necessary to place the Company beyond criticism with respect to the interests connected with it either financially or otherwise and, while malicious reports may be circulated as to the continuance of German interests in the Company, the directors are able to give an unqualified denial to any such statements.[8]

The statement did not mention that F.H. Goecker remained the New York representative of the company (until 1930), or that C.F. Bardorf remained the superintendent (until 1938). Both were probably German in origin.

For all their complaints about what a "most extraordinary and dangerous business"[9] sugar was, Canadian refiners did significantly more refining of raw sugar as the war progressed, surpassing the total production of any year between 1908 and 1913 by a wide margin. Moreover, in 1916 and 1917, Canada was a net exporter of sugar for the first time.[10] Yet it was not all clear sailing. By 1915, the war had completely disrupted the established purchasing practices of the refiners because it had also disrupted the established sources of supply. To make matters worse, the refiners showed themselves more competitive with one another in wartime than they had been under their pre-war arrangements.

For the first few months of the war, Canadian refiners were embroiled in a disagreement over pricing, with Canada Sugar keeping its price per pound stable in an effort to prevent hoarding; but with its competitors, St Lawrence and Acadia, raising theirs. Much correspondence ensued between Huntly Drummond of Canada Sugar, the chairman of the refiners as an industry in its dealings with the federal government, and Sir George Foster, the minister of trade and commerce. No agreement on stabilizing prices could be reached, however; and by the end of 1914 it was clear, in any case, that the pricing situation was beyond the control of the refiners either individually or as a body. Britain then set up the Royal Commission on Sugar, based in New York, to regulate the purchases of sugar for the entire empire, including Canada. With the entry of the United States into the war in 1917, a second body was created, the International Sugar Committee, which had the task of coordinating American and other non-British purchases by its members (including however Canada, which belonged to both bodies) with the Royal Commission on Sugar.

Only the acquisition of raw sugar was under control, in the sense that it was to be bought in New York by a representative of the refiners and then allotted among them by him. The wholesale price of the raw sugar sent to the refiners was negotiated between them and their representative in New York. The price to the ultimate consumer was not controlled at all. The chief variables here were two. First was the origin of the raw sugar being sent to Canada, particularly whether it was preferential or non-preferential, that is from within the empire, and thus subject to British preference, or not. And second was the cost of shipping through New York, or some other American port, to the two refineries in Montreal and the ones in Saint John and Halifax.

The issue of transportation became especially critical when in January 1918 W.G. McAdoo, the director general of railroads in Washington, placed an embargo on all shipments by rail from American ports to Canada. J.R. Bruce, the Canadian representative on the International Sugar Committee, told him that Canada hoped to obtain a third of its sugar requirements from the British West Indies and Demerara, with the rest from non-preferential sources, nearly all which had to go through American ports during the year. Moreover, the British government had more recently requisitioned two of the four steamers of the important line running from the British West Indies to Canada, and the two remaining small boats could make only one round trip every six weeks, which is why New York remained more important than ever for Canadian imports. Towards the end of January 1918, the Dominion food controller, H.B. Thomson, and McConnell went down to Washington to see Herbert Hoover, the American food administrator, about the embargo. Whether it was through McConnell's intervention is not clear, but the embargo seemed to be clearing up by 2 February.

Even with the embargo lifted, however, New York continued to prove to be a bottle-neck in February. Drummond pleaded with Bruce to try to retain the normal, pre-war channels of trade, but it now proved impossible to ship all sugar directly by steamer to Montreal. The supply also continued to be problematical, and the refiners were buying non-preferential sugars, that is those from outside the empire.

The situation became grimmer for the St Lawrence and Canada refineries because of chicanery by Atlantic, which was run by McConnell's enemy since 1914, Lorne McGibbon. As Drummond explained to Bruce: "Under present conditions, every pound of sugar that any of us [refiners] can get finds an immediate sale at a high price, and this fact is being taken advantage of by one of our competitors, who claim they can get all the sugar they want (while none of the rest of us is in that position) and are trying to make contracts for this whole year, based on this supposed advantage that they have in getting Raw Sugar."[11] On 26 February 1918 Drummond summarized the result of Atlantic's tricks to Bruce. Since the previous 1 December, the Canada refinery had been closed for thirty-six days and operated for fifty-two days; the St Lawrence had been closed for twenty-nine days and operated for fifty-nine; and, all the while, Atlantic had been running at full capacity.

As the role of purchasing commissions suggests, the war brought unprecedented governmental regulation of the economy, and businessmen were not just observers of this regulation but participants in it. The process gained momentum with the formation of the Union government of Sir Robert Borden in 1917. N.W. Rowell of Toronto, a former leader of the Ontario Liberal Party, became vice-chairman of a new War Committee, with Borden as the nominal chairman. The committee issued a declaration of war policy, which included the "adequate taxation of war profits and incomes, and limitations on excessive profits, hoarding, and rising prices" among its twelve points. In 1918 a War Committee subcommittee called the War Trade Board emerged, with Sir George Foster as chairman. The board was to control licences for import and export, to keep records of Canada's stock of raw materials and manufactured products, to distinguish between essential and other industries, to investigate and make recommendations on production and trade, and to cooperate closely with its counterpart in the United States. The order-in-council setting up the board directed it "to undertake and carry out such supervision as may be necessary of all commercial and industrial enterprises and by cooperation with producers to prevent the waste of labour, raw materials and partially finished products."

McConnell became a member of the board and also its director of licences, which made him responsible for allocating space on ships travelling the Atlantic between Canada and Europe. He also became involved in the sensitive and complicated question of whether to divert Canadian ships from the West Indies and the United States to transport raw sugar to Canada, as opposed to keeping up their scheduled transatlantic runs. This led to difficulties from three sources in March 1918, all to the same effect. First, the West Indian Transportation Committee, representing exporters in the West Indies, refused to accede to Canadian requests to divert special steamers for deliveries to Canada. It was irritated that the Royal Commission on Sugar was apparently indifferent to helping Canada, and that Canada itself was not pressing into service vessels of its own to transport sugar, while all American vessels were engaged in war service. Secondly, the Allied Shipping Board, charged with allocating space on Allied ships generally, refused to divert ships to Canada for the same reason. Finally, the American refiners, who were operating at no more than 70 per cent of capacity, resisted sharing their stock with Canada if Canada would not use its own ships.

McConnell arranged for the Department of Marine and Fisheries to hold a Canadian ship in New Orleans for deliveries of sugar to Canada. Drummond wrote to C.C. Ballantyne, the minister of marine and a former director of St Lawrence Sugar, to intervene by commandeering other Canadian vessels. Their appeals seem to have had an effect, for by the end of June the Canadian refiners had in sight their usual full supply. But then the American refiners began to complain that Canada had got most of its annual allotment of the raw sugar available already, and should cut back its annual consumption, as they themselves had cut back. They pressured the International Sugar Committee to act. In July, Bruce described the committee to Drummond as "autocratic and high-handed" in refusing to allocate any more sugar to Canada from Cuba, Santo Domingo, and the West Indies. Nonetheless, Ottawa soon followed the American lead and reduced Canadian consumption by one-half.[12]

Even apart from this decision, it was clear to Bruce that no sugar would be moving from the British West Indies and Demerara at least until mid-October. Moreover, the majority of the Demerara producers would hold out as long as possible "in the expectation of receiving an increased price based on the contemplated higher price for Cuban sugars." And, even if there were enough sugar available to Canada from these sources, it would be impossible to move it all owing to the lack of tonnage. Bruce could not even trust the Royal Commission, since it was reluctant to divert Cuba sugar to Canada before November. In any case, it might prove necessary for Canada to apply to the United Kingdom for relief from the decision by the committee. The strains on Canada in having to answer to both the Royal Commission and the International Sugar Committee were becoming intolerable.

More pressure was placed on the Canadian refiners in the autumn, with an attempt by the Americans to divert all sugar allocated to Canada to the Canadian ports of Saint John and Halifax. This move was designed to force Canada to find its own tonnage and thereby to cancel the Canadian allotment of tonnage allocated by the West Indies Transportation Committee. It was also designed to relieve the congestion at the railway terminals and piers in New York harbour.[13] F.C.T. O'Hara, deputy minister of trade and commerce, wrote to McConnell at the War Trade Board that such Canadian tonnage did not exist to implement this change, a fact that had already been determined by others, including McConnell himself.

Behind this American scheme, both Drummond and Bruce detected the hand of Lorne McGibbon of Atlantic Sugar. Drummond explained to Samuel Lee, a New York sugar broker, that McGibbon's real object "is to compel us [the other refiners] to pay 20¢ [per hundred pounds] more (the extra freight to Saint John over New York) on any sugar for Montreal [Canada and St Lawrence Sugar] or Chatham [Dominion Sugar]." Atlantic was "creating propaganda in spite of the protests of the Canada Food Board" because it wanted to close the other Canadian refineries down.[14] It could do this simply by destroying the traditional supply lines to the Montreal and Chatham refiners, namely, railways from New York, Boston, and Philadelphia.

The end of the war in November of 1918 did not bring about a relaxation of sugar controls. The world generally was in turmoil, with the displacement of people and pre-war patterns of trade and communication. The Canada Food Board arranged for Bruce and the New York broker A.R. Neill to purchase sugar for Canadian consumption in the first nine months of 1919, and they bought about 277,000 tons for allocation among the eastern refineries.[15] There was more than enough sugar to meet Canadian needs. The wholesale grocers, however, believed that prices would shortly fall, and they refused to contract at the prices agreed to by the Canada Food Board and the refiners. They purchased only small quantities from the refiners.

Early in 1919, the refiners were permitted to buy additional sugar at the market price and to re-export. They were also allowed to make contracts with the Royal Commission to refine sugar for the commission's needs within the empire but outside Canada. The export of sugar by the Canadian refiners continued from January to April. McConnell went personally to England in April and May to sell St Lawrence sugar to London dealers, both what he had reserved for export and any surplus, and he seemed to be making progress. As he wrote to his wife, he found himself "securing higher prices (privately) than I had ever dreamed of in this market." He had come "here at exactly the right moment, and by holding on to my available sugar have secured the highest prices paid."[16]

By June, however, it was apparent that there would be a world shortage of sugar, in the opinion at least of the brokers. The Indian crop had failed, Japan and India were competing for Dutch East Indies sugar, and a scramble broke out among the New York brokers. Southern European countries sent out orders almost regardless of price, and by August through October the sugar being delivered was much more expensive than the sugar that had been allocated by the Canada Food Board. By late July, it was clear that the reluctance of the Canadian wholesalers to buy, and the consequent export of sugar by the refiners, would make it impossible to fill a sudden surge in demand without interfering with the export contracts. There were no reserves, particularly to meet the increasing demand of western Canada, where sugar was needed for the making of jam and preserves.

From the point of view of the refiners, the main problem, during and immediately after the war, was security of supply. For the consumer, however, it was price stability. The evidence suggests that, apart from Atlantic Sugar, none of the refiners was in a position to hoard; but this was not apparent to the public, and, in any case, the popular clamour against war profiteering was tarring many big businesses, particularly established monopolies, with the same brush. It simply was not good enough for the refiners to say that the price of raw sugar, as opposed to the refined sugar sold to consumers, was determined by the world market. In the absence of government-sanctioned hoarding in anticipation of periods of want, it became possible to question whether the refiners were not hoarding when supplies were plentiful, to sell overseas refined sugar at high prices that they could not obtain at home.

On 27 July 1919 the new Board of Commerce began to regulate prices in a wide range of industries, including sugar, and the next day it issued an order restraining the whole sugar industry – wholesalers and retailers alike – from disposing of sugar "in such manner as designed or calculated to unfairly enhance the price or cost of said commodity." Refiners were prohibited from exporting sugar from Canada even if they had licences to export issued by the Canadian Trade Commission.[17] The function of the board was to set prices for political and not economic reasons so that – as in socialist command economies – both the cost of raw materials from abroad and the profit earnable through exports were essentially irrelevant to the domestic prices that it set.

On 2 September 1919 the Board of Commerce convened at the Windsor Hotel in Montreal. All the eastern refiners, except Dominion but including St Lawrence, which was represented by McConnell, asked permission to continue to export despite the domestic shortages. The board ordered the refiners to deliver 1,400 further tons of sugar to the west, in proportions agreed among them. They were permitted a net profit not greater than $^2/_5$ of a cent per pound.[18] The next day, McConnell appeared again before the board to say that he disagreed with the other refiners, who were claiming that they could not send sugar to the Canadian west because of fear of demurrage charges on ships, loaded with their sugar for overseas, that were delayed by having to meet Canadian demand.

In an effort to defend the right of all of them to export, which was much more profitable to them than domestic shipments, McConnell said that they had to meet the domestic emergency. Otherwise, they would have to raise their domestic prices, and "lend themselves to the impression that they were raising prices because they wanted to make more profit out of the urgent needs of the Canadian people" – an impression that would lead to a ban on all exports. McConnell asked for a recess, and after the hearing had resumed he reported that Acadia would ship 500 tons of granulated sugar at once to the west and that the Atlantic, St Lawrence, and Canada refineries would each ship 300 tons over the following week. He would ask the British Columbia and Dominion refineries to make up the difference.[19]

But the sugar shortage continued. Protracted strikes in Cuba had delayed the delivery of raw sugar ordered months before at comparatively low rates. The cost of refining had also gone up from two cents to four cents a pound more than in the United States. At the same time, throughout the control of profits by the Board of Commerce, retail sugar prices in Canada had been consistently lower than corresponding prices in the United States. In response, on 26 February, the board rescinded its order of 8 January, with the effect of leaving profits uncontrolled.[20] A few months later, however, it moved again to restrict "prices calculated unfairly to enhance the cost or price of sugar." To this end, it now permitted only selling by refiners to wholesalers, and it defined a fair price as one based on the "average invoiced cost of all sugar actually in stock at the time of sale," including freight, wholesaler, and retailer charges. All the eastern refineries and B.C. Sugar were also forbidden to sell any raw sugar, except to one another, until the end of September.[21]

Such was the rising market in Canada in the first six months of 1920 that St Lawrence found itself accused of withholding granulated sugar contracted for export, in order to reap higher profits by selling the same sugar at home. In October and November 1919, the company had entered into two contracts with the Nemours Trading Corporation of New York, a client of the Muller-Fox Brokerage of Chicago, to sell granulated refined sugar to it.[22] But then, in January 1920, St Lawrence failed to make its first delivery of five hundred tons to New York – owing, it later claimed, to the refusal of the Canadian Trade Commission to issue any permits to export granulated sugar. McConnell claimed that he had asked Rhys D. Fairbairn, a member of the commission, for an export licence, but only verbally.[23] This had been early in January 1920, at McConnell's hotel in Ottawa, but Fairbairn had refused. Muller-Fox claimed that McConnell and Fairbairn had struck an informal agreement by which the commission would not issue an export permit so that St Lawrence could sell the same sugar in Canada at much higher prices than those it had contracted for with the Americans.

McConnell underwent a preliminary interrogation in the case on 7 June 1922 in New York. The litigation was ultimately settled out of court – St Lawrence had, according to McConnell, "decided it was desirable to pay a comparatively small amount to clean the matter up and avoid the possibility of a long drawn out lawsuit, which might have dragged through the courts for another year or two"[24] – and so it is impossible to say whether McConnell was, as alleged, guilty of participating in a fraudulent conspiracy to avoid his contracts. In any event, whether the allegations of Muller-Fox were true or not, they are vivid testimony to the foetid atmosphere of the sugar industry in a rising market, and to the web of deceit into which all seemed to be drawn. What seems clear from McConnell's own records is that he made more than $400,000 by not shipping to the United States the sugar contracted for and by selling it instead to the Canadian market in the same period.

On 1 July 1920 all controls on sugar were officially lifted. In a supplementary directive, however, the Department of Trade refused to let the refiners export onto the world market, where they could now have obtained retail prices three to ten cents higher than at home. Meanwhile, the Canadian refiners were unable to keep up even with domestic demand, at least in the sense of producing enough profitably. They made various representations to government, and dispatched a deputation, which included McConnell, to Ottawa. On 12 October, McConnell and his associates met Sir George Foster, and the next day the Board of Commerce issued a new order. It decreed: "Refineries are restricted from selling sugar otherwise than to wholesalers, manufacturers or retailers, and such wholesalers, manufacturers or retailers are restrained from buying the sugar otherwise than from such refiners." Furthermore, "the wholesalers are restrained from selling to others than manufacturers or retailers and such manufacturers or retailers are restrained from buying such sugar otherwise than from wholesalers." It banned imports of sugar, and it ordered the refiners to sell sugar at 18½ cents a pound for the following seventy days. Although this was better than the prevailing American wholesale price, the government immediately raised doubts about the legality of the ruling, and the refiners decided not to press for its implementation.

On 20 October came the showdown. Prime Minister Arthur Meighen and much of the cabinet received McConnell and other industry representatives. According to the refiners, their situation was genuinely desperate but not because of a lack of raw sugar. There was indeed plenty, but it had been bought at extremely high prices at the direction of the Board of Commerce, while now the refiners were obliged to sell the refined product at much lower prices, as also ordered by the board. To be competitive with US prices, some were now suggesting that the Canadian refiners should charge wholesale 15 cents, or even less. But, were they to sell at 15 cents what it cost them 22 cents to produce, that would be a total loss to them of $19.2 million. In April 1920, the Board of Commerce itself had computed that it had saved the consumer $20 million thanks to its controls over the sugar industry, and so – the refiners argued – they had not been making colossal profits at all, and since April the board had saved the consumer a further $10 million.

As Drummond, who made the presentation, concluded: "The position of the refiners ... is unique in that their situation arises solely out of a system of Government control established, admittedly, for the benefit of the people, and that it furnishes no precedent for other claims. No other Canadian industry has been subjected in the same degree to have its inherent right to regulate its own affairs taken away from it

... However, the policy of providing Government support to assist native industries in overcoming difficulties is not without precedent ... in the United Kingdom, Newfoundland and Argentina."[25] The Meighen government listened carefully, but on 20 October, probably because of a mixture of political considerations – elections were looming – and financial ones, it refused the refiners aid. It also declared both an open market on sugar and the permanent suspension of the Board of Commerce.

On 25 October, the Montreal refiners agreed to reduce their wholesale price to seventeen cents.[26] Thus, their net loss per pound increased to five cents, for a total of $14 million, which was more than double the total net earnings of the refiners in the previous seven years. There was no point in continuing to produce at a loss, and the refineries shut down. On 6 October, the Canadian Bank of Commerce in Montreal had refused to extend a line of credit to St Lawrence or to make unsecured advances to the company.

On 2 November, McConnell announced to his St Lawrence colleagues that he had obtained a line of credit of $5,248,000 from the Bank of Montreal. In order to save the company from liquidation, he explained, he had agreed to pledge all his securities, British, Canadian, and foreign, to the bank for this loan. There was a further loan of $1,736,588 from the National City Bank of New York. McConnell had also decided to turn over to the company, as a gift, all income received by him in 1921–24. In consideration of all this, he asked to be given the right to take up and pay for at par all unissued preferred and common shares, at any time within a period of five years from 1 November 1920. His request was approved.

St Lawrence did return to profitability by the end of 1924, and it was able through its revenues to pay off the two loans that McConnell had arranged for it. He therefore exercised his option on 31 December 1924, buying at par 32,500 preferred shares and 45,000 common shares, and in payment he turned over securities with a market value of over $7,750,000. With this move and apparently through buyout of the other shareholders, he and his immediate family came to own all 60,000 of the common shares now both authorized and issued. This ownership made him and the company essentially identical.[27]

An analysis of this arrangement suggests that it may have been one of the most brilliant strokes of his career. He had used his own securities as collateral for two corporate loans, and when the company returned to profitability he simply took back these securities while transforming the company into a family property. The only cost to him of doing the latter was probability his inability to trade the shares that he had put up as collateral, between 1921 and 1924, which happened to coincide with an economic depression in any case. The only risk in this period was that the company might not return to profitability, but it did, and almost entirely to his benefit. This history of the company and of the sugar industry generally had been punctuated by failure, but the demand for sugar was constant if not growing; and McConnell must have calculated, entirely correctly, that there was every prospect of a recovery of prices after 1921. This calculation is in accordance with the oral tradition that Timothy Eaton had counselled him always to invest in what people needed, rather than in simply what they wanted. With total ownership of the company in his hands, he returned his portfolio of securities to it. Throughout the remainder his life, he would continue this practice of keeping securities and real estate also in the name of St Lawrence Sugar, where they were taxed at the corporate rate, thus reducing the tax liability of his personal fortune. Since he was the only decision maker in the company, there was no danger of losing his assets held in it owing to the decisions of others.

It was, however, not easy for St Lawrence to make a good profit between 1924 and the outbreak of a new world war in 1939. Although nobody could know in 1925 that the price of Cuban sugar, in particular, would not rise above four cents a pound over the following fourteen years, everybody realized that competition among exporters had returned. In January 1926 McConnell reported to the board that St Lawrence's "export business was taken without profit, as the margin was extremely narrow, but it was considered advisable to take the export business even at such a narrow spread, in order to help out on the cost of manufacture for domestic sugar."[28] In the absence of an international agreement limiting exports, McConnell wrote to Arthur Meighen in July 1926 to complain about the dumping of Cuban sugar onto the Canadian market. Because of its large inventory of refined sugar, the refinery was closed from December 1926 to May 1927, and there were no export orders received in this period.[29] Business did not apparently improve in 1928, and in 1929 Cuban refiners began to dump granulated, and not merely raw, sugar onto the Canadian market, which reduced very much the business of the Canadian refiners.[30] The international Chadbourne Agreement of 1931 reduced production in major exporting countries, but it failed to raise prices because production increased in the non-controlled British Empire and in areas with duty-free access to the United States. In 1937 twenty-one major exporting and importing countries, accounting for 85 to 90 per cent of world production and consumption, reached another international agreement, but Canada was not a party to it.

Difficult as the sugar business was from 1925 onwards, St Lawrence still made a modest profit. McConnell paid off the company's outstanding bond issue of $1.2 million, held by Imperial Trust and due in 1932, although he borrowed for this purpose $500,000 in New York. Yet he remained under considerable strain. The Depression was reaching its depths in 1931–32, and in 1932 alone the refinery operated only 170 days and was idle for 196 days. Then, in 1933, Canada imposed an excise tax on sugar of two cents per pound. This tax increased the price of sugar to consumers, and McConnell estimated a consequent shrinkage in sales in 1933 of from 10 to 15 per cent.[31] In 1933 as well, the plant was open for only 141 days.[32]

Through these years, St Lawrence continued to benefit from the Canadian preference accorded to British West Indian sugars, which was called the British preference and applied to all goods from within the empire. As McConnell explained in 1930, these sugars – together with other "British grown sugars" from Mauritius, Natal, and Australia – furnished most of what was refined in Canada. Yet McConnell did not rely on the British preference for all his supplies, since non-British sugar might still yield him a profit if demand for refined sugar and consequently domestic retail prices were rising.

At the same time, however, St Lawrence was facing growing competition from those sugar refiners who processed Canadian-grown beets and therefore paid no duty at all. Chief among these was Dominion Sugar in western Ontario, which was in the process of amalgamating with Canada Sugar in Montreal. In an appeal for further protection, McConnell explained to Prime Minister R.B. Bennett that refined sugar was selling for less in 1934 than in 1931. Then he summed up Bennett's dilemma as he saw it: "How much should the Canadian consumer pay for the purpose of bolstering one particular agricultural commodity [wheat or sugar beets] as against all others, or to what extent is there justification for pulling down an established industry with the hope of building up another of similar character, at a much greater cost to the consumer?"[33]

Bennett did nothing. Nevertheless, profits continued to flow to St Lawrence, partly because the refiners remained averse to ruinous price cutting and partly because people continued to see the product as a necessity rather than a luxury. In 1934 Canada reduced its excise tax on sugar by one cent per pound, and the year proved a little better for McConnell, with his refinery operating for 153 days.[34]

In 1934 business definitely improved, with sales for the first nine months being twelve million pounds greater than in the same period in 1933. But a confectionary company had opened its own refinery in Toronto in 1934, competing directly with the other eastern refiners. Its failure in the same year left an inventory of refined sugar in 1935 that cut into St Lawrence's market share in Ontario, which now formed almost half of its annual turnover.[35] In 1936 another competitor arose in Toronto, Beamish Sugar, which sold sugar for as much as thirty-five cents per hundred pounds less than the list price of St Lawrence. At first, St Lawrence matched Beamish's price, but, by the end of the year, it had decided to ignore the competition and thus lose more business to its rival.[36] Business seems to have been sluggish up to the outbreak of war in September 1939.

By then, McConnell had initiated plans to use St Lawrence as a source of income for his family and for the endowment of the charitable foundation that he was establishing in 1936–37. He began by redeeming all the preferred shares, for a total of $4 million, in other companies held by St Lawrence.[37] His next step, at the end of 1937, was to limit the number of shareholders to fifty.[38] McConnell eventually sold the securities that he had obtained through the redemption of his preferred shares, and with their cash proceeds he bought common stock. This stock he made over to members of his family and to Commercial Trust, the family trust company originally set up by Max Aitken. Possibly because of the outbreak of war in September 1939, he did not transfer his St Lawrence shares to Commercial Trust until 1941. These 33,000 common shares had a total value of $4,445,000.

On 10 April 1939 McConnell had pledged to Prime Minister King that, in the event of war, the St Lawrence refinery would "be placed unreservedly at the disposal of the Government." With this pledge in mind, and noting the establishment of government control of sugar, the board resolved in 1941 that "this Company devote its entire profits for the duration of the War to charitable purposes and to objects connected with the various types of War work."[39] Thus, all of the company's wartime profits, and some of its assets as well, went to McConnell's charitable foundation.[40] The first transfer of funds, in 1941, amounted to $4.5 million, which was followed by a further $2.5 million in 1943.[41]

Despite McConnell's promises to devote all the profits of St Lawrence to charity and war work, these profits did not escape criticism. M.J. Coldwell, the leader of the Co-operative Commonwealth Federation (CCF), was a frequent critic in the House of Commons, though the nature of his concern is not altogether clear.[42] Another critic was John H. Blackmore, leader of the Social Credit Party. On 7 March 1944, in the House of Commons, he demanded to know the nature of the relationship between the government and an alleged sugar combine and between the government and McConnell. He also challenged Prime Minister King to "rise and categorically state that the Liberal party has never received, directly or indirectly, from the St. Lawrence Sugar Refining Company, from J.W. McConnell, or from anyone representing either or both of these, or any other Canadian sugar interest any contribution of money for the campaign funds of the Liberal party." Replying on 10 March, King did not deny receiving such contributions, but he expressed his resentment at the suggestion "that the present government of Canada or any member of it would betray its trust at the instigation of any corporation, any special interest, or any individual." He also cited his exchange of correspondence with McConnell in April 1939, in which McConnell had offered to place the St Lawrence plant "unreservedly at the disposal of the government" in event of war. He explained that regulation had since enabled the government to avoid accepting McConnell's offer.[43]

During the Second World War, nobody wanted a repetition of the sugar crisis of 1920–21, even the refiners who had benefited from rises in prices in 1918–20.[44] An order-in-council on 21 October laid out the framework for confining purchases of raw sugar by the refiners to prices set by the Office of the Sugar Administrator. The refiners did not object. Their motivation was doubtless mixed, beginning with an unfeigned desire to help the war effort, as evidenced by McConnell's fulsome tributes to the troops in company publications. But they also felt, rightly, that comprehensive regulation would spare them the intense public scrutiny and criticism that they had experienced in the First World War, and that it might stabilize their prices and thus earn for them stable profits.

As early as January 1940, the procedures for price stabilization had fallen into place. Grant Dexter, the Ottawa correspondent of the Winnipeg *Free Press*, obtained a picture of the situation from Charles Dunning, the former premier of Saskatchewan and then the minister of finance under Mackenzie King. Dunning, who had now become a close business colleague of McConnell's and was soon to succeed McConnell as president of Ogilvie Four Mills, reported that the Wartime Prices and Trade Board, established at the very start of war four months before, had been "sitting in with all kinds of big business people, such as McConnell and Ross McMaster," the latter president of the Steel Company of Canada. This board "has done a magnificent job and completely possesses the confidence of the business community." From 1941 to 1949, the refiners obtained their raw sugar through two successive agencies of the Canadian government. For the first seven of these years, S.R. Noble, the sugar administrator (or controller) under the Wartime Prices and Trade Board, administered the supplies. The first problem was transporting the raw sugar by sea. In 1941 the St Lawrence stock of raw sugar reached, at one stage, the dangerously low level of just over 12,000 pounds, and at other times little more than a day's supply was on reserve. Noble arranged for stock to come by steamer to American ports and then by rail to Canada, and in August he announced the removal of duty on raw sugar entering Canada.

In February 1942 Noble permitted a rise in price of 25 cents per hundred pounds on raw sugar, and 26¾ cents on refined sugar, to offset rises in the cost of raw materials used in processing. The excise tax was also reduced from $2 to $1.50 per hundred pounds. In April the assistant sugar administrator suggested that the eastern refiners should form a committee to oversee the equitable distribution of their supplies. The Eastern Refiners' Sales Committee began its work swiftly, in June. It was therefore with the full knowledge and approval of the sugar-control authorities that the three eastern refiners exchanged their total sales figures on a weekly basis. These arrangements were essentially secret from the public, but the profits of the refiners were secure, at least in respect of traditional proportions, and indeed there were also governmental guarantees against losses occasioned by the falling value of inventory. They also spared the refiners scrutiny from investigation and the threat of prosecution under anti-combines legislation.

There was now in the form of the government itself, no less, a new barrier to the entry of new competitors, and so there was now no reasonable fear of any upset to the long-established divisions of the market. In C.D. Howe, the minister of trade and commerce, the refiners found someone who understood big business and would generally (but not always) protect them. Hector McKinnon and then Donald Gordon, the chairmen of the Wartime Prices and Trade Board, became reliable allies of the refiners, and McConnell had become close enough to S.R. Noble to invite him to Kit's wedding in 1945. With his fellow presidents among the eastern refiners, W.J. McGregor of Canada and Dominion (C&D) and L.J. Seidensticker of Acadia-Atlantic, McConnell maintained sufficiently cordial enough relations to send salmon to them from his fishing camp on the Restigouche.

The cosy relationship between government and the sugar industry that had thus developed lays bare precisely how much competition the refiners really wanted. Effectively, they were at least temporarily now parts of a state-sponsored monopoly. It may be tempting to describe this arrangement as a conspiracy among capitalists to promote their own welfare, to the detriment of the consumer. But sugar prices in the Second World War and afterwards never rose to the levels experienced in 1914–18. Indeed, governmental regulation of the industry in the Second World War was the only alternative to the unbridled price competition that had so harmed consumers during the First World War and afterwards.

The outbreak of war almost immediately meant shortages among both the consumers and the producers of sugar. Sugar rationing and a shortage of labour forced St Lawrence to shift from a double to a single shift in July 1942, releasing about a hundred employees for war work. St Lawrence was also grappling with increasing shortages of the fuel oil necessary for its operations. It considered converting to coal, but it found that the essential equipment was effectively unavailable. Henry Borden, nephew of Sir Robert Borden and a friend of McConnell's, was coordinator of controls in Ottawa. He suggested switching the operations of St Lawrence to C&D's Redpath plant on the Lachine Canal, which used coal, since there was excess capacity at C&D. McConnell proposed a "joint melt" to C&D, but the latter insisted on taking over the shipping, invoicing, and collection of accounts done by St Lawrence staff. McConnell refused, on the ground that this would mean St Lawrence's "retirement from business." Under pressure from Noble, and because of labour shortages at C&D itself, W.J. McGregor, the president of C&D, agreed to confine the cooperation between the two companies to a joint melt. The St Lawrence refinery had already closed down in December 1942, and it remained closed under the agreement with C&D that took effect the following February. It did not reopen until 1947.

Sugar rationing came into effect, on a voluntary basis, in January 1942, at ¾ of a pound per person per week. In May the quota was reduced to ½ pound, and in July coupon rationing was introduced. McConnell expected that rationing would reduce profits by 30 per cent in 1943 and estimated that profits for 1942 had been maintained only through the increase of twenty-five cents per hundred pounds allowed by Noble, as well as through the reduction in staff through the switching to a single shift.

McConnell was bitter about the increasing subsidization of beet sugar, particularly the setting up – by the Quebec government – of a beet plant in Saint-Hilaire, which he described as "a great conglomeration of junk" that would cost the taxpayer about $3 million. He would complain about this plant to the end of his life, even to his friend Premier Duplessis in the 1950s, only to find Duplessis's turning a deaf ear to him.

Still haunted by the insolvency of St Lawrence in 1920–21, McConnell was heartened when a 1942 amendment to the order-in-council setting up the sugar controls authorized the creation of a stabilization fund, for which he had been vigorously lobbying. It addressed squarely the complaint that McConnell had lodged earlier with Noble, namely, that there were doubts and fears among the refiners "as to whether or not [a] fund would actually be available in the hands of the Controller for the purpose specified, which reads – 'to the extent of the resources then in the Administrator's reserve fund.'" The "then" referred to the end of control; and now the refiners were to be fully indemnified for the prices that they had paid for raw sugar, either before or after the end of control, to the extent that they had bought the sugar from the sugar administrator and regardless of what amount remained in the reserve at the end of control. With this regulation, the ghost of 1920–21 was at last exorcized, and the refiners could feel much more comfortable that the price fluctuations occasioned by war would not destroy them again.

The years of the joint melt with C&D were tough ones for St Lawrence, with profits falling sharply in 1943 and in the second half of 1945 in particular. McConnell saw this as part of his contribution to the war effort, and the profits of 1943 were still given to his foundation. In 1945 industrial users of sugar faced increasingly stringent rations. From January to March, they were restricted to 70 per cent of what they had been permitted to buy in the corresponding period in 1941, a ration that was reduced to 65 per cent in April-June and 50 per cent in July-December. By the annual general meeting on 24 April 1946, McConnell was warning that, if some relief were not given, "we must be ready to see our profits from sugar operations eventually disappear." Sales had fallen since 1944 by over twenty-five million pounds. But McConnell saw a heavy backlog of demand building up, and he launched a program to update the facilities of the refinery in anticipation of future opportunities.

At the end of 1946, C&D terminated its joint melt with St Lawrence, over the objection of the latter. The supply of oil in 1946 was even worse than in 1943, when the joint melt had begun, but McConnell managed to obtain his requirements from McColl-Frontenac Oil. At least sugar control was still in effect, and the government would continue to ensure the supply of raw sugar by shipping by rail after the navigation season. Nevertheless, other costs were rising, including wages. McConnell warned Noble that profits in 1947 would completely disappear, and in April 1947 Noble reduced the price of 100 pounds of raw sugar by thirteen cents. McConnell protested that this was inadequate. In November 1947 the Canadian government abolished sugar quotas, but it retained full control over the purchases and the prices of sugar. Noble's powers were transferred to the new Canadian Sugar Stabilization Corporation (CSSC), which had begun functioning in February and continued in operation until 1949.

McConnell explained to the board that the corporation was "to give the indus-try such protection as it is politically possible to obtain against losses resulting from future price declines in the period of readjustment, which it is felt must inevitably follow."[45] To many, the future of privately owned refineries remained dim. Robert Miller, who joined St Lawrence as cashier in McConnell's office on St James Street in July 1947, had been working as an accountant with P.S. Ross just before. There, he had been warned that sugar was "not a good business. It's dead. It's going to be taken over by the government."[46] This judgment was wrong, and Miller himself eventually became a president of St Lawrence.

Although sugar rationing lasted only from July 1942 to November 1947, there were controls on price, distribution, and supply until March 1950. During the nine years of control, Canadian sugar production was only 70 per cent of pre-war production, but the sugar controller and the CSSC were at least still guaranteeing the refiners against loss on raw sugar. Furthermore, with the lifting of rationing or quota restrictions on 1 November 1946, the price of raw sugar rose by 75 cents per hundred pounds, and of refined by $1 per hundred pounds. The removal of the excise tax then reduced the cost of refined sugar. The sugar administrator duly transferred all the increased profits to the refiners, and it was to be expected that the demand for refined sugar was about to increase.[47] The future, therefore, looked bright. Prices of the raw material were stable; the market prices were permitted to rise; and there were still allocations of raw sugar among the refiners by the sugar administrator, now called the president of the CSSC, S.R. Noble.

Yet, even with this amount of regulation, a new competitive threat emerged in 1949 with the grant by Noble of a special licence to the Manitoba Sugar Company, essen-tially a beet company, to import 10,000 tons of raw cane at a price ten cents lower, per hundred pounds, than that paid by St Lawrence for its entire stock for that year, although there was to be no guarantee to it against a fall in prices. The problem was not so much the favourable price accorded to Manitoba Sugar as the implication that this company was entering into direct competition with St Lawrence to increase sales through refining imported cane in addition to its sales of domestic beet. McConnell protested to Noble that machinery for the manufacture of beet sugar had entered Canada free of duty, whereas St Lawrence had had to pay a 25 per cent duty on the machinery that it was importing. C.F. Elliott, deputy minister of national revenue, eventually forced Manitoba Sugar to pay duty on its cane-refining equipment.[48]

From August 1949 to the end of 1952, the British Ministry of Food was the sole seller from which the Canadian refiners could obtain supplies of Commonwealth sugar. Since the CSSC was still acquiring additional quantities of sugar, made avail-able to the refiners at fixed prices guaranteed against loss, it had a decisive voice in determining the sources of raw sugar for Canada. It was official Canadian as well as

British policy that the refiners should as much as possible buy sugar from within the Commonwealth, and Canadian tariffs favoured Commonwealth raw sugar.

In October 1949, anticipating the forthcoming removal of the British Ministry of Food as the sole source of Commonwealth sugar, the British sugar controller assured Canadians that the ministry would still reserve about 500,000 long tons[49] of Commonwealth sugar for them. This sugar would be sold, however, following the expressed desire of the Canadian government, at the world price, plus an agreed portion of the preference. This price structure was in accordance with a bilateral agreement between Canada and Cuba that the cost of Cuban imports should be equalized with that of Commonwealth imports. Discussions under the General Agreement on Tariffs and Trade (GATT) in Torquay in 1950–51 had led to this equalization of Cuban, and later of Dominican Republic and Haitian, sugar with Commonwealth sugar.

With regard to sugar from the Commonwealth, the three eastern Canadian refiners met at the end of October 1949. They agreed to form what was called a "central agency" for purchasing, although this was not to begin functioning until the following March, when sugar control in Canada, under the CSSC, came formally to an end. The refiners were, of course, still bound by the agreements entered into by Canada with respect to how much of their imports were to come from within the Commonwealth, and so – far from being a secret conspiracy – they openly assumed the function of implementing an obligation in international law undertaken by Canada such as had been fulfilled under wartime regulation by the Canadian government itself.

Despite the effective end, in December 1949, of raw-sugar purchases first through the Canadian sugar controller and then through the CSSC, the British and Canadian governments still wanted Canada to purchase as much Commonwealth sugar as possible. In the interests of both Canada and the Commonwealth, a central agency of the three eastern refiners was created in March 1950 to purchase Commonwealth sugar jointly from the British Ministry of Food, to average among its members the cost of raw sugar annually, and to divide expenses according to sales. This arrangement continued until 1953, when the refiners could deal directly with the producers rather than through the British Ministry of Food.[50]

The outbreak of the Korean War in June 1950 led to a sharp upward surge in world sugar prices, and on 6 July all the eastern refiners raised their base price by fifteen cents. There were two further advances on the base price in July, of twenty-five cents each. The crisis had led to an increase in demand among their customers, and this – combined with the turmoil on the world market – prompted the central agency in July to, in effect, take joint decisions on their sales as well as their purchase prices. Such blatantly premeditated coordination of sales prices was exceptional, but it was probably justified inasmuch as it was the double function of the agency to average the costs among its members of raw sugar and to divide their expenses according to sales.

Participation in the central agency did not deny McConnell personally the capacity to take initiatives in order to obtain favourable prices for all the raw sugar bought by St Lawrence, and indeed to lead St Lawrence to diverge from Acadia-Atlantic and C&D. Although Canada was obliged to purchase a definite amount of Commonwealth sugar, it appears that the three refiners were not obliged individually to participate in every purchase made by the agency. McConnell felt that the price then being paid for sugar by the central agency was exorbitant. Commonwealth sugar was being sold at the world price, and this was effectively cheaper to the Canadian refiners only to the extent that it entered Canada at the imperial or British preference rate, which still made it expensive in comparison with what it had been before the outbreak of war. McConnell therefore began to seek a source of sugar at less than the prevailing world price, and he found it in the United States.

In 1950 the United States announced that it would pre-empt all other countries and buy the entire Cuban crop, not yet sold, in order to curb speculation by producers and hoarding by American consumers. The US government saw this deprivation of other established customers of Cuba as temporary, but as long as it lasted both the United Kingdom and Canada would be without Cuban imports to meet demand. The British Ministry of Food was unable to change the mind of the Americans. But McConnell himself, on behalf of both the British ministry and Canadian refiners, lobbied the US secretary of agriculture, who relented. The secretary agreed that the United States should make Cuban sugar available from its reserves for the United Kingdom. There followed the important consequence that the Cuban imports now exportable to the United Kingdom would enable the United Kingdom to release some of its own share of Commonwealth sugar to Canada at a lower price that that prevailing on the world market. Canada, being part of the Commonwealth, would benefit from the imperial or British preference.[51]

The assurance to McConnell from the United States arrived on 23 August, but two days later both C&D and Acadia-Atlantic raised their base price by seventy cents. St Lawrence declined to follow them, and it was swamped with orders until 28 August, when it, too, raised its base price by seventy cents. This incident is a further illustration of how the refiners did not decide on their prices necessarily or perhaps even habitually together, notwithstanding the existence of their central agency. Instead, they waited to see how their competitors acted. In this crisis situation, it is probable that Acadia-Atlantic and C&D did take a joint decision, but clearly not with St Lawrence. And when St Lawrence did follow them in raising its base price three days later, it may have been because it could not fill the orders pouring in. In any case, at the beginning of September, the United States released 48,000 tons of raw sugar to the United Kingdom, then the United Kingdom released some of its Commonwealth-produced sugar to Canada, and the central agency was able to cancel its August orders.

Panic buying continued through September, when the beet crop began to alleviate the situation.

McConnell's actions between August and October 1950 demonstrate how much in charge and indeed independent he remained as a refiner. In January 1951 he resigned as president of St Lawrence and was replaced by his son Wilson, who had become a vice-president in 1939. Despite his resignation as president, however, he remained a director and the ultimate authority. He was thus still in charge a few months later, when the world price for Cuban raw sugar shot up again dramatically. Acadia-Atlantic and C&D raised their prices in May and June, but not St Lawrence, and indeed St Lawrence announced a price reduction on 6 September. On 4 May, C.D. Howe wrote to St Lawrence and the other eastern refiners that – in an effort to ease the panic – the cost of sugar bought from Cuba for consumption in Canada would be the same as that for Commonwealth raw sugar.

By June, the Canadian refiners were baulking at paying the extortionate prices still being demanded by speculators and, with the approval of the Canadian government, they held off from buying the quota to which Canada had committed them until the price of Cuba raw sugar fell. They also refused to buy Commonwealth sugar until prices fell. The year 1951 was a difficult one for St Lawrence, since it had passed on to the consumer the benefit of purchases of raw sugar made before the speculative bubble that had followed the end of the Korean War. It found itself in the course of the bubble unable to buy raw sugar at what it saw as a reasonable price.[52]

Purchases into the summer of 1951, when the market broke and prices fell on 25 June, left the Canadian refiners with overpriced stocks by the beginning of 1952. The central agency of the refiners agreed with the government on a program for the purchase of non-preferential raw sugar in 1952. In order to fulfil the Canadian commitment to Cuba for 1952, the central agency agreed that B.C. Sugar was to take 19,000 tons of non-Commonwealth sugar; Atlantic, 63,000 tons; C&D, 59,000; and St Lawrence, 32,000. In the second half of 1952, into 1953, there were actually thirteen price reductions by the refiners, to the benefit of consumers, four of these by St Lawrence, and in 1954 St Lawrence reduced its price again.[53]

A new problem arose in 1952. Cheap imports of Cuban refined, as opposed to raw, sugar began to hurt the markets served principally by the Canadian manufacturers of beet sugar, chiefly C&D. This company aggressively lobbied C.D. Howe to establish a quota for imports of Cuban refined sugar. St Lawrence and Acadia-Atlantic said nothing. In principle, they also were threatened by the import of refined sugar, but, unlike C&D, they produced no sugar from beets, and C&D stood to gain from the lower costs of its beet sugar whenever the cost of imported raw cane sugar went up on the world market. Howe went to Cuba and ten other countries in February 1953, and, to forestall further imports of Cuban refined sugar, he threatened not to renew the Torquay purchasing agreement of 1951 on its expiry in 1953. He returned to Canada with an assurance from the Cubans that they would ship no more refined sugar directly to Canada.

A new International Sugar Agreement in 1953, which was to extend for five years, was designed to stabilize prices between exporting and importing countries. The United States was not part of the system thus established; for much of the rest of the world, however, the 1953 agreement established basic export tonnages for the world free market and set a price range that was "equitable to consumers and producers." The participating importing countries agreed not to import annually more from non-participating exporters than they had imported from these exporters in any of the three years from 1951 to 1953. Canada joined this agreement in 1954.

At the end of 1952, the central purchasing agency of the refiners had disbanded upon the British government's announcement that all Commonwealth sugars were to be sold freely to Canada.[54] In the International Sugar Agreement of 1953, there was a provision for the Commonwealth countries to maintain export quotas to a slightly higher level in 1954–56 than that set out by the International Sugar Agreement of 1951. But this commitment by Commonwealth producers to restrict their exports would dissolve if there should be further bilateral agreements between a Commonwealth importer, such as Canada, and any exporting country, such as Cuba. Canada did not want to nullify the Commonwealth commitment in the 1953 agreement, and so it did not renew its 1951 bilateral agreement with Cuba. In 1958 a new International Sugar Agreement came into effect, to last until the beginning of 1964. This agreement provided for annual revisions of export quotas to take into account European beet sugar, while also giving exporters an incentive to declare if they could not fulfil their export quotas, in order to permit a redistribution of their crop to other exporters.

Cuba was essentially a producer of raw sugar rather than a refiner. But it wanted to increase its exports of raw sugar, and it saw that the Canadian refiners might be vulnerable enough to increase their purchases of this product if pressured. The Cubans accordingly began exporting their refined sugar to Canada again in 1954, potentially in direct competition with St Lawrence as well as with C&D. This time, McConnell and his right-hand man at St Lawrence, J.R. Crawford, were alarmed. They took the lead among the Canadian refiners to purchase more Cuban raw sugar in order to block completely the import of Cuban refined sugar. McConnell kept Howe fully informed, and in February 1954 Crawford and McGregor agreed that C&D and St Lawrence should buy 80,000 short tons of the Cuban crop by November, if the Cubans would refrain from exporting refined sugar to Canada.

Again, the goal of the Canadian refiners was to retain their shares of a market that was not shrinking, and they continued to keep Howe informed at every stage of the negotiations with the Cubans. Howe wrote to McConnell, however, that the British were afraid that this private agreement would lead to a breakdown of the International Sugar Agreement insofar as the latter incorporated commitments by Commonwealth producers to restrict their exports. McConnell telephoned Howe on 23 February 1954 to say that all the refiners had voluntarily reduced their prices by twenty-five cents, in order to meet criticism that they were merely fighting for their market shares.

Later, in September 1954, Crawford and McGregor returned to Cuba. There, they agreed, on behalf of all the Canadian refiners, including B.C. Sugar, to buy 85,000 short tons of raw sugar every year for three years, less an equivalent quantity of raw to 2,000 short tons of Cuban refined. The amount bought was to be shipped only to Newfoundland and British Columbia and not to be resold or diverted out of those provinces. Nevertheless, in October 1954 Howe wrote a disturbing letter to McConnell, denying that he had approved on behalf of the government the arrangement reached between the refiners and the Cubans, and warning that there might be an investigation under the Combines Investigation Act. McConnell telephoned Howe to express his astonishment.

McConnell had reason to be surprised, for the sugar industry had never been subjected to government investigation before. The first anti-combines legislation in Canada, the Combines Investigation Act of 1910, made it a crime to limit "unduly" trade, production, transportation, and storage of goods, or to lessen "unduly" competition. However, this legislation lacked teeth and it was not until 1923 that the act was amended to make it illegal to lessen competition by agreement, merger, or other means, where this was likely to operate to the detriment of the public. This law also provided for a permanent registrar who could launch a formal investigation or let a special commissioner do so. In 1935 the Bennett government amended the act, replacing the registrar with a tribunal and, in a move that reduced the scope of prosecutions, barring the use of documents submitted to the commission as evidence in other proceedings. These changes were reversed by the King government in 1937, through further amendments that also transformed the registrar into a commissioner with powers to enter premises and seize documents. Prosecutions of two industries with which McConnell was long associated – flour milling and rubber footwear – followed in the late 1940s, but the sugar industry remained untouched.

Then, in 1955, as threatened by Howe, the Restrictive Trade Practices Commission, operating under the Combines Investigation Act and under the chairmanship of C. Rhodes Smith, began to inquire into alleged collusion in price setting among the eastern Canadian refiners: Acadia-Atlantic, C&D, and St Lawrence. From the point of view of the commission, the problem was not that there had been no price reductions in 1952–53 – the evidence showed that there had been no fewer than thirteen. But these reductions had been swiftly coordinated, so that that there were no differences among the base prices of the three eastern refiners between September 1951 and January 1955, when the inquiry began.

Possibly under the pressure of this inquiry, but also because of new fluctuations on the world market, the pricing of the three companies suddenly became competitive from November 1956 to March 1957. This outbreak of competition underscores a point made by the refiners to the 1955 inquiry, namely, that their setting of prices was rooted primarily in their awareness of the *world* market price for raw sugar, which they were all obliged to pay. They all denied conspiring to fix their prices to their customer in advance. Crawford even suggested to the inquiry that they did not very much trust what each said it was going to do about pricing. They waited to see what each in fact had done, and then made ad hoc decisions on whether to match the actions of their competitors.[55]

In October 1958 St Lawrence served the commission with a notice of a petition seeking a writ of prohibition of its hearing, set to commence on 3 November 1958. But it withdrew the notice before this date, reserving its right to object to the jurisdiction of the commission later.[56] The commission submitted its report in 1960. Smith made several allegations. The first of the two principal ones was that Acadia-Atlantic, C&D, and St Lawrence had entered into agreements and arrangements to prevent or lessen competition in and substantially to control the manufacture, purchase, sale, transportation, and supply of sugar, to the detriment and against the interest of the public, contrary to the Combines Investigation Act. Secondly, Smith alleged that they had engaged in a conspiracy to prevent or lessen competition contrary to section 411 of the Criminal Code. The commission concluded further that these companies had tacitly agreed to have uniform basis prices and to maintain the division of the market that they had enjoyed under wartime and post-war controls. As the *Report* concluded: "It was expected that if the business of any one refiner in any period departed significantly from its historical position, the others, in the words of Mr. Crawford, 'will do something about it.'"[57]

After the release of the report, the Department of Justice laid charges against the refiners for conspiring to prevent or lessen unduly competition between January 1954 and January 1955. On 15 January 1963 all the refiners pleaded guilty and were convicted. Sentencing took place in March 1963, and each refiner received a fine of $25,000 – a penalty that, in comparison with the insolvency of St Lawrence and the other refiners after the First World War, was hardly lethal. Acadia-Atlantic alone pursued appeals until July 1967, when they were dismissed by the Quebec Court of Appeal.

By the time of the release of the Smith report, McConnell was fairly remote from the day-to-day affairs of St Lawrence, though it is probable that he was the one who authorized the company's guilty plea. From his vantage point, the anti-combines inquiries and prosecutions of the 1950s were merely part of another change in sentiment with regard to big business. In any case, he had other matters on his mind. In May 1963 there was a tragic explosion at the St Lawrence refinery, injuring fourteen and causing McConnell much grief.[58] But the business carried on in the refinery until it was sold to Atlantic Sugar, and at the end of the twentieth century the refinery became part of B.C. Sugar although retaining the name of Atlantic. Thus, St Lawrence was now part of a much larger sugar monopoly than it had ever been in McConnell's time.

One last inquiry into the industry, covering the last three years of McConnell's life (1960–63) but extending to May 1973, issued its report in 1975. In this case, Mr Justice Kenneth Mackay of the Superior Court of Quebec found no conspiracy on the part of St Lawrence, Atlantic, and C&D to maintain prices to the detriment of the public.[59] The minister of consumer affairs, André Ouellet, described the judgment as "a complete shock" and "a complete disgrace,"[60] and the Montreal *Gazette*, in an editorial entitled "Sweet Toothlessness," concluded: "If the nature of the sugar trade is such that legislation cannot ensure competition, the solution would be to make the sugar companies a publicly related utility, with public ownership as a possible option."[61] In any event, the ruling seemed to reverse the conviction of 1963.

In retrospect, it is easy to see McConnell as part of an oligopoly largely operating in tandem with government. Yet it is impossible to see him as a successful monopolist. The sugar industry, in Canada as in the United States and elsewhere, was incapable of producing monopolists because the largest cost of production for them, the raw sugar, was determinable only outside these countries, and not by the refiners as individuals or as an industry. In addition, there was throughout McConnell's time an ideological and legal aversion to corporate concentration. Weak as this aversion was, it did affect corporate behaviour, as did the power of the government to determine tariffs. Finally, there was often real if very limited competition among the sugar companies, and retailers determined the pricing of sugar to the ultimate consumer, also somewhat uncompetitively.

There is an argument – set out most cogently by the Marxian economist and German minister of finance under the Weimar Republic Rudolf Hilferding[62] – that an oligopoly is little more than a variety of monopoly. Yet, even if we accept this equation of monopoly with oligopoly, McConnell's record fails in every instance to meet Hilferding's definition of how a monopolist should operate. In the first place, corporate concentration – a key element of Hilferding's schema – was lacking from the sugar industry. So was the trend, in Hilferding's words, "in retail trade to eliminate the independent trader in so far as the producers in the consumer goods industries themselves take over the sale of their products."

Canadian sugar refiners, including St Lawrence, were never able to establish this sort of monopoly. They were beholden to governments for tariff protection and price stabilization, and subject to the interests of others in the chain of distribution for their product, notably the wholesale grocers. They never established a stable oligopoly, much less monopoly, except with government help and regulation. In the absence of this regulation, they did not hesitate to compete with one another, usually surreptitiously. The reason why they did not compete vigorously was not that they did not want to win profits from one another. It was that the chief determinants of their business were exogenous both to their efforts, collective and individual, and to any Canadian governmental regulation. These determinants were international market conditions, sugar brokers and speculators in London and New York, and weather and political conditions in sugar-growing areas.

There is much to be said for the contribution of anti-trust regulators in promoting business efficiency, particularly in the United States but globally as well.[63] But anti-trust ideology, or anti-combines ideology in Canada, was fundamentally misdirected in the case of the sugar refiners. The refiners were not a trust in the American sense, or even a combine within the meaning of Canadian anti-combines legislation; and they failed utterly to establish a monopoly. The only antidote to the often-fumbling efforts of the refiners to maintain their market shares was a state sugar monopoly.

McConnell kept close watch on St Lawrence almost to the end of his life. This was in marked contrast to his detachment from most of his other business interests, for which he depended more on subordinates. Crawford remained for most of the post-war period his trusted lieutenant at St Lawrence. For a period, as already noted, Wilson McConnell was president, but his father did not approve of various changes made by him, and Wilson quit in protest against his interference. As the controlling, and essentially the sole, shareholder apart from his foundation, McConnell loved the company and its employees, and many of them felt the same way about him. In his 1932 memoir, C.F. Bardorf paid tribute to McConnell's "dual interest" in the refinery:

> He has constantly entertained suggestions for the improvement of our technique as forwarded by the introduction of new appliances as well as the investigation of more or less scientific problems of the industry. Furthermore, under Mr. McConnell's administration the buildings and grounds have been so beautifully established and maintained in such excellent condition that the ensemble stands as an example that industrial activities and beauty can go hand in hand ... our president has encouraged and supported the social features of our establishment by giving to all employees greater opportunity to enjoy the hours for relaxation. Our social and athletic groups have brought men and officers in close touch. Our Bowling Alley, our Tennis Court, and our Annual Picnic are factors in cementing a desire cama[ra]derie highly beneficial to all.[64]

CHAPTER SIX

Keep the Home Fires Burning: Fundraising for the YMCA in Peace and for Canada in the Great War, 1909–19

If we, who remain at home, are to do our share towards winning the fight for Liberty and Empire, vast sums of money must be raised for the relief and support of the ever increasing number of families and dependants of those brave men who have sacrificed so much to fight our battles at the front.

J.W. McConnell to Montreal employers, 12 January 1916[1]

When McConnell returned to Montreal from Nelson in 1908, he already had begun to display his skills as a fundraiser both for the Trinity Church there and for the Douglas Church to which he was now returning. But in the following year he was to develop these skills on a much larger scale, helping to raise not merely money but, more important, the spirit of community in much of Montreal. He did this in the service of perhaps his favourite organization since his youth in Toronto, the YMCA.

Founded in 1851, the Montreal "Y" was the first to be established in North America and it was long to remain one of the most important. With hundreds of young immigrants arriving yearly at its building in Dominion Square, probably McConnell's own first home in the city in 1901, the YMCA decided in April 1909 that it was time to launch a campaign to raise $320,000 for an expansion.[2] Described as the "Y"'s "First Whirlwind Campaign," the effort mobilized local businessmen to work without pay in canvassing during the two weeks scheduled.

By now, word of McConnell's work for the church in Nelson must have leaked out. He chaired the young businessmen's division of the "Y" campaign, which included such figures as William Goodwin, with whom he was to work in Goodwins department store for several years, served as the captain of team no. 1 (which included G.B. and Hudson Allison), and sat on the executive committee chaired by J.W. Ross. Ross, one of the leading accountants of the city, had been not only president of the Montreal "Y" since 1905 but was also honorary treasurer of McGill. He was to remain one of McConnell's closest colleagues in fundraising for almost the next forty years, the two of them addressing each other in their letters as "Dear J.W."[3]

Cartoon of the 1909 YMCA campaign,
source unknown, private collection.

This YMCA campaign was the first major public effort at fundraising in Montreal and it was under the direction of C.S. Ward of the "Y"'s International Committee in New York. Teams of workers – in all, there were two hundred volunteer fundraisers – reported to the campaign headquarters on St James Street, and the daily newspaper coverage included cartoons, photographs of volunteers, and human-interest stories. The press called it a "Great Civic Movement." Its progress monitored by a large "clock" downtown, to measure the time for fundraising remaining, and by a large "thermometer" uptown, to measure the funds collected, the campaign's results exceeded everyone's expectations. In thirteen days, 3,419 subscribers pledged $321,749. The special-names committee – focused on soliciting donations from the rich and powerful – secured $127,350 of this; and McConnell's team, one of the ten in his young businessmen's division, ultimately reported over $43,487.

Along with similar efforts in New York and elsewhere, this campaign stimulated the building of YMCAs all over the world. The following year, John R. Mott, the secretary of the International Committee of the YMCA, convened two hundred Canadians and Americans at a "Million Dollar Day at the White House," to meet President Theodore Roosevelt. At this meeting, J.W. Ross and Gerald Birks (a son of the jeweller Henry Birks), representing Montreal, announced a gift of $40,000 to build

The Ross brothers, famous for their athleticism and close friends of the McConnells, including P.D. Ross of the Ottawa *Journal* and the accountants Brigadier-General James Ross and J.W. Ross (extreme right), who worked closely with McConnell on the YMCA and Victory Loan campaigns, n.d. Private collection.

Henry Birks and his sons (from left): Henry Jr, Henry Sr (seated), William, and Gerald, 1895. McCord Museum.

The central board of management of the Montreal YMCA,
1910–11, from Harold C. Cross, *One Hundred Years of
Service with Youth: The Story of the Montreal YMCA*
(privately published, October 1951).

a YMCA in Canton (Guangzhou) in China. In the campaign in Montreal to finance
this expansion into China, Gerald Birks and McConnell each secured $10,000 and
Henry Birks and J.W. Ross each secured $5,000. There followed a pledge from John
Penman of Paris, Ontario, of $50,000 for a "Y" in Hankow (Hangzhou), also in China.
A Moscow YMCA was also promised, and John D. Rockefeller, Jr pledged to match
donations for it of up to $540,000.

After the 1909 campaign, McConnell, speaking to the educational department of
the Montreal "Y," shared the secrets of his business success: "Work twenty-five hours
out of twenty-four if you want to succeed ... I believe a man can succeed in business
with common sense, hard work and a little ambition, providing he keeps a smiling
countenance. If he has common sense it will keep him from getting a swelled head
when he attains a little success. [If he] has courage it will permit him never to let

The new YMCA Building, Drummond Street, 1912.
McCord Museum, V12.641.

the others know when he is licked. With this combination a man can beat the world. 'Fear of failure,' as Carnegie said, 'makes countless millions poor.' Have confidence in yourselves, take off your coats, dig in and you will get there."[4]

Although the original plan of the "Y" in 1909 had been to remodel and enlarge its building in Dominion Square at its central branch in Montreal, Sun Life bought the site of the existing building for its own new headquarters at the end of that year. This effective expropriation of its long-standing headquarters suddenly forced the "Y" to buy lots from the Ogilvie family on Drummond Street, opposite the house of Lord Mount Stephen, for a completely new central branch. Simultaneously, the "Y" was building other new branches on Park Avenue and in Westmount on Sherbrooke Street, both of which were to open in 1912.

In 1910 McConnell became a director of the Montreal "Y" as well as chairman of the board of management for the Westmount branch building, aided by such men as D.A. Budge, the secretary of the Montreal "Y," and William Goodwin. With the organization's rapid expansion giving rise to budgetary strain, the work of the "Y" directors was not light. But McConnell was not deterred. As chairman of the first Joint Current Expense Canvass, in 1912 – joint fundraising of the three branches prevented duplication of time and effort – he raised $37,000 in three days, whereas the previous subscriptions had averaged $10,000 annually.[5]

During the campaign, Budge wrote twice about McConnell to J.W. Ross, who was in Europe, and his comments reveal the shyness combined with independence and selflessness that others were to notice throughout McConnell's fundraising career, although the shyness later sometimes gave way to peremptoriness. Reporting on the organizational meeting of 31 October 1912, Budge described McConnell as at first "very nervous," then as "more confident," but in any case feeling "that the best result was not the money only which was secured, but the service which it [canvassing] rendered some of the men."[6] At the conclusion of the 1912 campaign, Budge informed Ross that the board had passed a resolution of special thanks to McConnell because of his "splendid leadership": "He threw himself heartily into it, and did not spare time or effort in those three days. If he could only release himself from the fascination which business has upon him so as to give more time and personal effort to the promotion of Christian work how much greater blessing would come to himself, and what a large service he would render to the City! May we not hope that this will be brought to pass?"[7]

Although he never devoted himself full-time to the organization, McConnell's support for the "Y" was to continue through his life. In addition to his work for the campaign of 1912, in that year he also bought a site at Lake Desjardins, near Saint-Sauveur, for a new Camp Kanawana, which was renamed Lake Wilson after his first son.

Further, the YMCA campaign provided the model for a fundraising campaign of McGill University, also in 1912, which is described in chapter 17. But, whereas the McGill campaign was directed at the relatively wealthy, the effectiveness of the YMCA effort in mobilizing funds from the wider community would be replicated only two years later. Many of the same workers toiled in the campaigns of 1909 and 1912, and most did even more in much more ambitious campaigns all through the Great War, and none more than McConnell himself.

At the beginning of the Great War in August 1914, McConnell was thirty-seven years old. His brother Walter was to win the Distinguished Service Order, and nearly everyone of his acquaintance was either serving or related to someone serving at the front. Some questioned why he did not enlist, but he was the president of St Lawrence Sugar and Goodwins department store, and demonstrably far more talented in mobilizing funds than he was likely to be in fighting in trenches. His war was on the home front, and he immediately assumed high command on this front, wielding money as his sword. As the prospectus of the Victory Loans campaign of 1918, of which he was the executive chairman for Montreal, put it: "Behind the Gun the Man ... Behind the Man the Dollar ... Make Your Dollars Fight the Hun."

Almost immediately upon the outbreak of war, Herbert Ames, MP, of the shoe-making family of Ames-Holden-McCready and thus well known to McConnell, wrote

Distinguished Service Order recipients Walter McConnell, L. Martin, J. Cornwall, lieutenant-colonels in the Canadian Railway Troops, n.d. LAC, PA 7148.

to the governor general, the Duke of Connaught, proposing the establishment of a national Canadian Patriotic Fund. This was to support only dependants of soldiers overseas, but not disabled men and the widows and dependants of those killed, who would have to collect pensions from the government. Ames headed the national body as well as the Montreal branch, and, to emphasize that this was a country-wide effort, the king was the fund's patron, the governor general its president, and provincial lieutenant governors its vice-presidents. On 27 August 1914 McConnell sent Ames $10,000 on behalf of St Lawrence Sugar.

Early in September, within a day of the departure of Montreal recruits for Camp Valcartier, near Quebec City, the Canadian Patriotic Fund organized a national fund-raising campaign.[8] The Montreal canvassers were divided into twenty-two teams, McConnell being captain of team no. 14, which included many colleagues, such as O.W. Donner of St Lawrence Sugar, C.C. Ballantyne of Sherwin-Williams, and the coal merchant Lorne Webster. As in YMCA fundraising campaign of 1909, huge "clocks" and "thermometers" monitored progress, and on 14 September McConnell's team reported pledges of over $27,000 for that day alone. At the end of the first week, the leading team had raised about $114,000, with McConnell's trailing at $107,000.[9] Rising to the challenge, McConnell devised a different sort of canvassing. Attributing the idea to Sir Thomas Shaughnessy, president of the CPR, he began to canvass employees of companies for one day's pay. Within the first week of this canvass, in addition to donations from corporations and individuals, he had obtained pledges

Canadian Patriotic Fund advertisement, Montreal
Herald, 14 September 1914. Private collection.

of over $18,000 from employees of nine different companies, one of which was St Lawrence Sugar. By the end of the campaign, McConnell's team had collected a total of $227,000, leading *Saturday Night* to observe that his hand had not "lost its cunning."

The second Patriotic Fund campaign began on 21 January 1916 and was far more elaborate than the 1914 effort, with daily luncheons at Montreal's Windsor Hotel, in the first week, and the increasing participation of women and prominent French Canadians. This time, McConnell was not a mere team captain but rather led a special "One Day's Pay Committee." Besides writing to various companies saying asking for a contribution from their employees of one day's pay *every three months*, his committee held meetings at various factories, with Campbell Stuart, who was organizing a regiment of Irish rangers and would go on to be managing director of *The Times* of London, speaking at them. By 25 January, the two were able to report employee pledges of $57,000 from six different firms. One cleaning woman sent McConnell her "widow's mite" of $1.25, her day's wages.

Beyond McConnell's call for one day's pay from employees, the campaign concentrated on rich individuals and companies. J.P. Morgan of New York contributed

$20,000, and, in Canada, Herbert Holt of Montreal Power, Holt's father-in-law Hugh Paton and Charles Gordon, both textile manufacturers, and James Carruthers, "Canada's Wheat King," pledged $10,000 each. By 29 January, McConnell's team had collected more than $427,000 and all the other teams $1.3 million. At the closing dinner that night, the Scottish singer and comedian Harry Lauder was the guest of honour, but reports said that McConnell almost stole the show. He "electrified" the crowd by announcing several large last-minute pledges from workers at various companies totalling more than $162,000. By this stage, his team had signed up 85,000 workers in 769 firms.

The war dragged on. By January 1917, with no end in sight, the Patriotic Fund had to begin another campaign, this one with a national goal of $6 million. In Montreal, McConnell sat on the finance committee, and he also took the lead in responding to a charge that threatened to hobble the fund's efforts in the city. With the inflammatory crisis over conscription approaching, an Ontario MP asked in Parliament whether French Canadians were contributing their share to the Patriotic Fund. McConnell telegraphed his answer to Prime Minister Laurier, who read it to deafening acclaim in the Commons on 31 January. McConnell reported that his 1916 One Day's Pay campaign had yielded about $500,000, and at least half of this came from French Canadian workers.

On 9 February, the new governor general, the Duke of Devonshire, gave the opening address of the new effort at the Windsor Hotel. McConnell announced that he was naming his team "Bonne Entente" in recognition of the cooperation from French Canadians that he had been receiving. Now the Montreal teams were no longer each headed by both an English captain and a French captain; instead, they were divided cleanly between French and English, with a cup being promised to the best team in each category. The *Gazette* described McConnell as the "General Commanding the Day's Pay Army in the Patriotic Fund and Red Cross Campaign," the Red Cross having merged its effort with that of the fund.[10] McConnell's "army" planned to raise $1 million, out of a total Montreal goal of $2.5 million and a total national goal of $13 million. Deciding to visit 3,000 workplaces, as opposed to the 769 in the previous campaign, McConnell organized a corps of speakers, both English and French, to visit the factories.

Women played a more prominent part in the campaign generally, with Mrs Huntly Drummond, the wife of the president of Canada Sugar, taking charge of the first women's fundraising team. They also cared for the beneficiaries of the fund. The fund's headquarters was the Drummond Building on St Catherine Street, and since the beginning of the war over 10,000 Montreal families had applied for help, mainly there.[11] The women also organized teams to visit the dependants of recruits at home. They developed "case files" and ran statistical, filing, and ward-organization departments, thus foreshadowing the development of social work after the war.[12]

By the end of the campaign on 17 February, the fund had raised more than $4 million in Montreal, of which about $800,000 was attributable to McConnell's team, short of the $1-million goal. Contributions continued to arrive, however, so that the total by March 1919 was $7 million. About $3.5 million had been expended on 13,000 families and only 1.37 per cent of the subscriptions had gone to the raising, collecting, and distributing of the money.[13] Yet McConnell had only begun his fundraising for the war effort.

Although Great Britain had paid for the Napoleonic Wars by borrowing from the public through the issuing of bonds, and the United States had done the same during its Civil War, public loan subscriptions for waging war were unknown to Canada in 1914. To be sure, the time seemed hardly propitious for such subscriptions. The depression of 1913 had upset the London money market and dried up British loans for Canadian railway and industrial enterprises, which was one reason why McConnell had formally retired as a broker in 1914. Then, the coming of war ended trade with enemy countries, interrupted trade between Canada and Great Britain and its allies as shipping was requisitioned for war purposes. It triggered controls on imports and exports, and closed the London money market. Trade restrictions drastically lowered the customs duties collected by Canada, then the only source of government revenue, and depressed business and increased unemployment. In the first week of war, there was a run on the banks, which was stopped only by an emergency order-in-council increasing their liquidity.[14] Between the end of August and the end of December 1914, the government expected to spend $50 million on the war alone. Before this period, it had never borrowed more than $6 million on the London market.

With the London market closed, from September 1914 to the end of March 1915, Canada borrowed £12 million from the British Treasury to finance Canadian military operations, railways, and public works for the unemployed. Great Britain used the payments made on this loan to pay for munitions, wheat, and other Canadian products. In turn, the sale of these products enabled Canadians to subscribe to the war loans that followed, so that Canada soon was paying the cost of its military operations through its own production. Canadian goods and services repaid all the loans from the British Treasury, and by 1918 Britain actually owed Canada $400 million, half to the government and half to Canadian banks. The roles of creditor and debtor had reversed within four years.

War forced the government to devise new forms of financing. The 1915 budget levied special taxes upon financial services and luxury goods, and it increased general customs duties and British preferential rates. Its creditworthiness enhanced, in July of the same year, Canada issued $45 million in one- and two-year notes, ostensibly for public works and other capital expenditures. In November, the first Canadian domestic war loan was floated for $50 million, since the British Treasury could no longer lend to Canada. A bountiful harvest of wheat, combined with an increased demand for war materiel, did wonders for the Canadian balance of trade, transforming a deficit of $300 million in 1912–13 into a *surplus* of $200 million in 1915–16. A huge number of potential new investors had emerged in Canada within a few months.

Most Canadians in 1915 hardly knew what a bond was. Those with savings tended to deposit them in bank accounts. Businesses generally had trouble attracting investment from Canadians, which is why so many had been going to London in search of investors. The banks, therefore, offered to subscribe to $25 million of the 1915 Canadian war bonds "upon the understanding that all subscriptions from the public in excess of twenty-five million dollars should be taken in abatement of their subscription."[15] In other words, without remuneration they were to underwrite half the issue.

The banks, bond dealers, stockbrokers, and even churches promoted the 1915 war bonds and over $100 million was subscribed, twice the original issue, which the government increased to meet demand. With this public loan, Canada was actually able to lend Great Britain $50 million. The second war-bond issue, in 1916, was for $100 million, but $200 million was subscribed; and in 1917 the issue was for $150 million and $200 million was subscribed. The third domestic war loan was launched in March 1917, and in the summer Canada placed an issue of $100 million of two-year notes in New York. This failed because the United States had entered the war in April, and Americans were buying their own Liberty Bonds. The failure of the Canadian war-bond flotation in New York in 1917, the end of the Patriotic Fund campaigns in the same year, and the increasing demands of the British and Canadian war efforts called for a fundamental reorganization of fundraising for the war.

As Britain ran out of cash, to buy munitions and food supplies in Canada, it came to depend on loans from both Canada and the United States. In particular, it arranged to spend $10 to $15 million per month, of what it was borrowing from the US Treasury, on Canadian-made munitions, which helped the American suppliers of raw materials used by Canadian manufacturers of munitions. Canadian banks lent to Britain money to buy Canadian wheat, in particular, and in June, July, and August they advanced a total of $75 million to the British government in credits. This amount was hopelessly inadequate, for Britain announced that it required $40 million in credits to purchase its immediate needs in Canadian cheese alone. By the autumn, Britain was spending $40 to $50 million per month on Canadian munitions, and 200,000 Canadians were employed in munition factories, so that the economy was now largely dependent on war production. By mid-1917, Canada estimated that it would need to lend Britain about $500 million a year until the end of the war. Clearly, the country could no longer depend simply on the quiet selling of war bonds through financial institutions.

The government did have other sources of revenue. In response to charges of war profiteering, the finance minister, Sir Thomas White, had brought in a Business Profits War Tax Act in February 1916, but he saw it as a purely temporary measure and declared his opposition to taxation generally. Then, however, with "the failure of

McConnell as chairman of the Montreal Executive Committee for Canada's
Victory Loan, 12 November 1917. Private collection.

some well-to-do people to contribute as generously as they should have" to the Patriotic and other war funds provoking calls for the "conscription of wealth."[16] White, in 1917, increased the Business Profits War Tax and passed the Income War Tax Act. Complementing the legislation passed the same year for the conscription of men for the war effort, the latter was the first income-tax legislation in Canada and intended initially also to be temporary.

Notwithstanding these measures, McConnell knew instinctively from his stock promotions that there was still plenty of untapped money under the beds of Canadians and that it was not being conscripted through taxation. For him as a financier, sources of funds were the tools of his profession, and, under the aegis of Victory Loans, he was about to start selling the greatest issue of securities in Canadian history. In essence, the Victory Loan campaign expanded the techniques of the Patriotic Fund – while also using techniques developed in the US Liberty Loan campaigns – in order to sell war bonds. McConnell was the executive director of the first Victory Loan campaign in Montreal and vice-chairman of the second. The 1917 campaign, and those that followed in the next two years, not only saved and expanded the Canadian war economy: it reversed the tide of British investment in Canada on which McConnell and his contemporaries had made their fortunes by 1912. From this reversal, McConnell, as a substantial investor in Canada, became richer still.

Montreal Executive Committee, Canada's Victory Loan, 1917, from *Canada's Victory Loans Montreal 1917* (privately published). MUA, MG 4240, c. 33.

The first Victory Loan campaign in 1917 was also described as the fourth war-bond campaign, and its object was to sell bonds rather than solicit contributions of cash. When, therefore, the national organization pioneered by the Patriotic Fund was applied to this bond campaign, it was natural for bond dealers to predominate in it,

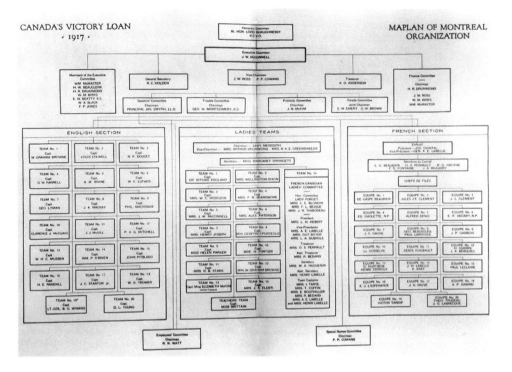

Montreal Victory Loan campaign 1918 organization chart. Private collection.

which they had not done in the previous, charitable efforts. McConnell was one of five Montrealers on the national committee.[17] The Quebec provincial organization was divided into two parts: Montreal Island and the rest. McConnell was the chairman for Montreal Island. There were twenty teams of English-speaking men, twenty of French-speaking men, fifteen of English-speaking women (including no. 15, captained by Lily McConnell), and one of French-speaking women.[18]

McConnell presided at the opening dinner of the three-week campaign on 12 November, and thereafter all the previously tried and proved techniques of the YMCA and Patriotic Fund campaigns, some originated by McConnell, were brought to bear upon the selling of the government bonds on a mass scale. In Montreal, 91 speakers gave 337 addresses to workers in munitions plants, department store, and factories – in English, French, Italian, Hebrew, Greek, Polish, Flemish, and Ruthenian. Four hundred and forty-five speeches were given to people in theatres. Churchgoers were canvassed, and 30,000 children in public schools received promotional pamphlets. Among the other groups visited were a hundred and twenty-five labour organizations, fifty-two Jewish organizations, and the Forester, Freemason, and Oddfellow fraternal societies.

There was also much more sophisticated publicity generally. R.N. Watt of the Employees' Committee, which had originated with McConnell's One Day's Pay

Executive Committee, responsible for raising $50 million for the 1918 Victory Loan, Montreal. Seated, left to right: H.R. Drummond, J.M. Wilson, J.W. Ross, P.P. Cowans, McConnell, Zephiron Hébert, R.T. Leclerc, A.D. Anderson. Top row, left to right: E.F. Slack, R.C. Holden, Brig.-Gen. A.E. Labelle, J.N. Dupuis, Lorne C. Webster, H.W. Beauclerk, J.N. McKim, F.W. Steward, James Carruthers. Canadian War Museum, 20030331-12.

The Special Names Committee, Montreal Victory Loan campaign, 1918. Seated, left to right: H.W. Beauclerk, J.W. Ross, James Carruthers, A.J. Brown, KC, P.P. Cowans, McConnell, W. McMaster, Zephiron Hébert. Top row, left to right: R.T. Leclerc, J.W. Kellam, F.W. Molson, Edwin Hanson, E.A. McNutt, J.M. Mackie, F.C. Fairbanks, J.M. Wilson, and A.P. Frigon. Canadian War Museum, 20030331-13.

Committee in the Patriotic Fund campaigns, issued thirty bulletins a day, and Montreal newspaper editors gave more than $58,000 in free space to the campaign. J.N. McKim (a pioneer in newspaper advertising) was chairman of the publicity committee, and, with the aid of J. Murray Gibbon, a writer for the CPR, he helped spread the message not only through the press but also through hoardings, windows, streetcars, automobiles, and office buildings and elevators. Clubs, hotels, and restaurants carried advertising on the menus. The Dominion Advertising Committee distributed over five million pieces of advertising in the country as a whole.

Although the campaign carried on into the beginning of December, its culmination was a great Victory Loan parade on 20 November, declared for the occasion a civic holiday, which took three hours to pass any given spot. The parade contained over 15,000 marchers and almost a hundred floats, and McConnell stood on the reviewing stand alongside the mayor and many others. On 3 December, McConnell presided over the closing dinner at the Windsor Hotel, and he announced with glee that Montreal had topped Toronto by $500,000, its total subscriptions being $76 million of the provincial total of $94 million.

The second Victory Loan campaign in 1918, also known as the fifth war-bond campaign, was very much a repeat of the 1917 one. Sir Thomas White opened the national sales effort in Winnipeg on 8 October, and McConnell, described in the press as the "Big Chief," served as the chairman for the Island of Montreal once more. The planning was more refined than ever, with Montreal divided into eastern and western districts, each of these divided in turn into twenty-five subdistricts, and each resident of each subdistrict noted for canvassing. The subscription lists were open from 28 October to 16 November.

In the week before the list opened, the Victory Loan organization was reeling from the influenza epidemic that was devastating much of the world. Public meetings were already banned and this included mass meetings of employees in large firms. As McConnell put it, "it means that our work is doubled, but our difficulties are nothing compared to those of the boys at the front."[19] He called on people to respond to canvassers over the telephone and by post, and reluctantly called off a mass meeting at the St Denis Theatre which was to have been addressed by White and Laurier. McConnell himself was reported as "plugging away, and in addition to his other work he addresses each of the 25 teams of canvassers, giving them an outline of the arguments they must use, and the methods they must employ to achieve success."[20]

Notwithstanding the epidemic, the organizational plans were more ambitious than for the 1917 campaign. Edward Beatty of the CPR undertook to borrow the "Avenue of the Allies" decorations for the parade, which had already transformed thirty-four blocks of Fifth Avenue in New York into the Avenue of the Flags of Freedom. In Montreal, St Catherine Street would be so honoured, with every building decorated from Guy to Papineau streets. The Eastern Townships Building in Place d'Armes, which

Victory Loan prospectus, 1918. Private collection.

was the headquarters of the Victory Loan campaign, the St Catherine Street department stores, and the Drummond Building were already being decorated, and work started on the construction of a victory arch in Phillips Square. There were 625 male canvassers and 200 female ones. On the first day, factory whistles were to sound, automobiles were to toot, and church bells were to ring for five minutes. "Put "pep" in Your Patriotism," newspaper advertisements urged. Individual companies also geared up to enable their workers to buy bonds through payroll deductions, which they had done in 1917.

Not everyone, however, approved of the Victory Loans. Some, for example, saw their tax-free feature as a concession to the rich. I.W. Killam, the head of Royal Securities and a bonds salesman himself, published two open letters, one to Sir Robert Borden and the other to Sir Thomas White, on 12 September, attacking the loans as a matter of public policy.[21] Although he acknowledged that the United States had issued tax-free war bonds, Killam proposed that it was "imperative that those who lend their money to the nation should do so on exactly equal terms … No sale of national secu-

Cartoon of a fat capitalist, Montreal *Daily Star*, 14 February 1917.
Private collection.

rities should be made, on terms that will result in an exempting from taxation the income derived from accumulated wealth, while placing a proportionately increased burden upon the earnings of the industry and labour of the people."[22]

The Victory Loans campaign opened notwithstanding the complaints of Killam and others. In Montreal on 28 October, the bells duly rang and the automobile horns tooted. McConnell's office was "a storm centre" and "a mecca for a stream of business men, team leaders and others," and he was described as "the busiest man in town." One newspaper touted Victory bonds as "the purest jewels you could secure," each being "a bullet or a bayonet or a bomb aimed at the Curse of the World."[23] By the end of the day, it was clear that no encouragement was necessary, for subscriptions already exceeded $6 million. All the while, the Victory Loan parade was being readied for 11 November. St Catherine Street was described as a riot of colour, with flags flying from every window and fifteen-paintings representing each of the allied countries.

By the end of the second day, a Miss Shea, who described herself, at under 2 and ½ feet tall, as the smallest woman in the world, appeared at the Victory Loan headquarters to offer herself as a window display in a store, but was regretfully turned down because of the prohibition against crowds. By the fourth day, St Catherine Street, temporarily renamed the Avenue of the Allies, was full of new window displays. Almy's department store on Bleury Street featured the life-size figure of a soldier throwing a hand grenade and a life-size figure of a Red Cross nurse holding a wounded soldier in her arms. In Phillips Square, Morgan's store featured the heroic figure of a bomb-thrower, a bronze statuette of Joan of Arc waving the French tricolour, and Britannia, with breastplate and trident, hailing Lord Nelson. McConnell's own Goodwins store depicted a "huge sovereign [who] surmounts a kind of throne, on which a Victory Bond, an ink pot and quill pen invite the spectator to buy the 'sovereign' remedy."[24] At the same time, a private showing was given at the Pathé Exchange on Bleury Street of special films made for the Victory Loan campaign. Douglas Fairbanks, "Canada's Sweetheart" Mary Pickford, Fatty Arbuckle, and Charlie Chaplain were among the actors in them. The campaigners made mistakes. A Chinese restaurant owner demanded that the Victory Loan organization replace the Japanese flag it had placed on his establishment with a Chinese flag or at least a Union Jack.

In November, with subscriptions becoming disappointing, Montreal would need to raise $5 million a day for the remaining twelve days if it was to meet its target of $80 million. McConnell urged every household that had subscribed, no matter how small the amount, to display in its window an "honour-flag" card. Inevitably, the conscription crisis, which was to involve riots in Montreal and Quebec City, affected sales. All the residents of Sainte-Anne de Beaupré, near Quebec City, who had subscribed cancelled their subscriptions.

By the happiest of coincidences, the guns of Europe fell silent on 11 November, the date already scheduled for Montreal's Victory Loan parade. With the ban on crowds temporarily lifted, at 6 a.m. a CPR engine left Windsor Station, its whistle shrieking, and then the whole city exploded with the sounds of other whistles, bells, and automobile horns. Windows opened all over Montreal, and hundreds, perhaps thousands, of Union Jacks and Allied flags were thrust out into the November wind, in a city already festooned with bunting for the Victory Loan parade. Sherbrooke Street, from Atwater Avenue to Lafontaine Park, was filled with hundreds of thousands of spectators and the procession began. Hundreds of veterans and returned soldiers led the parade past the reviewing stand, where McConnell sat alongside cabinet ministers and other dignitaries. Following the parade, there was a luncheon at the Mount Royal Club in honour of White and Lord Shaughnessy, and in his address McConnell declared the day to be the greatest in the history of the world. It was one of the most jubilant moments in his life.

The next day, 12 November, the campaign carried on, and McConnell was at his desk, declaring that Canadians should now buy Victory bonds in gratitude for the great victory vouchsafed to Allied arms. Montreal had actually just become the first city in the country to reach its official quota of $80 million. McConnell presided at two luncheons at the Windsor Hotel, the first on the 12th for all the Victory Loan

McConnell, C.C. Ballantyne, Percy Cowans, Sir Vincent Meredith,
and Sir Thomas White outside the Ritz-Carlton Hotel,
11 November 1918. Private collection.

Victory Loan Parade, 11 November 1918. From left to right: Sir Vincent
Meredith (president of the Bank of Montreal), Sir Thomas White (minister of
finance and acting prime minister), McConnell, and Mayor Médéric Martin
(wearing his chain of office). McCord Museum, M 2003.8.6.4.58.

workers and the second on the 15th. On the later occasion, he sat beside Lieutenant-Colonel D.R. McCuaig, DSO, of a well-known family of stockbrokers, who had been a prisoner-of-war for three years. McCuaig spoke of horrifying instances of German brutality and recounted the stories of Montreal officers whose loss at the Battle of Ypres in 1915 had so affected the city. Figures dressed as the ex-kaiser, the German crown prince, and Field Marshal von Hindenburg were led in chains to him.[25]

A dinner at the Windsor concluded the campaign on the 18th, with McConnell again presiding, and he announced total Montreal subscriptions of more than $143 million, out of a national total of over $676 million. Toronto had done better by over $1.5 million, but he explained that Montreal had still gone "over the top." Since Ontario had not been divided between two Victory Loan organizations, as had Quebec, with the Island of Montreal and the rest, non-Toronto residents in Ontario could appear on the Toronto subscription list. Moreover, because Montreal was the headquarters for most of the large Canadian corporations, many of these had divided their subscriptions among cities, to the extent of $7 million. Had this amount been included, it would have made Montreal's total $150 million, or $6 million more than Toronto's. To conclude the evening, a wide array of the Montreal business world rose with McConnell to sing the National Anthem, *God Save the King*.

The next day, 19 November, McConnell presided over the first meeting of another campaign, this time to raise $1,400,000 for the Canadian Red Cross Society, but the three-day campaign gathered only about a third of its projected subscriptions. There was another Victory Loan campaign in 1919, which raised $127 million in Montreal, out of a national total of $647 million. For this, McConnell served only as an honorary vice-chairman. When Lorne Webster asked him if he would help to underwrite any shortfall in the collections, McConnell replied from England, where he was selling sugar, by cable: "Have burdensome obligations. Treat me gently ... the spirit was willing though the treasury might be weak."[26]

In the published lists of Victory Loan subscribers, McConnell had been mentioned only once, for $100,000. However, in a statement of assets and liabilities dated 31 December 1921, McConnell stated the market value of his 1918 Victory Loan bonds to be more than $6 million, or $60,720,000 in 2008 terms. From his ledgers, it is clear that at least some of these bonds had been bought on the open market, between the close of the subscription list in November 1918 and the valuation as of December 1921. Whenever he acquired these securities, he had in acquiring them ensured a guaranteed tax-free income stream of 5½% until 1933, from $2.5 million of these bonds, and until 1937 from the other $3.7 million, or $341,000 a year in total ($3,656,819 in 2008 terms), at least up to 1933.

Whatever his personal investments in Victory bonds, the three campaigns had been a remarkable success – and McConnell had played an important part in all of them. No less an authority than Sir Thomas White summarized their significance.

Victory Loan Champagne, 1918, Forest and Stream Club, McConnell, top left;
Cowans, centre; J.W. Ross, bottom right, 17 December 1918. Private collection.

"The business of Canada," he said, "literally depended upon her ability to finance the greater part of her external trade. If we could finance it, the national gain would be sufficient to pay for the expenses of our army overseas and leave a large surplus beside. The people of Canada met the situation by their subscriptions to the three Victory Loans."[27]

McConnell went to Europe to sell sugar in the spring of 1919. Although he was disappointed to find "not many people of particular importance on board" the *Caronia*, and no dressing for dinner, things improved after his arrival. In May he met, for the first time, Lieutenant-General Sir Arthur Currie, commander-in-chief of the Canadian forces in France, thus beginning a warm friendship that was to last until Currie's death in 1935. The occasion was a luncheon hosted at the Mansion House by the lord mayor of London. Also there, McConnell met his old friend Brigadier-General Raymond Brutinel, whose machine-gun battery McConnell had helped to finance. Through Brutinel, Sir George Perley (the high commissioner for Canada), and Currie, McConnell was able to arrange a six-day tour of the Western Front. Currie asked Major Billy Bishop, VC, to accompany McConnell, and the two left London on 30 May. From Boulogne, Bishop drove him to see the ruins of Ypres, which had once boasted a population of 600,000. McConnell was struck by "the devastation and desolation of the entire country[side] in that district as far as the eye can see for miles and miles of motor travel ... There is not a living thing, or a living tree, or a living twig, or shrub. The land has literally been churned up with shell fire until one crater joins another, making the earth a series of holes and mounds. It looks like an utterly deplorable and unrecoverable piece of Belgium. And besides, the territory is full of unexploded, or 'dud,' shells, which renders ploughing or any other effort at levelling up the ground rather dangerous."[28] They went on to Passchendaele to see more of the same and, after touring Currie's headquarters in Mons, drove through Leus and Arras, almost totally levelled. The two parted at Paris, but their visit had left McConnell with indelible memories. He was to meet Bishop often in years to come and to invest in his aircraft company.

In comparison with the dead and the wounded and most of the survivors, McConnell had had a good war. About fifteen million had died in the conflict, in part because of the machine-guns invented by McConnell's friend Sir Hiram Maxim and the armaments sold by his friend Sir Basil Zaharoff, who was accused of making $6 for every soldier killed in battle. McConnell, however, had lost no relative and no close friend, and was even reaching the peak of his career. He was now the father of three children – Wilson, John, and Kathleen, the last born in July 1918 and, but for a delay in the end of the war, nearly named Victory.

McConnell's work as a fundraiser for the war effort raised him to the first rank of those serving on the home front. It certainly was the work for which he was best suited. It was also as essential to the war effort as fighting in the trenches, since it helped to generate the money needed to get the job done. So formidable did his reputation as a fundraiser for public causes become that, at the start of the Second World War in 1939, he would be offered the position of minister of war services, which was largely responsible for the voluntary sector.

As a wartime fundraiser, McConnell participated in a process that turned out to have significant effects for society as a whole. In selling Victory Bonds to people who had never owned a security in their lives, he made an effective case for thousands to buy them, and from their purchases, because he was no longer a broker, he made not a cent of commission. Despite the wide appeal of his Victory Loan campaigns, however, McConnell realized that income tax would make Victory Bonds harder to sell to the rich, the only people able to buy them in bulk. It is possible that to this end he helped to convince White to make tax-free the income from the bonds for 1917 and 1918. The rich did in consequence buy Victory Loans, and they did benefit particularly from the tax-free feature of their income from the interest on them. That the tax-free feature of these bonds was an advantage to the rich cannot be disputed. Neither, however, can the fact be denied that the sale of Victory Loans to very ordinary people created what McConnell declared that it would, namely, a society in which many more felt they had a stake.

The creation of what almost a century later would be called an "investor society" started with these war bonds, but it rapidly developed into a much more comprehensive view of social as opposed to merely monetary investment. The controversy over the tax-free feature of the bonds of 1917 and 1918 underlines the fact that they were bonds and not donations to traditional charities, in the sense of churches and foreign missions, societies for the blind and the lame, and so on. The repayment of their principal was guaranteed by the credit of all of Canada. The interest on them was similarly certain. They were marketable, in the sense of saleable to others. And so buying them was not a donation to charity at all. It was not a donation because the purchaser received tangible monetary returns. It was not for charity because it benefited the community as a whole, as opposed to some particular cause, however worthy, serving only part of it. This shift from a charitable cause to a community cause was what expanded the very notion of fundraising, in the First World War, into one for "social investment." It did not exclude fundraising for traditional charities, but it went well beyond them.

The First World War affected McConnell, like the rest of his generation, deeply. Yet his wounds were internal, and, as one of the most public cheerleaders in Montreal, he seldom displayed them. Largely perhaps because he wanted to consolidate public support for the Canadian Patriotic Fund and for the Victory Loans, he never made public his position on conscription, for example. He quietly supported the Union government of Sir Robert Borden in 1917, probably because he was more in favour of a coalition government to wage war than of conscription itself. He also developed a high respect for the individual, especially in the face of German militarism. His later loathing of Nazism and communism, which he saw as indistinguishable because they were both totalitarian, can be traced to his perception of the barbarism of the First World War.

The YMCA, which McConnell saw as the best route to a useful life for young men, and his work for it hardly ceased during the war. The organization extended its work to the soldiers overseas, especially through Gerald Birks. McConnell served, in April 1916, on the executive of the YMCA Military Service Campaign. The purpose of this effort was to raise $60,000, Montreal's share of the Canadian total of $300,000, to set up YMCA facilities with Canadian goods, particularly foodstuffs, which would be given or sold cheaply to Canadian troops in England and on the continent. In a similar campaign in June 1917, McConnell served as vice-chairman.

After the war, in May 1919, McConnell was to chair the special-names committee of the Red Triangle Fund campaign for the National YMCA and YWCA and to serve on the "Y" executive. In 1927 he was once again chairman of the executive committee of the "Y"'s annual current-expense canvass. In the following year, the Montreal YMCA launched its first capital campaign since 1909, with a goal of $1,300,000. McConnell was on the honorary and special-gifts committees, and he gave in that year $100,000 for the building of the "Y"'s Stanley Street residence. In 1933 he donated $10,000 to aid the "Y" in the Depression. With the onset of another world war, he served as an honorary co-chairman of the National YMCA War Services Campaign.[29] In some sense, this very non-violent and yet sturdily competitive man was never to cease to wage war – war against totalitarianism, suffering, poverty, and selfishness. He loved wealth and he loved success. But even more he loved sharing them and helping to build a stronger infrastructure for the exercise of practical compassion.

During the war, McConnell had brought his skills as a financier to serve the broadest and the most pressing of patriotic causes, and now he was beginning to bring them to the service of humanity generally. But as Budge of the Montreal YMCA had observed during the fundraising campaign of 1909, McConnell could not free himself from his "fascination" with business. In the same year, he had actually begun his most ambitious and controversial financing of all. This would occupy much of his time for almost a decade, and it is to this that we now turn.

CHAPTER SEVEN

Developing and Financing Tramways and Electricity, 1890–1925

The whole sorry story, gentlemen, is one of "high finance," of ruthless denial of justice, of flagrant disregard of the community's rights. You and your company are the custodians of a great public franchise … The watering of stocks, the division of profits, and all the juggling that goes on so merrily with regard to private interests, are so generally accepted as orthodox methods of making money, that the fact that they could not with safety be applied to a public service corporation may not have appealed to you.

> *Montreal Herald*, 3 January 1912, in an open letter to E.A.Robert,
> J.W. McConnell, Marcelin Wilson, W.C. Finley, F.H. Wilson,
> and J.M. McIntyre, who sued the newspaper for defamation.

In 1877, when McConnell was born, only people in rich cities enjoyed the luxury of gas and dim and isolated electrical lighting. Most people cooked and heated their houses with wood or coal. The best that urban areas could offer their burgeoning populations was horse-drawn trams. In the last years of the nineteenth century and the first years of the twentieth, however, electrical generating stations and electrified street railways became integral to the utilities industry, which had been long supplying gas and water to urban areas.

The rapid advance of both technological and financial innovation made investment in electricity central to any strategy for profiting from an economy previously fuelled almost exclusively by wood, coal, and gas. Lengthened transmission lines made electricity available, even in the countryside. And holding companies were being set up to own shares in other companies, in order to diversify the risks to investors. It was becoming increasingly easy to invest in the power that served vast tracts of North America and other continents.

For McConnell electrical utilities were more than businesses to promote: they were to form the bulk of his own investments from 1925 onwards. Electricity, he correctly grasped from his time in the Mackenzie-owned Standard Chemical Company, would

McConnell, c.1920. Private collection.

be the basic industry of the twentieth century, as it was making possible the growth of almost every other industry. Oil was about to perform a similar role, but the infrastructure to produce large volumes of electricity predated oil refining, so that oil came to complement and not replace electricity. McConnell never lost sight of the primary importance of electricity or abandoned it as part of his larger strategy to secure and to maintain wealth. Nor did he ever turn his back on the holding company as a vehicle both to develop electric power and to use it to operate urban transit, to light buildings and streets, to fuel domestic appliances, and to transform both heavy and light industries.

One early example of his interest took place in Saint-Timothée, near Beauharnois, to the west of the Island of Montreal. In May 1911, McConnell was photographed standing proudly beside an electricity-generating station that his new company, Canadian Light and Power, had pledged to expand in order to serve the Montreal transit system, which his syndicate of investors was hoping to take over. Potential investors had arrived by special train to inspect the new power station, started up in the previous September, with its capacity of 12,000 horsepower. McConnell laid out for his visitors the immense benefits that awaited both its expansion and the reorganization of the Montreal transit system to buy power from it. A steel tower, set in concrete in the middle of the St Lawrence, was already in place to bear a transmission line carrying up to 50,000 horsepower, and, by the following autumn, McConnell confidently declared, there would be an increase in its capacity to 80,000 horsepower. He had begun yet another career, that of a power executive, but he had already had five years of experience of investing in electrical utilities and a year of organizing their financing.

For McConnell, the Canadian Light and Power venture in 1911 was a way to make his own name, for, although his partnership with Johnston and Allison was not to end until the following year, his appearance at Saint-Timothée was the culmination of much work independent of them. It also was part of a much larger emerging story, one that featured McConnell's role as a financier of one of the biggest deals in the history of the country. In essence, this was to involve, with his syndicate partner Edmond-Arthur Robert, the takeover of the Montreal Street Railway by a new Montreal Tramways; the merger of Montreal Tramways with Canadian Light and Power; and finally the ownership of the two last by another company, Montreal Tramways and Power, popularly known as Tram-Power.

Almost simultaneously, McConnell and Robert were engaged in a similar venture to take over the Halifax Electric Tramways and merge it with a local power company to form Nova Scotia Tramways and Power. Curiously, these ventures were almost totally forgotten well before McConnell's death, even though he had been both vice-president of Montreal Tramways and a director of Nova Scotia Tramways for six years. The history of the Montreal and Nova Scotia tramways from 1909 to 1918 and beyond is full of dark intrigue, ferocious debate, and sheer farce. By about 1909, electrified tramways were reaching the peak of their popularity in North America. Less than a decade later, the internal-combustion engine was making them marginal and in some places obsolete. And although they have survived into the present day and may even be becoming popular again, today's tramways do not reflect the essential impatience and enterprise of an age, as they did up to about 1918.

The first horse-drawn tramway to be electrified was in Boston, the work of the financier Henry M. Whitney and the engineer F.S. Pearson in the early 1890s.[1] Then Whitney and Pearson electrified the Halifax Tramways, and through that venture as well as through Dominion Iron and Steel and Dominion Coal, they came to know Senator G.A. Cox of the Bank of Commerce in Toronto and Sir William Van Horne and James Ross of the CPR. Ross introduced Pearson to the Toronto financier William Mackenzie, who then turned to the idea of developing the utilities of Brazil. In 1899, just as McConnell was beginning his work with Standard Chemical, its founder, Mackenzie, incorporated Sao Paulo Railway (later Tramway), Light and Power. Two years later, this company won an exclusive forty-year streetcar franchise in Sao Paolo, the economic capital of Brazil, along with a perpetual franchise for the distribution of electrical light.

The Sao Paulo Railway remained thoroughly Canadian, if not Torontonian, in both management and outlook. In addition to its other franchises, it won the rights to sell steam, gas, electricity, and other forms of power and to operate telephone and telegraph services. Mackenzie presided over it, his Toronto Railway, and his Canadian Northern Railway, all out of the same office on King Street in Toronto. In 1903 Pearson also helped Mackenzie in the creation of the Electrical Development Company (EDC) to construct a power plant at Niagara Falls, a huge project comparable to Pearson's work in the United States, and in the construction of the Winnipeg Electric Railway. In the following year, Mackenzie and his associates set up Rio de Janeiro Tramway, Light and Power. Their goal was to replicate in Rio what they had established in Sao Paulo, a monopoly over the tramways combined with electrical power, and as much as possible to control all other utilities in the city.

Three years later, in 1907, the Sao Paolo Railway raised its capital stock to $10 million. It was at this stage that McConnell made his first investment in the venture, thus transforming himself from an employee of a Mackenzie company into a minor partner in the Mackenzie empire. When in 1912–13 Mackenzie united control of the Sao Paulo and the Rio de Janeiro utilities under the ownership of a holding company called Brazilian Traction, Light and Power, McConnell was one of its first subscribers.[2]

As a broker in 1910, McConnell bought $1.5 million of troubled Detroit United Railway bonds on the open market. Through his salesmanship, he raised their price from $50 to $80 and sold them largely to Montrealers. Within a year, the dividend on the railway's common shares had risen from nil to $5.

McConnell also joined Max Aitken, the CPR lawyer R.B. Bennett, and others in developing electricity in Calgary. Their primary object was to power the Western Canada Cement plant at Exshaw and the Alberta Portland Cement plant in Calgary, which Aitken had merged into his new Canada Cement company in 1910. Both plants required much energy, and previous promoters, operating as Calgary Power and Transmission, had also applied in 1906 for thirty-five-year franchises for both a power development for the plants and an electrified street railway in the city. Aitken now bid for the same franchises, and in 1909 he succeeded in taking over properties of Calgary Power and Transmission through a third company, Calgary Power, of which McConnell became one of the original shareholders.

Since they required the substantial investment of capital over considerable lengths of time, public utilities, including electrified street railways, were generally accepted as "natural monopolies." Investors in them demanded franchises, guaranteed by legislation to last a number of years, before they would risk their capital on them. If such utilities as power stations and street railways could be merged, the resulting larger monopolies would be even more attractive to capital. Thus, like the Sao Paolo Railway, Mackenzie's Winnipeg Electric Street Railway, in which McConnell seems to have been interested as early as 1907, eventually gained a complete monopoly of gas, electricity, and public transit in Canada's fastest-growing city. Similarly, Mackenzie's group controlled the street railway in Toronto, a generating plant in Niagara to its southwest, the transmission of electricity from Niagara to Toronto, and through Henry Pellatt, the distribution of lighting in Toronto.

Not everyone benefited from this arrangement, and Mackenzie and Pellatt held a stranglehold over the Toronto utilities for only a short time. When a major coal strike had broken out in Pennsylvania in 1902, Ontario manufacturers began campaigning for the provincial control of all electricity generated in their province, a campaign that led to the creation of the Hydro-Electric Power Commission (HEPC) in 1906 and then its transformation into a government monopoly of the electrical-power industry by 1921, roughly when Mackenzie's Toronto Railway become the city-run Toronto Transit Commission and both Mackenzie and Pellatt went bankrupt.

The story in Montreal was different. In 1892 James Ross, the former CPR engineer, and the broker Senator Louis-Joseph Forget took over the horse-drawn Montreal Street Railway, and they proceeded to electrify the system. With Forget's nephew, Rodolphe, and J.A.L. Strathy, they began to buy shares in Royal Electric, which was supplying electricity to the Montreal market. In 1901 Royal Electric sold its Montreal plant, its subsidiary Chambly Manufacturing, and Montreal Gas to Senator Forget, who reconstituted them as Montreal Light, Heat and Power, commonly known as Montreal Power.

The new firm was to enjoy a monopoly in the supplying of light, heat, and power to Montreal for ninety-eight years – a monopoly that included a long-term contract with the Montreal Street Railway (MSR) to supply it with 5,000 horsepower a year. Crucially, although Forget controlled both Montreal Power and the Montreal Street Railway, he did not incorporate the latter into the former as a subsidiary. This fact, combined with the fact that the MSR required more electricity than Montreal Power had the capacity to sell to it, created an opportunity for another supplier of electricity to compete aggressively with Montreal Power.

In 1901, as Montreal Power was being organized, the Robert family, manufacturers in the Beauharnois district, to the west of the island, had obtained from the federal government a lease of the disused Beauharnois Canal, with a view to developing it as a source of electrical power. This canal extended from Valleyfield, on Lake St Francis, to the town of Beauharnois, at the upper end of Lake Saint-Louis, about eleven miles. It was 200 feet wide at its top and 10 feet deep. At the beginning of the twentieth century, the four rapids on this part of the river were potentially one of the greatest sources of electricity in Canada. Power-generating stations at three of these were owned by Cedar Rapids Manufacturing and Power, Montreal Cottons, and Provincial Light, Heat and Power. To harness the power of the fourth rapids, at Saint-Timothée, Robert incorporated Canadian Light and Power (known also as Canadian Power) in 1904. Soon afterwards, in 1907, he obtained an extension of the 1901 lease of the Saint-Timothée rapids for sixty-three years. The lease required the provision of electrical light to the municipalities of Valleyfield and Beauharnois and the widening and deepening of the canal. There was to be no further leasing of the canal to or – most important – partnership or amalgamation with Montreal Power by the lessee.[3]

There was considerable public anxiety about the monopolistic potential of Montreal Power, but Robert had already convinced the city of Montreal in 1906 to undermine it by hiring him to lay cables to replace the electric wires that were strung out all over the business district, particularly at St James and McGill streets. This he did through Beauharnois Light, Heat and Power, which he had incorporated in 1902.[4] Then, an amendment in 1909 to the Canadian Light and Power franchise reinforced the exclusivity of its lease by precluding it even from doing business with Montreal Power and from acquiring or possessing any of its securities. The federal government of Sir Wilfrid Laurier and the provincial one of Sir Lomer Gouin both supported increasing competition in the development of hydroelectricity and the effect of the 1909 law was to make Canadian Power the direct competitor of Montreal Power. The potential of Canadian Power attracted Max Aitken as its possible promoter, and he agreed to participate, but only if his lawyer, C.H. Cahan, became president. Robert refused. The negotiations collapsed in June 1909, and McConnell became Robert's principal partner, with Johnston, McConnell & Alison acting as underwriters.

The Imperial Trust Company, which McConnell and Robert began operating in 1910, became their vehicle to attract the interest of major investors to Canadian Power. They almost immediately began making plans to take over the Montreal Street Rail-

The directors of Canadian Light and Power and Montreal Tramways,
c.1910. McCord Museum, 03262000.

way. By the beginning of the twentieth century, there had emerged a flood of new trust companies in the United States, which were gaining popularity as vehicles for investment, rather like mutual funds a century later, and by 1903 there were seventeen trust companies in Canada too. Like these other trust companies, Imperial Trust combined "every function of financial business," so that it resembled a "department store of finance."[5] It was effectively a bank that did not discount paper or issue banknotes.

It did perform the traditional trust functions of executor, administrator, assignee, trustee, and agent for individuals. What was much more important, however, was that it was also a corporate trustee and agent for other corporations. It promoted and reorganized other corporations, underwrote their stock, and offered them insurance and land titles.

In Imperial Trust, promoters such as McConnell became the most important shareholders. Its charter permitted it to issue shares, so that the beneficiaries of the trusts that it was administering were also its shareholders. Imperial Trust was thus a hybrid, something between a traditional trustee and a joint-stock company with limited liability. Consisting of a limited number of wealthy investors, it tended to resemble a mutual fund or unit trust, aiming for a controlling interest in companies, preferably in monopoly situations. Only incidentally did it serve the more traditional trust functions, such as taking custody of shares.

What trust companies did was give promotional sprees, like those of Johnston, McConnell, and Allison, momentum. They bought industrial securities directly from the promoters, changed their portfolios rapidly, and so indirectly they increased the money supply. Imperial Trust did all of this while also acting like an investment bank engaged in short-term business financing, actively underwriting and distributing securities as well as buying them. In short, Imperial Trust began life not as a traditional trust company at all but as a group of investors initially committed to developing the waterpower at Beauharnois through Canadian Power.

The charter of Imperial Trust had been granted in 1905, and the gap of five years before the beginning of the company's operations was probably attributable to Robert's inability to find financing for Canadian Power until McConnell undertook a sales campaign for him in England in 1909. Three men took over the charter of Imperial Trust in March 1910: Robert, J.G. Ross (brother of James Ross), and the paper manufacturer F. Howard Wilson.[6] The first shareholders included McConnell, Robert, G.F. Johnston, H.J. Allison, and Alfred Baumgarten of St Lawrence Sugar; Robert became president and McConnell vice-president.

Imperial Trust then organized Canadian Power, which it hoped to link with the four tramways operating on Montreal Island. Of these, the MSR was only the largest, although in practice it controlled the other three. There was a growing demand for urban transit among commuters, and this required both more electrical power and more streetcars, and so the prospects were good. In August 1910 the directors and officers of Canadian Power were announced. F.H. Wilson was named president and Robert vice-president; McConnell was a director. Among the underwriters, Johnston, McConnell & Allison were first, down for $750,000, and J.T. White was second, down for $500,000.[7]

In 1910, the decisive advantage of the Robert-McConnell syndicate over Montreal Power was its access to the rapids at Beauharnois. Another advantage was that

Shawinigan Power, based in Shawinigan Falls outside Montreal (which entered into a quasi-amalgamation with Montreal Power in 1909–10), was not permitted to build, own, or operate a tramway on the Island of Montreal, any more than Montreal Power was. Linking Canadian Power with the MSR and other tramways was therefore the keystone of the proposition.

The production schedule of Canadian Power promised 20,000 horsepower imminently and 200,000 to 250,000 horsepower within a year. The tramways, Canadian Power argued, could probably take 15,000 horsepower almost immediately and save money by allowing it to shut down its inefficient steam plant. With the takeover, the demonstrated earning power of the MSR would give solidity to the enterprise, and the new electricity from St. Timothée would increase the value of the railway by increasing its capacity for expansion.

McConnell gave an interview to the Montreal *Herald* that was published on 1 September 1910. He explained that Canadian Power could already supply over 100,000 horsepower a year. The company had leased the Beauharnois Canal from the federal government for sixty-three years on condition that it expended $4 million on it, and it could supply power at a much lower rate than Montreal Power. He also admitted that "we will not be satisfied with bare control."

This aggressive admission came as a surprise to many on St James Street, for, as *Saturday Night* explained, they had been assuming that the MSR might still somehow merge with Montreal Power. Since Forget and Sir Montagu Allan were leading shareholders both of Montreal Power and the MSR, and indeed Forget was the president of both, these two men seemed likely to be decisive in merging the two companies. But Forget was soon to die in France, and so, if McConnell had any single individual to convince not to vote for this proposed merger between Montreal Power and MSR, it was Allan, whom he had known since selling him Standard Chemical shares in 1901. McConnell seems to have succeeded. And over four more decades, the two men were to enjoy an unusually warm business and personal relationship.

But there were other MSR shareholders to win over. The speculative frenzy in the markets was proving a real challenge to Montreal Tramways. The *Star* reported on 27 September that McConnell had been canvassing Montreal Street shareholders in Ontario and Quebec, buying over 1,000 of their shares above their market price. He wanted to counteract any Street shareholders tempted to change the proxies that they had already given to him in favour of the proposed merger with Montreal Tramways. On 19 October the *Gazette* announced any proposed merger between Montreal Power and the MSR dead, which left Montreal Tramways as the only suitor for the MSR. McConnell's task was now to arrange to arrange the takeover.

McConnell succeeded in raising $3.75 million in Canada and a further $250,000 in the United States, all in less than a month. The precise origin of all this money was obscure,[8] but years later Senator Forget's former secretary learned that the hidden

A 'Power' in Finance

Head of M.S.R. System

JUST ARRIVED IN TOWN.

MR. J. W. McCONNELL.

MR. E. A. ROBERT.

(*left*) Cartoon of the battle among Montreal Tramway and Power, Canadian Power, Montreal Street Railway, and Shawinigan Water and Power. Private collection; (*middle*) Cartoon of McConnell, a "power in finance," Montreal *Daily Witness*, 8 March 1911. Private collection; (*right*) Cartoon of E.-A. Robert, "Head of M.S.R. System," Montreal *Daily Witness*. 17 March 1911. Private collection.

principal behind the Robert-McConnell syndicate had been James Ross, whose son J.K.L. Ross had been in a bitter feud with Rodolphe Forget. This had led to further feuding between the senior Ross and the senior Forget, and to the determination of James Ross to deny the inheritance of the MSR by Rodolphe Forget. This is plausible, since James's brother J.G. Ross was on the board of Imperial Trust. In any event, Montreal Tramways finally took over the MSR through an exchange of shares. Robert became the president and McConnell the vice-president of the reconstituted transit system. The shareholders of the Montreal Tramways included about twenty underwriters, including McConnell. Robert owned 1,545 shares, the Saint-Sulpice Seminary 1,530, and McConnell himself 1,250.

Press attention was now turning to McConnell, described by the Halifax *Morning Chronicle* as a "New Wizard of Finance."[9] At a meeting of the MSR the 1 November 1910 to approve the merger, the *Gazette* reported him sitting far in the back "looking as innocent as a schoolboy with his pockets loaded down with marbles won from his playmates." The replacement of the old board of the MSR by the new Montreal Tramways board took seventeen minutes.

The *Financial Post* marvelled at how McConnell had overwhelmed the opposition through sheer hard work: "An erroneous report has been circulated calling the present deal the 'Robert Syndicate.' It should properly be called the 'McConnell Coup d'Etat,' for while Mr. Robert had the property he could finance the Canadian Power Co. [only] with Mr. McConnell's aid, and in getting control of the Street Railway it was through Mr. McConnell's efforts and his personal magnetism that he secured the co-operation even of directors who were at first opposed to loss of control."[10] The *Witness* reported that McConnell had started "several months ago, almost single-handedly, to obtain control," and the Halifax *Herald* shrieked in a red headline: "Montreal Street Railway Directors, Like Davey Crockett's Possum, Come Down before the Power Gunners."[11]

On 9 December 1910, the syndicate registered a new holding company in London, Montreal Tramways and Power, or Tram-Power. As its name suggested, the purpose of this company was to break into the market for tramways in Montreal but also to take over electrical generating companies in addition to Canadian Power. It was McConnell's task to find new investors in England with H.A. Lovett, the general counsel to the Trust. Lovett was not merely one of the most respected corporate lawyers in Montreal: he was widely admired for his ability to draft documents, he was a veteran of other mergers, and he had worked with Max Aitken on several utilities ventures, including the street railway in Calgary, as well as with McConnell himself in Pacific Pass Coal. He had also worked for James Ross in Mexican Light and Power in 1903–6.

Even if there had been effective anti-trust or anti-combines legislation in Canada in 1910, which there was not, the use of Tram-Power as a holding company for Canadian Power and tramways companies would not have offended it. This was because the Tram-Power scheme involved no conspiracy in restraint of trade in the sense that say the American sugar trust was. It faced competition on Montreal Island in the form of Montreal Power and Shawinigan Power. And since all three companies essentially covered different territories, with little overlap, and their monopolies were perfectly authorized by legislation, they did not individually or collectively constitute a conspiracy.

Broadly defined, a holding company was one that held securities in any other company or companies, and this could include almost any large corporation, such as St Lawrence Sugar, that held shares in its own name in another company. More narrowly defined, the holding company often exercised considerable control over the companies whose securities it held, or it had the capacity to exercise such control. "Control" could mean simply legal control, in the form of the right to elect at least a majority of the directors, either through ownership of the majority of voting stock or through a voting trust. It was "working" control when there was an essential identity between the boards of a holding company and its subsidiary. It was working control that Robert and McConnell wanted Tram-Power to enjoy over Montreal Tramways.

The holding company made possible the development of such giant systems as American Telephone and Telegraph and Bell Telephone. It also made it possible for business to minimize or even to avoid regulation – by utility commissions and securities regulators, investment banks, commercial banks, and individual investors – and government legislation, particularly as it pertained to the linking of unrelated industries, such as coal and railways. Apart from this, the holding company generally was the easiest way of combining companies, of keeping control in the hands of the organizers, and of overcoming charter restrictions.

A holding company generally possessed no assets except for the shares of its subsidiaries, and it was these that owned tangible and intangible property. The most valuable asset of Tram-Power, after the takeover on 1 November 1910, was the MSR franchise, which was not due to expire until 1918. But the terms of the renewal of the franchise had to be clarified if McConnell was to obtain ongoing financing – chiefly in the form of bonds extending well beyond 1918 – for the tramways. Such bonds would typically be rolled over for the duration of the franchise. The length of the franchise determined might be twenty, thirty, or more years, or even perpetual.

Lovett having devised the corporate structure and McConnell having found initial financing for Tram-Power, it was primarily the responsibility of Robert to handle the politics of winning a franchise. By arguing that a new monopoly was the only effective way to rein in the Montreal Power monopoly, Robert managed to secure the crucial support of three declared opponents of monopolies generally. All of them had records of resisting Montreal Power: Godfroy Langlois, journalist, lawyer, and member of the Legislative Assembly, Joseph-Léonide Perron, lawyer, and Sir Lomer Gouin, premier and attorney general since 1905.

The terms of any proposed franchise were a delicate issue, involving municipal as well as provincial politics, with thousands of Montreal commuters now dependent on the trams. The struggle over Sunday tram service in Toronto, which McConnell had seen in the 1890s, revealed precisely how vital trams now were to the functioning of the local economy.

The chief argument in favour of Tram-Power was that both electricity generation and tramways were "natural" and thus in some sense inevitable monopolies. Canadian Power was the only source of electricity for the trams in Montreal apart from Montreal Power, an even bigger monopoly that was still failing to meet the needs of the tramways. The only alternative to any private monopoly would have been a government one, but neither the province nor the city could afford to buy out the private investors that owned Montreal Power or the Montreal Street Railway, while the demand for both electrical power generally and streetcars in particular was continuing to grow.

In January and February 1911, Robert tried to reach an agreement on a new franchise for Montreal Tramways with the Montreal Board of Control,[12] which was a committee of businessmen that oversaw the city council, but he met with no success.

While he proposed sharing profits on the whole system with the city, Robert refused to reduce fares for workingmen and schoolchildren, describing the existing fares as already "the minimum on the continent."[13] The city for its part wanted new routes, the improvement of existing routes, an end to the illegal hauling of freight on the system, less crowding, and new fenders and brakes on the streetcars.[14]

With the breakdown of negotiations between Robert and the Board of Control of the city, Robert tried to attain Tram-Power's ambitions in one stroke. Godfroy Langlois suddenly rose in the Assembly on 20 February 1911, at the end of the session and without the usual notice in the *Quebec Gazette*, to present a bill. Its principal object was to amalgamate four existing privately owned streetcar lines in Montreal, of which the MSR was only one, under the name of Montreal Tramways.

The bill provided that, if after its passage, the city and Montreal Tramways could not agree on the precise terms of the franchise, full jurisdiction was to pass to the Public Utilities Commission (PUC), which then had four or five weeks to decide. The PUC would fix the terms of taking over the four companies so as to avoid stockwatering. Most importantly, it provided for the extinction of the four existing franchises. Instead, section 18 sought "exclusive and perpetual rights" for the consolidated company "to acquire, equip, maintain and operate tramways and street railways in and through the Island of Montreal and the Isles Jesus and Bizard." The suddenness with which Langlois had presented his bill caught the legislative opponents of Tram-Power by surprise, but it was the proposed perpetual franchise that caused real alarm.

Resistance rapidly spread in Montreal. The *Herald* wanted the franchise not to be perpetual but only during "good behaviour," so that Montreal Tramways should have a perpetual franchise only if it was "perpetually good."[15] The city council passed a resolution describing the bill as "a direct menace against the autonomy of Montreal," while the *Witness* called it a "bombshell in civic circles." As municipalities fell under provincial jurisdiction, the outgoing mayor, James Guerin, expressed alarm and decided to go to Quebec City with various aldermen and business figures to protest.

A more formidable if unlikely adversary, Fred Wanklyn, a member of the Montreal Board of Control and an associate of McConnell's in Canadian Coke and other ventures, declared himself "not at all surprised at the attempt to spoliat [sic] Montreal; poor Montreal is accustomed to being despoiled of its rights. It is always the same story; it is the taxpayers; it is you and I who create the receipts of the big companies, but your representatives, those you elect to watch your affairs, have nothing to say, as these companies, as a rule, have charters which render them masters of your prosperity."[16]

Wanklyn spoke with authority. He was a railway engineer of wide experience and sometime manager of the street railways in both Montreal and Toronto under the existing Forget and Mackenzie ownership. In the previous November, McConnell had tried to present the prospective amalgamation of the various systems under Montreal

Tramways as a measure aimed at rationalization, "purely a business proposition." But now, in February 1911, seven aldermen were reported as declaring the bill "an attempt [by the province] to make away with the Board of Control and the City Council."[17]

Robert and a fellow Canadian Power director, the lawyer G.G. Foster, along with the lawyer J.-L.Perron, met the city controllers to reopen negotiations, and Robert suggested that he was now willing to accept a fixed term of years rather than a perpetual franchise, periodic revisions to the franchise, and other concessions, such as a reduction in fares and submission to PUC decisions.[18] But this offer did nothing to forestall a mass protest meeting on 27 February at the Monument National.

At this meeting, J.C. Walsh, who was to become the leading anti-Tramways journalist, recalled that Langlois had opposed the creation of the original Montreal Power monopoly in 1901. A.R. McMaster, a lawyer, described Montreal Tramways as asking "for about every probable right and privilege ever thought of on earth and above the earth" and expressed surprise that it had not asked for "aeroplane rights." The nationalist journalist Olivar Asselin, though seeing himself as a "partizan of monopoly," termed Robert's methods "so crude and so western" that the proposed measure should be called "the Buffalo Bill." The journalist Henri Bourassa observed that the bill permitted any line or company to be acquired by Montreal Tramways, including *Le Devoir* itself, and that it was worse than anything inflicted on the southern states by the carpetbaggers after the American Civil War.[19]

On 28 February, the *Gazette* reported that Montreal Tramways was now asking for an extension of its franchise by thirty-eight years, which, when combined with the twelve years of the unexpired contract, would mean an effective franchise of fifty years. At the same time, Montreal Tramways was offering the city a percentage of the earnings of the entire system, both urban and suburban, and car service every three minutes instead of every five. To Fred Wanklyn, these concessions seemed to be a victory for the Board of Control over the original "outrageous" and "preposterous" provisions of Langlois's bill, and so agreement seemed closer.[20] The *Herald*, however, rejected Robert's offer of compromise on principle. "Kill the Bill" was its reply. Why should the city compromise? It had a contract with the Montreal Street Railway and it was not seeking to change it: "There should be no negotiations with a man who orders you to break your contract and holds a pistol to your head to compel obedience."[21]

The sparring continued through much of March. At the end of February, McConnell had joined Robert and Foster in Quebec City for further negotiations with Premier Gouin. Although Robert had dismissed Wanklyn as "childish and absurd," it seemed that they were indeed willing to accept his conditions for a fifty-year franchise. On 2 March, a delegation from the Citizens' Association, a group intent on municipal-government reform, arrived in the provincial capital from Montreal. But Premier Gouin said that he could not kill the bill and that it would go to committee.[22]

In committee on the following day, Langlois confirmed that he wanted a fifty-year franchise. Gouin proposed forty rather than fifty years, and the committee decided on forty-two, so as to enable the company to place debentures on the market for forty years, as was normal although not inevitable.[23]

The *Herald* declared that the city's right to control its streets, and to make contracts for the transport of passengers over these streets, was about to be lost to a group of speculators "imposed through the willing agency of the Legislature" – "government by Messrs. Robert, Foster, Perron, et al. ... the most daring lobby which the Legislative halls of Quebec have ever witnessed."[24] Mayor Guerin called another mass meeting at the Monument National, describing the bill as "the most arbitrary piece of legislation that was ever presumed by any Government,"[25] while Henri Bourassa castigated the premier himself as "attorney-in-chief" for Montreal Tramways, which was now run by a "small gang of speculators."[26]

Wanklyn, no longer mollified by Robert's concessions, accused these financiers of having bitten off more than they could chew. As a former general manager of the Montreal Street Railway, he expressed particular outrage at the preamble of "this infamous bill," which claimed that people were clamouring for better service when in fact it was all a "put-up job": "Last year, steps were taken [by the new owners] to make the service worse, to aggravate the citizens and to stick pins into them. The so-called negotiations were commenced. We were simply being played for suckers while this bill was being prepared and taken over to England to show the financial magnates there what they might obtain."

The bill received royal assent on 24 March 1911.[27] There the matter rested until 5 October, when the *Star* published details of McConnell's arrangements for the financing of the new corporate organization. At a meeting of Tramways shareholders, Robert had announced that $9 million in bonds had been placed in New York. Over $1 million more had been set aside for the bond indebtedness of the Montreal Public Service Corporation, which was set up to sell electricity from Canadian Power to Montreal Tramways, and there was an additional $3 million in the Montreal Tramways treasury.

Under the new authority of Tram-Power, the shareholders would maintain their existing relations with the subsidiary companies; there was "no watering of stock" and the reorganization was "simply a matter of internal economy." But in essence the MSR shares had already, upon the takeover, been made exchangeable for Montreal Tramways debentures, cash, and bonus common shares. Canadian Power shares received one and a half Montreal Tramways shares for Canadian Power share they were holding, without exchanging it. Crucially, $10 million in MSR stock became $25 million in new bonds, and $6 million in Canadian Power stock became $10 million in new stock. In other words, the syndicate had enriched itself by $4 million and added $15 million to the debt of the company. McConnell personally held 1,250 Tramways shares and Robert held 1,545.

(*left*) Cartoon of Goldbrick Twin Ticket, *Beck's Weekly*, 28 March 1914, showing
E.-A. Robert and Sir Hugh Graham in support of Percival W. St George, a candidate for the
Montreal Board of Control who favoured a franchise of forty years for Montreal Tramways.
Private collection; (*right*) Cartoon of Lorne McGibbon. "A Hustling Financier,"
Montreal *Daily Witness*, 22 March 1911. Private collection.

All through the rest of 1911, there was growing disquiet about the implications of
the financing of Montreal Tramways. It appeared that tramways would be paying
more for electricity – to the benefit of Tram-Power and, by extension, Canadian
Power – than Montreal Street had paid under its arrangement with Montreal Power,
or would under another arrangement with Shawinigan Power.[28]

Nevertheless, Montreal Tramways seemed to be making some progress. In August,
it issued a report on its first nine months, claiming a 14 per cent return on common
shares on an annualized basis. With a view to expansion, Robert went to the city
council to ask for elevation of the Grand Trunk Railway tracks, more street routes,
and a tunnel under the Lachine Canal. By December, Sir Hugh Graham's land development, the Town of Mount Royal, was incorporated. Montreal Tramways got an

exclusive franchise from it for up to twenty-five years, which led to suspicions that Graham (soon to be elevated to the peerage as Lord Atholstan) was closely linked to Robert and McConnell. Montreal Tramways also obtained a franchise to serve the suburb of Saint-Laurent.[29] Canadian Power was also beginning to transmit electricity, and the Montreal Public Service Corporation received an exclusive franchise for fifteen years to supply electric power and light.

Despite the apparent triumphs of the Robert-McConnell group, the expansion of Montreal Power and Shawinigan Power had hardly been foreclosed by Canadian Power, which had yet to build its promised new plant. In February 1912 Montreal Power and Shawinigan Power bought from Lorne McGibbon control of Cedar Rapids Manufacturing and Power, operating north of Montreal, a company for which he had recently obtained a charter. It was to take a further nine years, but this was the start of the joint investment vehicle of Montreal Power and Shawinigan Power, known first as Civic Investments and then as United Securities, that was eventually to absorb Canadian Power itself.[30]

In addition to the competition that these two other generating companies posed to Canadian Power, the technological revolution that had been producing such electrified systems as Montreal Tramways was also facing two new threats, after less than a quarter century of development. The first was the automobile and the other was the bus. The enthusiasts for both of these new developments in transport tended to overlap, and the principals behind Canadian Autobus, which had been incorporated in April 1912, suggest also that Montreal Power had organized it to strike back at Robert and McConnell. Duncan McDonald, formerly general manager of the Montreal Street Railway and then briefly of Montreal Tramways, was president and managing director; and the board included Herbert Holt and J.S. Norris of Montreal Power, Fred Wanklyn, and Lorne McGibbon. McGibbon, who had recently been ousted from the presidency of Goodwins department store by McConnell, was by now a firm opponent both of Imperial Trust and of Montreal Tramways, and he had made a fortune by buying Cedar Rapids Manufacturing and Power and flipping it within a year to Montreal Power. If Canadian Autobus could offer bus service in league with Montreal Power, it would not be trespassing on the proposed Montreal Tramways monopoly so much as circumventing it, and, more importantly, it would not require any more electrical power, as opposed to petroleum, in order to operate.

On 29 July 1912, city council passed by-law 453, on the establishment of autobus lines; and then on 22 August it entered into a contract with Canadian Autobus, granting it a franchise for ten years. The agreement was disturbing to the fledgling Montreal Tramways, since the 1911 provincial legislation permitting the fusion of the various street railways had specified that any renewal of the franchise of the MSR, inherited by Montreal Tramways, was subject to the discretion of the city on "the operation, maintenance, equipment, establishment and extensions of routes."[31] The city had thus proved itself very favourable to Canadian Autobus, and its vehicles would probably cut into the existing tram routes, as would be confirmed by the new (or renewed) franchise for Montreal Tramways that was still pending. *La Presse* had already been predicting the end of the despised trams in favour of buses, and a war to the death by Canadian Autobus against Montreal Tramways.

To forestall the implementation of this contract between the city and Canadian Autobus, a close friend of McConnell's from the YMCA fundraising campaign of 1909, and a prominent shareholder in Imperial Trust, W.G.M. Shepherd, took legal action to nullify it. He sued for an annulment of both the by-law permitting autobus lines and the contract between the city and Canadian Autobus. Through J.-L. Perron, he claimed that the city (as opposed to the province) had had no right to grant a monopoly to, or to own shares in, or to appoint three directors of Canadian Autobus, as provided by the contract.

Whether by design or otherwise, throughout 1913 Montreal Tramways repairs effectively blocked traffic on St Catherine Street, Bleury Street, and Park Avenue, three of the most important thoroughfares in Montreal. All of these streets happened to be principal routes proposed for vehicles to be operated by Canadian Autobus, although initially only St Catherine Street was to be served by buses.

In its own defence, Canadian Autobus broadened its challenge to Montreal Tramways. It proposed in November 1913 to build from seven to eight miles of subway (an underground railway) at the cost of $20 million. It also offered the city half the profits from the operation of this subway, ownership and control of the subway proper, and construction of a tunnel under the joint supervision of the city and the company. Canadian Autobus would furnish all the capital for plant, cars, tracks, powerhouses, lighting and ventilation, and car equipment, or about a third of the total expenditure, and fares would be five cents, the same as that on other subways on the continent. Construction would take place between 1914 and 1918, and Canadian Autobus was willing to put its proposal to a referendum.

Apart from the autobus contract, the campaign against the proposed Montreal Tramways franchise continued. On 31 December 1912 the *Herald*, now apparently under the ownership of Lorne McGibbon, reviewed Robert's "pretext [of] the absolute necessity of being placed in a position to raise the money imperatively needed for the development of the street railway":

What did they do? Raise new capital for development work? Not they! They had other purposes to which they could put the money. Their own pockets were itching. So they put another mortgage on the property, and shoved the proceeds, nearly ten millions of dollars, into their trouser pockets!

That is what these gentlemen did, and they have ever since let Montreal hang by the straps when it wanted to get home nights. They have moved not a finger to improve the service; have not spent a dollar upon new central city routes, and have been cheese-paring the service in every way. Little bob-tailed hand-brake cars are being run; in cold weather many cars are not heated; and, in a word, what was ten years ago a reasonably efficient transportation service is now hideously inadequate, out of date and exasperatingly inefficient.

The Montreal Tramways directors, the newspaper continued, did not realize "the indefensible position in which the company has placed itself, by its jockeying with stocks and its indifference to the citizen"; a public franchise was a public trust, not a private enterprise "to be used as a pawn on the stock exchange chess-board." By January 1913, Montreal Tramways had sued the *Herald* for defamation, seeking damages of $600,000 ($100,000 for each director, including McConnell).

In the autumn of 1913, it was clear that under pressure Montreal Tramways was trying to improve service: since April, 1,000 men had been laying seven miles of new track and repairing twenty miles of old track, 250 new cars had been ordered, and improvements had been scattered over 270 miles. Heavier rails had been laid and already a hundred more cars were operating than last year.[32] But the animosity towards the company remained intense. The legislature had made the formal granting of the tramway franchise dependent upon the reaching of a new contract of service between Montreal Tramways and the city, and so attention shifted again to the city council.

In November 1913 Robert presented an ambitious plan to the city. In return for a forty-year franchise and the right to ship freight on Tramways trackage at night, he proposed building subways under steam-railway tracks and the Lachine Canal. Further, he proposed a new artery between Viger Square and Victoria Square or as far west as Windsor Street Station (later Windsor Station); a boulevard and a subway from Craig Street (later St-Antoine Street) to Mount Royal or Van Horne avenues; other subways under St Catherine, Notre-Dame, and St James streets; and the widening of Vitre Street.[33] The *Herald* was not favourably impressed, and it demanded whether Montrealers were to be "despoiled of their rights by this gang of franchise-robbers." Indeed, this was "one of the boldest gangs of buccaneers and strong-arm financiers" ever to seize control of the public utilities of any city.[34]

There were still weightier fears for the city to ponder. Robert's proposal gave Montreal the right to take over the system after forty years, but experience suggested that the city might not be able to exercise this right. A similar provision had been in an earlier franchise given to the gas company. But when, at the end of the gas franchise, Montreal had decided to buy the gas plant, it had to find money for this purchase from the legislature, where gas and electrical interests blocked it.[35] Moreover, upon examination, the Tramways proposal obliged the city to build new streets and to guarantee the bonds for any subways built by the company. These details, the *Herald* said, amounted to making the city build the subways itself, and would enable the company to traffic in the money market upon the faith and credit of the municipality.[36]

In April 1914 Mayor Médéric Martin ignored these fears and revealed himself as a supporter of Montreal Tramways. He proposed giving the company a thirty-year franchise over all sections of the current city of Montreal, exemption from paying percentages of gross earnings to the city, the right to run autobuses, freight-carrying privileges, and a conditional automatic renewal of its franchise. He would refer new surface lines to the PUC and not force the Tramways to lower fares. In return, the company was to abandon all its existing franchises, tax exemptions, and rights to franchises in adjoining territories as they were annexed to Montreal; to furnish equipment for the subways; and not to increase fares within the city while reducing fares to outlying areas.[37]

Debate over the franchise spread beyond city hall. The Trades and Labour Congress came out against any new or extended franchise, in view of the financial crisis and the general commercial depression.[38] The Board of Trade found itself divided. The general council declared that it viewed "with alarm" the proposed franchise. Then, under pressure from Robert and his friends, a general meeting of the Board of Trade reversed this stand and called for a new contract as soon as possible.[39]

By this stage, it appears that Sir Hugh Graham, owner of the *Star* and the new *Herald-Telegraph*, had bought the scourge of the Tramways camp, the *Herald*, effectively silencing that newspaper as a critic of the Tramways. The *Herald*'s Tramways critics seem to have moved to the *Daily Mail*, established in 1912, possibly by Lorne McGibbon. According to this latter paper, the Board of Trade meeting, called originally to consider the issue dispassionately, had been no more than a "love fest" for the Tramways. The Board of Trade had invited Peter Witt of Cleveland to discuss tramway problems in a disinterested manner. But then Robert had turned up at the meeting, in his capacity as a board member, with "a special plea for his private business interests, given with an appearance of authority, and not only specious but misleading as well."[40] The same newspaper suggested a coat of arms for McConnell, who had been publicly silent: "A man and a pump, a trough brimming full (labelled Aqua Pura); a long, long row of lambs 'lapping it up,' and a sheep-shearer awaiting their distension before starting to take their wool. Motto 'Feed my lambs' done in old biblical script."[41]

At meetings of the Board of Control, the franchise battle dragged on into 1915. The war had become very personal. In March, the journalist Edward Beck described the blackballing of two proposals for membership of the Montreal Club, a luncheon club one floor above McConnell's office in the Dominion Express Building, orchestrated by McConnell. The candidates who found their applications blocked were city controller Duncan McDonald, a Tramways critic on City Council, and Brenton A. McNab, the editor of the *Daily Mail*. Although it is impossible to verify the truth of his account, its publication further illustrated the bitterness aroused by the ongoing fight over the franchise, as well as how McConnell was seen by his critics.[42]

All the while, ongoing litigation continued to block implementation of the Canadian Autobus contract through 1915. One case made its way to the Privy Council, which upheld the Canadian Autobus contract; the other, Shepherd's, continued working its way through the courts; and even by 1917 Canadian Autobus had not managed to put one bus onto the streets of Montreal.[43] It was, however, not until 28 June 1917 that the Board of Control was able to declare the contract with Canadian Autobus null and void because of non-performance by the company.[44]

On 30 June 1915 the *Evening News* reported that a city controller, Napoléon Hébert – who had just taken his seat on the board of Canadian Autobus – had nevertheless accepted a bribe from the Tramways. It published a photograph of a letter to the Tramways, purporting to be signed by Hébert in which he accepted $200,000 in cash for supporting the Tramways in any vote on the franchise. Hébert denied that the letter was genuine, although later he admitted that it was his signature on it.

Following this revelation, the anti-Tramways camp swiftly made a successful application to the Superior Court to prohibit the Board of Control from dealing with the franchise question.[45] Chief Justice J.S. Archibald issued an interim injunction against the board to prohibit it from even discussing – much less acting on – this matter. But, notwithstanding this injunction, Mayor Martin and controllers Thomas Côté and Hébert rushed through approval of the franchise without permitting their opponents to speak on the franchise, read out the court order, or vote. Following this travesty, foes of the Tramways moved for a further injunction both to restrain the board from transmitting a report on its action on the franchise to the city council, and to restrain council from receiving and considering any such report.[46]

Eventually, in Practice Court, Mr Justice Panneton convicted Martin, Côté, and Hébert of contempt of court and imposed sentences on each of $2,000 in fines and six months' imprisonment. Upon appeal, the court simply removed Hébert from office and levied fines against the mayor and Côté. To the public and Premier Gouin, it was now incontrovertible that the controllers and probably the aldermen were unfit to decide the franchise issue.

A new franchise, negotiated by Perron and imposed by the provincial legislature, seemed to be the only way to accommodate both trams and buses. The city of Montreal was literally bankrupt and being administered by a provincial commission, and there was no alternative to direct provincial intervention. In February 1918 Gouin imposed a contract between the city of Montreal and Montreal Tramways which was to run until 1953.[47] In addition, he set up a Montreal Tramways Commission to manage the system. The contract annulled all privileges, rights, and franchises now possessed by Montreal Tramways in the city and in areas to be annexed to the city; it granted the commission the authority to construct, equip, maintain, and operate a system of surface tramways; and it required the commission to extend uniform tariffs to all of Montreal Island. The effect was to address nearly all the criticisms that had been levelled at the Robert-McConnell group since its takeover. Coincidentally, it shut out Canadian Autobus and similar applicants for a municipal bus franchise.

The benefits to the shareholders of McConnell's elaborate financing were brought under control. The company was to receive in quarterly payments out of gross revenues a sum equal to 6 per cent of its capital value of $36 million, including all physical assets added to the system to the end of 1917. Mortgages, mortgage bonds, and debenture stock could not be more than 75 per cent of the total additional capital then furnished with the contract. Any surplus was to be divided as follows: 30 per cent for the city, 20 per cent for the company, and 50 per cent towards toll reduction. A reduction of fares could be ordered when the tolls-reduction fund exceeded $1 million.

Montreal Tramways was therefore not expropriated in 1917, even if the definition and the administration of its franchise were placed in the hands of trustees. The company remained privately owned, but the tramways system became regulated by a public commission. Payments to the shareholders and bondholders, with certain deferrals, continued. As of 1918, Tram-Power, Canadian Power, and the Montreal Public Service Corporation were all continuing as privately owned companies as well. Their value, however, had lain since 1911 in their connection with Montreal Tramways. Now that the tramways had been wrested from their control, the function of these three companies was murky. Canadian Power and the Montreal Public Service Corporation could still function and in principle profit their shareholders, but they no longer had a guaranteed customer.

The provincially appointed Montreal Tramways Commission was empowered to decide how to purchase power for the Tramways and from whom, such as Shawinigan Water and Power or one of its subsidiaries, rather than Canadian Power. The Public Service Corporation had the right to distribute electricity on Montreal Island, but if the commission did not buy electricity from Canadian Power, this electricity could not go towards powering streetcars. The holding company of Tram-Power still owned Canadian Power and the Public Service Corporation, as it still owned Montreal Tramways, but only Montreal Tramways still possessed significant productive assets and a monopoly position, and Tram-Power had no influence over its decisions.

While Robert remained president of Montreal Tramways until 1924, McConnell himself appears to have lost interest in the company after 1915, though he did not resign as vice-president until about 1918, when the Montreal Tramways Commission took over effective control; and he remained vice-president of Tram-Power until probably 1922. As effectively a passive investor in Montreal Tramways, Tram-Power did reasonably well after 1918. By June 1921, it could report small increases in both gross and net earnings and a total surplus of over $900,000. Moreover, the company's deficit, which in 1918 amounted to $3 million, had been reduced by almost one-half. The new contract, therefore, seemed favourable to the shareholders of Montreal Tramways, and at the annual meeting of Tram-Power in September 1921 Robert was re-elected president and McConnell vice-president of the holding company. For all the failure of its machinations, Tram-Power was receiving steady payments from Montreal Tramways, and the question arose of how Tram-Power was now to expand without losing control in such a way again.

On 14 February 1922 Robert had two private bills passed by a committee of the Legislative Assembly. One effect of them was to remove the prohibition, inserted in the Canadian Power charter of 1909, on any amalgamation with Montreal Power. The bills also provided for the possible amalgamation of the Montreal Public Service Corporation, which was renamed as the Quebec-New England Hydro-Electric Corporation, with Canadian Power and three other electrical utilities. The Taschereau government, Robert argued, was most concerned to earn revenue by exporting surplus Quebec power, to either Ontario or the United States, and Robert saw an enlarged Canadian Power as a major step to this end. But apart from the change of name of the Montreal Public Service Corporation to Quebec-New England Hydro-Electric, this company did not merge with three others as provided. And it was still apparently held by Tram-Power.

At this time, Robert also saw opportunities in the region of Quebec City. In April 1922 he took over the presidency of the Quebec Railway, Light, Heat and Power (commonly known as the Quebec Railway), in order to effect an amalgamation not unlike that of Montreal Tramways and Power, but without any control of the tramways by a provincial commission. Electricity was more wanted than ever, and optimism about a still greater corporate consolidation in Quebec continued into the summer, with rises in the prices of the shares of both Canadian Power and the Quebec Railway. Despite the popularity of the automobile, Montreal Tramways showed a surplus for the financial year ending in June 1922, which it described as the "best in its history." Yet again, Robert and McConnell retained the presidency and the vice-presidency of Tram-Power.[48]

Ultimately, however, Robert's attempt to secure full control of the Quebec Railway failed, when he tried to double its capitalization, and he was even forced to surrender its presidency in June 1923. Shawinigan Power took over. Worse followed. Two weeks later, attacks began on Robert's administration of Tram-Power in Montreal. Work had not begun at Carillon as he had promised. Fifty shareholders signed a requisition for an extraordinary meeting to consider the company's financial condition, to elect directors, and to appoint inspectors. On 15 June, Robert issued a financial statement which revealed that W.C. Finley had succeeded McConnell as vice-president of Tram-Power, although the exact date of McConnell's resignation was not disclosed. The remaining directors included J.M. McIntyre and Senators Marcelin Wilson, G.G. Foster, Nathaniel Curry, and Lorne Webster.

On 3 July 1923 the first meeting of Tram-Power shareholders in nine years took place. It lasted over three hours, and two brokerage firms led the attack on Robert. The meeting resumed on the following day, and it began with questioning of the value of assets claimed by Tram-Power. T. Kelly Dickinson of the brokerage firm of Dickinson Walbank concluded that there were only $2 million of securities properly listed among the assets. This deductions necessary to reach this figure would increase the deficit from the nearly $2 million claimed by Robert to an estimated $16 million.

An in-house Tram-Power report, by C.J. Doherty, a retired justice of the Supreme Court of Canada, appeared in November 1923. It revealed that the shareholders of the holding company (Tram-Power) did not own, as they had been led to think, the Montreal Public Service Corporation, now renamed the Quebec-New England Hydro-Electric Corporation. Neither did they own Canadian Power, which they might reasonably have assumed they did. Although Canadian Power was historically a subsidiary of Tram-Power, it was actually now owned by Quebec-New England Hydro-Electric.

All these revelations led to the creation of a Shareholders' Protective Committee, which disputed Robert's claims that opposition to Tram-Power's bid for the tramway franchise, war conditions, and unsettled financial markets had all doomed the holding company. In December 1923, the committee announced a provisional slate to replace the existing Tram-Power board. The annual meeting of Tram-Power that followed went on for eighteen hours without break, in "tumult" and in "hysteria," on 19 and 20 December. Although the Robert group held only a small portion of the company's shares, Robert as chairman was able to disqualify many of the opposition proxies for technical reasons, and the board was re-elected. The opposition declared that it would go to court. McConnell, as usual, remained silent.

What had happened? In 1922, when McConnell probably resigned as vice-president of Tram-Power, Robert apparently decided to shift most of the assets of the holding company to a completely new venture at Carillon, on the Ottawa River, where he would build a new generating station much more promising than that at St Timothée. Several other directors of Tram-Power – Marcelin Wilson, W.C. Finley, K.B. Thornton, F.J. Shaw, and P.J. MacIntosh – backed Robert and joined the board of Quebec-New England Hydro-Electric. Henry Miles and his National Hydro-Electric Co. had already erected a small plant at Carillon in 1913. Robert and his confederates did not own Carillon yet, but were holding an option to purchase it. In view of its change of name in 1922, Quebec-New England was now clearly intended by them as an effort to develop power for sale to the US.[49]

At about the same time, the American tobacco magnate and investor in the Quebec aluminum industry, J.B. Duke, was finding himself with excess electricity to sell from his power plant in Isle Maligne, in the region of the Saguenay. In 1923, GE engineers advised Duke and New England Company Power (a group of utilities in New England not to be confused with Quebec-New England Hydro-Electric), that if they could combine power from Isle Maligne with power from Carillon, it would be economical to export it from these two plants to the US.

The new Duke investment would require power lines 500 miles long, twice as long as any erected up to that time, extending from Isle Maligne to Carillon and then into the United States. Even without selling electricity to New England, Quebec-New England Hydro-Electric was also holding valuable franchises for the distribution of power in Montreal and 250 miles of pole lines, and Montreal was on the route from Carillon to the States, and so Duke might benefit from these as well. Duke completed an all-Canadian strategy to sell his excess power in November 1923. He asked Frank Jones of Canada Cement to form a company to transmit power from Isle Maligne to the Montreal market and the St. Lawrence Valley.

With the support of the National City Co., the securities arm of the National City Bank of New York, Jones made a bid to take over Quebec-New England for Duke. National City had marketed the bonds of the collapsing Tram-Power, and it was concerned that there should be no default on these new ones. Despite Prime Minister Mackenzie King's veto of any power exports from Quebec to the US in 1922, the prospects for Carillon in 1923 were far from permanently blocked. The reason was the possibility of a joint development of power along the St. Lawrence River (which included the rapids at Carillon) by Canada and the US.

In the meantime, Tram-Power was continuing to collapse. Robert's victory at his board meeting at the end of 1923 was short-lived, for the threat of legal action soon forced his resignation as president of Tram-Power at a board meeting on 7 January 1924. Subsequently, he was also forced to resign from the presidency both of Imperial Trust and of Montreal Tramways, and Tram-Power was taken over by United Securities, a joint venture between Montreal Power and Shawinigan Power.

Apart from its shady origins, Quebec-New England suffered from very bad timing, as there were three separate developments that threatened the sort of export of electricity that it was contemplating. The first was any prospective joint development of the power of the St Lawrence River, already mentioned. Internal questions of jurisdiction over the river – among Ottawa, Ontario, and Quebec – had still to be resolved, and any such cooperation with the US required the further consent of Ottawa. In 1924 both Canada and the US set up separate committees, followed by a joint one, to study how to develop the river. And so an international joint development of the river seemed more than possible. And it would cut into, although not necessarily eliminate, the need by the US of power from Carillon, with or without cooperation between Carillon and Duke.

Secondly, at this stage, it was also the policy of the Ontario HEPC to develop its "eastern system," essentially disconnected from its central system based in Niagara, as Sir Adam Beck had made clear in 1923. Beck saw Quebec-New England Hydro-Electric as a private attempt to circumvent the governments of both provinces, and any possibility of export to the US as dangerous to the development of Canadian manufacturing. He estimated the maximum capacity of Carillon as 200,000 HP, while Quebec-New England Hydro-Electric had pledged itself to the production of double this amount, which he assumed would come from the Ottawa and St. Lawrence Rivers, rivers that he was planning to develop for the HEPC, as already described. In virtually his last public statement, in June 1925, Beck observed that a third of the estimated cost of Carillon was for transmission lines to the US.[50]

Thirdly, also opposing the proposed takeover by Jones and National City were the Aldred-Holt group or United Securities, the joint venture between J.E. Aldred of Shawinigan Power and Sir Herbert Holt of Montreal Power. It was roughly at this point, in June 1924, that the shareholders of Quebec-New England, led by Marcelin Wilson, sold what had been originally Robert's option to buy the Carillon site from Henry Miles to Lorne Webster and Oscar Dufresne.

Six months later, on 10 December 1924 at a general meeting of United Securities, which had taken over Tram-Power in January, it was revealed that Tram-Power had accumulated a deficit of more than $13 million. In the following year, a United Securities investigation concluded that Canadian Power could still not generate even 20,000 horsepower at Saint-Timothée, well short of the 80,000 horsepower that had been estimated, by McConnell among others, in 1911. Auditors, moreover, reported a deficit for Canadian Power of over $176,000. Canadian Power finally now admitted that it had never possessed sufficient working capital, and so the new directors reduced the capital of the company from $6 million to $600,000.

In 1926, Ontario and Quebec definitively agreed to block any attempt by the Dominion to lease or sell Carillon or any other Ottawa River site, and to block any export of power to the US more generally.[51] This decision also ended, for years to come, further discussion about a joint development of the St. Lawrence by Canada and the US. Carillon therefore went into a very temporary limbo just after the collapse of Tram-Power but not as a result of this collapse.

In the meantime, in October 1925, McConnell was elected to the board of Montreal Power, which ran United Securities, the new owner of Tram-Power, with Shawinigan Power. He had escaped the Tram-Power debacle by quitting as its vice-president just before its looting by Robert, Finley, Wilson and others in order to fund Quebec-New England. He had of course lost his vice-presidency of Montreal Tramways with the imposition of control over it by the Montreal Tramways Commission in 1917. He blithely took his seat at Montreal Power not merely unscathed but to fulsome acclaim of his sagacity noted in identical articles in newspapers all over Canada. The *Montreal Daily Star,* which he had just secretly bought from Lord Atholstan, led this chorus of praise.

To what extent McConnell was responsible for the failure of Tram-Power is difficult but not impossible to determine. He seems to have absented himself from meetings of the board from 1918 onwards, and yet from the beginning he had been vice-president, essentially for finance, and so he was presumably privy, if not central, to all the decisions made on financing and refinancing at least until the loss of the tramways franchise to the provincially appointed commission in 1917. As a financier, he had been spectacularly successful, especially in gathering the support among holders of the Montreal Street Railway for its takeover by Montreal Tramways. Even from 1911 onwards, his task as financier was limited, as no refinancing seems to have been required. For all its problems – which did not become public until after he had resigned as its vice-president – the Tram-Power group seemed highly attractive to investors, and this attraction, justified or not, was a credit to him.

Certainly, bad faith, bribery, and bad planning and execution seem to have dogged Montreal Tramways from its start. In consequence, all of Montreal and by extension the economies of Quebec and even of Canada as a whole suffered, along with the shareholders and the bondholders of Tram-Power and, of course, the city's commuters. Robert, against whom McConnell eventually joined other shareholders in a lawsuit, was undoubtedly the evil genius behind much of the chicanery and maladministration, but by 1924 his career was practically over.

McConnell's financing of Tram-Power had been aggressive, but no more illegal or unethical than those used in American utility amalgamations. What he did was not materially different from what tramway promoters in New York, Cleveland, Detroit, Boston, and Toronto, among other cities, had been doing. To observe that there was no law in place that he violated, or was accused of violating, is not to immunize him or indeed his predecessors elsewhere from all possible criticism, for example, for failing to respect the legitimate interests of a public that had conceded a transit monopoly as natural and necessary. But his essential function did not involve public relations or politics. It was to find what investors were demanding, and to consent to corporate decisions as long as they were consistent with what investors wanted.

This account of Tram-Power is a sketch based largely on newpaper cuttings collected by McConnell itself, as well as on other sources. The full story may never be known because it involved so many murky players with hidden and largely inscrutable agendas, such as Lord Atholstan (Sir Hugh Graham), Lorne McGibbon, James Ross, and Sir Herbert Holt. Edward Beck, the chief journalistic enemy of McConnell, seems to have developed his antipathy to the tramway promoters generally during McConnell's reorganization of the Detroit United Railway, which coincided with Beck's employment in Detroit. Duncan McDonald and Fred Wanklyn, who had done so well as managers of the MSR under Forget, seem to have quarrelled with Robert, and thus lost any role in Montreal Tramways. Forget and indeed Mackenzie, with whom they had also been associated, had been at least as aggressive as Robert and McConnell. Holt's creation of Canadian Autobus was no act of altruism to the Montreal commuters. Neither was it rooted in his declared belief in competition so much as in his resentment at losing to Canadian Power.

None of this serves to exonerate McConnell from responsibility for the failure of both Montreal Tramways and Tram-Power, but it is truly unclear to what extent if at all he was involved, say, in the apparent bribery of Mayor Martin and two aldermen to pass a franchise for Montreal Tramways through the Montreal City Council. A close study of the alleged bribery of controller Hébert suggests that he was actually working for Robert and trying to entrap Canadian Autobus by accepting a bribe from its president, Duncan McDonald, in return for previously pretending to accept a bribe from Montreal Tramways. This was why the notorious letter that he had signed had been addressed to Senator Forget, rather than Robert, while everyone knew that Forget was dead. It is probably impossible now to know the truth. All that is clear is that there were shifting, less than savoury alliances of businessmen vying to control transit and power in Montreal and Quebec City, led by such men as Lorne Webster, who may or may not have been in collusion with his friend McConnell while flirting with Robert in the Quebec Railway merger. None of them perceived any overriding duty to protect the public against free enterprise.

In the absence of contrary evidence, it is fair to conclude that McConnell may have been too busy to do more than condone dubious practices. He was one of many players, and known as a specialist in finance just as Lovett was a specialist in corporate organization. For all or nearly all the period from 1912 to 1925, he was also the president of Goodwin's and of St Lawrence Sugar. Canadian Power failed to develop as even McConnell had promised because of an overestimate of the capacity of the site at the start of the project. St-Timothée was never to fulfil its original promise, even after eventually falling into the hands of Montreal Power.

One reason Aitken had refused to work with Robert in 1908–09 was that he did not trust the estimates of the potential of St-Timothé made by J.G. White, a firm of New York engineers that had taken a big position in Canadian Power. It was an engineering misjudgment that led in the end to the transfer of Tram-Power efforts to Carillon, in addition to the loss of control over Montreal Tramways in 1917, the growing competition to tramways from buses and motorcars, and the growing technological capacity to export power far outside the province. McConnell's financing methods were not the cause of the Tram-Power collapse.

What McConnell was rumoured to have done in the tramway battles was in any case offensive to many, and when Montreal Tramways was finally expropriated by the city almost forty years after he had worked on its financing, even the old accusations of stockwatering surfaced. They were undermined by the conflation by his accuser, an accountant, of bonds with common shares, so that he spoke of vaguely of watered "securities," as though bonds as well as shares could be watered. This was nonsense, apart from the fact that even stockwatering was virtually obsolete as a criticism, in light of the demonstrated superiority of common shares (including those of Montreal Tramways) over preference ones as vehicles for capital appreciation. Fully aware of this, McConnell was to protest vehemently the low valuation of shares that served as the basis for compensation to the shareholders. He had felt likewise about the compensation to shareholders of Montreal Power and Beauharnois Power (another project near the old Canadian Power plant), including himself, in the course of their expropriation by Quebec in 1944 and 1951 respectively.

Despite its origins in the looting of Tram-Power, the ultimate fate of Quebec-New England Hydro-Electric was a separate one. Unlike Robert, Finley, and others, McConnell was not on its board. Even if evidence surfaces some day that he was somehow involved in the looting, notwithstanding the fact that he does not appear to have been blamed in any of the extensive coverage of it by the press, it will have to contend with the fact that he became a director of Montreal Power in 1925, almost at the time as its subsidiary Shawinigan Power, United Securities, was uncovering and publicizing the extent of the same looting.

That Sir Herbert Holt of Montreal Power was hardbitten there can be little doubt. But he did not invite, say, Robert to join his board with McConnell in 1925. It would require hard evidence of a prior conspiracy by Holt and McConnell to loot the Tram-Power assets with Robert, to prepare them for a takeover by United Securities, to substantiate any allegation of participation in the looting by McConnell. There is no evidence of such a conspiracy, while there is ample evidence that Robert and his colleagues at Quebec-New England genuinely wanted to sell power from Carillon, rather than let Holt and Montreal Power do so. Their failure was due to political forces beyond their control, and not for want of trying. Indeed, their destruction of Tram-Power, by shifting assets from it without authorization, suggests how desperate they were to sell from Carillon.

Simultaneously with their efforts in Montreal, McConnell and Robert turned to Halifax to set up a company similar to Montreal Tramways. McConnell himself did not spend as much time in Halifax working on this venture as Robert, but the methods of financing that they used in Halifax bear comparison to what they were doing in Montreal.

In 1909 Sir Frederick Borden, a cabinet minister in the Laurier government, had applied to the Nova Scotia legislature to incorporate Nova Scotia Power and Pulp. This company was to develop power on the Gaspereau River, disposing of it in the immediate vicinity of his home, fifty-five miles northwest of Halifax. Robert agreed to offer Borden advice and, once the charter had been passed by the Nova Scotia legislature, to pay $100,000 in cash for a share in the undertaking, in particular water rights, while Borden, in return for using his political influence, was to receive $250,000 in common stock.[52] In furtherance of his relationship with Robert and McConnell, Borden bought $20,000 in stock of Canadian Power and $20,000 in the Montreal Street Railway.[53] From Johnston, McConnell, and Allison he also bought fifty shares of Ames-Holden-McCready preferred stock and subscribed to $25,000 in preferred shares of British Canadian Lumber.[54]

As in the case of the bill in Quebec to incorporate Montreal Tramways, the bill to incorporate Nova Scotia Power and Pulp conferred power on the company to enter any municipality to string wires and erect poles without the consent of the local authorities. In response to pressure from the Nova Scotia Public Utilities Commission, Borden and Robert offered to confine their operations to the Gaspereau valley in return for exemption from the commission's jurisdiction. As agreed, with the passage of the act of incorporation, McConnell and Robert paid over $100,000 for the company's water rights and $250,000 in securities for the lands and timber it controlled.

Borden, Robert, and McConnell then turned their attention to taking over the Halifax Electric Tramway. Unlike Montreal Tramways, however, the shareholders in the new Nova Scotia Power and Pulp were not allowed to own stock in other undertakings or to use the streets of Halifax. The three promoters therefore applied to the legislature in 1911 for removal of these restrictions. They also wanted to change the name of their company to Nova Scotia Power and to increase its authorized capital from $6 million to $10 million. This increase in capitalization would provide securities to be used in a contemplated stock swap with Halifax Electric Tramway shareholders, along the lines of the offer made to shareholders of the Montreal Street Railway. Through Borden's lobbying efforts, the government obliged.

Then, however, the Borden syndicate found itself competing with a Halifax lawyer named John R. McLeod, who owned large blocks of Halifax Electric Tramway shares. A race between the two syndicates for Halifax Electric Tramway began, but it did not last long. While the stockholders in Halifax Electric Tramway did not seem interested in the offer of either group, a buyout of McLeod by McConnell and Robert was effected through the aid of Premier George H. Murray and the federal minister of finance, W.S. Fielding. The two syndicates formally merged their efforts on 5 April 1911. In the following January, as Halifax Electric Tramway shareholders began to resist the takeover, the directors solicited proxies and began to negotiate a renewal with the city of the company's exclusive franchise to run the street railway for twenty-five years. This franchise was due to expire in 1916, and by February the renewal had been agreed upon.

The Robert-McConnell syndicate, which by now was holding 38 per cent of the railway's shares, protested to the city council, but without success. The legislature refused to uphold the renewal, however, and simply prohibited an increase in the dividends and capitalization of the company, and the sale of its shares to other utilities, for a year. Before the end of that year, Robert and McConnell had acquired complete control. Then a new holding company, Nova Scotia Development, acquired all of the shares in Halifax Electric Tramway held by Nova Scotia Power (which had changed its named from Nova Scotia Power and Pulp in 1911).

On the day Robert became president, the city council voted to ask the province to acquire the street railway, subject to ratepayer approval. Robert began a publicity campaign against this and applied to the legislature to incorporate Halifax Tramways and Power to take over Halifax Electric Tramway and develop the power on the Gaspereau. In return for a forty-year extension of the exclusive franchise, Robert offered an increase in the company's annual payment to the city and promised to cut lighting rates by a third and power rates by a half. The city rejected the offer, since it would have permitted Halifax Electric Tramway, or at least its holding company, to develop hydroelectricity itself, thereby increasing capitalization and allowing securities to be handed to insiders at knockdown prices. The interest and dividends on these securities would have to be paid by transit riders, as in Montreal.

The Conservative Party, under Sir Robert Borden in Ottawa and Charles Tanner in Halifax, opposed the Robert-McConnell syndicate. But, with the help of a local MP, Edgar N. Rhodes, and his uncle, Senator Nathaniel Curry, Robert bought a potential hydro site on the West River at Sheet Harbour in the summer of 1913. A rival bid, by Halifax Development, to supply Halifax with electricity from St Margaret's Bay, seventeen miles west of the city, offered charges for electricity that would be less than half those currently demanded by Halifax Electric Tramway. The advantage that Robert and McConnell possessed, however, was control of the street railway, which provided demand for a large, steady base load and the right to use the existing distribution system. This control made available to them the earnings of the street railway, $270,000 in 1913. Armed with their charter, the promoters lost no time in trying to reap their profits.

In August 1913 Robert and McConnell, in the name of Halifax Electric Tramway, asked the Public Utilities Commission for permission to issue 6,000 ordinary shares at $100 each. These were to raise the $600,000 to retire the existing bonds, as required by the new Public Utilities Act. Effectively, the new issue might not take into account any rise in the value of the company since incorporation, and therefore the new stocks could be bought at the original book value but resold at market value. The commission, however, viewed this as a form of stockwatering, which, it said, was oppressive to both existing minority shareholders and outsiders. It then applied the principle that when a corporation increased its capital stock, stockholders were entitled to subscribe to the new issue in proportion to their original holdings, before subscriptions were received from strangers. It refused the application.

The promoters were more successful in November 1913. They returned to the commission with a new resolution endorsed by 90 per cent of the shareholders which authorized the directors to dispose of the bonds at no more than 105 per cent of the par value of the shares, as determined by an independent valuation of the company. The commission could not object to an increase in capital if convinced of the propriety of the redemption of the bonds at this time and at a premium. It accepted the application.

In February 1914 the Robert-McConnell syndicate took over the Halifax Electric-Tramway, Robert becoming president and McConnell one of three vice-presidents. They then asked the legislature for a charter for the new holding company, Nova Scotia Tramways and Power. This set off a war in the press. The Liberal *Chronicle* took the side of Robert and McConnell, while the Conservative *Herald* supported the city council. Lorne McGibbon bought up about $1 million of real estate in Halifax and pressed for public ownership of the tramway.[55] The Robert-McConnell group charged that, with confidential information from Sir Robert Borden about port and terminal railway plans, McGibbon had purchased land for sale to families whose properties would be adversely affected by the tramway under new ownership. On 10 June 1914 the Robert-McConnell group won, and Nova Scotia Tramways and Power was incorporated. During the stormy debate over the charter, one of McConnell's associates, the lawyer H.A. Lovett, gallantly described him "as a man of the highest personal character, and whose work for and contributions to educational and Christian institutions is not exceeded by that of any man of his age in the Dominion."[56]

In July 1915 Nova Scotia Tramways and Power applied to increase its capital stock to $10 million. The existing directors being still provisional, the Public Utilities Commission permitted only the issuance of $6 million of ordinary stock,[57] but on 14 February 1916 it reconsidered the application. At the hearings, the city of Halifax argued that if the commission approved the desired capitalization, "the hands of the Board will be tied for all time in so far as reducing rates is concerned."[58] For the promoters, Lovett argued that the commission was not required to take into account either the nominal capital of the company or even the amount of capital actually invested. The English courts were concerned with the "reasonableness of the rates charged apart from the investment or capitalization."

The commission decided that it could deal only with the proposed issues of securities at this stage, on the basis of whether these were reasonable for an approved purpose, as authorized by the legislature. It held that the securities were speculative by their very nature, and that an investor in a public utility was entitled to receive more for his money than an investor in a mortgage was on his. It concluded that it could approve the issue of bonds and shares but not any increase in the company's capital stock. On 19 September 1916 it authorized Nova Scotia Tramways and Power to issue $3 million of gold bonds, out of an authorized total of $5 million, 25,000 preferred shares, and 25,000 ordinary shares.[59] The total gross profit to the syndicate has been calculated as $1,001,265.50 or $17,345,008 in 2008 terms.

The Robert-McConnell syndicate delayed developing electricity from the Gaspereau property, obtaining in 1917 an extension on its obligation to do so until 1919. It then lent the funds for this project to Montreal Power and, before trying to meet its 1919 deadline, sold Nova Scotia Tramways and Power to American investors, the firm of Stone and Webster, a holding company for about fifty utilities. On this transaction, the Robert-McConnell group made an undisclosed profit, probably at least a further $820,000, or $10,726,279 in 2008 terms.

In sum, Robert and McConnell's efforts in both Montreal and Halifax were remarkably similar, from failed power projects, possibly not entered into in complete good faith, to holding companies. There was much chicanery in the background, on all sides, that may never be fully understood. In the end, the operations of Robert and McConnell in both cities were even virtually identical in duration, both beginning in 1909 and concluding in 1917–18, with none of the promises to the public fulfilled but the promoters richer.

McConnell kept the initial common shares that he had in Montreal Tramways at least until 1921. His portfolio for that year reveals holdings of $81,000 in that company, $24,000 in Montreal Tramways, and $20,000 in the Montreal Public Service Corporation. This total of $125,000, $1,340,480 in 2008 terms, constituted just over 1 per cent of his portfolio as a whole.

When once asked what he had done with the common shares that he had earned on his promotions, McConnell replied simply, "I kept them all."[60] This is not quite accurate in respect of Montreal Tramways, since he seems to have sold his 1921 holdings by 1929. McConnell, however, did not merely keep common shares generally for long periods; he also gave them to his own family as presents. Lil in particular would receive such shares each year on her birthday, and, near the very end of his life, McConnell gave a wedding present of common shares to his grandson Christopher's wife. Such presents were expressions of his continuing faith in the future, as were his many endowments of institutions with common shares.

There has never been the suggestion either that he was in later years in any way ashamed of his role in financing tramways and power. The evidence suggests that he had been brilliantly successful in it. In many respects, the Tram-Power venture was his most adventurous and most elaborate. If some argued that such financing gave private enterprise a bad name, he would never admit it.

CHAPTER EIGHT

The Rise and Fall of Holding Companies for Power and Paper, 1925–39

From coal he switched to selling bonds and his salesmanship was one of the main reasons for putting the Montreal Light, Heat and Power company on a paying basis. Supposedly still wet behind the ears in the financial field, he traveled to England with M.LH. and P. bonds and fooled all the wise fellows back home by selling a suitcase full.

"Sugar Baron," *New Liberty*, March 1949, 23

The Quebec government could have developed Quebec resources for the benefit of the Canayen people. It could have borrowed money to launch our economy. But it was prevented from doing so because it was dominated, through the Clergy and through petty Canayen politicians like Sir Lomer Gouin, by the Anglo-Saxon bourgeoisie. The provincial government was at the service of Anglo-Saxon capital. [...] With no trouble at all, the United States capitalists took hold of the primary sector of direct extraction – the entire pulp and paper industry, hydro-electric works, asbestos, gold and silver mines. [...] This legalized, institutionalized robbery makes us slaves in the lumber yards and factories of our own country.

Léandre Bergeron, *The History of Quebec: A Patriote's Handbook*
(Toronto: NC Press, 1975), 171–3

By 1925, McConnell could take comfort in being free at last of the Tram-Power imbroglio. Further, with the recession of 1921–24 over, both he and the economy were on the threshold of profiting from a period of unprecedented prosperity. And with the freeing of shares in his own portfolio from their use as collateral for the loans of St Lawrence Sugar, he had millions of dollars to invest in the market.

The following four years were economically among the headiest of the twentieth century. Most countries prospered in this period, and none more than Canada with its practically limitless trees and waterpower. Its industries based on them were attracting enormous investment, both internally and from abroad. There was growing demand, naturally, for electrical appliances and newspapers but also dramatic growth in such industries as that of motion pictures, all requiring advertisement in the press,

McConnell in the 1930s. Private collection.

which in turn required paper and the waterpower that produced it. New companies, thirsting for capital, were sprouting to supply what was becoming a massive new consumer economy. And there were thousands of new investors to slake this thirst, introduced during the First World War to investment through their purchase of war bonds. Corporate behemoths, both holding companies and investment trusts larger than ever before seen, emerged to absorb the money flowing in. Although McConnell had officially retired from promoting new or merged companies in 1913, he was now pursuing a new career as an investor, and he was also working to attract other investors to favoured ventures of his, nearly all of which involved electrical power.

McConnell was a director of a few of the major power corporations, but only the survival of some of his portfolios and ledgers enables us to see how extraordinarily extensive his interests really were. Even these records, moreover, cannot tell the whole story. It was impossible for him or anyone to own shares in Ontario's HEPC, for example, but he did invest in it indirectly, through its joint ventures with a company that he had helped to organize, International Power and Paper. He also invested in numerous American power companies indirectly through investment trusts. Through Niagara Hudson Power, based in northern New York State, he was by extension invested in Consolidated Gas, one of its chief customers, which served New York City. In addition, he invested directly in Consolidated Edison in California, and, through Brazilian Traction, his interests extended to Spain and Mexico as well as Brazil.

The economy of the interwar period was fuelled by oil as well as electricity, although both together could hardly satisfy its growing appetite for energy. By the end of the First World War, tramways were becoming technologically old-fashioned all over North America, and they were yielding the streets to petroleum-fuelled buses. In 1919 the new provincially appointed Montreal Tramways Commission introduced the first bus route to the streets of Montreal. In 1923 the city council noted that there was still inadequate electricity for the tramways, and so it called for more buses. In 1927 Montreal Tramways also acquired numerous regional bus companies and merged them under the name of Provincial Transport.[1]

In addition to buses, there was a fundamental shift from trams to private motor vehicles. Between 1910 and 1926, the number of tramway-track miles in Montreal rose by 35 per cent, but the number of road (bus and car) miles rose by an even more impressive 56 per cent. The lawyer for the Tramways under Robert and McConnell, J.-L. Perron, became a lawyer for the Automobile Club of Canada as early as 1913, a director in 1918, and finally provincial minister of roads in 1921. In the last capacity, he so expanded the provincial road network to encourage Americans to come to Quebec by car and to tour it the same way that the route round the Gaspé was named after him. Buses and cars were becoming so common that no power companies wanted to be tied predominantly, much less exclusively, to streetcars. It was therefore no great loss for McConnell to diversify out of his investments in tramways. Like Robert and everyone else in the industry, he also had seen that electricity was of much wider use, once it could be transported great distances, as they could by the time Robert was incorporating Quebec-New England Power in 1925.

Electricity generated by water power was now demanded for domestic as well as industrial use. Electric stoves, refrigerators, lights, and other appliances such as vacuum cleaners were spreading all over North America. Thus, with the invention of long-distance electrical-transmission lines, Quebec realized that it could sell its surplus power to Ontario, and this became provincial policy in the 1920s, spawning a new power industry along the Ottawa River between the two provinces.

More generally, as the electricity grid expanded, former locally defined "natural monopolies" over electricity merged into financial ventures of often continental dimensions. Holding companies became not merely appropriate but almost necessary in order to spread and manage the development costs and risks. Far from being chastened by his experience with Montreal Tram-Power, therefore, McConnell moved on to investing heavily in power in New York State and in Quebec. The provincially operated HEPC in Ontario – held up by admirers in the United States as the antithesis of the private utility companies that McConnell was investing in – was in fact integrating itself into the same power grid with them. In later years, electrical utilities would allegedly become a safe investment haven for widows and orphans, but in the 1930s they were a field for aggressive investors, many of whom were to be destroyed by their boldness. McConnell was not among those utterly ruined, but after the Crash of 1929 he did suffer heavy losses when the utility holding companies collapsed under the weight of their debt and mismanagement.

McConnell, though unaffected personally by the ban on power exports from Canada in 1926, looked south to invest in lucrative electrical markets extending to New York City. In 1925 a group of power companies in northern New York State had come together to form the Buffalo, Niagara and Eastern Power Corporation. Part of the northern border of New York State, of course, was the St Lawrence River, which was therefore American as well as Canadian. In 1926, before Ontario and Quebec had announced their decision to block exports to the United States, the New York State Water Power Commission began hearing applications by the Frontier Corporation and the American Superpower Corporation to develop power on the St Lawrence. The commission approved Frontier's plan, which involved the building of a dam at Barnhart Island. The HEPC, however, would have to give its consent for this plan to proceed, and it proved recalcitrant, as did the state governor, Alfred Smith. The ensuing deadlock provoked the creation in 1929 of an even larger power company in New York State, Niagara Hudson Power, which took over both Buffalo, Niagara and Eastern Power (Buffalo, Niagara) and the Frontier Corporation. In 1928 Buffalo, Niagara had been the largest utility in North America, but the formation of Niagara

Hudson in the following year made the latter the largest utility in the entire world, accounting for 20 per cent of all American production.

Niagara Hudson was a consortium of large interests, notably J.P. Morgan, and there were various personal connections between its board and the cabinet of President Herbert Hoover. McConnell was one of the earliest investors, his holdings in the company as of September 1929 exceeding $800,000, and in taking on this role – which represented probably his first major utility investment after the collapse of Tram-Power – he became a major investor in power for New York City, a far more important market than Montreal. He also was associated with some of the most powerful interests opposed to public ownership of power in the United States, a cause represented by Alfred Smith and his successor as governor, Franklin Roosevelt, to whom McConnell was to be firmly opposed until the Second World War. When Smith resigned as governor in order to run for the presidency against Hoover in 1928, Hoover's subsequent victory proved to be that of Niagara Hudson as well.

In 1929, at the state level, Roosevelt challenged the legality of the Niagara Hudson merger, but his attorney general declared it legal. The next year, Roosevelt established an exploratory St Lawrence Power Development Commission, which, in the absence of interest from Canada, achieved nothing. However, still obsessed with Niagara Hudson, Roosevelt in 1931 appointed the Power Authority of the State of New York (PASNY) to follow what he understood to be the HEPC model of expropriation of private utilities and rural electrification. With Roosevelt's support, PASNY asked President Hoover to enter into a St Lawrence treaty with Canada along lines similar to those proposed by Prime Minister R.B. Bennett, who had come to power in Ottawa in June of that year. Bennett had proposed that the federal government should pay for navigation works while the HEPC should pay for power development. The secretary of state, Henry Stimson, connected to Niagara Hudson, refused a parallel cost-sharing agreement between Washington and New York State; but the Joint Board of Engineers agreed on the Canadian plan for a St Lawrence project that would produce 2.2-million horsepower, and a treaty emerged for ratification.

Then, in 1932, Roosevelt won the presidency against Hoover, partly on a platform of full public regulation of the utility holding companies, such as Niagara Hudson, and at least a local-rights option on electrical development. He conceded a continuing function for private initiative and private capital for utilities, and thus excluded the HEPC model for the United States at the national level. But he continued to back PASNY's campaign for cost-sharing between Washington and New York, and he asked PASNY to launch an investigation of the public versus private costs of distributing St Lawrence power. The chairman of PASNY announced that it was involved in the greatest project since President Theodore Roosevelt had built the Panama Canal.

Niagara Hudson, for its part, was not standing still. In 1931 it extended its transmission lines to Westchester, New York, where it joined the terminus of New York Edison, a subsidiary of Consolidated Gas. Floyd Carlisle, formerly the manager of Niagara Hudson, became chairman of Consolidated Gas in 1932, and the first exchange of power between it and Niagara Hudson took place the following year. Carlisle's success, particularly his claim that his companies were distributing more than 75 per cent of all power sold in New York State, alarmed PASNY. It recommended municipal distribution and publicly owned transmission, using as its model the Tennessee Valley Authority (TVA) that President Roosevelt had just inaugurated.

Roosevelt appointed Morris W. Cooke, a PASNY trustee, as head of the TVA's rural-electrification administration, which was to operate along the lines developed by Sir Adam Beck in Ontario. Roosevelt was so taken with the TVA, the centrepiece of his New Deal, that he expressed the hope that it would be copied all over the country. But here he ran into the opposition of one of the most compelling politicians and ablest lawyers of the time, Wendell Willkie. As the leader of the opposition to Roosevelt's New Deal, Willkie commanded the allegiance of capitalists all over North America, especially McConnell, who lent him his warm support until Willkie's sudden death in 1944. In fact, McConnell's respect for Willkie may have been exceeded only by his respect for Joseph Chamberlain thirty-five years before.

After the First World War, Willkie had become chief counsel of the new Commonwealth and Southern Corporation (C&S). Bernard Capen Cobb had created C&S out of 165 other utility companies, worth $100 billion. It was a holding company with operating units in eleven states, from Michigan to Alabama. McConnell was one of its earliest investors, owning more than $2 million ($24,478,260 in 2008) of its shares in its first year of operation, a sum that represented over 4 per cent of his portfolio before the Crash of 1929, after which, in the space of two months, it lost almost half its value. It was also his second-largest utility holding after Brazilian Traction, and significantly more the value of his investment of $1.2 million ($14,686,957) in Montreal Power or MLHPC.

Cobb had built C&S consciously to avoid the chicanery of the utility empires of Harold Hopson and Samuel Insull, whose stock pyramiding and interlocking holding companies were then causing concern and even scandal, even though Insull himself – whose utility empire would collapse spectacularly in 1931 – was heavily invested in C&S.[2] Ill health forced Cobb to surrender the presidency of C&S to Willkie almost at the same time as Roosevelt was assuming office in January 1933, and in the following year Cobb gave Willkie the company's chairmanship as well. Shortly afterwards, in April, Congress began debating the development of Muscle Shoals under the new TVA. To Willkie, the swift passage of this bill was an assault on constitutional law, democracy, and free enterprise. He asked for compensation for the 300,000 investors in the six C&S operating companies, then providing 64 per cent of the power in the Tennessee valley but soon to be endangered by the TVA. He even offered a compromise, by which C&S lines should carry all of the power generated by government plants in the valley, and pass on any savings generated by the TVA to the consumer, all under a contract extending from fifteen to thirty-nine years. But his arguments could not prevail against the overriding need of the federal government to create jobs through the building of the TVA.

The ideological as well as corporate battle over the ownership of waterpower that had opened in Ontario a generation earlier had now arrived in the United States. McConnell keenly followed its progress, not merely as a shareholder in C&S but also – following the collapse of Tram-Power – as a shareholder in Montreal Power or MLHPC, which was likewise coming under increasing threat of government control. The Insull scandal inspired the Roosevelt administration to draft a bill in 1934 to limit holding companies generally, not merely in their ability to milk the profits of their operating companies but also in their geographic reach. All the utility holding companies were tarred in the eyes of the administration with the same brush, and C&S was uniquely vulnerable in finding itself in the same territory as that of the TVA and therefore potentially in direct competition with it.

Willkie decided to test the constitutionality of the TVA all the way to the Supreme Court. In 1939, however, the Supreme Court rejected C&S's claim that the TVA was guilty of coercion, duress, fraud, or misrepresentation in seeking to break the utilities in the Tennessee valley. For the *New York Times*, the way now seemed open for Washington to compete with private enterprise in any field, even on terms obviously unfair to business.[3]

Willkie, and McConnell too, foresaw the cost overruns, the political interference, and the general lack of direction that such large government monopolies as the TVA were to come to stand for,[4] and, partly in response to that body's creation and the Supreme Court's legitimization of it, he resolved to launch a political career in direct opposition to Roosevelt, to the immense delight of McConnell. Yet he also realized that it was time to sell at least parts of C&S to the TVA, and he obtained $78 million for its prize operating unit, Tennessee Electric Power, enough to pay its bondholders and holders of preferred shares. The common shareholders, including McConnell, got nothing. Five southern C&S operating companies remained, and Willkie obtained contracts for them to buy electricity from the TVA. In 1940 he won the Republican Party's nomination for the presidency, and was defeated by Roosevelt, now running for his third term.

McConnell believed that state ownership could be fought only with a reformed capitalism. Willkie had set out a defence of capitalism in language that McConnell understood, in accounting terms rather than in ideology, and with the same disarming moderation – at least in public – that McConnell himself had adopted as his own style. For Willkie and for McConnell, the problem was not that Roosevelt was a socialist much less a communist, although in unguarded moments they might attach extremist labels to him. The problem was that it was highly uncertain where Roosevelt's New

Deal, even apart from the TVA, might now lead. His attempt to pack the Supreme Court of the United States suggested a willingness to override the traditional separation of powers in the American constitution.

Furthermore, Roosevelt's reluctance to make hard decisions about the purposes of the TVA led to considerable vacillation in how it operated, to the detriment of the hydroelectric market generally. Eventually, critics were come to label this threat as "Big Government," but for McConnell personally, damaged and horrified as he was by the fate of most of the utility holding companies in the era of the New Deal, the antidote was no longer Big Business in any indiscriminate sense. By 1939, McConnell was largely retired from active business and becoming an active philanthropist, and he had lost millions to badly run utility holding companies. The task for him was how to reconcile free enterprise, which had raised him, Willkie, and so many others from almost nothing, with social responsibility.

Hydroelectric power was not the only industry that shone a spotlight on this issue. Another was an industry closely allied to hydroelectricity – pulp and paper. Producing paper out of pulverized woodchips and the cellulose that derived from them, pulp and paper had first emerged in Canada in the 1890s and by 1926 was the most important industry in the country and the largest of its kind in the world, utilizing waterpower and as well as a variety of woods, chiefly spruce. From shopping bags to the newspapers on which the new advertising industry was largely dependent, the products made from Canadian wood pulp outstripped those from the United States, Norway, and Sweden and helped to transform daily life in the early twentieth century.

Most pulp was the product of a mechanical grinding of wood, which retained relatively short wood fibre suitable only for newsprint. In fact, newsprint was by far the most important product of pulp, hence the term "pulp and paper industry." In Canada, the growth of demand for newsprint was directly tied to the growth of advertising in American newspapers especially up to the end of the First World War, when radios were rare and other electronic media unknown. American newspaper owners lobbied Washington for the free entry of Canadian newsprint, since it was the major factor in their costs of production and US forests were rapidly thinning out. In 1910 the Quebec government of Sir Lomer Gouin forbade the export of unprocessed wood pulp from trees cut on the province's crown lands, which forced the establishment of paper mills in the province, the most important Canadian source of newsprint. Ontario followed suit only in 1926. This prohibition of Quebec pulp exports in itself led to the import of Canadian newsprint into the United States free of duty, a fact confirmed by new US legislation in 1913.[5]

From 1913 to 1921, Canadian mills generally did well. In 1916, in the midst of wartime regulation, four (eventually five) of the mills set up the Canadian Export Paper Company to coordinate their sales efforts. Like the informal association of Canadian sugar refiners, it did not fix prices directly but "stabilized" them, so that the mills compensated one another when they sold special items at below established prices. In 1920–21 the US removal of wartime price controls on newsprint led to sharply increased demand for the product, rising prices for it, and eventually an overexpansion of the Canadian industry.

By the mid-1920s, the price-stabilization system run by the Canadian Export Paper Company was beginning to fall apart, and in 1927 it had completely collapsed. It had never in any case controlled more than 50 per cent of Canadian production, and so its collapse led to a comprehensive free-for-all among the Canadian producers. Eleven of these producers, including the five that had formed Canadian Export Paper, formed the Canadian Newsprint Company as their new selling agency.

By September 1928, however, the American newspaper owner William Randolph Hearst had destroyed Canadian Newsprint by forming secret contracts with certain of its members, notably International Paper (IP), based in New York since its creation in 1898 but operating the biggest mill in the world at Trois-Rivières, Quebec, to purchase newsprint at prices lower than the "norm."[6] In 1927 the official selling price had been $65 per ton, but in 1928 IP offered to sell to Hearst at $52 per ton, a price that would barely cover the costs of the members of Canadian Newsprint.

With price cutting proving ruinous to the industry as a whole, the premiers of Quebec and Ontario, Louis-Alexandre Taschereau and G. Howard Ferguson, helped to establish a new industry agreement in November 1928, by which at least initially all producers in their provinces were to operate at 80 per cent of capacity. A new Canadian Newsprint Institute emerged to enforce this rule. Under strong political pressure, IP agreed to operate its Canadian mills at the reduced capacity, but it used its mills in New England and Newfoundland (then not part of Canada) to produce at 100 per cent and it began to sell the product of these mills directly to Hearst and other American clients. It offered to reduce its production at its American mills if permitted to operate at more than 80 per cent of capacity in Canada, and it made plans to build mills in New Brunswick, outside Newsprint Institute territory. IP could afford to remain aggressive, since the US Federal Trade Commission, in light of the Quebec-Ontario agreement, recommended the building of additional mills in Alaska, and IP began to reopen antiquated ones in the United States, all of which threatened to take more business away from the Canadian producers. Under American pressure, three of these producers – IP, Ontario Paper (controlled by the Chicago *Tribune*), and Spruce Falls (controlled by the New York *Times*) – refused to participate further in the Canadian Newsprint Institute.

In addition to its efforts at price stabilization, the Canadian newsprint industry faced much reorganization. In 1928, IP bought a half-interest in the Bathurst Paper Company of New Brunswick, Price Brothers took over Donnacona Paper, and Abitibi Power and Paper took over Spanish River Pulp and Paper and four smaller mills, becoming for a while the largest paper company in the world. Sir Herbert Holt and

J.H. Gundy of Montreal decided to do even better, buying not only the Bay Sulphite plant at Ha! Ha! Bay, at the mouth of the Saint-Maurice River but also Saint-Maurice Paper and Belgo-Canadian Paper, and in 1925 they merged them into the St Maurice Valley Corporation, adding to their assets in the following year Canada Power and its mill at Windsor Mills.

It was at this point that McConnell entered the picture. When the St Maurice Valley Corporation approached the Laurentide Company, a paper mill controlled by the CPR and the Bank of Montreal, McConnell, already a director of the Bank of Montreal, briefly became a director of Laurentide, apparently to facilitate its merger with the St Maurice Valley. After the merger, however, McConnell resigned as a Laurentide director and had no ties to the huge new Canada Paper and Power that Holt and Gundy had just created out of the two companies. His refusal to ally himself with this venture coincided with a frenzy in trading the shares of the newsprint producers generally, which suggests that McConnell already knew what Holt and Gundy did not: that the bull market was about to end. He also added insult to injury by joining the board of IP, Canada Paper's rival and eventual nemesis, just after quitting the Laurentide board.

The market for Canadian newsprint began to break in October 1928, when it surfaced that IP had obtained a contract with Hearst to sell at $52 a ton, $13 lower than the price for newsprint of the Canadian cartel,[7] the members of which were reduced to less than 50 per cent of their capacity. The following year, the biggest paper company in the world was the troublesome IP; however, IP was unable to translate its size into increased market power through economies of scale, and by 1913 its market share had declined from 60 per cent in its first year to only 26 per cent, and its American stocks of timber had been depleted. The US Underwood Act of 1913, which abolished tariffs on newsprint imported from Canada, imposed further strain on the company, which could not find comparable cheap American wood to process, and it clearly had to consider manufacturing in Quebec (the prime source of Canadian pulp) or changing its business.

Under Philip Dodge, its president from 1914 to 1924, IP tried to meet its challenges in four ways. First, it changed from the production of newsprint in the United States to that of higher grades of paper. Secondly, beginning in 1922, it shifted its newsprint operations to Trois-Rivières. Thirdly, it diversified into hydroelectric power generation, also in Quebec. And, finally, it experimented with sulphate-pulp and kraft (smooth brown paper) production for bags and wrapping paper. By 1923, the first strategy, of moving into the production of higher-grade paper, had failed.

Presumably because of its size and his preference for investing in market leaders, McConnell owned IP shares at least as early as 1921, when his portfolio as of the end of that year recorded 500 common shares valued at $22,500. He was thus an interested observer in 1925 of the efforts of IP's new president, Archibald Graustein, a corporate lawyer from Boston, to pursue the company's three remaining strategies. Graustein bought and reorganized the bankrupt Riordan Paper of Quebec; expanded aggressively into the production of kraft; and established a Canadian subsidiary, Canadian International Paper (CIP), to take over both the forest reserves and the power facilities of Riordan and also the operations of St Maurice Lumber, purchased in 1910, at Trois-Rivières. In his first year as president, he asked Prime Minister Mackenzie King whether he should invite McConnell to join the CIP board. King, resenting McConnell for his active support of Arthur Meighen in the general elections of 1925, recommended Raoul Dandurand instead. Nevertheless, McConnell joined the board of CIP in 1926.

The CIP newsprint mill at Trois-Rivières was then the largest in the world, with a capacity of 240,000 tons. And by 1930, CIP, with an overall annual capacity of 800,000 tons, was second only to Canada Paper as a Canadian producer, controlling 17 per cent of the country's total capacity. Despite the fall in the price of newsprint from $78 a ton to $62 in the period from 1925 to 1930, Graustein also raised gross sales from $50 to $154 million. Nevertheless, because of the costs of its overexpansion, CIP was to accumulate the worst record of all the major pulp-and-paper companies that survived the 1929 Crash. Its net losses totalled $20 million for the first five years of the Great Depression, almost double the combined net losses of nine large competitors. In 1932 it was losing $7.50 on every ton of paper that it was producing.

With the continued depression of prices following the market crash of 1929, the consolidation of the Canadian paper industry continued. In 1930 Port Alfred Pulp and Paper, Anticosti Corporation, Anglo-Canadian Paper (of Newfoundland), and Wayagamack Pulp and Paper all merged into Holt's Canada Paper. Price Brothers cooperated with, but remained independent of, Canada Paper. Abitibi negotiated with IP for a merger, but their talks failed, and so there remained three distinct big newsprint companies in eastern Canada. Even this reduced number, however, could not stabilize prices. In 1928 the Canadian Newsprint Institute had raised the "normal" price to $55 per ton, which Hearst and IP agreed to abide by. In 1929 it raised the price again, to $60, but on this occasion IP ignored it and sold newsprint at less that that price to Hearst. After the market crash of the same year, there emerged a totally free market again, and John Price, president of Price Brothers, resigned as chairman of the Institute the following year.

In 1929 IP became a subsidiary of the new holding company of International Paper and Power, which capped IP's third strategy of expanding its operations into the generation of electricity. The first step towards this goal had been IP's earlier diversification, in 1925–26, into electrical power in New England.[8] In 1925 IP paid $20 million for majority interest in New England Company Power and related companies, and out of this purchase emerged the New England Power Association (NEPA).

A master at leveraging a small amount of equity, Graustein set up holding companies at two levels, and both of them were Massachusetts voluntary trusts, that is, incorporated in Massachusetts in order to circumvent the Massachusetts ban on the owning by foreign companies (such as IP) of utilities within the state. First, there was the International Hydro-Electric System (IHES), which turned over its common stock to IP for most of the common stock of NEPA and IP's other power companies. Then, in the summer of 1928, Graustein set up IP&P to hold the common stock of IHES and IP. In return, the former IP shareholders received a controlling share of IP&P. Since NEPA itself was a holding company, this led to a pyramid of corporations, from IP&P at the top to the NEPA subsidiaries at the bottom. From 1925 onward, NEPA went on a spree of acquisitions. Using its own stock, it paid prices that were a considerable mark-up from the book value of the local utilities.

In becoming a director of IP&P in 1928, McConnell was now effectively helping to block Holt's own effort to form one big Canadian company to challenge American incursions into the Canadian paper industry. He was also now allied to even greater interests than Holt and Gundy: the Phipps family and the Chase National Bank, representing the Rockefellers, owned most of IP&P. The full advantage of these interests was not initially apparent, however. In 1928 the paper industry seemed to be stabilizing and consumption was unusually heavy.[9] Canada Paper was not without its own utilities investments,[10] and its first year was actually better than IP&P's.[11] But its debt load was greater and it could find no contracts to match that between IP&P and Hearst. By June 1928, IP&P's consolidated balance sheet showed over $500 million in assets.

Newsprint prices continued to slide with the contraction of advertising during the Depression and with the collapse of the Institute cartel in 1930. Canada Paper in particular – burdened with the outstanding bonds and preferred shares of the several companies that it had absorbed – went into receivership. Its security holders, including the CPR and Sun Life, established a protective committee. On the recommendation of the president of the CPR Edward Beatty, Charles Dunning, who had been the federal minister of finance in 1929, became chairman of this committee. In 1931 the Dunning committee recommended a radical reduction of the capitalization of Canada Paper and the formation of a new company, Consolidated Paper, to absorb Canada Paper shares. Canada Paper had been a terrible failure for Holt, and disastrous for the Royal Bank of which he was president. In 1932 W.E.J. Luther, president of the Montreal Stock Exchange, took matters into his own hands. Distraught at his losses, he shot Holt at Holt's house on Stanley Street. Mistakenly thinking that he had killed him, Luther returned to his own home and successfully shot himself. Holt, wounded, hid at the Royal Victoria Hospital until recovered.

Based as it was in the United States, IP&P was much larger, richer, and more flexible than the Canadian newsprint conglomerates, particularly since it was from 1928 onward as much a power company as a paper one. Its power and utility interests formed about 55 per cent of its assets, and the net earnings from them had in 1927 (that is, even before taking over NEPA) exceeded those from its paper interests before depreciation, and these net earnings also exceeded them after depreciation.[12] Its output, from NEPA alone, increased by 26 per cent the following year. True, the IP&P paper companies incurred a deficit of almost $5 million in the year ending April 1929,[13] but, nevertheless, by that October IP&P had paid off more than $27 million of its current liabilities of $39 million.

In the 1930s, despite the shrinking demand for paper that accompanied the onset of the Great Depression, IP&P was one of the Quebec companies that were able to benefit from its contracts with the Ontario industry. The roots of these contracts dated to the 1926 Ontario-Quebec agreement, which not only banned power exports to the United States but also authorized the sale of surplus Quebec power to Ontario. Soon afterwards, Ontario accepted IP&P's offer of 260,000 horsepower, to be fed into the Niagara system between 1928 and 1931. This agreement led IP to set up a new company, Gatineau Power, to generate electricity along the Ottawa River.[14]

In the meantime, a threat to IP from Carillon, the project that had destroyed Tram-Power and Quebec-New England Hydro-electric by 1925, had been looming. Carillon was still in 1926 estimated to have a capacity of 300,000 horsepower, exceeded only by Beauharnois (a project described later in this chapter), in its initial stage, at 450,000. IP under Graustein began lobbying for its lease in succession to National Hydro Electric, which Robert and then Webster and Dufresne had failed to develop. Shawinigan Water and Power, which had rebuffed Henry Miles's invitation to develop the site in 1916, became alarmed by this new threat from IP. Premier Taschereau promised to lobby for a lease by Ottawa of Carillon to IP, after the expiry of the National Hydro Electric lease in May 1927, on condition that IP should not bid against Holt and Gundy – through Canada Power and Paper – to develop power in the upper St. Maurice Valley. It was Taschereau's policy to divide the resources of the province for development among different companies in different territories.

IP desisted as requested, and Canada Power won the right to develop St Maurice power, but apparently Taschereau failed to fulfil his undertaking to IP. He instead permitted Ottawa to renew the Carillon lease to National Hydro Electric, many of the shares of which were already owned by Aldred and Co., the brokerage house tied to Shawinigan, founded by J.E. Aldred, and to the Taschereau family. IP&P continued to insist on enforcing Taschereau's commitment to it or at least on compensation for his failure to meet it.[15] It also continued to lobby Ottawa, challenging its jurisdiction over the Ottawa River. IP&P seems to have been fairly successful, for it set up with Shawinigan in 1930 the General Development Co., to hold all the securities of National Hydro Electric until negotiations could be completed with the governments of Canada, Ontario and Quebec on how to develop the site. It was an uneasy relationship and it collapsed in 1933 under the weight of the Depression.

At the federal level also in 1926, IP was facing a threat from Carillon. The King government had been supportive of development there in 1923–5, as described in the last chapter. But a new Conservative government was no more inclined to stop this development. According to the chief biographer of Howard Ferguson, the election of Arthur Meighen as Prime Minister in 1925 merely provoked Meighen to solicit bribes from alleged Tories invested in Carillon, to finance his campaign in the general elections in August of that year.

These Tories presumably included Holt, who stood to profit most through the approval of any project by National Hydro Electric, which was now owned by United Securities. But although about to become a director of Montreal Power and therefore also connected to United Securities, and a fundraiser to boot of Meighen's, McConnell was probably not among them, in view of his directorship of IP and CIP. In any case, the re-election of King and the Liberals in September, 1926 resulted in the cancellation of any arrangements between Meighen and United Securities.

King's election led to the non-renewal, also in May 1927, of an even more threatening lease that two sons of Sir Clifford Sifton held in the name of the Georgian Bay Canal Company, which had been making claims on the Ottawa River alleged to be even more extensive than those of National Hydro Electric. Ferguson of Ontario and Taschereau at Quebec had campaigned against the renewal of this lease by Ottawa in the name of provincial jurisdiction over interprovincial streams.[16] Unlike the Siftons and United Securities, IP seems to have convinced the two premiers that it would not interfere with this jurisdiction, and so its 1926 contract with Ontario survived. HEPC engineers actually went to the Quebec side of the Ottawa River to build the Gatineau Power plant and its 220 KV line for transmission to Leaside near Toronto. In October 1928, it inaugurated its supply from Gatineau.

In 1927, with its potential competition on the Ottawa River from the Siftons at Georgian Bay and from United Securities at Carillon removed, IP entered into a further contract to supply electricity to Ontario. In 1928, Ontario also contracted with the Ottawa Valley Company (controlled by I.W. Killam of Royal Securities), at Chats Falls, to buy 192,000 horsepower, and with MacLaren Quebec Power for 125,000 HP. By 1928, IP&P had 1,032,600 horsepower developed or under construction, and a prospective capacity of three million horsepower.[17]

The future of IP&P as a supplier to Ontario brightened further when the report of the National Advisory Committee on the St. Lawrence Waterway, appointed by King four years before, reported in that year. The Committee, dominated by Sir Clifford Sifton and W.L. McDougald, recommended that all development of the St. Lawrence should begin in Quebec, with the Ontario or so-called international section to be later developed by American interests. This report stymied the hopes of Ontario to develop more power for itself from the St. Lawrence in the foreseeable future, and it actually recommended further Ontario purchases from such companies as Gatineau. It led directly to McDougald's Beauharnois power project, with R.O. Sweezey, to sell power to Ontario, a project that won the support of both Ferguson and Taschereau. By 1931, Ontario contracts with Quebec utilities totalled 721,000 horsepower, and

250,000 of it was from Gatineau; by end of the 1932, Gatineau supplied 20 per cent of the power used by the HEPC's Niagara system.

But, for IP&P, the good times were coming to an end. Not only did it, like other utilities, start to suffer greatly from the sharply reduced demand for power in the Depression, but in 1935 Ontario's political landscape changed to its detriment. The new premier, Mitch Hepburn, and his attorney general, Arthur Roebuck, were vehement foes of Ontario's contracts with Quebec power companies, partly because these companies had allegedly supported the Conservatives in the recent provincial election. Whatever the truth of this charge, Hepburn and Roebuck made an economic case as well, claiming that the HEPC's Quebec contracts saddled Ontario with over a 600,000 surplus horsepower at a cost of millions of dollars – and might soon even bankrupt the HEPC itself. After much haggling between the government and the Quebec companies, Hepburn introduced a bill declaring the contracts "illegal, void and unenforceable," and, despite threats from Premier Taschereau and warnings from the Canadian Bankers' Association and the Chamber of Commerce, the bill passed. The Bank of Montreal promptly threatened a cut-off of credit to Ontario, and there were also warnings that bondholders might refuse to refinance Ontario bonds. Then, however, the federal government stepped in, and, at its strong urging, the banks and investment dealers bought a new issue of Ontario bonds.

By this time, IP&P had decided to make a separate peace with the Hepburn administration. Apparently in return for Hepburn's help in curtailing price cutting in the paper industry, IP&P agreed to supply emergency power under the table. This was only a ploy to gain time; the company's real goal remained the reinstatement of its old contract, or the negotiation of a new one with favourable terms. But, for IP&P, time was running out. In the United States, the passage of Public Utility Holding Company Act of 1935 threatened its very existence, and while the company fought the legislation in the courts for a few years, its efforts ultimately proved futile. The company's US operations were broken up in 1939, and its Canadians ones soon followed.

By then, McConnell had done well from his investments in IP&P. By 1928, he owned $613,900 in the company's common shares, and his portfolio showed IP&P dividends of $20,925 in 1927, $12,500 in 1937, and $180,000 in 1941.[18] In 1937 he began transferring shares in the company to his foundation, which, after a stock split in 1949, owned 100,000 shares with a market value of $5 million or $46,528,926 in 2008 terms.

Much the same was true of another of McConnell's investments that was closely tied to hydroelectricity, this one not in Canada or the United States but largely in Brazil. By 1928–29, Brazilian Traction was the largest and most successful "British" company left in South America, the others having fallen victim to either rising nationalism in the region or American competition. It was the first major Canadian corporation run from Toronto but operating entirely overseas. McConnell, one of the first investors in the company on its creation in 1912–13, became a director in October 1925, replacing Sir Henry Pellatt, who had gone into bankruptcy. Two years earlier,

Sir William Mackenzie, the founder of the companies that had evolved into Brazilian Traction, had died virtually bankrupt as well, his Toronto Railway having been sold and his Canadian Northern Railway taken over by the the Canadian National Railways.

As a member of the Brazilian board, McConnell was closest to E.R. Wood, one of the company's six vice-presidents, who had nominated him to fill the seat of the disgraced Pellatt. Wood and McConnell had been associated at least since 1909, when they both bought shares in Aitken's Calgary Power.[19] It was a talented, experienced board, and his new colleagues in turn were impressed with McConnell, regarding him as a member of the "Montreal group," a clear reference to another director, Andrew Holt, who since 1924 had been representing his father, Sir Herbert, the only individual with more shares in the company than McConnell himself. Brazilian was known globally as a sound investment, and the presence on the board of Holt and McConnell lent weight to the already strong Toronto directors.

Yet the finances of both Brazilian Traction and its component predecessors had not been uniformly strong, and now a cloud was hanging over Brazilian itself in the form of a possible takeover bid by one of its most successful boosters, Alfred Loewenstein of Brussels, one of its bond salesmen. Loewenstein was one of the most flamboyant figures of a very flamboyant era. He claimed to be the third-richest person in the world, and he travelled about with nine secretaries, dramatically dictating and scribbling memos. He was the first to use private aircraft. He held parties in Biarritz and Barcelona, flying in caviar from Moscow, and, through his genius for publicity, he captured the imagination of vast numbers of investors not merely in Belgium, where he was based, but throughout Europe and North America. His almost-clownish antics made many, including McConnell, doubt his sanity as well as his honesty, but he was far from a complete fool, and he struck anxiety if not fear in most of the directors of Brazilian.

Possibly with a view to a takeover of Brazilian, Loewenstein proposed to Sidro, a holding company that he had formed in 1922, that it merge with a new company holding shares in electricity companies, Hydro-Electric Securities, which he had incorporated in Canada in 1926. He was soon claiming that Sir Herbert Holt had put his Brazilian holdings into Hydro-Electric and that these alone constituted a quarter of Brazilian's common stock. Through Hydro-Electric, Loewenstein bought up 167,500 Brazilian shares, pushing the price of the stock up from $50 in mid-1925 to $115 in August 1926, which made his holding in the company about £3.5 million. In October, he also suggested to Brazilian that it should purchase his holdings in Sidro, another holding company, to avoid a takeover by the latter. McConnell and most of the rest of the Brazilian board refused, believing that Loewenstein would ruin the company.

Nevertheless, speculators were raising the stock price of Brazilian and thus causing Sir Alexander Mackenzie, the company's president, much grief in dealing with the Brazilian government for a renewal of tramway and telephone concessions necessary to ensure profitability. The higher stock price also made it difficult for him to demand an increase in rates and threatened an increase in the corporate income tax to be paid. The Montreal broker Percy Cowans told his clients that the stock was overpriced at $120, and Montreal investors sold off 40,000 shares through him. But Sir Herbert remained silent and joined the board of Sidro.[20]

Loewenstein's strategy seems to have been to float $20 million or more in Hydro-Electric bonds, secured by its holdings in other companies, and to use Hydro-Electric Securities to gain control of Brazilian Traction's Mexican, Brazilian, and Spanish entities and then make lucrative operating leases with them. In October 1926 he offered to sell to Brazilian his 15,000 French bonds for the market price of the true sterling bonds, before putting them into Hydro-Electric. The board, including both McConnell and Andrew Holt, rejected Loewenstein's offer on 4 November, on the ground that he was then suing Brazilan in a dispute over bond sales.

Then, as an alternative to selling his bonds to Brazilian, Loewenstein proposed to exchange shares in Hydro-Electric for shares in Brazilian. Mackenzie wrote privately to Loewenstein, explaining that his scheme was "a negation of everything we have maintained for many years," that the Brazilians were already discriminating against foreign-owned utilities, and that there would be an "outburst of feeling" if they learned that the company was allied with other foreign interests, even though in fact it always had been.[21] The Holts were still refusing to pronounce on Loewenstein's plan, but to avoid the resignation of Mackenzie they permitted the board as a whole to warn against "fusion" with Loewenstein on 25 November.

On 11 February 1927 the Brazilian Traction vice-president, E.R. Peacock – an Ontarian formerly with A.E. Ames, now immensely distinguished in England as a banker and one of McConnell's closest friends – strongly recommended that the company buy the disputed bonds from Loewenstein, on the grounds that its case in the pending litigation was weak and Lowenstein's price was below par value.

With no apparent progress in the year following, Loewenstein put his preference shares into Brazilian's Barcelona operations and all his Sidro shares into Hydro-Electric, and he called for representation for his new company on the boards of Brazilian's Spanish and Mexican ventures. He also induced Andrew Holt and George Montgomery and J.S. Norris of Montreal Power, among others, to join the Hydro-Electric board.[22] The same three, with the Montreal lawyer Frank Common, joined the board of Loewenstein's International Holding and Investment, which actually was a holding company for Hydro-Electric.[23] The effect of these moves was to change the centre of Loewenstein's operations from Brussels to Montreal, in alliance with the Holts. Investors raised the price of International's shares from $65 in January 1928 to $352 in May.

McConnell did not share the fears of others at Brazilian. He wrote to another board member, Miller Lash, on 11 April 1928 that the more that Loewenstein became "interested in buying and salting down the shares of Brazilian Traction, the better we should like it, as it will only put the new stock to $100.00 per share at any earlier date than anticipated." He doubted that Loewenstein had "any idea in his head" of taking over Brazilian, and that his chances in any case were "slim." At a meeting of his Belgian investors in Brussels on 16 April, Loewenstein announced that he had bought shares in Brazilian in 1926 when they were worth $110 and now they were worth $262 – an increase of $190 million in value in the company as a whole. His investors were now holding $78 million in Brazilian shares.

Peacock reported on 20 April that Loewenstein was planning an exchange of Brazilian shares for Hydro-Electric shares, which would have avoided the proxy fight that McConnell did not think Loewenstein could win. Lash in Toronto felt that Peacock and Malcolm Hubbard, the Brazilian director in London, were weakening in the face of the repeated attacks. But even Lash himself was somewhat afraid of Loewenstein, whom he described to Wood four days later as a "trained boxer."

On 27 April 1928 McConnell noted that "King Loewenstein" had arrived in New York and was coming to see him in Montreal. McConnell remain unperturbed after their meeting on the 30th, and he told Lash on 1 May that Loewenstein's shareholders were in fact only warrant holders not entitled to board representation, and that Andrew Holt and Peacock, being resident in London, were themselves sufficient international representation on the board. The Belgian shareholders were no more entitled to special representation than Chinese ones would be. McConnell said that he had not spoken to Sir Herbert about his intentions. In any case, McConnell and Lash agreed to resist any exchange of shares with Hydro-Electric. Unlike most of his fellow directors, McConnell seems to have concluded that Loewenstein was so unstable, or so lacking in voting shares, as to be harmless.

According to a cable apparently from Lash to Hubbard, dated 2 May, McConnell did not feel that Holt would support Loewenstein; and even if Holt did, McConnell was "absolutely prepared to come out in opposition" to a takeover bid. By the 23rd, Peacock was reporting to Lash that J.H. Gundy had assured him that he and Sir Herbert did not intend to join Loewenstein in launching a takeover bid for Brazilian. Nevertheless, towards the end of June, the Brazilian management was quietly gearing up for a proxy fight with Loewenstein, in case he should instigate one. The fight never came, for, on 6 July, Loewenstein fell or was pushed from his aircraft while flying over the English Channel.

At the beginning of August, McConnell seems to have been behind Mackenzie's replacement as president by Miller Lash. From the middle of that month to October 1928, he accompanied Lash on a tour of Brazilian Traction projects in Brazil, which was effectively their new kingdom now that Mackenzie and Loewenstein were gone. Among their colleagues, one published a poem about the trip, describing McConnell as the "King of Finance" and the "Beau Brummel of the troop, as all the world could see." In Barbados, they watched "the diving niggers," and the "coin McConnell threw away" would total to "big figures."[24] For McConnell himself, the journey over 1,600 miles of bad roads – through more than twenty towns with "strange sounding and unpronounceable names" – was exhausting. But he was impressed by the daring river developments, the old mule-car lines now electrified and crossing deep gorges, and the cable cars, coffee plantations, and orange groves, and he was never to give up his investments in the company.[25]

On his return to New York from Brazil, on 17 October, McConnell gushed about the prospects of both Brazil and Brazilian Traction. The company's net total earnings for 1928 were expected to be $25 million, with profits of $14,500,000. In 1924 McConnell had owned 11,000 Brazilian shares; by September 1929, he owned 75,000, and in the following month his total holdings in the company amounted to almost $5 million or $61,195,652 in 2008 terms.

The Loewenstein story ended so abruptly that it is almost disappointing. Yet it was revealing in various ways. It showed that almost nobody at any stage could determine what Sir Herbert Holt was thinking, even McConnell, except perhaps Gundy and Andrew Holt. It turned out that he was probably not thinking much, since his investments in Hydro-Electric and International Holding and Investment could not have been part of a secure strategy as long as Loewenstein was in charge. Through his withdrawal from these companies in March 1929, on the ground that they had moved from Montreal, it may be deduced that he was hoping to take over from Loewenstein at some point and perhaps even converting the companies into his own global empire, and so it was rumoured. In any case, it seems clear that Holt and Gundy, despite rumours to the contrary, had no intention of trying to take over Brazilian, for they had confidence in its management.

McConnell shared this confidence, and he emerges from the voluminous Brazilian files that have survived as supremely unflappable, often amused, and extremely lucid, if not penetrating, in his analysis of character and in his grasp of voting strategy. All McConnell wanted was a secure, profitable investment, and, after Loewenstein's death, he was the largest individual shareholder. Nonetheless, although he had been one of the original shareholders of Brazilian, and remained a major shareholder in it for his remaining twenty-five years, McConnell played little part in its daily management. Instead, he was rather like a constitutional monarch, with the power to be advised, to advise, and to warn – a power that he exercised to the full until his resignation from the board in 1938.

Back at home, McConnell was an important player in still another enterprise: Montreal Light, Heat and Power Consolidated (MLHPC). The story of how this company came into being, and of McConnell's involvement in it, begins in 1916, when Herbert Holt established Civic Investment and Industrial, a holding company for Montreal Power and the companies associated with it since 1901, when it had been formed by Senator L.-J. Forget, whom Holt had succeeded as president in 1911. In 1918 Civic changed its name to Montreal Light, Heat and Power Consolidated (MLHPC), which by 1923 was operating several subsidiaries.

Then, with the final collapse of Montreal Tramways and Power (the Robert-McConnell holding company for Canadian Power and Montreal Tramways) in 1924, the MLHPC joined Shawinigan to pick up the pieces.[26] The two companies formed United Securities to control Canadian Power and the Quebec-New England Hydro-Electric Corporation (formerly the Montreal Public Service Corporation), two components of the old Tram-Power looted by Robert and certain confederates.

The Montreal Public Service Corporation had been formed originally by McConnell, in 1910, out of the Saraguay Electric and Water Company, and then merged with the Central Heat, Light and Power, a small company belonging to Canadian Power. Until 1924, on the Island of Montreal, the Montreal Public Service Corporation had been the only competitor to Montreal Power in distribution. Within two years, United Securities was to eliminate all the unnecessary plant of its successor, Quebec-New England Hydro-Electric, which it had bought from Senator Lorne Webster and Oscar Dufresne in 1926, but it retained the promising site of Carillon

These arrangements bound together MLHPC and Shawinigan in some respects inextricably, although Shawinigan continued to develop separate businesses, chiefly in Trois-Rivières and the Eastern Townships, and remained jealous of its exclusive control over territory not exclusively controlled by MLHPC. In 1923, after Robert's ouster from the Quebec Railway, United Securities took over its assets through a new Quebec Power company, which meant that, in the province generally, in the place of cutthroat competition, there was now a sharing of profits and an amicable division of the market – in effect, an oligopoly or perhaps more precisely a duopoly. The prices these companies charged were not necessarily to the benefit of the domestic consumer, in Montreal in particular, where critics alleged that high rates subsidized the lower ones charged to the industrial entities in which such men as Holt and McConnell held enormous investments.[27]

Any discussion of MLHPC must recognize its political as well as economic significance, as it was the very symbol to most French Canadians, and many English Canadians as well, of everything they hated about McConnell's world. In January 1926 McConnell joined the MLHPC board, which reunited him with the remnants of the Tram-Power that he had abandoned in the course of the debacle of 1917–22.

Already so vague, however, was the public memory of his partnership with Robert that the *Star* now proclaimed McConnell as "a man of long-distance vision, with an alert mind, sound judgment and public spirit." It was, moreover, "to be hoped that he will impress his fellow directors with a fuller sense of their duty in catering to the citizens." The most vitriolic critics of Robert and Holt could not have sounded more public-spirited or fulsome than Lord Atholstan's *Star*, which editorialized: "Men of public spirit like Mr. McConnell can be influential in establishing a 'fair play,' 'give and take' policy, so that privileges granted to the companies – privileges that constitute an important franchise, their most valuable asset in fact – would give the citizens the right return, and that should be represented in the very lowest price for light and power, consistent with a modern return on the investment."

Was the *Star* was being tongue-in-cheek or was McConnell himself behind its refurbishment of reputation? Only a few months before the editorial, he had secretly bought this newspaper although he was not to assume complete control until after Atholstan's death. On the same day as the *Star* editorial, newspapers across the country reinforced McConnell's vaunted promise with the following press release: "Mr. McConnell's thorough grasp of the inwardness not only of the enterprises in which he is directly interested, but of Dominion and international affairs, is bringing him more and more into prominence, and his counsel is sought in great and small financial and business matters outside of his own companies. His keen business acumen in the past year has solved several particularly knotty problems for local commercial and industrial enterprises, with the result that what threatened to be routs have turned into victories."

These references are obscure, but in any case, all while the fiasco of Canadian Power and the Montreal Tramways had been unfolding, MLHPC was becoming by far the greatest power monopoly in both the province and – apart from the HEPC in Ontario – in Canada. McConnell himself had long been investing in it, with 4,000 shares in MLHPC valued as $320,000 in 1921, as opposed to just over $83,000 in his own Montreal Tramways and a little more than $20,000 in his own Montreal Public Service Corporation. In other words, he had in 1921 invested more than double in MLHPC what he had in his own Tram-Power group. And his MLHPC's holdings only grew. In 1929 he had $1.2 million invested in MLHPC; in 1939, $6.9 million. In 2008 terms, these investments translate into $14,986,957 and $102,228,947 respectively.

Notwithstanding the collapse of Tram-Power and Quebec-New England Power by 1925, the wraith of Robert persisted. Although he and McConnell had failed to develop the Canadian Power plant at Saint-Timothée, as promised in 1909, Robert and his family continued to own rights to develop the Beauharnois Canal generally.[28] In 1912, Max Aitken's Royal Securities began investigating its possible exploitation. R.O. Sweezey, was Aitkens' agent, but war intervened and it was not until 1920 that Sweezey concluded that a huge power station could be built near the town of Beauharnois, generating two million horsepower. The Beauharnois Light, Heat and Power Company, originally incorporated in 1902, generated several subsidiaries for construction, transport and transmission. Sweezey claimed that there was an initial capacity of 670,000 horsepower to be developed at the Beauharnois site. In 1926, he agreed to sell the Ontario HEPC 86,000 horsepower, with annual increases up to a limit of 320,000 horsepower, and then he promised a further 250,000 horsepower, beginning in 1932.

Just after the market collapse in 1929, but as a result of the federal report, in the previous year, recommending that Ontario should buy power from Quebec, Sweezey's own securities firm and Dominion Securities launched the sale of shares in a holding company, the Beauharnois Power Corporation. Controversy broke out about whether the project had the right to divert the waters of the St. Lawrence, and a complicated scandal emerged involving accusations of bribery of public officials by Sweezey, Senator W.L. McDougald and others.[29] McConnell, probably preoccupied with advising IP on the establishment of the rival Gatineau Power, was not involved in the two syndicates that were set up to finance Beauharnois Power.

But in 1932, in order to forestall competition from Beauharnois for its established customers, MLHPC – which by then included McConnell as a director – contracted to buy 150,000 horsepower from the new project. Sévère Godin, Jr. and George Montgomery, representing United Securities, joined the Beauharnois Power board. In 1933, Beauharnois Power built a high-tension transmission line connecting stations at Cedar Rapids and Beauharnois with its Atwater substation in Montreal, and the MLHPC underwrote $9 million of Beauharnois Power bonds.[30] McConnell had owned Beauharnois shares just after the Crash valued at $225,000, or $2,753,804 in 2008 terms. But he increased these holdings considerably after the effective takeover by the MLHPC, so that they totalled $972,000 ($8,167,701 in 2008), or 5% of the shares outstanding by 1951, shortly before the expropriation of the company by Quebec.

By the time of McConnell's retirement from its board in 1938, the MLHPC had effective but not formal control of Beauharnois and had long before – in 1911–16 and 1927 (through United Securities) respectively – gained control of the two older and smaller plants, in the Soulanges section of the Beauharnois district, erected by Cedar Rapids and Canadian Power (at St. Timothée). The Beauharnois power station was then the greatest project that Quebec had seen, and it reaped considerable profits for McConnell, who saw it a triumph of risk taking. In a sense, it more than fulfilled the promise of Saint-Timothée, except not in the same place along the Beauharnois Canal.

McConnell retained a large holding in the MLHPC until its expropriation in 1944, for reasons that are not hard to understand. From $4.3 million in 1920, the MLHPC's net earnings after bond interest increased to $10.2 million in 1931, which was the worst year of the Depression. During the same period, the company paid out $51.6 million in dividends and interest, and it increased its retained earnings from $3.5 million to $25.8 million.

The profits of the MLHPC were such that, at one stage, a special, supplementary dividend was declared to divert attention from how fat they were. Even during the Depression, its investors had no complaint. Its workers and customers felt otherwise, however, and the company entered Quebec folklore as the ultimate symbol of English dominance of the province. As a history of electricity distribution in Quebec put it as late as 2004, the "money-makers" at the MLHPC were characterized by "le vague à l'âme": that is, they were without soul, heartless in their treatment of workers as well as of defaulting customers.[31] Stories of Holt's cutting power off from widows and orphans in the middle of winter have entered into the mythology of Quebec. Their accuracy cannot be evaluated here, but they do not seem ever to have included, at least by name, McConnell – who was in any case only one of several directors and not a manager. Nevertheless, McConnell as a businessman has been compared in importance to Holt by men from Prime Minister Mackenzie King to Conrad Black. They further describe McConnell as Holt's successor – as the most prominent businessman in the country – after Holt's death in 1941.

It is perhaps fitting here to turn from a description of holding companies to consider what these men, so often caricatured, probably believed as individuals and together. Though widely seen as comparable in wealth and in influence, the backgrounds and the careers of the two were in reality quite different. Holt was a formally educated engineer of a thoroughly middle-class background, and it is probable that in consequence he was also a more ideological capitalist than McConnell. Unlike Holt, a construction engineer preoccupied with solving problems and not a salesman, McConnell found a great variety of associates for a great variety of purposes, and he seems to have loved the sport of making money as much as he loved giving it away. Holt, notoriously short on small talk, was the quintessentially solitary empire-builder, preoccupied with control more than with his own fortune. McConnell was quite the opposite in all these respects. It is also probable that McConnell was considerably richer in money just as Holt was considerably richer in directorships.

They were alike in many ways, however, not least in their thorough pragmatism and corresponding lack of sentimentality in business, and they developed a wide-ranging partnership. Holt's experience of government-subsidized railways and their failures led him to seek as much independence as possible from government for his businesses. His creation, the MLHPC, was to all appearances the antithesis of Ontario's HEPC: whereas it was privately owned, the people of Ontario were theoretically the owners of the HEPC. Yet, in practice, both companies were monopolies run by powerful men, especially Beck in Ontario, largely beyond public scrutiny, and with close ties to government.

As Holt saw, the real difference between the situations in Ontario and Quebec was in ultimate accountability. If a company such as MLHPC failed, it was the shareholders who lost; if the HEPC failed, it was the taxpayers who lost. In Quebec, as in Ontario, power projects depended at their start on government land and other concessions, and the cultivation by promoters of government officials was standard practice. But, once the projects were running in Quebec, they sought private capital and not provincial to keep them running. Most of them were very successful, and so they were exemplars of the success of free enterprise, even if "private" monopolies.

McConnell, promoter and fundraiser par excellence, would have subscribed to this view as heartily as Holt. Faced with the Tennessee Valley Authority and Roosevelt's New Deal in the 1930s, he became much more robust in his opposition to publicly owned companies on the basis that in practice they were insufficiently accountable to their owners, the taxpayers. But in the end, McConnell, dependent as he was on tariffs to protect St Lawrence Sugar, was much less the pure free-enterpriser than Holt. Since working with Peuchen for government business at Standard Chemical, he had always been open to government aid, an attitude that would blossom into his guarded support for the welfare state in the 1940s and 1950s and to his securing of provincial support for McGill University, in the teeth of much opposition, from 1946 to 1956.

To the extent that Holt and McConnell were divergent in tactics, they were also probably complementary in strategy. Despite their differences in background and emphasis, where McConnell and Holt probably agreed most fundamentally was in their position towards the development of Quebec. The accusation by Léandre Bergeron in 1975, reproduced at the head of this chapter, that the takeover of Quebec's natural resources by American capital was no more than legalized, institutionalized robbery is not new.[32] Quebec nationalists in the 1920s and 1930s made similar accusations, except that they referred also to English, Jewish, and even Belgian capital in addition to American. Few mentioned the MLHPC, in particular, as Canadian. Yet all its directors were evidently both Canadian and Quebecers, although not necessarily French-speaking ones. The composition of its shareholders is unclear, but it is unlikely in this period that many were British, and American investors had many similar companies in the United States to invest in.

A comprehensive and dispassionate history of the MLHPC has yet to be written, and there is as yet little to suggest that McConnell played a dominant role in its affairs, although this possibility cannot be ruled out. Yet, also because he, Holt, and the MLHPC became symbols of "anglo" power, the question arises of their true significance in Quebec history, and of their relations with French-speaking Quebecers. The four Quebec premiers with whom Holt and McConnell dealt – Sir Lomer Gouin, L.-A. Taschereau, Adélard Godbout, and Maurice Duplessis – all fundamentally understood and ultimately accepted that English-speaking capitalists were indispensable to the development of Quebec, even though Duplessis was to attack in the 1930s, and Godbout was to expropriate in 1944, the MLHPC.

They also all accepted that Quebec must remain firmly part of Canada, although, of the four, Duplessis was the most blatantly nationalist and anti-federalist. One of the ironies of McConnell's career is that he has often been depicted as Duplessis's puppet master, even though his probable lobbying of Duplessis, from 1944 onwards, either to reverse Godbout's expropriation of Montreal Power or to increase the compensation of its shareholders, like his lobbying of Duplessis to shut down the provincially run beet-sugar industry, seems to have been thoroughly rebuffed.[33]

These four premiers all wanted Quebec to benefit from English-speaking technology, business practices, and legal expertise, in addition to capital, and thus to increase employment in the province. This can be seen in their robust use of tax dollars to fund such institutions as the École des Hautes Études Commerciales. They all struggled with the fears of the church that industrialization and modernization might threaten the faith and the culture of French Canada. And, with the possible exception of Godbout, they have all attracted considerable opprobrium both from their contemporaries and from subsequent commentators for their alleged willingness to accommodate St James Street, if not grovel to it.

With many others, Holt, McConnell, and the four premiers were effectively heirs of Sir George-Étienne Cartier, one-time *patriote* and then a baronet and a father of Confederation, who had declared in 1866 that "property is the element which must govern the world."[34] A strong defender of the blessings of the English constitution, the British Empire, and the monarchy, he was also responsible for dismantling the seigneurial system of the ancien régime and for the codification of the Civil Code of Lower Canada, embodying French legal concepts and eventually coexisting with the English as embodied in the Criminal Code of Canada. He was the sort of man with whom nineteenth-century English Montreal could and did do business, particularly the developers of the Grand Trunk. Cartier's measured modernization provided more than an example of how a French Canadian could act as broker. He provided the ideology for a productive coexistence between the French majority and the British minority in the province, and a powerful framework for business growth.

In the next generation, for English-speaking interests, Holt in particular "personified" this so-called Cartier compromise, which functioned as an alliance among church, state, and business in the province. All three parties to the alliance believed in the need to entrust natural resources to private enterprise for development. Private, effectively English-speaking, enterprise was expected by all to create jobs for French Canadians, and thus to discourage their emigration to the United States. It would provide a strong tax base to support established rural communities, and the "colonization" of new districts.

Although Quebec nationalists, including even McConnell's alleged intimate Duplessis, have long bitterly criticized the province's French-speaking elite for being toadies to McConnell, Holt, and their like, they have never implied either that the *maudits Anglais* could have obtained their stranglehold over Quebec without French-speaking help, or that there was any hostility among the English against the French, or conspiracy among them to repress the French. They could not, moreover, readily make such a case on the basis of the evidence. By 1919, when Taschereau was articulating a strong industrial strategy in succession to Gouin's, probably most French Quebecers recognized a clear need for local resource development to overcome unemployment and emigration to the United States. They saw local industries as the only serious alternative, even though their capitalization depended on the import of English-speaking capital.

Thus, as early as 1922, there had been a chorus of virtual unanimity in the French press in favour of this industrialization with the aid of imported capital.[35] Under this optic, we can now perhaps better see why Holt, McConnell, and their friends on St James Street were in their heyday far from simply the bugbears that they were to become to Quebecers in the 1960s. The Conservative Montreal newspaper *L'Événement* saw the processing of aluminium in Quebec, with the aid of English and American capital, as integral to the survival of French Canada. It enthusiastically supported the Liberal Taschereau in the provincial elections of 1923 precisely because his industrial strategy involved the increased importation of this capital. *Le Soleil* and *La Presse* – essentially Liberal newspapers – agreed.

The Cartier compromise was articulated by St James Street perhaps even more loudly. Perhaps unsurprisingly, the English-language Conservative Montreal *Star* in 1923 called for a reinforcement of the Liberal Gouin's ban on the export of pulpwood from Quebec crown lands. More remarkably, it was the *Star* – hardly the voice of French Canadian nationalism – that also declared, in ringing tones, in 1923: "We surely have the right to rescue [Quebec] from the old reputation that it was the home of 'hewers of wood and drawers of water' for the luckier people to the South."

In sum, the difference between Liberals and Conservatives in the 1920s was not over whether English-language capital was needed for industrial investment, but over no more than whether British investors should be more assiduously cultivated as a counterweight to American ones. And, despite his American directorships and investments in the 1920s, it seems that McConnell was not averse to this sort of "nationalism," which was simply complementary to his active support of the Tory, imperialist, and protectionist platform federally of Arthur Meighen.

The compromise worked to some extent even in the boardrooms of St James Street. The tension in Quebec before 1960 was over not language but religion – and was largely internal to Roman Catholics and French speakers, who were diverging on the degree of secularization necessary for the accommodation of Quebec to modernity. Holt and McConnell eagerly embraced those French-Canadian Roman Catholics that were prepared to work with them. Indeed, it appears that many of the leaders of St James Street were highly sensitive to French opinion, if only because their employees, and less commonly their neighbours and colleagues, were French, and because their provincial and municipal politicians tended to be French. Nearly every board had a French-speaking member, usually a prominent lawyer, and J.-L. Perron, Eugène Lafleur, Aimé Geoffrion, and Louis St Laurent were fixtures on St James Street. The peculiarities of the Quebec Civil Code, and the overwhelmingly French element on the bench, in the legislature, and in the civil service all made it often advantageous to employ French lawyers. This is not to say that English-speaking lawyers could not speak good French or be masters of the local legal system. McGill specialized in turning out such French-speaking English lawyers, and with considerable success, but it also produced Geoffrion, and so the bar and the notarial office were always natural places for the two linguistic communities to meet.

Moreover, there were French Canadians without legal background that also prospered on St James Street. Holt's right-hand man at Montreal Power was Sévère Godin, and Beaudry Leman was president of the Banque d'Hochelaga (later the Banque Canadienne Nationale and still later the Banque Nationale) and a key figure in Shawinigan Water and Power. These were much more than the usual notaries and advocates appointed to Montreal boards essentially for their linguistic abilities and local political connections. Godin, who was a protégé of McConnell's since his boyhood, had been Holt's chauffeur from 1906 and then secretary from 1915, and he went on, at least in part with McConnell's advice, to become a power on St James Street in his own right. He became chairman of Claude Neon General Advertising, in which McConnell held a particular interest, and president of such diverse enterprises as Montreal Trust, British Columbia Power, United Amusements, and Belgo-Canadian Realty. Leman, an engineer married to a daughter of Senator F.-L. Béique (a director of the CPR and vice-president of Canadian Cottons), had been educated at McGill and the Université de Lille, and, in addition to his work at Shawinigan Water and Power, he was mayor of Shawinigan, vice-president of the Canadian Bankers' Association, and member of the National Advisory Commission on St Lawrence Waterways. His son became vice-president and treasurer of Alcan, another particular interest of McConnell's and a company for which Aimé Geoffrion and his own son both acted as counsel.

No definitive judgment on these issues belongs here. It is enough to point out that English Montrealers, including McConnell and Holt, were not a separate caste. At the highest as well as the lowest levels, many worked daily with French Montrealers. For religious reasons, they seldom intermarried, but the leading French families often did, and yet they did not form a caste either. English was indeed the working language, particularly on St James Street and west of Bleury Street or St Lawrence Main, but the reality is that there were symbiotic relationships running through the population of the city. Jews from Eastern Europe, Italians, Greeks, and others, as well as French, all spoke English, because English was the working language of Canada, North America, and the British Empire.

In fact, the split that emerged in the early 1900s was only incidentally along lines of language and more between two groups of monopolists, each of which contained both French and English businessmen. Both Montreal Power and its rival, Canadian Light and Power, were led by French-speaking capitalists, the Forgets and Robert respectively. Holt and McConnell initially played only subordinate roles in these groups respectively, but they were undoubted competitors in the bids for the Montreal Street Railway in 1910. They were formally to ally themselves only in 1925, when the notion of monopoly in Montreal as being English-speaking reached its fullest expression.

The political divisions among businessmen were more pronounced than the linguistic and religious ones long before 1925. McConnell was from 1901 to about 1907 associated in business largely with the Forget group, particularly with Rodolphe Forget but also with the Greenshields and the Henshaws. The Forget group was aligned with the Conservatives. After Rodolphe Forget had broken with his uncle Louis-Joseph in 1907, and concentrated his own railway and power interests in Quebec City, McConnell continued to help in his promotions. But in Montreal, McConnell also came to associate himself with the Robert group, which was associated with the Liberals. The subsequent acquisition of the Tram-Power assets by United Securities left power in Quebec essentially in the hands of Holt and McConnell when they had become not very effective Conservatives. The result by 1925 was that no political party, federal or provincial, was fundamentally against monopolists generally, and indeed all were to some degree working with them, at least until Godbout and his expropriation of the MLHPC in 1944.

McConnell was not concerned, therefore, to maintain the dominance of English-language capital in Quebec. What interested him was that his businesses were reaping profits. The MLHPC was essentially merely a distribution system for an urban area, but, since that area was Canada's richest, the company was an excellent investment for McConnell and its other shareholders. It was so successful in generating dividends that even its stock splits could not conceal its profitability to its shareholders, which its critics saw as being at the expense of the consumers. By the mid-1930s, the MLHPC was a major issue in provincial as opposed to merely Montreal politics, and it was becoming a major irritant not only to French-Canadian nationalists but also to socialists, English- as well as French-speaking. Facing calls for its expropriation, the company continued to claim that private investment was necessary to expand the economic infrastructure of Quebec and that competition kept down the cost of power to the consumer.

Tram-Power scarcely proved these claims under McConnell and Robert, but creative accounting, including distributions of shares rather than dividends, disguised some of the MLHPC's profits. The company's dividends rose from 5 per cent in 1920 to 10 per cent by 1929, a figure that was maintained throughout the 1930s, while its earnings increased from $25.8 million in 1931 to $35.6 million in 1944. The book value of its capital was $58.5 million in 1944, at the time of its expropriation, of which $42.5 million was described as "water," representing no assets, but $25.3 million had still been paid in cash. Its investors received over $200 million, in constant dollars, over forty-three years, in dividends and interest.[36]

From 1925 to 1930, Premier Taschereau implemented a policy of industrialization and electrification based on the division of territories leased from Quebec to various developers of power and paper. Although there was real, sometimes ruthless, competition for these leases and other concessions, the developers agreed to abide by the division of their territories; they had no choice, since their common lessor was still the province. Not everyone, however, was convinced that Quebecers were paying less than Ontarians for their power. Under public pressure, Taschereau appointed Ernest Lapointe in 1935 to report on the possibility of a new regulator to replace the Public Utilities Commission.[37] In particular, the report was to address the possible nationalization or municipalization of local utilities, and the effects of this expropriation, by definition in urban centres, on rural districts. It was also to address the existing charges for electricity and the possibility of reducing them, and generally the electrification of rural areas.

Lapointe held hearings in Montreal, Quebec, Hull, Rimouski, Chicoutimi, and Trois-Rivières, and he interviewed Charles Magrath, the chairman of the Ontario HEPC. In his report, he noted that, since electricity was a natural monopoly, it was essential for it to be controlled and regulated by the state in order to safeguard the public interest. It would, however, be too expensive for Quebec to nationalize or expropriate its private electricity companies. In Ontario, large municipalities had founded the system in the absence of electrification; in Quebec, the power companies possessed numerous legal rights in a relatively mature market, and determining the future value of these rights might be an interminable process and overburden the municipalities.

Partial expropriation was possible, but Quebec was already producing more power than it could consume, and partial expropriation would demand much capital investment, effectively simply to create ruinous competition between the provincially run and the privately run companies. According to the Lapointe report, everyone admitted that the electrical service in each community should be run by a monopoly. What was needed in Quebec was an alliance between private enterprise and the municipalities, which would operate a joint commission to pass regulations and control (among other matters) the amalgamation and the capitalization of companies. The new Electricity Commission that Lapointe recommended would coexist with the Public Utilities Commission, from which it would differ by operating through consensus alone.

Despite his platitudes, Lapointe revealed how dramatically the energy situation had changed since McConnell was financing coal companies and Lorne Webster was establishing his monopoly on coal distribution in eastern Canada.[38] In 1932, 98 per cent of the energy produced in Canada was waterpower, and about half the horsepower used by Canadian industry came from Quebec. Of the total sale of electricity in Quebec, 61 percent went to large factories, not including what was exported. In the same year, Quebec exported 17.1 per cent of its electricity production to Ontario. Further, Quebec attracted to its electrical industry 43.04 per cent of all capital invested in electricity in all of Canada.

With the passing of the "death sentence" on American utility holding companies in 1935, although they did not cover local monopolies, and with the death of Holt in 1941, the resistance to the "nationalization" of his utilities empire crumbled. The vision of Sir Adam Beck in Ontario, of a provincially run power company excluding all privately owned utilities, became more plausible in Quebec than it had been to Lapointe in 1935. The vision became real in 1944, when Quebec finally expropriated the MLHPC. Premier Godbout and the minister responsible for the new Quebec Hydro-Electric Commission, Wilfrid Hamel, and the first president of the commission, T.-D. Bouchard – all long enemies of the MLHPC – were, however, accorded only a few weeks in which to savour their victory. After winning the subsequent provincial elections, Maurice Duplessis formed a new government on 30 August, with Johnny Bourque as minister of Lands and Forests responsible for the commission, and L.E. Potvin as president. Nevertheless, the accountant George McDonald (and McConnell's most determined enemy) and John W. McCammon were to remain two of the four commissioners, McDonald until 1947 and McCammon until 1956, both English Montrealers but neither of them sympathetic to the old St James Street of Holt and McConnell.

The subsequent takeover of the remaining private companies in 1962–63 by the Liberal government of Jean Lesage, with René Lévesque as minister of Natural Resources, has become central to the myth of the "Quiet Revolution" in Quebec. The takeover was not complete until 1 May 1963, a few months before McConnell's death, when the provincially run Quebec Hydro-Electric Commission absorbed the last seven privately owned companies. These included Shawinigan Water and Power, Gatineau Power, Quebec Power, Southern Canada Power, Saguenay Power, Northern Quebec Power, and the Lower St Lawrence Power Company.

The place of this second stage of nationalization in political myth has tended to obscure the significance of Godbout's expropriation in 1944, as well as of his other legislation, such as women's suffrage. Myth has also insinuated that McConnell and Duplessis were holding back the forces of reform and nationalism more generally through the 1950s. In fact, the takeover of MLHPC in 1944 had already marked a momentous break with the patterns of power development and ownership in Quebec. These had prevailed since the establishment in 1901 of Montreal Power as its first "trust" by L-J. Forget, himself a French Canadian. McConnell did little or at least nothing effective to resist the calls for further nationalization after 1944, although he seems to have initially hoped that the expropriation of that year might be reversed, or that compensation to him as a shareholder of the defunct MLHPC might be increased.

The Ontario HEPC was not as different from MLHPC as Hamel and others imagined. In principle, it was a state monopoly subject to political influence as opposed to competitive interests. In practice, it was so big, and its securities formed such a large part of the Ontario debt, that it proved itself largely immune to provincial oversight, time and time again. Increasingly powerful critiques of the Beck model that became Ontario Hydro have painted it as a disaster from the financial, as well as environmental and technical, points of view. It is possible that eventually Quebec Hydro will be judged likewise. McConnell's view that the expropriation of MLHPC was wrong is therefore not obviously absurd. Privatization of electricity in Ontario and of transit in Toronto were live issues for debate even at the end of the twentieth century, to say nothing of a revulsion against public ownership in much of the world.

A lingering question is what McConnell may have learned from his experience of holding companies and monopolies generally. Commentators have claimed that Roosevelt "saved" capitalism with his legislation against the holding companies in 1935. McConnell, who hated Roosevelt until well into the Second World War, would not have agreed with this conclusion any more than his friend Wendell Willkie.

All three men did agree that capitalism must be reformed, so that the shifting of assets and debt among the subsidiaries of holding companies, such as Insull was accused of, was prohibited. There is no reason to think that McConnell and Willkie were against fuller disclosure in the issuance of securities – more "transparency," to use a later concept – for the benefit of investors. But they believed in the ongoing discipline of the market to ensure viability. For McConnell in particular, the TVA was reminiscent of the CNR in Canada, with its heavy governmental subsidies that rendered accountability and profitability at best moot.

To break up the C&S or the MLHPC in favour of state monopolies beyond the scrutiny of private investors was not for him to "save capitalism." If the TVA or Quebec Hydro could be seen as instruments of state capitalism, as capitalists they enjoyed, through tax subsidies, an unfair advantage over private investors. Their bonds were, in American terms, ensured by the "full faith and credit" of the state, an advantage that encouraged inefficiency. Quebec Hydro became even more of a monopoly than the MLHPC that it succeeded, just as the HEPC of Ontario had in taking over private utilities.

It is unnecessary to agree with McConnell and Willkie on these matters in order to conclude that many private holding companies were not so much wrong in principle as subject to fraud and abuse, and further to presume that state monopolies are not necessarily exempt from the same. Whether or in what sense Roosevelt saved capitalism is therefore hard to prove, which we ought to bear in mind as we explore McConnell's own ambivalence about socialism, despite his professed loathing of it, later in this book.

CHAPTER NINE

Almost a Jack of All Trades, 1911–39

Incidentally the efforts alluded to in the Nickel matter will have meant perhaps as much as $200,000,000 to Canada when the story is finally told. The same interests were also responsible for the retaining of control of Brazilian Traction in this country, another market operation which has meant many millions to the investors of this country, for if the local financier had not had the vision to take hold of Brazilian Traction at the time he did, it would unquestionably have gone to the United States … these two are the greatest market operations Canada has ever seen, and have spelled millions and millions for Canadian investors, and have been of material advantage to the country at large. The foresight and courage of one man has been mainly instrumental in both instances.

Montreal Gazette, 24 October 1928

As we have seen, by 1911, McConnell had already become one of the richest men in Canada. He had made a fortune in his promotions, was vice-president of the transit system of Canada's biggest city, and was on the way to taking over one of the largest sugar refineries in the country. He might well have contemplated spending the remainder of his life playing golf and tennis, skiing, entertaining, and being entertained. In fact, he was already doing all this even before 1911, and he would continue doing it over the almost half-century to follow. But retirement held no allure for him, and he was in 1911 on the verge of a new, multifaceted career as an investor, an industrialist, an entrepreneur, a fixer, and a company director.

What made him run? Robust health and his famous "flaming energy" certainly contributed. His restlessness actually proved the undoing of his health in his sixties, when he suffered from sleeplessness. This was his stated reason for declining office in the government of Mackenzie King and the chancellorship of McGill. Nevertheless, a ferocious appetite for both challenge and achievement was probably the origin of his insomnia, not demons. Possessing money for its own sake was *not* a chief motivation, although making enough to give huge amounts to worthy causes – and maintain his very comfortable way of life – was.

McConnell in his office, n.d. Private collection.

Apart from his desire for doing good, McConnell liked being "in the game." Certainly, it was hard work to create, preserve, expand, repair, and distribute a great fortune. But it was also fun. Hard work enabled him to continue to grapple with some of the most interesting challenges and people of his time. It was compulsive rather than boring. As a financier acutely sensitive to the effects of inflation, deflation, and taxation, as well as of speculation and technological innovation, he was not inclined to a fixed view of wealth. The business world for him resembled a chessboard, with players and moves in constant adjustment. Others might object to one aspect or another of his businesses, whether it was his participation in oligopolies or his hostility to trade unions. Each of these criticisms might hold merit, but his was a bigger picture than what troubled his detractors. He dealt with the world as he saw it, not as anyone, including himself, preferred it to be. In this untidy picture, there was at least as much failure as success, and nothing was secure for long.

The full range of McConnell's business interests was enormous, especially in the years between the two world wars. During this period, he owned substantial – sometimes huge – interests in companies with products as diverse as rubber, milk, nickel, rayon, neon lights, liquid air, and insurance. Often but not always, his investments led to his appointment as director. In his lifetime, McConnell may have held more than two dozen directorships, many of them simultaneously, most of them of the major companies of Canada and some of global significance, and he held on to the majority of them until 1937–38.

His directorships do not define the full range of his investments, but they signal some of his principal ones. From 1912, he occupied high positions in three companies simultaneously – Montreal Tramways and Power, of which he was vice-president until 1918; Goodwins department store, of which he was vice-president until 1914 and president until 1925; and St Lawrence Sugar, of which he was vice-president until 1914 and president for almost a half-century afterwards. But for the unexpected longevity of Hugh Graham, Lord Atholstan, McConnell would have become president of the *Montreal Star* at any time after 1925, as he did eventually become after Atholstan had died in 1938.

The heyday of McConnell's parallel career as both investor and director was, like that of most other interwar businessmen, between 1925 and 1929, a period that extended from the regaining of his portfolio from the Bank of Montreal, where it had been pledged as collateral in 1921 in order to save St Lawrence Sugar, to the Great Crash of 1929.

Membership of company boards, of course, was not the same as managerial control. Apart from the periods in which he was briefly chairman of the Borden Company of Canada and president of Ogilvie Flour Mills, McConnell was not involved in the day-to-day running of the companies in which he was merely a director.

Furthermore, his directorships varied considerably in duration and in significance. Some he held for only a year or two or less, ranging from the early lumber ventures to Canadian Tube, Sherwin-Williams, Quebec Railway, Light, Heat and Power, and, perhaps surprisingly, the Canadian Pacific Railway. Apart from the CPR, he generally accepted these appointments merely to lend credibility to a new venture that he had promoted. In other companies, he held on to his directorship for years, such as Dominion Manufacturers, an amalgamation of coffin makers that he had helped to arrange, although this was an insignificant part of his portfolio.

He was by contrast also a director of huge international concerns based in Toronto and New York, such as Brazilian Traction, International Nickel, International Paper and Power, and the Borden Company, often chiefly because he was a major shareholder. He took a directorial interest also in certain Canadian companies, such as Canada Steamship Lines, Dominion Bridge, Ogilvie Flour Mills, Holt Renfrew, and Montreal Light, Heat and Power Consolidated, in each of which he held a substantial stake. Their boardrooms and those of Sun Life, the Bank of Montreal, and Royal Trust offered the advantage of being minutes from his office. Although Sir Herbert Holt held more directorships, McConnell's covered a wider swathe of the economy, and to this extent he may have been the most influential businessmen in the Canada of his time.

One of McConnell's business interests in these years – retailing – harked back to his days at Goulding's in Toronto. As both imports increased and local industries developed towards the end of the nineteenth century, there had emerged big dry-goods stores in cities. These were larger versions of the general stores that were to survive longer in rural areas. They displayed piles of goods in settings not unlike that of a warehouse, either within or behind counters. The interior of the store was hidden from the street behind windows that had been painted over, so that competitors were unsure of what their rivals had in stock. Several Montreal families well known to McConnell had made their fortunes with dry-goods stores in the nineteenth century, such as Greenshields', established in 1801, and Carsley's.[1] Another, perhaps the most famous, was Morgan's, established itself near the harbour in 1845, distributing consignments of goods from England. By the time that Morgan's had moved to Victoria Square in 1866, it had become noted for carpets, oilcloth, household furnishings, millinery, mantles, silks, tweeds, and broadcloth.

One of the first department stores in the world, the Bon Marché, opened in Paris in 1852. With its goods divided into departments rather than jumbled together, it was a landmark in the evolution of consumerism. It has also been described as the very embodiment, or at least a central institution, of bourgeois culture.[2] Other such stores were soon started in Paris, while, in the United States, Marshall Field in Chicago and Macy's in New York were almost contemporary, followed by Wanamaker's in Philadelphia and Jordan Marsh in Boston – pioneers in the use of iron and steel construction, telephones, electric lights and lifts, pneumatic tubes, cash registers, marketing, and advertising. In the same period, in London, H. Gordon Selfridge, an American who had begun his career at Marshall Field's, opened Selfridges, to be followed by Whiteley's and Harrods.

Bigger than the typical dry-goods store, the department store was designed to seduce the customer into buying on impulse, rather than out of some preconceived need. Commentators described it in religious terms as a palace of consumption and a temple to the creation of want. Its customers might still buy wool for knitting, for example, but increasingly they bought finished products made by unknown hands. The painted windows disappeared in favour of picture windows to display goods. Gone were monotonous rows of counters, which gave way to model rooms to showcase both furniture and fashionable clothing in particular. Those department stores that did not belong to chains became effectively collections of shops, still called departments but each an independent profit centre, with directors and a general manager for the store as a whole. After its move to Phillips Square in 1891, Morgan's became the first department store in Montreal. In addition to the medicines, textiles, clothing, and household goods that it had stocked as a dry-goods store, it now sold perfumes, books, stationery, and antiques. In time, it offered manufacturing, storage, automobile maintenance, rug washing, realty, and even trust-company services. It supplied panelling to the new Parliament Buildings in Ottawa and the Royal York Hotel in Toronto.

In Toronto, two department stores owned by Methodists with Ulster roots, Timothy Eaton of Eaton's and Joseph Flavelle (and later J.H. Gundy and C.L. Burton) of Simpson's, were soon spawning chains of affiliates across the country. In the 1880s, almost accidentally through its distribution of a booklet at the Canadian Industrial Exhibition, Eaton's developed a mail-catalogue department to serve the needs of farmers far from Toronto.[3] Nor was this its only innovation. From its start, Eaton's shocked Torontonians by selling for cash only, as opposed to the credit that nearly all other stores extended to their customers. Its cash policy permitted the much readier calculation of its cash flows and thus of its ability to fill inventory needs. Other stores adopted the same policy. The superior inventory control thus established enabled them to develop links with counterparts abroad, out of which emerged a global culture of department stores. This culture manifested itself in the wide range of goods that they offered, typically from all over the world. Although they might still retain their own buyers overseas, as dry-goods stores had done, they now could share wholesalers and buyers and other agents, and sell to one another.

McConnell had acquired an intimate knowledge of haberdashery from his years at Goulding's in Toronto, and he possessed an unusually keen appreciation of luxurious dress for women as well as for men. All his working life he looked remarkably well turned out himself, up to date and debonair. With his habitual boutonniere, his beautiful clothes were part of the persona that he created for himself as a successful man. On his first trip to Europe in 1904, he had made a point of going to the spectacular Galeries Lafayette in Paris to shop for Lil, and he became a great admirer of Harrods in London.

Thus, when an opportunity to enter the world of department-store retailing came his way, he was not about to pass it up. In about 1909 A.E. Rea and Company had established department stores in Ottawa and Toronto as well as Montreal. The Montreal store occupied land at the corner of Victoria and St Catherine streets, owned by the dry-goods-store owner Samuel Carsley, whose own business was on Notre-Dame Street. By 1910, however, Rea had overextended himself and was unable to pay his rent to Carsley. McConnell and Lorne McGibbon, who had been a purchasing agent in the west and was of an established Montreal family, bought the land from Carsley, but it took months to evict Rea. Afterwards, the Carsley property, separated from Morgan's only by Christ Church Cathedral, became the site of their new project, a larger department store. They had several competitors already – nearly all on St Catherine Street along with Morgan's – but McConnell and McGibbon decided that their store must be the most luxurious of all.

It was called Goodwins, after its managing director and one of its vice-presidents, W.H. Goodwin, an extremely severe Methodist who had been general manager of Murphy's, a rival store, and had worked for Eaton's in Toronto. To finance the venture, McConnell had to sell to investors at least $1 million in new preferred shares.[4] Evidence on the investors is fragmentary, but in April 1911 McGibbon, the store's president, is reported as owning 1,492 shares ($149,200) and McConnell, vice-president, as owning 6,250 ($625,000).[5] The store opened on 20 April 1911, and, by

Goodwins Department Store, St Catherine Street, c.1925.
McCord Museum 84105004.

the first annual meeting of its shareholders in 1912, it boasted a surplus of $229,519 and assets of over $4 million, including prime real estate. Its site covered over 100,000 square feet, equal to that of Gimbel's in New York and larger than that of Marshall Field's in Chicago.[6] At this meeting, McGibbon was re-elected president, and McConnell and Goodwin vice-presidents.

In Goodwins, McConnell and McGibbon created a store to cater to Montrealers very much like their wives, who were both known for their beauty and elegant dress. They were about as far removed as can be imagined from, say, the mothers of both Lil and Jack, who typically wore jet-black and no jewellery. Goodwins was a new shrine to luxury, gentility, and refinement, and in this respect quite different from Eaton's in particular. On 25 March 1911 the *Herald* quoted Goodwin: "We want to spread this idea of the dignity of service … The old idea of the vulgarity of trade, the ignominy that has always been implied in the word 'clerk' is fast disappearing." As a reflection of a changing society, the *Witness* revealed on 19 April that male clerks, the norm in dry-goods stores, were to be largely replaced with women, as they had been in other department stores. "To instil into the ordinary sales clerk the joy of service, and to use her as a force to radiate an influence for good throughout the city, is the goal which Mr. W.H. Goodwin, the managing director, has set himself in this great enterprise." In the French Room, decorated in "dainty grey," a female clerk offered "a

Advertisement for Goodwins, Montreal *Herald and Daily Telegraph*, 9 November 1911. Private collection.

small, instantly renewed, stock of the finest articles of ladies' attire." And, in order not to repel society ladies, "willing to pay hundreds of dollars for costumes," the French Room would not "push itself blatantly before the public."

During the First World War, Goodwins devoted a day to raising money for the Imperial Order of Daughters of the Empire and the Soldiers' Wives League. For this day alone, the saleswomen were the wives of men well known to McConnell in other spheres of business, and precisely the sort of clients that Goodwins cultivated. They included Lady Allan (general sales manager for the day); Mrs F.N. Southam and Mrs Percy Cowans (linens); Mrs C.B. Gordon (books); Lady Graham (laces and ribbons); Mrs Huntly Drummond (millinery); Lady Forget (furs); Mrs J.G. Ross (house furnishings); and Mrs Herbert Holt (pastry). The other departments of Goodwins included costumes, hosiery and gloves, drugs, fancy goods, men's shoes and clothing, ladies and children's shoes and clothing, corsets, carpets, house furnishings, wallpaper, crockery, grocery, pictures and photo supplies, music, toys, hardware, electrical goods, and mail order.

In depicting itself as being at the forefront of women's liberation, Goodwins may have incidentally been aiming to save on wages, since the women were not paid as much as men would have been. This qualification apart, women were becoming more important generally as consumers, and shopping was "integral to the identity of the new woman."[7] For Montreal in particular, Goodwins was innovative in consciously employing women to help other women shop. The employment of even relatively genteel women, even in industry, was rapidly expanded in the Great War to come; but even before, the intimate association of luxury with productivity and consumption at Goodwins was pure McConnell. He was deeply attached to the Goodwins venture, as vice-president for three years and then as president for almost eleven. From 1912 onwards, Goodwins would place a daily advertisement in the Montreal press, and McConnell's name would proudly appear at the head of it.

The store's second annual report was less satisfactory than the first. It revealed that McGibbon now held 25 per cent of the shares of the company, now called Goodwin's (so spelt as opposed to the store "Goodwins") Montreal, and that the return was 13 per cent on preferred stock and 4 per cent on common stock. The company then had a net surplus of $60,738, barely more than a quarter of what it had been in the previous year.[8] Difficulties increased over the summer of 1913 and, by May 1914, McConnell had won a proxy fight, with the aid of the investors he had recruited in England, to oust McGibbon.

It is not clear whether the difficulties at Goodwins were the cause of McGibbon's departure from Imperial Trust and Montreal Tramways as well. What is clear is that these ruptures were to poison the relations between McGibbon and McConnell in the years to come. It seems almost as though they were leaders of different camps, with important followers in each. This can be seen in their fight over newspapers in Halifax and Montreal and street railways in both cities. McConnell may also have had a hand in the departure of McGibbon from Canadian Consolidated Rubber, which McGibbon had cobbled together from various smaller companies. It was McConnell who became a director of the new Dominion Rubber that emerged from Consolidated. As recounted earlier, the rivalry between McConnell and McGibbon grew particularly nasty after McConnell had become president of St Lawrence Sugar and McGibbon president of Atlantic Sugar, as they struggled with dwindling supplies during the First World War.

By June 1915, Goodwins was in trouble. Still, the total assets were almost $4 million, as against total liabilities of just under $2 million. Difficulties notwithstanding, business improved. McConnell's last full year as president, 1924, was the most successful of all, in sales and net profits.[9] In February of that year, Goodwin retired as managing director and was replaced by W.K. Trower, who had joined McConnell's Montreal Securities Corporation in 1919, after working with him in the War Trade Board in 1918. Later, in 1925, McConnell sold Goodwins to Eaton's. The three hundred shareholders did well, receiving more than $5 million.[10] Eaton's promptly erected a new building on the site of Goodwins, which stands to the present day and which, under the Eaton's name, remained a major retail operation almost until the end of the twentieth century.

While Goodwins claimed to be modelled on Harrods but to possess a French touch, its suppliers were almost wholly based in New York City and largely German in name, even at the end of the First World War.[11] In its very goal of providing luxuries to the new middle classes that had hitherto been reserved to the aristocracy, it was essentially a distribution centre for the luxury products created by machines fuelled by newly available coal, steam, gas, and electricity. Much as he delighted in the details of ladies' clothing and housewares, it probably mattered little to McConnell what Goodwins sold as long as it was for a profit. The store, like so many of his enterprises, was an engine for transforming money as capital into money as commodities and then back to money as capital.

Thus, Goodwins fitted well into the industrial consolidation that was the theme of this stage of McConnell's career. It combined with other businesses dependent on investment capital to create a culture in which consumption became a good in itself, whether it was ladies' frocks, men's boots, sugar, transit, electricity, or paint. As the chief financier of Goodwins, McConnell had found himself at the confluence of some of the most powerful streams of this new culture of desire. Yet, although dedicated to his work at Goodwins, he was no marketer or retailing innovator. He never really abandoned his role as a financial broker for the store while president.

McConnell did not withdraw from retailing entirely with the sale of Goodwins to Eaton's. At this time, one of the most venerable names in Canadian retailing was Holt Renfrew, which traced its origins to 1860. Changing its name from G.R. Renfrew and Company to Holt Renfrew in 1901, it evoked high fashion, luxury, and above all furs. Sir Herbert Holt, apparently unrelated to the store's founder, John H. Holt, was behind the reorganization of the new Holt Renfrew in 1919. Lorne Webster, the coal merchant, and McConnell joined him in this effort, reincorporating the company provincially. Webster was the principal individual shareholder; McDougall and Cowans and the Montreal Securities Corporation held 5,500 of the preference shares and 3,750 of the common. On his own account, McConnell himself bought 500 preferred shares for $45,000 and 125 common shares for $11,555. Webster became president and McConnell vice-president. At the end of October 1919, McConnell resigned as vice-president. By the annual meeting of 1920, however, he was one of the major individual shareholders, with 2,002 of the 4,355 common shares and 625 of the 3,460 preference.

In its political make-up, the new Holt Renfrew board was very Conservative. Webster had been and was to remain one of the chief Conservative Party fundraisers in the province. Another director was to be Arthur Meighen. After the defeat by Mackenzie King's Liberals of Meighen's Conservatives in December 1921, Meighen paid tribute to McConnell's support. "There are few," he wrote, "indeed one could count them

Holt Renfrew, the new store on Sherbrooke Street,
ad in *Passing Show*, 1937. Private collection.

on the fingers of one hand, who contributed so much as you to the success of our cause. Indeed I regard the personal relationship which has been established between us as one of the results worth while out of the worry and toil of the last seventeen months."[12] Subsequently, despite much assistance from both McConnell and Webster in the general election of 1925, Meighen lost to King again and thereafter was to remain in the political wilderness over the almost four decades that remained to him. McConnell had him elected at director of Holt Renfrew, and they were to sit together on the board of Meighen's Canadian and General Investments in Toronto as well.

Under the stewardship of McConnell and Webster, Holt Renfrew was never strong financially, and indeed sometimes it was a financial disaster. But it was a property of enormous prestige. Their social triumph was secured in 1937 by the move of the store from St Catherine Street to a new Art Deco building on Sherbrooke Street, beside the Ritz-Carlton. It was a handsome building in the smartest modern style, the Royal Arms above its door proudly surmounted by the Union Jack. Described in the press as the beginning of the transformation of Sherbrooke Street into Montreal's answer to Fifth Avenue in New York, it was a bold intrusion into the residential heart of older money.

A portrait of Lil, in furs probably from Holt Renfrew,
n.d. McCord Museum M2003.8.68.67.1.

With the Depression, the dismal performance of Holt Renfrew was reflected in its shares. By September 1929, through St Lawrence Sugar, McConnell was holding preferred and common shares, for a total of $546,100. Within less than five years after the Crash, his shares had declined in value to $60,940 or by 89 per cent. The fact that he remained a director until 1938, and that his son John took over as a director after him and even became president of the company, suggests strongly that McConnell's interest in Holt Renfrew was very personal and not simply for investment. Indeed, he bailed out the company from a crisis as late as 1953.[13]

If retailing was a passion of McConnell's, banking and railways were less so. Conrad Black views McConnell as the embodiment of the traditional hegemony exercised by Montreal, describing him as "the doyen, in wealth and influence, of the Canadian Pacific-Bank of Montreal-Royal Trust group by the end of the First World War."[14] The Bank of Montreal had played a central role not only in the expansion of Montreal but also in the expansion of Canada more generally under the influence, if not the control, of the city. It therefore became the very symbol of the economic strength of Montreal, and a seat on its board was a sign of ultimate acceptance by St James Street. Often this seat coincided with membership of the board of governors of McGill, and with membership of the Mount Royal Club, which McConnell himself held. For twelve years, but not beginning until 1925, McConnell was a director of the bank and of its affiliate Royal Trust.

He was, however, a director of the CPR for less than one (1937), and he attended only six of its board meetings. While the two enterprises were practically inseparable in the eyes of many, such that the president of the railway was almost ex officio a director of the bank, McConnell's directorships of those did not even coincide for all of 1937, since he had resigned both before the end of it. To some extent, McConnell's short tenure on the CPR board was due to the lack for some time of a vacancy among the directors and his decision to retire from nearly all his directorships in 1937–38. But it also suggests that prestige in Montreal was no longer unequivocally identified with this old alliance between the railway and the bank.

The overcapacity of the rail network in Canada hung like a millstone round the necks of the CPR and, by extension, its traditional financier, the Bank of Montreal, through the interwar period. McConnell himself saw the government-owned and tax-subsidized Canadian National Railways as one of the chief blocks to the return to prosperity in Canada in the Depression. The Bank of Montreal was also facing competition, notably from the Royal Bank of Canada, under Sir Herbert Holt and others from 1905 onwards.

Although he could not own shares in the CNR, McConnell did invest in the Royal Bank and maintain many links with its board. With Holt in particular, its president, he sat on the boards of Brazilian Traction and Montreal Power, as well as Holt Renfrew. In 1929 McConnell actually had more invested in the Royal Bank than in the Bank of Montreal, and the same applied to their affiliated trust companies, Montreal Trust and Royal Trust respectively. If we merge his investments in the two banks and their trust companies, he had invested in the Royal Bank and Montreal Trust $612,975 and in the Bank of Montreal and Royal Trust $494,404.

The men whom McConnell joined at the Bank of Montreal board in 1925 included at their head two established colleagues of his in fundraising, Sir Vincent Meredith (president) and Sir Charles Gordon (vice-president). Among the others, he was particularly associated with C.R. Hosmer, through Ogilvie Flour Mills; William McMaster, through the steel industry; Sir Lomer Gouin, the retired premier of Quebec, through Montreal Tramways; the lawyer F.E. Meredith, D. Forbes Angus of Standard Life Assurance and BC Sugar, and F.W. Molson, through personal acquaintance; H.R. Drummond, through the sugar industry; Lieutenant-Colonel Herbert Molson, through fundraising; and Sir Arthur Currie (principal) and E.W. Beatty (chancellor, and president of the CPR), through McGill. The bank still resembled a

Montreal club, and only sixty-six men attended its annual meetings of shareholders in 1925, of whom McConnell knew the vast majority, if not everyone.

By 1937, McConnell seems to have regarded his fleeting membership of the CPR board as a rather dubious honour, as reflected by the amount that he had invested in the company: he had $125,000 invested in it in 1921, and apparently nothing by 1929. Nevertheless, his short formal association with the railway cannot disguise the fact that he was very much a CPR-type of man. Most of the directors were close colleagues of his on other boards, especially either the Bank of Montreal or McGill or both. To save the time of the CPR's chairman and president, Sir Edward Beatty, the meetings of the McGill governors were frequently held in the CPR boardroom.

McConnell had a much more long-lasting interest in another mode of transportation, ships, holding a directorship in Canada Steamship Lines (CSL) from 1926 until 1937. CSL was the product of successive consolidations of transport companies in the Great Lakes as well as of other ventures, assembled by the Anglo-Canadian financier Grant Morden operating in conjunction with Vickers, McConnell's old friend since 1904 Sir Trevor Dawson, and the British Maritime Trust. A "fully integrated shipping provider,"[15] it ran bulk, freight, and passenger services. Through the Montreal General Hospital, on the board of which they both sat, he had also known the grain dealer James Carruthers, president of CSL in 1913-19, who had links with Ross McMaster's Steel Company of Canada (Stelco), one of CSL's most important clients.[16]

CSL was in dire straits by 1921, principally because of poor management, and it was reorganized the next year. All members of the new board were well known to McConnell, and his investment in it, by 1929, of $1,338,450, made him one of its principal owners. He seems to have been on particularly good terms with William Coverdale, CSL's president, who though from Kingston had been a consulting engineer and adviser to railways and other enterprises in New York. McConnell joined the CSL board in 1926 and retained his seat for the next two years – a boom period for the company. Then came the fall. The wheat glut of 1928 and the subsequent Depression were ruinous to Great Lakes shipping. In 1929-35 CSL's gross earnings averaged only 55 per cent of what they had been in 1928, and by 1935 the company was insolvent. McConnell worked on a restructuring in that year with the broker A.J. Nesbitt; the lawyer Senator A.J. Brown, who was a director of the Royal Bank and Holt Renfrew; and Coverdale. They agreed to withhold payment of interest and dividends to investors (including themselves) until 1943, at which point all investors would then receive new common shares. In 1937 CSL showed its first profit since 1928.

The company continued to prosper into the Second World War, and it resumed the payment of dividends and raised the salaries of workers. Nevertheless, before the war, the conditions of most of the CSL crews had been abysmal, and there was growing discontent with the authoritarian methods of the Canadian shipping companies generally. In 1937–38 CSL made a pact with the Canadian Seamen's Union (CSU), and this contract was renewed in 1938. Labour peace then prevailed until just after the war, when management-union relations deteriorated markedly, the workers themselves became fragmented between two unions, and Ottawa intervened to control inland shipping through the National Emergency Transitional Powers Act. For help in stabilizing the situation, CSL eventually turned to the Seafarers' International Union (SIU), affiliated with the American Federation of Labor (AFL), an action that led to the emergence of Hal Banks as head of the SIU. Concern about the communist affiliation of the CSU led Ottawa to decertify it and embrace Banks despite his criminal record.

By this time, McConnell was largely retired from business, apart from St Lawrence Sugar, and trying to stay free of further commitments. There is no doubt, however, that he was deeply troubled by the labour strife encountered by CSL from 1946 onwards, as he saw it as communist and threatening to a crucial sector of trade both in Canada and what was coming to be called the Free World generally. Although the extant evidence is slim, it seems that McConnell, even when confined to bed with pneumonia and no longer a director, remained a power at CSL as late as 1951 and probably to the end of his life.[17] It is clear that he played a crucial role in the takeover of the company by Sir James Dunn in 1951. The following year, the company's new president, Rodgie McLagan, ushered in an era of considerable growth. One of his achievements over his sixteen-year tenure was to replace most of the CSL fleet with much larger vessels capable of benefiting from the deeper and wider St Lawrence Seaway that was being built in the 1950s.

On the day before the opening of the seaway in 1959, McConnell dined for the last time with Queen Elizabeth II, on the Royal Yacht *Britannia*. He might have been forgiven for marvelling at how much had changed on the Great Lakes over the last fifty years. The queen was about to sail smoothly through locks – reduced from twenty-two to seven – on deepened and widened canals almost unimaginable to Morden and Dawson, to say nothing of Rodolphe Forget, McConnell's early mentor and the owner of the Richelieu and Ontario Navigation Company. The new standard for the remaining seven locks was that of the fourth Welland Canal, opened by Lord Bessborough in 1932. Now the queen could proceed on *Britannia* all the way to Toronto, where she was to have her final meeting with her senior privy councillor from the empire, McConnell's old ally, Arthur Meighen.

McConnell's interest in CSL was closely tied to another of his businesses, flour milling. Like retailing, flour milling had first attracted his attention many years earlier: one of his first jobs had been with Christie's Biscuits in Toronto, and one of his early stock-promotion ventures was Canadian Cereal and Milling, later part of the International Milling Company of Canada. Thereafter, he invested in one of the best-

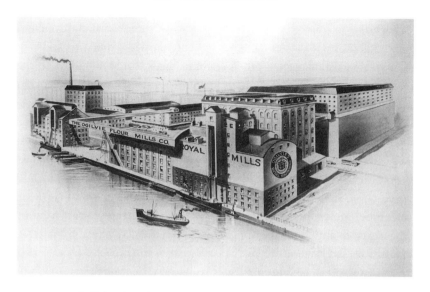

Ogilvie Flour (Royal Household) Mills, Montreal, 1924.
McCord Museum V21094.

known flour businesses in the country, Ogilvie Flour Mills, and he later joined its board in the same year, 1926, that he became a CSL director. The two companies were a good fit, since, along with the transportation of steel, the movement of grain from the prairies to Montreal constituted one of CSL's core businesses.

Ogilvie Flour Mills, which bore various other names before its incorporation in 1902, originated with Alexander Ogilvie's founding of a Quebec City mill in 1801. It had grown spectacularly in the early nineteenth century owing to several factors: the opening of the Lachine Canal in 1825, which brought supplies of grain to Lower Canada from Upper Canada; the invention of the McCormick reaper, patented in 1834, which halved the costs and risks of harvesting; the advent of the grain elevator, which permitted grains to be precisely graded, assuring industrial classifications and standards; the introduction of Galician wheat, called Red Fife, which became the standard of wheat quality in British North America; and the introduction of the process of stone-and-roller grinding.

When the Crimean War broke out in 1854, cutting off continental supplies of wheat to Great Britain, and reciprocity was agreed upon with the United States in the same year, the fortunes of the company substantially improved. By 1895, grain and cereals had replaced timber as the country's leading industry, and, by the time of the time of its incorporation in 1902, Ogilvie had become the largest milling company in Canada and one of the largest in the world, exporting not only to Britain but to Africa, Latin America, the Caribbean, Scandinavia, and even Asia. Its growth became even more spectacular in the years afterwards, as immigrants poured into the Canadian west and wheat production soared, triggering a period of extraordinary profitability for Ogilvie that did not come to an end until the Crash of 1929.

In 1921 McConnell owned only 500 common shares in Ogilvie, worth $90,000. Just before the Crash, however, he owned 5,760 common shares in it worth nearly $3.5 million, to which he gave a book or purchase value of $600 each, which suggests that he had bought most of them when they were near their peak in market value. In the short term, his new investment in Ogilvie, presumably in 1928–29, did not prove wise, since wheat was grown all over the world and subject to intense international competition. In the twelve months ending on 31 March 1929, for example, Canada's agricultural exports, mainly wheat, to Germany fell from $35.4 million in value to $2.18 million.[18] And the situation only grew worse after the Depression had set in. In September 1931 Great Britain abandoned the gold standard, which impaired its ability to import food. By the end of 1932, No. 1 Northern wheat had dropped to 42 cents a bushel, the lowest recorded price for wheat since the Middle Ages. In 1937 drought struck Saskatchewan's wheat crop and its yield fell to a seventh of normal. Five years later, in the midst of the war, Ogilvie suffered another blow with the loss of the royal warrant that it had held since 1912. This was not a minor matter, since the royal arms were a prominent part of Ogilvie packaging and marketing, and both its Montreal mill and its most prestigious brand was called "Royal Household."

In 1935 McConnell assumed the presidency of Ogilvie, a post he retained for five years. The company records for this period are missing, but McConnell's 1935 speech accepting the presidency has survived. He began with the good humour that often characterized his public addresses: "I appreciate the fact that you have elected me to a highly honourable position – and for that, I must thank you. I have grave doubts, however, as to whether or not the job is a thing to be thankful for, as you must know from the stories so frequently told that the 'ranks' of the flour milling companies are filled to over flowing with pirates, liars and highwaymen. However, these new associations will be – at any rate – a complete change for me, and may add a little spice to life." After describing the company's growth since its founding in 1902, he concluded: "I shall endeavour to uphold the fine traditions of the 'old Company' and in doing so, I must not forget the lessons so well taught by my esteemed predecessor – that above all, I must be pessimistic; the flour milling business is never good. I must never complain that flour is being sold at less than cost; that we have a tough lot of competitors, and that the milling business is a damn rotten business at best."[19]

McConnell left the day-to-day operations of the company in the hands of the vice-president, G.A. Morris. He also seemed to depend a good deal on C.A. Dunning, formerly premier of Saskatchewan (and thus an expert on wheat pools) and then the federal minister of finance under Mackenzie King. Dunning, elected director and vice-president in 1939, was to succeed McConnell as president in 1940 and serve until 1947. McConnell remained a major investor, however, and a major voice in the company's management, despite significant losses in the market value of its shares of about 83 per cent between 1929 and 1939.

Together with St Lawrence Sugar and the Montreal *Star*, Ogilvie is generally considered to have been one of McConnell's core assets. By 1926, he owned 5,255 shares in the company through St Lawrence Sugar, yielding a dividend of $51,488, and, just before the Crash of 1929, he owned 5,760 shares with a market value of $3,456,000. Of the 75,000 common shares outstanding, his interest constituted 13 per cent. By 1939, however, the market value of his holdings had declined to $574,146, and he continued to dispose of shares until 1947, when a purchase of 450 new shares brought the market value of his interest to $612,771. In 1949 and 1952 he transferred to his Foundation 30,000 shares, with a total value of $317,600.

Despite the long-term decline in the market value of its common shares, what is clear is that Ogilvie did much better under McConnell's presidency than it had done under his predecessor, and McConnell's leadership coincided with a gradual recovery from the depths of the Depression. In 1929 Ogilvie's profit had been $366,741. It fell to $12,436 in the following year, and it reached a low of $3,498 in 1935, the year in which McConnell took over. From then on, profits rose rather erratically, but rise they did, to over $160,000 in 1940. By 1947, however, Ogilvie was no longer the largest milling company in Canada but the third-largest, behind Maple Leaf Milling and Robin Hood Flour Mills.

McConnell also found gratification in a much different sort of business, one that appealed to his abiding interest in technological innovation. He had been educating himself in science since his time at Standard Chemical, and in later years chemical and manufacturing processes became an essential part of his evaluation of potential investments, and even more their application from one industry to another – so much so that he grasped that a new industrial revolution, based on metals, was under way after the First World War. His interest in liquid air, which was used in welding metal, was part and parcel of his fascination with the new world of science, and coincided with his investment in industries using huge amounts of steel as well as nickel.

The origins of liquid air dated to 1889, when the Frenchman Georges Claude invented a process to distribute acetylene in steel cylinders. Thirteen years later, two French engineers developed, from stored acetylene, the first practical oxy-acetylene welding torch. Almost simultaneously, in 1902, Claude had successfully liquefied air, and three years afterwards he was able to extract pure oxygen from air in industrial quantities. Paul Delorme established Air Liquide to commercialize Claude's inventions, and he opened its first oxygen-producing plant in France in 1905 and four more there within a year. Canadian research also contributed. In 1900 Ernest A. LeSueur, of Consolidated Lake Superior in Sault Ste Marie, had crucially determined that the initial liquefaction from air contains over 40 per cent of oxygen, and then he developed a liquefying apparatus, the patents for which he later sold to Claude.[20]

A decade later, in the Montreal industrial suburb of Maisonneuve, R.J. Levy, an engineer who had set up British Liquid Air in 1906, established a factory for Air Liquide to manufacture oxy-acetylene torches for cutting steel and welding various metals. Until the opening of Levy's plant in Maisonneuve in 1911, oxygen had been imported into Canada in cylinders from England or Buffalo, New York, but in its first year the new Montreal factory produced 592,000 cubic feet of oxygen, and by 1913 it was producing four million cubic feet. Although Levy perished on the *Titanic* in 1912, Air Liquide had expanded across the country by 1915. The relevant corporate records are inaccessible, but it seems that in 1923 McConnell reorganized the Canadian operations of the company with Sir Herbert Holt.

By 1929, he had invested $66,000 in Air Liquide and $6,500 in Canadian Liquid Air, the subsidiary that had emerged from the reorganization. In addition to torches, liquid air lent itself to another new industry, that of neon lights. By the 1920s, they were lighting up the "Great White Way" in New York and the city of Las Vegas in particular. By 1929, McConnell's investments in the Claude Neon Corporation totalled $925,000.

McConnell remained a director of Canadian Liquid Air long after he had resigned most of his other directorships in 1937–38, apparently because he saw it as an essential war industry. With the fall of France to the Germans in June 1940, the director of the foreign department of Air Liquide and its research technician fled to New York, but they found themselves barred from settling there. Montreal therefore became the world headquarters of all of Air Liquide beyond Nazi control. It established six new plants in Canada alone, as well as operations in the Middle East and Argentina. Ships, tanks, guns, and airplanes were all products of flame-cutting and production-welding techniques developed by Air Liquide.

The welding of steel and nickel made possible by liquid air was one of the basic operations of other big investments of McConnell's, including INCO, described below, Dominion Bridge (one of the chief engineering companies in Canada), and the automobile industry.[21] In 1929 McConnell had $565,998 invested in Studebaker Corporation, $650,000 in Evans Auto Loading, and $303,310 in Chrysler Corporation.

McConnell was similarly successful in his investments in what many saw as a "mature" industry, textiles. The textile industry was one of the big employers of Canada, and particularly of Quebec, its total workforce numbering over 50,000. Because of the tariff protection that it enjoyed, it was one of the favoured fields for investment not merely of McConnell but also of his colleagues Sir Herbert Holt and of Sir Charles Gordon. But the industry was not about to rely on tariff protection alone to safeguard its future. Various consolidations in the Canadian textile industry took place from 1882 to 1905, culminating in the formation of Dominion Textile. After the First World War, the various surviving firms divided the market by specializing, with only one major firm in each product line, and in the 1930s they formed a joint monopoly run through their Primary Textile Institute. Among its members, it exchanged statistics of production, arranged prices, and defined "fair trade" practices, although the Depression had stymied its activities by 1938.[22]

In 1929 McConnell owned almost $2 million in common shares of Dominion Textile alone. At the same time, his investments in other textile firms – Canadian Cotton, Penmans, Tooke Brothers, Dominion Woollens and Worsteds, Wabasso Cotton, and Belding-Cortecelli – totalled a further $2.6 million. These firms used, mainly but not exclusively, the traditional fibres of wool and cotton like that produced by Dominion Textile, so that McConnell's total investments in manufacturers of primarily traditional textiles was $4.6 million just before the Crash of 1929.

But "artificial silk" or rayon, respectively the dominant English and American terms in the 1930s, in the forms of either viscose or Celanese, had been capturing much of the textile market as well, and even Dominion Textile operated a rayon plant, although Courtaulds (Canada) and Canadian Celanese manufactured about 90 per cent of Canadian needs. In 1929 McConnell's holdings in Courtaulds in England, Canadian Celanese, and the Belgian Tubize Artificial Silk totalled $1.6 million, almost 65 per cent as much as he had invested in traditional textiles. Since he was invested in both kinds of rayon – through Courtaulds, Tubize, and Canadian Celanese – McConnell benefited from the global rise in the use of both viscose in women's stockings and acetate in women's underwear, especially after the entry into production of dull lustred yarns in 1926. Aided by advertising, women's liberation after the First World War had led to an almost universal shortening of skirts and the use of underwear as a source of sexual attraction. Other artificial fabrics such as nylon followed, and viscose in particular became mixed with cotton in clothing and furnishing fabrics, while acetate went into taffeta and satin for dress fabrics.

Through marketing techniques such as those of Goodwins and other department stores, the incorporation of women into a massive social revolution in consumer behaviour and fashion was one of the great sources of McConnell's increasing wealth, even during the Depression. Courtaulds, his only English holding, never failed to pay a dividend in the 1930s, which averaged 8.3 per cent from 1929 to 1939. In 1929 McConnell's income from Courtaulds was about £50,000, and, even a decade later, in 1939, it was more than £11,000.[23] This unbroken, if uneven, income stream, on one of his many investments explains how he survived the Depression so comfortably.[24]

During the 1930s, the Canadian textile industry came under scrutiny by a royal commission chaired by Mr Justice W.-F.-.A. Turgeon. The inquiry followed the sudden closure by G. Blair Gordon, president of Dominion Textile in succession to his father Sir Charles, of its rayon plant in Sherbrooke, in January 1936, ostensibly because of Japanese competition. Although the closure lasted only twelve days, it appears to have been a tactic by Gordon to overturn an agreement between Canada and Japan to end a trade war that had been going on in 1935. Moreover, although the agreement, reached on 1 January 1936, had left Canadian manufacturers stronger in relation to Japanese rayon manufacturers than they were to Americans ones, Gordon rejected any relaxation of protection against Japanese imports.

Turgeon concluded that the closure was "not justified by the situation as it then existed, and as it has developed since without the desired action [of heavier tariffs on Japanese imports] having been taken."[25] He found that the industry as a whole had, by 1938, come through the Depression "in a manner which many other industries might envy," and he referred to rumours of "secret industry reserves," "improper charges to operations for depreciation," and "true profits" that were "hidden," although all these matters had been referred to tax authorities.[26] He was scathing about the stockwatering of Dominion Textile, and about the alleged need of the industry for perpetual protection, even though it had long grown out of its infancy.

Turgeon also attacked the monopolistic practices of the Canadian textile industry, following on the sort of research done for the Royal Commission on Price Spreads in 1935, but his was not an investigation under the Anti-Combines Act, which would probably have involved closer analysis of whether a monopoly really existed. McConnell in any case believed in investing in companies that were dominant in their industries, if not outright monopolies.

How difficult it was to maintain this sort of investment over time can be seen in the period under consideration here. Canadian Celanese exercised a virtual monopoly over acetate production in Canada, and so even if the textile industry was a monopoly, there was another monopoly within it. Courtaulds (Canada) exercised a similar monopoly over viscose production in Canada, but McConnell's shares were in the parent Courtaulds in England, which – although it belonged to a European cartel – derived roughly half its income from its American subsidiary, AVC. The latter company, moreover, was operating in what was clearly an oligopolistic rather than monopolistic situation in the United States. It faced numerous serious competitors – such as the Celanese Corporation of America since 1925 and DuPont and Tubize from 1929 onward. Between the establishment of AVC in 1911 and 1939, the price of natural-fibre yarn generally fell, and so did that of rayon fibre, which enabled the substitution of one fibre for the other, and which complicated price leadership by any firm, including AVC. Thus, even if the American rayon was an oligopoly, the oligopoly itself was part of a larger competitive situation.[27]

Competition affected still another of McConnell's business interests, the manufacturing of chemicals. After the First World War, the collapse of demand for chemicals gave rise to new cooperation among chemical firms in Europe and America, something that was absolutely necessary if they were not all to go bankrupt. The cooperation of chemical firms in price fixing led to their actual amalgamation into larger firms, which, in Canada as elsewhere, were now operating as international entities.[28] In December 1926 Imperial Chemical Industries was formed, directly in response to the challenge posed by the German firm IG Farben. It emerged from the marriage of four companies known to McConnell since his sales trip to England in 1904. Created by Sir Harry McGowan (later Lord McGowan) of Nobel Industries, ICI was a holding company with an initial capitalization of £56.8 million, roughly the same as the initial capitalization of IG Farben. As it turned out, however, ICI was to experience considerable and prolonged difficulty in rationalizing the operations of its constituent companies. Nor did it pose a serious challenge to IG Farben. In 1931 ICI joined the international cartel of chemical manufacturers, in which the Germans had a quota of 66 per cent and the British only 7 per cent.

With the incorporation of ICI in 1926, DuPont, the family-owned chemical company based in Delaware since 1799, found itself obliged to set up a new Canadian holding company with ICI to replace Canadian Explosives Limited (CXL), which DuPont had owned with Nobel, now part of ICI. This development gave rise to Canadian Industries Limited (CIL) in 1927, when Arthur Purvis, president of CXL since 1925, in succession to William McMaster (father of Ross McMaster of Stelco), became president of the new Canadian operation. Purvis and his successors as president of CIL until the 1960s were all close to McConnell, especially James Eccles, who for long managed the investment portfolio of McGill and sat on its board. Eccles may have first met McConnell as early as 1910, when he was a banker for Harris Forbes and involved in the financing of Montreal Tramways. McConnell was never a director of ICI or CIL. But as early as 1929 he had $250,000 invested in ICI, and to this extent he was indirectly an investor in CIL.

CIL was an effort both to exploit the Canadian market and to avoid competition between the English and the American giants. It had its own plants, production and marketing departments, and research and development facilities. Its assets tripled between 1927 and 1942, largely through the aggressive leadership of Purvis, who played ICI and DuPont off against each other and tried, largely successfully, to create a successful Canadian enterprise distinct from their strategic needs. In 1944, however, the US government launched an anti-trust suit against ICI and DuPont, alleging that CIL was a co-conspirator in "throttling the growth of industry within the dominions of the British Empire."[29] As a result of the suit, DuPont sold its shares and set up its own subsidiary in Canada, and ICI retained 74 per cent of the voting shares of CIL, so that the latter was now a subsidiary of ICI alone and became ICI of Canada, with Eccles as its chairman and president.

The formation of ICI in 1926 was the prelude to the refinancing of International Nickel in 1928–29, in which McConnell was intimately involved. Apart from Brazilian Traction, of all the companies in which McConnell held a substantial interest, INCO was probably the one that sustained his interest the longest.

The nickel industry is one of the greatest of Canada, chiefly because most of the nickel deposits in the world are found here.[30] In 1886 the Canadian Copper Com-

International Nickel of Canada advertisement, 1933,
origin unknown. Private collection.

pany, run from Ohio, began the mining of nickel ore from its Copper Cliff mine near Sudbury, and within a few years it was clear that nickel was likely to become one of the most valuable resources of Canada and the British Empire, its chief use being as an alloy in reinforcing steel for armaments.

Canadian Copper did not refine its nickel in Canada but shipped it to Orford Copper of New Jersey. In about 1900 Orford approached the financier J.P. Morgan to finance its expansion. Morgan undertook to support Orford's purchase of Canadian Copper while destroying the Nickel Copper Company of Hamilton, Ontario, a company that could have refined the ore in Canada. With his backing, in 1902 R.M. Thompson of Orford and Charles Schwab of Carnegie Steel incorporated International Nickel as a holding company for several firms, including Canadian Copper and Orford Copper. Ambrose Monell became the first president of INCO, and his successor, Robert C. Stanley, developed "Monel" nickel-copper alloys, the elements of which were in the same proportions as those in nickel-copper ore. Monel alloys were to prove one of the major products of INCO in years to come and key to its retention of supremacy amid stiff competition.

In the meantime in England, Ludwig Mond, of the firm Brunner, Mond that was to become part of ICI, had invented a carbonyl process for producing completely pure or primary nickel. Mond began buying nickel deposits in Ontario not owned by Canadian Copper, and his Mond Nickel Company started mining and smelting near Sudbury in 1901. Mond's company, along with Le Nickel, a Rothschild-owned French firm operating in New Caledonia, and Thompson's INCO, were soon to divide the global market for nickel. Demand for nickel grew steadily up to the outbreak of the First World War, and during the war all the nickel that Canada could produce went into armaments. In 1914 Ontario produced over 45 million pounds of nickel, a figure that approximately doubled by 1918.

Just before the outbreak of the war, in 1913, the New Brunswick financier James Dunn, since 1905 based in London, had begun to challenge the monopoly established by INCO and Mond.[31] With the American engineer and street-railway promoter F.S. Pearson, E.R. Wood, Z.A. Lash, and others, Dunn set up the British American Nickel Company (BANCO). All four of these principal colleagues were also directors of Brazilian Traction, set up in the year previous, and Pearson was president of Brazilian. The purpose of BANCO was to develop a new electrolytic method of nickel smelting which BANCO hoped would be cheaper than the Orford process. BANCO was on the verge of collapse within a year, however, partly because of opposition to its financing by Morgan and INCO.

Help from BANCO came from a besieged Great Britain. In 1915, at the request of the British government, Dunn bought a Norwegian syndicate in order to direct Norwegian supplies of nickel away for the Germans, and also to purchase for BANCO control of a new smelting process. Yet, although he obtained a British government guarantee for $6 million of BANCO shares, Dunn was unable to impose unified control over supplies and production. British interest in BANCO also ended with the conclusion of war, and by 1924 the company had collapsed, and with it the gravest challenge to the worldwide monopoly enjoyed by International Nickel and Mond Nickel.

By now, pressure had been building for the refining of its nickel to be done in Canada, pressure that only increased in 1916 when INCO was accused of dealing with the Germans, who were at war with the British Empire but not with the United States. Canada passed an order-in-council placing an embargo on nickel exports outside the empire. Such was public hostility to the action of the Americans that INCO formed a Canadian subsidiary, the International Nickel Company of Canada (INCO Canada), with headquarters in Toronto, in an effort to defuse it.

Both the Ontario government and the federal government created commissions of inquiry to consider the future of nickel, the first in 1917 and the second in 1920, and each called for refining to be done in Canada. In response to these two reports, INCO finally opened a refinery at Port Colborne, Ontario, but then, in the three or four years following the end of war in 1918, the world market generally for nickel more or less collapsed and demand fell back to what it had been in 1900.

Furthermore, in 1923, Great Britain, the United States, France, Italy, and Japan entered into a Naval Disarmament Treaty that provided for the scrapping of large numbers of battleships and armoured cruisers, and the cancellation of similar vessels under construction or being planned. As a result, the United States and Great Britain alone suddenly found themselves possessed of about thirty-six million tons of nickel scrap. By then, however, INCO had become the industry leader in research and development, which in the long run were to prove its salvation. By 1933, 20 per cent of world production was going into nickel-alloy steel for automobiles, trucks, and buses, and, in preparation for the next world war, the rearmament of Germany and other countries further increased demand from 1933 onwards.

With competition between INCO and Mond Nickel for the deposits near Sudbury also increasing, the two reached an agreement in 1928 to exchange their shares for stock in a recapitalized INCO based in New Jersey, to be renamed the International Nickel Company of Canada. The principal impediment to the merger was the threat of American anti-trust law, which would not permit a monopoly over nearly all the nickel in the world to be held by an American company. Although this threat was real, it appears that no anti-trust action was imminent, and that the more important motivation for the merger was to make the company "British," which would only incidentally shield the company from anti-trust action.[32] Under the reorganization that effected the merger of the old INCO and Mond, there was to be ownership by a Canadian corporation (the new INCO) of the old INCO's assets.

The roles of International Nickel Incorporated in New Jersey and its Canadian subsidiary, International Nickel of Canada, were thus reversed. This reversal yielded two results. One was to circumvent definitively the threat of American anti-trust legislation. The other was to overcome the qualms of the Mond board, which did not want nickel production to fall totally into American hands but to remain largely if not entirely within the empire, in particular in Canada. As the Montreal *Gazette* crowed on 24 October 1928, the nickel mines of Ontario had at last passed into "British control, a control which will be as effective in time of war as well as in time of peace as a means of averting war."

The reorganization of 1928 had brought McConnell and the grain dealer James A. Richardson of Winnipeg to the board of the old INCO in March, to help effect it. Notwithstanding its nominally Canadian character, however, the new INCO remained based in the United States, its headquarters in New York City, and possessed of factual but not legal control of the Canadian INCO.[33] Not surprisingly, therefore, Robert C. Stanley, an American, became president. McConnell's directorship brought him to New York once a month, and through it he came into regular contact with such powerful figures as the corporate lawyer John Foster Dulles, who represented INCO at the time and later became the American secretary of state under President Eisenhower.

Sir Herbert Holt in Montreal and James A. Richardson had worked with McConnell to make a Canadian market for the shares of the reorganized company. Over months and in anticipation of the reorganization, there developed feverish demand in the stock markets for shares of the old INCO, and McConnell's broker, Percy Cowans, was the principal dealer in INCO shares in Montreal, reaping a huge fortune. McConnell began by buying 5,000 shares for himself. Then, shortly before the merger took place, in August 1928, the old INCO issued 167,338 common shares to its existing common shareholders and 35,650 common shares to its existing preferred shareholders at $60 a share, when the market price was about $150 a share.[34] Next, the shares of the old company were split, six for one, as part of the reorganization, so that McConnell soon owned 30,000 common shares in the new company. These shares rose from $58 to $63 each before they were even traded, and within six months they went to $75. They declined, however, to a market value of $55 each, or $1,650,000 in total, by 3 September 1929.

In 1928 McConnell became a member of the management committee of the new INCO, and his fellow Canadians on the board were confident that a forthcoming expansion of the American naval program would entail an outlay of $800 million and increase orders for copper. Despite the troubles of the 1930s, International Nickel remained supreme in its near-monopoly situation, with economies of scale and large profits; indeed, it proved to be one of the most successful Canadian companies globally. Yet, to the extent that McConnell and the other Canadians involved in the reorganization of 1928 had consciously been acting patriotically, in defence of British interests, their work was a failure. They had been unable to sell enough INCO securities to make the company really controlled by Canadians. International Nickel thus almost inevitably remained dominated by the Americans and likely to deal with a Germany hostile to the British Empire.

Indeed, that was exactly what happened in 1934, when Dulles arranged for INCO to supply unrefined nickel to IG Farben and the latter agreed to act as INCO's agent in selling refined nickel. Three years later, Dulles arranged for an increase in Farben's quota of unrefined ore for domestic use in the thriving German armaments industry. When Canada, in contemplation of war, attempted to enact legislation prohibiting the Canadian export of nickel to such potential adversaries as Germany, Japan, and Italy, Dulles successfully lobbied to suppress the legislation. INCO continued to export directly to Germany, and it secretly supplied through intermediaries even more ore to IG Farben than it was obliged publicly to admit.[35] Thus, until Germany declared war on the United States at the end of 1941, Canadian nickel was being exported to the chief enemy of and threat to the British Empire, Germany.

The record is silent as to what McConnell thought of INCO's actions with respect to Germany, whether before his resignation from the company's board in 1938 or afterwards. It is inconceivable, however, that, as a fervent supporter of the British Empire, he consciously supported the strategic threat that INCO posed to the British and Allied cause. To have done so would have be a betrayal of his deepest beliefs, and would have also have flown in the face of many of his actions, such as his financing of a shipment of Spitfire aircraft to Britain in 1940. In any case, it is clear that, as an investor, McConnell retained his faith in INCO for a remarkably long period of time. Even after the second market crash of October 1929, his INCO shares were worth $900,000 in total, which still was almost three times the $315,000 that he had apparently paid for them in 1927. He bought more shares after the Crash, and in 1930 he held about 50,000 shares through St Lawrence Sugar. Ten years later, however, he had only 25,000 shares, valued at $246,870. In 1952 he transferred to his Foundation 5,000 shares, then valued at $210,000, and profits from dispositions of shares of $145,000. Through his sales of INCO shares from 1927 to 1954, McConnell made total profits on his investment in INCO of about $815,000. He also earned INCO dividends, which rose from $5,000 in 1927 to $56,600 in 1937.

If INCO was one of McConnell's most enduring business interests, among the companies of which he was a director, the closest to his heart was probably Borden's. Dating to the 1850s, Borden's made daily deliveries of milk safe to drink to millions of children, and it made millions of dollars in the process. The company's association with Canada began with its acquisition of a small firm in Ingersoll, Ontario, in 1899,[36] and the Borden Milk Company was incorporated in Canada in 1912, changing its name to the Borden Company in 1920. The first headquarters of the new company were in Place Royale in Montreal, but it moved to Toronto in 1931, eventually occupying the ugly if picturesque City Dairy Building, on Spadina Circle, in 1938. Acquisitions of many other companies followed.

McConnell joined the board of the American parent, the Borden Company, in 1928 and served on it for ten years. Its chairman and majority owner was Jeremiah Milbank, the treasurer of the Republican Party, and a great friend who would give him much advice on philanthropy. Within a year, McConnell owned 2,000 common shares worth $180,000; nine years later, he owned 4,600 common shares worth more than $100,000, all of which were sold by 1944.

In the context of his portfolios, these were not large sums. But the Borden Company was probably the sole owner of Borden's of Canada, of which McConnell served as chairman, again until 1938. Borden's of Canada was important but only in eastern Canada. It bought its raw material from cartels of producers, and it seems to have been even less critical in determining its price than St Lawrence Sugar was in determining that of raw sugar. McConnell's role in pricing at Borden's of Canada was therefore either limited or non-existent, and the studies that have documented the restrictive trade practices of anti-combines aspects of the Canadian milk industry mostly relate to the years after McConnell's time with Borden's.

McConnell found through Borden's of the United States another business that was much more important to him than Borden's milk products. A subsidiary of the Borden Company was Corn Products Refining, in which McConnell held a much larger interest than in its parent – more than $1 million in 1929. This was actually another sugar company, as it manufactured fructose as well as cornstarch, one of the most important food products of the twentieth century.

And so what are we to make of a business career as wide-ranging as McConnell's in the period before the Second World War? To critics of corporate elites, McConnell may seem an ideal case study in conflicts of interest, the oppression of minority shareholders, and other crimes. But, in fact, his surviving financial records suggest that he was the steadiest of long-term investors, generally but not exclusively in conservatively run and dominant companies. As for his influence in these companies, the very breadth and number of his investments would have made it impossible for him to control all or even most of them, even if he had wanted to do so. True, businesses that he was invested in sometimes dealt with one another, but they did not necessarily do so to exploit either minority shareholders or consumers. As far as McConnell himself was concerned, he was already a very rich man before the speculative mania of the late 1920s, the very picture of new money, and by the early 1930s he was becoming at least in part the very image of old money, lavishly dispensing charity, administering family trusts, and bestowing his patronage on good causes. One of his main concerns was now how to conserve capital, rather than make it out of nothing. Accordingly, he simply had no need to engage personally in many of the self-serving practices banned by American securities legislation in the 1930s, practices that, in any case, had caused him considerable losses.

In itself, McConnell's almost steady rise in wealth from about 1909 to 1929 does not establish that he did not benefit from "interlocking" directorships, although this term suffers from the image of wildly different businesses, all marching in highly implausible lockstep. It also ignores other basic facts: that his ownership of various companies was, proportionately to the issued capital, overwhelming in some but almost negligible in others; that his investments fared variably over time, especially during the Depression, when many of them had little or no market value; and that McConnell, like all investors, made decisions as an individual, not as part of a cohesive group. On the last point, one should remember that, compared to most of his friends, he survived the Depression relatively unscathed, chiefly because he had not personally borrowed in order to buy securities.

In his personal life, the McConnell of the interwar period was, like the version that preceded and followed it, very Canadian. He never wanted to live in England or the United States, much less anywhere else. He could easily have maintained secondary residences in these countries but he did not. Towards the end of his life, he tried to escape the Canadian winter to the sun of Georgia, Florida, Bermuda, and the Bahamas, but he was content with staying in hotels, some very modest, in those places. His business interests in Canada always drew him home, which is how he had regarded Canada since his first trip to England in 1904.

Yet his home was never economically wholly self-sufficient. He and his contemporaries realized that even Canada, vast and rich as it was, could not and should not be self-contained: they wanted to sell the products of Canada abroad, and to sell the products of abroad in Canada. McConnell's businesses are therefore remarkable not merely for their variety of products, but also for how variously they defined Canadian business. Two of McConnell's major Canadian businesses, Goodwins and St Lawrence Sugar, catered almost exclusively to the Canadian market, the first, however, marketing mainly finished goods from other countries, and the second marketing raw sugar from overseas refined in Canada. Holt Renfrew and Ogilvie Flour Mills sold both within Canada and abroad. McConnell did not hesitate to serve as a director of Dominion Rubber, which traced its thoroughly Canadian origins to Lorne McGibbon and but already been bought by United States Rubber. McConnell also aided in the takeover of much of the dairy distribution in eastern Canada by the Borden Company of the United States. At the same time, McConnell's view of business as inherently international assumed the flows of investment capital, including Canadian capital, in various directions. If opportunities arose to encourage growth in the Canadian economy with outside investment, McConnell was happy to ally himself with American companies to take advantage of them. He would not have recognized any easy equation between American investment in Canada and the automatic shifting of Canadian resources to American head offices and investors.

In 1928 the *Gazette* claimed that McConnell had saved Brazilian Traction and International Nickel for Canadian investors and from takeover by foreigners.[37] This is an overstatement. Even after his defence of Brazilian Traction and having become its largest individual shareholder in 1928, the company remained largely in the hands of the European owners of Sidro. And, even after his refinancing of INCO in the same year, it remained largely in the hands of Americans. It is true that he helped to preserve the Canadian management of Brazilian, and that he increased Canadian ownership of INCO, but he did not "save" the enterprises for Canada. Probably no individual could have performed this salvation single-handed. But, in comparison with anyone else, he probably did the most to this end, not least by investing his own money in them. For him, patriotism was not an absolute. It was to be practised as circumstances allowed, not to be trumpeted about. As in his work as a financier and as a philanthropist, patriotism in business was the art of making limited ends possible.

The political conservatism associated with his ventures was nothing in comparison with the financial conservatism of his prudent management, and yet neither form of conservatism could compare to his fascination with new products and technologies. He was invested widely in the economy of his time, and no detail, technical or financial, was too small for him. Nor was any effort towards tangible productivity too large, or any reverse in his investments discouraging, much less fatal, to more investment. This business philosophy was to be tested by the Depression of the 1930s, but ultimately it survived intact.

CHAPTER TEN

Insecurities: McConnell's Investments, 1921–39

"There's one indication of how smart he is," one employee said recently. "He deals in staples – newspapers which everyone must continue to read to find out what's going on, and sugar and flour which everybody must buy to live."

"Sugar Baron," *New Liberty*, March 1949, 23

Both in Canada and internationally, the business world between the two world wars sparkled with a galaxy of financiers and captains of industry. In the company of only a handful or so other Canadians, McConnell was a major player on Wall Street just as he was on St James Street. Such flamboyant colleagues as Lord McGowan, the chemicals manufacturer, Lord Kemsley, the newspaper proprietor, A.R. Graustein, the utilities magnate, Sir James Dunn, the mining executive, and Alfred Loewenstein, the Belgian takeover artist, embodied his age as surely as the Prince of Wales and Hollywood stars in other spheres. They were powerful personalities, self-made but consciously harking back to a swaggering past. The anonymous grey-flannel suit and the corporate credos of the post-1945 executive were not their style.

Neither McConnell nor any of his colleagues, however, even remotely resembled the so-called robber barons of the late nineteenth century, to whom they have been wrongly compared, in appearance, or manner, or even business strategy. These essentially interwar businessmen were enriching themselves in new ways, because many of the pre-war industries were facing bankruptcy, American anti-trust legislation was changing the ways by which businesses generally could grow big, and the First World War's legacy of regulation, taxation, and product innovation to meet ever-shifting consumer demand was posing new challenges to business growth all over the world. In breaking up international cartels, such as among chemical manufacturers, the Great War had also opened up new patterns of investment, while innovations in accounting, engineering and management, and technology seemed to lend an almost scientific basis to finance.

Many of the interwar businessmen were audacious speculators, and many of their fortunes were fleeting or ill-fated. Among the more respectable, McGowan, for example, saw the collapse of his investments, Graustein saw the dismantling of his power-and-paper empire, and Loewenstein either jumped or was pushed from the airplane in which he was flying. Though associated with these and many others, McConnell somehow avoided falling with them, and indeed at least in Canada he was one of the few to survive the Crash of 1929 as still a very rich man, even if one still decidedly diminished in his wealth.

The fact that McConnell himself was a generally successful investor demonstrates both his maturity and his flexibility. There was no room among investors for unthinking loyalty. McConnell showed no hesitation in joining the board of International Paper and Power (IP&P), an increasingly successful rival of Sir Herbert Holt's Canada Paper, while sitting with Holt on the boards of Holt Renfrew, Sun Life, and Montreal Light Heat and Power. Sentiment was irrelevant beside an instinct for self-preservation, if only because the interests of such men were ultimately so interconnected. They themselves had set up the rules of the game of high finance, and when the house in which they were playing was being blown down by a hurricane, they would prop it up as individuals.

Unlike Holt, McConnell remained studiously in the background in the interwar years with their increased insolvency. Although not part of the Royal Bank board that bailed out Holt, Brown and Gundy after the collapse of Canada Paper, he had been part of the Sun Life investment committee that approved the investments that led to its theoretical incapacity to meet all Sun Life's obligations. In the world of politics, he, like most of his friends, supported Prime Minister Bennett, partly because Bennett, as a close colleague of Max Aitken's, a CPR lawyer, a director of the Royal Bank, an owner of E.B. Eddy Paper Mills, and an investor in Calgary utilities, was cut from the same cloth. Critics might complain about Bennett's heartlessness, amid all the suffering. But he was in fact pompous rather than heartless. Even more of a devout Methodist than McConnell, he gave much from his own fortune to relieve cases of hardship, and eventually he came to pledge himself to a Canadian equivalent of President Roosevelt's New Deal. McConnell accepted Bennett's policies, with all their contradictions and their ultimate rejection by the electorate, probably more than those of any other prime minister. He himself saw the challenges of the Depression as unprecedented, and, despite Bennett's failed strategies in response, McConnell could not believe that any of Bennett's opponents had anything better to offer.

In his investments, McConnell was probably neither better nor worse than many of his associates after the Crash, but, unlike them, he himself never came close to insolvency. The extent of the anguish on St James Street generally during the Depression is a rich source of anecdote but it has never been quantified, and it may never be. Suicides and bankruptcy were common among the former rich as they were among the traditionally poor, perhaps because of the perceived need in Westmount, where many of the stockbrokers were now living, to keep up appearances, rather than because they were actually starving. For most people of means, however, the Depression meant economizing rather than suicide. Every family faced its own challenges. McConnell's did not suffer materially, but he was acutely aware of the suffering on St James Street and well beyond.

To Patrick Ashley Cooper, the governor of the Hudson's Bay Company, it was McConnell's charity during the Depression that made the greatest impression: "He will head any important subscription-list with $50,000 [about $740,800 in 2008], and his minor gifts to all sorts of small deserving cases are legion. All sorts, great and small, have been saved from disaster. They say that, in the financial slump of 1929/31, he placed his wealth at the disposal of many important people. His financial generosity is only balanced by the generosity of his services, for he has headed innumerable financial drives to help the University, Hospitals etc., and there is scarcely anything in either English or French Montreal that he has not assisted."[1]

Various brokerage houses failed in the "Dirty Thirties." One of the most spectacular examples was that of McDougall and Cowans, which operated offices across Canada. This firm found itself insolvent in October 1931 not because of trading losses but because Britain had abandoned the Gold Standard, which resulted in the loss of a quarter of the value of collateral it had put up in the US. But McConnell, rather than see it wound up or reorganized, lent Percy Cowans, one of his closest friends since 1901, the money to meet his losses, which were said to amount to $2 million ($26,490,000 in 2008 terms). The result was that McDougall and Cowans was the only one of the three failed brokerages on St James Street in 1931 to revive, and McConnell himself remained loyal to the firm and to Cowans's descendants even after Cowans's death in 1954, vowing to give it business as long as there was a Cowans "on the Street."[2]

How rich was McConnell, so that he could make such a loan?[3] In 1921, as we have seen, McConnell took out loans for $7 million ($75 million in 2008) to bail out St Lawrence Sugar. He secured these loans with securities held in his own name and valued at more than $10 million ($107,240,000 in 2008), including all his shares in St Lawrence valued at $1, even though their par value was $100 each. Of this $10 million, $6 million was in tax-free Victory Loans, or 60 per cent of the total. Of the remaining 40 per cent, there were large holdings in a wide range of enterprises, among them: Cuba Cane Sugar ($381,000) and Cuban American Sugar ($234,000); the Bank of Montreal and the Royal Bank of Canada, totalling $450,000; various utilities, including the MLHPC, totalling $492,094; railways, including the CPR and Brazilian Traction, totalling $405,153; textiles, including Dominion Textile, totalling $728,579; mining, totalling $55,001; Ogilvie Flour Mills ($90,000); oil, totalling $50,748; cement, totalling $135,000; property and investment management, totalling $150,000; and paper, including IP&P, totalling $165,500. About 32 per cent of his capital was invested in companies that he did not own control. Relatively modestly, he was invested in companies over which he probably exercised significant managerial control. These included Dominion Manufacturers, Goodwin's, and Holt Renfrew, totalling $331,184, or slightly more than 3 per cent of the total.[4]

In summary, by the end of 1921, McConnell was able to keep 60 per cent of his assets in tax-free government bonds, and over a third more (including the minor holdings) in corporate bonds and stock outside the companies that he was actively invested in. With over $340,000 in tax-free annual income from Victory Loans, and income from other interest, dividends, director's fees, salaries, and rents, his financial situation was more than secure, so long as his sugar business recovered. To put his annual income, which may have approached $6,730,000 in 2008 Canadian dollars, into some perspective, the average wage rate in Canada in 1921 was $1,140 or $12,225 in 2008 dollars. His annual tax-free income from Victory Loans alone was almost 178 times the average wage.

At any rate, McConnell's sugar business did turn round, and by 1925 he had paid back his bank loan of $7 million. It is not clear whether he did this in instalments or in one payment. But in either case the effect was that his personal stock portfolio was no longer frozen as collateral for the loan. He could now use it as he wished, and – as already recounted – in 1925 he applied it to the purchase of all the unissued shares of St Lawrence Sugar, and he bought out the other shareholders as well. The tax advantages of the new private company and its portfolio were considerable; income from the securities hived off into the family trusts was taxable in the hands of the beneficiaries under the trusts, thus spreading the tax burden beyond McConnell personally. Under existing law, moreover, the vesting of the rest of the portfolio in St Lawrence rendered the Canadian dividends from it free of tax.

The same was not true of McConnell's American dividends, which were subject to American tax. But when McConnell set up his charitable foundation in 1937, and for several years afterwards, he endowed it overwhelmingly with American securities, and he ultimately obtained a tax ruling from the United States that dividends from his American shares paid directly to his Foundation should be free of American tax. Thus, a good part, probably the bulk, of the income from his assets was sheltered from tax. This fact did more than make McConnell richer than ever. Insofar as it enabled the Foundation's endowment to grow without tax consequences, it significantly increased his capacity as a philanthropist.

All that said, McConnell remained, as Prime Minister Mackenzie King was to observe in the 1940s, the largest individual taxpayer in Canada, despite his aggressive efforts to minimize his taxes.[5] He liked taxes no more than any taxpayer, but he came to support government funding, particularly of health care and of education, if private funds were inadequate, and to see taxation as a necessary complement to, though not a replacement for, private giving. In any event, McConnell's actions in reorganizing St Lawrence and the trusts that emerged from it were not merely legal ploys: they also demonstrated his continuing talent as a financier. So beautifully do the parts of his new structures dovetail into one another that it is hard to avoid surmising that he probably was developing in his mind, as early as 1921, a comprehensive plan for the long-term employment of his capital. Such a plan, whenever it emerged, was a necessary outgrowth of his view that capital must be used productively, not merely hoarded.

The onset of the wrenching period called retrospectively the Great Depression would test McConnell's business philosophy, to say nothing of his investment skills. It began with the collapse of the stock market in New York on 24 October 1929, followed by a worse collapse five days later. As in the case of failure of the Knickerbocker Trust in New York in 1907, leading bankers headed by J.P. Morgan tried to stem this crisis, but this time they failed. Not everyone was immediately affected by the Crash; most did not own shares sold in the market, and so they lost nothing. Those most affected were purchasers of shares on margin – meaning the borrowing money on investments – and they numbered about 600,000. According to oral tradition, McConnell, at least after the First World War, never borrowed money in order to invest in securities. This is likely to be true, since he was never personally short of cash, even after taking out his bank loans to rescue St Lawrence Sugar. He was also profoundly conservative in valuing his assets in downturns, as is evident from his ledgers. Even so, in the single month following the Crash, McConnell's portfolio declined from $45,223,000 to $16,644,000.

As the Depression rolled on, other disasters unrelated to the Crash befell the American and, by extension, world economy. One was a drought that blighted the American Midwest and the Canadian prairies, destroying crops and bankrupting farmers. Then, protectionist policies stifled world trade, which delayed recovery. By 1931, the Depression had reached its lowest point, and, within two years, recovery was in sight for various sectors of the economy. But it took the demands of a new world war, which began in September 1939 for the British Empire, including Canada, to shake off the Depression for good – a development that also banished the Depression in the United States, which, however, did not officially enter the war until December 1941.

On the day of the first of the two crashes in October, McConnell was at Mercy Hospital in Chicago, having surgery done on his hand. While turning a tap at his former house on Redpath Street, he had twisted the tendons in the hand and had developed a condition known as Dupuytren's contracture. This was an extremely painful condition, as was the surgery necessary to release the tendons, known as Z-oplasty after the z-shaped incision that it necessitated, and recovery was slow. McConnell was to have surgery again on this same hand in 1933, and in 1929 he was in hospital from 19 to 29 October. Forty-one floral arrangements arrived at his room, from his employees at St

Lawrence Sugar, his office staff on St James Street, and assorted friends, including Herbert Molson and R.B. Bennett. The upshot of the hospital stay in 1929, however, was that he was probably unable to do anything at all to salvage his portfolio as the markets were collapsing.

It has been said that McConnell had known some time before that a severe market "correction" was on its way. Yet it is more probable that he did not foresee the market crash, since he had been investing heavily, particularly in investment trusts, for several months leading up to October 1929. McConnell's advice to the governor general, Lord Willingdon, both before and after, the Crashes of 24 and 29 October (now usually conflated as "the Crash"), seems to confirm McConnell's optimistic view. Because of the strains on his purse and of the gyrations of the stock market in the late 1920s, Willingdon, even before the Crash, had been growing increasingly worried about his finances. As early as February 1928, he had written to his son Inigo that the New York market had been "rotten of late but McConnell keeps smiling so I hope my affairs are going well."[6] By September, he was lamenting to his son and daughter-in-law, with reference to the personal expenditures necessary to keep up Government House: "Unless stocks & shares go brilliantly well in the next 3 years, I shall be completely broke from excessive entertaining & shall want you both to feed & house yr. ancient parent during his declining years."[7]

But Canada, in Willingdon's view, still held out the promise of prosperity. As Willingdon saw it: "This country is certain to go ahead in all its industrial concerns during the next few years, & I want to make what I can in some ventures ... I have now in my private acct: here 10,000£ much of wh: I have made & which is invested in good industrials wh: will go higher. I have also 15000£ whc: McConnell is looking after for me and whc: shows up to date a profit of 20000£ making my total holding there [sic] 35000£ which by the end of the year shd: be considerably better."[8] On the assumption that Willingdon had given McConnell the £15,000 in 1927 or 1928, its rise to £35,000 in a few months shows how much was becoming expected by Willingdon of McConnell's expertise. In the summer of 1929, the McConnells joined the Willingdons for a four-day cruise on Georgian Bay on the yacht of the shipowner James Playfair, during which they reviewed Willingdon's portfolio. McConnell had bought the governor general shares in Brazilian Traction and pronounced himself on the cruise "sanguine" about them, though no "spectacular" rise was likely.[9] Then came the Crash in October.

By 16 November 1929, Willingdon was calculating that he still had $150,000 invested in North America at post-Crash prices: "The one thing I am anxious about is McConnell and his investments for me. He did, as you know, a great deal of his business in New York, & unfortunately for him he was away sick in California [sic] at the time of the crash, & I've not been able to hear anything of him yet. However, I hope he weathered the storm all right."[10]

Then, early in January 1930, the governor general was hopeful that the harvest would be good "& I hope to come back with something to the good as a result of my life here": "I went to play tennis with J.W. McConnell in Montreal the other day, & he was in good form & had just given his wife a new Rolls-Royce as a Xmas present. Not much sign of difficulty there, though I think my account with him is back a bit. Still he is quite confident he'll pick it all up again ere long. Poor chap he was in Chicago having an operation performed on him the 1st day of the crash whc: was a little hard."[11] In August 1930 Willingdon was finding everyone, including presumably McConnell, "supremely confident" of economic recovery, but the situation remained grim. "I haven't," he reported to Inigo, "seen McConnell for some time but think he's saved something from the wreck."[12] This correspondence between Willingdon and his son shows in what high esteem McConnell's ability was held by the governor general, but it is also suggestive that McConnell himself was far from "out of the market" at the time of the Crash. And there is more evidence to the same effect.

There is a also long-standing myth that McConnell, like Joseph Kennedy, Charles Merrill, and Bernard Baruch, had sold substantial stocks before the Crash, anticipating the collapse of their values. Conrad Black, for example, says of Sir Herbert Holt that he "did not weather the Great Depression as handily as McConnell, who had foreseen it and largely withdrawn from the summer of 1929, awaiting the debacle with tens of millions of dollars in cash."[13] Although this is correct about Holt, a surviving portfolio of McConnell's disproves the claim that he had anticipated the Crash by withdrawing from the market. It not only describes his holdings as of 23 September 1929, about a month before the first of two collapses of the market in October; it also gives the prices of these securities in November 1929 and in July 1936. It can be seen from this portfolio statement that some of his holdings declined to nothing in value, and that the total assets declined by about 40 per cent at the depth of the Depression.

From McConnell's own portfolios, overwhelmingly in common shares, we know that he held, in the name of St Lawrence Sugar, $48,520,990 in securities as of 23 September 1929, and that this total had declined to $29,806,432 by 26 November 1929.[14] This was a loss of about 39 per cent, which mirrored the decline in the market as a whole in these two weeks. Though such was the common experience of holders of common shares at the time, it raises the question of McConnell's expertise as an investor. By his later years, particularly in the 1940s and 1950s, McConnell had developed the reputation of a legendary investor, and his close colleague Peter McEntyre is said to have declared that McConnell could have written the bible of "value investing," *Security Analysis* by Graham and Dodd, published in 1934. But, if McEntyre was right, why did McConnell's portfolio not do better than those of others in the month following the Crash? Why had he not withdrawn at least partially from the market in anticipation of the loss of almost $20 million in a few weeks? And after the Crash, why did he not see the downward trend of market values over the next few years and cut his losses, at least more than he did? Owing to the fortuitous survival of McConnell's portfolio from the Crash and its aftermath, a fairly firm answer to these questions, in some respects, is possible if not simple.

The principal component of McConnell's losses took the form of utility holding companies and investment trusts (the latter would be later called leveraged mutual funds though within a holding-company structure). The practice of investment trusts was to borrow money, using as collateral securities held by them. This meant that, insofar as he invested in these trusts, McConnell – despite his reluctance to borrow – *was leveraged*. He may not have personally taken out loans to buy shares, but the managers of the investment trusts that he was invested in did; and, to this extent, McConnell was subject to the losses caused by leverage, more precisely to the inversion of the borrowing process as the value of the collateral for loans was collapsing.

There are other examples of disaster. By 1929, McConnell was heavily invested in Power and Consolidated Gas (later Consolidated Edison) of New York, companies put together by Floyd Carlisle in that year. Carlisle had allied himself to J.P. Morgan, head of the quintessential investment bank, which took on as clients only the rich.[15] Morgan and Carlisle set up a holding company, the United Corporation, to take over the assets of various operators who together produced more than a third of the electrical power in the eastern states. United was not formally linked to Carlisle's Niagara Hudson Power and Consolidated Gas of New York, in which McConnell was also invested. But, at the time of the Crash, for reasons unknown, in his 1929 portfolio, McConnell listed holdings amounting to $1,350,000 in the United Corporation under the name of one of its subsidiaries, the Public Service Corporation of New Jersey. This was one of the largest holdings in his utilities portfolio, exceeding the $1.2 million that he had in the MLHPC at the time of the Crash. The investment had declined to $790,000 by November of the same year, and to $72,000 by 1939.

Another Morgan-sponsored holding of McConnell's was in the Alleghany Corporation, which may, before the Crash, have been fairly profitable for Morgan, although it brought down upon him the wrath of the public. Alleghany was a holding company for the highly leveraged railway and real-estate empire of Oris P. and Matnis J. Van Sweringen, who in 1929 controlled the fifth-largest railway system in the United States, and was one of the most infamous pyramid schemes of the time. Unlike others, McConnell did not make a big profit on buying and selling shares in Alleghany shortly before the Crash. He was not on the Morgan list of favoured clients for its shares, any more than he had been for United shares. McConnell had only $12,000 in Alleghany at the time of the Crash; it declined to $10,000 a month later, and it fell more sharply in the autumn of 1930, when each share sunk from $56 to $10. By 1935, the stock had declined further to 37.5 cents a share.

McConnell's instincts again led him astray when it came to the American Founders Corporation, one of the most ambitious holding companies in this period. Incorporated in 1922, it included four subsidiary investment companies and in 1929 became part of the United Founders Corporation, which also held substantial interests in other ventures. McConnell personally held a direct interest in only one of these firms. And he did not have a direct interest either in the Founders-related Hydro-Electric Securities Corporation, incorporated by Alfred Loewenstein and Sir Herbert Holt in Canada in 1926. Still, his holdings in the Founders group totalled just over $1 million in September 1929, which fell to $611,119 by 16 November.

Then there was Sun Life. If the Montreal of McConnell's heyday could be symbolized by a single company, that company would surely have been Sun Life Assurance. The Sun Life Building, facing Dominion (later Dorchester) Square and built over the course of two decades, from 1914 to 1933, projected such a grandiose, luxurious, and permanent presence that it was effectively a monument, as well as one of the principal office buildings of the city. At twenty-six storeys, it was known as the tallest building in the British Empire, and it seemed to embody all the solidity of the English-speaking enterprise that had transformed what had once been a small settlement of a few thousand souls into a powerhouse of global commerce.

In London, too, Sun Life's headquarters projected great symbolic weight, standing as it did, alongside the CPR building and Canada House, the office of the High Commission, as a proud representative of the Dominion in the heart of the empire, Trafalgar Square. That seemed only fitting, for the company's reach traversed the globe. Almost wherever McConnell the Sun Life director went in his travels – from Bombay to Cape Town to San Francisco – he was met and escorted by the local Sun Life representative. If there was a local representative of the Bank of Montreal, of which McConnell was also a director, McConnell would meet him too. The identity between the boards of the major Montreal banks and Sun Life created a consensus among big investors, to which McConnell was not immune. They agreed that Sun Life hired the sharpest stock analysts and portfolio managers in Montreal, if not in Canada as a whole.

The history of Sun Life dates back to 1865,[16] when Mathew Hamilton Gault incorporated the Sun Insurance Company of Montreal. In 1871 Sun Insurance organized itself as the Sun Mutual Life Insurance Company, with Gault as managing director, and ten years later, in order to distance itself from other companies that had failed while being called "mutual," the company renamed itself Sun Life Assurance. With shareholders rather than policyholders now owning it, Sun Life grew impressively through the 1890s onward. By 1891, it could boast that it provided the shareholders with the potential profits of a joint-stock company, in addition to the safety to policyholders of a mutual one. Its assets had risen six times in three years, and in later years it expanded territorially as well as through acquisition. In 1894 it opened an office in London, and in 1895 one in Detroit; it took over nine Canadian competitors, one Chinese company, and two American companies. By 1900, Sun Life seemed to embody the soul of probity combined with a capacity to set the pace for the insurance industry as a whole. It was famous for hiring dour Scots accountants and actuaries, and thus for projecting the essential financial soundness of Montreal.

By the end of the nineteenth century, as have seen in connection with the career of McConnell's early partner G.F. Johnston, the managers of insurance companies were beginning to use the accumulated premiums of policyholders to invest in the stock market, in order to increase the value of their companies for shareholders, as opposed to policyholders. In an era when few but the very rich invested in stocks and bonds, far more people apparently saw the insurance policy as a safe vehicle for investment, as well as a source of protection, since a life policy in particular guaranteed a return on premiums paid on the death of the policyholder. Once the investment departments of insurance companies strayed from their investment in bonds with low return into potentially more lucrative common shares, their losses on the latter potentially threatened the solvency of their companies.[17]

Under the ascendancy first of Robertson Macaulay (president from 1889 to 1915) and then of his son, T.B. (president from 1915 to 1934), Sun Life's growth seemed inexorable. But, by the time of the Royal Commission on Life Insurance in 1907, the aggressive investment practices of the insurance companies were becoming painfully obvious. Nothing much changed thereafter. Three months *after* the Crash of October 1929, Macaulay declared: "We believe in the future of Montreal, of New York, of Chicago ... we believe even more in the future of our entire nations – both Canada and the United States. We have hitched our investment policy to the star of this continent."[18] By this time, 52 per cent of Sun Life's investments were in common shares, which in 1900 had been considered speculative and dangerous.

McConnell appears to have made his own first investment in an insurance policy in the 1890s, and he was to continue to insure his life heavily, particularly after his marriage.[19] Nor was he just a policyholder. In December 1928 he joined the board of Sun Life. In addition, he bought shares of Sun Life between 1921 and 1929, for an average price of $2,500. His portfolio for 1929 showed that he now owned 300 shares. This made the total purchase price (between 1921 and 1929) of his holdings about $75,000. In September 1929 these were worth $3,500 each for a total of $1,050,000 in market value. The same shares fell to $2,300 each, or $690,000 in total, by November. By July 1936, they were worth $500 each, for a total market value of $150,000.[20] The performance of his shares reflects the essential collapse of the value of the company from 1929 to 1932 by 96 per cent, with a faint recovery evident by 1936. Much of its losses were in the investment trusts of Samuel Insull, once Thomas Edison's secretary and a brilliant builder of utilities in the American Midwest, which he financed through a pyramid of holding companies, all of which collapsed. Although Insull was found innocent in court of any crime, a fact often forgotten, his financial collapse was one of the greatest scandals of the Depression, and it led directly to Roosevelt's Public

Utility Holding Company Act of 1935, which placed severe limits on what holding companies might do.

The crisis over the Sun Life investments came to a head with ferocious attacks on the company by J.J. Harpell, author, publisher, and editor of a sporadically published newspaper called the *Journal of Commerce*. Harpell had been a policyholder of Sun Life since 1914 and the president of the Policy-holders' Association since 1929. Though he did know enough about insurance and economics to cause Sun Life acute discomfort, he did not know enough about business and the law to sustain as seriously plausible, much less to prove, his wilder accusations. These reached a crescendo in 1932, when he claimed in his newspaper that – in an era riveted on such gangsters as Al Capone – T.B. Macaulay was one of the two greatest crooks in the world, the other being Ivar Kreuger, the so-called Swedish match king, who had committed suicide and in whose collapsed empire Sun Life had invested. The essence of Harpell's more substantial accusation was that the value of the accumulated premiums of Sun Life was at least theoretically inadequate to pay out its policyholders, should all its policyholders die under present market conditions. This theoretical deficiency was just theoretical, since nobody could predict when all the existing policyholders might die, or when market conditions might improve to increase the ability of the company to pay out. This accusation was not litigated, but his claim that Macaulay was comparable to Kreuger led to criminal charges.

When Macaulay laid a criminal information with the police against him, leading to Harpell's trial for criminal libel, most of Harpell's accusations were found in court to be so extravagant in nature that they were in the preliminary proceedings struck out as incapable of proof, and thus as unworthy of litigation. Macaulay had indeed framed his information well, focusing on Harpell's claim that Macaulay was one of the world's greatest criminals, rather than on claims examinable in the discovery process. Chief Justice R.A.E. Greenshields took the view that this allegation in particular was unprovable, and he convicted Harpell of criminal libel and sentenced him to three months in prison, after which he was obliged to post a bond of $1,000 to keep the peace, with a further surety of $1,000.[21] His appeal was denied and he served his sentence.

The immediate effect of this ruling was to quash any judicial consideration of Macaulay's conduct and, by extension, of the business practices of Sun Life. Nevertheless, it is clear from the court record that there was initially considerable interest, at least among Harpell's counsel, in Sun Life investments in the bankrupt Insull utilities empire. Insull, though not mentioned by Harpell in his newspaper in the same breath as Macaulay and Kreuger, was by this time seen well beyond North America as more than Kreuger's equal in venality. Macaulay seems to have invested much of his own fortune in the Insull enterprises and to have induced Sun Life to do the same, perhaps to shore it up as it came crashing down, which was a clear conflict of interest.

Harpell may have initially hoped that demonstrating such breach of fiduciary duty would save his case. Depositions were taken of employees of Insull, and correspondence between Sun Life officers and Insull was entered into the evidence, but the conviction of Harpell of criminal defamation precluded any examination by the court of Macaulay's possible breach.

In the end, however, Prime Minister Bennett, concerned above all with the long-term credit of Canada, permitted through legislation the revaluation of the Sun Life portfolio to what it had been before the worst of its declines. So the crisis passed. But, with regard to McConnell, the question arises as to his role in the debacle. He spent a decade on the Sun Life board and as a member of its investment committee, from 1928 to 1938, and the investment portfolio that rendered the insurance company insolvent during that time to some extent mirrored his own personal holdings, although he owned no part of Insull's businesses. When T.B. Macaulay personally came to be criticized for the investments – indeed these criticisms and others would force him to retire from Sun Life in 1934 – he raised in his own defence the point that the investment committee had approved all of them, and the directors likewise. McConnell also appears to have made no effort to resign from the committee or the board before the situation became clear. The similarity of his portfolio and the company's, then, suggests that Sun Life and McConnell shared the same point of view towards investing, and strongly influenced each other.

In contrast to the accusations made against Macaulay with regard to his Insull shares, or against Lord McGowan with regard to General Motors shares – which McGowan induced his Imperial Chemical Industries to buy to support the value of his own holdings in General Motors – it seems that McConnell was never accused of a conflict of interest. Macaulay and McGowan had apparently propped up the values of their personal investments by either preventing their own companies from selling corporate investments in their personal investments or by forcing their own companies (particularly Sun Life) to buy shares in companies in which they had personally invested, in a declining market. McConnell held most of his investments in a portfolio nominally owned by St Lawrence, a company of which he was the sole owner, and so no possibility of conflict of interest arose. He had genuinely believed in his investments and he accepted his losses, and his sounder investments pulled him through. There was no reason, therefore, for him to conclude that common shares as such were bad, although the leveraging of the investment trusts and the utility holding companies had been.

What lessons did McConnell draw from his staggering losses in 1929 and afterwards, particularly in his utilities investments? He seems to have left no evidence of his views, but his conduct through the 1930s and 1940s provides some clues. First, he does not seem to have accepted that holding companies were in principle bad. Brazilian Traction was a very successful holding company, which he knew well as probably its largest individual shareholder. In any case, he embraced the "reformed" holding-company structure put forward by Wendell Willkie, and by implication he rejected the feverish shifting of assets and borrowing in which Insull had been engaged before his fall. But, especially since Insull was not convicted of any crime, it is likely that McConnell saw his collapse as essentially the result of misfortune rather than misfeasance. Be this as it may, all efforts by Willkie and others to present a newly acceptable face for holding companies failed with the passage of the US Public Utility Holding Company Act, with the resultant shrinking or even dissolution of many huge corporations, including Willkie's own Commonwealth & Southern.

McConnell thus appears to have been fairly unrepentant about the frenzied financing of the 1920s, despite his own immense losses. He was tough not because he was intransigent but because he was flexible, and because he adhered to the principle that timing is the essence of successful investment. It does not follow that he believed in what certain "value" investors call the fallacy of "market timing," reduced to "day trading" in some cases. It appears, rather, that he grasped that valuation and therefore marketability were bound to fluctuate, sometimes irrationally, and that it was part of a good investment strategy to discount these fluctuations and to aim at the long term, as long as the "underlying" value of the security remained. He held on to his stocks, perhaps all of them, through the Depression, and in 1951 his portfolio retained many of the same holdings that it had had in 1929. Since by then many of them had returned to their 1929 valuations, his own portfolio demonstrated the worth of his strategy of holding onto "good" stocks.

To this extent, McEntyre was correct in surmising that McConnell was a "value" investor who "could have written Graham and Dodd," the bible of such later successful investors as Sir John Templeton and Warren Buffett. This is also why McConnell almost undoubtedly supported the initiatives of Sun Life, the Royal Bank, and others to attach "fictitious" values to their portfolios in the early 1930s. These values were based on historical experience, but also on some notion that there was a fundamentally "sane" and irreducible market value that would eventually be restored to take into account the assets underlying the securities, even if some had to be written off. It was an optimistic belief because it assumed the return of "normality." It was also optimistic in implying that there would be growth rather than mere stability or even further decline in future valuations, although it was silent about when normality might return.

By 1935, even though McConnell believed that the worst of the market collapse was probably over, he foresaw a continuation of serious problems in some of the industries in which he was most interested, namely, newsprint, flour milling, and textiles.[22] And what was his opinion of common stocks after all his losses? His 1939 portfolio reveals total holdings of $23,907,000, of which $18,260,000 or 76.3 per cent was in common stocks, and his 1951 portfolio amounted to $82,137,000, of which $75,606,000 or

92.05 per cent was in common stocks.[23] From these proportions, it is clear that he remained an optimist about economic growth. After all his market losses during the Depression, he retained his faith in holding equities, though not in investment trusts and holding companies.

Even before the Crash, McConnell never showed much interest in either corporate or government bonds, at least after 1921, when tax-free Victory Loans comprised more than half of his portfolio. Despite the fact that he was entitled to tax-free income from some of his Victory Loans up to 1933, in 1929 he held no government bonds whatever; and only $169,000 or 0.37 per cent of his portfolio was in corporate bonds. In 1939 he held $3,485,000 in government bonds, making up 14.5 per cent of his total portfolio, but all of these were segregated in the family trusts. Also in 1939, he held $2,132,000 in corporate bonds in the St Lawrence portfolio, and $30,000 in the Foundation port-folio, but at that stage he had made up his mind to transfer, over time, securities from the first portfolio to the second. The 1951 portfolio confirms his lack of interest in fixed-return investments, since it held only $3,433,000 or 4.18 per cent in corporate bonds and $3,098,000 or 3.7 per cent in government bonds. In that year, the Founda-tion held $2,177,000 in corporate bonds, and $1,963,000 in government bonds, while he personally held $314,000 in company bonds and $837,000 in government bonds. Even in the Foundation's portfolio in 1951, the bond holdings were paltry in compari-son with the $40,385,000 that it held in shares of companies.

One remarkable element of the growth of his portfolio was his investment in Canada Cement. It was true that in 1912 he was a modest investor in Max Aitken's controver-sial amalgamation, but he was not central to Aitken's scheme. In 1921 McConnell held only 2,000 common shares in the company, worth $110,000 or 4.6 per cent of his port-folio, figures that had increased by 1939 to $490,000 and 2.6 per cent. By 1951, he held $8,453,000 in its shares, which was still only 11.18 per cent of his portfolio. Yet, at this point, he may have been the largest individual shareholder in the company. McEntyre became president, which suggests that McConnell's influence was substantial if not preponderant. Much popular opinion even in the 1950s suggested that Aitken had "got away" with some fraud, in looting the assets of the companies that he had amal-gamated into Canada Cement forty or so years before. It did not acknowledge that the company had actually grown in value ever since its amalgamation, apart from the Depression when almost no companies grew.

Some, including people who knew him fairly well, speculated that McConnell him-self had got his start with Aitken by defrauding the public through Canada Cement, or at least Sir Sandford Fleming, of what had been rightfully theirs. McConnell's internal records, and the records of the company, do not support such an accusation. What the records do show is that McConnell became a large investor in the company long after Aitken had retired from it. They also show that all of Aitken's amalgamations, including Canada Cement, in any case rewarded their investors handsomely in the four or five decades following his move to England. Critics said that Aitken's move was an effort to escape prosecution, although he was to return to Canada at least annually for much of the remainder of his long life. Time had disproved the many vociferous critics of stockwatering, at least in McConnell's estimation. His commitment in later years to Canada Cement, the most scandalous victim of stockwatering of all in the eyes of the enemies of promotions, reaped for him rich rewards.

The one luxury that his wealth afforded him, even in the pit of the Depression when he had lost so much, was patience in investing. Time was to catch up with him, as much as with anyone else, but he laid solid investments aside for his family trusts, for his Foundation, and for the numerous institutional and individual beneficiaries of his gifts of stock. Time likewise disproved the most sweeping vociferous critics of holding common stock, a practice for which he always counselled patience. The rising value of his portfolio, from 1939 to 1951, suggests that his judgment here was also correct. As a result of his enormous losses, he grasped the importance of fundamental stock analysis. He also saw a fundamental difference between value and price, which was the basis of Lawrence H. Sloan's famous book on "the long pull," a term used by both him and McConnell.[24]

Substantial as McConnell's pre-Crash portfolio was, its significant decline following the Crash does not demonstrate that McConnell was a talented investor in every respect. Not only had he not taken his profits on time, he had caught the pre-Crash speculative fever and invested in some of the worst securities available. But, after the Depression, he was fortunate in his investments. He was also much more intelligent. On occasion, he freely acknowledged the excesses of the 1920s, presumably in reference to the investment trusts and the holding companies in particular. His was a supremely pragmatic sort of capitalism, and his own experience could not fail but to teach him to rely on himself for investment decisions rather than on the promises of others.

After the Second World War, McConnell would make more money than ever. In this period, too, he developed a theory of value investing, and his belief in common stocks remained firm. In 1952, twenty years after his grimmest period as an investor and forty years after he had first become seriously rich, he wrote a memorandum to Premier Maurice Duplessis on the "value of water and forests in great national development" and the religious dimensions of "private risk capital" as the application of faith in works. He doubtless had in mind the compensation, then being negotiated by his friend Duplessis himself, after the expropriation of Beauharnois Power, along with Montreal Power, a compensation that infuriated him. As a distillation of his investment experience, and as an expression of his almost evangelical faith in capitalism, and especially in common shares, it deserves to be quoted at length:

How did Quebec manage to develop its immense natural resources; the greatest single one being Arvida?

The answer is, through the courage, resourcefulness and faith of leaders in private enterprise.

Examples – The waters of the Saguenay flowing unnoticed and unused; the waters of Shawinigan and the waters of the St. Lawrence.

By the use of the waters of the mighty St. Lawrence, Beauharnois – the greatest of all hydro-electric powers, through courage[,] far-sightedness and capital risk – Beauharnois, "the greatest of all," was developed.

True, *the waters were leased from Governments*, but "private risk capital" through the issue of debentures, with common stock as a bonus to represent future earnings, did the job.

… It can be said likewise of other great developments … well! *faith with works* was the challenge to which private investors responded. But always the lure was *common stock* which, although issued free, was also the lure to buy bonds or debentures in undeveloped fields.

Outstanding examples are the great pulp and paper mills which, like the power companies, were supported wholly by the natural forest resources leased from Governments.

Has anyone ever heard it said that the *forests* should be considered as having very little value to the pulp and paper industry because they belonged to the respective Governments. Nevertheless, we have witnessed the great pulp and paper companies right here in Quebec go into liquidation in times of depression for lack of customers to buy the products of their mills, built at great cost by "private risk capital."[25]

A more succinct expression of how McConnell justified capitalism to himself can hardly be imagined. Although it contains no explicit reference to God, it certainly implies the existence of providence, first in providing natural resources for development but also, more importantly, in guiding private investors generally, not just him, to wealth. As he said in other contexts, faith "without" works was worthless. By this he meant that people had to invest their faith in actions for the benefit of others. By defining investment as faith "with" works – and by discounting the ability of governments to exhibit the prescience, or at least to assume the risks, of private investors – he was articulating the role that he saw for freedom generally. Freedom led to taking risks and to taking losses, but its exercise was integral to the unfolding of the economy of divine grace.

CHAPTER ELEVEN

Wider, Ever Wider, Shall Thy Bounds Be Set: Social Life in Montreal, 1901–63

Twelfth hole. [Sir Arthur] Currie drove a beauty down the right side of the course. "What a beauty. Nothing the matter with that one except you can't quite use your brassie with it," L.G. [Lloyd George] said admiringly. McConnell drove a screecher straight down the fairway. "That evens us up General," L.G. said.

Ernest Hemingway, "On the Golf Course with Lloyd George"[1]

One of the most remarkable aspects of McConnell's life was how fast he rose socially, to become almost a symbol of the established order in the ten years following his arrival in Montreal. That a dirt-poor son of barely literate failed farmers from Ontario should come to mix so easily, as an apparent equal, with the most privileged of Montreal – and indeed of Canada, Great Britain, and the United States – tells us much about the city and even more about McConnell himself.

Montreal always lacked the wealth, the ostentation, and the numbers to rival London and New York in social glitter. Although it retained an acute sense of class and indeed inequality, it boasted no high society in the Victorian or the Edwardian sense. After the First World War, ballrooms fell out of fashion in the city's private houses, to the point that there was only one left.[2] That was Lady Allan's at Ravenscrag, and she gave only one ball before the outbreak of the Second World War, which eliminated private ballrooms for good. Lil McConnell never tried to emulate Lady Allan, and she did not give even one ball since she had no ballroom. The closest equivalent in Montreal to Mrs Astor's balls in New York City was one given by Percy Cowans in 1924, and he held it at the Mount Royal Hotel.

Its lack of high society notwithstanding, Montreal was self-consciously British, with a hefty admixture of old France, and inclined to class-consciousness. It is possible, however, to overestimate the depth and the effect of these attitudes. To later generations, much of the English-speaking enclave of Westmount looked indisputably "British," with many of its houses in the "stockbroker Tudor" style and others being twentieth-century variants in the manorial tradition. But McConnell did not live in Westmount. The slightly older Square Mile, where he did live, was in fact a pastiche of buildings in various revived styles, from Moorish to Beaux-Arts, and not particularly "British" at all, including his own small version of an Italian palazzo. The country houses of his circle were similarly eclectic, his own two being Norwegian and English in inspiration.

Nowhere in Montreal was there a hint of the grandeur of London's Belgravia. And nowhere outside Montreal in Quebec was there the equivalent of a grand English country house, except perhaps Sir Herbert Marler's, which was "stockbroker Georgian" and inspired by colonial Williamsburg in Virginia. The inspiration for much of English Montreal remained British, but it was becoming impractical even to attempt to sustain grand English style except on special occasions, such as the visits of governors general.

McConnell's way of life, nevertheless, remained almost Edwardian in its opulence well into the relatively subdued 1930s and 1940s. Even after 1945, he remained among the very few in Montreal who moved in the highest levels of English society, yet all the while eschewing special marks of royal favour, such as titles. With advancing age, he seemed to become more royalist than ever. At the heart of his increasing social conservatism was a contradiction found among those in Great Britain of inherited wealth and status with whom he associated. These people were of two minds with regard to him and other rich industrialists, especially from overseas. Self-made businessmen still did not fit comfortably into their ideal of a traditional society, but these same businessmen were precisely the people it was necessary to cultivate in order to extend and maintain British interests.

The task of governors general and the like, then, was to cultivate such men as McConnell as much as they were willing to be cultivated. And McConnell, being amiable as well as ambitious, was quite amenable. Within Canada, he would cheerfully do his duty to the British Empire but seek no recognition. In the mother country, he would receive his due in hospitality, while recognizing the lingering suspicion of "tradesmen" like him there. In any case, his closest friends in Britain, including such peers as Lords Camrose, Kemsley, Iliffe, and McGowan, were all as self-made as he, even if they lived even more grandly; and others such as Lord Melchett were not much better established. He was in effect part of a new aristocracy ennobled through industrial money, like his model, Lord Brassey, who was Lady Willingdon's father. It was almost impossible for his circle to imagine a world without aristocracy and inherited wealth. Thus, their imagination, their self-understanding, and their self-presentation were imbued with historical consciousness.

Mingling with the elite of the empire was more possible in Montreal than elsewhere in Canada, for in the interwar years it was the only even remotely cosmopolitan metropolis in the country. Few could have been more aware than McConnell of the pervasiveness of its shocking poverty and lack of sanitation – with its rate of tuberculosis in the 1920s three times that of Toronto. But for him the city was also a wholesome, fun-loving place. For others, it was frenetic in its entertainments and its vices. And so it attracted often glamorous visitors from afar, many of whom became his guests and friends.

Underlying the gaiety, however, were certain inescapable facts. First, Montrealers were increasingly a minority in a province in which political power was in the hands of the French majority. The majority and the minority did accommodate each other, but neither was much interested in the other, and many in each group wanted to be as self-contained as possible. Moreover, because of its fundamentally commercial history since the Conquest, Montreal, unlike its rural hinterland, was not divided into classes fixed beyond a generation or two. Its sense of inherited privilege was strained, almost an affectation. The Scottish merchants of the nineteenth century had either disappeared or were fading in the face of new money such as that of McConnell and Sir Herbert Holt and Percy Cowans, which further underscored the distance of Montreal from London. The result was that the Square Mile and Westmount only looked impregnably traditional, while in fact they were remarkably open to social leadership by new money, and this money was still overwhelmingly English-speaking.

In its organized sports and entertainments, its balls and its race meetings, the social round of McConnell's Montreal resembled that of the British community in India before 1947. But there was an important difference. Few English Montrealers saw themselves as being on a tour of duty, to be followed by a return home to England. Many had ancestors who had arrived in 1759, and nearly all expected their descendants to remain in Montreal. They had no fear of the "natives" because they were natives themselves. In this respect, they more closely resembled the British settlers in South Africa, who had soon come to identify with their new country, than the English in Shanghai or Cairo, who were clearly there to make fast money and then go home.

In Montreal, the very separate social lives of the French and the English constantly reinforced their differences. These lent themselves to caricature but a few generalizations may help to explain how the communities were able to fashion a modus vivendi. Among the French, religion – with its constant demands upon their time, their conscience, and their purse – held pride of place; among the English, a preoccupation with sports relieved the stress that proved impervious to release by alcohol. The intellectual habits of the English were stoutly pragmatic, the very antithesis of those of their classically educated French neighbours. Neither tradition inclined Montrealers to open conflict. The tension in McConnell's time rather stemmed from those French who wanted to "catch up" with the English – in hospitals, universities, business, and indeed wealth. This is why McConnell's Montreal was far from simply a cultural relic and instead a challenge to others to emulate and exceed.

In 1901, when McConnell arrived in Montreal, the majority of French Canadians were still living on the land and this remained true for most of the rest of his life.

For the English, who accounted for one-half of the city's population, there were tiny vice-regal courts to frequent in Quebec City and Ottawa, and the court in London on special occasions, but urban social life was essentially an isolated, provincial one enlivened by visits by the rich, the noble and the royal, and politicians and entertainers from Europe and the United States. Despite the impression that Montreal gave to some of a French town dominated by the Catholic Church, it was a bustling, commercial, and bourgeois place, a manufacturing as well as a trading centre and full of English-speaking immigrants from elsewhere in Canada and farther afield.

Its Britishness, moreover, was rooted as much in opportunism as in nostalgia and romanticism. The Americans who rushed into Montreal after the collapse of French rule ensured a hard-bitten, commercial underpinning to sentimental links with Great Britain. The propensity of St James Street to be politically reactionary came from its clannishness, and from its assertion of its ongoing and profitable British and American links in the face of the relative limitations of their French-speaking colleagues, rather than from a mindless desire to ape England. Since their riots over the Rebellion Losses Bill and the Annexation Manifesto of 1849, the loyalty of the Montreal merchants to England was at times equivocal, suspect, and contingent. But when England was in peril in both world wars, Montreal responded with the Royal Highland Regiment of Canada, the Royal Canadian Hussars, the Royal Montreal Regiment, and the purchase of Victory bonds.

After their marriage, as we have seen, Jack and Lil first lived at 4074 Tupper Street. In 1911 they moved to 400 Elm Street, at the corner of Sherbrooke Street in Westmount, where they remained until 1915. Their next house, at 87 Redpath Street, was between Pine Avenue and Sherbrooke Street, south of what was to become MacGregor Street (later Dr Penfield Avenue). They were to remain there for ten years, until 1925. During that time, Jack had initially intended, it seems, to build a new home near the summit of Mount Royal, at the southeast corner of Sunnyside Avenue and Edgehill Road in Westmount, on land he purchased in 1912. He commissioned Herbert Raine to design a house for the site, but, for reasons unknown, this house – which would have been enormous and reminiscent of the Gilded Age "cottages" in Newport, Rhode Island – was never built. McConnell did, however, hold the property for a further twenty years before giving it to his son Wilson at the time of his marriage and erecting a very different house for him on the site.[3]

From the mid-1920s onwards, the McConnells maintained three residences simultaneously. The principal one was a house at 1475 Pine Avenue, at Cedar Avenue, that Jeffrey Hale Burland had begun constructing in 1910. Burland died suddenly in London in 1914, and his widow decided not to complete the construction, leaving the house empty. McConnell bought the property in 1919 and hired Kenneth Rea of Montreal and Charles A. Platt of New York to complete the building. He also began acquiring surrounding land so that eventually the estate was to cover twenty-two lots.

1475 Pine Avenue West, exterior view, n.d. Private collection.

McConnell on his Irish chestnut horse Lightning at Pine Avenue, c.1931.
Private collection.

Stables behind the Pine Avenue house, facing Cedar Avenue.
Private collection.

Interior of the Pine Avenue clubhouse. Private collection.

The interior of 1475 Pine Avenue West, as designed and furnished by architect Charles Platt and interior decorator Julia Whitcomb. Private collection.

A Christmas tree in the high room at Pine Avenue, n.d.
McCord Museum, M2003.8.6.9.70.

On its completion in 1925, the house may have been the largest one in the Square
Mile apart from Ravenscrag. Unlike Ravenscrag, to the east and along the same street,
however, it was never a glittering social centre, for all its formality and size. It was
indeed a quiet place, set inside its own little park, high up on Mount Royal and surrounded by trees. There was no house higher on the southern slope of the mountain,
and no house with more commanding views of the city sprawling below. Inside, it was
a scene of considerable splendour, with tapestries and ornate furniture all conveying
a muted opulence.[4]

The Square Mile of Montreal had become the favoured quarter of the rich in the
1890s, with their move up Mount Royal from Dorchester Street and then Sherbrooke
Street. Its bounds were Côte des Neiges Road to the west, University Street to the
east, Pine Avenue to the north, and Sherbrooke Street to the south. It was just to
the north of the commercial heart of the city, where most of the fortunes had been
made and were still being made, and it did not acquire its mythic cachet until it had

McConnell's children and friends at Pine Avenue, dressed for the
Antiquarian and Numismatic Society of Montreal ball, May 1939.

been largely abandoned by its original settlers in the 1930s. It was then that it came
to be described as the Square Mile, and it was only in the 1950s that it began to be
described as the Golden Square Mile, which suggests that its wealth and exclusivity
were chiefly in the minds of realtors. Nevertheless, in McConnell's time it remained a
heavily treed, almost bucolic place, with orchards and gardens and its own shops and
hospitals and private schools, many of which were the best of their kind in the country. The Mount Royal Club and the Ritz-Carlton Hotel were its social centres.

McConnell was amiable but not by nature gregarious and he appreciated the quiet
of Pine Avenue. He cherished his solitude and he typically retired early each evening
in order to read, being asleep by 10 p.m. Yet, in comparison with such contemporaries
as Sir Herbert Holt and Sir Edward Beatty, he was sociable and accessible. Some
described him, particularly in his later years, as engaging and loquacious while basically serious, characteristics that were most pronounced when he was speaking on the
telephone. He especially enjoyed quizzing young people on their plans and activities.
Although, like Jack, Lil was shy in her own way, she loved parties and entertaining,
so that large numbers of people did pass through their houses, but often informally.

Some McConnell grandchildren and their friends at grandson
Murdoch's birthday party, Pine Avenue, c.1950. Private collection.

Over and over again, their guests commented on the McConnells' warmth, openness,
and generosity.

Several kinds of people belonged to their social circle. First were their children
and their friends and their other relatives. Apart from his brother Walter, who lived in
Toronto for several years, and Walter's sons, Jack's relations were nearly all in California. But he sent them train tickets for Montreal, and they came on occasion, almost to
the end of his life. Lil's relatives in St Thomas and Toronto, particularly her mother,
her brother Con, her brother-in-law George Kennedy, and their families, were always
welcome. There were also various almost honorary members of the family, mainly
single people. During the Second World War, refugee children from England came
to stay, in some cases for years, and airmen with Ferry Command, especially its commander-in-chief, Air Chief Marshal Sir Frederick Bowhill, and his wife, were frequent visitors. Then there were their neighbours, most of them business associates as
well, such as the C.C. Ballantynes, the Lorne Websters, the Victor Drurys, the Ross
McMasters, the James Eccles, and many others. Their closest neighbours on Pine
Avenue were also among their friends. These included, in the 1920s, for example,
Norman Dawes and his family to the west and Sir Frederick and Lady Williams-Taylor
to the south. They seem to have had little to do with Sir Henry Thornton, president
of the CNR, to their east, and they had difficulty in luring the shy Sir Edward Beatty,
president of the CPR, almost across the road. On occasion, they travelled abroad with
close friends, such as Dr and Mrs C.A. Peters and the Ross McMasters.

Baron Robert Silvercruys (the Belgian minister to Canada), the McConnells, Peggy Douglas, Principal Lewis Douglas of McGill University, and Paul van Zeeland, a former prime minister of Belgium, at Pine Avenue, December 1938. Private collection.

Every Christmas at Pine Avenue, the McConnells would give a reception for their friends, with an enormous tree in the High Room (the latter decorated by the artist Campbell Tinning, who was giving Lil lessons in painting). They would also hold a Christmas party for their own children and the children of their friends. Every child would receive the same present. McConnell had none of the inhibitions, common to those of inherited wealth, in talking about and displaying money, as well as in giving it away. Thus, at Christmas, he would shake coins in his pockets, which would fall through holes down his legs for the children to retrieve. There would be other coins in the Christmas pudding, and he would watch eagerly to see which children might be interested in retrieving them.

They sponsored smaller events as well, such as a concert at Pine Avenue by the Kedroff Quartette, singers exiled from Russia, in 1930. The house saw frequent luncheons and dinners; surviving place-cards for dinner in the 1920s include the names of Sir Charles Gordon, Sir Montagu Allan, Colonel Herbert Molson, Sir Herbert Holt, R.B. Bennett, and Sir Arthur Currie. One of their most frequent guests was Baron Robert Silvercruys, the Belgian minister in Ottawa and later the Belgian ambassador to the United States. A very energetic diplomat fluent in both English and French, he was a constant source of information from Ottawa, Quebec City, and well beyond. His sister Suzanne was a sculptress, generally resident in the United States, and McConnell commissioned her to create busts of Lord Tweedsmuir and of himself.

By the 1930s, McConnell was reluctantly permitting alcohol to be served in his houses, although he ostentatiously persisted in refusing any for himself, turning his wine glass upside down at dinner. Lil did not share his abstinence. In her cabinets could be found a variety of glasses for wine, beer, and hard liquor. Her "bar" in the High Room was hidden behind a screen, and from it she would dispense the refreshment expected by the vast majority of their friends.

Until after the Second World War, the McConnells seldom left Montreal in cold weather, which extended from October to May. To keep themselves warm, they were loyal customers of Holt Renfrew, Jack owning a raccoon coat, a mink cap, and two buffalo coats, and Lil a large number of fur coats, capes, stoles, and muffs. Their houses and their cars had rugs of leopard, polar bear, musk-ox, tiger, and raccoon. Lil collected a great variety of jewellry, for which she became much admired. She wore rings of emeralds, diamonds, sapphires, rubies, gold, and zircon. At the opera, she sported a lorgnette of platinum and diamonds with a diamond-set sautoire. There were brooches of diamonds, coral, and jade, all carefully coordinated with her outfits by Paris and London couturiers, and she wore earrings of pearl and coral and clips of jade and diamonds.

Social life demanded of both of them several changes of clothes in the course of the day, especially if tennis, golf, tea, and a formal dinner were involved. Both Jack and Lil , with the aid of his valet and her lady's maid, were always immaculately turned out. Even Jack was swathed in fur in winter, in plus fours on the golf-course, in white tie at balls, in black tie at dinner, and in eighteenth-century dress at costume balls, where no detail was omitted, whether it was powdered wigs, parasols, or walking sticks.

McConnell maintained stables with a groom behind the house on Pine Avenue and frequently rode up the mountain, and later Lil had an indoor tennis court built for him to the east of the house, which he used almost every day. One of the most exclusive clubs in Montreal consisted of about a dozen men who played there, including Judge Gregor Barclay and Ross McMaster. Grand motor cars, including Packards and Rolls-Royces, joined the horses in the stables. Ultimately, however, the house was too grand and sophisticated to serve as a satisfactory retreat from the pressures of urban life. That function was performed by the McConnells' country house in Dorval.

The name "Dorval" refers to three islands and the south shore of Montreal Island facing Lake Saint-Louis, between Lachine and Pointe Claire.[5] Its history goes back to beyond European settlement, but it began to assume its present residential shape with the sale by the Meloche family of the three islands, in 1854, to Sir George Simpson,

Ashburton exterior, mid 1920s. Photograph by Rice Studios.
McCord Museum M 2003.8.6.9.174

for forty years the governor of the Hudson's Bay Company. In 1860, with Sir Fenwick Williams, commander-in-chief of British forces in Canada, Simpson welcomed the Prince of Wales (later King Edward VII) – attended by a representative of every rank of the nobility and greeted by Indians in canoes – to the islands. With this royal visit, Dorval became highly desirable as a place of residence for professionals and was eventually linked to Montreal by the Grand Trunk Railway. It was incorporated as a village in 1892 at the request of Hartland St Clair MacDougall, first president of the Montreal Stock Exchange, who became its first mayor. McConnell's neighbours there were also among his closest business colleagues, such as C.C. Ballantyne and members of the McLean and Knox families.

From 1911 to 1921, McConnell bought various lots in Dorval from the estate of Samuel Carsley, the dry-goods merchant, and he probably occupied the Carsley house, later rented to his lieutenant from 1912 to 1940, Frank Knox. He acquired other property in Dorval in stages, merging it all into an expanded version of Ashburton, the estate of Hartland St Clair MacDougall, who had died in 1917. The first and largest part was bought two years later from MacDougall's son Hartland Leonard, who had lost the property through alcoholism and moved to a small apartment, a fact that McConnell later noted ruefully to Mackenzie King.[6]

While McConnell was awaiting the completion of his new house on Pine Avenue, in 1919–24, Ashburton was being expanded and renovated as the McConnell coun-

Ashburton terrace. Private collection.

Ashburton gardens, designed by Ormiston Roy. Private collection.

Meeting at Ashburton of the Canadian Medical Association, 1927. Private collection.

try residence. Even five years later, he was buying further lots on St Joseph Street to ensure greater privacy. The original house had been built in 1899 by Edward Maxwell of Montreal and George C. Shattuck of Boston, and it was in the English Arts and Crafts style, with classical ornamentation on the exterior. Edward Maxwell, with his brother William, was coincidentally to design the Dominion Express Building on St James Street, which McConnell was to occupy for fifty years from its opening in 1912. Kenneth Rea, who was also altering the Burland house for McConnell, was to make major changes to Ashburton in the early 1920s.[7]

Ashburton was the McConnells' favourite house. Although it lacked a distinctive character, it was a big house in the English tradition and set in what was effectively a large park, with a big swimming pool and gardens full of trees and fronting Lake Saint-Louis. Lil frequently made changes to the interior, which was distinctly relaxed in comparison with the palazzo atmosphere of the Pine Avenue residence. It was a contemporary house but full of antiques. It made no studied references to the past, however, unlike the Scottish baronial or French Renaissance or Beaux-Arts houses of their neighbours in town and out of it, or indeed their own house on Pine Avenue. To design the gardens, the McConnells began an association of over three decades with Ormiston Roy, superintendent of the Mount Royal Cemetery. Roy was a specialist in peonies, and he built a peony garden for Lil. Cleveland Morgan, their friend in Senneville, built them a rose garden.

Above all, Ashburton was a house designed not for show but to be lived in, and most guests seem to have found it both supremely luxurious and exceedingly comfortable. The McConnells held receptions for hundreds there in the 1920s. Most

Patrick Ashley Cooper, governor of the Hudson's Bay Company,
his wife and two daughters, and Kit at Ashburton, c.1938. McCord
Museum, M2003.8.6.72.

notably, in June 1926, they invited three hundred delegates to the General Council of
the recently formed United Church of Canada, who were regaled with music from the
band of the Royal Highlanders. The new moderator, the Reverend James Endicott,
was there, as were such old Methodist friends as Sir James Aikens from Winnipeg
and Sir Joseph Flavelle from Toronto, and delegates from all over Canada and Newfoundland and missionaries from Korea, China, Japan, Africa, and Hungary.

Ashburton, like Pine Avenue, provided ample opportunity for tennis, on outdoor
courts that McConnell had built. Tennis, indeed, was not just a pastime for McConnell but a passion. Family and guests at McConnell's houses in Dorval and on Pine
Avenue, including governors general, especially Lord Willingdon, who had a been
a favourite partner of King George V, were pressed into service as partners, and
McConnell even overcame his Methodist aversion to Sunday entertainment by playing on the Sabbath. He played tennis everywhere, whether at Pine Avenue or on the
Empress of Britain in 1936. When his friend Herbert Bruce, the lieutenant governor
of Ontario, came to call, McConnell demanded to know why his son Maxwell, who
was a godson of Lord Beaverbrook, could not play, since it would be of inestimable
social benefit to him.

Often business, pleasure, and social life mixed, as at the opening of the new Manoir
Richelieu in Murray Bay, east of Quebec City, by W.H. Coverdale, the president of

W.H. Coverdale (president, Canada Steamship Lines), Mrs Coverdale,
Lord and Lady Willingdon, McConnell, and Mary Coverdale, at the
reopening of the Manoir Richelieu, Murray Bay, June 1930.
McCord Museum M2003.8.6.2.84.

McConnell and Lady Willingdon, flanked by two aides-de-camp, on the tennis
courts of the Manoir Richelieu, June 1930. McCord Museum M2003.8.6.2.88.

An external view of Saran Chai in winter, n.d. Private collection.

Canada Steamship Lines, of which McConnell was a major owner. This magnificent hotel overlooking the St Lawrence replaced one built by Sir Rodolphe Forget, McConnell's pre-war colleague, which had burnt down, and the Willingdons joined in the festivities. The apparent ease of McConnell, Coverdale, and their associates, near the very nadir of the Great Depression, gave no hint of the near ruin about to befall CSL, which they called "Steamers."

Along with their Pine Avenue house and Ashburton, the McConnells maintained a large log house, usually called his "camp," at Val David, in the Laurentian Mountains north of Montreal. The Laurentians were sufficiently distant from Montreal to serve as a weekend retreat while still being closer to the city than, say, Muskoka was to Toronto. Like Muskoka, they were magical in the summer, but, unlike Muskoka, in winter they were also exceptionally suited to skiing. Starting in 1876, a train joined Mile End (Jean Talon) station in Montreal to the village of Saint-Jérôme, and before the end of the century the line had been extended through Shawbridge to Sainte-Agathe. It was not until the opening of the Laurentian Autoroute in 1964, just after McConnell's death, that the mountains became accessible to mass tourism. In McConnell's time, the family continued typically to go by private railway carriage to Sainte-Agathe. There, cars in summer or sleighs in winter met them, and, once on their own property, there was no hint of tourism. The silence was almost deafening and the air profoundly refreshing.[8]

The McConnells with the king and queen of Siam at Saran Chai,
August 1931. McCord Museum, M2003.8.6.9.184.

Designed to resemble Canarasset, the nearby Norwegian-style residence of his
friend Ross McMaster, the McConnell house in the Laurentians was also reminiscent
of some of the large log hotels in the Muskoka of Jack's youth. Social life there, and at
other Laurentian houses like it, took place in the setting of extended families, supplemented by invited guests who came mainly from Montreal and Ottawa. On special
occasions, there were parties on weekends. These were particularly agreeable to visitors from Government House in Ottawa, accustomed as they were to country-house
parties in England. The fact that many of the Laurentian houses were also themselves
very large, often with outbuildings, permitted guests to bring servants to supplement
the regular staff on site, and the amenities available to skiers and bathers and boaters
were often superior to those on offer even at the grander English houses.

McConnell acquired the Val David property in four stages from 1929 to 1938, so
that he owned all that he could see from his house.[9] A gravel road a mile long led
to the two-storey cabin, which in 1931 was to be given the Siamese name of Saran
Chai, or "Serene Happiness," by one of its most illustrious guests, King Prajadhipok
(Rama VII) of Siam. The sloping roof was covered with sod, and there were eight
bedrooms for the family and guests, all decorated in reds, yellows, and greens and
with natural wood. Lady Tweedsmuir, a writer like her husband and her sister-in-law
Anna Buchan, and her friend Virginia Woolf, visited the McConnells there as Hitler

John, Wilson, Lil, and Jack on the tennis court, Pine Avenue, c.1930.
McCord Museum 51392.3.

Mrs Jack Watson, Phoebe Campbell, and Cleveland Morgan
(of Morgan's department store and the Montreal Museum of Fine Arts)
at Saran Chai, March 1935. McCord Museum M 2003.8.6.5024.16.

Party at Saran Chai in the late 1930s. In back: Marjorie
McConnell at the left and Jack Watson, McConnell's jockey
friend, on the right. Private collection.

Mrs George Pape (lady-in-waiting), Principal Lewis Douglas, Kit, Lieutenant
Robin Scott, RN (aide-de-camp), Lil, Lord and Lady Tweedsmuir, David,
McConnell, and Mrs Lewis Douglas at Saran Chai, 16 March 1938.

McConnell's bookplate for Saran Chai. Private collection.

was absorbing Austria in 1938. She recorded, amidst "the utter fear and terror of the news": "The air was quite beautiful. The mountains rolled away in every direction and have queer, enormous toad-shaped boulders standing at intervals – the remains left by some glacial upheaval. The silver birches looked like filigree against the sky, and suddenly you come on a patch of orange dogwood in this utterly colourless land-scape, which is most lovely."[10] In the years to come, until its destruction by fire in 1952, Saran Chai was to become as much home to the McConnells as Pine Avenue or Ashburton.

In addition to these three houses, McConnell also owned a fishing camp, given the name Tom's Brook by its previous owners, consisting of seven lots of land on the Restigouche River, near the border between Quebec and New Brunswick. The McConnells and their guests went from Montreal by train to Matapedia and then by barge or canoe along the river, towed by horses, since the river was shallow. The house on the Restigouche was a simple wooden affair, not large enough for more than a few guests, usually close friends. But the family loved it and, from the time they acquired it in 1932, they typically spent as much of the summer there as they could. The property required frequent repair and in 1950 suffered a major fire, but McConnell continued to visit it until 1956. Although fishing at the camp was often poor, the atmosphere was

Tom's Brook on the Restigouche River, n.d. Private collection.

profoundly relaxing in the absence of telephones. When there was salmon to spare, McConnell would send it to colleagues in Montreal, to Princess Alice in Ottawa, and to Mrs Roosevelt in Washington. It was relaxation at a price, however, including fees to the Restigouche Salmon Club and the Restigouche Riparian Association, about four staff, and the rental of a cow, presumably for milk, which together cost almost $4,000 between January and September 1941 alone, or $55,000 in 2008 terms.

There were permanent grounds people at each of the McConnell houses, while the other servants tended to move with the family from one house to another. The family did move a good deal, typically spending weekends in Val David and the summers in Dorval and at the fishing camp, and not everyone moved at the same time. All their houses were very formally run in comparison with others in Montreal. Staff stood in attendance during meals and visiting ladies had their own maids. This was part of the attraction for visitors from Government House, accustomed to such service but finding it increasingly scarce in England as well as Canada.

There were about ten servants at a time, apart from gardeners, and they very seldom changed. At Pine Avenue, the cook was Mrs Rendall, so styled although she was unmarried. She was a plain cook from the Orkneys but had had expert training as a decorator of cakes. Tina, an Irish Canadian kitchen maid, assisted her. Lil had a Scottish maid named Ina Wallace. Chapman, an Englishman, served as the butler and as Jack's valet. Walter Adams was the Irish footman and occasional valet, and he was responsible for polishing the silver. Arnold was the caretaker at Pine Avenue and Dorval. The upstairs maid was Florence Weston, also known as Winnie. There

Jack, Lil, and Ross McMaster, president of the Steel Company
of Canada, at Tom's Brook, 1940s. Private collection.

McConnell and the governor general, Viscount Alexander, probably at the
Royal Victoria Hospital Ball, circa 1950. Courtesy of Earl Alexander of Tunis.

were two nannies, Marcella Heaslip for David and Margaret Hinton for Kit. In 1943 Antoine Lefebvre was the chauffeur at Pine Avenue, and there was another chauffeur at Dorval, Antoine Boyer. There were at least five gardeners at any time at Dorval. For the month of December 1943, household expenses totalled $5,419 ($69,339 in 2008 terms), which seems to have been about the monthly average for that year.

Although the McConnells did entertain at home, most of their mixing with local people was in various clubhouses, as was the entertaining of visitors from Ottawa, Toronto, and farther afield. This was not unusual, for few city houses – including McConnell's – were large enough to provide the facilities for sporting activities offered by the flourishing clubs. Even McConnell did not possess his own golf course, although he had his own tennis courts. The various clubs, moreover, tended to serve particular purposes. The McConnells, for example, often dined with friends on Christmas Eve at the Mount Royal Club, in order to let the staff at home enjoy a night off.

McConnell's clubs were very social, in contrast to many of the London clubs, which could serve as retreats from people. They were not, with such exceptions as the Montreal Club, intended to be suitable to the conduct of business. The Montreal Club, located on the top floor of the Dominion Express Building and above his office since 1912, was the only club to which he belonged by 1915, and it served luncheon to businessmen. Five years later, he belonged also to the Beaconsfield Golf Club, the Mount Royal Club, and the Royal Montreal Golf Club, as well as the York and National clubs in Toronto. By 1927, he had added the Montreal Hunt, the Montreal Indoor Tennis, the Montreal Racquet (often called the "Racquets"[11]), the Mount Bruno Country, and the Royal St Lawrence Yacht clubs. Since their purpose was social, most if not all these clubs expressly forbade the doing of business within them, taking notes in their dining rooms, and tipping the staff.

McConnell seems to have used all of his clubs frequently, chiefly in the 1920s and 1930s. Yet he was not "a clubman," in the sense of spending much of his time in club activities, and he appears never to have been an officer of any of his clubs except the Royal Montreal Golf. But he enjoyed their social amenities, and each served a somewhat distinct purpose, even though the memberships formed overlapping circles. Collectively, these clubs formed the framework for the social life of McConnell and his circle.

The Mount Royal Club had been established in 1899 and it instantly became the most exclusive club in the city. Nearly all of its founders were to be associated with McConnell, although he did not become a member until 1918. With the exception of one doctor, they were all businessmen. The first home of the club was at Sherbrooke and Stanley streets, in a house previously occupied by Sir John Abbott. After a fire in 1904 totally destroyed this building, a well-known firm of New York architects, McKim, Mead and White, designed its replacement for the same site, which opened

Montreal Hunt Horse Show, Mrs J.L. Todd, Miss Shirley Walker,
Mrs Anderson from Hong Kong (niece of Mrs Todd), Mrs Gordon-Ives
(secretary to Lady Bessborough), Miss Wilde, Col. Herbert Molson, and
McConnell, 12 June 1933. Montreal *Gazette*.

in 1906. McConnell's generation of members tended to be sons of the founders,
such as Huntly Drummond and Forbes Angus, and his business colleagues such as
Markland Molson, Alfred Baumgarten, Sir Herbert Holt, Sir Herbert Marler, and
Henry Joseph.

Forbiddingly chaste in its exterior and almost chillingly official inside, the Mount
Royal was reminiscent of Government House in Ottawa. It was highly suitable for
formal entertaining, and larger than nearly any house in Montreal, including McConnell's own. In the spring of 1931, probably at the request of his friends Prime Minister
Bennett and Herbert Marler, then the Canadian minister to Japan, he gave a luncheon
in it for Prince and Princess Takamatsu, recalling a reception given for Japanese royalty by Sir Montagu Allan at Ravenscrag in 1907.

If there was a summit to Montreal club life, however, it was probably the Montreal
Hunt, which was more social than the other sports clubs.[12] Its prestige was rooted in
its venerability, since it had been founded in about 1826. It derived prestige also from
its association with the British regular troops stationed in Montreal for 110 years,
from 1760 to 1870, and the lofty social connections of many of their officers. Hunting
was a way for members to associate themselves with the favoured sport of the English
aristocracy and gentry, and with their aspiring counterparts elsewhere in Canada and

Oil portrait of McConnell in hunting dress.

The ball to celebrate the coming-out of Anna Cowans at the
Mount Royal Hotel. Lil in front, holding a bouquet, 1924.
Private collection, courtesy of Mrs David Mackenzie.

in the United States. It attracted as members women as well as men of private means,
as opposed to simply rich men of business.

With the departure of imperial troops in 1870, the Hunt entered a period of decline
but then gradually built itself up again, with a distinctly business orientation. Above
all, the Hunt benefited from the mastership of Alfred Baumgarten, of St Lawrence
Sugar. Baumgarten established new kennels and the first clubhouse on what became Delormier Avenue, complete with a banquet room, billiards room, swimming
pool, library, and ballroom. In 1898 the Hunt moved its clubhouse to Côte Sainte-
Catherine Road, where it remained until gutted by fire in 1938.[13] Its dining room,
tearooms, bowling green, quoits ground, toboggan slide, and golf course made it a
centre of social life, and by the time McConnell became a member in 1924 the Hunt
was as noted as much for its club facilities as for the magnificence of its meets.

McConnell enjoyed riding but not hunting, although he had himself painted in
hunting dress. Among the members of the Hunt was McConnell's close friend Percy
Cowans. Cowans and his relations were at the heart of McConnell's social world.
They were well established when he arrived; he employed many of them once he

Unknown, Sir Arthur Currie (principal of McGill), David Lloyd George
(former British prime minister), J.J. McGill (golf professional), McConnell,
and caddies at the Royal Montreal Golf Club, 1923. Private collection.

was well established. Cowans's ball to mark the coming of age of his daughter Anna,
in 1924, was perhaps the most spectacular social gathering since war had begun a
decade before.

Although he never owned a yacht, McConnell's house in Dorval was just opposite
the clubhouse of the Royal St Lawrence Yacht Club[14] on Lake Saint-Louis, and he
almost inevitably became a member. Just west of the Yacht Club, about half a mile
from Ashburton, was the Forest and Stream Club, in a modest house originally built
for Senator A.J. Brown, a lawyer and bank director close to McConnell.[15] McConnell
was proposed for membership in 1914 but for some reason not then elected, and it was
only in 1921 that he became a member. Because it was so close to his house, he did not
spend much time there, apart for receptions, but the club attracted nearly all his circle
as members.

The Royal Montreal Golf Club was founded in 1873 and claimed to be the oldest
golf club in continuous existence in North America, receiving the prefix of "Royal"
from Queen Victoria in 1884. From 1896, the club was at Dixie, in Dorval. In 1957 it
would move to Île Bizard in the Lake of Two Mountains. For all practical purposes,
therefore, it was one of McConnell's Dorval clubs, like the Forest and Stream and the
Royal St Lawrence Yacht.

"SINCE YOU INSIST, GENTLEMEN I'LL TRY IT — BUT YOU CAN SEE HOW HARD ITS GOING TO BE TO FILL 'EM"

J.J's SHOES

Mount Royal Club
JAN 18th 1924

Mr. J. W. McConnell —

Mount Royal Club cartoon by Le Mesurier,
apparently concerning McConnell's assumption of
the presidency of the Royal Montreal Golf Club,
18 January 1924. Private collection.

Its course stretched from Lakeshore Road, bordering Lake Saint-Louis, to the
CPR tracks, and the Grand Trunk tracks also ran through it, which made it easy for
members to come from Montreal. During the Great War, matches were played for the
Patriotic Fund and other causes. In 1923 the former British prime minister, David
Lloyd George, toured Canada and stopped in Montreal. As club vice-president,
McConnell played with Lloyd George against Sir Arthur Currie and J.J. McGill, the
club professional as well as president. George pronounced McConnell a "magnificent
player," politely adding that if he could make a drive like McConnell, he would "quit
politics."[16]

McConnell himself became president of the club in 1924–25, when it was experiencing considerable financial difficulty. At the close of 1923, there was a capital debt of more than $90,000 and a current operating deficit of just over $4,000. The members were assessed $150 each in the form of a loan, redeemable on the death or resignation of a member. McConnell pronounced this "most equitable, inasmuch as it becomes merely a temporary burden upon the present members, and ultimately is passed on to incoming members, thus becoming a liability without maturity and without interest." He praised one Carth Thompson, "a typical, far-sighted Scotchman," for the innovative finance, which had resulted in cash payments of $94,043 by the end of the current financial year, the total assessments amounting to $104,100. With total revenue in the current year from all sources amounting to $110,264 and expenditures of $109,102, there was a surplus of $1,162. Thus had the future of the club been secured through McConnell's as well as Thompson's wizardry.

Another golf club of which McConnell was very fond was the Mount Bruno. Founded in June 1918 by Edson Loy Pease, the managing director of the Royal Bank of Canada, it occupied almost a thousand acres on the top of Mount Bruno, about a twenty-mile drive from Montreal, near Montarville on the south shore of the St Lawrence. It was modelled on Tuxedo Park, in New York State, which had a residential colony as well as facilities for golf, tennis, rackets, riding, swimming, and other activities, but its terrain was pre-eminently suited for golf. McConnell, later a director of the Bank of Montreal, was one of its original shareholders and more enthusiastic members. The club was chartered to provide facilities for more than golf – tennis, skating, badminton, squash, and indoor and outdoor games generally were mentioned in its letters patent. In 1940 the important Lend-Lease agreement – involving the transfer of US war materiel to Britain and its allies – was negotiated, at least in part, in the bungalows owned by the club.

The 1920s marked the end of a golden age of amateurism in athletics, which McConnell and his circle epitomized. Even before then, however, the Montreal Amateur Athletics Association (MAAA), which encompassed a wide range of amateur sports, had found its domination of athletics in Montreal challenged. Sports were becoming in part a big business, and McConnell was naturally a part of this transformation. Here again business mixed with social life inextricably, so that the Montreal Forum was to become yet another form of club for him. Various developments had led to the formation of the wholly professional National Hockey League in 1917 and the opening of the Montreal Forum in 1924. With its indoor ice rink, the Forum permitted the scheduling of games without regard to the weather. William Northey, longtime president of the MAAA and former manager of its Montreal (Westmount) Arena, became manager of the Forum, and just after Christmas the Montreal Professional Hockey Club (soon to be renamed the Maroons) played its first game there, against a

French-speaking team, the Canadiens. Northey was also behind the formation of the Maroons. And behind Northey in this venture was, among others, McConnell.[17]

The Montreal society of this era – dominated by white English-speaking business-men – welcomed McConnell as one of its own. Although he had nothing against other peoples, he was living in a world arranged superbly for someone of his background, and he took full advantage of what it had to offer. This was not all to the good for any of them, for an air of effortless self-satisfaction, even self-congratulation, clung to this world between the wars, whether through habit or arrogance or blindness, or through some combination of them. The same people who belonged to any one of McConnell's clubs seemed to belong to nearly all the others. And so, despite the superficial variety of his social life, he seldom encountered in Montreal anyone with views fundamentally contrary to his own. He was, to be sure, aware that there were threats, chiefly in the form of communism and socialism, throughout the world, but he never understood them except as threats, or even to let them have their say, as his own son John complained.

A wide range of critics echoed John's complaints. Alan Lascelles, the acerbic pri-vate secretary to the Prince of Wales (Edward VIII), to one governor general, Lord Bessborough, and later to King George VI and Queen Elizabeth II, found that McConnell's crowd was as individualistic as a "pack of beagles." Montreal social-ists such as Frank Scott and Eugene Forsey found them unspeakable. To some Torontonians who lived in Montreal, such as J.M. Macdonnell and B.K. Sandwell, the poverty of imagination, self-satisfaction, philistinism, and stultifying conformity that they encountered in English Montreal were shocking and did not bode well for its survival. None of these critics, however, articulated a viable alternative vision for English Montreal. And none of them was in practice half so adept at accommodating French Canada as McConnell himself and other businessmen.

Despite its limitations, and particularly its lingering traditionalism, McConnell's Montreal was extremely well informed about the latest developments in politics, finance, economics, and technology outside Quebec as well as inside. Even as early as the 1920s, it was probably no less up to date than a major American city, and no less open to innovation. The very capacity of its social structure to embrace such men of humble origin, and producers of results, as McConnell seemed to confirm its continuing success. The ultimate failure of this society was a failure of imagination, a failure to comprehend why many of the people beyond its ranks harboured different aspirations and how pressing these aspirations were.

In a sense, McConnell's Montreal was a victim not of its failure but of its success. McConnell and his circle stood for a modern, technical society based on an essen-tially secular education system. They yearned for a new, similarly educated French Canadian generation to cooperate with them in building the province and the country. This was the shared vision of premiers Gouin, Taschereau, Duplessis, and God-bout, in all of whom McConnell placed considerable hope. The French Canadians who followed them in the 1960s were equipped with just the sort of practical educa-tion that McConnell had in mind, but they no longer wanted acceptance by St James Street. They wanted to replace it.

Today, decades after his death, McConnell's clubs are all functioning, many rein-vigorated. But they enjoy little of the homogeneity of membership that he knew. Many descendants of the families whom he knew remain prominent in them, but they now include many French Canadians and people of other racial and national origins. Tra-ditional criteria of acceptability for membership, explicit or unspoken, such as reli-gion, race, and even gender, are either illegal or almost so. More important, clubs and sports no longer exert the preponderant influence that they did in McConnell's time as instruments of socialization. The MAAA is now more a French-speaking health club, professional sports outside clubs are much more followed than amateur, and the British sporting ideal is almost forgotten.

As they advanced in years, the McConnells saw that their elaborate and labour-intensive daily lives and entertainments were becoming hard to maintain, particularly after the Second World War. In his will, McConnell left the Pine Avenue house to Lil for life, and then to the McConnell Foundation to dispose of. Before his death, Saran Chai had burnt to the ground, and Ashburton was to share the same fate shortly after his death. The fishing camp, Tom's Brook, alone among McConnell's houses, remains in family ownership, though even it has been rebuilt. It is a remarkable survival of the McConnell legacy to architecture, a simple wooden structure not all that removed from the little cabin in which McConnell was born on the Butter and Egg Road.

CHAPTER TWELVE

For King and Empire, 1927–39

We can be national patriots, loving our own country with passion, deeply attached to its soil, dreaming of its future, and at the same time Imperial patriots, believing with all our hearts in the wider fellowship and brotherhood of the Empire, not only for the sake of our own country, not only for the sake of all the other nations associated with it in the Empire, but also for the influence which it exercises upon the world as a whole.

Leo Amery, secretary of state for Dominion affairs and the colonies, 30 January 1928[1]

The years 1927 and 1928 marked a pinnacle of McConnell's success, above all socially. Other years, such as 1929 until the market crash in October, and 1938, when he took over management of the *Montreal Star*, were landmarks in their own ways. But by 1928 he was settled in his house on Pine Avenue, he was engineering his International Nickel reorganization, and he was collecting directorships. He also was named chairman of the Royal Victoria Hospital Charity Ball, and he was becoming the confidant of Lord Willingdon, the new governor general who arrived in 1927 and the first of several governors general whom he would befriend. He was now firmly placed in the highest social and business circles of Canada, the United States, and England. Among the well informed, he was recognized as a major newspaper publisher in waiting as well as a governor of McGill, a sugar refiner, the chief individual shareholder of Brazilian Traction, and much else. Such were his dynamism and influence that he seemed to be now almost an imperial figure, rather than simply a Canadian one.

Canada itself, having reached unprecedented prosperity, still saw itself as part of a great empire, although there was only a little more than one decade of uneasy peace left to run before the Second World War that was to finish it off. For McConnell and his generation, the empire was weakening alarmingly, but it was far from dead. It remained a work in progress. Until about 1927, McConnell himself had had little opportunity to concentrate on imperial affairs, but now his new-found eminence pretty much obliged him to do so. That empire covered a quarter of the surface of the earth, and yet it had no formal beginning and no formal end. It was a chimera, encompassing another empire, a subcontinent in the middle of it, the Indian. From Gibraltar, Cyprus, and Malta – all colonies in the Mediterranean – it stretched to Palestine, in the Near East, and informally over Iraq, Persia, and Afghanistan before reaching India and what became Pakistan, Sri Lanka (Ceylon), Myanmar (Burma), and, farther east, Hong Kong, Shanghai, and other Chinese cities.

Japan, an empire in its own right, was not part of it, but McConnell's friend, Sir Herbert Marler, the Canadian minister in Tokyo, thought of it as England-in-Asia, rather as others were describing Chile and Argentina as Englands-in-South America. Africa was largely British still, from the Cape to Cairo, even though South Africa gained Dominion status in 1910 and Egypt was nominally an independent kingdom that nominally controlled the Sudan with England. Kenya was not wrested from the Germans until 1919, but it was both no more anomalous and no less exotic than Zanzibar, Swaziland, Bechuanaland, the Gold Coast, Nigeria, the Gambia, and the princely states of India not formally controlled from New Delhi. The whole continent of Australia, not to mention New Zealand and Fiji and the Solomon Islands, was British, as was most of the Malay Peninsula including Singapore, and countless possessions in the Americas, from Newfoundland and Bermuda to British Guiana and the Falklands.

Surviving sepia prints and jerky photographic montages of the empire in this period depict proconsuls laden with gold or silver braid and medals, stars and sashes, all topped with luxuriantly plumed helmets. Like them, the recorded voices of royalty all bespeak a now-vanished hierarchical, deferential, and traditional society. Yet, even when these records were being produced, disturbing nationalist movements, particularly in Ireland, India, and South Africa, were fatally undermining this picturesque vision of timelessness, authority, and effortless superiority. The empire was a cauldron bubbling with resentments, from which a direct line can be drawn to many of the most intractable problems in the world of the twenty-first century – such as those involving Palestine, Iraq, and Afghanistan. The apparent unity of the empire was fragile at best and delusory at worst, though not so insubstantial that imperial possessions around the globe would not soon rush into yet another world war to defend the mother country and its ideals.

For McConnell and his generation, it was almost as hard to make sense of the empire as it would be for later generations, and the difficulty only increased as it became apparent that the empire would never recover the unity and the power that it had enjoyed before the First World War. Few, however, found it possible to obtain much personal experience of what was happening over such wide swaths of the earth. Before commercial air travel, most of these far-flung places – though all tied to England in a variety of ways – were practically inaccessible to Canadians, even to those who fervently believed in the empire as a source for good. For them, the empire in practice consisted of Canada, Great Britain, and those favoured spots – such as Bermuda and the Bahamas – where the McConnells and their friends went to bask in the sun.

For others such as Churchill, India remained paramount in their imperial vision. Through Willingdon, who had been governor of Bombay and Madras and who was to return to India as viceroy after his posting in Ottawa, McConnell developed a sense of the strategic significance of India to Great Britain. He subsequently reinforced this sense through acquaintance with Willingdon's predecessor as viceroy, Lord Irwin (later Halifax), when Halifax stayed several times in Montreal while posted to Washington as ambassador during the Second World War. And, through his directorships of Sun Life, which operated in India and South Africa, and of US Rubber, which bought rubber from Malaya, McConnell paid regular attention to the economies of the British possessions overseas. To this extent, the empire was not an abstraction but deeply personal to him.

For his part, through close acquaintance with British industrialists, newspaper owners, financiers, and politicians, McConnell was to buttress his ever-broadening social and political connections to the mother country with a deep appreciation of its economic and strategic challenges within the empire and indeed beyond. Yet, although moving in the loftiest circles, McConnell never managed to influence British policy making, or perhaps even sought to do so. Such Canadian friends of his as the high commissioners in London and the former politicians Vincent Massey and Howard Ferguson were far more influential in this regard. Nothing that McConnell did would alter the course of imperial affairs, and yet, because he was perceived as an influential opinion maker, the men in charge of directing those affairs were well aware of him and of his views.

Although initially converted to imperial centralization through his meeting with Joseph Chamberlain in 1904, McConnell seems afterwards to have held no new coherent view of how the empire should develop.[2] At heart, he remained firmly a mid-Victorian, and, throughout his life, he would consistently eschew the term "Commonwealth" in favour of "Empire," leaving it to others to define the shape of the empire of the future. For others in Canada in 1904 and for almost fifty years afterwards, however, debate over the future of the empire was inescapable. Moreover, because Canada was the senior and the most developed Dominion, one that was on its way to some sort of nationhood, what Canadians said and did had considerable influence over those interested in the empire in England.

There were Canadian proponents of both closer federation and fundamental decentralization, and with many vacillating between these extremes. Among those known to McConnell, there were, in the 1920s for example, the centralizers Stephen Leacock and Sir Andrew McPhail at McGill; the decentralizers Mackenzie King and Sir Robert Borden in Ottawa; and the temporizers Vincent Massey in Toronto and Huntly Drummond in Montreal. The last two were members of the Round Table group, a debating society devoted to the dispassionate study of the future of the empire but, objectivity aside, determined to make it "work" as some sort of cohesive body. Headquartered in London, the group probably never had more than a few dozen members in Canada, though branches of it in Montreal, Toronto, and Victoria held regular "moots."[3] It exercised its greatest influence from 1909 to 1920 and then it declined slowly up to the outbreak of war in 1939, although it was still publishing its journal in the 1960s.

McConnell was no intellectual, and he took no part in the Round Table movement. Yet he was by nature deeply loyal and emotional, and he typically acted decisively and effectively for what he believed in. Unfortunately, the interwar period offered little coherent or even credible imperial policy in which he could place his faith. If he could not see his way clear to embracing empire-wide tariffs, for example, he was hardly alone. Ultimately, the empire was for him a probably unattainable ideal but nonetheless deeply inspiring. Its hold was on his heart rather than on his head.

The McConnells spent a great part of their lives with royalty, vice-royalty, aristocrats, and political and business leaders of England, largely because they had established most of their English friendships in the decade ending in 1914, when self-made wealth such as their own was at last not merely respectable but also widely admired and rewarded. McConnell was sentimental and loyal, but not much of a romantic. He was indulgent of aristocrats and courtiers rather than interested in them. But he profoundly respected them collectively as the representation of order, which he always valued, and so he was punctilious in according them the expected deference. The fact that most of the peers whom he knew best had been just as modest in birth as he was confirmed to him the genius of the British in adapting to the modern world without losing their civilizing habits and institutions.

In common with the Masseys, the Eatons, Canadian Methodists all, and a handful of other Canadian families, the McConnells were almost as at home in England as in Canada. For them, the empire made sense, as it did for few other Canadians, because its traditions conveyed ongoing reassurance that could comfortably accommodate both their own rapid rise and their enduring aspirations for the future. More than that, the empire was a living, modern reality, still a global power to be preserved for the sake of humanity. Their Methodist and evangelical world-view envisioned all peoples as one under God, with the subjects of the British Empire as specially favoured among them but not inherently superior to any. Perhaps the greatest strength of the empire, in their eyes, was its Christian legacy, since it retained a special duty to spread the good news of the Gospel among its non-Christian subjects. Christianity was also part of a much wider process of modernization, of humanization, and, to this extent, its evangelical spirit was not confined to its religious message. The empire, in short, was a force for good. As Leo Amery, colonial secretary and then dominions secretary from 1924 to 1929, and a friend of McConnell's, described it, "the Empire is not external to any of the British nation. It is something like the Kingdom of Heaven within ourselves."[4]

Well into the 1950s, people talked of the British Commonwealth, evolving out of the empire, as an imperial "family." There was the notion of young colonies growing into adulthood as Canada had done, taking their place beside their mother, England. Any characterization that involved family and children held profound power for McConnell. With his McConnell relations nearly all in California, he and Lil readily took young people, such as aides-de-camp from Government House[5] in Ottawa, under their wing as members of their extended family, a process that intensified when they housed several English refugee children during the Second World War. The McConnells did not travel extensively within the empire outside England, but wherever they did – to such places as India, South Africa, and the Bahamas – they met old friends and business associates and made new acquaintances with whom they kept up through the horror of the Second World War and its impoverished aftermath.

At another level, because McConnell was a businessman, not a theoretician or an academic, the empire was an economic power to be revived and sustained, for strategic as well as sentimental reasons. Of course, he could hardly remain aloof from an empire that directly affected his businesses. Much of the sugar processed by St Lawrence Sugar came from the empire, though increasingly more from Cuba. Sun Life Assurance, while based in Montreal, sold policies all over the empire and beyond it, and invisible earnings more generally – in the form of dividends, service charges, and interest – flowed to Canada from all over the world, partly because of admiration for Sun Life as a recognizably "British" company. In the interwar period, McConnell's Ogilvie Flour Mills still claimed to be the largest miller in the empire, and it proudly traded on its royal warrant.

At the same time, McConnell, as a director of INCO and other American companies, was acutely aware of how not merely Canada but even the empire as a whole was being eclipsed economically by the United States after the First World War. But he did not yield to the inevitability of this eclipse, and, with such friends as Lord McGowan of ICI, he struggled to keep Britain and the empire as a partner of the United States rather than as its client. In doing so, he was not motivated by nostalgia, for Great Britain remained still a great economic power. It seemed reasonable to hope that it would rise to meet the American challenge, but it was never clear when this might happen.

Within Canada, American investment after 1918 had replaced British investment as the chief source of capital, probably by 1920, but in many respects British goods remained very competitive with American. They were often competitive with Canadian goods as well, a fact that led to ambivalence about the empire throughout the Canadian economy. Similarly, McConnell was painfully aware that the mother country itself was turning against the empire, and that the cause of imperial free trade, which he had so eagerly espoused from the time he met Joseph Chamberlain in 1904, had lost almost all direction by the 1930s. Britain, for example, never took reciprocal action after Canada granted preferential status to British goods from 1897 to 1907, provisions that were still in place between the world wars. Preferential duties represented a real sacrifice on the part Canadian manufacturers, and they helped lead, for instance, to the closure of Canadian woollen mills that were unable to cope with British competition.[6] Nor was Britain shy in declaring Ogilvie flour overpriced in comparison with its competition from outside the empire. All in all, it was hardly surprising when, following the 1930 imperial conference in London, Sir Charles Gordon of the Bank of Montreal concluded that "free trade within the Empire is not a practical possibility."[7] Moreover, statistics, which counted for much with McConnell, did not encourage hope for a renaissance of the empire as an economic force. Shortly before the imperial economic conference of 1932 in Ottawa, Gordon reported that only 22 per cent of Canadian imports had been drawn from within the empire, and less than 40 per cent of its exports had gone to other parts of it.[8]

The 1932 imperial conference, in fact, exposed how conflicting the interests even of fervent Canadian imperialists were. Perhaps the hardest-working of them, and the chairman of the conference and McConnell's close friend, Prime Minister Bennett, caused tremendous offence in his attempts to browbeat the British delegation, headed by Stanley Baldwin and Neville Chamberlain, respectively the prime minister and the chancellor of the exchequer. Towards the end of the conference, Walter Runciman, president of the Board of Trade, had a showdown with Bennett. He had felt "hotly about the bullying manner" adopted by Bennett towards them, with his "insulting references to U.K. businessmen and their 'lack of enterprise.'" Runciman complained that Bennett was "doing nothing for cotton or woollens – all the things that mattered were left out of the list of benefits he proposed to confer." British manufacturers and exporters, Runciman continued, "were the most enterprising and successful in the world and had achieved their success and won their way (even over tariff walls) without assistance from tariffs, and that was in striking contrast with the Canadians who had been nurtured in a protective hothouse." After an hour's conversation with Bennett, Runciman was struck by the prime minister's "shallow restless mind."[9]

Bennett, with his close ties to Sun Life, the Royal Bank, the CPR, and McConnell, Beaverbrook, Holt, and Gordon, was indeed speaking for St James Street, as well as for Dominion Textile and St Lawrence Sugar and all the other enterprises dependent on protective tariffs. Clever compromises and reciprocal agreements were reached at the conference, but, while they eased tensions, they fell far short of a comprehensive imperial policy. And the atmosphere was poisonous. Dreams of a closer union, held by McConnell and many others, effectively collapsed forever. Alan Lascelles, the private secretary to the governor general, radically changed his mind about the future of Anglo-Canadian relations in the course of the conference, and even came to see the empire itself as a sham. As he reported to his wife: "It was not about Tariffs or Schedules of Currency, but just a general and bitter lament on the shortcomings of the British ... the impression one carries away from Ottawa is that Canadians and British are really as distinct from each other, nationally, as French and Italians, that the whole Empire, in fact, is more of a myth than a reality. What is the use of pretending that we are blood-brothers, and members of a great partnership, etc etc, if our chosen representatives cannot foregather to talk business, without losing their tempers and any regard they may have had for each other."[10]

Initially, many disagreed with Lascelles's assessment. Gordon reported to the Bank of Montreal that the various agreements reached on "mutual preference" between various parts of the empire, which he had advocated since 1929, might yield "highly beneficial results."[11] The subsequent failure, however, to implement many of the decisions of the Ottawa conference, largely as the result of the Great Depression but also because of loopholes in the agreements, marked the practical end of efforts to unite the empire economically through internal reform, so that the imperial unity displayed at the outbreak of war 1939 would be based more on sentiment than on practical advantage. McConnell was acutely aware of all of this, and fearful of the future.[12] Increasingly in the interwar period, he abandoned the term "mother country" in favour of "old country," with its suggestion of senescence.

In their social lives, the McConnells remained personally devoted to the crown. They met and to some extent knew every governor general from the Duke of Connaught to General Georges Vanier, from at least 1914 to 1963. The attachment of Canada to the British crown changed profoundly in this period, and so did the relationship between Canadians and the vice-regal occupants of Government House, evolving from an attitude of automatic deference to one rooted in an appreciation of the alliance between two countries, Britain and Canada. Yet, insofar as there was a high society in Canada, the crown remained at its summit, and an invitation to Government House was among the most prized tokens of prestige and status. McConnell, and even more his wife and daughter, was probably as readily received by every governor general and his wife as any Canadian, from 1927 onwards, just as he warmly welcomed vice-regal representatives into his homes. To understand why is to penetrate some of the deeper layers of the relationships between crown and country, and between McConnell's patriotism and his prestige.

In private houses and schools before the First World War, much of the English-speaking community, and some of the French-speaking, of Montreal had cultivated a devotion to England probably inferior to none elsewhere. Thereafter, however, the cultural pre-eminence of English Montrealers seemed to be shrinking, as were their homes. Most Square Mile houses employed fewer servants than before, if any at all, since the demands of the conflict had opened new employment opportunities in industry. Some grand houses closed down completely long before the Crash, such as that built on Peel Street and Pine Avenue by James Ross. (The Ross house stood empty until 1942, when McConnell bought it and gave it to the Faculty of Law at McGill as Chancellor Day Hall.) By 1918, the houses of lords Strathcona, Mount Stephen, and Shaughnessy had been abandoned by their owners or were about to be. Even Ravenscrag, the vast Victorian stage for Montreal society, entered into a sort of twilight, with the wartime deaths of three of the four children of Sir Montagu and Lady Allan.

In earlier years, governors general had regularly come to Montreal to host lavish entertainments, such as balls and tobogganing and snowshoeing parties. Now there were few houses large enough, or with sufficient staff, to accommodate more than cocktail parties. Even very prosperous people were moving into flats. Moreover, the few houses that were built after the war tended to be smaller and simpler than the pre-war ones. The most conspicuous exception to this trend towards reduced circumstances was McConnell's own house on Pine Avenue. This was by far the largest of the new post-war houses, and as such was one of the most fitting in which to entertain vice-royalty. Undertakings on this scale demanded practicality as well as dignity. Vice-regal parties travelled with ladies-in-waiting, aides-de-camp, secretaries, and servants, all of whom had to be accommodated, fed, and entertained. McConnell was happy to put all of his houses – not only the one on Pine Avenue but those in Dorval and the Laurentians – at the disposal of visitors from Government House.

During the Great War, the Duke of Connaught, as governor general, tried to overcome his family's German origins by participating in such efforts as the Patriotic Fund, in which McConnell himself worked. The duchess improved her English from broken to quite acceptable, and even repudiated her cousin, the kaiser of Germany, Wilhelm II. But the war years were too grim for much entertainment at Government House and indeed there was to be little fun or glitter there in comparison with that under previous regimes. Things improved somewhat when the ninth Duke of Devonshire succeeded the Duke of Connaught in Ottawa in 1916. His wife was the daughter of the fifth Marquess of Lansdowne, who had himself been governor general of Canada from 1883 to 1888. Unfortunately, the duke was extremely shy, and his eyes seemed perpetually hooded, which rendered his mien languid if not somnolent. On his wildly successful visit to Canada in 1919, the Prince of Wales (later King Edward VIII) had to spend much time at Government House. The duke, he admitted, was popular, but "he's got almost as little brains as your boy angel, he is a B.F. [Big Fart] and so slow!!"[13] What most isolated the place, however, was the sheer grandeur and remoteness that had attached for centuries to all Dukes of Devonshire.

Richer and more feudal by far than the royal Connaughts, the Devonshires arrived with a retinue of servants in the family livery. After their six great houses in England and Ireland, Government House was hardly more commodious to them than a workman's cottage, a view that echoed the assessment of the first governor general,

Lord Dufferin, who described the building as no more imposing than a "suburban villa," and of the Duchess of Connaught, who had called it "a gymnasium flanked by a riding school."[14] Still, though there was a standing Colonial Office directive that the governor general should accept hospitality only from members of the nobility and the diplomatic corps, the governor general marked out his own path in this regard, entertaining those he deemed to be members of Canadian high society. In practice, these were the established Ottawa families, since travel to the capital, even from Montreal and Toronto, was not undertaken casually.

There was nothing grand about Lord Byng of Vimy, who succeeded the Duke of Devonshire in 1920. He was impatient with ceremony and had in any case won huge popularity among the Canadian troops whom he had commanded during the Great War. He preferred being called by his nickname, "Bungo," by Canadian intimates, such as his aide-de-camp, Henry Willis-O'Connor, and Georges Vanier and Sir Arthur Currie – all Canadians whom he had befriended before coming to Canada. In 1926 Byng refused Prime Minister Mackenzie King's request to dissolve Parliament, and he sent for Arthur Meighen to form a new government. When Meighen was defeated in the ensuing election, King returned as prime minister. The relationship between King and the governor general now degenerated into mutual loathing. McConnell was not particularly close to the Byngs, although in her widowhood, largely spent in Ottawa and Victoria during the Second World War, Lady Byng came to depend heavily on his assistance.

After the Byngs, the McConnells found real and warm friends in Ottawa in Viscount and Viscountess Willingdon. She was the daughter of Earl Brassey, who had befriended McConnell during the Standard Chemical sales campaign of 1904 and was a mentor thereafter. Lord Willingdon, previously governor of Madras and Bombay and now governor general of Canada from 1927 to 1931, could exude suavity and charm, with an air of disarming superiority. He was also modest, humorous, and amiable – which was just as well, for he was charged with a role both less powerful and more iconographic than governors general had played before. It was the heyday of jazz, and the Willingdons' Government House nimbly adopted a breezy, unpretentious style. Lady Willingdon organized dances for young people at the Château Laurier Hotel, and he cultivated his image as a vigorous sporting type. Their love of fun notwithstanding, they were absolute professionals in running their operations like clockwork, since they conceived it their duty to show themselves publicly as much as possible, "to keep the people loyal."

Byng's principal Canadian aide-de-camp, Henry Willis-O'Connor, was a link between many Canadians and Government House from 1921 to 1945, and he was probably responsible for introducing the Willingdons to the McConnells. At any rate, they were all firmly connected by 1928, when a granddaughter of Sir Sandford Fleming, Margot (Margaret) Fleming, married Caryl Hardinge, the fourth Viscount

The wedding reception of Viscount Hardinge ADC and Margot Fleming, attended by
the Willingdons and the McConnells. Front row, from left: Margaret MacDougall, David
McConnell, Raymond Willis-O'Connor, Viscountess Hardinge, Viscount Hardinge,
Pamela Erwin, Lilias Ahearn, Cora Kennedy, and Louise Fitzhugh, September 1929.
(Private collection, courtesy of Mr and the Hon. Mrs. Worsley and Willa Worsley.)

Hardinge, who was an aide-de-camp to Willingdon. At the wedding in Ottawa, the
boys Raymond Willis-O'Connor and David McConnell served as tiny pages. Like the
guests from England, the McConnells stayed at Government House for the occasion.

Like other vice-regal couples, the Willingdons found Montreal a glamorous retreat,
and the Citadel in Quebec City, a charming one, in comparison to Ottawa. Various
causes brought them frequently to Montreal, and they became bound to the McConnells. Their first son had fallen in action in 1914, and their surviving son, Inigo, was
mainly in England. The Willingdons thus developed a particular fondness for Kit
McConnell, the daughter they had never had. Lady Willingdon, the most exacting of
mistresses of household staff, shared with Lil a passion for decorating, and she and
her husband were among the earliest visitors to McConnell's new house in Val David,
starting in October 1930.

Willingdon, as recounted earlier, put McConnell in charge of his money. Despite
reverses in his investment, the Crash of 1929 and the Depression did not sink him,
and he remained grateful to McConnell, consulting him on investments at least as late
as 1936. He remained in Ottawa until 1931 when, to his surprise, he was offered the
most glittering office in the empire, the vice-royalty of India. As their ship sailed from

The Governor General and Viscountess Willingdon with their staff, before the opening of Parliament in Ottawa:, probably 1928. From left: Captain Fiennes ADC, Colonel Henry Willis-O'Connor ADC, Col. Humphrey Snow (comptroller of the household), E.C. Miéville (secretary to His Excellency), Miss Phyllis Egerton (niece of Her Excellency), Captain R.J. Streatfield ADC, and Captain R.W. Rayner. Private collection.

Halifax on their way back to England, Lady Willingdon with characteristic exuberance scribbled "Goodbye, my darlings!" to the McConnells. The friendship between the two families would continue even after the death of Willingdon in 1941.

According to the charter of McGill University, the governor general was to be the visitor, fulfilling the historic role of the crown in overseeing institutions of higher learning. And, according to the charter of the Royal Victoria Hospital, the principal hospital attached to McGill, he was also to be its visitor. These two roles solidified the connection between McConnell – who was a dominant voice on the boards of both institutions for over thirty years – to the governor general of the day, whoever he might be. The duties of the visitor encompassed subsidiary roles, such as that of patron of the annual Royal Victoria Hospital Charity ball, which was McConnell's creation. Nor was the governor general's wife omitted, since she was patroness of the Victorian Order of Nurses (another favourite cause of McConnell's) as well as of the ball.[15]

McConnell served as chairman of the ball for about a quarter-century. This event, dating back to 1847 and, after a hiatus between 1852 and 1897, held annually, usually at the Mount Royal Hotel, was one of the most important of the social season in the city, and McConnell's assumption of its chairmanship signalled his ascent to the

McConnell (fourth from left) with Captain Robin Stuart-French ADC (third),
the Earl of Bessborough (fifth), and Sir John Child ADC (seventh) on the *Sir
Hugh Allan*, n.d. McCord Museum, M2003.8.6.2.97.

highest ranks of Montreal society. By 1922, its local patronesses were all friends of the
McConnells and included Lady Currie, Lady Gordon, Mrs D. Forbes Angus, Mrs
C.C. Ballantyne, Mrs A.J. Brown, Mrs P.P. Cowans, and Mrs Lorne Webster.

With the departure of the Willingdons, the McConnells lost real friends at Government House, but these were replaced by equally good friends in the Earl and
Countess of Bessborough, whose house, Stansted Park in Hampshire, was to become
the McConnells' English home away from home. The Bessboroughs tried hard to be
non-partisan, mindful of the hatred between the Byngs and King, and between the
Willingdons and R.B. Bennett. But, as a Tory, Bessborough seems to have been a real
admirer of Bennett and relatively distant from King. McConnell was probably one
of the few men equally acceptable to Lady Byng, the Willingdons, and the Bessboroughs. He would remain so with their successors, and he may have been unique in his
close and real friendships with prime ministers Meighen, King, and Bennett as well,
three men who hardly spoke to one another.

Although forearmed and forewarned by Lady Byng, the Bessboroughs endured a
harder time in adjusting to Canada than either the Byngs or the Willingdons. The
McConnells, by now quite at home at Government House, probably saw this from the
start and, no doubt equipped with an introduction from the Willingdons, showered

The governor general and the Countess of Bessborough before the opening of Parliament, 1932. Back row, from left: Sir John Child, ADC, A.F. Lascelles (secretary to His Excellency), Lt.-Col. Henry Willis-O'Connor ADC, the Hon. Mrs Gordon-Ives (secretary to Her Excellency), Lt D.A. Fuller RN, ADC, Captain R.F.H. Stuart-French ADC, Major Eric D. Mackenzie, pages J.F. Loveless and John McLaren. Private collection.

them with kindnesses. Lord Bessborough was immensely dignified, conscientious, and ever mindful of being the representative of the king. He was initially taken aback by the manners of the New World, as when McConnell marked the Bessboroughs' first visit to Val David by flicking butterballs into the air with his knife. The drill at Government House was stiffer, with curtsies and bows even when the McConnells were dining privately with the Bessboroughs. Lord Willingdon had always insisted that the ladies should precede him, but under the new regime the governor general – as was established protocol for the representative of the sovereign – always proceeded first. Even when passing her father in the corridor, his daughter Moyra felt compelled to curtsy.

It was actually Moyra who first brought the two families together. She was of exactly the same age as Kit and isolated from most Ottawa girls by having to be educated exclusively by a governess. Kit was designated as one of her playmates and had to spend weekends at Government House keeping her company. Moyra also spent a good deal of time with the McConnells in Montreal, as did one of her brothers, Eric, who was formally styled Viscount Duncannon. Through the daughters, the mothers became the best of friends, and Roberte (Lady Bessborough) wrote to Lil several times a week for years. The whole Bessborough ménage, including the household staff of secretaries, aides-de-camp, ladies-in-waiting, visiting relations, and friends and notables, became central to the social orbit of the McConnells. Aide-de-camps tended to be young, rambunctious men, and they lent a leisurely "Tennis anyone?" tone to the life of the McConnells, in which the mischievous McConnell himself, a devotee of tennis, was more than happy to join.[16]

Between McConnell himself and Bessborough, there seems to have been a correct but not particularly close relationship. Bessborough's deafness tended to make him seem remote, and Vincent Massey complained that he was never relaxed but rather always "buttoned up." Still, thanks to the wives and daughters of Bessborough and McConnell, the families spent much time together. The Bessboroughs' youngest son, George St Lawrence Neuflize Ponsonby, born at the Royal Victoria Hospital in Montreal in 1931, was practically to be adopted by the McConnells during the war. So was George's cousin, Edward Cavendish. In various ways, therefore, the two families were extraordinarily linked, and, especially through the Bessboroughs, the McConnells became more familiar to the higher reaches of English society. During the Depression, Bessborough reduced the scale of his official entertainments in keeping with the austerities of the time. But the vice-regal life that the Bessboroughs shared with the McConnells remained punctuated by traditional levees, drawing rooms (receptions), dinners, and country pursuits. The McConnells did their best to help Lady Bessborough survive her tours and the Canadian winter. Overcoming his Methodist aversion for the theatre, McConnell even agreed to become a governor of the Dominion Drama Festival, the governor general's most innovative project.

Bessborough's principal adviser was his private secretary, Alan Lascelles, "Tommy" to his friends, whose acerbic letters and diaries convey a vivid picture of Anglo-Canadian relations of the period, as seen from Government House.[17] Lascelles, who usually accompanied the governor general to the McConnells' and elsewhere, was a pivotal behind-the-scenes figure in the maintenance of the monarchy more generally in the first half of the century, serving as private secretary to George V, Edward VIII, George VI, and Elizabeth II. Although to all appearances a classic courtier, he concealed a dyspeptic, querulous, and sceptical side, to the point where he could find the empire ridiculous and the flummery surrounding royalty distasteful. He did not particularly warm to the McConnells, although Jack gave his daughter, Lavinia, a set of golf clubs. The "château McConnell," as Lascelles called the house on Pine Avenue, was "a typical example of a house that is luxurious without being comfortable, & an utterly unsuitable background for the worthy creatures that live in it."[18] He wearied of the dinners that he had to attend with the governor general and McConnell, both in Ottawa and in Montreal.

The arcane rituals of the court at Ottawa were now as familiar to the McConnells as to any Canadians, perhaps more so. Their visits to England consisted of an almost endless round of even more formal socializing. Smart luncheons, teas, dinners, royal receptions, and switching from town to country life demanded several changes of clothes each day. For Jack, it might mean tweeds or even knee-breeches; for Lil, every item of dress was carefully coordinated with jewellery; and for both, there were special outfits for tennis and golf, transatlantic voyages, and the various seasons in various climes. His valet and her lady's maid travelled everywhere with them, with enormous steamer trunks, and their stately progresses by train or ship made any journey an occasion for socializing. They became almost royal or at least vice-regal in appearance themselves.

Jack and Lil travelled to England and the continent probably every year of the interwar period, but unfortunately little record remains of their journeys. One exception occurred in 1936, when they were away for over four months, from January to May, with Kit and their youngest son, David, on a journey that took them to England, South Africa, India, Singapore, Hong Kong, Shanghai, Japan, Hawaii, and then back to Canada, with the first stop in Vancouver and then a cross-country train trip to Montreal. Lil and David, at least, kept a great collection of souvenirs of their trip, and Jack himself, like them, kept a diary. Essentially, it was a cruise no different from that taken by many in the 1930s, leisurely and pampered. But the McConnells took the opportunity to visit friends in India and Japan, and they made other friends with whom they were to keep up in the years to come. Jack brought along a movie camera to record it all in colour. Unfortunately, it had been improperly repaired in Montreal and it failed to work so that little photographic record exists of the trip. His friends thought that he had forgotten to take off the lens cap throughout, but that was not true!

It would be wrong to suggest that McConnell thoroughly enjoyed the trip, although his wife and children certainly did. He was not a particularly hardy traveller, and he had no deep interest in other cultures, but as usual he gave his full attention to the task at hand. He assiduously cultivated new friends and acquaintances, and stored memories that were to last him for the rest of his life. This was a unique experience for him, but it encapsulated three major themes of his life generally: money, prestige, and the British Empire. It summed up for him the intimate interconnectedness of the far-flung empire, bound by business, blood, and friendship as well as political power. It was the longest holiday ever taken by so much of the family together, and they never forgot their weeks in India in particular. The fragmentary recollections of it that survive offer a tantalizing glimpse of the place that McConnell had attained even outside Canada.

Before leaving, McConnell made the final preparations for the Royal Victoria Hospital Charity Ball.[19] With his characteristic punctiliousness, he wrote to every important purchaser of tickets and arranged for floral decorations for the luncheon for Lord and Lady Bessborough at the Mount Royal Club preceding the ball. In a frenzy of activity in the first four days of January, he delivered a "personal remembrance" to

Mrs W.A. Black on the death of her husband, the president of Ogilvie Flour Mills, whom McConnell had succeeded. He sent McGill $25,000, an instalment of his $100,000 subscription towards deficit elimination. To Sir Edward Beatty he sent a cheque of $5,000 to clear the deficit of the Shawbridge Boys' Farm. To the Mission and Maintenance Fund of the United Church, he sent $15,000; and there were many other cheques in respect of his businesses, as well as at least one stock option to exercise. His chauffeur Lefebvre had to take the car for repairs, and the butler Chapman to send boxes to the vault. He approved the final payment on the construction of his son John's house on Redpath Crescent. On 4 January, various friends came to say goodbye, his last visitor being R.B. Bennett, the defeated prime minister.

On the following day, McConnell, Lil, Kathleen, and David departed by train from Windsor Station for New York. Ina Wallace, Lil's Scottish lady's maid since 1932, and Walter Adams, Jack's valet, were accompanying the McConnells on the trip, joined by Dr Edward Archibald, who was in the party to operate on Lil's gallstones should this prove necessary.[20] On the 6th, in New York, McConnell managed to attend a meeting of the board of International Nickel before returning to the Plaza Hotel. He was uncharacteristically exhausted, and Lil was bedridden with an infection and her gallstones.

On the 7th, the family at last boarded the *Empress of Britain*, a ship so familiar to them that Lil greeted the officers by name. Launched in 1930 by the Prince of Wales, later King Edward VIII, the liner was twice the size of any other designed for world cruises, 760 feet in length and the pride of the Canadian Pacific fleet. Howard Ferguson, former Conservative premier of Ontario and latterly high commissioner for Canada in London, was aboard with his wife. McConnell, an old acquaintance from their Canadian International Paper days, spent his first evening at sea with him, discussing both the departure of Bennett from Canada and the arrival of Lord Tweedsmuir, the new governor general. The McConnells particularly spent time with Colonel Henry Cockshutt, who had retired as lieutenant governor of Ontario in 1927 and had been well known to McConnell long before, being a fellow director of the Bank of Montreal, the CPR, and International Nickel. One important person McConnell was to meet on the ship was the American financier Floyd Carlisle, in whose Niagara Hudson utilities empire McConnell had been heavily invested. Tennis, mainly with the Cockshutts, ping-pong, bridge, films, much dancing, and the casino filled their days until the landing at Majorca a week later. Dr Archibald wrote in his diary that the McConnells were "very kind and jolly" and Jack "like a boy playing truant & kicking up his heels. Full of small practical jokes."[21] At a fancy-dress ball attended by eighty, McConnell arrived richly attired and bewigged as a lord high chancellor of the eighteenth century.

Then, on 20 January, came the news of the death of King George V on the previous evening. McConnell still wanted to play tennis but was informed that all games had

McConnell (dressed in black as a lord high chancellor) at a fancy-dress ball
aboard the *Empress of Britain*, 1936. Private collection.

been cancelled out of respect for the late king. The McConnells attended a memorial
service in the Mayfair Lounge of the ship. The entry of the entire empire into mourning, and the rigorous curtailment of ceremonies and pomp, was to render the visit, at
least in India, suddenly a relatively sombre affair.[22] McConnell wryly noted that one
woman had boarded the ship with eighty trunks of colourful dresses for her visit to
the viceroy, but none of them was now suitable because of the mourning. The *durbar*
– a great gathering of India's princes – planned to mark George V's silver jubilee and
intended as the highlight of the trip – was, of course, to be cancelled. So was the
Royal Victoria Hospital Charity Ball in Montreal. Life on the *Empress* nonetheless
went on for the travellers.

Five days later, they landed in South Africa for a stay of eight days. Lil found
Cape Town majestic, and she and Jack went to have tea with their old friend Sir William Clark, the former British high commissioner in Ottawa and now high commissioner in Pretoria, and his wife. The Clarks took them shopping in search of suits
and dresses for the hot weather and black mourning clothes. As always, there were
diplomatic niceties to be observed. In Cape Town, McConnell called on Lady Mackenzie, daughter of the Toronto lawyer S.H. Blake and the wife of Sir Alexander Mackenzie, former president of Brazilian Traction. She told McConnell that Mackenzie
would gladly return to the presidency of Brazilian if asked, an admission that shocked
McConnell, who thought that Mackenzie would have been also shocked. Other busi-

The McConnells and Kit arrive in Durban, 1936.
Associated Screen News, private collection.

ness intruded, such as a call to the local representative of Sun Life and a letter to be sent to Ogilvie Flour Mills about salaries.

Durban was a thrill too. Crowds cheered at the arrival of the ship, and there were old friends to visit there as well. McConnell found the Zulu dances put on for them interesting but "not [e]specially warlike." He thought that the natives were "contented, childlike people" who liked the British but not the Dutch. While Lil bought a zebra skin, Jack bought books, including *Jock of the Bushveld*, which was to become one of his favourites.

Then it was on to India. By the time of the McConnells' visit, the previous viceroy, Lord Irwin (later Halifax), had promised India eventual dominion status, and so there was bound to be a faintly elegiac quality to their stay in the country. Like everyone else, the McConnells themselves sensed that the days of the Raj might be numbered, although no one knew how fast change might come, or how far it might go. In 1931 General Sir Arthur Currie, the greatest Canadian commander of the First World War and principal of McGill, and a close friend of the McConnells, had visited India. On his way home, he wrote:

> I am not saying it for publication my dear Jack, but I am beginning to think that Europe's day is done, and that she no longer dominates the world. The hope of England herself lies in the Empire, but she herself does not yet appreciate that fact. Before the war she was on top of the world and beheld her ships sailing the

seven seas and back again carrying raw products one way and manufactured articles the other. That day is gone and will never return. Her losses in the war were so great in men and money that it seemed to leave her benumbed and stupefied, she acted as if she were in a dream, hoping to wake up some morning and find that all was well again. She seems to have lost her grip besides which she saddled herself with some strange policies notably the "dole." They delude themselves by thinking that they have a genius for governing. We no sooner became an Empire than we lost a valuable part of it i.e. the United States, through bad governing. The present Dominions are in the Empire solely because they want to be. They like the freedom they enjoy, but they have won freedom by their own efforts and not because the Mother Country willed and wished it so to be.[23]

McConnell's response is not recorded, but he was no doubt mindful of such a weighty judgment from a friend whom he held in great esteem.

On 12 February, the *Empress* finally docked at Bombay and the McConnells proceeded to the Taj Mahal Hotel. After luncheon with a local representative of Sun Life, they embarked on an automobile trip to the Towers of Silence, where the Parsees dispose of their dead through sky burials. Then, it was on to New Delhi by train, in a carriage lent by the viceroy. They proceeded to the palace that served as Viceroy's House, the most resplendent building in New Delhi. An earlier visitor thought that nothing but the piazza of St Peter's in Rome could compare to the setting, and the house itself, designed by Sir Edwin Lutyens, was "the first real vindication of modern architecture … really modern, [though] not cubist or skyscrapery."[24] He added that the house was "one of the great palaces of the world, and the only one erected within the last hundred years. Its architecture combines the grandeur of Bernini and the subtlety of Palladio with the colour, shade and water of Mohammedan Asia … The fusion between East and West is only incidentally one of the architectural motifs. It is a fusion also of tastes, comforts, and conceptions of beauty, in different climates … Lutyens has combined the gorgeous façade, coloured and dramatic, of Asia, with the solid habit, cubic and intellectual, of European building. Taking the best of East and West, bests which are complementary, he has made of them a double magnificence."[25]

For McConnell in 1936, therefore, the house and the new city that it dominated were not a mere architectural curiosity, much less a historical relic. On the contrary, he could not help but see it as a bold feat of engineering, enterprise, and faith. The Willingdons were the second full-time occupants of Viceroy's House, with its 4,000 servants and 2,000 troops. It covered an area larger than that of the Palace of Versailles and had cost £2 million. Its architect, Lutyens, actually had designed much of the city of New Delhi in the 1920s.[26] He planned it for a population of 60,000, and the whole

The Viceroy and Vicereine of India at a costume ball just before the
arrival of the McConnells, December 1936. Private collection.

venture had become the most grandiose and ambitious project of the empire in Asia,
with Viceroy's House as its jewel. Its marbled interior remained frigid even under the
Indian sun, and it formed the central part of a governmental complex so overbearing
as to suggest an impenetrable defence to the pretensions of Indian nationalism.

On their arrival at Viceroy's House, Lady Willingdon received them warmly in a
cavernous entrance hall and then they went up to see the viceroy, whom they found
looking extraordinarily well. The Willingdons even greeted Walter, McConnell's
valet, as an "old friend." They seemed unusually delighted to see the McConnells
and personally escorted them to their bedroom suites, which were enormous and lavishly appointed, with servants sleeping outside each door in the passages for security.
After tea, there were tours of the gardens and the state rooms. The visitors found that
the State Dining Room alone was more than one hundred feet long and could seat as
many people, with a servant standing behind each chair.

Viceroy's House, New Delhi, c.1936. Private collection.

The Viceroy and Vicereine of India enthroned, c.1936, photograph by Kinsey
Bros. Private collection.

On the following day, Kit played tennis with one of the aides-de-camp against her
father and a Mrs Gosling. Lady Willingdon was attired completely in mourning, even
on the tennis court, down to her black tennis shoes. At dinner, through which a band
played, they met the Aga Khan III, who had just celebrated his golden jubilee as imam

LUNCHEON PLAN.

Captain Freeman-Thomas.

Captain Pearson.	Captain Khurshid.
Master McConnell.	Captain Daubeny.
Flight-Lieut. Johnson.	Mr. Stileman.
Dr. Pavry.	Miss Pavry.
Rajah Sir Vasudeva Rajah, of Kollengode.	Mr. Schwaiger.
Miss Sifton.	Sir Alexander Gibb.
The Hon. David Lloyd.	Mrs. Carlisle.
Mrs. Elliott.	The Earl of Caledon.
Mrs. Carlisle.	H. H. the Maharaja Scindia of Gwalior.
The Lady Margaret Alexander.	
THE VICEROY.	**HER EXCELLENCY.**
H. H. the Khan of Kalat.	The Hon. Sir Maneckji Dadabhoy.
Mrs. Strettell.	The Mother Rani of Kalsia.
Sir Victor Sassoon.	Major-General Strettell.
Miss Dadabhoy.	Mrs. Evans-Gwynne.
Sir James Irvine.	Sir Abdul Halim Ghurnavi.
Miss Norah Hill.	Mrs. Pam.
Brigadier Evans-Gwynne.	Brigadier the Hon. H. R. L. G. Alexander.
Colonel Sir Hassan Suhrawardy.	Miss Schwaiger.
Mr. Duke.	Captain Elliott.
Staff Officer to H. H. the Maharaja Scindia of Gwalior.	Mr. L. Carlisle.

Captain Stocker.

ENTRANCE.

GUESTS.

	L.	G.
His Highness the Maharaja Scindia of Gwalior	–	1
His Highness the Khan of Kalat	–	1
The Hon'ble Sir Maneckji Dadabhoy, K.C.S.I., K.C.I.E., President, Council of State, and Miss Dadabhoy	1	1
Major-General C. R. D. Strettell, C.B., Deputy Adjutant-General, Army Headquarters, and Mrs. Strettell	1	1
The Mother Rani of Kalsia	1	1
Rajah Sir Vasudeva Rajah, Member, Legislative Assembly (Madras)	–	1
Sir Abdul Halim Ghuznavi, Member, Legislative Assembly (Bengal)	–	1
Brigadier A. Evans-Gwynne, D.S.O., Commandant, Senior Officers' School, Belgaum, and Mrs. Evans-Gwynne	1	1
Colonel Sir Hassan Suhrawardy, O.B.E., Hony. Surgeon to the Viceroy	1	1
Mrs. Pam (wife of Lieut.-Colonel E. Pam.)	1	–
Dr. Jal Pavry, Author	1	1
Miss Bapsy Pavry	–	1
Captain A. C. Elliott, and Mrs. Elliott	1	1
Miss Norah Hill, Organising Secretary, Indian Red Cross Society	–	1
Miss Sifton	–	1
Mr. I. Schwaiger, Art Expert, and Miss Schwaiger	1	1
Mr. Carlisle, Stock Broker, and Mrs. Carlisle, and Mr. L. G. Carlisle	1	2
Staff Officer to H. H. the Maharaja Scindia of Gwalior	1	–
Captain S. M. Khurshid, Staff Officer to H. H. the Khan of Kalat	–	1

HOUSE PARTY.

	L.	G.
The Earl of Caledon	–	1
Sir Victor Sassoon, Bart.	–	1
Sir Alexander Gibb, O.B.E., C.B.	–	1
Sir James Irvine, C.B.E.	–	1
Brigadier the Hon. H. R. L. G. Alexander, D.S.O., M.C., Commander, Nowshera Brigade, and the Lady Margaret Alexander	1	1
The Hon'ble David Lloyd	–	1
Mr. C. G. Stileman	–	1
Master McConnell	–	1

THEIR EXCELLENCIES & STAFF.

	L.	G.
The Viceroy	–	1
Her Excellency	–	1
Mr. C. B. Duke, I.C.S., Assistant Private Secretary to the Viceroy	1	1
Flight-Lieut. J. C. E. A. Johnson	–	1
Captain R. G. Daubeny	–	1
Captain R. B. Freeman-Thomas } Aides-de-Camp	–	1
Captain F. F. Pearson	–	1
Captain A. C. Stocker	–	1
	13	30
		43

Guest list for a luncheon at Viceroy's House, 1936. Private collection.

of the Ismaili sect of Islam in Bombay. The next day, the McConnells went to a polo match in the afternoon with the Willingdons and with the Carlisles of New York, and then to the New Delhi Air Station, to see the viceroy open it and name it after himself and to observe the conclusion of an air race from Bombay. Among the guests whom McConnell met at tea was the representative of Sun Life in India, Sir Phiroze Sethna, who was also a member of the governor general's council.

On Sunday, the McConnells accompanied the Willingdons to the Cathedral Church of the Redeemer adjoining Viceroy's House. Afterwards, they met the bishop of Calcutta and watched the viceroy take the salute at the church parade, McConnell noticing Willingdon's "very snappy style." Jack and Lil then went to luncheon with Sir James Grigg, the finance member of the council, following which they had a motor-car tour of the city. Grigg expressed considerable doubt about the future of the Raj, his views on the subject being thus summarized by McConnell: "Thinks it difficult country, and wonders why British want to bother with it."

On Monday, the McConnells attended the first morning of the Imperial Delhi Horse Show with its patron, the viceroy. At dinner, one of the guests was Mohammed Ali Jinnah, who within eleven years and upon the partition of India was to become known as the father of Pakistan. On the following day, they returned to the Imperial

Painting of the same luncheon at Viceroy's House, 1936, David at right in an
Eton suit. Private collection, courtesy of Peter McConnell.

Horse Show in the afternoon. Their last day in Delhi, 15 February, was not demanding. After luncheon, there was a polo match at the Durbar Grounds in old Delhi, followed by tea with the maharani of Gwalior and her nineteen-year-old son for whom
she acted as regent. The maharani agreed to arrange a tiger shoot for the McConnells
when they reached Gwalior. Then the McConnells departed for Peshawar.

Lord Willingdon had provided them with a vice-regal railway carriage for their use
on their journey to the northwest of India. It contained four double bedrooms, a large
room for dining and sitting, a kitchen, and rooms for four servants. Peshawar was on
the Northwest Frontier with Afghanistan, a potential flashpoint in the long-standing
"Great Game" between Great Britain and Russia for hegemony over Central Asia,
and there they stayed at Dean's Hotel. Then they travelled on through the almost
mythic Khyber Pass, where they saw long lines of camels laden with merchandise.

By the 24th, they were in Lahore, staying at Government House as the only guests
of Sir Herbert Emerson, who was to remain a friend in later years. The domed dining
room of the house was also the upper story of the tomb of Mohammed Kasim Khan, a
cousin of Emperor Akbar the Great, dating from about 1635. The McConnells toured
the governor's train, with its thirteen carriages, capable of carrying a complete office
staff and seventy servants, and Jack played billiards after dinner. The highlight of
Lahore was the mosques and tombs in the Shadra Gardens, and the next day Jack and
David went on an ineffective hunt of vultures and parrots using air-guns.

Back at Viceroy's House in New Delhi on the 26th, there was time for another tea
and dinner before McConnells were off again on a train. Though not himself con-

Lady Willingdon presents an award at the 1936 Imperial Horse Show in
New Delhi, which the McConnells attended. Private collection.

spicuously wanting in staff, Willingdon remained impressed by the equipage of the
McConnells, describing Jack and Lil as "very rich with a surgeon they have brought
out with them, paying him 1000£ and all his exs. [expenses], for he was to be ready
with his knife in case she required an operation."[27] Early on the 27th, they arrived
in Jaipur for breakfast at the Rambagh Palace, and then toured other palaces and
shopped. After tea with the chief of police, they proceeded to the Sawai Mohodpur
shooting camp, about a hundred miles away, where the maharaja of Jaipur was waiting. A tiger hunt began the next morning. Jack, Lil, and Kit went up on machans,
elevated platforms, and David rode an elephant. The beat started and various wildlife
appeared, but no tigers. The next day was spent looking at jewels back in Jaipur and
on an elephant ride up to Humbur. A visit to Udaipur took up 2 and 3 March. The
ruler of the state, styled the maharana, boasted a more exalted ancestry than even the
Sun King of France, Louis XIV. He did not merely compare himself to the sun but
claimed to be in direct descent from the sun, like the Egyptian King Tutankhamen.
Thus the McConnells may have noticed splendiferous golden disks with rays adoring
the palaces, each decorated with eyes, a nose, a handlebar moustache, and a mouth
– a solar face with what seemed a mysterious smile. The following three days in Agra
covered, among other things, the Taj Mahal by moonlight, and then they went on
to Gwalior for dinner with the Maharaja Scindia, whom they had recently met in
New Delhi.

Lil on an elephant, 1936. Private collection.

In Gwalior, the McConnells stayed at the modern State Guesthouse. With Archibald, they climbed up to the great fort of Gwalior, about three hundred feet above a plain, with an eleventh-century temple at the top. Then they had dinner at the palace, a heavy, ornate structure. McConnell was by this time thoroughly weary of tombs and temples, taking his shoes off for sacred sites, and eating spicy food. He gloomily composed ditties. Nevertheless, he impressed the maharaja enough for the maharaja to ask to stay with the McConnells in Canada.

The next morning, 7 March, McConnell at last bagged his tiger. The shooting party drove into the countryside, sat on wicker stools, and waited for the seventy-five or so "beaters" and two elephants to drive the tiger to them. There was no elevated perch, or machan, as there had been in Jaipur. Instead there was a small stone wall on the edge of a cliff, overlooking a river, along which, in due course, a tiger was seen ambling. Since McConnell was the guest of honour, and only one tiger might be shot in a day, the animal was his. He shot twice, and both bullets reached their mark, but the tiger continued to struggle until others finally dispatched it. On 8 March there was more hunting, and this time Jack killed his own tiger. Its skin for many years adorned Saran Chai.

Dinners at the palace followed over the next two days, after which Archibald summed up his impressions of Lil and Jack: "She is clearly very ambitious, a trifle emotional, very feminine, can't bear failure. Socially I imagine that she is more ambitious than Jack. She is a good talker in company, keeps things moving, but is not so

McConnell and his tiger, Gwalior, 1936.
Private collection.

entertaining as he – has not much humour, but does keep up her end. He impresses everybody – as I see all along in India – with his look of keenness and decision, in spite of his gaiety. He is full of stories, incidents of the trip, light talk, but strength behind it. He was consulted on finance matters by His Ex & Her Ex, & by the Aga Khan at Delhi. I like them both very much indeed. They are both generous and straightforward."[28] McConnell must in the end have enjoyed his stay in Gwalior. Three years later, in 1939, he presented the maharaja with a .470-calibre double-barrelled rifle.

After Gwalior, it was on to Mysore, where the McConnells went up to Chamudi Hill to see a famous stone bull, nine hundred years old, before dinner. Before breakfast the next day, they went to see His Highness's zoo and then the royal stables, then to the Technical Institute and to Seringapotam, where the fearless Tipoo Sultan, whose emblem was the tiger, had fallen while resisting the British. Still more sightseeing followed over the rest of the day. On the 15th, Jack went fishing in the morning, and then for all there was a tiresome journey to Dhanushkodi, from where they sailed for Ceylon.

Once in Ceylon, they boarded a train for Colombo. Their stay there was short, just long enough to do some sightseeing, shopping, and swimming before heading off first to Singapore and then to Hong Kong, where, as previously in Durban, the McConnells were pulled by rickshaws. They made the rounds of the compulsory stops for all visitors to these colonies, and then they left Hong Kong on the *Empress of Canada*. On reaching Shanghai, they toured areas bombed by the Japanese in 1932, and then they were off to their next stop, Japan. They arrived first at Kobe and Kyoto, where they saw a cherry-blossom dance, following which they left for Yokohama, Nikko, and Tokyo.

In Tokyo, the McConnells found themselves among very old friends, the Canadian minister, Sir Herbert Marler (within a few weeks, the new Canadian minister to Washington) and his wife Beatrice, who was a cousin of Sir Montagu Allan and a niece of Lady Meredith, the widow of Sir Vincent Meredith of the Bank of Montreal. Marler had hired Kenneth Rea – who had designed his houses in Senneville and Westmount and outbuildings for his former estate in Drummondville, in the Eastern Townships, as well as McConnell's Pine Avenue residence – to design the Canadian Legation, which also served as the Chancery. In the teeth of the Depression, the Bennett government was reluctant to authorize the construction, and so Marler largely undertook the work at his own expense. For the McConnells, it was as close to Montreal as they had been since setting sail.

The Legation had opened in 1933 and was to be officially designated by Canada as Marler House in 1972. It is widely regarded as the one of the best erected in Tokyo in the twentieth century, another being the Imperial Hotel where the McConnells were staying. Yet, for all its charms, life in the Legation was not easy. Almost two months of mourning for Princess Victoria had ended at it on 18 January 1936, to be followed by weeks of deep mourning for King George V almost immediately. At the end of February, there was an attempted coup d'état in Tokyo, in which the prime minister, the minister of finance, and the lord privy seal were assassinated, all of which led to the imposition of martial law. These events still dominated conversation when the McConnells arrived in Tokyo early in April.

The Marlers invited Jack and Lil to dinner on 13 April. As Lady Marler recorded, Lil appeared "in white satin with such lovely puffed sleeves and gorgeous diamonds, and with her white hair she looked lovely." Lady Marler surveyed the Canadians at her table and pronounced herself immensely "proud" of all of them.[29] Among the other thirty-six diners were the London hostess Maggie Grenville and the American ambassador and his wife (the Joseph Grews), all of whom were to become good friends, in addition to the Howard Fergusons from Toronto, and several high Japanese officials. Later the McConnells called on Prince Takamatsu (brother of Emperor Hirohito), to whom they had given a dinner in Montreal in 1931.

After leaving Japan, the McConnells arrived in Honolulu on 22 April. This was a real vacation, with sun and lessons in surfing, and a close study of the sugar industry by McConnell. Then it was time to go home. Leaving Honolulu on the *Aorangi* on 8 May, they reached Victoria on the 14th and three days later, in Vancouver, boarded a train to Montreal, a trip that included a short stop in Winnipeg so McConnell could inspect the Ogilvie Flour plant there. On arriving home on 23 May, McConnell gave a rare interview. He agreed with Willingdon that there was no reason for concern about the nationalist cause in India: "There was no sign of any political disturbance in India … it seemed that the people as a whole were happy." Willingdon, McConnell felt, "must be feel happy and contented with the results of his work." In India, "I hear nothing of Ghandi [Gandhi] and there was no mention of Japanese competition." In Japan itself, McConnell had seen "no sign of any financial stringency" despite the recent Japanese conquest of Manchuria. Marler he praised for "extraordinarily good work." He reported improvement in business in South Africa, where the mining industry was enjoying "great prosperity," and described Ceylon, Singapore, and Honolulu as flourishing.[30]

Although McConnell was not as insightful about politics as he was about business, his visit to India in 1936 gave him a better appreciation of the strategic importance of India to Great Britain. Six years later, in 1942, he was to chide his American friend, Wendell Willkie, for daring to suggest that the British should immediately grant independence to India. He urged him to consult his friends Lord Halifax, the former viceroy and now British ambassador in Washington, and the Indian minister in Washington, Sir Girja Shankar Bajpai, whom he had come regard as "extremely well posted on the Indian situation." "Those," McConnell continued, "who are best informed on this subject declare that freedom for India to-day would be tantamount to handing the country to the Japanese on a platter."[31]

The McConnells were not back in Montreal for long when they began to hear ominous rumours. By the autumn, the abdication of King Edward VIII was only weeks away, and, although unknown to the bulk of the British public, the impending constitutional crisis was a subject of fierce debate in the McConnells' English circles. The McConnells themselves anxiously followed the news. McConnell wrote to Kit, who was at school in London, of King Edward: "I presume that he will do the right thing in the end and all the people who have anything against him will forgive him and everybody will be happy again, and he, I hope, will regain his old time popularity."[32] If McConnell thought that the king would give up Mrs Simpson, this was not to be. Through it all, the McConnells had an exceptionally well-placed source at court to keep them informed. Colonel Eric Mackenzie, formerly comptroller of Government

Lil attired for presentation at court in Buckingham
Palace, 1937. McCord Museum, M2003.8.6.8.120.

House in Ottawa and now in attendance as equerry to the new King George VI, wrote
to Lil: "What eventually happened was all for the best. King Edward had probably
never really wanted to be King; his mind was certainly not on his work and he could
hardly have been worse in the execution of his daily duties." He concluded: "If the ex-
King had decided otherwise & given up the Lady for the Empire, it would have been
a temporary lull by which I mean that even if there were not another Lady with whom
he became infatuated, there would have been some sort of trouble."[33]

The McConnells did not receive an invitation to the coronation of George VI on
12 May 1937, but they decided to travel to London both to witness the festivities and
to attend the presentation of Kit at court. Once back in Canada, they resumed their
active social life of visiting and entertaining. Of all the governors general known to
McConnell, Lord Tweedsmuir, appointed to the post in 1936, probably was the most
astute and the most thoughtful. Although best remembered as a writer, John Buchan

Lord Tweedsmuir and McConnell, c.1938. McCord Museum.

(as he was known before 1936) was a barrister by training and a fervent imperialist. He had served as director of information under Prime Minister Lloyd George in the last year of the Great War and later was a Conservative Member of Parliament.

Tweedsmuir's household staff, all single, joined the extended McConnell family while in Canada, and they often became devoted correspondents thereafter. As with the Willingdons and the Bessboroughs, the McConnells were most involved with the Tweedsmuirs in the Royal Victoria Hospital Charity Ball held every January. The drill was invariable, and one example will suffice to capture its flavour. In 1937 Lord and Lady Tweedsmuir arrived with their son William and a few of their staff at Windsor Station, where they were met by McConnell. They then proceeded with a motor-cycle escort to his house on Pine Avenue. There followed a luncheon at the Mount Royal Club tendered by the executives and directors of the Quebec Provincial Division of the Canadian Red Cross Society. McConnell, an honorary vice-president of the division, accompanied the Tweedsmuirs. The ball itself, in the evening, followed a private dinner given by the McConnells at home. The next day, the governor gen-

The governor general and Lady Tweedsmuir before the opening of Parliament, February 1936, Art Gravure Corporation, New York, *Standard* photograph, Montreal *Gazette* Archives.

The governor general and Lady Tweedsmuir at the Royal Victoria Hospital Charity Ball, McConnell third from left, c.1939. Private collection.

eral lunched with the board of the Royal Bank, and Lady Tweedsmuir at Pine Avenue with Lil.[34]

Between the Tweedsmuirs and the McConnells, ceremony inevitably alternated with private meetings. On 28 January 1938, for example, Lil and Kit watched the governor general preside over the opening of Parliament and attended the presentation of debutantes in the Senate chamber, which was called the "Drawing Room." As the Montreal *Star* reported, Lil wore a "handsome gown of white lace, over lame of the same color with a court train of lame of the off white shade embroidered in diamante." On her head was "a pearl and diamond tiara and ornaments." Kit was "attractive in a Victorian gown of white slipper satin with wide shoulder straps" and she carried a "Victorian bouquet."[35]

As mentioned in the last chapter, in the following March, in the midst of the crisis over Hitler's takeover of Austria, the Tweedsmuirs spent a weekend with the McConnells at Val David. The governor general found it "a wonderful place, built by Norwegians on the Norwegian model, high among wooded hills," and he did "a good deal of ski-ing and show-shoeing." He particularly enjoyed driving up from the Val David railway station in sleighs with tinkling bells and covered by buffalo robes, and the great reception from the French Canadians – "I really think I am on good terms with that most interesting race." At Val David, however, the vice-regal party was "besieged by telephone messages the whole time about the European situation." Lady Tweedsmuir admitted that it had been "a pretty agonising week-end listening to the wireless," with McConnell declaring, "The fat is in the fire." "Really," she continued, "life is now just one prolonged nightmare of fear and horror." Nevertheless, she found the weekend "very lovely" and "the hush and stillness of everything was delicious." She thought McConnell "a very able, far-sighted, public-spirited man," and Lil "a dear, a very selfless sort of person, thinking of everybody else's comfort and happiness before her own."[36]

In May 1939 there occurred the first visit of a reigning British monarch to Canada and the United States. On 15 May the *Empress of Australia* arrived at Wolfe's Cove in Quebec bearing not only King George VI and Queen Elizabeth but also, secretly in its hold, the gold reserves of the Bank of England, to be held in Canada for the duration of the impending war. Most of the McConnell family went to Quebec City to see the royal visitors, and Jack and Lil and John attended the official welcome by the province of Quebec in the chamber of the Legislative Council. After a night at the Citadel, the king and queen proceeded first to Trois-Rivières, the home of Premier Maurice Duplessis, and then to Montreal. On the afternoon of the 18th, the McConnells watched the king unveil the National War Memorial in Ottawa, and Lil went on to Toronto to watch the running of the King's Plate at Woodbine on the 22nd. Both followed the royal progress thereafter with rapt attention. The visit to North America as a whole was a roaring success, particularly in establishing links and goodwill that were to be tested in the global conflict to come.

King George VI and Prime Minister Mackenzie King
enter the Parliament Buildings, Ottawa. International
News Photos, private collection.

Early in February 1940, the Tweedsmuirs came to Montreal, principally to preside
over the charity ball of the Montreal Maternity Hospital Social Service Department
and its outdoor clinics. As chairman of the organizing committee, McConnell met the
Tweedsmuirs. As usual, the ball was held in the Mount Royal Hotel. Four days later,
on 6 February at Government House, Tweedsmuir suffered a thrombosis, slipped in
his bathroom in Ottawa, and suffered a concussion. He was immediately paralysed
in a leg and an arm, and fell into unconsciousness. His condition deteriorated and
he underwent surgery by doctors brought up from the Montreal Neurological Institute. On the 9th, the vice-regal train brought him to Montreal, where he underwent
further surgery at the institute itself. McConnell seems to have been involved in the
extraordinary efforts to save the governor general, and it was probably on this occasion that he discovered that the Institute urgently needed a new elevator, which he
was to provide later. Tweedsmuir died two days later, of a pulmonary embolism. Even
the surgery of Dr Wilder Penfield and his colleagues had been to no avail. Despite his

having been in ill health for some time, Tweedsmuir's end came as a shock to everyone, and the McConnells rushed a box of mourning clothes to Government House for his widow to wear.

By then, of course, Canada had greater things to worry about than the death of a governor general. It, and the empire of which it was a part, was in the midst of another world war, one that, even more than the Great War of 1914–18, seemed to threaten the future of civilization itself. The McConnells, as we shall see, were keenly sensitive to the stakes of this conflict, which they perceived through the lenses of the late Victorian era that had formed them.

Jack and Lil were accustomed to a level of wealth and luxury almost unimaginable to those who remembered only the world after 1914. Nevertheless, they remained very contemporary in the 1930s, even moderately modernist. And by associating so much with the most sophisticated, though not the most avant-garde, of the English, the McConnells moved well beyond the colonial reflexes of their Canadian friends. They understood these reflexes thoroughly, of course, and they did not demur when they found certain of their friends hankering after knighthoods. Although McConnell himself did not crave one, he did not share the growing Canadian opinion that imperial titles of honour were unsuitable for Canadians, and he was both fully aware of rank and scrupulous in his observance of it. The empire for him was a deeply felt personal experience, with old friends in every part of it that he visited, and new friends made in them as well.

Although personally very simple in his tastes, McConnell spent much of his time in the 1930s in settings that in retrospect might seem thoroughly reactionary and plutocratic. Under scrutiny, however, these settings prove to be thoroughly up to date for their time. The *Empress of Britain*, one of the great prides of Canada, was twice the size of any other steamship serving the St Lawrence, and the only liner ever built with a full tennis court, of which McConnell took full advantage, sometimes several times a day. Viceroy's House in New Delhi was the last word in modern British architecture when the McConnells were staying in it, and the Canadian Legation in Tokyo was just six years old in 1939. The favoured occupants of such houses still displayed exuberance about the imperial enterprise, isolated as they were from the deep depression gripping both England and Canada. At home in Montreal, their wealth maintained the McConnells in a style not dissimilar, while armies of the unemployed slept in the streets and queued up for soup.

Through his own efforts, McConnell had come to personify St James Street and the British Empire in Montreal, but some, quite wrongly, saw him as standing for the inherited privileges of both places, to which he would have been the last to lay claim. For reasons largely beyond his control, such as his good looks and distinguished bearing, McConnell came to embody the curiously North American mystique of the monied WASP. Betty Reitman, a daughter-in-law of the Montreal clothing retailer Sam

Reitman, was to recall seeing him by chance in Grand Central Station in New York, shortly after the beginning of the Second World War. Emerging from the train from Montreal to tip a line of expectant porters as was his custom, he appeared immaculately attired in a camel-hair coat, his manner that of a royal personage or a film star. He was, she felt, "the King of Montreal."[37] Even Lord Willingdon, accustomed as he was to hundreds and then thousands of servants at his call in India, was amazed by how regal McConnell was. In the midst of the Depression, McConnell would on occasion take a drive in his 1930 Rolls-Royce Phantom, with Lefebvre the chauffeur sitting exposed in the front, and a cabriolet top in the back for the occupant to roll down in clement weather, much like motor cars used by the royal family.

In an era that virtually equated film stars with royalty, McConnell exuded an aura of privilege and taste and glamour that attracted both hatred and admiration. He had wanted to occupy this realm, and he had succeeded. His manner was studied, but as a tycoon he was now the genuine article, and the public mask had become the man. The private man, however, was still the boy from Muskoka, giving away at least half his money systematically to those not so fortunate. How did he reconcile the ostentation and the selflessness in his life? To some extent, he genuinely believed his success to be due to luck or divine favour, or a combination of the two. The violent disruptions of the Depression merely reinforced his tendency towards fatalism. More positively, he remained deeply grateful for his opportunities to receive recognition and to do good. The British Empire was, for him, providential, and he saw his position of virtual equality with leading figures of British life as a sign of the success of Canada.

Many Canadians – such as J.W. Dafoe, Hugh Keenleyside, and Lester Pearson – found the trappings of imperialism distasteful and ridiculous. Others – such as Vincent Massey, Herbert Bruce, and W.M. Birks – revelled in the minutiae of coats of arms, titles, and other distinctions of rank. McConnell was between these two groups. He personally had no interest in hierarchy or deference or lineage, but he fully accepted them as integral to the empire of which he was so proud. In any case, titles and other such marks of honour notwithstanding, people of all walks of life were absolutely equal in his eyes, and he saw them all as members of the same community if not of the same family. This was a view both profoundly Methodist and profoundly Muskokan, and it was to enable him to survive the wrenching political and social upheavals to come.

CHAPTER THIRTEEN

Faith and Works: From Charity to Social Welfare and from Fundraising to Philanthropy, 1922–45

Money is a necessity, but that alone can bring no true happiness. For that must come from an inner feeling of happiness with family surroundings, good warm and faithful friends built up through the years. Acts of unselfishness and consideration for the poor and needy to the extent of your needs.

Charity suffereth long and is kind. Charity is at the root of all true religion, because without religion there can be little charity. The spirit of the Good Samaritan is needed in these days with materialistic and ungodly communists endeavoring to overcome this poor old world.

We must put ourselves into action to bind up the wounds of the injured and helpless, and give aid to the suffering wherever it is in our power. Such acts will be reflected in happiness and will bring their own reward.

J.W. McConnell to Mrs F.B. Wasserboehr, 11 December 1956[1]

McConnell's story as a financier, patriot, and philanthropist does not reflect a simple linear development. The three roles were facets of one personality. For at least the last fifty-six years of his life, McConnell demonstrated himself, over and over again, as playing all of them. At any one time, one of the roles would predominate over the other two, but it never overwhelmed them; and he was always able to switch emphasis very swiftly to meet changing circumstances. What made this possible was the simple fact that raising money and applying it to good causes were not in the least difficult for him – indeed, they were his two favourite activities. Almost every aspect of his business and social life was to be rooted in them. McConnell himself saw no magic in doing what he simply enjoyed doing, or any exceptional virtue or talent on his part. He constantly urged others to do the same, and he would accept recognition of his achievement only if his example would encourage others.

While consistently dismissive of praise for himself, McConnell was genuinely inclined to respect for others. As he knew, among his contemporaries and colleagues, there were bolder corporate strategists, more adept politicians, and profounder thinkers. Yet among them there was probably no better salesman, and sales skills were the key to effective fundraising. Whether his selling was of acetone or bonds or a charitable cause, his goal was to make the sales "prospect" part with money. A charitable cause, however, was harder to sell than consumable goods or even the promise held by an investment. It offered no more than the assurance that the contributor to it was doing something right and good.

Here is where McConnell's sincerity and probity gave him an advantage over other salesmen. As he had learned from both salesmen's manuals and his own experience, the essence of his job was to overcome resistance to purchasing by understanding the needs and the fears of his customers. It was not enough for him to believe in his own product. He had to make the customer believe in him and through him in his product, and he had to tailor his sales pitch to meet changes in the environment in which both he and his customers were living.

The most important of these changes was the introduction of the War Income Tax in 1917. Before then, McConnell had somehow engendered confidence in others to give to worthy causes, such as the Canadian Patriotic Fund, when there was no tax advantage to giving. With the introduction of income tax in 1917, the taxpayer might deduct his or her contributions to charity, but McConnell still met with considerable new resistance to giving from heavily burdened taxpayers. The tax system was a progressive one, so that the richer were taxed more as their income increased. Only the relatively rich paid income tax, and, since they had never paid it before, they sensed unprecedented insecurity. McConnell realized that people with modest, fairly fixed incomes were not faced with this issue of progressive taxation or with taxation at all. Cumulatively, therefore, their contributions might be relatively more significant to fundraising than those of the rich benefactors before 1917.

It was a time when the reform-minded were calling for the conscription of wealth, to correspond to the conscription of men to serve as soldiers. Even the Methodist Church was joining in this call, which at one level was potentially threatening to the wealthy but which at another could be interpreted as the mobilization of the resources of the entire community, including those not rich. McConnell, as probably a quiet supporter of the conscription of men as soldiers, was hardly in principle able to oppose the forced enlistment of private funds for the war effort. Neither were businessmen generally. To have part of their wealth conscripted was a small price to pay in comparison to that paid by the soldiers in Europe.

Although among the richest of big businessmen, McConnell was thus no fat industrialist in a silk hat who simply wrote cheques to keep the poor and the needy at bay. He was no ideologue and no outright rebel either. Instead, he worked for change and adaptation within existing systems, which made him all the more formidable and effective.

And to reinforce his earnestness, he gave unstintingly of himself, of his own money as well as of his time and energy, to the same worthy causes that he was canvassing others to support. He had done this from a very early age, and before he attained great wealth he sometimes contributed more than the richer people whom he was canvassing. He threw out to his "prospects" a challenge, "If you give, I will give," by which he meant that he would match the generosity of others.

He did not charm everyone. Not everyone looked forward to his calls, whether in person or by telephone; he had developed a reputation for being particularly vociferous and demanding over the telephone. Many did not enjoy being told how much he knew, with alarming certainty, about what they could afford to give, a subject already thoroughly researched by the caller himself. With regard to corporations in particular, he could reel off their profits, historical and prospective, their annual taxes, and a precise recollection of how much, if anything, they had given to him in previous fundraising campaigns. He followed even the progress of other rich individuals, clipping out newspaper notices of their good fortune and carefully verifying gossip. Despite his aggressiveness, many were still won over and did give, for his causes were only the most respectable but also of obvious value to the community as a whole.

Another reason for his success in fundraising had become clear in the Nelson campaign, as described in chapter 4. McConnell not merely could recite the merits of a good cause. He was able to demonstrate in detail to doubters how the funds contributed would be applied to reach a defined goal. As his own business experience increased, his appeals for good causes assumed an authority that those of no mere canvasser could claim. He understood far more than most how to finance a project and, more important, how to bring it to a successful conclusion, because he constantly cared about every detail, and he monitored the steps necessary to reach a goal. In the very process of fundraising itself, nothing was too small or too big for him to focus on: from the flowers for the Royal Victoria ball that he chaired to thank-you notes that he carefully wrote to canvassers, he left nothing to chance. He did almost everything in his own hand, such as keeping a file card for each of his prospective donors, recording how much he thought they could give and how often he had approached them, and even the date on which he had convinced them how much to contribute.

His intense research, into even very technical matters well beyond what his meagre formal education might have prepared him for, rendered his appeals to others for help essentially irrefutable. Although a shaky speller, he was strikingly effective and even commanding, in speech as well as in writing, as he exercised his persuasive skills on those from whom he solicited funds. He was more than persuasive, however. His business and investment success had made his capacity to see far into the future, to anticipate both financial and other practical issues and possibilities to follow – long after a project seemed "complete" – legendary. This is why he was so eagerly sought for various campaigns. He subscribed to the view that in investment of any kind timing is crucial, and almost no one matched his personal success as an investor.

Throughout his life, McConnell's fundraising and philanthropy were rooted more in his conscience than in his mere success as a businessman and as an investor. What he did and what he stood for, in both raising money and giving it away, was an integral part of the way of life that had produced him, of his Methodist conscience. As he wrote to his niece, Mrs Wasserboehr, in 1942: "It seems to me that the way of the Good Samaritan is the very bedrock basis of Christianity. He who can live up to this example of good works will do well indeed."[2] His claim that charity was at the root of all true religion, cited at the head of this chapter, goes back to St Paul's definition of the three Christian virtues as faith, hope, and charity, of which the last was the greatest (1 Corinthians 13).

Charity here is generally understood as derived from the Greek *agape*, as translated into the selfless love that Christians should have for another. Even towards the end of McConnell's life, Christian thinkers were exploring this theme. Thus, C.S. Lewis in 1960 published *The Four Loves*, a book on affection, friendship, eros, and charity, in which he defined charity as an unconditional love towards one's neighbour not dependent on any lovable qualities in the beloved. The implementation of precisely this sort of charity was for McConnell almost a form of worship, for it was the way of proving the love of God as opposed to simply helping others. Charity for him was not an expression, therefore, of pity or of guilt. Neither was it a method of righting the wrongs of inequitable political and economic systems. It was demanded by his sense of decency and self-respect, and it involved the daily exercise of "looking out" for the welfare of others, such as he had known in Methodist Bands of Hope and the Epworth League.

For adult Methodists, method in giving as well as watching out for others was at the heart of their spiritual formation. In Canada, the Methodist preacher James Woodsworth, father of the CCF politician J.S. Woodsworth and, from 1886, superintendent of Methodist missions in the Canadian west, had become famous as the "Apostle of Systematic Giving."[3] Systematic giving referred to the Methodist injunction, dating from 1882, for each member of the church to give one cent a day for missions. It led to the Methodist innovation of duplex collection envelopes, with one pocket for local church work and one pocket for missions, a practice imitated in the United States and continued by the United Church of Canada after 1925. Thus, methodical giving and, by extension, fundraising were at least a weekly part of the life of every churchgoing Methodist. It made giving to others a habit and indeed a rule of life.

Emboldened by their success in business, Methodists had, by McConnell's youth, started to convert their fundraising into mass organized campaigns, first among themselves and then in the community at large, as in the Montreal YMCA campaign of 1909. And as believers in credit, they did not shrink from borrowing money in order to extend their work. Thus, in 1885, while the Presbyterians were anguishing over their mission debt of $5,000, the Canadian Methodist Foreign Mission Board saw its own debt of $20,000 simply as an exciting challenge and a confirmation of divine favour. It was for them "a proof that God is opening for us ever wider doors of opportunity and is summoning us to ever larger responsibilities."[4] This sort of optimism about providence was one of the driving forces behind McConnell's own business career.

After the First World War, McConnell did eventually give up the Methodist prohibition on dancing, for example, as did most Methodists. He also bought shares in tobacco companies and befriended Gooderhams, Molsons, and Daweses, all prominent in the production of drink; but he never, in his heart, gave up his opposition to alcohol or, more important, his methodical, Methodist habits.[5] Through the turbulence of the decades to come, his Methodist character was like a sheet anchor. It endowed him with an unwavering sense of the purpose of life, and particularly of the obligation of the fortunate to help those less so.

The more radical and anti-capitalist manifestations of the Social Gospel – which began to take firm root in Canadian Protestantism after the First World War – held no appeal for McConnell, but he could never oppose them in principle, since one of his bedrock convictions was that every Christian had a responsibility to play a part, small or large, depending on their means, in transforming this earthly world into something more closely resembling the Kingdom of God. Still, proponents of the Social Gospel, and in particular the socialist Co-operative Commonwealth Federation, under J.S. Wordsworth, ferociously attacked such businessmen as McConnell, and they made the achievement of the Kingdom a political as well as religious goal.

The Christian message admitted of various interpretations and emphases, and such rich Methodists as McConnell, Lorne Webster, Sir Joseph Flavelle, and A.E. Ames made their peace with it by seeing is as non-political and non-socialist, while not necessarily anti-socialist. Love, for McConnell in particular, could be best expressed through service to others, but short of political and economic revolution. The clearest link between his business career and his philanthropy was his conscious effort to demonstrate that capitalism, for all its drawbacks, could certainly produce wealth, in the form of social as well as individual capital. His philanthropy was not an effort to apologize to his critics. It was to set an example for his fellow citizens in a capitalist society, to encourage them to give according to their own means, as a way of working towards their own redemption.

As he constantly said, faith without works was nothing. Giving for him was an obligation but not a burden, and as he said to his wife in 1907, when he had arranged the financing of the Nelson church, giving of his money as well as of his time made him happy and was "its own reward." Through the decades, many noticed his boyish delight in perfecting every detail of his gifts, a habit that persisted to his last years, when he was constantly upgrading the facilities of the McConnell Wing of the Montreal Neurological Institute. Almost a century after she had first met McConnell, the daughter of his lifelong friend Tim Curtis was to recall how McConnell had to her "radiated Christian joy."[6]

McConnell's disinclination to engage in abstract thought meant that he seldom expressed publicly, in writing or otherwise, the basis of his Christian faith.[7] In one of his engagement books, however, he drafted what seems to have been a speech, although it is unknown whether it was ever delivered. It is a reflection on the words of a burial service, "I am the resurrection and the life – if any man [doubt?] that, let him take up his X [cross] and follow."[8] McConnell wrote:

It is not enough to believe. No it is not enough to believe in anything. Good thoughts are useless unless you put those good thoughts into action. Take up your X. You are on the threshold of life. You will have many Xs [crosses] to face and take up in following along the road that inevitably leads to success and happiness. Now that is the ambition in life of any sane human being. What does he seek? What does he desire to achieve? – *happiness and success* of course above all things. How shall he achieve these things? Only as a result of *right* thinking, decisive *action* – as a man thinks with his heart so is he – then action enters upon the scene. He would be master must first be servant of all. Service therefore is the key note to a successful and happy life. Service to humanity, what a privilege, and you need not want to obtain any definite job. You can start at once along the unselfish path of service to your fellow men. You can give of yourselves. The Boy Scouts have the right slogan – a good action every day – you need not acquire money for this service. You can radiate good nature, you can radiate goodwill, you can carry an inspiring countenance and extend the firm hand grasp of [friendship?]. You can give the cup of water. You can visit the sick. You can bring [calm?] and comfort to the distressed. I repeat [that] success and happiness can be found only in right thinking & [applied?] action.[9]

Already in this book, we have seen McConnell's work in raising money for the Methodist church in Nelson, for the YMCA and McGill and the Wesleyan Theological College in Montreal, and for the war effort in 1914–18. No sooner had the McGill Centennial Endowment Campaign of 1920, which will be described in chapter 17, been concluded than he became involved in raising money for the teaching hospitals attached to McGill. These hospitals were almost as integral to the university as all the academic buildings on the campus, since all of them were staffed with McGill professors and medical students. They were also central to the city as a whole, for they delivered health care to English- and French-speaking people alike.

McConnell became interested in hospitals, medical research, and nursing for various reasons. He was even in childhood acutely aware of the lack of medical care in Muskoka, which did not build its first hospital until after the First World War. The death of his sister Sue, from typhoid in 1902, had affected him deeply, as had her nursing care. Two of his brothers-in-law were physicians, and one was a dentist, and he was close to all of them. For most of his life, he counted doctors among his close friends, such as the dermatologist Charles Peters at the Montreal General; the founder of the Wellesley Hospital in Toronto, Herbert Bruce; the anaesthetist Wesley Bourne; the oncologist Edward Archibald; and the neurosurgeon Wilder Penfield. Like the details of industrial processes, the details of medical treatment and of advances in medical technology never ceased to fascinate him.

McConnell's connection with the hospitals affiliated with McGill appears to have begun with his appointment to the board of the Montreal General in 1913.[10] The General, as it was popularly known, dated from 1819–21 and thus was slightly more venerable than McGill itself. Located on Dorchester Street (now René Lévesque Boulevard), it was, from its start, open to people of all religions,[11] but all the governors were English-speaking and Protestant, the first board including three members of the Molson family alone. It always depended overwhelmingly on charitable donations and public subscriptions, since token annual grants from the province did not change much from 1857 to 1921. From 1890 to 1913, the General underwent major rebuilding and expansion, costing over $1 million and paid out of private donations.

McConnell's appointment to the General in 1913 had been made as part of its plans for a fundraising campaign, following his dazzling effort for the YMCA in 1909. Financial conditions and the outbreak of war, however, led to the cancellation of this campaign, and at the end of 1914 the General's president, Sir Montagu Allan, was forced to ask the governors to give $150,000 to cover the deficits expected for the following two years. Its position was not unique, for the other hospitals of the city were similarly experiencing financial stringency.

Like the General, the Royal Victoria Hospital was one of the central institutions of Montreal. Successive generations of the same families served it, as doctors, nurses, volunteers, and benefactors. And successive generations were born and cared for and died in it. Owing its creation to the efforts of the cousins Lord Strathcona and Lord Mount Stephen, the "Royal Vic" – designed in flamboyant Scottish baronial style – was situated between the Allan house, Ravenscrag, to the west, and University Street to the east.[12] Its construction at the end of the nineteenth century was a pledge by the English-speaking community to keep Montreal at the forefront of medical research and care. It would do this by continuing to attract some of the best doctors trained in

The Royal Victoria Hospital, Pine Avenue, n.d.
McCord Museum, v6210.

Great Britain and the United States, including Montrealers themselves, and to provide comparable facilities for training locally at the Faculty of Medicine at McGill,
largely endowed by Strathcona and in the 1920s by the Rockefeller Foundation at the
instigation of Sir William Osler.

The founders and governors of the Royal Vic covered its early deficits, and on the
completion of its pathology wing in 1895 they invested $270,000, what was left of
the original endowment, as a continuing endowment, to which was added $25,000
from R.B. Angus and $5,000 from other sources. By 1914, however, the governors
would no longer agree personally to cover the deficits of the hospital, although two
years later they added a further million dollars to the endowment, which now totalled
$1,300,000. During the Great War, the hospital received bequests from the estates of
Lord and Lady Strathcona, totalling £125,000, and $50,000 from James Ross, with a
further $250,000 from J.K.L. Ross to equip the Ross Memorial Pavilion.

As at Montreal General, the future of the Royal Victoria had become pressing by
1922, when the funding and needs of Montreal hospitals were studied in a comprehensive survey by the American Hospitals Association known as the Davis Report.[13]
The results were not encouraging. They showed that Montreal maintained a ratio of
2.9 hospital beds per thousand people, while Toronto had just over 4 and Vancouver
and Boston just over 5. Neither was the distribution of beds proportionate to the sec-

tors of the population that required the hospitals. Protestant English-speakers, who formed 23 per cent of the population of Montreal, provided 65.6 per cent of its beds, while French-speakers, who formed 62 per cent of the population, provided only 33.6 per cent, and Jews, forming 7 per cent of the population, provided 0.8 per cent. Thus, English-speaking Protestants, less than a quarter of the population, were providing almost two-thirds of hospital and outpatient facilities for the entire city. Furthermore, the infant-mortality rate in Montreal, at 192 per thousand, was "double what is now regarded as a reasonable rate for a Western city," and the tuberculosis death rate was "50 to 75% above what is now generally prevalent."[14] Municipal medical and nursing services outside hospitals were non-existent, and there were only 150 nurses in the entire city, one for every 4,000 of population, half of what was desirable.

The report recommended a central body for coordinating the policy and administration among the English hospitals, with no administrative power but with uniform standards for reporting medical, administrative, and financial statistics for guiding policies. It also recommended a central financial organization, not necessarily the same as the central body for statistics, to deal with standards, policies, and procedures, and to allocate budgets to the various hospitals. Most of the matters addressed by the report demanded long-term planning, since they implicitly projected future needs as well as describing present ones.

But present conditions were bad enough, and they required immediate action. In May 1922, with operating deficits of the hospitals growing alarmingly, two of their presidents – Sir Vincent Meredith at the Royal Victoria and Herbert Molson at the General – launched a combined Emergency Appeal on behalf of the Montreal General, Montreal Maternity, Royal Victoria, Western, and Alexandra hospitals. (The Maternity was about to be amalgamated into the Royal Victoria, and the Western into the General, and the Alexandra was administered already jointly by the Royal Victoria and the General.) In the case of the General alone, the rising costs of fuel, labour, and supplies, combined with the rapid growth of the population, had already forced the hospital to close as many as a hundred beds, and $750,000 in total was needed immediately to avoid further reductions of service.

In the 1922 campaign, McConnell's principal stockbroker, Percy Cowans, was in charge of canvassing the wealthy, McConnell and J.W. Ross were the vice-chairmen, and Edward Beatty was treasurer. Progress was initially slow and disappointing, but after an extension, and with last-minute contributions from the Grand Trunk Railway, among others, the goal was reached and then exceeded, so that the money raised totalled $777,000.[15] Despite their success, however, the organizers had come to realize that the hospitals could not be funded on an ongoing basis by such sporadic campaigns. The so-called War Income Tax was becoming permanent, and there was now an inheritance tax as well, and so the traditional support of hospitals by the rich was drying up.

McConnell had grasped this trend from his chairmanship of the first Victory Loan campaign in 1917, the year of the introduction of the income tax. Meredith and Sir Herbert Holt, the presidents respectively of the Bank of Montreal and the Royal Bank of Canada, on the board of the Royal Victoria, were also swift to perceive that the tax system was ushering in a fundamental reallocation of wealth. All three men – far from blindly fighting the taxation of their fortunes – began to rethink how taxes could be extended to supplement, if not largely to replace, the private funding of hospitals, particularly of patients who could not afford to pay for their care. Although far from foreseeing state medicare, they furthermore began reconsidering the funding of public institutions, such as universities, more generally.

McConnell's thinking on the financing of hospitals – the crucial issue, in his eyes, being how to harness the power of taxation without depriving the hospitals of their independence or discouraging any impulse to private giving – began to crystallize as he considered the plight of one hospital in particular, the Montreal Maternity. Located since 1905 at the corner of Saint-Urbain and Prince Arthur streets, the Maternity became a life-long commitment of McConnell's, especially after Lil had had a miscarriage, and he was a life governor of it by 1925. With the birth in 1923 of his youngest son, David, he was now also the father of four children. The hospital was unusual in being founded by women for women and indeed run by female directors from 1844 onward. The doctors were male and were headed by a male medical superintendent, since there were almost no women doctors in Montreal; but there was always a strong nursing staff led by women superintendents. McConnell had probably been introduced to the hospital by Percy Cowans, whose sister Amy (Mrs George Cains) was its president. She was also the mother-in-law of Captain Herbert Holt, a son of Sir Herbert. Lady Holt was the hospital's vice-president, and Mrs Huntly Drummond and Lil McConnell were among the women most active in its management.

The post-war period was one of considerable optimism at the Maternity, with new developments in ante-natal and post-natal care, decreasing maternal mortality and morbidity, and increasing admissions and confinements. The Child Welfare Association and the Victorian Order of Nurses were supplementing its work, and women of thirty-two nationalities were served in 1925 alone. The following year, the Maternity merged with the Royal Victoria. With the sale of its building on Saint-Urbain Street and of its securities, probably arranged by McConnell, the Maternity was able to contribute assets of over $400,000 to the Royal Victoria, which were used for the building of a facility – known as a "pavilion" – for the new maternity wing of the merged institution. McConnell described the pavilion as "a wonderful new hospital, the finest of its kind to be found in the world and upon a site unequalled for attractive and wholesome environment – having three and one-third times the capacity of this [the former] hospital."

McConnell "doing the Lambeth Walk" at the Royal Victoria Hospital
Charity Ball, February 1939. Private collection.

With the move of the Montreal Maternity to its new building at the Royal Victoria,
McConnell – who had probably seldom or never danced before – became chairman
of the annual Royal Victoria Hospital ball, which was in reality the successor to the
Montreal Maternity ball. The ball was now described as being in support of the new
maternity wing and of the ladies' auxiliary of the hospital. This was widely considered the most glittering event of the Montreal social season, and he was to continue as
its chairman for over twenty years.

In a scene that was to repeat itself almost annually for two decades for McConnell,
the 1926 ball was held at the Mount Royal Hotel, under the patronage of the governor
general and Lady Willingdon, with all the proceeds going to the poor and needy. The
nine hundred guests faced a dais erected at one end of the ballroom, "banked with
palms and potted sword ferns with azaleas in wicker baskets lending a bright touch of
color, with a background of tall palms and basket stands of Ophelia roses, over which
a huge Union Jack was suspended." At this event as at the others, the festivities began
at about 10 p.m. A bugle sounded and everyone stopped dancing to stand for the
playing of *God Save the King* and the arrival of the vice-regal party. As one reporter
recorded: "Their Excellencies advanced along an aisle, formed by white ribbons held
by members of the committee, to the dais, Lord Willingdon walking with Sir Vincent
Meredith and Lady Willingdon with Mr. J.W. McConnell."

The receiving line at the Royal Victoria Hospital Charity Ball, January 1947.
From left: Mrs H.M. Pasmore, Mrs W.A. Bishop, Mrs Norman Prentice,
Mrs F.T. Rea, Mrs T.H.P. Molson, Mrs W.C.J. Meredith, Mrs A.F. Culver, Miss
Mona Prentice, Mrs W.M. Stewart greeting Mrs North Winnship, McConnell
(chairman), North Winnship (US consul general), Mrs A. Sidney Dawes,
Mr Dawes, Mrs Sydney Dobson, and Mr Dobson. Private collection.

By now, the Maternity's financial problems were ones of current expenses rather than capital. The 1922 Emergency Campaign had led to the elimination of accumulated deficits amounting to more than $25,000, but by 1925 there was again a deficit of $17,000. It was a matter of pride to the hospital that no woman had ever been turned away from it in the previous twenty years, regardless of her origin or her ability to pay, but the fact that it was continuing to struggle financially, while the demand for its services was growing, was a source of much worry.

Shortly before the move of the Maternity took place, Beatty, Holt, McConnell, and others decided that there needed to be radical change in the method of covering current expenses of the hospitals generally. At a meeting of the Montreal Maternity, on 3 February 1926, McConnell launched a campaign to unite the English hospitals of Montreal under a Joint Hospital Board, as recommended by the 1922 survey, and to have hospitals in Quebec funded, at least in part, out of tax revenues. This did not involve a physical amalgamation of all the English-speaking hospitals, such as would be proposed at the end of the twentieth century. But McConnell and his associates did think that coordination of resources under the direction of a joint board would accomplish "the greatest possible economy," the "maximum use of all current hospital facilities," and "the advance of sensible expansion in the proper direction when necessary."[16]

The statistical findings of the 1922 survey had summarized the extent of the challenge. As McConnell pointed out in a speech in 1926 – the same year in which he became a governor of the Royal Victoria – more detailed statistics from only two years before confirmed that the English hospitals of Montreal were still catering to far more than the English population. They had cared for 19,626 patients in total. Of these, 9,857 were English, 6,478 were French, 2,695 were Jewish, and 496 were of other origins. There were also 286,665 "outdoor" or outpatient cases. To every indoor indigent patient, the city of Montreal contributed 67 cents and the Quebec government contributed 67 cents, for a total of $1.34, but there were no contributions at all for outpatients. By contrast, in Toronto, the city contributed $1.50 for every indigent patient, outdoor or indoor, and the provincial government contributed 50 cents to each public-ward patient, or effectively $2 for each indoor indigent. Ontario also contributed 32 cents for each outpatient, or effectively $1.82 for every outdoor indigent. In addition, the city of Toronto was making a yearly grant to pay down hospital deficits.[17] How was the shortfall experienced by Montreal's English hospitals to be covered? McConnell observed that the Quebec Liquor Commission had made total sales in 1925 of $18 million. A tax of 2 per cent on these sales would yield $360,000. There were also 100,000 automobile licences issued annually in Quebec, and a similar tax on them would yield $200,000.[18]

The proposal of a new tax for hospitals was startling enough. But McConnell and his friends then followed it up with public agitation. Holt, in a rare interview with the Montreal *Star*, cited taxes in Germany, used for hospitals, as a precedent. Other businessmen in support of the idea included G.H. Duggan of Dominion Bridge, Sir Charles Gordon of Dominion Textile, Sir Vincent Meredith and Sir Frederick Williams-Taylor of the Bank of Montreal, and Lord Atholstan of the *Star*. The Montreal Trades and Labour Council agreed. McConnell joined Holt in circulating a petition sent to Premier Taschereau, signed by hundreds and calling for the imposition of "a small charge upon such luxuries or semi-luxuries as in your judgment you might be made to bear this impost, so that this plan of financing our hospitals may be given a fair and reasonable trial." In addition, over 9,000 employees of companies across the city sent similar petitions to the *Star*, between 12 and 19 February, to the same effect, while the *Star* itself organized other petitions with 100,000 signatures.

Soon, the campaign for a hospital tax spread to cover the funding of the French-speaking hospitals, then largely run by unpaid members of Roman Catholic religious orders and yet even more strapped for funds. Dr Eugène Saint-Jacques, a surgeon at the Hôtel Dieu, warmly endorsed McConnell's proposal, as did the Board of Trade and the Chambre de Commerce of Montreal, which both made representations to Quebec City to have the total grants to indigent patients increased from $1.34 to $2, in French-speaking as well as English-speaking hospitals.[19] McConnell's focus, however, was the funding of hospitals generally out of taxes, and not merely the costs of the indigents whom they served. In this vein, Holt called for the funding of all hospitals, Roman Catholic as well as Protestant, with "a fixed sum per average number of patients to be paid each hospital, the whole to be administered by a central body."[20]

Not all manufacturers and distributors of liquor, or indeed owners of automobiles, were so smitten with McConnell's proposal for the subject, as opposed to the purpose, of the new tax. One wag wrote to the Montreal *Gazette* that the proposed tax should be on hundred-pound bags of sugar. The Montreal Motorists' League held an emergency protest meeting. McConnell himself later clarified that he had not really asked for a tax on any specific commodity and had used automobiles and liquor merely by way of illustration. The point was "the desirability of obtaining revenue necessary from those who would feel it the least," in contrast to the practice of Glasgow of taxing the workingman a penny a week for hospital purposes. He concluded, "As every penny would be devoted to sick and suffering humanity in our Province it could surely be called a popular tax."[21]

Premier Taschereau initially expressed sympathy but pleaded lack of funds. Then Beatty went to see him on 19 February, and Taschereau agreed to legislate by amending the Public Charities Act to include funding through a tax on meals. The legislative process, however, did not proceed smoothly. Hoteliers and restaurant owners objected strongly. C.E. Gault, an MLA for Montreal-St George who had earlier antagonized McConnell with his comments on French-Canadian participation in the First World War, again raised the "racial" issue as he expressed his opposition to the care of such "strangers" as Jews and French people in the English hospitals.[22] Nevertheless, the meal tax did pass in the end, and so began tax-funded provincial aid to hospitals. It was formally called the "hospital duty" and applicable to all hotels and restaurants. The tax was 5 per cent on meals costing $1 or more, including beer and wine. The law left it to cities, towns, and municipalities to choose whether to impose the tax or not.[23]

In early 1927 the deficits of the hospitals generally were still accumulating, and expansion of both services and buildings was continuing. The Royal Victoria Hospital in particular had built the first stage of its new maternity wing, and it now urgently required about $1,500,000. The restaurant tax in aid of hospitals was in place, and the joint hospital board was to follow, first meeting in September 1927. But neither the tax nor the joint board was about to solve the deficit issue. Negotiations were held with Premier Taschereau, who undertook to cover future hospital deficits on condition that another fundraising campaign should seek to cover existing ones.

To meet immediate needs and to ensure ongoing funding, a new Joint Hospital Campaign was called for April and May 1927. The stated purposes of this canvass were: to raise money to complete and equip the new Royal Victoria Hospital Maternity Hospital Wing; to complete and furnish the Montreal General Nurses' Home, which would cost about $700,000; to provide for accrued deficits for the Royal Victoria and the Montreal General to the end of 1926; and to build a new Private Ward Wing for the Montreal General. The goal was initially $3 million, a sum later raised to $4 million, of which $2.5 million alone was needed to cover deficits.

McConnell and his colleague W.K. Trower, at Montreal Securities, were involved for months in planning the campaign. They studied the subscription lists of the annual Federated Charities Campaign, the McGill Centennial Endowment Campaign, and the 1922 Emergency Fund Campaign for the General and the Royal Victoria. McConnell assumed the chairmanship of the 1927 campaign, which was to run from 25 April to 2 May. Just before it began, on 22 April, he addressed a rally of eight hundred volunteer workers, all businessmen who had pledged themselves to devote their services, without pay, exclusively to the campaign. One report noted that McConnell's speech struck "the keynote of cheerful confidence" with "scintillating wit."

On the first day of campaigning, McConnell presided over not only the daily canvassers' luncheon at the Windsor Hotel but also a dinner for two hundred and fifty at the Montefiore Club, in honour of the steel manufacturer Mark Workman, who was in charge of the Jewish division and had personally given $20,000. Workman's Jewish special-names committee had raised $100,510 on the first day. McConnell was lavish in his praise: "Mark Workman stands today in this great work as the 'Moses' who will lead his people into the land of golden promises. His people will be willingly led by Mr. Workman, not only to the promises but into the fulfillment of the promises in hard cash. This has been our pleasant experience in the past with all the Jewish citizens of Montreal. They have always taken a leading and generous part in all patriotic and charitable movement."[24] Doubtless recalling his efforts to recruit employees for Victory Loans, McConnell launched other incentives attempted to keep up interest during the week. He presided over the luncheon for Scotsmen's day, seated with "representatives of the McCall, the McInnes, the Ogilvie, the Paton and the Mackay clans." Since J.T. McCall had sent in his cheque for $100,000, McConnell arranged a special reception for him. As McCall rose to speak, "the skirl of bagpipes was heard at the rear of the dining room, and while a big Highlander strutted up and down Mr. McConnell proceeded to invest Mr. McCall with a plaid of the McCall tartan and a tam o' shanter."[25]

At a luncheon at the Windsor Hotel on another day, McConnell directed his efforts to more modest donors, telling the story of the contribution of an ex-guardsman named Charles, who earned $25 a day to maintain his family of six. "Two quarters lay in the extended, calloused and toil roughened hand – his tobacco money." It was, McConnell declared, "a grand gesture worthy of the traditions that made Charles what he is." It "merited greater thanks than the goodly cheque which represented his employer's contribution."[26] Towards the end of the campaign, the Chinese com-

McConnell, campaign chairman, and the honorary chairmen of the
Four Million Dollar Joint Hospital Campaign – Sir Vincent Meredith,
Col. Herbert Molson, E.W. Beatty, and Sir Herbert Holt,
The Passing Show, April 1927. Private collection.

munity scraped together $770 and the Greek and Syrian Orthodox community over $7,000.

When the final tally was made in May, it was found that the campaign had collected over $4,735,000, or $58,589,121 in 2008 terms. The biggest contributor was the CPR, which gave $250,000, followed by the Bank of Montreal with $200,000 and Sun Life and Montreal Tramways with $100,000 each. Among individuals, Herbert and F.W. Molson jointly, Sir Herbert Holt, and McConnell (anonymously) gave $100,000 each ($1,237,363 in 2008 terms). There were prizes of a silver jewel case, a walking stick, a golf club, a pistol, fountain pens, tobacco, a chain, cufflinks, a trumpet, a bugle, and a sword, all presented by McConnell to exceptional canvassers in tribute to their individual personalities.

McConnell himself received a loving cup. W.G.M. Shepherd, who presented it, declared McConnell "the first citizen of Quebec province." He continued: "There is not a man in Canada, nor in North America, who could have produced this magnificent result in this period, He has spread lustre on the name of the great city of Montreal." An even more important tribute came from Herbert Molson, whose family had been the mainstay of the Montreal General for over three generations: "I consider him one of the greatest philanthropists we have ever known in Canada." Premier Taschereau cabled his congratulations and pledged to Beatty and McConnell that the provincial government would come henceforth to the aid of the hospitals in covering their annual deficits.[27]

The spirit of congratulation was not unchallenged. The 1927 Joint Hospital campaign brought to a head opposition to fundraising from corporations that had been brewing for some time. A rather strange combination between a disgruntled hospital, left out of the campaign, and disgruntled shareholders of the Bank of Montreal sued the directors of the bank for breach of fiduciary duty in contributing $200,000 to the campaign. The nominal plaintiff was John Hamilton of Quebec City, in the name of several shareholders of the bank. It was a battle employing the foremost lawyers of the city. The Jeffery Hale Hospital and Boswell's Ltd, of Quebec City, were joined as plaintiffs and represented by the future prime minister Louis St Laurent; George Montgomery and H.H. Hansard represented the Royal Victoria and Montreal General; A.R. Holden and F.T. Collins represented the Bank of Montreal and its directors; and Aimé Geoffrion served as counsel to all the defendants. The trial took place in May 1928 and resulted in a victory for the Bank of Montreal – and for McConnell and his associates in the fundraising campaign.

McConnell's testimony at this trial – he was unequivocal in stating that directors had no alternative but to subscribe generously to charitable causes, in the best interests both of their companies and of the community[28] – was described as trenchant and striking. It was, he said, impossible for the bank to be held immune from bearing a share of the burden, while all others were being called upon for the necessary relief of the sick and the suffering of the community. Goodwill and good judgment were the chief factors in the success of a bank, and the goodwill of the community was its very lifeblood. Historically, the Bank of Montreal had already supported the Montreal General Hospital, and in this campaign alone five corporations had contributed $800,000. Moreover, the subscription by the bank had been the key one, on which other corporate subscriptions depended. In short, taking big subscriptions from big corporations was like "painless extraction," and the shareholders never felt it. More precisely, the bank's subscription of $200,000 over four years, or $50,000 a year, meant 16⅔ cents per share per year, on a share valued at $300.

The fact that his arguments won the day is one of his two principal contributions to ensuring the continuance of corporate donations to charitable causes. The other was his obtaining of the recognition of corporate donations as tax-deductible, as will be discussed in chapter 17 in connection with the special McGill fundraising campaign of 1943.[29] Had McConnell lost either of these battles, the future of corporate giving in Canada would have been quite different. Instead, he ensured the active participation in community welfare by corporate businessmen such as himself. He would have been the last to claim credit for doing more than what he saw as the duty of every citizen, and yet his decisive influence can be seen in the aftermath of the 1928 judgment. Corporate donations, as he had seen as early as during the Great War, would form the bulk of all funds collected by most campaigns, as they remain to this day.[30]

The triumph of the Joint Hospitals Campaign of 1927 secured McConnell a unique and somewhat paradoxical position in Montreal society. Within twenty years of his first campaign in Nelson, British Columbia, his rise in the metropolis of Canada had been so spectacular and aggressive that many felt threatened by him. And yet his charitable work was so patently practical, necessary, and effective that he had become indispensable. As someone named "M.E.W.", who described himself as an "old friend," wrote in a magazine called the *Spur* after the 1927 campaign:

> Early in May some six hundred representative Montrealers, women and men – gathered at a dinner at the Mount Royal Hotel – gave John W. McConnell one of the greatest ovations ever bestowed upon a citizen of Montreal. All the week before volunteer workers of the city had been canvassing for the hospitals, with four million dollars as the objective. Mr. McConnell was the main driving force behind the campaign and when, at the dinner, it was announced that the total was nearer five million than four, the works made the welkin ring. But it was "Jack" McConnell they cheered, because it was well known that this irresistible collector had single-handed raised over three million dollars of the total …
>
> There have been many notable money-raising campaigns in Montreal, and particularly in the Great War period, when it became necessary to float the huge Victory Bond drives and also build up the Patriotic War Fund. Canada's greatest salesman, "Jack" McConnell, was the dynamo behind them all.
>
> When a Montreal citizen decides to give five thousand dollars to a good cause he gives five thousand dollars, providing an ordinary collector calls upon him. If, however, the Montreal citizen encounters the hypnotic eye of "Jack" McConnell, he gives ten thousand dollars. And should he object too strenuously and start to plead poverty, Mr. McConnell gets mad and makes the victim scream with anguish as he signs for fifteen thousand dollars. Should a rich man try to pacify Mr. McConnell with a measly check for two thousand dollars, Mr. McConnell as likely as not will tear the check up and notify the rich man that it must be five times that amount or nothing.
>
> Mr. McConnell is jolly and good-natured, but when he encounters a parsimonious plutocrat he is not a bit jolly. Just the opposite. Sometimes the

parsimonious plutocrat fails to do his duty to his fellow man, so Mr. McConnell in a few well chosen words tells the miser in private what he thinks of him, and then, if he happens to be particularly annoyed with the defender of money bags, he most likely arises at some public gathering, delivers Mr. Plutocrat a withering shaft and reads him right out of good society. It is no joke to get read out of society by Mr. McConnell. It makes your right ear burn.

Once embarked upon a campaign, this dynamic doer of good deeds slaves day and night. He has an iron constitution, with an enormous capacity for work. His friends, in commenting upon his untiring effort, frequently ask one another: "How does he stand it?" And yet he does not come out unscathed, as he found when he stepped upon the scales at the conclusion of the recent hospital campaign. He had lost eight pounds.

Mr. McConnell is lithe, tall, erect, clean-shaven and does not look his fifty years. He romps around with his children, plays like a boy and has the same genial smile for an obscure office boy that he has for the president of the Canadian Pacific Railway. And best of all, I think, he is genuinely modest.

The 1927 Joint Hospital Campaign was the last of the several great public subscriptions that McConnell was to head. He was an increasingly honorary participant in other campaigns well into the 1940s,[31] but it was the period from 1909 to 1927 (or 1928 if we include the Bank of Montreal trial) that saw the peak of not merely his fundraising efforts but also those of the community as a whole. With the assurance from Premier Taschereau to cover future hospital deficits, and the institution of the hospital tax, the way was now established for increasing governmental support for health care, although it would be over thirty years before a comprehensive system was to be put in place.[32]

Almost bizarrely, the beginnings of what became the welfare state in Quebec, and in Canada generally, can thus be traced in part to Beatty's CPR, Holt's Montreal Power (MLHPC), Meredith's Bank of Montreal, and Sun Life, as well as to such businessmen as the Molsons and McConnell, all pillars of private enterprise. The new hospital funding emerged not simply out of their coffers but also out of their minds. And their fight against their own, in the form of the Hamilton suit against the board of the Bank of Montreal, confirms how innovative and determined they were prepared to be. But it took McConnell to articulate at the trial precisely the reasons why private enterprise needed, in its own interest, to support social welfare and how it could do so.

As a fundraiser and donor, McConnell did not confine his efforts to the YMCA, McGill University, and hospitals. After the First World War, already the father of three and with another child on the way, he shared a special interest in children with the National Council of Women and the Federation of Women's Institutes. He also became, in 1923, a governor of the Iverley Settlement, founded in 1919 to provide a

Luncheon at the Mount Royal Hotel to mark the opening of Crescent House, new home of the Girls' Counselling Centre. From left: Mrs J.H. Dougherty (vice-president of the Centre), McConnell (chairman of the advisory board of the Welfare Federation), H.R.H. Princess Alice Countess of Athlone, Morris W. Wilson (chairman of the Board of Governors of the Welfare Federation and chancellor of McGill), Mrs H.V. Driver (president of the Centre), and unidentified man. Montreal *Daily Star*, 29 June 1944. Montreal *Gazette* Archives.

centre for the improvement of living conditions among the poor and to maintain a child-health centre.[33] The settlement worked closely with the Child Welfare Association and with the Montreal Maternity Hospital. It ran pre-natal clinics, a Little Mothers' League for mothers in their teens, a Baby Welfare Camp, a Girls' Club (divided by age into Happy Hearts, Merry Maidens, and True Blue girls), a Homemakers' Club, a Christmas Thrift Club, a Boy Scouts' troop, a Girl Guides' company, a kindergarten, a milk station, and a library.

Turning to children without parents and unwed mothers, McConnell became a life governor of an orphanage, the Protestant Infants' Home on Queen Mary Road. At the start of 1923, it was looking after fifty-four children and five women. McConnell also sat on the advisory and building committee of the Ladies' Benevolent Society, founded in 1841, the purpose of which was to provide a home for orphans, half-orphans, or children whose parents were simply unable to provide for them. There were beds for one hundred altogether, some admitted under the Quebec Public Charities Act, some private charges, and some kept free of charge. The home was on Ontario Street West and closely connected to the Anglican church of St John the Evangelist.

Poor but essentially intact young families particularly troubled McConnell, and he became one of the first life governors of the University Settlement, organized in 1891 and incorporated in 1912. The chief inspiration behind it was Dr Milton Hersey, a close friend and a scientist. Operating on Dorchester Street near Richmond Square, from houses owned by St John the Evangelist, this settlement complemented the work of the church in the neighbourhood. Primarily serving immigrants in the St George and St Lawrence wards, it ran a kindergarten, a women's social club, a Boy Scouts' troop and Wolf Cubs, a Girl Guides' company and Brownies, a library, a gymnasium, a handicraft guild, shower baths, a dental clinic, a dance club, a lunchroom, a dental station, a milk station, a summer camp, baby clinics, and pre-natal clinics. It was only natural, too, that McConnell should in 1928 join the Financial Federation, which oversaw the fundraising of the Montreal Council of Social Agencies, and to serve as honorary chairman of its successor, the Welfare Federation.[34]

All of this charitable work was fuelled by McConnell's religious convictions, as became clear at the time of the formation of the United Church in 1925. In a period in which he was still involved with business mergers, McConnell, not surprisingly, supported church union – and he did so for both idealistic and practical reasons. Seeing the United Church as another vehicle for consolidated fundraising, he delivered what must have been his standard talk to fundraising workers, adapted to promote the new religious enterprise:

> The time has arrived when a united effort must be made for the purpose of providing the funds necessary to carry on effectively the greater work in the interests of humanity for which it [the United Church] was brought into being.
>
> We have had plenty of talk about the wonderful prospects in store for the United Church. What we want now is action, not words only. Let us, therefore, "suit the action to the word." Let us bend every effort in the direction of achieving the results so urgently needed to crown the effort of unity with financial success – thus enabling the executive officials to fearlessly carry out their carefully planned programme for increased service.
>
> It is earnestly hoped that every worker in this campaign will do his utmost in his own way to obtain results. Small subscriptions in large volume are of vastly greater importance than a few large ones. There is an opportunity for all to help and the help of all is so much needed. A little service, and a little sacrifice, and success is assured.[35]

Then – as though to underline his business approach to religion – he came out strongly for building stores in front of the enormous St James United Church, on St Catherine Street. Formerly known as St James Methodist Church, this had been Montreal's Methodist "cathedral." It was a flamboyantly late-Victorian reinterpretation of a Gothic cathedral, complete with flying buttresses and a simulated chapter house.

Shortly after the inauguration of the United Church in 1925, McConnell or some-one else had proposed to erect a purely commercial and nondescript brick building in front of St James that would obscure the view of its front, apart from the steeples, destroy its front lawn, and virtually conceal its principal entrance, except through a short arcade running from the street through the commercial building. It would also, however, put the church on a sound financial footing.

Many of the trustees of the St James United Church were appalled by the prospect. At a public meeting, a Mr Bourke (probably George Wesley Bourke, later president of Sun Life) declared that three-quarters of the congregation would "refuse to worship in a hall back of stores." McConnell indignantly demanded to know whether Bourke had "advanced one single, sane and sensible argument" and whether he would accept responsibility for refusing $30,000 a year, in rental income, for thirty years. He brusquely dismissed Bourke's "stentorian" objections as "rot, piffle and twaddle" and "urged the sanity of placing a church on a business basis." Buildings around the church would not keep people away if the church provided good preaching. He urged the trustees to "take a leaf from the moving picture people" who "brought their invitation to the front street in an attractive manner."[36] McConnell won over those whom he regarded as sentimentalists. The commercial building went up and – in spite of its architectural hideousness – was still collecting rent over seventy years later, thus probably ensuring the physical survival of the church exactly as McConnell had foreseen and ensured. (The commercial fronts were largely removed in 2005 and the splendours of St James's front again became visible.)

The organization of the new United Church led coincidentally to the absorp-tion of McConnell's Douglas Church into the Dominion-Douglas United Church in Westmount. The Dominion had already moved from Dominion Square to a new site on Westmount Boulevard, between Lansdowne and Roslyn avenues, in 1914. But it did not erect a new church there until its union with the Douglas in 1925. The new Dominion-Douglas held its first service (in a church hall) the following year. It appears that the McConnells initially migrated in 1925 to the Dominion-Douglas church with much of the old Douglas congregation, uniting themselves in worship with such families as the Goodwins from the old Dominion. In 1925 Lil erected the handsome and enormous window in memory of Thomas Griffith in the new church, as described in chapter 3.

But closer to Redpath Street, where they were living in 1925, and to Pine Avenue, where they moved about 1928, was Erskine United Church (which became the Ers-kine and American United Church in 1934), at the corner of Ontario (later du Musée Avenue) and Sherbrooke streets, beside the Art Association of Montreal, later known as the Montreal Museum of Fine Arts. In June 1928 the McConnells joined this church, and it was to be from here that he would be buried thirty-seven years later.

Their children Wilson, John, and Kit also joined, but not David, who was confirmed as an Anglican while a student at Bishop's College School in Lennoxville.[37]

In 1934 the American United Church merged with Erskine United, thereby concentrating many rich members of the United Church in Montreal in one place. For the first time, it brought together in worship such old friends as McConnell and W.M. Birks, the latter having come from the American Church. In March 1938 Birks began raising funds for renovations of the church. When his brother Henry, after some difficulty, reached McConnell, who was ill at the time, McConnell said: "Don't spend a cent, put the money into Government Bonds."[38] The Birks brothers did not give up, however. They eventually induced him to give $10,000 and thus to become the most generous single donor to the project, by the end of June.

At the heart of the renovations was the removal of the huge central pulpit in favour of the incorporation of a richly decorated but restrained sanctuary, with a great Greek cross on the wall and symbols from the catacombs in the choir stalls. Rigorously excluded therefore was any reminder of Methodist preachers writhing with celestial fire in the fields and the forests. Gone, too, was the emphasis on the Sunday school. Expunged indeed was the Victorian sensibility that had suffused both the Methodism and the Presbyterianism of the amalgamating congregations. In place of the old pulpit and "concert choir seats," and even the once-controversial but soaring and gleaming organ pipes – which Birks found "distracting" – the marble communion table, virtually indistinguishable from an altar, surrounded by a marble chancel rail, became the focus of worship. The mystery of Holy Communion now vied for the attention of worshippers with the preaching of the Gospel. The marble floor and spotlights also highlighted the new prominence of the Eucharist, and the new, handsome but smaller pulpit stood to the side. The new airy chancel was more reminiscent of Byzantine Ravenna than of Calvinist Geneva, or indeed of Methodist Bardsville. The church admitted light through twenty-four magically coloured windows – many by the studio of Louis Comfort Tiffany in 1902 and rescued from the abandoned American Church. The renovated Erskine and American was actually the culmination of a tradition of Protestant church embellishment that had been developing since the 1870s among richer congregations. With the Tiffany windows and the Birks renovations, the church now conveyed some of the Byzantine-inspired lushness of the 1890s Sherbourne Street Methodist Church in Toronto, where Ames and Flavelle had taught Sunday school.[39]

It is unlikely that the renovations meant much, if anything, to McConnell, even though he had been the principal single financial contributor to them. The communion roll for 1933-35 reveals that he and Lil attended only one of the twelve communion services held at the Erskine and American in those years, and it is unlikely that their attendance was to improve after the renovations, since they spent nearly all their weekends, when not abroad, in Dorval and Val David, where they never went to church on Sunday, much less other days. God for him was found in helping others, and not in buildings. Eventually, McConnell himself took to playing tennis on Sundays and even to serving alcohol to guests to his house, dancing and playing cards, and attending the theatre. At his core he remained as Methodist as ever, but the culture of Methodism had disappeared almost utterly from his religious as well as his social life.

In hindsight, it is tempting to attribute the attrition in the traditional Protestant preoccupation with salvation in the next life to "secularism." Yet this is too simple to explain why, within McConnell's lifetime, charity workers became social workers, and why his charitable fundraising broadened into philanthropic giving through a foundation. Even by McConnell's youth, the Epworth League was preaching that salvation was open to all, and that even sin could not destroy moral choice, so that forgiveness and renewal were available to all who repented.

Methodism had almost lost its preoccupation with conversion and thus become secular in the sense of overwhelmingly oriented towards justification by works as well as faith, or even by works alone. McConnell himself never deviated from this view. Neither did the churches that he belonged to. The Methodists had a department of moral and social reform until 1902, when it became a department of evangelism and social service. The Presbyterians followed suit in 1907, and in the following year the two denominations cooperated in the Moral and Social Reform Council of Canada. In 1914 the Social Service Council of Canada in turn replaced it.

But in a multicultural, bilingual city such as Montreal, even Methodism was insufficiently broad to address all needs, as was the United Church from 1925 onward. The minister of the Erskine and then of the Erskine and American United Church from 1925 to 1946, Leslie Pidgeon, was in the 1930s moved to support the Moral Rearmament Movement. Founded by an American Lutheran, Frank Buchman, but also very popular in England as the Oxford Group. Much of English Montreal, including the B.M. Hallwards (son-in-law and daughter of Lord Atholstan) and even briefly the McConnells themselves, found this very personal kind of evangelism attractive. In merging psychology with public confession, it superficially harked back to an earlier kind of Protestantism, but its popularity did not last, and Alcoholics Anonymous was probably closer to its teachings than John Wesley. Pidgeon, whose brother George had been elected the first moderator of the United Church in opposition to S.D. Chown, a Social Gospeller especially close to McConnell, saw his special mission as being to businessmen.

What characterized McConnell's Protestantism in the years between the world wars was not the dilution of dogma, which had never played much part in his life. It was the triumph of pragmatism. Even if he could not understand any better than most the powerful forces that were undermining the bases of a society that professed itself Christian, he remained supremely numerate. If probable results were measurable, if the numbers added up, he could be convinced that a cause was worthy of his support, since he was always above all a bookkeeper. Numbers, from the YMCA campaign of 1909 through his wartime fundraising to the Joint Hospital Campaign of 1927 and to the very end of his life, provided him with an ongoing education in social as well as demographic change.

More personally, McConnell's political conservatism was in some sense undermined by his piety as well as his pragmatism, so that he lacked any clear philosophical objection to say unemployment insurance or even the welfare state. In another sense, his piety as an individual reinforced his belief in free enterprise and capitalism, which others saw as conservative or reactionary. This ambivalence, which resulted from his fundamental belief in the individual, left him less than articulate when it came to some of the most pressing social issues of his time. He was all in favour of social workers, but it is less clear that he was in favour of social work leading to central state planning and universal, undifferentiated entitlement to tax-funded services. It is unlikely that he was, since he always wanted to leave open the opportunity for individuals to contribute time, money, and ideas on their own initiative, which is what he did even while campaigning for increased government funding of hospitals and universities in particular. He never abandoned the old-fashioned notion of charity, in the sense of helping the less fortunate, even after he had set up his own foundation as an instrument of philanthropy, which literally means love for all men.

McConnell was the survivor of many upheavals in religious belief and social thought. He was as buffeted about by these as much as anyone else, probably more than most. Profoundly loyal by nature, he found his own church turning politically against nearly everything that he stood for, and yet he remained profoundly typical of that church, particularly its transformation of faith into something essentially private – rather than a collection of dogmas demanding public adherence. This aspect of his religion immunized him against the sermons of United Church socialists. Yet even with them he could share at least hope and also the belief that faith must be manifested through works. His primary aim was to bring help if not salvation to all regardless of religion, but his efforts in this direction – whether as an individual fundraiser and philanthropist or later as the head of a philanthropic foundation – were far from exclusively secular in inspiration and purpose.

There have been certainly richer financiers than McConnell whose wealth funded sprawling empires, such as E.H. Harriman of the Union Pacific Railroad. There have been certainly also richer people whose philanthropy has left a deeper mark on the world, such as the Rockefellers. But possibly no single person anywhere in his era ever merged money making with money giving so consistently and wholeheartedly, and over such a length of time, as McConnell. The wealthier he became, the more he gave away, from the very start of his career, when he was making a few cents a day, until he became probably the richest man in Canada. Although he kept much for himself and his family to live on very well, there was almost a cause-and-effect relationship between his making money and his giving it away.

This fact is what makes his life unusual although not unique. If what McConnell did was within a tradition of the gospel of wealth – practised also by, for example, Andrew Carnegie, Hart Massey, and Bill Gates – he still did it probably as well as anyone else, not merely in Canada but also beyond. And he did it with both enthusiasm and single-mindedness perhaps seldom equalled. His contemporaries certainly gave, sometimes in huge amounts, but sporadically or posthumously or with ulterior motives or with very distinct agendas. Although McConnell did have a few cherished causes, he gave without strings and widely, simply to the three traditional objects of charity: religion, education, and medicine. This expansion of his view of charity as applying to the community as a whole is clearest in his advocacy of a hospital tax, but it would become clearer still in his support of education, as described in chapter 17.

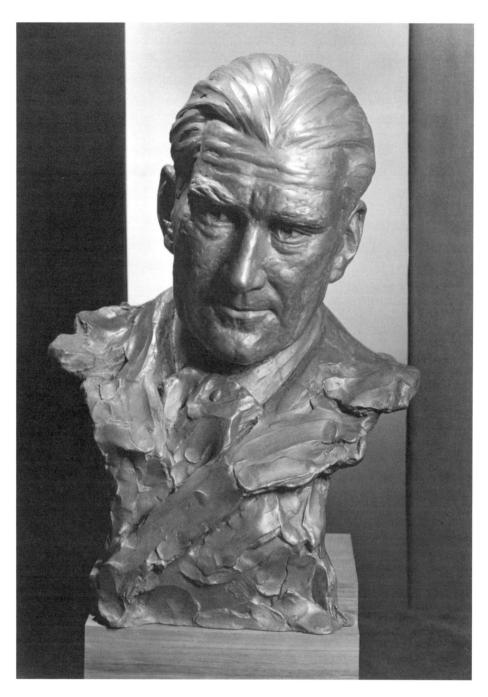

Suzanne Silvercruys's bust of McConnell, n.d. McCord Museum M 2003.8.6.8.84.

There'll Always Be an England:
The Second World War, 1939–45

Hitler, the apotheosis of paganism, has challenged our Christian civilization to a duel to the death. We have no choice but to take up the challenge … Public money will be more than absorbed in public effort. Such institutions as the Red Cross, the military hospital units, the various organized schemes to keep up the boys' morale, even direct gifts of machine gun units or tank corps, all sorts of moves by private patriotic generosity to support and assist the forces in the field, will depend upon the purses of individual citizens.

– Editorial, Montreal *Star*, 1 September 1939[1]

It is unthinkable that there should be at this time any lack of co-operation, any manifestation of failure to realize the urgent need of the Allies, any movement calculated to create outside even the idea that discord prevails within our borders.

We must preserve UNITY; we must avoid discord; we must co-ordinate our efforts with the rest of the Dominion; we must play our part, do our fair share, discharge our manifest duties to Canada and the Empire to the best of our capacity and our understanding. […]

The hope of this lies in a religion that is fully alive to the realization that the service of God and the perfection of humanity are matters of the most practical importance. The New Testament is a book of the world's greatest religion, written at a time when religion was vital. In that Book two things are clearly set forth – the democratic idea and the instinct for personal perfection. The religion of the New Testament is the religion of the poor and the meek. Every page is permeated with the thought of the possibilities of the common man. Slaves are brethren and common-folk are kings and priests before God.

Editorial, Montreal *Star*, 3 September 1939, "Quebec Must Be United."

Like nearly all Canadians, McConnell dreaded the onset of another world war from every point of view. He was sixty-two years old and somewhat tired and frail. His sons might have to face injury and death in battle. His business interests would probably nearly all suffer, particularly St Lawrence Sugar. The whole British Empire, including Canada, and democratic countries everywhere faced mortal danger. Friends and colleagues, employees, and perhaps civilization itself were confronted with possible extinction. For the Square Mile and indeed for McConnell's friends everywhere, the declaration of war seemed to guarantee the end of an entire way of life, one already devastated by the First World War.

Unlike the First World War, the Second was not to be a "good" one for him. He had already retired from most of his boards and he lacked the energy for selling war bonds, for example, although he did heroic work for McGill. He did his best of course, day after day, for the war effort, playing several different roles. Thousands, from royalty to refugees, and sometimes royal refugees, benefited from his help, directly and indirectly; and he was constantly looking to do more. Although he was sometimes frustrated that he was not doing more, the war actually brought out new facets of his humanity, and his relative lack of influence laid bare the moral simplicity that had been at the root of his fiery ambition of earlier years.

Great Britain declared war on the German Reich at the start of September 1939. Many Montrealers were in the Laurentians or elsewhere on holiday. McConnell was at Saran Chai, and he followed with horror the unfolding story. Like the king and queen and nearly everyone else in Great Britain and the empire, except for the circle of Winston Churchill and Anthony Eden, he had probably been in favour of appeasement before the war, seeing Germany as a bulwark against Soviet expansion. During the war itself, however, neither subtlety nor doubt undermined his belief in the rightness of the cause of fighting Hitler and later also the Japanese. Like Lord Beaverbrook, he was more supportive of Soviet Russia than he probably would have been glad to recall in later years. His strong views on the Suez crisis eleven years after the end of the war, in favour of the Anglo-French intervention and against both the United States and the Soviet Union, were to be an apparent atonement for both his pre-war appeasement and his wartime sympathy for Russia.

Whether his views over time were correct or not, McConnell worked tirelessly to raise money for innumerable causes related to the war effort. Humbled by the selflessness and the sacrifices of those in combat, he saw his own work on the home front as minor by comparison. But each was obliged to do his or her part, for the stakes could not be greater. As he wrote at the end of 1942:

> The story of this life and death struggle with U-boats, floating mines and Nazi raiders will perhaps never be told. Apart from the miraculous defence of Great Britain where the R.A.F. smashed the much vaunted Nazi Air Force, the story

of sea mastery by British and Canadian Navies, and the great Merchant Marine, is beyond the powers of comprehension. It is the most incredible story of heroism and achievement the world has ever known.

To me, Hitler is the personification of Satan at work on earth, bringing trials and suffering worse than death to innocent people wherever his evil hand is felt. Our fight is surely a righteous crusade against the powers of darkness.[2]

This sort of evangelical fervour and conventional patriotism held little allure for those charged with the actual direction of the war. He gained no access to Churchill and Roosevelt, although he managed to cultivate their wives. As will be seen, such a worldly woman as Mrs Churchill was puzzled by his lack of guile in offering her a fur coat and assistance to her favourite charities. But after due inquiry she concluded that he held no hidden agenda, and she relented in respect of the charities. This is a theme that carried on into the post-war years when, accepting no rebuff, he successfully offered material support to Princess Marina, Anthony Eden, and the charities of Princess Elizabeth. His insistence might be perplexing, but he was so eminently successful in business, and so patently simple as well as rich, that it was hard not to succumb. In the end, through his unstinting generosity with his time and his money, he did no harm but rather much good.

For countless other less privileged Canadians and their families, the experience of war on the home front was similar to that of the McConnells. They, too, took in refugee children and generously gave clothes and money to the war effort, in addition to their toiling in factories and offices and on farms. Unlike the McConnells, they also lost husbands and wives, children, and other relatives. But for the McConnells, it was still an exhilarating and even a liberating period. Kit became a voluntary nurse; John, disqualified for active service because of water in his knees, became responsible for controlling publicity for the Royal Air Force (RAF) Ferry Command and for raising money for Londoners bombed out of their homes by the Germans; Wilson, after leaving St Lawrence Sugar, joined the Royal Canadian Artillery in 1941, teaching at the training centre at Eastern Passage in Halifax and in Vancouver and also becoming one of the country's first radar specialists; David was at university for much of the war but then joined the Royal Canadian Air Force (RCAF) and served in Trenton, Ontario.

In comparison with the fierce struggles in Europe, Africa, and Asia, life in Canada during the war was almost placid. There were restrictions on the consumption of butter and sugar, but no real food shortages; no rockets fell from the sky; and no armies of occupation came to rape and pillage. The news from overseas was often harrowing despite the censorship, but most people, including the McConnells, carried on many of their pre-war patterns of life, to which they added their wartime activities. Lil and Jack were busier than ever. There was an enormous amount of entertaining to be done, of British and foreign royalty, governors general, ambassadors, politicians,

Brig.-Gen. E. de B. Panet hands over a cheque for $4,038, collected through the dimes of thousands of Montrealers, to John G. McConnell, chairman of the Queen's Canadian Fund for Air Raid Victims. At extreme left is Lt.-Col. K.M. Perry, assistant adjutant and quartermaster general of Military District No. 4, and at extreme right is Col. George P. Vanier, joint chairman of the special recruiting committee. Montreal *Daily Star*, 6 August 1941. Private collection.

Wilson (centre front) in training, n.d. Private collection.

Kit in Red Cross uniform, n.d. Private collection.

air marshals, and raw recruits. The sugar industry was under government control, and the St Lawrence refinery was closed for much of the war. Yet tennis continued at Dorval and skiing at Val David, with friends both old and new, and there were receptions at Pine Avenue.

On about 26 June 1940, rumours surfaced that Mackenzie King had approached McConnell, among other businessmen, to be minister of war services in Ottawa. But he refused to join King, who then turned to another candidate, J.T. Thorson, later a judge of the Exchequer Court of Canada. Why McConnell in particular refused is not clear. He pleaded age and health, but the remaining years of the war were to see him almost as energetic as ever, and indeed apparently, at least to the American minister to Ottawa, Pierrepont Moffat, frustrated by the lack of a major position to fill in the war effort. On the other hand, even King noted that McConnell looked "delicate" when they did meet, and in November 1941 McConnell was to decline even the national chairmanship of the Joint War Services Campaign offered to him by King at the urging of Thorson. McConnell pleaded ill health owing to sleeplessness.[3]

Although McConnell's *Star* pledged its support for the King government in 1940, it is possible that McConnell himself was still dubious about King, and about his own ability to back him. King was unlikely to institute compulsory registration for

David receiving his wings, 1945. Private collection.

national service, such as might be used for the conscription of troops. McConnell felt strongly that every province, including Quebec, must pull its weight, and his presence in the cabinet might proved awkward for King if conscription arose as an issue. It is also possible that King's offer was not serious. McConnell possessed no base of political power in Quebec or anywhere else, and he could bring no significant support to King. In any event, it is hard to see why it was so necessary to add more businessmen to the ones already in the cabinet. The offers to McConnell and the others may thus have been simply window-dressing, to give the appearance of creating a "national" government of unity without the reality of sharing government with the established parliamentary opposition, as had just happened in Britain.

Whatever his reasons for not going to Ottawa, McConnell found more than enough to occupy him in Montreal. As the German Blitzkrieg rolled through Western Europe in the spring of 1940, it became clear that English children might not be safe simply by being moved to the countryside outside London. Even the young princesses, Elizabeth and Margaret Rose, who were largely sequestered in Windsor Castle, might have to be moved to Canada. Although these were denied, there were plans to remove the entire royal family to Canada should Britain fall. This removal, with that of the British cabinet, would have made Ottawa the wartime capital of the British Empire, as Algiers was of Free France. The gold reserves of the Bank of England had already arrived with the king and queen on their visit to Canada in the spring preceding the outbreak of war. Now the gold was safely in the vaults of the Sun Life building in Montreal. Even the location of the highly secret hiding place of the Stone of Scone, which was normally lodged under the coronation chair at Westminster Abbey and was thus a sacred symbol of British sovereignty, was held in Ottawa.[4]

In June 1940, in anticipation of a German assault on Britain, there was a mass evacuation of children from England. In total, about 3,000 English children came to Canada or the United States in 1940, half with governmental aid but the other half through private arrangements with such families as the McConnells. More would have come later, had not a ship carrying fleeing children, the *City of Benares*, been torpedoed by the Germans in the summer of 1940, killing 83 – or 77, the accounts vary – of the 90 children on board, and 256 passengers in total.

Lady Tweedsmuir asked Angela (Mrs Herbert) Bruce to find homes in Canada for the children of a hundred of her friends, people who could afford to pay the fares across the Atlantic, and McConnell and Sir Edward Beatty helped with the transport.[5] The Bessboroughs decided to send their younger son, George St Lawrence Ponsonby, born in the Royal Victoria Hospital in Montreal, to stay with the McConnells and he arrived with his cousin Edward Cavendish. Two days earlier, two of George's neighbours, the two sons of the Duke of Richmond – Charles, who then bore the courtesy title of Earl of March, and Nicholas, known as Lord Nicholas Gordon Lennox – had arrived from Goodwood in Sussex. The McConnells had met the Duchess of Richmond in 1936 in New Delhi, where they all were guests of the Willingdons at Viceroy's House. An aunt, Molly Hudson, accompanied the Gordon Lennoxes.

The Ashley Coopers also sent their son James, known as Jim, to stay. He arrived with his sister Pat and a daughter of Geoffrey Dawson, the managing editor of *The Times* – both on their way to Australia. Rosemary Kelsey, half-sister of Lieutenant Robin Scott, formerly aide-de-camp to Lord Tweedsmuir and now in the Royal Navy, also arrived, on the *Duchess of Atholl*, but she did not stay for long. Pine Avenue and Dorval were filled to capacity, with Lil at one stage reduced to sleeping on the porch at Dorval. She had been in Georgia when the children suddenly arrived and so McConnell himself met most of them at the quayside and entertained them. He found the Gordon Lennoxes "extremely nice," and a letter from their father, the young duke, only thirty-seven, was enough to make him weep.[6]

Wilson and John were now married with their own houses, and David was at McGill. This left only Kit spending much time at home with her parents, and the

The arrival of English children in Montreal, 3 July 1940. From left: Angus James, Venetia Fawcus, Jeremy James, the Earl of March (Charles Gordon Lennox, later 10th Duke of Richmond and Gordon), Lord Nicholas Gordon Lennox (later British ambassador to Spain), Edward Cavendish and George St Lawrence Ponsonby. Private collection.

addition of five new boys enlivened the McConnell houses for several months, until the threat of an imminent invasion of England was over. Lil kept her staff, but she found herself taking the children to the doctor and the dentist. McConnell himself generally found it fun to have the house full of young children again. Charles (who was to become the 10th Duke of Richmond) and Nicholas scampered up and down the servants' staircase at Pine Avenue, finding the house dark, "opulent," and forbidding and McConnell himself "benignant." All in all, they seemed quite content, but Molly Hudson and Lil turned out to be wholly incompatible and after Christmas 1940 McConnell moved Charles, Nicholas, and Molly to a house in Westmount. Subsequently, the boys proceeded to Washington, where their father had been appointed air attaché in the British embassy.

After the Battle of Britain, and with the threat of invasion receding, the other three boys at the McConnells' returned to England, although such returns proved difficult to arrange. Early in the autumn of 1941, it took the efforts of McConnell and Air Chief Marshal Sir Frederick Bowhill, commander-in-chief of the Royal Air Force Ferry Command in Dorval, to arrange for Jim Ashley Cooper to hitch a flight home with the Duke of Kent, who had come to Canada on a tour of inspection.[7] George Ponsonby and Edward Cavendish were to stay with the McConnells for considerably longer – Edward until the end of 1942 and George until July 1943.

Apart from these refugee children, the popular novelist Barbara Cartland, known in private life as Mrs Hugh McCorquodale, also had reason to be grateful to McConnell. She arrived in Canada with her children, armed with an introduction from Lord Ratendone, the son of Lord Willingdon. She recalled that McConnell was "exactly what I had expected a great Canadian to look like – very tall, handsome, clean-cut, with vivid blue eyes, which were exceedingly alive."[8] His "simplicity and directness" impressed her, and she told him that she did not feel it right to live such a privileged life in Canada while so many were suffering at home. When she asked him to help her return to England, he warned her that Canada had prohibited ships from carrying women and children in war zones, but he promised to see what he could do and offered money. "I went away from J.W. McConnell's office, as so many other people have done, walking on air," she recalled. Within about a week, McConnell had arranged passage for her and her children through the Department of External Affairs, and by November she was off, profoundly thankful for Canadian hospitality.

Jews of course felt particularly at risk with the fall of France, not least members of the most renowned of Jewish families, the Rothschilds. Rita Flower (a former sister-in-law of Lord Bessborough who had visited the McConnells in Montreal a year before), Vincent Massey (high commissioner for Canada in London), and Baron Silvercruys (the Belgian minister in Ottawa) all appealed to the McConnells on behalf of the Austrian Baron and Baroness Alphonse de Rothschild. The Rothschilds arrived in 1940 with only the clothes on their backs, accompanied by their two little girls, a nephew, and the younger son of Lionel de Rothschild. The McConnells were quick to help them and invited them to Pine Avenue from time to time. Even after the war, in September 1945, they put the now-widowed Baroness up at the Ritz-Carlton.

For friends remaining in England, the news was increasingly desperate, and the war became personal for the McConnells. The south of England, where the Bessboroughs and many of their friends and relatives were living, was in "bomb alley" – the route of German aircraft from France across the English Channel to London. In the terrifying autumn of 1940, the country house of the Bessboroughs, Stansted, was badly damaged in three separate incidents. The McConnells had known it well since 1932, when they accompanied the Bessboroughs to England on home leave. A little later, in November, the *Empress of Britain*, the pride of the Canadian Pacific fleet, on which the McConnells sailed to India in 1936, was sunk.

McConnell's generosity was not confined to British subjects. The Italians had invaded Greece in October 1940, followed by the Germans in April 1941. In connection with the Greek War Relief Fund that had been incorporated in November 1940, King George II of the Hellenes (Greece) came with his mistress, Mrs Joyce Britten-Jones, to Pine Avenue in June 1942.[9] When Greece fell to the Nazis, Greek Canadians, like Greek Americans, rushed to organize aid for their compatriots. Assistance came from the wider community in the form of a local committee of the Greek War Relief Fund, of which McConnell immediately accepted the honorary presidency; Sir Edward Beatty was its patron. From November 1940 to March 1941, the committee raised over $415,000.

With the German occupation, which led to the requisitioning of all available food, starvation soon gripped Greece. By April 1942, the population of seven million seemed doomed to extinction, as typhoid, cholera, and dysentery spread with the famine. Prince Charles of Sweden arranged with the occupiers for the shipment of relief supplies to Greek civilians under a neutral commission made up of Swedish and Swiss nationals. At the time of the visit of King George II, McConnell had personally helped to arrange for Canada to send 15,000 tons of wheat per month to Greece. The first three ships full of medical and other supplies, as well as wheat, left Montreal in July 1942. They were part of a large international effort shared with the Red Cross in Canada and the United States, the Greek War Relief Association of the United States, the American and Canadian governments, and eventually, in 1944, the Argentine government. By the end of the war, the Canadian committee of the Greek War Relief Fund had sent over $2.5 million in supplies. In the meantime, in June 1943, the committee had launched a second appeal, with McConnell again as honorary president. The goal was $500,000, but this second campaign for funds raised over $1 million. Later in 1943, the committee, with the help of other organizations, sent over 600,000 pounds of supplies out of Montreal to Greece.

Britain's plight early in the war was no less dire than that of Greece. When, under Churchill, the British began to stiffen their resistance early in the summer of 1940, Hitler decided to soften them up by destroying the RAF. Almost at once and in the face of opposition from the king, Churchill appointed his great friend Lord Beaverbrook, known as Max Aitken when he was a competitor of McConnell's in Canada, as minister of aircraft production. Beaverbrook's task was to speed up the production of aircraft for the Battle of Britain, which was expected to begin at any minute – and in this he received much assistance from McConnell. Immediately after Beaverbrook's appointment, McConnell cabled his congratulations and pledged to give his announcements the "widest possible circulation"[10] in Canada. The relations of the two had warmed with the stress of war, and, in the days that followed, McConnell continued to send a stream of encouraging messages, including material to be passed on to Churchill.

In the air conflict that was inevitably to dominate the war, two distinct but related shortages faced Britain: qualified pilots and aircraft. McConnell contributed to the Canadian efforts to address both of these. With regard to pilots, almost four months after the outbreak of war, in December 1939, Britain, Canada, Australia, and New Zealand decided to create an Empire Training Plan. Later renamed the Joint Air

Training Plan, and finally the British Commonwealth Air Training Plan (BCATP), its mission was to coordinate the preparation of pilots from all over the empire for its air defence.

Prime Minister King had been reluctant to permit even this measure of preparation for war, but Senator Arthur Meighen, who had given a ringing speech on the matter at the recent Conservative leadership convention, pressed McConnell to support the scheme in the *Star*. McConnell sent Meighen's letter to Dr A.R. Carman, the editor-in-chief, who explained to McConnell that his paper had been playing down the British air-training plan in Canada because of the hatred of Meighen in Quebec.[11] McConnell had no sympathy with this hedging, and he ordered Carman to publish Meighen's letter in the *Star* and assured him: "You may not, I sincerely hope, have any reason to feel that The Star is in sympathy with the inaction of the Ottawa authorities and their failure to co-operate with Great Britain in matters of such great importance."[12]

Canada was to be the principal location for the scheme, and RAF officers from Britain were to train with officers of the Royal Canadian, the Royal Australian, and the Royal New Zealand air forces. From April to August 1940, trainees from Canada and Britain gathered in Toronto, and, with the beginning of the Battle of Britain that summer, twenty-three RAF schools moved out of Britain to Canada, all of which were eventually brought within the plan. The training courses were shortened and the facilities in Canada were filled to capacity: at its peak, in 1941–42, the BCATP was to run 359 schools and depots, and during the war it was to train 136,849 airmen.[13]

In the early days of the Battle of Britain, McConnell wrote to Vincent Massey, the Canadian high commissioner in London: "Our admiration for the courage and spirit of the people in the British Isles is beyond words. We have just had the report of the mass air attack of 1,000 planes, and the number brought down by the R.A.F. compared to our own losses is almost unbelievable. At the moment, it would appear as if the enemy would try to break down the R.A.F. resistance, with the hope of winning the 'Battle of England' by Air rather than by invasion, but if the score keeps up at yesterday's rate as reported here of approximately 5 Nazi to One British brought down, the Nazis will be compelled to sacrifice thousands of planes in the attempt."[14] But, notwithstanding such successes, the situation remained critical. Even though empire pilots were being trained in Canada, as early as 1940 and particularly after the retreat from Dunkirk, there never seemed to be enough experienced pilots to wage the life-and-death struggle against the German Luftwaffe.

Since it seemed clear from the start that air power would probably decide the war, it fell to McConnell and Sir Edward Beatty, among others, to work to find seasoned pilots while waiting for the new ones to be trained, more than a year before the US entry into the conflict. Many Americans wanted join the struggle to save Britain, and, with their own country maintaining its neutrality, they were prepared to join the RAF and the RCAF. To help to capitalize on their eagerness, McConnell offered his services. He and Beaverbrook worked with J.P. (Jack) Bickell, president of McIntyre-Porcupine Mines in Toronto but now based in England, to coordinate their recruitment. Beaverbrook had initially asked for only about a hundred pilots, but McConnell swiftly found between 200 and 250 Americans. The men recruited were to be flight-tested in Canada before being sent to England.

In Montreal, McConnell further worked on the recruiting with Morris Wilson, president of the Royal Bank, and through the Clayton Knight Committee, later called the Canadian Aviation Bureau. This committee had been originally set up to assist the men in the BCATP, but was now being expanded to recruit Americans. It maintained fifteen offices in the United States. McConnell remained in particularly close contact with Clayton Knight and Wing Commander Homer Smith, who were discreetly supervising the office in the Waldorf Astoria in New York, so as not to contravene American neutrality law.[15]

Although many of the very first recruits proved unsuitable, Beaverbrook was apparently impressed by McConnell's success. On 26 September, as much of London was burning under relentless German bombing, he wrote encouragingly to him: "On you we rely completely to furnish the pilots who are so necessary to us. My confidence in you is absolute. And we are delighted with the improved quality of the men who have come over lately." Through the autumn, with continuing fears of an invasion of England, or at least of a submarine blockade, McConnell persisted in his search for new pilots, both those already qualified and civilians wanting to train to fly for the RAF. Finding these new pilots – who now included Norwegians, Poles, Belgians, Free French, Czechs, Englishmen, Australians, New Zealanders, and South Africans, as well as Canadians and Americans and others – was a desperate, exhausting task for all involved, but McConnell did what he could. The search took months, and by the following summer he would also be working with Captain (later Air Vice-Marshal) Donald Bennett, an Australian with the RAF, to ensure the adequate training of the recruits.

The need for aircraft in Britain was no less acute than that for pilots. McConnell made his first contribution in this area directly after Beaverbrook's appointment as minister of aircraft production, when, on 24 August 1940, he offered Beaverbrook a million dollars ($14,253,000 in 2008 terms) "for most vital immediate airforce needs." Churchill cabled to McConnell that this singular act of generosity had honoured Canada and sustained "our common cause," reflecting "a magnanimity matched to this hour of purpose and resolve." "Hard-tried and enduring," Churchill concluded, "the people of Britain know well that their brothers are numerous, powerful and true." McConnell replied to Churchill: "In these difficult days your own courageous and indomitable leadership thrills and inspires us all. May you be given health and strength to continue irresistibly to glorious victory."[16] Beaverbrook himself described the whole British nation as "filled with gratitude and admiration" for McConnell's

An aircraft in McConnell's Squadron, n.d. Private collection.

gift, the generosity of which was, "like the valour of our pilots," "a true reflection of the unconquerable spirit of the race."

McConnell had not specified any particular use for the $1 million, but Beaverbrook decided that it should be used for building more Spitfires.[17] McConnell initially refused to have a squadron of new Spitfires named after him. He had tried to remain as anonymous as possible from the start by depositing the money into Beaverbrook's trust account in the name of Morris Wilson. But, as newspaper owners, both McConnell and Beaverbrook soon realized that public recognition of the $1 million was necessary to encourage others to contribute towards the production of Spitfires. McConnell therefore relented in October, and the planes his money produced came to be named the McConnell Squadron.

After McConnell's gift of $1 million was made public in October 1940, the reaction was electric, particularly, of course, in Britain. The Willingdons cabled from London: "SPLENDID MAN CHEERS BLESSINGS." Other cables were just as effusive. The Duke of Richmond declared: "YOUR MAGNIFICENT PATRIOTISM RAISES OUR ALREADY OVERWHELMING GRATITUDE TO SPITFIRE ALTITUDES [.] YOU HAVE INSPIRED THOUSANDS." Lord Rothermere, the press lord, cabled simply: "SPLENDID, SPLENDID, SPLENDID," while Garfield Weston, a Canadian manufacturer and British MP, proclaimed: "ALL ENGLAND STOOD AND CHEERED WITH THE WESTON FAMILY WHEN YOUR PRINCELY GIFT WAS ANNOUNCED." Sir Kingsley Wood, Sir John Reith, Vincent Massey, Sir Campbell Stuart, Sir Beverley

Baxter, and many others joined them. From the Carlisle Memorial Methodist Church in Belfast, the Rev. James Smyth, formerly of the Wesleyan Theological College in Montreal, wrote. So did J.D.D. Lloyd, formerly of Goulding's in Toronto and now in Hemel Hempstead. Calvin Bullock, the financier, wrote from One Wall Street, as did people from Kansas, California, Brazil, South Africa, and elsewhere, many of whom said that they rejoiced in bearing the name "McConnell."

It has been asserted by a biographer of Beaverbrook that the Spitfire Fund, of which McConnell's million dollars had been the nucleus, was an "irrelevancy" because "the shortage was in productive capacity, not in money, and even £13,000,000, the sum finally raised, was not a serious stroke against inflation."[18] But it does seem clear from other evidence that money was indeed urgently required for the war effort, even as early as August 1940. The Churchill government had decided to create and equip an army of fifty-two divisions and expand aircraft production to 2,782 units a month by December 1941. The necessary purchases from the Americans for this expansion would, according to the chancellor of the exchequer, total $3.2 million over the twelve months extending from August 1940. In the meantime, the remaining British resources in foreign exchange and American securities amounted to only £490 million, which meant that Britain would exhaust her gold and dollar reserves by December 1940. In fact, Britain was able to remain solvent for a few months beyond that, but bankruptcy was postponed not avoided, occurring in the spring of 1941. It was also in March 1941 that the US Congress passed the Lend-Lease Act, which authorized the continued flow of American supplies to Britain without payment until the end of the war, although the total loan to Britain under this arrangement was to reach a crippling $27,023 million by 1945.[19]

In the context of war expenditures generally towards the end of 1940, therefore, it seems to follow that McConnell's gift of $1 million was far from negligible, much less irrelevant. Its importance lay in its timeliness and in the example that it set for other friends of Britain overseas. It is true that the McConnell squadron had not been built by the time of the Battle of Britain, but it was able to replace in part the Spitfires lost in that battle and thus to aid in the further prosecution of the war effort. Moreover, had the Lend-Lease agreement not been achieved by the following March, such contributions as McConnell's would have remained Britain's only source of foreign exchange.

The new Spitfires were welcome, but they did not come close to meeting Britain's aircraft needs. Before the outbreak of war, Canada had virtually no industry to produce munitions or aircraft for use in battle. Outside the Dominion Arsenal, only the National Steel Car Corporation was producing shells for Britain by the start of the conflict. In any case, the principle throughout the empire had been that all arms and ammunition used by imperial troops should be standardized and interchangeable, and so any aircraft ordered by Britain from Canada must be at least predominantly established British types, made to British engineering standards. Thus, Canada was to come to produce Hampdens, Bolingbrokes, Hurricanes, Ansons, Lancasters, Mosquitoes, Lysanders, and other types of aircraft for Britain, distinct from those shipped from the United States.

The production of these aircraft in Canada proved initially difficult, because in peacetime Canadian industry had become geared to American standards. In all, Canada built over 4,000 aircraft by the end of the war on the British account, and almost 12,000 on its own account, most of them trainers vital to the air crews being produced under the BCATP. Nonetheless, the Canadian production of aircraft quickly proved wholly inadequate for growing British needs, and, as early as the middle of 1940, it was clear that Canadian production capacity was already stretched to its limits. Britain had to look elsewhere to place new orders, in particular to the United States.

As late as that autumn, however, the Americans still seemed to believe that the British needed pilots rather than aircraft. The British under-secretary of state for air, Captain Henry Balfour, met Henry Morgenthau, the US secretary of the treasury and President Roosevelt's point man on the Lend-Lease agreement, at the Seigneury Club in Montebello, Quebec. Balfour explained that the only prospect of maintaining a transatlantic link between Britain and America during the winter to come was through Canada. For this, Britain required the early provision of six four-engine CB-30 bombers designed for the US Army, to serve as a ferry service. Morgenthau, however, relayed the army's concern that any aircraft shipped to Britain from the United States would be stockpiled and bombed. To this Beaverbrook replied that a large part of the British training organization was now secure from enemy attacks by being scattered across Britain or relocated to Canada and that new aircraft were urgently needed for the pilots currently being trained.[20]

Beyond training pilots in Canada and building aircraft in Britain, there remained two further issues. The first was the procurement, and the second the transport, of the primarily American-made aircraft to Britain. The question of how to find and ship US-made aircraft and other supplies to Britain had arisen even before September 1939, when it was becoming apparent that the United States would for the foreseeable future remain neutral even in the event that Britain found itself at war. In 1938 Sir Henry Self, the head of a British Air Ministry mission to North America, had bought American aircraft and explored the possibility of the Canadian production of British-designed aircraft under licence. In November 1939, shortly after the British Empire had gone to war with Germany, the Americans revised their Neutrality Act to repeal their embargo against the sale of arms to Britain. Days later, a British Supply Board in the United States and Canada was established, with its headquarters in Ottawa, to order both Canadian materiel through the Canadian Supply Board and American materiel through the British Purchasing Commission in Washington. Arthur Purvis, of Canadian Industries in Montreal, headed the latter mission.

There was then the question of transporting aircraft. As the so-called phony war had given way to real battle in the spring of 1940, German U-boats began destroying the convoys making their way across the North Atlantic. With this increasing danger, it was becoming clear that aircraft from North America could no longer reach Britain aboard ships, as originally planned, but must fly across on their own power. With arrangements for the procurement of these aircraft generally secured by the summer of 1940, Beaverbrook sent Australian Captain Donald Bennett to Sir Edward Beatty of the CPR to organize the delivery of Hudsons and other aircraft from Lockheed in Burbank, California. Beatty arranged the logistics of ferrying these Hudsons to Britain under the auspices of his Canadian Pacific Air Services.

The amended US Neutrality Act still forbade Pan American Airways, the first commercial transatlantic airline, from delivering even parts for aircraft, much less fully constructed aircraft, directly to Britain, a belligerent. To avoid this prohibition against such direct transport of war materiel from the United States, considerable imagination was demanded. It was decided to fly the American-made Hudsons from Burbank to near the Canadian border, south of Winnipeg, and then to drag them across this border. From Canada (or Newfoundland, which remained a British colony until 1949), they would fly directly to the British Isles.

Until November 1940, however, the North Atlantic had never been flown in winter. Captain Bennett himself had piloted the first direct flight from the British Isles to Montreal in a seaplane in 1938. Now, in the middle of November 1940 and to widespread astonishment and delight, he led the first flight of bombers, seven Lockheed Hudsons fitted with long-range petrol tanks, safely across the Atlantic to Northern Ireland from Gander in Newfoundland. In the following two weeks, two more groups of seven Hudsons made the trip, with only one aircraft lost. At almost the same time, the Transatlantic Ferry Pilot School began operations in Montreal. Six British Overseas Airways captains, pilots from the British Air Transport Auxiliary, Americans, Canadian bush flyers, Free French, Dutchmen, Australians, South Africans, and even Egyptians received training there. Through the remainder of the winter, more Hudsons, B-24s, Liberators, Boeing B-17s, Catalinas, and other aircraft crossed the Atlantic, with only four lost out of 185.[21]

In August 1941, having been summoned to New Brunswick by Beaverbrook, Arthur Purvis, the president of Canadian Industries Limited in Montreal, a governor of McGill, and the chairman of the British War Purchasing Commission in North America, was killed when his aircraft hit a bridge while taking off. He had been a close friend and a colleague in fundraising, and the McConnells felt his loss deeply. Jack attended his funeral at Christ Church Cathedral, the grandest there since that of Sir Arthur Currie.[22]

Purvis had epitomized the crucial role played by Montreal businessmen in helping to keep Britain free of German occupation, at least up to the entry of the United

Frank Knox (US secretary of the navy), McConnell, and Adhémar
Raynault (mayor of Montreal) in Montreal promoting war bonds,
Montreal Daily Star, 17 June 1941. Montreal *Gazette* Archives.

States into the war in December 1941. His death led to several changes in procurement for Britain. The British Supply Board in Ottawa was wound up, and British orders from Canada were placed directly with the Canadian Department of Munitions and Supply. Sir Henry Self returned to Washington as director general of the British Air Commission, an arm of Lord Beaverbrook's Ministry of Aircraft Production, now separate from the British War Purchasing Commission. In January 1942 a British Supply Council in North America was set up under Colonel J.J. Llewellin, a former minister of aircraft production. He held the rank of resident minister for supply in Washington until 1943.[23] In Montreal, Morris Wilson, the president of the Royal Bank and another close friend of McConnell's, assumed Purvis's job of procuring aircraft for Britain in North America. He became the representative in Canada and the United States of the British Ministry of Aircraft Production.

In March 1941, with Sir Edward Beatty, the British Ministry of Aircraft Production becoming increasing incapacitated because of ill health, Wilson, representing Lord Beaverbrook, and H.M. Long, seconded from the CPR, in Montreal took over the ferrying of aircraft from Canadian Pacific Air Services. Until May, it operated under the name of the Atlantic Ferry Organization (ATFERO). In the first half of 1941, J.P. Bickell handled ATFERO from the British end. By 9 June 1941, when he handed its administration over to the Air Ministry in London, ATFERO had transported 170 aircraft to England. There were now 900 employees in the ferry organization, including

The head table at the Canadian War Services Fund opening campaign dinner, March 1941. From left: Chief Justice R.A.E. Greenshields of the Superior Court of Quebec, Senator C.P. Beaubien, McConnell, Samuel Bronfman, Group Captain E.R. Owen, Miss E. Meredith Hodgson, the Reverend Malcolm Campbell, and Mrs E. de B. Panet. Private collection.

537 flying personnel. Their gravest disaster had occurred in February 1941, when Sir Frederick Banting, the co-discoverer of insulin from the University of Toronto and a co-winner of the Nobel Prize in medicine in 1923, was killed in an air crash.[24]

With the passage of the Lend-Lease Act in March 1941, the direct delivery of US-produced aircraft to Montreal became possible. The US Air Force set up its own Air Transport Command to coordinate this delivery with ATFERO. Because American-made aircraft had, by American law, ultimately to be handed over to a military organization for deployment, the ad hoc, essentially civilian-run arrangements for ferrying were abandoned and Captain Bennett, who had quarrelled with Long, was sent back to England.

ATFERO was transformed into the RAF Ferry Command, under Air Chief Marshal Sir Frederick Bowhill, the commanding officer of RAF Coastal Command, in July 1941. In May, Bowhill had sunk the deadly German submarine, the *Bismarck*, which had previously devastated British morale by sinking HMS *Hood*. Appointed by Churchill to express gratitude to Roosevelt for Lend-Lease, he did not disappoint, applying his formidable powers over the following two years to making Dorval a bastion of the air defence of the empire. RAF Ferry Command existed until March 1943, when it became the RAF Transport Command. In Canada it became known as

Ashburton, in Dorval, during the war. From left: Jack Watson, John G. McConnell,
Wing Commander Dizzie Deane (seated), Mrs Jack Watson (Margaret Yuile), Lil,
unknown, Norman Dawes, Air Chief Marshal Sir Frederick Bowhill of
RAF Ferry Command, unknown, and McConnell. Private collection.

the No. 45 Group, RAF, under the command of Air Vice-Marshal R.L. Marix, with
Bowhill as commander-in-chief in England until his retirement in 1945. The ferry
service was at first confined to the transport of aircraft, but, as the war continued,
it came to carry passengers and freight as well. By the time it had become Transport
Command, it was towing gliders and dropping paratroops during the Normandy and
Arnhem landings.[25] Even as early as September 1941, Ferry Command was transporting Fortresses and Liberators as well as Hudsons, and it had been obliged to move
from Saint-Hubert Airport to a new, bigger airport at Dorval.

Dorval (later Trudeau) Airport stood on the site of the old Bel-Air racetrack to
the north of the McConnell house, Ashburton. Through the many officers and pilots
who visited Ashburton, McConnell became better informed on the progress of the
war than ever. Bowhill came to play tennis almost every day, and there was a constant stream of the pilots under his command. One of the most frequent visitors was a
French pilot, Count Richard de la Rozière, known as Dick, who had come to Canada
to be with his lover, the actress Madeleine Carroll, and suddenly found himself ferrying aircraft from Dorval to Scotland. De la Rozière and McConnell regularly played
Chinese checkers.

Over time, Ashburton, and the houses at Val David and on Pine Avenue as well,
assumed the role of a hotel for passengers as well as pilots on the vital route between

Britain and America. Lil had to entertain everyone from Major Victor Cazelet M P and Field Marshal Sir John Dill, former chief of the Imperial General Staff, to Lord Knollys, the governor of Bermuda (and an adviser to INCO, later chairman of BOAC and Vickers, and a long-standing friend), amusing the latter with brandy-snap ice-cream and ping-pong balls.[26] And although McConnell was not directly involved in civil aviation, any more than in military aviation, in the years after the war he was also closely to follow the development of Montreal, largely through Ferry Command, as a centre for the expansion of commercial air travel and transport. The International Civil Aviation Organization, an agency of the United Nations charged with overseeing this development globally, was to make its home in Montreal in 1946. Its first director general was an old friend of McConnell's, Sir William Hildred, who himself had served in the British Air Ministry and with R A F Ferry Command as the first financial adviser to Bowhill.

John G. McConnell was involved in the war effort, chiefly in his capacity as publisher of the *Standard*. In February 1941 he sent Davidson Dunton, the editor of his newspaper, to England to gather material for articles on "Britain's fight for freedom" and to represent the Canadian Fund for Air Raid Victims (soon to be renamed the Queen's Canadian Fund), in aid of bombed British civilians. Over forty daily newspapers across Canada backed this cause in an ongoing appeal. When, in June 1941, Canadian Pacific Air Services became ATFERO, the centre of the ferry operations moved from the Windsor Street Station to Morris Wilson's office in the Royal Bank headquarters on St James Street. John McConnell himself was put in charge of its public relations.

The beginning of the Battle of the Atlantic in January 1941 had made the need for additional aircraft more urgent than ever. Morris Wilson, Huntly Drummond, and McConnell began to organize the Wings for Britain Fund, its goal being to raise money for new aircraft from individuals and communities in the United States as well as Canada. Through contributions to this fund, aircraft could be named after their donors. Photographs of the named aircraft would be released when they joined units, and announcements of gifts would be made in both Britain and Canada. Five thousand pounds would entitle a donor to have a fighter in his name, and £20,000 would be enough to name a bomber. In December, Beaverbrook authorized McConnell to set up a representative committee of Americans in Canada to receive donations from Americans, although US neutrality laws prohibited canvassing in that country.

The previous November, Beaverbrook had gushed to McConnell, "My confidence is complete that, whatever can be done in the cause, you will accomplish it." His words were sincere. Until his replacement at the Ministry of Aircraft Production in May 1941, he continued to rely on McConnell personally not only for pilots and bombers sent through Ferry Command but also to raise money for new aircraft. As for McConnell, in the days leading to the establishment of the Wings for Britain Fund, he was

A.R. Doble, honorary secretary of Wings for Britain, asks for contributions
to a cigarette and tobacco fund for overseas employees of Canadian Car and
Foundry, Belmont Park, 21 July 1941. Seated under a Hawker Hurricane
donated by the company are Brig.-Gen. E. de B. Panet, McConnell, Marguerite
Shaughnessy, Huntly Drummond, and Mrs Adair. Private collection.

sceptical of working through government, and he merely informed Prime Minister
King of what he and his associates intended to do. King complained to the war committee of cabinet of the "the danger of private industries trying to become governments in themselves" and of McConnell's refusal to consult J.L. Ralston, the minister
of national defence, before setting up the fund.[27]

Nevertheless, on 15 April 1941, McConnell (as chairman), Drummond (as vice-
chairman), and others arranged for the fund – which had been registered in February
under the War Charities Act, 1939 – to be incorporated under letters patent.[28] The
fund raised $615,642 in its first year for the British Ministry of Aircraft Production
and the RAF Benevolent Fund (set up in 1919). The sources of funds included a fashion show at Holt Renfrew, the St Jerome Horse Show, and the sale of special "Wings
for Britain" merchandise at a shop on Peel Street and in other departmental and retail
stores. In all, by May 1946, through a wide range of fund-raising activities (many
using the Dionne quintuplets in their advertising), the fund had collected $875,682
($10,835,682 in 2008 terms).

Wings for Britain emphasized McConnell's role as a volunteer. Indeed, his reputation for voluntary work was so well known by 1939 that he became the honorary

chairman of the entire Canadian YMCA War Services Executive Committee, organized by James A. Tory of Toronto. McConnell was not involved in the day-to-day operations of this committee, but he kept abreast of its activities. Another venture that McConnell supported was the Beaver Club, run by Alice (Mrs Vincent) Massey in Spring Gardens, near Canada House in London. The Canadian YMCA had run the Beaver Hut in the Strand in the First World War. This was a demobilization centre, equipped with dormitories for 160 men, a dining room, and even a theatre.[29]

There had also been a Beaver Club in Mayfair from 1915, in a house contributed by a friend of the McConnells, Maggie (Mrs Ronald) Greville, and run largely as a convalescent hospital for Canadian soldiers. But, through the Massey Foundation, Alice Massey made this new effort into a social centre for Canadian and Commonwealth non-commissioned officers on leave throughout the war, and many of her friends in London, both English and Canadian, helped her, while her husband presided over a men's support committee. In August 1940 McConnell sent £500 to Mrs Massey to help launch the facility, after having sent a large sum to Lord Bennett (as the former prime minister had become) for Canadian Red Cross work in London.[30]

Meanwhile, McConnell's own houses continued to serve as a haven for distinguished visitors. In wartime, there was naturally no thought of balls or glittering receptions, and, in any cases, none of his houses was equipped for such. But, for even very prominent guests, a hot meal and a warm bed could be welcome enough. In summer, the McConnells could offer tennis and swimming as well, and even in winter there was an atmosphere of relaxed hospitality and luxury which by now was but a memory in occupied Europe. Especially to those important officials huddled, or about to be huddled, in the holds of the freezing cargo planes that did the hazardous North Atlantic run, the blazing fireplaces of the McConnells must have been a glorious sight. Jack loved quizzing his guests and offering them his own opinions.

The heavy traffic of aviators, old friends, the McConnell children and their friends, and visiting dignitaries lent all three of their houses, at times, the air of an exclusive transit camp, where guests might stay even when the McConnells were absent. Diplomats being stationed in Ottawa or Washington were among the more regular visitors, particularly when they were obliged to use the Dorval airport in flying to or from England. Several consulted him regularly, for his wide contacts in England and the United States, as well as Canada, equipped him with knowledge, authority, and access well beyond those of most businessmen. In turn, through them he followed the progress of the war with unusual insight.[31] In 1941, at the urging of John Bassett and others, McConnell was briefly considered for the post of Canadian minister in Washington, in succession to Loring Christie, who had died suddenly. J.L. Ralston, the minister of national defence, seems to have vetoed this proposal. McConnell was in fact qualified by neither experience nor personality to be a diplomat, although he would probably have made a greater impression than the man that was appointed in his place, the lawyer Leighton McCarthy.

The most senior diplomatic visitor to the McConnells was the former British foreign secretary, Lord Halifax. By August 1941, Halifax had become the British ambassador in Washington. Having waived his claims to the premiership in favour of Churchill, and yet still suspect because of his continued advocacy of appeasement or at least a negotiated peace with Germany, Halifax was effectively in political exile. During the war, his new position involved stopping several times in Dorval and at Pine Avenue on his way between England and the United States. At Dorval, it was necessary to change aircraft, and so McConnell's Ashburton became a sort of rest house for him as for others embarking on that then-perilous route. On his first visit, he found the McConnell house in Dorval "quite a nice place on the river – though it might be made much nicer." To his surprise, he was "turned into a bedroom to 'rest' before dinner, where I read my book, which I had had the forethought to take!" "My host," he sighed, "though very kind, revealed himself as rather a bore."[32]

Far different from Halifax was the British high commissioner in Ottawa for most of the war, Malcolm MacDonald. At first blush, MacDonald seemed even less likely than Halifax to endear himself to McConnell. He was the son of Ramsey MacDonald, the first Labour prime minister of Great Britain. McConnell had supported the "national government" headed by Ramsey MacDonald in 1931, a government that led to MacDonald's expulsion from the Labour Party and that is generally seen as Conservative in all but name. The younger MacDonald, often unkempt and resolutely egalitarian, as well as mischievous and rambunctious, was the very antithesis of the traditional British cabinet minister, diplomat, and proconsul, although, like Halifax, he became all three, even while resolutely refusing all titles of honour. Indeed, as a representative of Great Britain, he could not have presented a greater contrast to Halifax.

In what was then a tiny community in Ottawa, MacDonald found himself isolated and yet not even the sole representative of the United Kingdom. After the sudden death of Lord Tweedsmuir in 1940, the Earl of Athlone and his wife, Princess Alice, took over at Government House. A veteran of the Boer War, Athlone was sad and taciturn but dedicated to his duties and capable of shrewdness. Since he was a brother of Queen Mary and since the princess was a granddaughter of Queen Victoria, he naturally felt that he could speak for Great Britain as well as for Canada. Moreover, although rather nervous, he was far from decrepit, and he exhausted McConnell on at least one of his daily one-hour walks.[33] Very royal and austere, the Athlones were as much a contrast to MacDonald as Halifax.

MacDonald's superior at home, the dominions secretary, was Lord Cranborne (later the Marquess of Salisbury), a grandson of Queen Victoria's long-serving prime minister. In demeanour he was not much warmer than Athlone. Halifax, as MacDon-

Recipients of honorary degrees in front of Redpath Hall, McGill University, 29 May 1941. Front row, from left: Dr Hu Shih LLD (Chinese ambassador to the United States), the Earl of Athlone (visitor of McGill), Princess Alice, Dorothy Thompson, Malcolm MacDonald (British high commissioner). Second row from left: Dr F. Cyril James (principal and vice-chancellor of McGill), Ariel Baird (lady-in-waiting), McConnell, Dean C.J. Mackenzie, Dr Muriel V. Roscoe (warden of Royal Victoria College). Back row from left: Captain T.C.R. Goff (aide-de-camp) and Sir Shuldham Redfern (private secretary to the governor general). MUA, PR009561.

ald's opposite number in Washington, was geographically and strategically his closest associate. Finally, MacDonald's lover, Dorothy ("Dot") Hyson, an actress then married to Robert Douglas and later to the actor Sir Anthony Quayle, had decided to remain in England.

Although his sister, Sheila, joined him at Earnscliffe to act as his hostess, MacDonald was condemned to leading the life of a lonely, restless bachelor, but also as a confidant of another lonely, restless bachelor, Mackenzie King. King was an old friend of his father's, and it was Malcolm MacDonald's brief to cultivate the prickly prime minister on behalf of Churchill.

It was probably at King's suggestion that, in April 1941, MacDonald made one of his first visits out of Ottawa to the McConnells. Afterwards, he described them to Dot as a "delightful, unassuming couple" who lived in "a miniature Italian palace built high on the side of Mount Royal."[34] Over the next five years, MacDonald was to stay with the McConnells so often as to be almost an honorary member of the family. A month after his first visit to Pine Avenue, he was at Ashburton in Dorval, "a rather sumptuous place, standing in the midst of beautiful lawns and a small park of most stately trees ... The lilacs were in full bloom, and scented the whole air. There were banks and banks of them, many-coloured. There is also a large marble open-air swimming bath built on a princely scale. I suppose it is there just in case the lake, which laps the very lawns of the garden, and stretches placid and beautiful almost as far as the eye can see, is not large enough to accommodate all the guests of the McConnell house parties."

To this shrewdly observant man of the world, the McConnells were "charming." He was touched by stories of Jack's boyhood, "without a penny in his pocket or to his name," and by his marriage "in those distant humble days." But, he noted, "neither of them has been in the least spoilt by riches. They are simple in character and taste, and yet gloriously hospitable and generous. Their friendship is a comfortable and delightful experience."[35] Towards the end of October 1941, MacDonald was back at Pine Avenue, where he "wallowed in the double luxury of their riches and their sweet kindness." He found them not merely "simple, warm-hearted and open-handed" but good-looking too. As for Lil, MacDonald could not guess her age, "but she looks younger than her snow-white hair would indicate, and she too looks a healthy specimen," sparkling "with humour and fun, and there is always about her too the sparkle of one or two bits of exquisite jewelry." He enjoyed talking to her about art and French Canadians.[36]

By the end of that month, however, MacDonald confessed that he was "restless" and that his job was not "invigorating or testing enough any longer." The office work was "mostly unexacting routine" and the inspections of munitions factories and training schools "mere parades." Even talks with Mackenzie King "don't use up one's energy or creative facilities," and the cocktail parties were "a maddening waste of time when civilization is being threatened and there is work and fighting to be done to save it." There was indeed little for the high commissioner to do, for "Canada is in the war wholeheartedly; [and] her government and people are tackling their problems with zeal and considerable success."[37] The 30th of October was "a typically awful day, with six and a half hours of luncheon, tea, cocktail and dinner parties – a most criminal waster of time." Dinner at King's Laurier House was a bizarre experience, MacDonald feeling himself to be in something resembling "the apartments of a small museum ... filled to choking point with sentimental nick-nacks and historical relics gathered during his long career as a magpie statesmen ... an assortment of cheap china, souvenirs and trophies ... as though the whole house were an obstacle course."[38]

It was with real relief that MacDonald returned to Pine Avenue in February 1942: "Jack McConnell said rudely at breakfast that he didn't like my looks and that I should send for my skis from Ottawa and come and get rest and fresh-air with them up on the Laurentian Mountains for the week-end." It took two and a half hours by train to go from Montreal to Val David. On arriving there, it was dark "but there were a young moon and all the stars were glittering in the sky overhead and underfoot the ground was covered with deep snow." In the intense cold, made even colder by a keen wind, they all put on large fur coats and hats and piled fur rugs on top of themselves in an open sleigh. The "gay red sleigh was drawn by a pair of beautiful piebald horses" and the McConnells and their guests "looked like a family of bears going out for a drive." For over forty-five minutes, "the sleigh glided silently over the roads, but the bells of the horses tinkled merrily all the time as they trotted along" until they reached McConnell's huge log house among the firs. A "rather incongruous cross-breed of French-Canadian with Norwegian," Saran Chai stood "in magnificent solitude at the head of a fair-sized lake with hills climbing away from it on all sides, and no other habitation in sight." The weary high commissioner crawled gratefully into his bedroom, with its "gaily carved and painted timber work."

After Jack's death, MacDonald would write to Lil of McConnell's "wonderful presence." He recalled "all those merry times we had together in Montreal, at Dorval, and in the Laurentians, in Ottawa, and elsewhere." He talked of "peaceful hours beside the lake at Dorval; of agitated minutes on Hell's-a-Poppin [a ski jump] in the mountains." "Those memories," he concluded, "will abide with me fresh and evergreen, as long as I remain on this Earth. I have had many friendships with all sorts and conditions of people, but I have never had a better one than with the McConnells."[39] He was deeply fond of and grateful to the McConnells for giving him a refuge from the drudgery of official life and the strains of the war. He found them almost parental without being interfering.

In 1945 the new Labour prime minister, Clement Atlee, offered MacDonald the embassy at Washington, in succession to Lord Halifax, or the vice-royalty of India, in preference to Lord Louis Mountbatten. MacDonald chose instead to administer Malaya and Singapore, and he spent his last night in Canada at the McConnells' before returning to London and then to Asia to take up his new posting. Kit had made for him a sarong with the initials "G.G.," which he actually wore as governor general of Malaya and Singapore. Over the course of his subsequent career – he would go on to serve as high commissioner to India and governor and then governor general of Kenya – he was a key figure in the transition to the post-war Commonwealth. A determined opponent of racism, he befriended Prime Minister Jawaharlal Nehru of India and Zhou Enlai (Chou En-lai) of communist China, and he sported his MacDonald tartan kilt amidst the tribespeople of Borneo "to show them that they were not the only wild men in the world."[40] And, through all these years, he kept in contact with the McConnells.

Unlike Halifax and MacDonald, the American minister in Ottawa in 1941–42, Jay Pierrepont Moffat, the third of McConnell's diplomatic contacts, was exclusively a diplomat by calling. His father-in-law was Joseph Grew, the last pre-war American ambassador to Japan, whom the McConnells had first befriended in Tokyo in 1936. In his hundreds of surviving memoranda of conversations in Canada, Moffat noted the nuances of shifting opinion in the country and beyond towards the war, and he seems to have missed little. On several occasions, he met McConnell. The first visit of the Moffats to Pine Avenue seems to have been at the end of April 1941 Jack and Lil gave Moffat "the impression that they wished Mr. McConnell had more political power or importance, or else could play a leading role on a larger stage than Montreal."

A cold spell in Ottawa in December 1942 led to Moffat's sudden death there a few weeks later, at the age of only forty-six.[41] Ray Atherton, who – as acting chief of the European division, had been in charge of Canadian affairs at the State Department – took over from Moffat in Ottawa for the next five years, assuming, however, the rank of ambassador.

One other diplomat in McConnell's circle has already received mention. Baron Robert Silvercruys was a classic continental diplomat – smooth, sleek, charming, and ingratiating, almost equally fluent in English and French. Like Moffat, he made a special study of opinion in French Canada, and often exchanged views with McConnell on the participation of Quebec in the war effort. Silvercruys served as the Belgian minister to Canada from 1937 to 1944 and then as ambassador until 1945. Thus his posting covered the years of the German occupation of Belgium, and some the many books in McConnell's library on Poland, Czechoslovakia, France, and Germany probably came from him. The McConnells continued to see him after he had gone on to become ambassador to the United States and to the United Nations. Like Mac-Donald, he was bachelor who did not marry until fairly late in life. In consequence, he especially enjoyed the diplomatic circuit, and he happily mixed with the McConnells and other distinguished Canadians – so much so that he was one of the best known of the few diplomats then posted in Ottawa, particularly at Government House, where the McConnells themselves were so often to be found. Silvercruys was immediately captivated by Lil, around whom, he told her, there was "a halo of cheerfulness and radiant happiness."[42]

The war, finally, brought McConnell into active cooperation with a man whom he had long admired, Wendell Willkie. Impressed in the 1930s by Willkie's effective defence of free enterprise and the Commonwealth and Southern Corporation, McConnell became even more taken with Willkie's internationalism. The single most important American politician opposed to US isolationism, Willkie was very narrowly defeated by Roosevelt in the presidential elections of 1940. Thus unfettered by political office, he became more openly supportive than Roosevelt of aiding Brit-

McConnell hands over a cheque to Wendell Willkie, probably in aid
of Russia, at their meeting in Toronto, 1942. Private collection.

ain, although still not of sending American troops overseas. Like McConnell, Willkie
became a supporter even of Stalin after Hitler's sudden invasion of the Soviet Union
in 1941, and it was this cause that brought him to Canada in 1942.

In England, Beaverbrook, apparently seeking to endear himself to the trade unions
and the Labour Party, schemed for months to have a second front opened in Russia
against Germany. McConnell does not seem to have gone so far, at least publicly.
Moffat described McConnell as "very close" to Beaverbrook, who had on occasion
asked McConnell to "cut corners" on his behalf by making trips to Washington,
apparently to press the cause of a second front. Lord Halifax and Mackenzie King,
however, had warned McConnell against "giving any impression that McConnell was
speaking either at their instigation or with their foreknowledge and consent."[43] The
result was that McConnell never managed to see President Roosevelt in Washington
but was confined to talking with Mrs Roosevelt in the hope that she would pass on
Beaverbrook's concerns.[44]

In the meantime, at home in Canada, some of the most established citizens, including McConnell, joined such committees as that of the Canadian Aid to Russia Fund,
incorporated in November 1942 after Hitler's invasion of the Soviet Union. It was a
most curious cause, uniting big capitalists with socialists and communists, and Jews
with Gentiles. The president and national chairman was McConnell's old friend (and
Lil's old beau, as well as the brother of McConnell's lieutenant, Herbert McLean) J.S.
(Stanley) McLean, president of Canada Packers. A national campaign, which ended

in January 1943, raised over $1 million, or $12,795,455 in 2008 terms. It claimed the patronage of all the provincial lieutenant governors and religious leaders, including Cardinal Villeneuve, the archbishop of Quebec; Archbishop Derwyn T. Owen, primate of the Church of England in Canada; the moderators of the Presbyterian and United churches; and Sir Lyman Duff, the chief justice of Canada. In Quebec, Allan Bronfman was the executive chairman and McConnell sat on the advisory committee. Many of the same people, but not McConnell himself, joined the Russian Aid Medical Committee (Montreal). McConnell did give, however, $25,000 ($319,886 in 2008) for medical aid to the Russians, and he attended a meeting in aid of the Soviet Union in Maple Leaf Gardens in Toronto, on 25 November 1942, at which Wendell Willkie was the speaker and which McConnell found "immense fun."[45]

McConnell shared Willkie's vision of a new post-war world. This vision encompassed a reformed but rejuvenated capitalism, much as their battle for Commonwealth and Southern and against the Tennessee Valley Authority had done. But for a healthier capitalism to emerge, it was necessary first to establish a healthier society. This was totally consistent with McConnell's lifelong preoccupation with medicine, hospitals, and the alleviation of suffering more generally. He wrote to Willkie approvingly of the Beveridge report in Britain, describing its call for "better living and working conditions for all" as "the first positive and practical step pointing in the right direction." Sir William Beveridge himself had come to McGill to present his vision of a welfare state, and McConnell kept a copy of his report, a blueprint for the post-war welfare state, and presumably studied it.

He also told Willkie of his support for the abolition of high tariffs. "Production everywhere," McConnell declared, "of those essential things for the masses must be ample, and the distribution must be unimpeded and equitable." In words that might have warmed the heart of the socialist Frank Scott, he concluded: "Plenty of everything for everybody, that this good old earth can produce should be the post War objective when she is finally permitted to enjoy unhampered by past evils, comparative peaceful and happy surroundings."[46]

There was little overt support in Britain or Canada for a reformed capitalism as integral to the welfare state. Full-scale socialism, if not communism, seemed a more likely prospect. In the two years that followed, McConnell grew yet closer to Willkie, who he still hoped would succeed Roosevelt as president, sharing information on Canadian politics, especially the performance of the CCF in elections in Ontario, which he analysed with close attention. He reported that the socialist David Lewis had lost in a by-election in Montreal to someone even worse, the communist Fred Rose. The result was being contested by the Bloc Populaire, described by the *Star* as appealing to "racial and religious prejudices" which made it all the more distasteful to McConnell.[47] It was this injection of socialist and communist ideology into state planning, combined with the outbreak of the Cold War in 1945, that turned McConnell against what he described as collectivism, putting a brake on his enthusiasm for the welfare state. It was the racist and religious nationalism of the Bloc Populaire and similar groups that turned him into a supporter of a much milder nationalist in Quebec, Maurice Duplessis. For all the tendencies to dictatorship that Duplessis seemed to exhibit, he was no fascist or communist, and like his Liberal predecessors as premier – Gouin, Taschereau, and even to some extent Godbout – he was a firm supporter of capitalism.

After Willkie's narrow defeat for a fresh presidential nomination for the Republicans in 1944, McConnell described him as "a young man yet, and the country will still be in need of an Abe Lincoln."[48] Two years before, Willkie had won support for his renewed presidential aspirations from at least one non-American much better known than McConnell, Madame Chiang Kai-shek, wife of the Chinese president, with whom Willkie had recently had a very public affair in Chungking. In June 1943 the McConnells dined at Government House in Ottawa with Madame Chiang. It is unknown whether McConnell discussed Willkie with her. In any case, a few months after Willkie's political aspirations were dashed again in 1944, he died suddenly of a heart attack apparently related to his alcoholism. McConnell kept up with Mrs Willkie, but with Willkie's death McConnell seems to have lost his interest in American politics, President Truman being no more to his taste than Roosevelt.

At home, the key political event of the war years was the crisis over conscription that emerged towards the end of 1941. From the beginning of the war, Mackenzie King had desperately sought to avoid the bitter divisions between French and English Canadians that had torn the country apart in 1917. McConnell was very aware of King's fears, and he suggested in May 1941 that the prime minister should "educate public opinion" by using the term "selective national service" in place of "conscription."[49] As the pressure for conscription, however termed, became increasingly unavoidable, Pierrepont Moffat, the American minister, sought to keep track of Canadian opinion on it.

In November 1941, the McConnells went to the American Legation for two days as houseguests and to dine with the Moffats and the Halifaxes. Moffat found McConnell "violent" about the postponement of conscription by King. McConnell explained that the *Star* appeared milder about conscription than he himself felt, because he believed that there was a better chance of persuading King to change his mind through reasoning than by antagonizing him. In McConnell's view, either a plebiscite or an election would be extremely divisive.

Three months later, in January 1942, Moffat noted a sharp rise in McConnell's disenchantment with Mackenzie King, who was now promising a plebiscite to release the government from its promise not to introduce conscription. The *Star*, Moffat recorded, had previously come out editorially for a plebiscite on the matter, but now McConnell himself was taking a much harder line against it: "To my surprise, his attitude has completely changed and his whole tone was one of bitterness against Mr.

King for what he considered his pusillanimity that was reminiscent of the comments of the average New Yorker against Mr. Roosevelt in '34 and '35. He considered that far from uniting the country the plebiscite would split it wide asunder. When the true figures of enlistments are given and the country realizes that in the Province of Quebec four times as many British Canadians have volunteered for overseas service as French Canadians there will be an outcry."[50]

McConnell, Moffat reported, expected Quebec to vote No by a very large majority, and the other provinces to vote Yes by equally large majorities, which would leave a legacy of hate throughout the country. McConnell lamented the "national indignity" and "disgrace" of the situation, and he was effectively "indifferent to the feelings of the French Canadians and thought with their unsatisfactory recruiting record their opinions should not carry any weight."[51] This was not to say that McConnell was anti-French or had given up on ultimately bringing the French Canadians around to conscription. His hopes were with Premier Godbout, who he hoped would enter the federal cabinet once Ernest Lapointe had died. He felt that Godbout had given Quebec the best administration in many years and was honest. If he accepted conscription, Godbout would be "immediately attacked, smeared and knifed by the Old Guard, led by Casgrain, the present Secretary of State," and it would be a battle to the finish.

After the plebiscite had yielded the results predicted by McConnell, his mood did not improve. In November 1942, in an effort to ascertain the mood of English Montreal, Moffat went to Montreal to meet him and his friends, including Sir Edward Beatty, Ross McMaster, Senator Charles Ballantyne, Dr Wilder Penfield, Morris Wilson, and others. He found that they nearly all spoke "with unconcealed bitterness" about the French Canadians and their attitudes towards the war and towards the rest of Canada, and no sign whatever that McConnell's group was willing to compromise. They blamed the Roman Catholic prelates for not controlling their priests. In particular, they believed that Cardinal Villeneuve, the archbishop of Quebec, who had spoken out loudly in favour of the war effort, was duplicitous in failing to discipline the lower clergy, who tended to be against the war.

Even more boldly, McConnell's group declared themselves as wanting to break the hold of the church by emphasizing its "fiscal tyranny" over the population. Indeed, they noticed that those French Canadians who had gone into war work had already largely severed their ties with the church, and this was a trend to encourage. But they also feared that such emancipated French Canadians were flocking to the CCF. Lapointe and fellow Liberal cabinet minister P.-J.-A. Cardin, in their view, had been largely responsible for Quebec's "poor attitude on the war," and Godbout had proved a disappointment.[52]

In 1944 McGill held a special convocation in Quebec City to confer honorary degrees on Churchill and Roosevelt, the only time in the history of the university that the chancellor, the principal, and the members of the board of governors had left Mon-

McConnell with Prime Minister Winston Churchill, President Franklin D.
Roosevelt, the Earl of Athlone (visitor of McGill University), Morris W. Wilson
(chancellor of McGill) and Dr F. Cyril James (principal of McGill), at the
special McGill Convocation in Quebec City, 1944. Private collection.

treal so to confer such degrees. The event revealed much about McConnell's place in
the war and in public life more generally, which was largely private and peripheral
and brought him only momentarily into the public eye. McConnell's critical role in
creating the event consisted of making a single telephone call. Cyril James and others
at McGill had for some time wanted to confer degrees on the two leaders, but they had
never been able to arrange it. As was so often the case, it was McConnell who possessed the necessary connections, and he called Sir Shuldham Redfern, the private
secretary to Lord Athlone, at Government House.[53] Redfern had the event arranged
on the same day, for a few days following, to considerable consternation, as well as
delight, at McGill, where the principal organizers of the ceremony had to scramble to
find the gowns and prepare the diplomas in short order. It was all somewhat frenzied
as Roosevelt was to return to Washington the same evening as the convocation.

When the day arrived, McConnell probably met Roosevelt and Churchill, for the
first and only time in each case. Churchill was bored and irascible and generally
refused to speak to anyone. Athlone drew him out from reading a book in public by
saying, "Manners, Winston." But McConnell reported to Kit that Churchill had still
been "very gruff." Mrs Churchill, moreover, was initially taken aback when McCon-

McConnell with Mrs Winston Churchill, Quebec, 1944.
Montreal *Gazette* Archives

nell offered her and her daughter Mary fur coats and to contribute in her name to her favourite charities. She was sorry to tell McConnell that she was forbidden to accept gifts, but eventually she did relent and accept cheques for her charities, £5,000 for them generally in addition to £2,000 for her to give to the YWCA.[54] As she wrote to her family, McConnell was "tactless" but "generous" and she was "much overcome by such kindness."[55] Although it wonderfully publicized McGill's war effort, the ceremony was simply one of many events of a not particularly successful conference.

Under another optic, however, the ceremony summed up much about McConnell's view of the world and his role in it. He was indeed something of an impresario, in the sense that without him the occasion would not have arisen. Other images of the leaders at Quebec would have remained, of course, but without any reference to McGill. More important, for McConnell, the event encapsulated the part that he and most Canadians saw their country playing in the emerging world order, that of a linchpin between Great Britain and the United States in a North Atlantic Triangle. Particularly as a newspaper publisher, McConnell knew the value of good pictures. But he was hardly by nature a publicist, and few could have been less inclined to imagery to the detriment of substance. The substance underpinned by events such as this one was

McConnell with Princess Alice, Countess of Athlone, and Anthony
Eden, the British foreign secretary, Quebec, 1944. Private collection.

the continued geopolitical significance of the empire in a world increasingly dominated by the United States, with Canada as an honest broker that was both American
and British. This was probably a view shared by Mackenzie King. The ceremony was
therefore symbolic of a conscious work in progress, to affirm a distinctive but useful
role for Canada.

The ceremony was important for McConnell in another sense. Although it bore
the sobriquet of the "ancient capital," Quebec City was very much for McConnell a
modern, living place, not least because of its miniature version of St James Street in
its Lower Town. He had known the city from about 1901, and it seems from his correspondence that he attended its great tercentenary celebrations in 1908, with Lil.
He had attended sessions of the Legislative Assembly in 1910 to ensure the passage
of the Montreal Tramways bill. He had in 1939 attended the welcoming ceremonies
for the king and queen in the Legislative Council chamber. He had stayed often at the
Citadel, with its commanding view of the St Lawrence from the King's Bastion from

which flew an enormous Union flag. Driving across the parade ground of the Cita-del, past the Garrison Club, through the Kent Gate, down Saint-Louis Street, past the Boer War monument, the Price Building, and Kent House to Dufferin Terrace, McConnell could be forgiven for believing that the city had reached its fulfillment as a centre in a new Anglo-American order.

The province more generally, even outside Montreal, was for McConnell and his circle their home. Critics might snipe that this was because they owned it, not to say exploited it. But that was unfair. McConnell and those like him not only loved Quebec and its past, they were both building it and helping it to interpret itself. W.H. Coverdale's Manoir Richelieu in Murray Bay was an example of their work. Cover-dale, from Ontario and largely based in New York, not only erected a grand hotel in French-inspired style but also filled it with one of the most important collections of Canadian art ever assembled. As we have seen, the McConnells and the Willingdons were among the first to stay there, being at its opening in 1930. Similarly, the Seigniory Club, originally called Lucerne-in-Quebec and later the Château Montebello, was a Depression-era project of the CPR, of which McConnell was very fond. Designed with remarkable flair, it recalled some of the great luxurious log hotels of Muskoka. It was an equally magnificent tribute to French Canada, even in its incorporation of Louis-Joseph Papineau's manor house and gravesite.

It did not matter that many if not most of McConnell's circle could not speak French. They saw Quebec and French Canada as moving not into the past but into a future that was already dominated by the English language. Language was therefore not an issue for them, for any issue of it had been long settled. What mattered were the prosperity and progress of Quebec. The McGill special convocation at the second Quebec conference may have been a high-water mark of the anglicization of the city and the province. But, for McConnell, it also signalled the strategic role that Canada should undertake in the post-war world.

It was ideas such as these – along with his continuing attachment to the British Empire and all that it symbolized – that inspired McConnell in the darkest days of the Second World War. His efforts to help the Allied cause in whatever way he could spoke to his most basic values as a subject of the empire, as well as a proud Canadian. These same values, moreover, were inextricably linked to his view of the place that his country should occupy on the international stage once the horrors of the war were a thing of the past. The one could not be separated from the other.

CHAPTER FIFTEEN

The Dilemma of
Conservative Politics, 1911–63

Vous avez entendu les hurlements sur la rue Saint-Jacques, vous avez vu les articles des journaux; "Duplessis fait fuir les capitaux." "Duplessis nuit aux investissements." Avez-vous remarqué qu'aussitôt qu'un gouvernement de Québec relève la tête puis demande à être respecté, les capitaux s'en vont, les investissments fuient. Il y en a qui voudraient qu'on vive à genoux, qu'on se mette à genoux devant le Parti libéral, à genoux devant Ottawa, à genoux devant les impérialistes, à genoux devant Basset [sic], McConnel [sic]. Bien moi, je vous dis ceci, c'est que l'Union Nationale a juste un maître, puis ce maître-là, il est pas sur la rue Saint-Jacques, il est pas à Ottawa, puis il est pas à Londres, il est ici ce soir et c'est le peuple de la province de Québec. C'est le seul maître qu'on a jamais eu puis qu'on aura jamais!

The character Maurice Duplessis addressing
Paul Sauvé (his successor), priests, and dignitaries in
scene 27 of *Duplessis*, a play by Denys Arcand[1]

If you were a Czar and were looking for a man to handle the finances of Canada to the best advantage of the Country, I am quite certain you would pick J.W. McConnell. I trust when you are in the position of Premier that you will select him. It would also have a great influence on Quebec, because Quebec would have received the most important portfolio in the Cabinet, and I am absolutely convinced that McConnell would make the best Finance Minister Canada has seen in generations and would relieve you of an immense amount of anxiety and work. The difficulty is that he would not want the job, but I am satisfied that he can be forced to take it.

F.P. Jones, president of the Canada Cement Company,
to Arthur Meighen, 30 October 1925[2]

In politics as in much else, McConnell was a thorough-going pragmatist. He never even pretended to be a straight party man, even when his closest business colleagues were anguishing over their party loyalties, and indeed he was always ready to shift party allegiance when it seemed expedient to do so, whether for economic or other reasons. At both the federal and provincial levels, his choice of which individuals and parties to support was based on his assessment of their abilities and their records, never on considerations of ideological purity. Yet loyal he also was, to individual politicians whom he respected and more particularly to party leaders whom that he found effective. And although not ideological, he was by inclination deeply conservative as well as pragmatic. From about 1937 onward, he found the federal Conservative Party of Canada insufficiently conservative, and the leader of the Liberal Party, Mackenzie King, much more to his taste.

In federal politics, McConnell's pragmatism was evident as early as the election of 1911, fought mainly over Laurier's proposed reciprocity treaty with the United States. In that contest, most among McConnell's associates in business were firmly against reciprocity, which they believed threatened British and imperial investment and markets. The anti-reciprocity forces included T.A. Russell, president of the Canadian Manufacturers' Association (CMA); Z.A. Lash, about to become president of Brazilian Traction; Sir Edmund Walker of the Bank of Commerce; and Thomas White of National Trust. All were friends of McConnell. In addition, McConnell's partner, G.F. Johnston, stood as the Conservative, anti-reciprocity candidate in Westmount. Johnston openly represented the interests of the protectionists who dominated the CMA. He lost. Another close friend of McConnell's, C.C. Ballantyne, had been a Liberal until Laurier's adoption of the policy of reciprocity. He stood for Parliament as a Conservative candidate pledged to the promotion of the CMA's interests and won. Ballantyne spent the remainder of his political career as a Conservative cabinet minister. He became a senator through McConnell, who had declined the offer of a Senate seat from Bennett and recommended Ballantyne in his stead.

With such close colleagues as Johnston and Ballantyne in 1911, it may be expected that McConnell should have supported the Conservatives too. But such was not the case. Montreal was bitterly divided over the issue of the tramways franchise, and in that year the takeover of Montreal Tramways depended largely on the tacit support of the Liberal Laurier at the federal level and of the Liberal Gouin at the provincial. Moreover, McConnell's associate E.-A. Robert had been close to Laurier for some time, and McConnell himself had just broken with Lorne McGibbon, a prominent supporter of Borden. It seems also that McConnell severed his ties with Rodolphe Forget, the Conservative politician whose expansion of the Quebec Railway merger in 1910 he had aided. This was in order for McConnell to become associated with Robert – and by extension with Laurier and the Liberals – the following year.

In a letter to Laurier during the elections of 1911, McConnell described himself as "a very warm admirer of your excellent ability and the great work which you have done for Canada in the past." "You have," McConnell continued, "my sincerest wish for the success you so richly deserve and to which you are certainly entitled and which I feel confident will be yours at the conclusion of the coming, political campaign." But, apart from personal regard, the other reason that McConnell mentioned for his support was his disagreement with certain Conservative newspapers, which had claimed that "the proposed Reciprocity agreement will kill Canadian securities in the English market or, at least have a very damaging effect on Canadian issues in that market." In reply to this charge, McConnell cited his friend Arthur Peuchen, "a Conservative," as being behind a recent successful issue of Standard Chemical preference stock in London, notwithstanding the threat of reciprocity, and – at the suggestion of E.-A. Robert – he invited Laurier to use this fact in the campaign. He also noted that, in a prospectus, Peuchen foresaw the profits of his company increasing by $110,000, "particularly in view of the benefit likely to accrue to the lumber business from the probable Reciprocity arrangements." In short, McConnell's rationale for supporting Laurier was almost purely pragmatic: he simply did not see reciprocity as a threat to his own business of stock promotion.[3] As yet, he owned no part of St Lawrence or any other sugar refinery, and he was deeply involved with the takeovers of the Montreal Street Railway and the Halifax Tramways, which were unaffected by tariffs.

The victory of Borden's Conservatives in 1911 ensured a continuation of protective tariffs. And, even though Canadian tariffs upon imported refined sugar had not been threatened by the reciprocity agreement proposed by Laurier, the Conservative victory probably emboldened McConnell to acquire a big stake in, and later complete ownership of, St Lawrence Sugar in 1912. McConnell thus became for the rest of his life a manufacturer vitally dependent on tariff protection and government assistance. It was partly for this reason, but also because of his probable support of conscription during the First World War, that McConnell – despite his admiration for Laurier – seems to have switched his allegiance quietly to the Conservatives in 1917.[4] Mackenzie King was to recall, with bitterness, McConnell's switch as late as 1940, when Senator Raoul Dandurand lobbied him unsuccessfully to try to buy McConnell's support, and thus that of the *Star*, with a knighthood.[5]

Though the unwillingness of Borden's successor, Arthur Meighen, to ignite public outrage in 1921 by rescuing the sugar refiners, who were widely seen as war profiteers, led to the effective insolvency of St Lawrence Sugar and all its Canadian competitors, McConnell's support for the Conservatives and for Meighen himself remained firm. He worked hard for Meighen against Mackenzie King in the general elections of 1921 and 1926,[6] likely because of Meighen's protectionist principles, which favoured many of his investments, as opposed to the generally free-trade views of King and the Liberals. The investments of McConnell that would benefit most from Conservative protectionism, apart from St Lawrence Sugar, were in the Quebec textile industry. As we have seen, he had an enormous investment in Quebec textiles, particularly in Dominion Textile. It is, however, unduly narrow to attribute McConnell's Conservative allegiance solely to that party's inclination to protect his economic interests. If only protection had been at the basis of McConnell's politics, he would never have switched his support to King and the Liberals in 1939, by which time they were still essentially hostile to what King at least perceived as McConnell's profiteering.

McConnell and Meighen remained business associates until the 1950s, particularly until 1938, when they sat together on the boards of Holt Renfrew and of Canadian and General Investments. At first sight, the reasons for their closeness are obscure, especially in view of claim by Meighen's official biographer that the CPR and most of St James Street were bitter about Meighen's role in the formation of the CNR. After the sugar crisis of 1921, however, it is clear that McConnell and Ballantyne, at least, took comfort in Meighen's maintenance of the moderate tariffs necessary for the recovery of the refiners. Moreover, an erroneous and malicious attack by Mackenzie King on Ballantyne for retaining a directorship of St Lawrence Sugar, while a minister in Meighen's government of 1920, really left McConnell with little choice but to see Meighen as preferable to King. In fact, Ballantyne had resigned his directorship before joining Borden's Union government of 1917 and never resumed it. Even more offensive to McConnell, however, was King's ill-disguised hatred of the refiners generally, whom he saw as an evil "combination."

Apart from all of this, there seems to have been genuine personal esteem between Meighen and McConnell. For McConnell's part, he, like many others, admired Meighen's exceptional ability. Meighen exhibited a brilliant mind in parliamentary debate, and he was honest, hardworking, fearless, and both willing and able to tackle the thorniest of problems. And, despite his electoral failures, he was decisive, not a ditherer like King. With the retirement of McConnell's friend Sir Thomas White from federal politics, there was probably nobody left in the Commons more able or promising than Meighen.[7]

Unfortunately for Meighen himself, he was also a corrosively sarcastic and abusive debater who inspired hate, particularly in Quebec after the introduction in 1917 of conscription, a measure with which he was closely associated as both architect and champion. This legislation, because of its disruptive consequences, had not endeared the Conservatives to much of St James Street, despite the adherence of nearly all of English Montreal to the war effort. It also destroyed Conservative support in nearly all of the French-speaking population, particularly in rural areas. At least among the French Canadians, his much-criticized but misunderstood intransigence over conscription had laid him open to caricature as an enemy of French Canada, which he was decidedly not. Nor was his unpopularity confined to Quebec. In the west, which he represented in the Commons, Meighen was attacked for being in the hands of eastern big business, especially in his support of tariffs.

Meighen himself laid the blame for the defeat of the Conservative government in 1921 squarely at the feet of Hugh Graham, Lord Atholstan, editor of the Montreal *Star*, who had spread the fictitious story that the government intended to move the head office of the Grand Trunk Railway to Toronto, in preparation for the establishment there of the CNR's new headquarters. This would have cost hundreds of jobs in Montreal, and the result was that the Conservatives lost every seat in the city.

Meighen described Atholstan as "a political intriguer in a class by himself; a circuitous gumshoe sort of person … who could turn a corner so fast that you could hear his shirt-tails snap." Moreover, "aside from the moral aspect of his course, the degree of sagacity and judgment used by its owner in public affairs has been a converging minimum which long ago passed the zero point." As for the *Star* under Atholstan, Meighen confessed: "I cannot think of any institution in Canada whose history is more uniformly despicable than that of The Montreal Star."[8]

Existing literature on Meighen and St James Street concludes that the Conservatives lost in Quebec in the next federal election, in 1925, and therefore their majority in the Commons partly because of the opposition of the business magnates of Montreal led by Lord Atholstan. However, Meighen's biographer, Roger Graham, cannot identify any of these magnates except Atholstan and perhaps, faintly, Edward Beatty.[9] Whether McConnell was among the "bigger bigwigs of Montreal," to use Graham's term, may be questioned, but his support of Meighen cannot, any more than his friendship at the time with Beatty. Neither can his alliance with the Toronto financial interests behind the CNR, chiefly Sir Joseph Flavelle, Sir Thomas White, Z.A. Lash, and E.R. Wood, all of whom he was about to join on the board of Brazilian Traction. It is quite possible, too, that by 1921 McConnell was on good terms with the former Liberal Premier Sir Lomer Gouin, who ran as a Liberal candidate in the federal elections, despite Meighen's efforts to persuade him to stand for the Conservatives.

Such a wide range of associations casts into grave doubt any generalizations about the class loyalties of McConnell and his circle. Neither McConnell nor Atholstan had been born into any "class" of Montreal moguls, and neither had Beatty. The class postulated seems to be reducible to Atholstan alone, a class of one, described by Borden as "a singular mixture of cunning and stupidity."[10] In any event, relations between many Montreal Conservatives and Meighen did not improve before the general elections of 1925. There seems to have been deep divisions among Montreal Conservatives and Liberals over the moderation of Meighen's tariff policy, a moderation designed to win over such protectionist Liberals as Vincent Massey.

Following a Conservative defeat in a Montreal by-election in 1924, both the *Gazette* and the *Star* demanded the replacement of Meighen as the Conservative leader. McConnell, however, continued to support Meighen and even tried to convince Atholstan, with whom he was becoming connected through their joint ownership of the *Star*, which began in 1925, to change his mind about the Conservative leader. As the stockbroker Murray Williams reported to Meighen late in September 1925, "I refereed a one round match between Jack McConnell and Lord Atholstan. If ever a man fought a good battle for you it was McConnell on that occasion. Lord Atholstan is heart and soul in the fight, but we certainly have great trouble ironing out some of his kinks."[11] Meighen replied that McConnell had "contributed zealously" to "party integrity," for which he was "under a tremendous debt of gratitude to him."[12]

McConnell had reasons for hoping that Meighen might be able to revive Conservative fortunes in Quebec. In 1920 Meighen had appointed as his unofficial Quebec lieutenant E.-L. Patenaude, who had resigned as his colleague in the Union Government of 1917 because of conscription. In taking this step, Meighen was signalling a determination to win Quebec back to both Canada and the Conservative Party. Patenaude was a moderate Quebec nationalist, not unlike Henri Bourassa in his insistence on the official use of French as well as English, and on equality more generally between the two linguistic communities. He did not, however, share Bourassa's blanket opposition to the empire, and he had been in favour of the war effort up to the imposition of conscription. He and Meighen struck an alliance on the basis of an agreement that pledged the federal government to respect the role of French Canadians in Confederation and the rights of French and Roman Catholic minorities outside Quebec, as well as to provide proportional representation according to "race" in the cabinet, the Senate, the judiciary, and the civil service.[13]

In anticipation of the general elections of 1925, McConnell and Lorne Webster purchased the newspaper *La Patrie* to give the Conservatives a voice in Montreal.[14] During the campaign, McConnell and probably Webster approached J.N. Ponton, the owner of a newspaper for French-speaking farmers, offering to cover his costs for his support of Meighen.[15] In English Montreal, McConnell sought the support of Howard Smith, the paper manufacturer, Arthur Purvis of Canadian Explosives, and H.L. Rutherford of Canadian Bag for the Conservatives. He probably worked with Webster to convince C.H. Cahan to stand in the riding of St Lawrence, in succession to Ballantyne. Although Meighen even tried to persuade McConnell to join him on the hustings, McConnell declined.[16] Behind the scenes, however, McConnell provided financial support to the Conservative journalist Gratton O'Leary, in O'Leary's futile campaign to win a seat in the Gaspé.

But Atholstan was still up to mischief, having decided that Patenaude could win in place of, rather than in support of, Meighen in Quebec. McConnell and Webster were working hard with Patenaude and Conservative cabinet minister Sir George Perley to discourage protests against Meighen[17] when Patenaude himself, seizing upon Atholstan's strategy, decided to distance himself from Meighen. In the end, Patenaude failed to deliver even one Quebec seat to the Conservatives, including his own. McConnell had apparently contributed $30,000 to the Conservative campaign in Quebec, and there has been the suggestion that Patenaude simply pocketed it. According to Meighen, however, McConnell "had the same opinion of Atholstan as I had" and was "always entirely loyal and helpful," and "in no sense did he sit in any conclave with Atholstan."[18]

To what extent McConnell agreed with Atholstan on Meighen or Patenaude, or otherwise, is unknown, but it seems logical that all three men thought that Meighen without Patenaude was a lost cause in Quebec. Yet, although it was quite clear what

Patenaude was not, it was unclear what he was. It was therefore dangerous for Atholstan and McConnell alike to read into him what they wanted to see, and indeed the election campaign was to prove that he was essentially standing only for himself. In any case, the tactic of using Patenaude was bold, but probably doomed to failure, not so much because of Atholstan's betrayal as because French Quebec electors refused in any case to see Patenaude as anything except a mouthpiece for Meighen.[19]

Notwithstanding their debacle in Quebec, the Conservatives as a party did win the largest bloc of seats in the Commons in the elections of 1925. But Mackenzie King, prime minister since 1921, clung to power with the aid of the Progressives from western Canada. When King lost the support of the Commons as a result of a scandal in the Customs Department, he asked Lord Byng, the governor general, to dissolve Parliament and thus permit new elections – a request that Byng refused. King thereupon resigned, and Byng sent for Meighen to form a Conservative administration, which fell the same year, necessitating the elections denied King and resulting in King's return as prime minister in 1926. The discontent with Meighen, in Montreal in particular, grew.

With Premier Howard Ferguson of Ontario managing his campaign, R.B. Bennett succeeded Meighen in 1927. As a rich businessman himself, Bennett had known McConnell at least since his protégé Max Aitken's amalgamation of the utilities in Calgary in 1909, and Bennett as prime minister was to find no more stalwart supporter than McConnell. Bennett was slow to respond to the Great Depression that began with the Crash of 1929, but he did win the general election of 1930. McConnell seems not to have participated actively in the 1930 campaign, and it is even unclear whether he backed the Conservatives financially, but the *Star* did support Bennett. So did McConnell's friends on St James Street, with lavish donations.[20] They were not disappointed. Bennett and the Conservatives were elected.

But, instead of the prosperity that Bennett had promised and St James Street had been hoping for, the Depression deepened. In response, the Bennett government appointed in 1931 a royal commission to consider the profits made by such retailers as Eaton's. The commission interrogated neither McConnell nor his close business associates, but its work deeply disturbed him. The profit motive was at the heart of the system of free enterprise, and, in the context of the 1930s, any attack on it raised the spectre of a collectivist alternative, at least in the sense of big government. Yet McConnell did not abandon Bennett. The prime minister came to dinner at Pine Avenue, and he seems particularly to have warmed to Lil. And, although McConnell was later to tell Prime Minister King that he had never really liked Bennett – which is possible, since very few did – he was actually a warm supporter and confidant of Bennett as a politician over several years.

Even when almost all of St James Street, led by Beatty, turned against Bennett because of his adoption of New Deal ideas from the United States and his refusal to bail out the CPR, Senator Ballantyne assured Bennett that McConnell, almost alone on St James Street, still supported him.[21] In November 1932 McConnell acknowledged Bennett's thanks for some favour: "What I have done has been out of esteem and admiration for you, and for the wonderful job you are doing every day in this country to protect her citizens against the demoralizing influence of present worldwide conditions to which they are exposed on every side."[22]

Whatever his own misgivings about Bennett may have been, McConnell was a firm Conservative until Bennett's defeat in 1935. For example, on 5 December 1935, he organized a luncheon at the Mount Royal Club in honour of R.C. Matthews, the minister of national revenue. This appears to have been a private meeting of leading Montreal Conservatives, and on the guest list is scrawled, in McConnell's hand, "not a liberal guest at this table," "muzzle the press," and, in an apparent reference to the Bennett government, "every one here has some knowledge of the very excellent job." As the host, McConnell was trying to rally even Bennett's fiercest critics on St James Street to the Conservative cause. Those present included Sir Edward Beatty of the CPR, Sir Charles Gordon of Dominion Textile and the Bank of Montreal, Sir Herbert Holt of Montreal Power, the lawyer F.E. Meredith, R.H. McMaster of Stelco, Herbert Molson of Molson's Brewery, W.A. Black of Ogilvie Flour Mills, Morris Wilson of the Royal Bank, Senator C.C. Ballantyne of Sherwin-Williams, and the publisher F.N. Southam. This was probably the very last meeting in history in which so many leaders of St James Street met in support of the Conservatives, and it underlines McConnell's role as a loyal Conservative and a mediator until the end of Bennett's leadership.[23]

How devoted McConnell was to Bennett may be seen in a letter that he wrote during the 1935 election campaign. He had been unable to hear Bennett speak at the Atwater Market, but, if he had been able to introduce the prime minister, he would have called him "a constructive force – a man of the highest intelligence with unusual wisdom – and what is more, a man of action":

> No words of mine can add fresh lustre to his name; he, himself, with every new pronouncement makes that lustre more apparent.
>
> No man in Canada who is desirous of conducting his business in a fair and equitable manner need feel alarmed in the slightest degree because of any reforms that may be considered necessary by Mr. Bennett.
>
> Just, resourceful and swift of action, if reforms are needful, let us by all means have them under a Statesman of his wide experience and well known fairmindedness to all concerned in the development of this country.[24]

But Bennett went down to defeat, the victim of the Depression, his own mistakes, and Conservative divisions.[25] His successor, the Liberal Mackenzie King, was perhaps the most successful Canadian politician in the twentieth century and the longest-serving prime minister in history of the British Empire. He had long hated McConnell, as far back as the general elections of 1921. King blamed him, the Bank of Montreal, the CMA, and the CPR for "the Patenaude fiasco in Quebec and corrupting constituencies in Ontario" and for having "self-interest as their dominating impulse," their goal being "to get control of Govt."[26]

The two men met socially, and King came to see Lil, whom he seems first to have met at the wedding of Lord Hardinge, an aide-de-camp to Lord Willingdon, to Margot Fleming in 1928, even more. The Willingdons were very close to both the McConnells and King and, according to Lady Byng, blatantly Liberal, and Government House provided common ground for them. But, because of McConnell's unstinting public support of Bennett, who cordially hated King, there could be for long no meeting of minds between McConnell and King.

Nevertheless, McConnell did his best to cultivate the new prime minister. He sent King books, complimented him on a speech in 1937, and expressed the hope in the same year that he could do something to rein in Premier William Aberhart of Alberta, restoring that province to "political sanity and stability."[27] In the summer of 1937, the two men reached a sort of rapprochement on their way to the coronation of George VI on the *Empress of Australia*.

While they were at sea, the news came through of the dismissal by Chancellor Edward Beatty of Principal A.E. Morgan of McGill. McConnell reminded King that Beatty had offered King the McGill principalship before Morgan's appointment, and, presumably authorized by Beatty, he renewed the offer. As an alternative, McConnell also offered King the editorship of the *Star*, if only King could have Atholstan "*shuffled off this mortal coil.*"[28] King found both of the McConnells "exceedingly pleasant throughout the voyage," with McConnell pledging to further landscape "beautification" throughout Canada.[29] The reasoning behind McConnell's efforts so to ingratiate himself with King is puzzling. King had no intention of relinquishing the post of prime minister soon, if ever, and a successor to Morgan at McGill had to be found urgently. Offering him the editorship of the *Star*, long a Tory paper, was likewise strange, especially since it was not clear over the summer that Atholstan had only a few months to live. In any event, McConnell did make these offers, and they underline the difficulty of characterizing his conduct as reflective of any naked self-interest.

In October 1937 the McConnells visited King at his Kingsmere retreat. McConnell offered to build King a new residence there, incorporating King's collection of ruins from other buildings. King was warming to him and he confessed to his diary: "I wd. like to enjoy with him the sort of friendship I had with Mr. Rockefeller, Jr., – which was based on my not having allowed him to do anything for me – except in the human relationship we enjoyed, & had asked him for nothing, nor sent people to him etc." But suddenly, as King reminded himself of Laurier and reciprocity, he recalled wrongly that it was McConnell who "had done so much to defeat us, and that it was through *sugar* that he had made his money, – the tariff, special privilege, etc."[30] On the following day, he reflected on a vision that he had had of a pile of sugar cubes, and on the reference in the Book of Joshua in the Old Testament to "the accursed thing," which he associated with McConnell's "loot" from St Lawrence Sugar. He determined never to compromise with McConnell on his own independence or that of the Liberals. He would, he decided upon reconsideration, never forget McConnell's "antics, in going about the ruins [of Kingsmere], suggested how this could be constructed, and that, etc., trying literally to thrust a house upon me, – and to make Kingsmere a second Chequers."[31] The blossoming friendship suddenly seemed blighted.

As late as January 1939, King suspected that McConnell was probably at least tangentially involved in plotting with Mitch Hepburn of Ontario and Maurice Duplessis of Quebec against the re-election of King's Liberals in the forthcoming general elections. Hepburn was bidding, in return for the projected alliance, for Duplessis's support in opposing a new St Lawrence waterway and any scheme of imperial defence. In King's mind, this plot was associated with the threat made to King two years before by J.S. Norris, the president of Montreal Power, of a "show-down" with the Liberal government if King refused his company a licence to export power to the United States, a licence that, as McConnell claimed to King, had been approved by Prime Minister Bennett. King believed that, behind Hepburn, Duplessis, and, by implication, Norris, McConnell was representing American private interests, and he instructed Sir Herbert Marler, the Canadian ambassador in Washington, to inform President Roosevelt of his suspicion.

Gradually, however, King's opinion of McConnell, and vice versa, improved. Bennett's successor as Conservative leader was Robert Manion, a Roman Catholic physician from Ontario, married to a French Canadian and possessed of bilingual children. As minister of railways and canals under Bennett, he, and the prime minister, had earned the enmity of Edward Beatty by opposing unification of the CPR and CNR, a position that was to prove fatal to financial support for the Conservatives from St James Street. Furthermore, Montreal business perceived Manion as a social reformer, a pacifist, and at best a tepid imperialist if not an anti-imperialist. When elected as federal Conservative leader in August 1938, Manion had called for social reform as the only alternative to anarchy and revolution. The *Star*, now firmly under McConnell's control, chided "Revolution! Tush, tush, Dr. Manion. Turn over. You are sleeping on your back."[32]

In March 1939, with the coming of war almost inevitable, both Manion for the Conservatives and Mackenzie King for the Liberals declared themselves against conscription. By August, Manion and his Conservatives at the federal level had entered into an alliance with Maurice Duplessis's Union Nationale in Quebec, which was firmly against even registration for national service. After the declaration of war in September, Duplessis called a snap election and declared his opposition to all participation by Quebecers in the conflict. The only man who could defeat Duplessis was Adélard

Godbout, the leader of the provincial Liberals, who was allied to King. Godbout was no less cautious about forcing the participation of Quebecers than Manion or King, but at least he did not campaign actively on non-participation. With the fate of the empire at stake, McConnell had to weigh the fact that provincial Liberals were allied to the federal Liberals, and that at least King had brought Canada into the war and hated Duplessis.

Once Duplessis had called his election in September, just after the declaration of war, King was relieved. He described Duplessis's call as "a diabolical act on his part to have made the issue of provincial autonomy versus Dominion Government, taking advantage of the War Measures Act, to have it appear that Ottawa is encroaching on freedom of individuals in Quebec." Hepburn, King judged, was now "left out on a limb" and the Quebec-Ontario axis "smashed," since in Ontario it was impossible to make federal interference an issue in war.[33] Any further flirting by McConnell with decentralizing provincial politicians would have to await the conclusion of the war. He was now in King's corner.

By this time, the Conservative Party, both federal and provincial, was effectively dead in Quebec, and, with Duplessis's election call, McConnell believed he had no choice but to support the Liberals at both levels of government. On 5 October he went to see King, who recorded in his diary that McConnell felt that Duplessis had been "a thorough traitor ... spoke of the way in which he had run the province into debt. Then went on to speak in highest terms of Lapointe, Cardin and others, saying that he believed that Lapointe would succeed in defeating Duplessis; and that it would be an appalling thing for the future of the province if Duplessis could win on isolating it, were the campaign that Duplessis was waging to be successful. He said he himself was ready to help financially the [Liberal] committee on organization, and to get other Conservatives in Montreal to the same."[34]

McConnell did not personally become a Liberal, but he pledged the backing of the *Star* for both King and Godbout. In March 1938 McConnell had already told Lord Tweedsmuir that he intended to run the *Star* "as supporter of whichever government might be in office – pretty much the attitude of 'The Times,'" as Tweedsmuir reported to King.[35] This stance did not apply to the Duplessis government, still in office in October 1939. But, as a result of McConnell's pledge to King, who was in office, McConnell had his newspaper ask in an editorial, "Will Duplessis Go on Fiddling with a World in Flames?" The *Star* attacked Duplessis for saying that the forthcoming provincial election was "a fight for the liberties and rights of the people of Quebec, a fight for the survival of the French-Canadian race in this Dominion of Canada." What was objectionable to McConnell was not so much Duplessis's position on non-participation in the war as his "deliberate appeal to race hatred, designed to stir up racial animosity at a time when all patriotic Canadians of both races are agreed there should be no discussion of racial prejudices." The newspaper continued: "No Britisher in this Province, or in any other Province of the Dominion, will be able to hold up his head if such evil counsel prevails. Canada must be stoutly and without reserve united for the prosecution of the war and the overthrow of the twin evils [communism and Hitlerism] against which it is directed until Victory crowns the Allies' efforts."[36] In a letter to the Liberal Vincent Massey, then high commissioner in London, McConnell called Duplessis simply a "wild man."[37]

As the *Star* itself noted, though the federal and the Quebec provincial Liberals were equally opposed to conscription, the three Quebec Liberals in the federal cabinet – Chubby Power, Ernest Lapointe, and P.-J.-A. Cardin – declared that they would resign from the cabinet if Duplessis were elected premier. Their resignations, they implied, would open the door to a conscriptionist government in Ottawa, and so they presented the provincial Liberals, under Adélard Godbout, as in effect more likely to prevent conscription than Duplessis himself. It was a contorted rationale for supporting the Liberals, but it worked. As for McConnell, he seems to have given $10,000 to the successful Liberal campaign in the provincial elections.[38]

By now, McConnell was highly attuned to the twists of Quebec politics, and his position was that it was better to choose the lesser of two evils. He had chosen to support King not because King shared his support for the war effort at all costs but because King was ambivalent, which was in McConnell's view better than Manion's active opposition to the war effort. Likewise, Godbout was essentially against conscription, but otherwise he was much more open to the war effort than Duplessis. King was never to abandon his suspicion of what he saw as big business, and throughout the war he consistently refused any offer from McConnell of financial aid and rejected all appeals for political intervention in aid of business interests. Nevertheless, King was gratified that there was now a generally Liberal newspaper in Montreal, especially since John Bassett's *Gazette* remained so implacably Tory and opposed to him.

In winning the provincial elections of 1939, the provincial Liberals killed Conservative hopes, at the federal as well as the provincial level, in Quebec for pretty much the remainder of the war. In the aftermath of the Liberal victory there, Manion seemed so hapless that in December 1939 the *Gazette* called for Bennett, who would doubtless have been very aggressive in support of the war effort, to resume the leadership of the federal Conservatives in Manion's place. The *Star*, now cultivating King, remained silent. In his own way, McConnell was becoming as cagey as Duplessis and Godbout. He was personally in favour of the full-scale prosecution of the war, but his knowledge of Meighen's disastrous career made it pointless for him or his newspaper to go so far as to press for anything like conscription; and, in any case, it was far from clear in 1939 that conscription, with all the hatred that it would stir up in Quebec, would be necessary.

Despite the switch of the *Star* to the Liberals, McConnell formally joined neither the federal nor the provincial Liberal Party. Privately, he remained hopeful that the traditional Conservative loyalty to the empire and to tariff protection would revive, and he quietly gave money to Conservatives to the end of his life.[39] If McConnell had any non-Conservative political inclinations at this time, they may have disposed him to favour a national, or coalition, government, involving liberal, socialist, and conservative politicians alike. On the day Germany attacked Poland, 1 September 1939, the *Star* called for a national government in Canada,[40] and the idea was to be tested in two different ways the following year.[41] In January 1940 the Liberal premier of Ontario, Mitch Hepburn, joined the provincial Conservative leader, George Drew, in attacking King's war leadership and in obtaining a resolution of the Ontario legislature to this effect. In response, King called a snap federal election for March. The shocked Manion was forced by his party to pledge the formation of a coalition government should the Conservatives be elected. Almost undoubtedly, this idea still appealed to McConnell, particularly since it had been openly advocated by Beatty and other big businessmen since 1935, as well as by McConnell himself through the *Star*.

Manion's preference for Conservative candidates to stand as National Government, rather than Conservative, candidates in 1940, however, alienated traditional Conservative supporters without gaining any support from non-Conservatives. During the campaign, Meighen reported to McConnell that Conservatives remained "quite frigid" to Manion,[42] an attitude that was reflected in the closed wallets that greeted the Conservative leader on St James Street: the CPR, the Bank of Montreal, and others in Montreal had contributed $500,000 to the Conservative campaign in the election of 1930, but in 1940 they gave the Conservatives absolutely nothing. The results were predictable. In all of Canada in 1940, the Conservatives won only 40 seats as opposed to 184 for the Liberals. All the Conservative candidates but one lost in Quebec, including McConnell's old associate from Tramways days, C.H. Cahan. Manion himself lost his seat and thus the leadership of the Conservative Party. His replacement as Conservative leader was R.B. Hanson, a New Brunswick lawyer, who, like his predecessor, pressed King for a coalition government.

King initially saw no reason to invite Conservative MPs to join his cabinet, but, as recounted in the last chapter, in the summer of 1940 he did offer a cabinet post to a number of businessmen, one of whom was McConnell. Since none of these men were Conservative politicians and all were certainly outside the Conservative caucus, their acceptance would not have created a true coalition government, but at best a broader-based one. All those approached eventually declined King's invitation. McConnell offered to place a fund of $100,000 in trust for King to use for war needs, but King refused.

George McCullagh of the *Globe* and Cahan then pressed again for the return of Meighen as leader, and Meighen was so elected in succession to Hanson. Meighen's subsequent defeat in a by-election by the CCF candidate was important for several reasons: it marked the effective end of his political career, as well as of Conservative Party's prospects for more than a decade; it underlined the disappearance of big-business

Toryism as a political force, at least at the federal level; and it accelerated the decline of St James Street and Montreal in both the Conservative Party and federal politics, in favour of the Liberals. Finally, it left the Liberals as the only effective opposition to the tide of socialism that seemed to be advancing.

The depth of McConnell's hostility towards the CCF cannot be overstated. As he wrote to relatives in California at the end of 1943:

> The war seems to offer a good excuse for many short comings. The C.C.F. is not asleep: their leaders everywhere in Canada are on the alert to make the most of all the short comings and all the weaknesses of past regimes. The C.C.F. Star is rising but if it ever brings them into power that will be a sorry day for all Canadians – that is – when the real force behind the present leaders gets into action. This force: undisguised and stripped of glowing promises, for the working people is, simply National Socialism of the type advocated by Hitler, when he was on the rise in the early thirties.
>
> The German people thought it meant for them the promised land, – ease and plenty for all. But it has brought them instead anguish – suffering, death and destruction.[43]

At the close of the Second World War, McConnell's hostility to socialism did not soften. He saw the election of a CCF government in Saskatchewan, and a strong showing by the CCF in Ontario elections, as omens of much worse to come.

With the effective end of Meighen's political career, King was far more threatened from within his own party than by any of the opposition parties. In these circumstances, McConnell could hardly avoid concluding that cultivating King was the best way to bring about conscription if it should prove necessary. As already noted, McConnell deplored King's decision to hold a plebiscite on conscription in 1942, seeing it as an abdication of leadership that threatened to divide the country rather than hold it together, but even then he continued to see King as the best man available to lead the country in wartime. King, moreover, had proved himself most amenable to assisting the sugar industry through wartime regulation, and McConnell could not but be impressed by his political sagacity and electoral success.

During the remainder of the war and afterwards, McConnell's relationship with King increasingly developed into a cordial but still not a political one. They talked of the Rockefellers, mission work, McConnell's business affairs, medicine, spirituality, the afterlife, charitable foundations, and even art. In 1946 McConnell offered King the chancellorship of McGill, which King declined.[44] Jack and Lil recommended their landscape architect at Dorval, Ormiston Roy, who was also the superintendent of the Mount Royal Cemetery, to design the grounds at King's estate in the Gatineau Hills, Kingsmere, apparently satisfactorily to King. McConnell paid for all the landscaping, which astonished the prime minister, who thought that McConnell was overpaying. Their confidence in each other blossomed, and King was a frequent guest especially at the McConnell house in Dorval. On one night there, a servant left an iron on before going to bed, and the house nearly went up in flames, which caused King to muse on how history might see his perishing together with McConnell. As King recorded of another stay at Dorval on 13 June 1948:

> The stories McConnell told me simply amazed me. In the course of the conversation, Mrs. McConnell said I was the only man her husband would listen to. He wanted to do all the talking himself with anybody else.
>
> I certainly enjoy the talks with McConnell. Find him exceedingly pleasant. A man of fine noble purpose. I noticed he always tries to pass on a nice word about others. He is not given to being critical – is rather kind.[45]

McConnell, however, was "very emphatic in saying I had more than done my work and must not think of staying on." In the months of King's declining health that followed, McConnell was tireless in working to secure him the best medical care, at the Montreal Neurological Institute and elsewhere, and he proved himself to be what King now thought of him, namely, King's best friend along with John D. Rockefeller, Jr. In making his funeral arrangements, King had named McConnell as one of his honorary pallbearers, a duty that McConnell undertook in the extreme heat of July 1950, accompanying the body from the funeral in Ottawa to its burial in the Mount Pleasant Cemetery in Toronto, where McConnell's own parents and a sister had been buried. John D. Rockefeller, Jr had sent his son David to represent him, and McConnell accompanied David on the journey by car from the cemetery, a fitting conclusion to King's friendship with the two great philanthropists.[46]

The same patterns evident in McConnell's association with federal politics – a decided preference for the pragmatic over the ideological, coupled with a shrewd sense of economic self-interest as well as a keen sensitivity to needs of both Canada and the British Empire – were apparent at the provincial level. In Quebec, McConnell set himself apart from much of English Montreal by supporting – not during the Second World War, it is true, but both before and after that conflict – a man whom many in his community loved to hate: Maurice Duplessis. Like many in the business circles in which he moved, he did so partly for reasons of intellectual affinity but also for, again, pragmatic considerations.

As in Canada more generally, the interwar period in Quebec was politically full of movement. But, apart from the Union Nationale government of Maurice Duplessis in 1936–39 and then from 1944 to 1960, the Quebec governments that McConnell knew were Liberal ones, first under Sir Lomer Gouin from 1907 to 1920 and then under

Funeral of Mackenzie King, McConnell as an honorary pallbearer, fourth from
the end of the line, Ottawa 1950. McCord Museum, M 2003.8.6.4.1.

Louis-Alexandre Taschereau until 1935. In its dealings with these governments, English Quebec had long acknowledged its minority status. By language and generally by
religion, it was isolated from the intellectual salons, the noisy press, and the church
that were the dominant voices of politics in French Montreal. And, outside Montreal
itself, although there were pockets of English influence in Quebec City and the Eastern Townships in particular, the English point of view counted for even less. Out of
habit, therefore, English Quebec was largely detached from provincial party politics.
It did not need the patronage of any provincial government, and indeed it was largely
much more interested in London and New York than in Quebec City. It had even lost
control of municipal politics in Montreal, and all that remained to it was economic
power, which was still formidable and centred in St James Street.

Although generally uninterested in provincial party politics, the businessmen
of English Montreal could not be equally indifferent to their economic interests as
defined by the political agenda of the government of the day in Quebec, particularly
since decisions of the Judicial Committee of the Privy Council produced a decided
shift of power from Ottawa to the provinces in the period from the 1890s to the 1930s.
St James Street was divided between Liberals and Conservatives on the federal stage,
at least until 1925. But there was no effective provincial branch of the federal Conservative Party after then. And, with the gradual fragmentation of the federal Conserva-

tive Party that followed, Montreal business had little choice but to support the long Liberal reign in Quebec City. Indeed, many Montreal businessmen supported the Liberals even during the brief Union Nationale interregnum of 1936–39.

The interwar years, then, were ones of accommodation between the Street and government. The Street marketed provincial bonds, which were a more important source of revenue than taxes, and ran much of the province's industry, from textiles to mining and pulp and paper and waterpower. For these reasons, the province was obliged to accommodate the Street, rather than the opposite, while the Street, for its part, was happy to offer provincial leaders a place in its boardrooms. Thus, Gouin, on his retirement, became a director of the Bank of Montreal and Sun Life, and Taschereau, his successor, remained a director of Sun Life even while he was premier. It was a cosy, almost symbiotic relationship.

Generations of French-speaking Quebecers, however, were to revile Premier Taschereau for his nepotism and for his closeness to St James Street. For his part, Taschereau was committed to the industrialization of the province, at least in the foreseeable future through English-speaking capital. Together with electrification, industrial development promised, in his view, a higher material standard of living to French and English Quebecers alike. The most obvious interest threatened by his policies was the Roman Catholic Church, which saw traditional rural life as more conducive to the maintenance of the faith. McConnell and English-speaking Quebec did not share the church's fears, and neither did they feel threatened by the rise of new French Canadian managers and professionals – particularly after the founding by Gouin of the École des Hautes Études Commerciales – whom they may have seen as exemplified by Gouin and Taschereau themselves.

Moreover, when Duplessis came to power, ostensibly in opposition to the corruption of Taschereau and the power of the English-speaking monopolies, he essentially adopted the same view as Gouin and Taschereau, that progress in Quebec must be promoted through private, often foreign, investment and through the provincial funding of education. Thus, to St James Street, there was not a significant difference between the Union Nationale and the Liberals, since both parties were led by men with whom English Quebec could do business. It is true that Duplessis had campaigned against St James Street in order to court some of the nationalists to join the provincial Conservatives in forming his Union Nationale. But he promptly turned against them. Thereafter, the only real threat to English Quebec came from the extreme anti-modernist clericalists, who eventually merged with nationalists, in some cases to become separatists.

During the First World War, as chairman of the Victory Loan campaign for the Island of Montreal, McConnell was careful to distance himself from the accusations of disloyalty levelled against French Canadians. Accustomed as he was to working with French Canadians, he had no inclination to caricature. But conscription was an issue on which nobody could be neutral, and, like nearly all moderate English Canadians, he was shocked by the failure of the vast majority of French Canadians to do their "share" and volunteer. The elections won by Borden's Unionist government near the end of the 1917 bitterly divided English from French Canadians; the Unionists did not include a single French Canadian, and the Liberal MPs under Laurier counted only sixteen English Canadians from outside Quebec. The perception grew among French Canadians that the conscription legislation was vindictively directed against them. Riots broke out in Quebec City for four days, beginning on 29 March 1918 and ending with the shooting of at least four innocent civilians by English-speaking troops and injuries to both soldiers and civilians.

After the war, McConnell regarded Taschereau as not a bad premier. He was corrupt, like most of his predecessors and his successors. But he was also a modernizer, in tune with St James Street and trying genuinely to provide a better future for Quebec through modest legislative steps in education and health. Later, with the emergence of Duplessis in the mid-1930s, McConnell had every reason to remain supportive of the Quebec Liberal Party, particularly after Duplessis's Union Nationale administration came out in opposition to Canadian participation in the Second World War. Despite the provincial expropriation of Montreal Power in 1944, which horrified him, McConnell continued to back the Liberal Godbout government during the remainder of the war, but then, with the return to power of Duplessis, he reconsidered his options.

In 1944 McConnell was caught in the same dilemma as his Conservative friends, in both Ontario and Quebec, who were facing a seemingly interminable Liberal regime in Ottawa combined with the increasing threat of socialists provincially. After 1948, McConnell was able to like personally King's successor, Louis St Laurent. But his innate conservatism left him open to the appeal of a strongly conservative provincial leader. With Duplessis's defeat of the Godbout government, and the strong showing of the CCF in Saskatchewan and in Ontario in the same year, the provincial Liberals fell apart as an electoral force. At the same time, McConnell sensed that Duplessis was strong enough to prove a brake on the growth of socialism in Canada through his assertion of strong provincial autonomy, such that, in the event of a CCF government in Ottawa, at least Quebec, and possibly other provinces, would prove to be a countervailing force.

The relationship between McConnell and Duplessis after the war has intrigued commentators. In book after book, the same stories are repeated, all to the effect that McConnell through the *Star* and John Bassett through the *Gazette* were vital and uncritical pillars of support for the Duplessis government. Then there are elaborations: one that McConnell in particular bankrolled Duplessis's election campaigns with thousands or even millions of dollars in unmarked banknotes; another that the two talked by telephone every day; and still another that they met at a bar (of all places) in the Ritz-Carlton once a week to decide on how to run Quebec. According to this tradition, McConnell was the éminence grise behind the throne throughout the *grande noirceur* – great darkness – that enshrouded Quebec under Duplessis. In return for his corruption of the political process, it is implied that McConnell gained, among other things, valuable timber rights for his interests in pulp and paper, as well as preferential treatment on newsprint costs. The price that Quebec, and indeed Canada, allegedly paid for McConnell's silence, even conscious complicity, in the face of an evil, reactionary dictatorship was the trampling of civil liberties. So often praised as the greatest philanthropist in Canadian history, McConnell has curiously also become a symbol of all that was wrong with Quebec before 1960.

The fullest and most influential description of the relationship between McConnell and Duplessis is by Conrad Black.[47] Black depicts an unusual and indeed unbroken cordiality between the two men from January 1946, when, perhaps at the instigation of Antonio Barrette, they were reconciled. Barrette, minister of labour in the government formed by Duplessis in 1944, had first met McConnell at the dinner for the king and queen given by the Quebec government in 1939, and now they met again at a Canadian Club dinner. It was McConnell – having observed Duplessis's stand against communism in the year and a half since resuming the premiership – who took the initiative, asking Barrette after the health of Duplessis. Referring obliquely to the part that the *Star* had taken in opposition to Duplessis in the provincial elections of 1939, McConnell assured him that now "the hatchet is buried."[48] Shortly after his meeting with Barrette, McConnell wrote to the premier, congratulating him on sending twenty provincial police to the Valleyfield plant of Montreal Cottons (a subsidiary of Dominion Textile), apparently breaking a strike by members of the United Textile Workers of America. According to Black, this approach proved decisive. Duplessis and Barrette had branded the strike as communist and illegal, and McConnell sent the premier a copy of the coverage of it by the *Star*, as well as an editorial on strikes against Ford in Windsor, Ontario, and by the Canadian Seamen's Union in Cornwall.[49] Duplessis replied, recalling the *Star*'s support for his Padlock Law of 1939, the constitutionality of which had been upheld by Chief Justice R.A.E. Greenshields, and he continued:

> Don't you think that the lack of energy shown by the federal authorities is most harmful? The United States may be suffering from "delerium Truman," but this is an additional reason for us to stop and prevent the spread of the dreadful disease in our economic life.
>
> You have certainly noticed that centralization of powers has always been the "sine qua non" condition of Bolshevism, Fascism, Hitlerism and Communism. Just imagine what would happen to this country of ours if we had only one government for the whole of Canada, directed by the C.C.F. people or by other

radical socialists. It is bad enough today with the insidiously socialistic regime we have.

Provincial Legislatures, the Legislature of Quebec in particular, are the essential bulwark against Communism and Socialism. When we are fighting for the safeguard of provincial autonomy we are fighting in favour of democracy and democratic institutions as against the forces of disorder and tyranny so well represented by Communism and Bolshevism.[50]

In response to another pronouncement by Duplessis in August, McConnell telegraphed: "Again I congratulate you upon forthright democratic stand and determination to enforce Quebec laws which are capable of rendering justice to everyone."[51]

Then McConnell donated $100,000 anonymously to the victims of fires at Rimouski and Cabano, as well as raising donations from other sources.[52] He also started giving Duplessis little gifts, such as cigars, a gold coin, photographs, paintings by Cornelius Krieghoff. There were "supplementary" contributions too, but the context of these suggests that they were to charities named by the premier, rather than to the premier himself. Thus, Duplessis directed $15,000 from McConnell to the Carmelite monastery in Trois-Rivières, his constituency, and the Hôtel Dieu in Quebec City, while a further $285,000 of McConnell's money was devoted to the building of a boys' club in Trois-Rivières.

Another boys' club that was started with the help of McConnell money was in Montreal. On 30 May 1953, when McConnell was in England for the coronation of Queen Elizabeth II, the premier laid the cornerstone of the Point Saint-Charles Boys' and Girls' Club on Ash Avenue. This was to provide recreational facilities for 5,000 children of the impoverished district, combining the work of the 79th Battery Boys' Club and the Griffintown Club. In the words of the *Star* – words that reflected McConnell's own feelings – Duplessis remarked that if "the state controlled everything, a trend that had occurred elsewhere and unfortunately was appearing in this country, there would be no place for philanthropy, no place for freedom, no place for success or ambition or real achievement."[53] McConnell was delighted to be able to attend the actual opening in February of the following year. He had taken a personal interest in the details, including choosing the coloured tiles for the swimming pool. There were twenty-four hobby rooms, a woodworking and machine shop, and a games room, all designed to serve about eight hundred families in perhaps the poorest district of Montreal.[54]

McConnell's generosity did not stop there. Black claims that "if McConnell's bequests [sic] to the French charities were generous, his gifts to his favourite projects, and particularly McGill University, the Montreal General Hospital, and the Royal Victoria Hospital, were immense, amounting to tens of millions of dollars." He further notes that "Duplessis was genuinely flabbergasted at McConnell's great generosity, and almost equally so at his insistence on anonymity ... Duplessis insisted that the beneficiaries know who the angel was, that he might receive their expressions of gratitude. McConnell was adamant that the reverse be the case, but in this gentle tug-of-war Duplessis generally prevailed and snitched on McConnell, to the latter's consternation."[55] McConnell's lavish giving was such that even Duplessis, accustomed as he was to receiving financial aid, seemed overwhelmed, and he publicly called McConnell "Big Heart," the greatest philanthropist in Canadian history.

All of Duplessis's biographers agree that he did not personally benefit from McConnell's contributions.[56] For McConnell's part, what did he want or receive from Duplessis in return? To quote Black again:

> Provincial government support of these causes and others that McConnell particularly championed were the principal, though not the only *quid pro quo* that McConnell sought for his many attentions for Duplessis. And Duplessis replied with an official generosity toward those and other English-language institutions in Quebec that was unprecedented.
>
> Every request that Mr. McConnell made for provincial government assistance was acceded to at Duplessis's instructions, immediately and completely. In the more modest budgets or circumstances of Gouin, Taschereau, Godbout, or the pre-war Duplessis term, there had certainly been no discrimination against English institutions, but from 1946 to 1959, in the life of the Duplessis-McConnell arrangement, the largesse of the provincial government flowed in a river, as never before and not since.[57]

In summary, Black confirms that McConnell's chief benefit from his philanthropic contributions during the Duplessis era was provincial funding of English-language institutions. Apart from special consideration in the granting of timber rights, concessions on newsprint prices, and intervention to prevent the widening of Notre-Dame Street so as to encroach on the St Lawrence Sugar site in 1957, Black does not specify any other advantage that McConnell gained for his private interests through his philanthropy.

With respect to political contributions, McConnell, in Black's account, made donations to the Union Nationale only in the elections of 1952 and 1956, when Georges-Émile Lapalme was the Liberal leader. These donations "arrived within 48 hours of the dissolution of the Legislative Assembly in 1952 and 1956 and consisted of from $50,000 to $100,000 in wads of fresh bank notes delivered in cartons for the Prime Minister's own attention."[58] Lapalme has been depicted as precursor of the Quiet Revolution that began under his successor, Jean Lesage, in 1960. But he was not notably in favour of labour, and generally English Quebec supported him as unanimously as it had supported his three predecessors – Gouin, Taschereau, and Godbout.

The overwhelming and consistent support of English Quebec for the Liberals shows not merely that the *Star*'s support of Duplessis had little effect on its readers, but also that McConnell was hardly representative of the English community in his personal support of Duplessis, any more than he had been in his support of Meighen and Patenaude in 1926. It seems to follow that McConnell helped Duplessis not out of fear of Lapalme but because, like most Quebecers, especially French-speaking ones, he simply thought Duplessis to be the abler leader, as was confirmed several times by Duplessis's victories in provincial general elections. In any case, organizationally the federal and the provincial Liberal parties were one until 1964, and if McConnell sent money to Mackenzie King and Louis St Laurent, which has been on occasion hinted but never substantiated, he was effectively also enriching Lapalme's electoral coffers. If this is true, there is no obvious general personal advantage that McConnell had to gain from a renewed Union Nationale government, and he probably could have put up quite comfortably with a Liberal one.

The question, then, is whether there was some general quid pro quo that McConnell obtained from his political contributions, apart from those already discussed, and, if there was, whether this can be understood in the context of party financing more generally, which has been described as evolving from the "cottage industry" of the Taschereau years into the "mercantile venture" of the Duplessis era.[59] The chief fundraising method used by Duplessis was unofficial taxation, in the form of the sale of licences and permits, particularly liquor licences. Duplessis had no licences or permits that could have been of use to McConnell – least of all, of course, liquor licences. Another method was kickbacks, through which the prices of goods bought by the provincial government were jacked up. McConnell's products in 1952 and 1956 were newspapers and sugar, neither of which was of interest to the provincial Department of Colonization and the Government Purchasing Service, whose kickback activities between 1955 and 1960 were the subject of an official inquiry. If the province was to buy sugar from any Quebec refinery, it was the beet refinery at Saint-Hilaire, which Duplessis refused to close despite a plea by McConnell to do so.

It has, however, been maintained that licences and kickbacks were merely supplementary to the contributions by large corporations.[60] Since there seems to be no published figures of the relative amounts obtained by Duplessis from these three sources of funding, it is impossible to evaluate this allegation in detail. But, even if large corporations did contribute largely, there is no evidence that they did this through McConnell, and indeed a survey of McConnell's major investments in the 1950s does not disclose which, if any, stood to gain favours from Duplessis. Indeed, as will be described in the following chapter, with regard to timber rights and newsprint prices, we find that Duplessis – by interfering with the market to lower the cost of newsprint – was potentially threatening the profits of McConnell's one major investment at the time in pulp and paper, Consolidated Bathurst, ostensibly in order to help the *Star*.

Favouring a pulp and paper investment of McConnell's by giving it timber rights, and then reducing the price of newsprint sold by the same corporation, was a best a contradictory strategy for winning alleged bribes from McConnell. It made no sense.

It should also be pointed out, first, that political donations were not limited by legislation until the Quebec Election Act proclaimed in 1964, the year after McConnell's death, and, second, that the kind of contributions made by McConnell, as described by Black, were not prohibited by law until fourteen years later, in 1977. None of this is to suggest that McConnell's contributions are not mysterious. But they were not illegal, and they took place in the context of substantial giving to causes from which he could never have dreamt of deriving advantage, such as McGill, or to individuals, and not merely through his Foundation, who were clearly in no position to help him in return.

With the possible exception of Black, commentators on McConnell's relationship with Duplessis have engaged in no more than innuendo.[61] Nobody has so far alleged any specific favours granted by Duplessis to McConnell. In fact, there are substantial reasons for thinking that McConnell was indeed giving to Duplessis's "good works," and no more. The first is McConnell's relationship with Jean Lesage. The Liberal Premier Lesage prided himself on breaking the Duplessis mould, on rooting out all the corruption associated with the Duplessis era and the Union Nationale government that he had replaced. He indeed became known as the father of the Quiet Revolution that led to the destruction of the English-language domination of the Quebec economy and to at least half a century of profound instability in the Canadian federation. Yet Lesage opened one of the last of McConnell's big charitable projects, the Griffith-McConnell Home for the elderly in Côte-St-Luc, and he also vigorously asked McConnell to make donations to various charities on his behalf.[62] The recorded requests were for $200,000 and $150,000, and both were complied with, the latter amount increased by McConnell himself to $175,000. Eventually, this $375,000 seems to have grown to $1,030,050, a sum that probably exceeds all the money paid by McConnell to charities on behalf of Duplessis. No allegation has yet been made that McConnell personally benefited in any way from these donations at the request of Lesage, which did not differ materially from the donations to Duplessis's charities, except that Lesage's were generally more specifically Catholic.

Secondly, in order for it to make sound economic sense for McConnell to bribe Lesage, it would, as in the case of Duplessis, have to be proved that there was some correspondence between the amounts of the alleged bribes and the benefits alleged to have been gained, or indeed a distinct monetary advantage in the benefits over the bribes. It would have to be shown that the charities thus benefited by McConnell in some way offered some political advantage to Lesage as the notional recipient of the bribe, even apart from any advantage demonstrably gained by McConnell. There is no evidence whatsoever for any of this.

A few other comments on McConnell's relationship with Duplessis are in order. First, many of Duplessis's policies were hardly unique in the Quebec context. As we have already seen, most twentieth-century Quebec premiers were in favour of greater autonomy for their province. Even Taschereau, and certainly Godbout, were hardly pawns of Ottawa. Duplessis, moreover, was clearly a father of Quebec nationalism, his proudest achievement being his provincial flag, with which he replaced the Union flag on the Legislative Buildings in Quebec City. His relationship with English-speaking Quebec grew increasingly cordial, but never to the point where predominantly English-speaking constituencies would vote for his party. His relationship with Ottawa, particularly Louis St Laurent, was often frosty.

Unlike most businessmen, inside or outside Quebec, McConnell was very familiar with Duplessis's nationalism, particularly through his cultivation of Judge Thomas Tremblay, who was officially charged with the valuation of shares in the expropriation of Montreal Power and then of Montreal Tramways, of which McConnell was a shareholder. McConnell was deeply hostile to what he saw as the insufficient compensation awarded by Tremblay. It is unlikely that he was pleased either with the Tremblay Report on relations between the federal government and Quebec, which offered an elaborate defence of the uniqueness of Quebec as a society within Confederation. More perhaps than any other official document, the Tremblay Report foreshadowed the nationalist debates that would be unleashed for decades after the death of Duplessis in 1959.

Yet, since he saw provincial authority as a bulwark against the centralization that an election of the CCF in Ottawa would bring, McConnell was much more in favour of provincial autonomy than probably most English Montrealers. He was acutely aware of Duplessis's aggressive assertion of exclusive provincial jurisdiction over McConnell's two chief interests, health care and education. He was also aware that far more extreme nationalists, such as André Laurendeau, were waiting to assume power, which must have inclined him to be tolerant of the relatively mild aspirations of Duplessis and Tremblay. When Tremblay became a patient at the Montreal Neurological Institute, McConnell became a frequent visitor, and they are said to have friendly enough later to go fishing together.

Duplessis's relationship with St James Street was generally much better than with Ottawa. This suggests that the Street, although the centre of Canadian business at least until the Depression, was something of a world unto itself, curiously unrepresentative politically of even English Montreal, to say nothing of the rest of English-speaking Canada. It could have no rational or even natural affinity with the suspicious and even hostile stand towards French Quebec of many Toronto Conservatives. Its own politics were, for historical reasons already outlined, more pragmatic. Thus, much of the Street perceived that Duplessis was probably the best bet for stability and a policy of laissez-faire, although English Montreal generally never voted for him.

McConnell himself was an oddity on St James Street itself, however, just as St James Street was sui generis in the contexts of Quebec and Canada. He had left Toronto to work in Montreal, and, unlike many others who took this path, he stayed. Like many Ontario immigrants, he never spoke French. This was not because he refused to learn, but because he had no linguistic gifts and managed well enough without learning it. As early as 1904, it may be recalled, he had confessed to Lil how much he admired some multilingual German Jews whom he had met, and how they made him feel "small" by comparison. He certainly was no linguistic chauvinist or racist; the names of Dick de la Rozière, E.-A. Robert, Rodolphe Forget, and Robert Silvercruys readily come to mind as French-speakers with whom he had had long association. Nevertheless, the established English families of the province, such as the Prices and the Dunns of Quebec City, and the Molsons and the Drummonds of Montreal, by contrast, largely spoke French to some extent, sometimes extremely well. They had chosen to stay over generations, and they felt that they belonged in Quebec as McConnell could never feel.

Finally, the picture McConnell as the power behind the throne during the Duplessis years fails to take into account certain basic facts. From 1945 onwards, when not bedridden with illness, McConnell was often abroad. He held no public office, he turned seventy in 1947, and in 1953 he gave the position of publisher of the *Star* to his son John. How could such an old man, increasingly crippled with arthritis and eventually stricken with leukemia and numerous other afflictions, and seldom seen in public after 1955, been such a powerful and sinister figure? Moreover, how could nearly everything that he is alleged to have stood for disappear in hardly more than a decade after his death? Without answers to these questions, McConnell critics may be well advised to think again.

So much for McConnell's politics on the national and provincial stages. Internationally, he was very much the same man, particularly in his deep and abiding antipathy to socialism and communism. As an example, take McConnell's close ties to one of the leading British politicians of the mid-twentieth century, Anthony Eden. McConnell had known Eden since the 1930s – when he and Churchill were two of the few voices against the British government's policy of appeasement towards fascism – and he met him again at the Quebec Conference of 1944. With the onset of the Cold War, Eden's strong anti-communist stance won McConnell's warm admiration, and the two became close at a personal level as well. Eden stayed several times at Pine Avenue when on his way to or from Ottawa or Vincent Massey's house near Port Hope, Ontario, and it was almost undoubtedly McConnell who arranged for an honorary degree to be presented to Eden by McGill in November 1950. When Eden received an honorary LLD at Columbia University in 1951, McConnell enthusiastically fired off copies of the *Star*'s coverage of Eden's address on that occasion all over the world.

La cité entre bonnes mains

"J'allais justement te confier la direction de mes affaires"

Cartoon from *Le Devoir*, depicting J.M. Savignac of the Montreal
city council, with a picture of Duplessis in the background, coming
to deliver the business of the city into the hands of a woman
representing McConnell interests in the *Star*, sugar, flour, etc.,
6 December 1951. Private collection.

In 1953 Eden succeeded Churchill as prime minister. His administration is now
most remembered for its role in the Suez Crisis, when British and French forces
invaded Egypt in October 1956 to wrest control of the Suez Canal from President
Gamal Abdel Nasser, who had seized it from the Anglo-French company that had
built it. McConnell naturally supported Eden's effort: for him, the invasion represented a defence of capitalism against communism and Soviet imperialism. When
George Ferguson wrote a less-than-enthusiastic editorial on the invasion in the *Star*,
McConnell summoned him to Pine Avenue for a rare dressing-down.

Unsupported and indeed opposed by the United States, whose policy on the matter
was largely determined by Secretary of State John Foster Dulles, McConnell's former
colleague on the board of International Nickel, the invasion stalled and failed.[63]
Lester Pearson, the Canadian minister of external affairs, proposed a United Nations
peacekeeping force to extricate the British and the French from the situation. The
proposal was accepted, and Pearson won the Nobel Prize for Peace.

But many in Canada and elsewhere in the Commonwealth saw Pearson's intervention as tantamount to a betrayal of imperial interests. Soon, indeed, the Suez Crisis
came to be widely seen as the last nail in the coffin of the British Empire, the begin-

ning of Britain's final retreat from overseas and the end of Britain itself as a great power.[64] There can be no doubt that McConnell was appalled by the fiasco of Suez and by the humiliation of Britain, the empire, and Eden in particular. For Britain and the empire he could do little. But his sympathy for the plight of the prime minister, within months to be driven from office by illness and shame, was immediate.

In the midst of the crisis, Eden had suddenly decided to retreat to Jamaica for a rest of several months. At the beginning of May 1957, McConnell invited him to stay in Montreal before he was due to sail back to England on the 28th. Eden accepted the invitation but stayed with McConnell only a night and remained exhausted and ill on his return home. Their surviving correspondence in the Eden papers reveals a relationship of remarkable trust. It also demonstrates how closely McConnell was following both world affairs and the stock market until almost the very end of his life. In fact, it offers about the only extant evidence of how he advised others on how to invest.

In the first of the surviving letters between them, after Eden's visit, McConnell recommended vegetable salt from Harrods and sent Eden a copy of a *Star* photograph of him with the Masseys at Port Hope. By July 1957, Eden had finally been ousted from office and was looking for a new house. McConnell offered him a gift of £4,000, tax free, to help, which Eden accepted. "Rest Eat – and Sleep all you can," McConnell urged.[65] They discussed John Diefenbaker, the new Canadian prime minister, whom they both liked.[66] Eden proposed to put his new house in the name of his wife, Clarissa, and McConnell replied: "It is high time some friend would show appreciation for your wonderful public service and how better can I show mine [than?] through Clarissa?"[67] To Clarissa herself, who told him of Eden's improving health, McConnell wrote: "This assurance brings me great reward for what *little* I have done. He has done *so much*: in such a selfless manner, and at what cost to his health!"[68]

In November, McConnell sent Eden £1,000 to cover his expenses for travelling to Bermuda. Then McConnell himself was confined to bed for several weeks with a cold, and he would remain ill with influenza for over three months. The Edens invited him and Lil to join them for a holiday in Cornwall, but the McConnells themselves went instead to Nassau. He invited Eden to write a few articles for the *Star* and also offered to arrange for the purchase of Eden's serial rights for his memoirs.[69] It was, however, Suez and its consequences that dominated their correspondence. On this episode, the two men resembled two old lions licking their wounds. Both were well past their prime, Eden defeated and discredited, and McConnell with no comparable expertise in politics or foreign affairs. Eden, nevertheless, shared with his "trusted friend"[70] some of his frank opinions in retirement, not least because of his self-imposed silence in England and because McConnell was so far away.

By the beginning of 1958, Eden had found a house in Wiltshire, and McConnell offered him £1,000 for furnishings. Through that year, the two corresponded on the security of oil supplies for Western Europe and on Eden's Canadian investments. Eden compared Nasser to Mussolini and likened Nasser's relationship with the Russians to that between Mussolini and Hitler. Particularly concerned that Nasser controlled the oil pipelines as well as the Suez Canal, he wanted Western Europe to get "the larger share of its oil and gas supplies from Canada and maybe Nigeria." He noted that the question of exporting Canadian oil through Montreal was being canvassed. Were it not for currency problems, "it would be very good business for us to fetch it from there across the Atlantic."[71] McConnell advised that Shell Oil could probably solve the oil problem by drawing oil from Venezuela and elsewhere where the freight rates were not exorbitant, using large tankers recently turned out by British shipyards. Western Canadian oil, he added, could not be soon shipped through Montreal because the Trans-Canada Pipeline could not start delivering until 1959. Dulles, he felt, was reaching the conclusion that the United States had made a mistake in hoping to replace British influence in the Middle East with its own.[72] Eden replied bitterly that the United States now had hardly a friend left: "I assign a good deal of this to Dulles personally. I would only write this to you. He does not give an impression of candour in his dealing. I think that is an English understatement. With a stronger President [than Eisenhower] that might not matter but, as it is, it is something near a calamity."[73] To this McConnell responded: "The views you hold, and have expressed in confidence concerning Dulles are, alas I fear, very generally held, but he is 100% down on Communism and that must stand to his credit."[74]

In July 1958 McConnell offered his final judgment on Eden's place in history, bearing in mind the brutal suppression of the Hungarian Revolution that occurred simultaneously with the Suez Crisis and the Soviet offer to build the Aswan High Dam in Upper Egypt: "It is now known to the whole world how thoroughly justified your action was when you saw clearly, before anyone on this side of the water, that the Russians were preparing to enter, but the United Nations cease-fire resolution, followed by the Eisenhower doctrine, put Nasser in the saddle, and it may be that the Russians will gang up with him now."[75]

With regard to his investments, Eden told McConnell that he has been advised to sell his holdings in the CPR while McConnell was in Florida and unable to offer an opinion. Eden had divided the proceeds between Shawinigan and the Hudson's Bay Company. McConnell regretted that Eden had sold his CPR holdings at a loss, but he noted that the entire market had receded on average in excess of the decline in CPR shares. Nonetheless, he approved of Shawinigan, which was well managed and operated a profitable chemical company, and the HBC had extensive oil and mineral rights in the West. He and Eden agreed that the CPR always had to contend with "the menace of the nationally-owned Railway [the CNR] whose deficits are absorbed by the tax-payers."[76] Eden wanted McConnell to review his portfolio. "It sounds like an impertinence," he admitted, "but it is a result of my unbounded faith in your advice and the good results of the earlier investments in such things as Aluminium, B.A. [British American] Oil, and Howard Smith Paper."[77]

In 1959 McConnell reported to Eden that Beaverbrook had had a nasty fall but was still asking him for donations to the University of New Brunswick. When the Conservatives won the elections that October, McConnell wrote: "Cheers for [Harold] Macmillan and the good judgment and sound common sense of the British people," who were assured of "five more years of efficient and capable Government."[78] By now, the end of their long friendship was approaching. Afflicted with arthritis and anemia, McConnell was unable to holiday with the Edens in the West Indies or even to accept Beaverbrook's invitation to inspect his Art Gallery and other gifts to the university in Fredericton. In March 1961 he reported to Eden that Lil had had a bad fall in the attic of the house on Pine Avenue, tripping on a roll of carpet while looking for magazines to send to the Boys' Clubs. She broke a wrist, bruised her ribs, cracked a kneecap, and splintered her teeth, necessitating a stay of three months at the Royal Victoria Hospital, where she also had a gallstone removed. Nevertheless, by the end of July 1963, only four months before his own death, McConnell told Eden that he and Lil were in "pretty good shape" despite the unprecedented heat, which was making even Dorval oppressive. He also told him of the new subway under construction in Montreal, "so you will see Montreal is progressing."[79]

Along with the Suez Crisis, which it overlapped, the Hungarian Revolution and its aftermath gave McConnell an opportunity both to vent his anti-communist views and to demonstrate the extent of his concern for people in need. When the revolution was crushed by Soviet tanks on 4 November 1956, to the horror of much of the world, 200,000 refugees flooded into Austria, 39,000 of whom were permitted to settle in Canada. As the Quebec Provincial Division of the Red Cross was to report the following year, in the month of December 1956 alone, 4,000 arrived in eastern Canada by ship. Of these, 700 were processed in Quebec City. Five planeloads arrived in Montreal and others by train, and 350 were immediately "clothed with funds donated by a well-known citizen of Montreal."[80] McConnell, entirely anonymously, financed this program of humanitarian relief, the full dimensions of which are unknown. As J.W. Knox, son of Frank Knox and later the president of the Canadian Red Cross, recounted in a letter to Lil in 1963: "When reports of the exodus of Hungarian Refugees to Austria reached Canada, Mr. McConnell took action immediately. Before any of the free nations or international organizations reacted to the emergency, he instructed us to ensure that refugees arriving in Austria should be properly fed and clothed at his expense. As this situation developed and Hungarian refugees arrived in Canada, we were further instructed to see that they were met at both ports and airports and adequately clothed to face a Canadian winter. This task involved thousands of refugees and lasted many months ... It was largely, totally in Quebec, his unsolicited generosity which underwrote most of the cost of this operation."[81] The amount that McConnell gave to the Hungarian refugees included at least $10,000 from the McConnell Foundation, but he may have given more out of his own resources.[82]

Such were the patterns of McConnell's political involvement, both domestically and internationally, from just before the First World War to the early 1960s. At this point, it is useful both to summarize the main features of that story and to relate them to the larger picture of McConnell's personality and career. In the first place, it must be emphasized that, though McConnell was a conservative both temperamentally and intellectually, the precise content of his conservatism is difficult to define. Certainly, as someone who enjoyed almost meteoric economic and social success early in his career, and never lost it, he had ample reason to see much to conserve even beyond his material assets, especially the political and the social systems that had made it possible for him to flourish. The capitalism that he exemplified was not a theoretical construct for him but the context in which he functioned best. And so he fought to defend his money and what it could buy. But it is facile to attribute his conservatism purely to economic self-interest. It is misleading, too, if only because he gave away probably most of his money, often anonymously, for the use of others.

Canada in the twentieth century witnessed unprecedented social mobility and economic upheaval, and McConnell was merely one example of how these changes shaped an individual. The question thus arises: If he was instinctively conservative and yet constantly evolving with his society, what was there left for him to conserve? This question of what to conserve was a central one for those of his contemporaries whose views McConnell found most sympathetic. Their answer lay not in party platforms, in ideologies, or in dogma. In the face of ferocious challenges, McConnell and his business friends in particular had no choice but to be pragmatic even about capitalism – unstable and creatively destructive as it might be – itself.

McConnell himself believed that the reform of capitalism was essential in the wake of the Depression, in order for capitalism to survive. Specifics about which things he believed needed to be reformed are, unfortunately, wanting. But, like many of his friends, he came to espouse elements of what was later known as the welfare state, such as unemployment insurance, and he personally took initiatives in promoting state intervention in health care and in higher education. With all his staggering stock-market losses during the Depression, it may be presumed that he was also not fundamentally opposed to regulation of the excesses of holding companies and investment trusts, and his preoccupation with funding war, hospitals, and universities implies that he supported the introduction of income tax in 1917 and its imposition for the remainder of his life, notwithstanding its heavy burden upon him. There is certainly no record of his opposition to either of these measures.

While narrowly defined self-interest was not what motivated McConnell and his friends, something more fundamental may well have. This was their mid-Victorian sense of order, which they had seen largely shattered by 1918. Without idealizing life in the last quarter of the nineteenth century, they understandably looked back on their childhood as a time of relative peace, free of world war and economic collapse. More significantly, in their recollection although perhaps less in fact, the Victorian period was one of emotional security, in which social, moral, and religious norms seemed to reinforce a belief in steady progress, as opposed to fanatical reaction or revolution or cataclysm. Others might preach continuing revolution, but it was not fundamentally irrational or perverse for McConnell and his friends to seek equilibrium in the restoration of what was familiar as they faced the first half of the twentieth century, with its unprecedented bloodshed and destruction.

Yet, if peaceful progress was what they were trying to restore, it is a mistake to assume that they had a clear vision of the interests of their class, however defined, to defend at all costs. Most of them were essentially self-made, and none more than McConnell himself. They clung to no ideological investment in a fixed social and economic order. What they were fighting to conserve and to restore was the orderly and the peaceful society that had given them their start and that was free enough to permit the sort of rise that they had known in their own careers. It was this notion of freedom that was central, and that enlisted them to the defence of democracy and capitalism in the face of central planning and socialism.

In retrospect, theirs seems to be a largely, though not an entirely, doomed vision, chiefly because the underpinnings of their Victorian memories of order were relentlessly but not irreversibly eroding throughout their lives. The fate of two pillars of the Conservative legacy of Sir John Macdonald, which McConnell embraced for almost his entire career, captures this decay. One was Canadian industry protected by tariffs. McConnell worked hard and successfully, for almost fifty years, to preserve tariff protection for St Lawrence Sugar. But he lived to see the sugar industry successfully prosecuted for violating anti-combines law, under the same government that had shielded the sugar industry from criticism and ruin throughout the Second World War. Then there was the British Empire, which McConnell spared no effort in supporting only to see, six years before the end of his life, Canadian troops act to help separate the British from their enemies the Egyptians, during the Suez Crisis. It is true that new forms of equilibrium were emerging, and likewise new assets and visions to conserve, and most of all new opportunities for the enterprising. It is also true that the sugar refiners remained protected by tariffs over the half-century that McConnell was president of St Lawrence Sugar, and that the empire likewise survived in shadowy form. But the mid-Victorian certainties never were to revive, and McConnell could only dimly perceive a newly emerging order, and faintly hope for the best from it.

It did not help that there was a noticeable lack of institutional support for the conservative cause. McConnell's own religion turned against capitalism before he was forty. The Methodist Church called for the "conscription of wealth" as early as 1917, and for a centrally planned economy as early as 1918; and its successor, the United Church, which McConnell generously supported, increasingly embraced the idea of democratic socialism in the decades that followed. The Conservative Party of Canada itself, under various names, produced policies and leaders from 1911 to 1956 that contradicted one another. In the face of Macdonald's firm support of the CPR, Arthur Meighen introduced the legislation creating the CNR, to the hostility of most of St James Street. Meighen also introduced military conscription in 1917, but, by the Second World War, both conscription, Meighen himself, and his firm imperialism had been largely rejected by his own party. From the First World War onward, then, Canada lacked a successful political party with a coherent conservative vision.

There were, however, many conservatives, some of whom belonged to and even led parties not called Conservative, such as Mackenzie King and Maurice Duplessis. Much more depended on the personalities of individuals than on party labels, and McConnell, ever the salesman, adopted this fact as an operating principle. King, the longest-serving of Canadian Liberal prime ministers, would have bridled at being called conservative, but he was no activist; and despite his mixed loathing and admiration of the rich, he did less to confront conservative businessmen than R.B. Bennett, himself a successful and rich businessman of the most Tory hue. Bennett exacerbated many of the contradictions of Canadian conservatism, and he could not even agree with his lifelong conservative friend Lord Beaverbrook on imperial free trade. In England, Winston Churchill switched parties three times, and Beaverbrook was not much sounder as a party man. The maxim that in politics there are no friends, only allies, applies to McConnell as it does to all of these politicians.

Although he had several friends with whom he took holidays, engaged in sports, and invited to his houses, McConnell did not associate with politicians except formally. Probably the only exceptions were Anthony Eden and Mackenzie King, to whom he became close only when he was in his late sixties. Nevertheless, at various times, McConnell cultivated many of these politicians – especially Meighen, Bennett, Duplessis, and indeed King – largely because their opponents were to him more distasteful. As the politicians whom he favoured often disagreed with one another, and as he himself left such a sparse record of his political views, it is difficult to determine when and to what extent he agreed with each. Yet, since he had no desire to determine the course of high politics, and since he in fact exercised no such influence, this difficulty does not matter. What is more interesting perhaps is why he and other rich and conservative businessmen were so marginal. In McConnell's own case, an aversion to open confrontation was one reason, while, for him as for others, the extremely limited and gradually declining influence of St James Street and English Montreal in Quebec was another.

Despite his conservatism, by instinct and in action, McConnell tended to favour non-partisan, coalition governments in times of crisis, Ramsay MacDonald's in Great

Britain as well as Borden's in Canada. His changes in political allegiance did not affect his close friendships with both Liberals and Conservatives over many decades, through war and peace. And, despite his quiet switch to support of the Unionist Government of 1917, he revered Laurier even decades later, as seen in his agreement to serve as honorary vice-chairman of a fundraising campaign to erect a statue of Laurier in Dominion Square in Montreal. Always conscious of a possible change of government, McConnell also cautiously cultivated that bitter enemy of Meighen and Bennett, Mackenzie King.

McConnell's pragmatism did not extend to socialists, Social Creditors, communists, or fascists. He was always in the mainstream of politics, in the sense of supporting one or the other of the major parties. Essentially, he was what in a later day might be called a compassionate conservative in matters of social policy, and a largely unapologetic capitalist economically. As a publisher of a major newspaper from 1938 onward, he tried to shape public opinion along similar lines, leaning towards the parties of the governments in power in Ottawa and Quebec City, not because he was a partisan but because he thought he would be more likely to achieve his non-partisan goals through sitting governments. Pragmatism in political allegiance among newspaper owners had, of course, hardly been begun with McConnell. Lord Atholstan was a pragmatist par excellence, owing a Liberal newspaper (the *Herald*) and a Conservative one (the *Star*) simultaneously.

Yet McConnell perceived his personal interests very differently from the way Atholstan did. There was, it is true, probably no man more assiduous in defending and in developing his businesses than McConnell. But his personal interests extended also to a high regard for certain individual politicians and an unwavering devotion to political freedom and free enterprise. Above all, they focused on a keen sense of the public weal and on the untidy practical compromises necessary to the evolution of community as he saw it. It was this that was at the core of his political pragmatism.

Given his close association in later years with such fierce Tories as Herbert Bruce, George Drew, and Gratton O'Leary, as well as Meighen and Bennett of the older generation, it is hard not to speculate that, had McConnell never left Toronto, he might have become a lifelong Toronto conservative and imperialist businessman. Such friends of his as J.S. McLean, Sir Joseph Flavelle, C.L. Burton, and Sir John Eaton were such. Toronto conservatism, however, was much influenced by the Orange Order, and even where it was not, it displayed little or no sympathy for French Canadians or their aspirations. McConnell lived in Quebec for most of his life by choice, and apart from the two world wars his interests were overwhelmingly local. He was not an Orangeman or in the least hostile to Roman Catholicism, and he attracted a wide range of French Canadian admirers. McConnell was probably closest politically to the moderate conservative Methodist J.M. Macdonnell, the representative of the Toronto-based National Trust in Montreal in the 1920s and a friend of McConnell's even while serving in the cabinet of John Diefenbaker, except in respect of the empire, about which Macdonnell was tepid.

Imperialism for McConnell was thus distinct from Orangeism and from disdain for French Canadians and Roman Catholics, and so he was not in the least apologetic as one of the most outspoken imperialists in Montreal. Although he changed his position over details, he never wavered from the stirring ideal of imperial unity after his meeting with Joseph Chamberlain in 1904. In the context of Canada, McConnell's imperialism inclined him to the Conservative Party, which had been devoted to the empire since the time of Macdonald. British incompetence during the Great War had, it is true, turned Prime Minister Borden from a fervent imperialist to a decidedly sceptical one, if not an outright Canadian nationalist. In this respect, Borden was in advance of the views of most of the Conservative Party, including McConnell; but in Borden's successor, Meighen, McConnell found an imperialist soulmate. Bennett's imperialism, following Meighen's, was almost equally fervent, and so the imperialism of the Conservatives can account, at least in part, for McConnell's apparent allegiance to them throughout the interwar period, or at least until Bennett's defeat by King in 1935.

Nevertheless, imperialism was a cause fundamentally hobbled by profoundly differing economic and political interests in Great Britain and Canada. There was some meeting of minds at the imperial economic conference in Ottawa in 1931, but not much. Although there seems to be no record of McConnell's precise opinions on this conference, his strong support of Bennett at this time and afterwards suggests that he must have shared Bennett's firm defence of Canadian manufacturing interests. He probably shied away as much as Bennett from Beaverbrook's empire crusade of 1930–31, which called essentially for Great Britain to impose taxes on foreign food in order to favour foodstuffs from Canada and the rest of the empire, in return for which the empire was to buy British manufactured products. McConnell had moved considerably from his starry-eyed espousal of Joseph Chamberlain's vision of a highly centralized empire in 1904. Likewise, he had moved considerably from Laurier's reciprocity proposal of 1911. Nevertheless, in matters of foreign policy and unquestioning loyalty to the mother country in the face of threat, he remained, like probably most Canadians in the interwar period, unswerving, as he would confirm after the outbreak of war in 1939.

In contrast, King, the Liberal leader, was conspicuously anti-imperialist, and his refusal at the imperial conference of 1926 to countenance a common foreign policy for the empire has been widely interpreted by historians as one of the most decisive events in the eventual dissolution of the empire. Even McConnell's coming to support King and the Liberals in 1939, however, seems motivated by imperialism, in the sense of the paramount necessity to defend Great Britain in an hour of need. By then, with the replacement of Bennett first by Robert Manion and next by R.B. Hanson, the

Conservative Party was even less united in favour of fighting to save England than King and the Liberals themselves. The calamitously ineffective John Bracken, Hanson's successor, backed by Meighen and Toronto Tories, was more pro-British than Manion but also more of a progressive than a conservative. What McConnell cared about most was effectiveness, and King seemed to him to be more likely to organize Canada effectively for the British cause than any other politician, certainly among the Conservatives.

Whether it is was globally, imperially, federally, provincially, or even municipally, McConnell exhibited distinctly conservative reflexes. But he was constantly reacting to political and economic change with some imagination as well as often-surprising flexibility and sagacity. Nearly all of his specific causes are now of purely historical interest, but his preoccupations with two broader themes, the freedom of the individual and the practical welfare of the community – as opposed to any other collectivities, such as social classes – ran through them all. So did his loyalty to individuals whom he respected, and his cultivation of former or potential foes. To have been such a confidant almost simultaneously of Bennett, Meighen, King, Duplessis, and Eden, among many others not known for their friendship with one another, must have been unique.

CHAPTER SIXTEEN

Press Barons, Publishers, and Editors: The *Montreal Daily Star* and Other Newspapers, 1925–53

The advent of Mr. McConnell [in 1938], a gargantuan figure in the financial community, exorcised a good many of the ghosts which had frequented the building at 245 St. James Street. The first winds of change affected the payroll. All manner of injustices were corrected. We felt, and liked, the McConnell presence from the outset. There was no ambiguity about him.

David M. Legate[1]

Apart from St Lawrence Sugar and McGill University, McConnell was most often associated in the public mind with the Montreal *Star*, which was actually called the Montreal *Daily Star* for most of the period of his ownership. Affiliated in ownership with this newspaper were the *Standard*, the rural *Family Herald and Star*, and, more distantly, the Montreal *Herald*, also all published in Montreal. From the 1940s, his newspaper company also published *Weekend Magazine*, a Saturday supplement distributed widely with various newspapers through Canada.[2]

In 1925 Lord Atholstan, who as Hugh Graham had been one of the two founders of the *Star* in 1869, sold it and its affiliated newspapers to McConnell. By then, the English press in Montreal was more consolidated than it had been before and during the Great War. The White family owned the morning *Gazette*, and Atholstan owned the evening *Star*. Through his Montreal Star Publishing Company, Atholstan also published the afternoon *Standard* and a rural newspaper called the *Family Herald*. He did not own outright, but he had since 1914 and through a company that he owned called British American Publishing, maintained a considerable stake (72.5 per cent) in the Montreal *Herald*. Unlike the *Star*, this second *Herald* had been historically, and still remained, a supporter of the Liberal Party. Atholstan, a strident if erratic supporter of the Conservative Party, permitted it to remain Liberal and to be run largely autonomously. He reasoned that it was better for him to be the passive owner of the only Liberal paper in English Montreal than to permit Liberals to be the active owners of it. And although he did not interfere in its editorial policy, he ensured that there was no direct competition with the *Star* from the *Herald* for advertising revenue.

Lord Atholstan (Sir Hugh Graham), n.d.
Private collection.

With the bitter battles over the tramways over by 1918, the English press in Montreal seemed now rather staid. The *Gazette* had been long overtly Conservative and
the sober, austere voice of St James Street. The *Star* was more populist in flavour, but
seldom radical. Generally and often noisily, it was in support of the same Conservative Party. Its opposition to the leadership of the Conservatives by Arthur Meighen – a
close friend of McConnell – kept it lively and unpredictable, but such campaigns were
peculiar to Atholstan, and McConnell must have felt that he could abandon them
once he had taken over, as in fact he did abandon them, although not until 1938.

The circumstances of the McConnell purchase in 1925 were unusual and never
publicly known for thirteen years, and they are not well understood to this day. An
unpublished history of the *Star* records that, at the age of seventy-seven, Atholstan decided that after his death his paper should be left to a board of trustees.[3] He
approached McConnell to act as "ambassador" to these trustees, but for what purpose is unclear. There is the suggestion that Atholstan asked McConnell for a loan to
keep the paper in operation, and that McConnell responded with an offer to buy the
paper outright. At the time, Atholstan had one daughter and he wanted neither her
nor her husband to take over his businesses.[4]

In actuality, McConnell agreed to take over full control of the *Star* and its affiliates on Atholstan's retirement, incapacity, or death, while leaving Atholstan absolute discretion in both management and editorial policy in the meantime. On 23 June 1925 a new company, the Montreal Star Company Limited (MSCL), was incorporated by McConnell to replace Atholstan's old Montreal Star Publishing Company. The composition of its board, however, reflected the fact that control remained in the hands of Atholstan and the same nominees of his who had controlled his old company. McConnell did not sit on the board but he was represented on it by W.K. Trower, who was also working for Montreal Securities, one of McConnell's private investment vehicles.

Six days after incorporation, McConnell's new MSCL bought Atholstan's company for $2.5 million ($30,597,826 in 2008 terms), in the form of bonds and shares. In return, McConnell received the *Daily Star*, the *Standard*, the Montreal *Herald*, and the *Family Herald and Star*, with a total readership in excess of 450,000. (By contrast, the *Gazette* had 32,254 readers and *Le Devoir* 14,645.) The preferred shares of the MSCL yielded an annual dividend of 7 per cent or $105,000 (in 2008 terms $1,285,109). In the first three years of the agreement, this sum was divided between McConnell and Atholstan, the latter's share declining from $87,500 in 1926 to $27,500 in 1928. From 1928 to 1939, all the preferred dividends went to St Lawrence Sugar. These dividends then ceased except for 1947, when St Lawrence received $105,000 for the last time. As for the dividends from common shares, it appears that Atholstan received all of these up to 1928 when they were split into two, one half going to Atholstan and the other to the MSCL and St Lawrence Sugar.[5] From the records of St Lawrence Sugar, it is clear that this company, from 1926, held $100,000 of the $150,000 in gold bonds in its name. The interest on these bonds, amounting to $60,000, went from St Lawrence to Atholstan as part of the 1925 agreement, probably until Atholstan's death in 1938. At some stage before 1937, the remaining $500,000 of authorized bonds was issued to St Lawrence, and all $150,000 of the bonds were redeemed in 1941.

The thirteen years that Atholstan controlled the *Star*, after his sale of it, were increasingly frustrating to McConnell. The issues between them were dry and largely related to accounting. But they suggest much about McConnell's principles, and about how he differed from Atholstan, who was an immensely successful businessman in his own right. Expansion continued after 1925 under Atholstan's continuing management. In his report to the board for 1927, he noted a growth in advertising and circulation, the installation of new equipment, the occupation of a new building, and the conversion of deliveries to news dealers totally by truck rather than horse-drawn vehicles. By October 1928, business had so increased that the facilities could not accommodate the staff necessary, particularly in the editorial and composing rooms. Advertising had increased, too, from over twelve million lines in 1924–25 to sixteen million in 1927–28. Atholstan had, however, was failing to invest adequately in the plant, thereby limiting the prospects for further expansion.

McConnell, who was very concerned about any limits to the growth of what was really his investment, appeared before the board on 1 November 1928. He had visited the existing facilities, including a space next door in the old Standard Life Assurance Building, owned by Atholstan, which was being rented by the *Star*. He suggested bridging over Fortification Lane, between St James Street and Craig Street, for the entire width of the existing building, to enlarge the composing rooms without a large capital expenditure. He did not wish to erect a new building on the site of the decaying Standard Life building, since he "had in mind the erection of a great newspaper building some years hence." Atholstan agreed, but he rather lamely complained that without a new building the company would have to beg large advertisers, such as Eaton's, to withhold their orders for "splurging advertisements" as he was afraid of a loss of life among the workers in the present space.

But then the superintendent of the proofreading room said that the bridge would not materially relieve the congestion, and the director of the Montreal Public Works Department refused a permit for the bridge. McConnell's friend, a printer and fellow newspaper owner Fred Southam brought the foreman and the manager of the Hamilton *Spectator* to survey the problem. In the composing room, they found 80 people occupying 5,500 square feet, or 69 square feet per person, whereas good practice required from 85 to 100 square feet per person.

Still disturbed, McConnell and Atholstan met privately and there then followed a special meeting on New Year's Eve, 1928. Atholstan had the company revoke its option to purchase the old Standard Life property, a step that permitted the purchase of the property by another owner, who could then erect a new building in which the necessary space could be leased – the arrangement originally rejected by McConnell. It is not known who this prospective buyer was, but in February 1929 Atholstan reported to the board that negotiations had fallen through and that the printers' and typographical unions were threatening to strike over working conditions. He arranged for the company to buy the old Standard Life property, but nothing came of this and, by the end of the year, the site had been sold to a syndicate.

The Standard Life Building thus became the Star Building and a lease for space in it had been entered into by the *Star*. It is not clear from the board minutes whether Atholstan had any interest in the new syndicate, or whether he had been the undisclosed owner of the Standard Life Building from the beginning, but he had at least nominally sold the site; and if he was behind the syndicate he would be receiving rent under the new lease. Apart from these difficulties, the 1925 arrangement seemed to go reasonably well until 1931.

Atholstan's continued editorial independence from McConnell was clear in the *Star*'s raucous campaign against Lorne Webster's purchase of Montreal Water and Power, which ran the municipal waterworks, for $10 million, and his resale of it to

The Star Building, St. James Street, probably in May 1937, decorated
for the coronation of King George VI and Queen Elizabeth.
Montreal *Gazette* Archives.

the city, at a profit of $4 million ($49,494,505 in 2008 terms) to himself. Atholstan's
barrage of criticism was reminiscent of the *Herald*'s campaign against the takeover by
McConnell and Robert of the Montreal Street Railway, and it extended from February
1927 to August 1928. It did not involve McConnell this time, but Georges Beausoleil,
Imperial Trust, J.-L. Perron, and even Hudson Allison's brother George were implicated. Atholstan accused Webster of bribing the city council, and, although eventually Webster was acquitted of wrongdoing and was awarded even more money by an
arbiter, Atholstan's aspersions were central to the victory of Camillien Houde over
Médéric Martin in the mayoral elections of April 1928.

   Two years later, troubles internal to the newspaper began. They were highly technical in nature, and there seems to be a story behind them not revealed by the surviving
documents. The scent of this story suggests that McConnell believed that Atholstan
was manufacturing issues as an undisclosed beneficiary of their resolution, a resolution that Atholstan could arrange through his continued control of the MSCL.

In his annual report for 1933, Atholstan noted a general and continuous decline in advertising since that July. On the other hand, the paper had not reduced its advertising rates, while some of its competitors had reduced theirs by as much as a third, and now the outlook for local advertising, particularly by department stores, was better. At the end of May 1932, using the decline in revenues as his excuse, Atholstan announced that a general reduction of staff salaries was to be effected, as it had been at American newspapers.

Much more serious than even advertising revenue, according to Atholstan, was the potential of a new competitive threat posed by the *Herald*, which the MSCL controlled through its arrangement with British American Publishing, the nominal owner of the *Herald* since 1914 but controlled by Atholstan. In July 1931 Atholstan proposed a new agreement with British American to ensure the continued paramountcy of the *Star* in the Montreal market. Under this new agreement, British American was to surrender the *Herald* plant to the *Star* in the event of fire or some other disabling event at the *Star* plant, even to the exclusion of the use of the *Herald* presses by the *Herald* itself, at least until the *Star* editions came out. Furthermore, the *Star* was permitted to call upon the aid of the *Herald* in the event of a strike at the *Star*, and the *Star* might establish a school for printers on British American premises without compensation to the *Herald*. Finally, the *Herald* would govern the size of its issues, its advertising rates, and its subscription price according to the desires of the *Star*. Although the *Star* was to choose the managing director of the *Herald*, the *Herald* would be free to determine its own policy with regard to federal, provincial, and municipal politics. In consideration of all of these provisions, the *Star* would make good any deficits incurred by the *Herald*.[6]

McConnell was suspicious that British American was simply a front for Atholstan and was afraid of more self-dealing. Acting on his behalf, Trower immediately objected to the proposed arrangement, but the rest of the board overruled him and the contract between British American and MSCL was signed on 3 August 1931. Then, on 2 November of the same year, there was an important postscript to the renewed contract, stipulating the continuation of the monthly payments of $2,000 by the *Star* to the *Herald*, as instalments towards covering the deficits of the latter, which had been the practice since 1925.

On 21 March 1932 McConnell wrote to British American, with a copy of his letter to Atholstan. He said that he had obtained a legal opinion to the effect that the purported agreement of 3 August 1931 and the postscript to it of 2 November 1931 were "in no way binding upon the Montreal Star Company, Limited." Accordingly, "you [British American] will in due course be required to account for, and pay over to The Montreal Star Company, Limited, all moneys received by you from that Company under such writing [i.e., the purported agreement on the $2,000 monthly subsidy]."[7] Atholstan produced this letter to the board together with a legal opinion that affirmed the legality of the agreement.

Meanwhile, Atholstan was increasingly concerned that the share of advertising claimed by the *Herald* had grown permanently larger. In the spring of 1934, he proposed converting British American from a public company into a private one and buying out the *Herald*. McConnell immediately objected to the proposed purchase. Atholstan nevertheless ordered an appraisal of the *Herald* from C.M. Palmer of New York, who reported at the end of September 1934 that the *Herald* was worth up to $1,500,000. Trower retorted that these findings were "absurd" and complained that Palmer "comes to Montreal, spends four days and then attempts to tell the owners of the Star that it should become the purchaser of the Herald. It is extremely unlikely that he knew anything of newspaper conditions in Montreal before he arrived here … Mr. Palmer's statement that the Herald, which has had an unenviable reputation in Montreal for many years[,] should become a serious competitor to the old-established Star is unthinkable, provided the management was keen and alert and safeguarded its interests. This letter of Mr. Palmer's does not influence Mr. McConnell or me in any way towards changing our opinion that the Star should not become the purchaser of the Herald."[8]

Atholstan then proceeded to remind the board than, in his sixty-five years of running the *Star*, he had produced a paper whose earnings had been continuously twice those of any other paper in Canada. The dilemma that the paper now faced was either to increase circulation or to reduce advertising rates. At present, the paper had a circulation of 120,000 out of total English-speaking population in Montreal of 400,000. It was still making a profit of 1½ times that of the Toronto *Star*, at least in part because of its influence over the *Herald*. Still, the *Star*'s circulation had declined by 16,000 since 1932.

Trower noted that profits in 1923 or 1924 had been the same as in 1933. The profits were now due not to increased advertising or circulation but to a decline in the price of newsprint, the savings on newsprint prices totalling over $350,000 between 1926 and 1934. Trower's own figures did not support Atholstan's opinion that earnings of the *Star* were 1½ times those of the Toronto *Star*. Finally, if Atholstan was contending that the decline in circulation of the paper, since April 1932, of 16,000 copies per day, was due to the competition of the *Herald*, the *Star* controlled the circulation of the *Herald*. Atholstan immediately read out the agreement with the *Herald*, which showed that the *Star* controlled only the size of each issue, the rate for advertising, and the subscription price.[9]

In the midst of all this controversy, McConnell returned to Chicago for another operation on his hand. The enforced rest permitted him to pen a few poems. One was on Lord Atholstan and sums up his views at this stage, which also seems to disclose much about McConnell's views of ethics in business more generally. It reads:

> Lord Atholstan the fearless
> Who hides behind himself,

His way through life is cheerless,
Despite his power and pelf.

True courage seeks no cover,
And yet, tis fair always
While frankness like the sunshine
Illuminates the way.

In dealing with one's fellow men
Courage and frankness win,
Whilst guile, intrigue and shamming
One's troubles all begin.

When mighty riddle you do pose
And challenge me to guess,
Then perchance if the truth arose,
Have courage, answer 'yes.'

Oh Atholstan, how foolish
That you should thus behave,
Your actions are but mulish
Instead of being brave.

Face right about good Baron,
Turn squarely to the task,
For he who would the truth reveal,
Must first rip off the mask.

Let children play at make believe,
To them it is no sin,
But seriously, the game you play
You cannot hope to win.

And you are eighty-six my Lord,
Your days are short and few
Why not make haste to win accord
In place of troubles new?

Shall these long years so ill be crowned
Throughout the live long day

> By such deceitful scheming round
> What shall the Reaper say?[10]

The question of advertising dominated the next board meeting, on 3 November 1934. Advertisers had been complaining about the *Star*'s high rates, particularly in view of its declining circulation and the fact that Toronto papers, with higher circulation, were charging them less. Atholstan announced that, having been unable to increase circulation, he had decided to lower rates. Four days later, McConnell himself appeared at the next meeting, to protest against both the lowering of advertising rates and Atholstan's proposal to buy the *Herald*. Trower added that his figures showed that circulation was actually now increasing over that of the previous year, but Atholstan quoted rival figures in refutation.

On 18 April 1935 Atholstan announced that the *Star* had bought the *Herald* in March, following a meeting between him and McConnell. The meeting, on 5 March, was intended to establish peace between the two men, and it provided for arbitration of future contentious issues. The price for the *Herald* was $637,500 ($9,969,792 in 2008), for which the *Star* received all the shares of British American. British American owned all the shares of Herald Publishing and of the Herald Press, and these other two companies also came now to be owned by the *Star*.

But the *Herald* building – bounded by Juror (Vitre), St George, and Anderson streets – had been owned by Grand Central Park, a company owned by Atholstan himself. Atholstan arranged for British American, now owned by the *Star*, to take the title to this building from Grand Central Park, and also to assume his mortgage of $100,000 from the Standard Life Assurance Company, as part of its purchase price of $215,000 for the building. Whether or not Atholstan was an undisclosed beneficiary of the purchase by MSCL of British American, his ownership of Grand Central Park was not in dispute, and so he personally benefited from all these rearrangements by $115,000, the purchase price less the mortgage repayment.

With the purchase of the *Herald*, the situation of the *Star* seemed to improve. In May 1935 the University of Missouri awarded the newspaper a bronze medal for distinguished service in journalism, as a link between England and North America, between Canada and the empire, and between Canadian Roman Catholics and Protestants.[11] Atholstan announced to his board that circulation had increased substantially. But then the question arose of the appraisal of the *Herald* building, with a view to establishing the capital structure of British American for insurance and income-tax purposes. On 12 July, Trower lodged a protest against any change of the value of the fixed assets of the Montreal Star Company and its subsidiaries from book values, as determined by the agreement of 1925. The only qualification to this was new equipment and machinery, which had been entered into the books at cost. With this protest, a bigger battle than ever began. It was a bizarre fight, Atholstan's last after decades of self-righteous crusades. He seems to have confused book valuations on the balance sheet with depreciation allowances for income-tax purposes that yielded undepreciated capital costs. There may well have been motives now not clear, but, after besting McConnell over and over again since 1925, the old man was now losing his grip at last.

At the meeting of 7 September, Atholstan returned to the question of the necessity for new appraisals for income-tax purposes:

> From what I know of Mr. McConnell's views on ethical matters I venture to say that nothing would be farther from Mr. McConnell's mind than to deprive the State at this critical time in its history of any money to which it is fairly entitled ... Although in our balances it has been overlooked, it is true that a part of our machinery has been depreciated out of existence, some of it far below zero, and it is anything but fair to go on depreciating it further ... I maintain that the condition of the country makes it impossible to be over scrupulous. I maintain too that deliberate overvaluation of plant as a basis for depreciation would in any court of law be considered decidedly wrong ... To risk the question to the whims and caprices of two men as arbitrators would be highly improper because it would prove that we were willing to commit a wrong provided that two men could be induced to condone it ... In the discontinuance of the making of our depreciation allowances on a false basis of valuation, we are correcting a mistake without affecting the real value of our plant and buildings. We will be making our depreciation allowance on [an] actuality instead of a sham ... I am willing to enter into an agreement with Mr. McConnell to the end that any profit accruing to the stockholders of the company by rectifying the basis of value for depreciation shall be donated to the Salvation Army, the most needy, the most worthy, the most self-sacrificing of all our charities. If Mr. McConnell does not approve of such an agreement I will give every cent accruing to me.

On 27 September McConnell wrote to Atholstan that he emphatically protested against his proposed changes to the balance sheet: "There is no warrant for these changes either in law or under established accounting practice. The Balance Sheet cannot at will be changed by writing up the item of copyrights and goodwill and by writing down fixed assets as you propose to do ... the proposed changes would contravene my [1925] arrangements with you." They also, McConnell continued, violated a clause in his agreement with Atholstan of the previous March, reaffirming the present rates of depreciation as fixed: "I had hoped that the agreement of the 5th of March, 1935, marked the end of all controversy between us and that our future relations would be harmonious. Your proposed action, however, is such a flagrant disregard and violation of vested rights that I have no alternative but to resist it with all the means at my disposal, and to hold you, your heirs and legal representatives, as well as your nominees on the Board of Directors of the Company, personally responsible for all loss and damage which may be suffered by me as well as for all claims which the Company may have."[12]

Atholstan replied to McConnell in a letter dated 8 October: "You refer to an agreement of March 5th which provided that the annual rate of depreciation allowance should be 5% for plant and 2½% for buildings. It meant that and nothing more. It did not stipulate, nor did it mean, that we were not to change the capital figures to take into account wear and tear. If your views were to have precedence over those of the managers we would be treating some of our plant on the basis of a value that has been depreciated below zero, which would be not only ridiculous but flagrantly dishonest."

Trower retorted that he had not had time to study Atholstan's letter before the meeting, but there were things in it that were quite incomprehensible: "Either Lord Atholstan has very little knowledge of accounting practice with respect to depreciation or else he has been badly advised. The system of depreciation which the company has followed for the past ten years is sound in principle and one that is followed by all chartered accountants in preparing Balance Sheets and Profit and Loss statements … Why are we at this late date after following the old system for ten years changing it now? … The agreement [of March 5] seems to have established for all time the basis upon which the assets of the company were to be depreciated." The board voted to accept the appraisals, but on 16 January 1936 McConnell prevailed.

This is the last recorded controversy between the two men. Atholstan died on 28 January 1938 and McConnell at last gained control of the paper. By then, there had been a change of the guard in other major newspapers as well, in both Montreal and Toronto. At the Montreal *Gazette* in 1936, Senator Smeaton White, son of Richard White and president of the paper since 1910, died and was replaced by John Bassett, who was to remain president of the *Gazette* until 1956. At about the same time, George McCullagh took over the *Globe* and the *Mail and Empire* and merged them into the *Globe and Mail*. McCullagh was to control the *Globe and Mail* until 1952, when R. Howard Webster, a son of Senator Lorne Webster, bought it. McConnell was president of the Montreal *Star* from 1938 to 1953, and thus he, McCullagh, and Bassett were essentially contemporaneous in heading the three major newspapers in English Canada, apart from the Toronto *Star* and the Winnipeg *Free Press*.

Although the concentration of newspaper ownership was to become a political issue after McConnell's time, he never aspired to build a newspaper empire. He inherited the *Standard*, the *Family Herald*, and the *Herald* with the *Star*, but these were not his own acquisitions, and he seems not even to have made a bid for another newspaper. This made him very different from his friends among the English press lords, in particular Kemsley, Beaverbrook, Camrose, Rothermere, and Iliffe. It also

Financial Post cartoon showing George McCullagh of the *Globe and Mail*
watching McConnell take over the *Star*. B. Grassick, 5 February 1938.
Private collection.

made him different from the Southams in Canada, to say nothing of such people as
William Randolph Hearst in the United States. Moreover, although he was called by
some a press baron, McConnell had never been a journalist or built up a newspaper.
For him, the *Star* was a mature property in a mature industry, and he was to run it
with the same mature expertise as he was running St Lawrence Sugar. The newspaper was merely one of his interests, and, although he kept a close eye on it, he did not
disturb Atholstan's staff arrangements or influence editorial policy significantly.

McConnell, who was sixty when he gained control of the *Star*, was far too conscientious to see it and the fading *Standard* and *Herald* as mere playthings for his
retirement. But he was largely in retirement by 1938, at least from his other business
interests apart from St Lawrence Sugar, and there was the element of simple prestige in his being the president of the newspaper. Had Atholstan died or relinquished
his authority ten years before, McConnell's tenure of the newspaper might have been
very different.

On the last day of January 1938, McConnell solemnly walked behind the coffin
containing the remains of Lord Atholstan as it made its way from Atholstan's house
to his funeral at the Church of St Andrew and St Paul. Walking with him as honorary pallbearers were the leader of the opposition, R.B. Bennett, Chief Justice R.A.E.

John G. and J.W. McConnell enter Lord Atholstan's house before
his funeral at the Church of St Andrew and St Paul, 1938. Private collection,
courtesy of Mrs John M. Hallward.

Greenshields, Mayor Adhémar Raynault, Sir Edward Beatty, Dr Edward Archibald,
C.H. Cahan, and Sir Charles Gordon. McConnell dutifully published a fulsome tribute to his predecessor in the *Star*.

At the first meeting of the board under McConnell as outright owner, however,
on 31 May 1938, there was no mention of Atholstan. Although the chief bane in
McConnell's life was now removed, the new president swiftly announced that not a
single employee or member of the executive staff, "from office boy to Editor-in-Chief,"
was to be replaced. He also announced the conversion of the MSCL into a private
company, with the number of shareholders limited to fifty and the number of directors reduced from five to three. This action paralleled what he had done at St Lawrence Sugar the previous December, and it opened a way to creating an endowment of
the Foundation that he had established in 1937.[13] McConnell was, of course, the new
president, A.R. Carman the vice-president, and E.R. Whitrod (soon replaced by J.D.
MacKinnon) the secretary-treasurer. McConnell's son John became a director, and
the appointment of H.G. Brewer as general manager, in August 1939, completed the
partially new team, with Wilson McConnell joining the board in 1940 in succession
to Carman.

McConnell received congratulations from old friends and a wide variety of admirers. Dr Edward Archibald wrote:

You are giving up a great deal – the well-deserved fruit of hard work plus brains, both pushed to the limit for many years. You are giving that up in order to take on the job, as a public and high-minded citizen, of trying to lead public opinion and form public decisions in the way which you think right, and which all men of knowledge and of good will think right. That, I feel sure, must be your ambition. You will influence politics, from Dominion down to municipal, and you will influence individual life, through the daily written word, in the paths of rightness and sanity and humanitarianism. For that is your character. Atholstan did well; but you will do better; for you have finer qualities and your sincerity can never be doubted.[14]

Echoing these sentiments was Charlotte Whitton, executive director of the Canadian Welfare Council: "The Star has always been a powerful force in the advocacy of humane treatment of the causes of need and distress and in the development of community consciousness on behalf of those who are not able to be their own advocates. It can only be a cause of great gratification, therefore, to those who have benefited from its wise and sympathetic leadership in the past to know that its destinies pass into the hands of one whose generous and intelligent appreciation of human need and suffering have already been of such inestimable value to Canada as a whole, to scores of its social agencies, and to thousands of its citizens."

Few were explicit about what McConnell might actually do at the newspaper. Arthur Meighen reported to McConnell that "our old friend, H.B. Thomson," had described the succession as "a step in the right direction, as J.W. is full of horse sense and looks upon things in a practical way, even though he has not been a university professor." McConnell was "flattered, encouraged and highly amused" by Thomson's statement.[15] In response to Sir Joseph Flavelle's congratulations, McConnell made clear how well aware he was that economic power was already shifting from Montreal to Toronto. He recalled how Atholstan had launched a campaign in 1921 ostensibly to prevent Flavelle – as chairman of the Grand Trunk Railway and in anticipation of its absorption into the CNR – from moving the CNR headquarters to Toronto. As Flavelle had said to McConnell at the time: "J.W., two things I promise to leave in Montreal – the St. Lawrence River and the Montreal Star." McConnell now observed: "You faithfully kept that promise, and I shall now try to hold it [the Star] 'steady' at its Montreal moorings."[16] To demonstrate his commitment to his new role, he resigned nearly all his directorates in other companies.

The former premier of Quebec, L.-A. Taschereau, speculated that McConnell would now be studying political, social, and religious problems, and he invited him to join the Roman Catholic Church or the Liberal Party! Senator Raoul Dandurand wrote that, with the death of Atholstan, "all of a sudden, you discard 'le vieil homme' [Atholstan], your financial garb, your industrial and commercial associations and

Lord Tweedsmuir visits press room in the *Star* Building, McConnell at centre left, 24 October 1938. Montreal *Star* photograph, Montreal *Gazette* Archives.

– buckling on a brand of new armor – you step into the arena as a leader or moulder of public opinion rather than its invariable follower." A.D. Anderson, honorary treasurer of many fundraising campaigns in Montreal, urged him to fight "for clean living, high ideals in home and business life, the value of the Church in the Community and all its stands for." In October 1938 the governor general, Lord Tweedsmuir, honoured the *Star* plant with a visit.

What seems clear is that McConnell took his responsibilities as a newspaper owner very seriously, perhaps, paradoxically, too much so to make much of an impression as one. Probably to mark his new position, his friend Fred Southam gave him a copy of George Seldes's recent book *Lords of the Press*, which criticized some owners for turning their newspapers into vehicles of propaganda and distortion. With the book, Southam enclosed "The Creed of C.P. Scott of the 'Manchester Guardian'": "A newspaper is of necessity something of a monopoly, and its first duty is to shun the temptations of monopoly ... Neither in what it gives nor in what it does not give, nor in the mode of presentation, must the unclouded face of the truth suffer wrong. Comments are free, but facts are sacred. Propaganda, so-called, by this means is hateful. The voice of opponents no less than that of friends has a right to be heard. Comment also is justly subject to a self-imposed restraint. It is well to be frank; it is better to be fair."[17]

McConnell did not need any encouragement in this regard. Though the rise of the yellow press in England, the United States, and elsewhere in the late nineteenth century had started transforming the business of journalism into an enterprise with new dimensions of sordidness, serious newspapers continued to be seen as instruments for the mobilization of public opinion rather than simply as records of events or a source of entertainment, much less as mere vehicles for advertising. Their publishers and editors, accordingly, regarded themselves as custodians of the public trust, or so they said, even if they personally proved incapable of defending this trust except through the eyes of their political parties and their personal interests. In Montreal, this was the ethos of the White family's *Gazette* and Hugh Graham's *Star*, both of which, while adhering to the Conservative cause in the political arena, professed to be and generally succeeded in being guardians of the public virtue and promoters of public welfare rather than mere muckrakers or party broadsheets. Furthermore, many of those who came to own newspapers grew more sedulous than their predecessors in affirming themselves to be above party politics as the twentieth century wore on.

Of profound aid to this trend was the decline of the Conservative Party, as a force in both government and opposition after the First World War, and the rise of new parties such as the Progressives and the CCF. These developments deprived such big businessmen as McConnell of what had been their natural political home and permitted the emergence of the Liberals as the "national party," transcending the sharp divisions that had prevailed before Borden's Union government of 1917. Finally, even the "yellow" press, with its coverage of crime and sex, tended to transcend strict allegiance to party politics. Both *La Presse* and *La Patrie*, like the *Star*, were following a recipe – devised by the Scripps family, Joseph Pulitzer, and William Randolph Hearst in the United States – that called on newspapers "to forsake the pattern of narrow partisan advocacy for a new diet of entertainment."[18]

Thus, where the ownership of the press was involved, there never disappeared the ill-defined dimension of the public trust. This implied that a newspaper was not blind to changes in political realities. Atholstan, for example, was not an inflexible Conservative. He switched from Borden to Laurier and back to Borden, probably for personal advantage but possibly also sincerely out of principle. His successor as publisher of the *Star*, McConnell, began by supporting the Conservatives federally but then came effectively to support the Liberals. Provincially, as publisher, he began by supporting the Liberals but then switched to the conservative Union Nationale. In public, he claimed that his paper was non-partisan. He would probably have said that his paper supported whatever party was in power, which, in retrospect, basically turned out to be true. But his notion of the public trust did not entail blind support of all authority, even of the democratically elected variety. His principle was that a newspaper possessed the right to publish only all the news that it saw fit to print. It was not obliged to accept advertisements from those whom it opposed or to give uncritical coverage to them.

Of the major Canadian newspaper owners, McConnell alone owned significant businesses outside his newspaper, principally St Lawrence Sugar and Ogilvie Flour Mills. These companies, in both principle and practice, equipped him financially to take the notion of his public trust as publisher with great seriousness, an attitude to which he was predisposed in any case because of his perception of himself as a man of high morality. As probably the richest newspaper owner in the country, McConnell enjoyed an independence from others that may have been unique. He simply did not need the revenues of the *Star* to attain any material goals that he could conceivably desire. Nor did he have any specific economic interests that demanded defence in his newspapers. He often said that he wanted to transform the *Star* into the Canadian equivalent of *The Times* of London, which was then both the very symbol in his circle of probity and accuracy.

After the death of Atholstan, McConnell immediately did all he could to ensure the loyalty of the staff. Apart from sacking nobody except the directors related to Atholstan, he raised salaries and wages by $80,000, and he ordered alterations and improvements to the company garage as well as new wire-carrier equipment in the press room, reading machines for the composing room, and cameras and photographic equipment. On the journalism side, he changed the typeface and generally cleaned up the *Star's* appearance, and, because of a rise in the price of newsprint, he raised the paper's price from two cents to three cents. He appointed A.E. Whiting as manager of the *Family Herald and Weekly Star* and contributed $10,000 to advertise in these two papers.[19] As the weeks went on, he added more improvements and equipment, including Dodge trucks, a Studebaker coupe, and hoods and exhaust fans for the press, ventilation facilities, rubber rollers, mailing equipment, and much else, while also handing out Christmas bonuses totalling more than $25,000. In his annual report dated 31 August 1939, he announced that gross advertising revenue in 1938 had increased by $8,870 over that of 1938 and that circulation income had increased by $125,852.

Doubtless mindful of the extreme difficulties suffered by dependants of servicemen in the First World War, McConnell was ready to take care of his employees at the start of the Second.[20] On 18 September 1939 he announced that all employees of the Montreal Star company who enlisted for service would receive employment (though not necessarily their previous positions) after the war, and that for the duration of the conflict they would receive part-payment of their regular salaries while serving. Current salaries were to be paid for two weeks after enlistment. Following this, married men would be paid monthly the difference between their regular salary and their service pay. Single men and widowers without dependants were to receive a monthly sum, which, plus their service pay, would be equal to two-thirds of their regular salary. Single men and widowers with dependants would receive a sum not more or less than the provisions above, to be determined by the nature and extent of the dependency. The families of those who enlisted or were conscripted would be

Kevin and Paul O'Connor, *Montreal Daily Star* delivery boys,
buying $100 Victory Bonds from their own earnings.
Photograph by Lew McAllister, *Montreal Daily Star*,
26 April 1940. Montreal *Gazette* Archives.

eligible to benefits in the case of death, in accordance with the insurance plan already in effect.

In June 1940 McConnell announced that more than $40,000 was to be spent on alterations and improvements of the offices, plus another $25,000 on Christmas bonuses. The number of working hours in the composing room was reduced from forty-four to forty per six-day week, retroactively to January. As the war progressed, he periodically arranged cost-of-living bonuses for the workers, to conform to the adjusted cost-of-living index, in accordance with a general order of the National War Labour Board and the Wartime Wages Control Order of 1943.

After the war, in December 1946, McConnell announced the purchase from the Island Land Company of the property across from McGill University on which had previously stood the house of Sir George Drummond. This was on Sherbrooke Street, between Mansfield and Metcalfe streets, and it had cost $4,500. It was to serve as the site of a new building for the *Star* and its subsidiaries, replacing a car wash and gas station there.[21] As it turned out, however, McConnell was never to erect this building. It was left to his son John to construct a new facility on Craig (later Saint-Antoine) Street in 1961, which later became the home of the *Gazette*.

The rise in salaries, the provision of Christmas bonuses, and the signing of agreements with unions, as well as annual improvements in the machinery and equipment and offices, all point to McConnell's considerable care for the staff. The Christmas bonuses were particularly appreciated since it had been Atholstan's practice to dock pay for time taken off for Christmas and New Year's. In addition, McConnell would often look after the medical expenses of individual employees and their families and readily grant compassionate leave, and he also established a pension plan for the *Star* workforce in 1947.

Many of these efforts are attributable to McConnell's own values and character. But the country was changing as well, and the setting-up of the pension fund in particular was prodded by broader social trends. There were no strikes at the paper under McConnell's ownership, despite minor union activity.[22] Much as McConnell resented the largely American unions, and particularly what he perceived as the communist agitators within them, he had had years of experience of his own as a worker and as an employee. His attitude towards unions was therefore defensive rather than blindly hostile. Although he was prepared to permit the clerical staff to unionize, he was determined to resist the Newspaper Guild.[23] When he sniffed the possibility of more aggressive union organization, he demanded of his staff whether they really wanted John L. Lewis, the American labour leader, to run their paper.

Editorially, the most notable feature of the transition from the Atholstan era to that of McConnell was the *Star*'s shift from the Conservatives to the Liberals, in both Ottawa and Quebec City. This change of allegiance was confirmed by the divergence between the *Star* and the *Gazette* in 1940 on the issue of national service. In August of that year, the *Gazette* called on the King government to have Mayor Camillien Houde of Montreal arrested, under the War Measures Act, for having publicly urged a boycott of the National Resources Mobilization Act. The government declined on the ground that there had been no publication in print of Houde's words to give cause for this arrest, although the content of Houde's speech was well known. Government censors, furthermore, would not permit the publication of Houde's speech in newspapers, citing the Defence of Canada Regulations, which prohibited the publication of any document "intended or likely to cause disaffection to His Majesty or to interfere with the success of His Majesty's forces ... or to prejudice the recruiting, training, discipline or administration of any of His Majesty's forces." The *Star*, while not opposed to Houde's arrest, was decidedly less enthusiastic than the *Gazette*. A memorandum, apparently from John G. McConnell to his father, on the subject refers to the blatantly partisan stance that the *Gazette*'s John Bassett was taking on the matter.[24] This memorandum concluded that the *Star* had always found government censors "very co-operative," and that while the *Star* "understands and sympathizes with the

Gazette's desire to expose Houde and cause action to be brought against him," it felt that the attitude of the censors in this case was legally justified.

Frustrated by the censors, Charles Peters, the owner of the *Gazette*, then arranged for the Conservative leader, Richard Hanson, to read Houde's speech in the Commons. Once the speech was published in *Hansard*, where it was protected by parliamentary privilege, the government had no choice but to arrest and intern the mayor. The incident confirmed that the *Star* was increasingly falling into the Liberal camp and, while never flagging in its support of the war effort, was unwilling to support the shrill Toryism of the *Gazette*.

Apart from the change of party allegiance by the *Star* over national service, McConnell interfered surprisingly little with the editorial policy. He customarily discussed editorials daily with the editor, and we can probably safely conclude either that he approved of what was published or that what was published was thought to be in conformity with his desires. He appears also to have written or dictated certain editorials himself, chiefly about the war effort and philanthropy and religion.

Critics, such as Frank Scott, a McGill law professor and a prominent figure in the CCF, charged that McConnell used the *Star* to advance his own economic interests. But the charge is false. Acutely sensitive to any accusation of conflicts of interest, McConnell virtually forbade any mention of his other companies in his paper. The business section of the *Star* was notably skimpy generally, the similarly uncritical but more informative *Gazette* being in any case preferred by businessmen because it appeared in the morning. The *Monetary Times* and the *Financial Post* of Toronto, and the *Financial Times* of Montreal, as well as British and American publications, served those more seriously interested in business.

McConnell himself lacked journalistic experience and any interest in abstract ideas. He generally thought in neither party nor ideological nor philosophic terms. He was no Walter Lippman or J.W. Dafoe, but neither probably was anyone else in English Montreal. His retention of Atholstan's editorial as well as other staff at best maintained the editorial mediocrity of the old regime. Probably it did worse, inasmuch as the peppery Atholstan often wrote his own editorials and, for all his faults, possessed a keen sense of what would appeal to the public. McConnell was no Atholstan, in this as in other ways. It was inconceivable that the newspaper under McConnell's direction would publish an exposé, as the *Star* had in January 1914, exposing the corruptibility of the Quebec legislature.

The aged if respected Albert Carman, son of a superintendent of the Methodist Church, remained editor-in-chief in the transition from Atholstan to McConnell. On Carman's death in 1944, Samuel Morgan-Powell became editor-in-chief, a post he held until 1946. He was a poet rather than a gutsy journalist, and in later years he served as the *Star*'s theatre and arts critic. He described modern art, such as paintings by the Group of Seven, as "swill, not fit for pigs" and was known to throw typewriters down stairwells and to break up office furniture.[25] His very differences from McConnell suggest McConnell's essential tolerance, but they did nothing to create out of the *Star* the Canadian version of *The Times* that McConnell held out as his ideal. If the *Star* had wished, it could have explored the avant-garde poetry, novels, and painting – to say nothing of exuberant nightlife – for which Montreal was then known. But McConnell, like Bassett, had no interest in any of this. Furthermore, his retention of Englishmen, such as A.J. West as well as Morgan-Powell, failed to inject the liveliness of the English press into the *Star*, such as Lord Beaverbrook was offering up in his *Daily Express*, a newspaper that McConnell found vulgar and sensationalist.

The story was different at another newspaper that was part of the *Star* family, the *Standard*. On purchasing the *Star* in 1925, McConnell had planned to turn it over, one day, to his son John, born in 1911, who had long shown an interest in newspapers. Unlike his father, he was to become well educated, cultured, and a connoisseur of the arts. In 1931, after John had spent only two years at McGill, McConnell arranged with Sir Arthur Currie and Lord Bessborough for John to attend Trinity College, Cambridge, where John's Montreal contemporary Bartlett Morgan was also studying. Bartlett's father and the most cultured friend of the McConnells', Cleveland Morgan, of the department store and the Museum of Fine Arts, had also studied there. To act as a steadying influence on John, McConnell looked to Davidson Dunton, whose father, a Montreal notary, had died, and whom McConnell had first seen reading a lesson in church.

The two boys went to England with him and Lil. Within a few months, John surprised his family by marrying Evelyn Margaret Henderson, known as Peggy, one of the three daughters of George Henderson of Montreal, president of Brandram-Henderson, a paint company. The Hendersons were from Halifax and were close friends of the family of Victor Drury, who in 1937 was to become president of Canadian Car and Foundry and was already connected to McConnell through Gatineau Power and other International Paper and Power interests as well as Sherwin-Williams.

Drury's sister Gladys had married Max Aitken, later Lord Beaverbrook, and Peggy's mother had been her bridesmaid. It is said that Beaverbrook himself had approached McConnell to buy the *Star*, should McConnell's interest in it wane. He had also been trying to lure John to work for the *Daily Express* in London, although eventually it was Dunton whom he hired. At any rate, a new generation of McConnells was coming of age. Peggy had been at a finishing school in Lausanne with Mimi (Marjorie) Wallis, also of Montreal, who was to marry Wilson McConnell in 1935.

In 1938, having gained complete control of the *Star* group of papers, McConnell made John the publisher of the *Standard*, then a floundering weekly newspaper published on Saturday. At the time, John was a relative novice in the business, his only experience consisting of a short apprenticeship of a few months at *The Times*

Jack, Lil, and John McConnell with Davidson Dunton on
the *Empress of Britain*, 1931. Private collection.

of London and three years as a *Star* reporter. But he proved himself a quick learner, and, with the assistance of two close associates, Davidson Dunton as editor and Mark Farrell as assistant promotions manager, he soon turned the *Standard* around. Both Dunton and Farrell were radical in their political sympathies, by McConnell's standards. John was less political, while being sensitive, kind, and popular with the staff. Farrell had known John at Selwyn House School and was the son of Gerald Farrell, a stockbroker associated with Aitken. Through his uncle G.W. Cook of Westmount, McConnell's first landlord, Farrell was related to the Countesses of Minto and Haddington and through Lady Minto to Lady Violet Astor, whose husband owned *The Times*. All of them were friends of McConnell's. For a year, however, McConnell knew nothing about Farrell's joining the *Standard*. At a social gathering, he asked Farrell's mother what her "communist" son was doing, and she replied, "He is working for you now."

A former member of the CCF and the League for Social Reconstruction (LSR), treasurer of the Ontario CCF, and managing editor of the LSR's *Canadian Forum*, Farrell was in many ways an odd recruit to the McConnell empire. He had articled in the accountancy firm of George McDonald and been a chauffeur to Senator Adrian Knatchbull-Huggesson, McConnell's two most determined foes on the McGill Board of Governors. Moreover, his socialist connections were even more hostile to McConnell's big-business point of view. Frank Scott had founded the LSR in 1933, with

J.S. Woodsworth as honorary president, Frank Underhill as president, and the Reverend J. King Gordon, of the United Theological College, as the local president in Montreal. Its work was the basis of the CCF Regina Manifesto of 1933, pledging the party to the eradication of capitalism and the implementation of "a full programme of socialized planning."

But Farrell was also a professional, and, to do his job at the *Standard*, he abandoned his formal association with the CCF, though not his political views. During his tenure, the *Standard* published articles exposing the corruption of Duplessis's private constabulary, the Quebec Liquor Police, just as McConnell was establishing an alliance with the premier. At the end of the war, to the chagrin of the McConnells, Dunton relocated to Ottawa to become chairman of the Canadian Broadcasting Corporation, whereupon Farrell, as the new general manager, replaced Dunton as John's closest associate.

From the beginning, the *Standard*'s already-established pictorial emphasis suited John very much, and the royal visit to Canada of 1939 gave him an opportunity to produce a lavish special number full of photographs in sepia. Apart from this special number, the *Standard* was produced in Toronto in tabloid form, assembled in the week before the publication date, and distributed essentially in eastern Canada, separately from the Saturday editions of local papers. In Montreal, a broadsheet news section, published by the McConnells in Montreal, was wrapped around it.

On 14 December 1945 John sent a memorandum to his father, announcing that in 1946 the *Standard* would be taking its first steps to build national circulation.[26] Since 1938 it had added 35,000 readers west of Ottawa and 112,000 east of Ottawa, making its total circulation 220,000. John expected readership to rise above 300,000 the following autumn and urged increasing circulation rapidly early in 1946 so as to set advertising rates for 1947 on the basis of this number. In addition, John, his father, and Farrell all saw the need for colour photographs to replace sepia ones, and for faster and more efficient presses. They were already having the *Standard* printed on rotogravure presses in Toronto, which combined high speed with a high quality of illustrative engraving. But, in order to compete with the *Star Weekly*, published by the Toronto *Daily Star*, the *Standard* required greater control over its scheduling, organization, and quality of production. Accordingly, the paper now decided to operate its own rotogravure plant. In 1946 John went to England, France, and Belgium in search of rotogravure presses and to re-establish links, ruptured by the war, with English press agencies for the exchange of news and photographs.

The paper took other huge steps forward in the late 1940s, first with the hiring of the writer Greg Clark in 1947 and the cartoonist Duncan Macpherson in 1948, two men destined to become legends in Canadian journalism, and then with the building of a new plant. McConnell had been keeping the property on Sherbrooke Street for joint presses for the *Star* and the *Standard*, but in 1948 he bought land for the plant

Mark Farrell, John G. McConnell, and Maurice Field (manager
of the rotogravure plant) examining the *Standard Magazine*,
1949. Private collection, courtesy of Mr and Mrs Mark Farrell.

near the Blue Bonnets racecourse, exclusively for the printing of the *Standard*. Farrell presided over the construction of a $1.75-million facility, using technology from Chicago, which was completed in 1949. Serious start-up problems hampered operations. One day J.W. McConnell came to inspect the plant and found it not yet running. He asked Farrell when it would begin operations, and Farrell promised that this should be within two weeks. With typical precision, the older McConnell – to Farrell's surprise – visited the plant again exactly at the end of two weeks, when it had just begun printing, only to shudder to a sudden stop immediately after the visit of the owner.[27]

Even with the solution of its equipment problems, the new plant proved too large to make money, and, if the paper was to earn a profit, an essentially new product was necessary. Montreal alone could not support an English-language weekly, and the distribution of the *Standard* in eastern Canada had stagnated at 300,000. Could it now take the form of a well-illustrated magazine distributed with various newspapers across the country? Newspaper supplements in the form of picture magazines could increase advertising revenue through their larger distribution. If sufficiently wide in appeal, supplements might, moreover, be included in newspapers far from Montreal, indeed all over the country and beyond.

Following the success of such American newspaper supplements as Hearst's *American Weekly*, and then *Parade* and *This Week*, the McConnells decided that a shortened version of the *Standard* should appear within the Saturday editions of other leading Canadian newspapers. These papers would raise their weekend prices to cover their purchase of the supplement. Once circulation and advertising increased to cover production costs, they would share the profits from increased advertising with the *Standard*. In 1951 John and Farrell developed out of the *Standard* a new colour supplement, to be sold with high-circulation newspapers all over Canada. For its first three years, it was called *Weekend Picture Magazine*, then renamed *Weekend Magazine*. It proved to be a considerable success. In addition to a photo-news section, it contained a condensed novel, a colour-comic section, and a magazine section with short stories, feature articles, and columnists.

Weekend Magazine incorporated the magazine and picture sections, but not the news, of the *Standard*. It was included initially in the Saturday editions of the Toronto *Telegram*, the Vancouver *Sun*, the London *Free Press*, the Montreal *Daily Star*, and the *Standard* itself (which remained a Montreal newspaper), with a circulation of 775,000 in Canada as a whole. Craig Ballantyne became its editorial director. The various small newspapers belonging to Roy Thomson joined in 1952, when the circulation of the *Weekend Magazine* reached almost a million. When the *Standard* disappeared as a separate newspaper, the *Star* itself adopted *Weekend* as its Saturday supplement. By 1959, *Weekend* – with a staff that had grown from 40 in 1938 to 400 – was also appearing in French, under the title *Perspectives*. In Montreal, this French version appeared with *Dimanche-Matin*, and within two years it was being distributed also in Quebec City, Trois-Rivières, Sherbrooke, Granby, and Ottawa-Hull. The total circulation was 2,098,987 – 1,714,388 for *Weekend* and 384,599 for *Perspectives*.[28] This was more than double the circulation of the *Star Weekly*. McConnell was enormously proud of his son, not least because John's success represented a victory over the legacy of Joe Atkinson of the Toronto *Daily Star*, who owned the *Star Weekly* and who was a fierce sympathizer with Soviet Russia and other causes horrifying to McConnell.

On 29 March 1944 John submitted to his father an elaborate memorandum on how to plan the future of all the four newspapers within the *Star* family – the *Star* itself, the *Standard*, the *Family Herald & Weekly Star* (as it had been renamed), and the Montreal *Herald*. This was a crucial document in determining the course of the transition that the two men had been planning at least since 1932. In writing to "J.W. McC., Esq.," John was diffident, beginning with the words: "I am taking the risk of sending you the enclosed memo before having time to finish it. Many of the ideas expressed

I know run counter to your own ... We don't have many opportunities to talk about these very pressing problems."[29] John urged first the establishment of objectives over five to ten years for circulation, "editorial character, i.e. (field of reporting, features, picture coverage, etc.), physical appearance, syndication and pooling of facilities." Secondly, he wanted policies put in place for the publication of news, letters to the editor, and advertisements.

One of the catalysts of John's memorandum – possibly the decisive one – had been a spat between his father and the socialist Frank Scott a few weeks previously. One of the most enduring popular memories of J.W. McConnell concerns his alleged refusal to give publicity to the CCF and its leading spokesman in Quebec, Scott, in the *Star*, a memory that has been elaborated to the effect that the newspaper even refused to mention the CCF at all. As Eric Kierans, a McGill economist and a provincial minister of revenue, was to recall, McConnell "was not a man of broad intellectual tolerance, and ordered that the CCF party never be mentioned in the pages of his newspaper."[30] A similar recollection is to be found in the memoirs of the socialist Eugene Forsey.[31]

Scott likewise saw McConnell's refusal to publicize CCF views as an abuse of power. But Scott himself also disproved the story that McConnell refused *all* mention of the CCF in a pamphlet that he published privately in 1944, *The Montreal Star and the C.C.F.: Another Monopoly at Work.* Far from complaining of a blanket ban on comment, the first sentences of Scott's pamphlet read: "Everyone has read the vicious attacks upon the C.C.F. conducted by the Montreal Star. Nearly every day, sometimes twice a day, it has been accusing the C.C.F. of plans to establish a dictatorship in Canada, and of a desire to abolish democratic processes including freedom of the press. Everyone [sic] of these charges is demonstrably false."[32]

Kierans's allegation of a blanket refusal by McConnell to acknowledge the existence of the CCF in the newspaper is therefore wrong and reckless if not malicious. As Scott himself explained, his objection was to McConnell's refusal to give *publicity* to the party, even though the *Star* was willing to accept advertisements even from Stanley Ryerson, a communist: "For some time past the Montreal Star, under Mr. McConnell's direction, has followed a different policy with respect to the C.C.F. Party. It has barred all news about C.C.F. activities in Montreal. It will not report C.C.F. meetings. It will not accept paid C.C.F. advertisements. It will not print official letters from C.C.F. leaders. Meanwhile it carries on its attacks upon the C.C.F. and gives full reports to C.C.F. opponents. Mr. McConnell is using his monopoly power to prevent his readers from learning the truth about one of Canada's major parties."

Scott said that, through McConnell's ownership of the *Star*, the *Herald*, and the *Standard*, he had "acquired a monopoly control over the evening news distribution in English in the Montreal area." With his franchise from the Canadian Press, which in turn held exclusive rights for Associated Press and Reuters, McConnell had "exclusive use of these press services between the hours of 9:30 A.M. and 9:30 P.M."

McConnell "alone is able to decide what part of this news to release to the Montreal public and what to withhold from them." He also controlled the only English-language outlets in Montreal, during the same hours, for the British United Press and the American United Press, which placed him "in the position of district controller of public information," "responsible only to himself."

In his pamphlet, Scott reproduced a letter that he had written to Samuel Morgan-Powell, the editor of the *Star* – which was dated 18 February 1944 and which McConnell declined to publish – describing the CCF as "the strongest defenders in Canada of freedom of speech, of association and of the press." Morgan-Powell's right "to criticise us in your editorials we freely admit." But this right "goes with a correlative duty which you owe to the public, and that is the duty of fair reporting of public meetings, including C.C.F. meetings, and of equal access to all political parties to your advertising and letter columns on equal terms." Failure in this duty, Scott asserted, made it "hypocritical to preach democracy in your editorials, or to claim to you are defenders of a 'free' press."

McConnell's reply made clear that he saw his role as a gatekeeper, even a censor, for the reading public.[33] It read in part:

> The STAR certainly sifts the news. It is on guard constantly against untruths, half truths and deception. Promises incapable of fulfilment must be carefully watched. Readers have a right to expect that of the Press. The STAR has a responsibility to its readers and it has a duty to perform in separating the wheat from the chaff, truth from falsehood and sound news from misleading statements.
>
> Despite the wailing of Mr. Scott the STAR is not disposed to allow him to dictate its Editorial or news policy or the news it shall print; or indeed just what news is fit to print. Readers are ofttimes misled seriously by flashing headlines of socalled news. Have the people not the right to expect guidance and leadership from the Press or the exercise of discretion in selecting and printing news? If professional newspaper men are unable to do this or fail to do it, then they fail utterly in their duty to the reading public who have neither the time nor the opportunity of checking the news.

McConnell was in truth obsessed with the CCF, and he frequently discussed it with his correspondents and dispatched reporters to its meetings. The day after receiving John's memorandum, McConnell sent a reporter named Macfarlane to report on a meeting of the Montreal branch of the General Alumnae [sic] Association of Queen's University. M.J. Coldwell of the CCF was the speaker. Coldwell, who had been attacking St Lawrence Sugar, launched a general attack on cartels which were, in essence, "private economic supra-national governments, which divide and rule the world on the basis of economic privilege." Their effect was "to restrict production and trade," "to limit competition," to "restrict output through production quotas," "to control the use of new inventions and retard technological advances," and "to fix prices so as to raise profits to the highest possible levels." In particular, he attacked Alcoa/Alcan, CIL, and Phillips/GE/Westinghouse, as well as rubber, magnesium, munitions, tungsten carbide, and dental-plastic cartels, some of whom impeded the war effort through their links with German companies.

The row between Scott and McConnell continued after the election in June 1944 of a CCF government in Saskatchewan, which Scott was advising on constitutional matters. As the country prepared for a general election, George Ferguson attacked the CCF in Winnipeg *Free Press* editorials, and he taunted the party for not replying to his attacks. Scott did reply with two letters, which McConnell refused to publish, and it is at *this* stage that McConnell was later said by Scott to have banned mention of him (but not of the CCF) in the *Star*.[34]

It is therefore unduly limiting to see the alleged repression of Scott as simply an aspect of a personal vendetta between Scott and McConnell. McConnell hardly knew Frank Scott except by reputation, and McConnell's views of him were no more extreme than those held by Frank's own brother, William. The background to this dispute of 1944 was the sensitive conscription crisis that threatened the survival of the Liberal government in Ottawa, which was supported by Ferguson and McConnell as well as the Canadian people generally. Thus, the *Star's* denial of coverage to Frank Scott was in fact probably in accordance not merely with McConnell's opinion but also with the dominant public mood, certainly in Montreal and probably in the country.

McConnell's keen interest in the CCF combined with his effective censorship of its views in his newspapers must also be understood within the context of wartime censorship and the emerging Cold War. In associating himself with the policy of the New York *Times* to publish only "all the news that is fit to print," McConnell was not being disingenuous, since discretion to decide on newsworthiness is logically implied by that slogan. Scott, with his preoccupation with rationality and fairness, could properly have disputed the way in which McConnell exercised his discretion, but not the principle of such discretion itself. For his part, McConnell believed that the CCF was at best a fifth column, bent on establishing a dictatorship in Canada, and to that extent indistinguishable from the Nazis. In the context of the Cold War, his position was not extreme or irrational even if it was still peculiar and rooted in misapprehensions about the CCF's true character. It was his failure to appreciate Scott's originality and sincerity that led to McConnell's reputation in some quarters as stupid and reactionary. Given, however, McConnell's very open opposition to the CCF, it scarcely makes sense to accuse him of refusing to see the threat posed by the party. His fault was not that he did not take it seriously: it was that he took it too seriously because in fact it was not a serious political force, particularly in Quebec.

Finally, Scott's reference to McConnell's monopoly in the English-language press was not correct. McConnell did not control the *Gazette*, even if he was much in sympathy with its owners and managers. Furthermore, the two Montreal newspapers were far from identical in their coverage, and the *Gazette* remained unrepentantly Conservative while the *Star* offered barely covert support to the Liberal Party.

Such was the background to John McConnell's 1944 memorandum. With regard to the issue of the C C F and labour, John attached to his memorandum several articles – including one from the *Star* itself dated 14 January – that demonstrated his view of the need for a distinctly more measured approach in the future. The *Star* article contained a speech by McConnell's close friend Morris Wilson, made at the annual meeting of the Royal Bank of Canada, which amounted, in John's words, to "a temperate reasoned statement on the C.C.F." John also attached an editorial from the *Gazette*, dated 18 March, which attacked "American leftists," especially the New Dealers, and, of course, the C C F, but also the "old guard" in Canada that "would maintain themselves in power only on a program of berating the C.C.F. and going back to the 'good old days.'" It urged this old guard "to do a lot of constructive and progressive thinking if it intends to play a part in the future of this country."

Rather boldly, John articulated to his father a fresh and a coherent plan for dealing with both the C C F and labour. His plan was essentially both a repudiation of what he saw as the narrowness of his father's world-view and a reinvigoration of its free-enterprise principles. Though abandoning what, in John's eyes, was the elitist and *parti pris* approach adopted by the *Star* to that time, the plan was also a vindication of his father's instinctive humanism, particularly his cautious but genuine openness towards social and economic reform. It offered a strategy for making a fundamentally conservative position palatable, and even attractive, to what John anticipated to be the changing readership of post-war society. As he put it:

In our approach to the C.C.F. the first thing to remember is that in Canada now hundreds of thousands of decent Canadians are leaning towards the C.C.F. … Their hopes can be summed up generally as looking to better standards of living in the widest sense. And their fears – a repetition of depression days with lights cut off, furniture thrown in the street, children poorly fed.

They see in the C.C.F. leaders an idealistic group who intend to do their best … to bring about a fair distribution of opportunity and well being. In attacking the C.C.F. extreme care must be taken to respect these feelings … and confine condemnation of the party to exposing the real faults of its operations and bad political practices … At the same time a constructive policy must be worked out to show that the editors are equally concerned with decent living conditions … The mass of our readers are antagonized by wholesale attacks on the C.C.F. This attitude is felt to reflect fear on the part of the vested interests. It should be shown that free enterprise working with government planning agen-

cies genuinely wants to build a better society, and that we recognize the failings
of the capitalist system in the past.

...

The reader responds to carefully reasoned argumentation. He doesn't
believe the c.c.f. is all black, and he doesn't believe the capitalists are all white.
Let us show him without ranting where the c.c.f. is all wrong, and how we
intend to work constructively for a better world for the *average man*.

To implement this approach, John proposed that editorials on the CCF be "few in
number but very effective"; that "most editorials concerning the political and economic organization of the country should concentrate on constructive criticism of
the government in power and a constant stream of advice to the party favoured by the
paper"; that all feature articles "avoid special pleading"; that the letters-to-the-editor
section "should encourage controversy, and make the readers feel that views will be
published contrary to the editorial policy of the paper"; and that "the necessity for
objective reporting on labour strife ... should be constantly in the minds of the editors ... our editorial policy should emphasize the need for the cooperative working of
all sections of society for the furthering of better government."

McConnell was thus confronted, probably for the first time in his life, with a
demand for intellectual nuance. His response to John's memorandum is unknown.
Editorially as well as financially and otherwise, however, it is clear that McConnell did want to improve the *Star*. The problem was that neither John nor Davidson
Dunton was even remotely ready to edit the *Star*, and, even if McConnell had been
convinced by John's memorandum, Morgan-Powell and A.J. West remained largely in
charge, and so little was done to alter editorial policy for two years. Then, with the
arrival of George Ferguson from Winnipeg in 1946, this situation changed.

Before his firing that year by the Winnipeg *Free Press*'s owner, Victor Sifton,
George Ferguson had been the principal lieutenant and heir apparent of the widely
recognized dean of Canadian journalists, J.W. Dafoe. As the long-time editor of the
Free Press, Dafoe, from beyond the grave, was to influence – both positively and neg-
atively – the evolution of the *Star* over the quarter-century that extended from the
appointment of Ferguson as editor in October 1946. This was partly because Ferguson had been his disciple, but it was also because Ferguson was working to overcome
what he saw as the antipathy of his master towards French Canada, in particular its
Roman Catholicism.

With regard to Ferguson's relationship with McConnell, the two men's views
were considerably different. To begin with, before the war, McConnell's imperialism struck Ferguson as akin to Meighen's "ready, aye ready" internationalism, which
focused on the defence of the mother country as the essence of Canadian external
policy, "the butler type," of subservience as Ferguson described it. When war broke

The editorial board of the *Star*, with Samuel Morgan-Powell (seated) and
George V. Ferguson (holding a cigarette) behind him, probably 1940s.
Private collection.

out, imperialists such as McConnell and Meighen, who were inclined to see conscription as necessary, continued to be at odds with such internationalist-minded Canadian nationalists as Ferguson, who feared that conscription would threaten Canadian unity but eventually came to support it, albeit reluctantly. Then there was the issue of the CPR. Ferguson was a long-time critic of the CPR president, Sir Edward Beatty. Like opinion in the west generally, the *Free Press* had since 1921 consistently supported the CNR as a competitor to the CPR and firmly opposed any amalgamation between the two. Ferguson grimly reported to Dafoe that McConnell had been "in charge of propaganda" for such an amalgamation even before assuming control of the *Star* in 1938.[35]

Yet, for all his drawbacks, Ferguson had a sterling reputation based on over twenty years of experience under one of the most demanding, and revered, of Canadian journalists. Moreover, reform-minded as Dafoe had been, he had never sided with the CCF, and Ferguson was as hostile to the CCF as McConnell himself. Ferguson was also shrewd and, in the opinion of Lord Tweedsmuir, a first-rate businessman. One lesson that he had imbibed from Dafoe – despite the latter's rows with, and near dismissal by, the Sifton brothers – was the necessity for the editor to accommodate the owner at least on small matters, and sometimes on big ones. It was a lesson doubtless reinforced by the recent antipathy of Victor Sifton for Ferguson himself.

With the advent of Ferguson, the *Star* became more unequivocally a Liberal paper, whereas before it had been largely Conservative, at least until 1939. It was not overtly partisan, but it was effectively so, especially since neither McConnell nor Ferguson saw merit in the Conservatives or the CCF. Provincially, from 1946 onwards, it also supported the Union Nationale rather than the opposition Liberals, as was decidedly in accordance with McConnell's preference rather than Ferguson's. The allegiance of the paper to Maurice Duplessis put it at odds with probably most of its readers, though not with the *Gazette*, which supported both the Conservatives federally and the Union Nationale provincially, seeing the latter as the provincial Conservative party. These allegiances bound the *Star* as long as McConnell remained in charge, and even afterwards they changed slowly.

The divergent political allegiances of the *Star* were distinctly awkward for Ferguson. He was a liberal philosophically and a qualified supporter of the Liberal Party of Canada, and the Union Nationale was hostile both to the federal Liberal Party and to liberalism itself. Moreover, although McConnell was avowedly a friend of Mackenzie King's, and cool at best to the Conservative Party, he was fundamentally and temperamentally closer in many respects to King's bitterest Tory enemies, Arthur Meighen and Herbert Bruce. Ferguson suffered, too, from acute guilt about what he saw as Dafoe's failure to understand or even to tolerate French Canada, to accommodate what Ferguson now saw as the legitimate and pressing claims of the French Canadians on Confederation. This was not a guilt shared by McConnell. Ferguson himself possessed no particularly intimate understanding of French Canada, but, unlike Dafoe, Victor Sifton, and indeed McConnell, he did speak and understand some French. At the same time, of course, McConnell was the only one of these four men who had spent most of his life in Quebec, worked closely with many of the big French Canadian businessmen, and come to know well most of the leading French Canadian politicians, from Laurier and Gouin to Dandurand and Duplessis.

As a result of McConnell's somewhat equivocal support for the federal Liberals, combined with his support for the provincial Union Nationale, the *Star* under Ferguson remained essentially ambivalent in matters political. If he was to avoid a personality clash with McConnell, Ferguson had little choice but to walk the tightrope set in place by his publisher. In any case, as editor, he adhered to a simple credo, namely, that "the ultimate direction of a newspaper's course should rest in the hands of its responsible ownership," with the irresponsible owner answerable to the marketplace or silenced by death.[36] This principle survived even McConnell's departure as the *Star*'s president. During the campaign preceding the federal elections in August 1953, Ferguson explained the strategy of the *Star* in these terms: "We comment … with some degree of impartiality [and] I fancy … will come down for St. L[aurent] ab[ou]t the beginning of Aug[ust] … as J[ack] Pickersgill remarked to me earlier this year, 'we appreciate y[our] 70 p[er] c[ent] support.'"[37] The newspaper duly endorsed "Uncle Louis" on 1 August and thus retained its Liberal credentials, at least federally.

On the other hand, after McConnell had left the *Star*, Ferguson felt able take a franker line against imperialism and the Union Nationale. Yet his political stance – with its openness to French Canadian aspirations combined with a more assertive Canadian nationalism – remained ambivalent. No better than McConnell was Ferguson able to overcome the idea that Quebec, in Ferguson's words, was "Canada's club foot." In the end, the *Star* could not reconcile the centralism inherent in Ferguson's Canadian nationalism with the emerging separatist tendencies of Quebec nationalism. By contrast, McConnell was able to draw upon a longer and more varied experience of conflict between Ottawa and the provinces. Likewise, as we will see in the next chapter, he was to prove himself considerably shrewder than Ferguson – and such MPs from English Montreal as D.C. Abbott, the minister of finance, and Brooke Claxton, the minister of national health and welfare – in his understanding of the balance of power between Quebec and Ottawa in the area of university grants. In an apparent reference to McConnell, Ferguson publicly recalled knowing publishers whose general rules were "reactionary" but who supported the Liberals. They had "even gone to the length of putting in a strong plea for family allowances, and old age pensions, on the ground that, if any other party but the Liberals introduced them, they would either be higher, or less well administered."[38] If this in fact is what McConnell told him, Ferguson could have been under no illusion about McConnell's unsentimental toughness about the Liberals.

One respect in which Ferguson early asserted his independence as editor was in attacking Duplessis over the Roncarelli affair. At the end of 1946, Duplessis, acting in his capacities as premier and attorney general, withdrew the liquor licence of the Montreal restauranteur Frank Roncarelli in an effort to stop his posting of bail for imprisoned Jehovah's Witnesses. Duplessis had promised a war without mercy against the Witnesses, who had been condemned by the Roman Catholic Church. In common with the *Gazette*, the *Herald*, and the *Standard*, the *Star* attacked the premier for weakening the tradition of tolerance that was at the basis of the Canadian state. The *Standard* even compared Duplessis's techniques to those adopted by the Third Reich.[39] Almost alone in Quebec, the English press of Montreal fought against Duplessis's authoritarianism in this long affair, which ran through the courts until 1958. *Le Temps*, *Montréal-Matin*, and *L'Action Catholique* all defended Duplessis, and only *Le Canada* attacked him, but it was to cease publication in 1951. Even *Le Soleil* and *Le Devoir* were at best equivocal, although the latter, under the new editorship of André Laurendeau, turned bitterly against the premier in 1959, just after Frank Scott's victory in the Supreme Court of Canada on behalf of Roncarelli.

McConnell did not in fact impose the details of his broadly conservative views upon the *Star* with a heavy hand, particularly after John's confrontation with him over its lopsided political coverage in 1944. A survey of the newspaper suggests that he confined most of the editorials that he wrote himself to such uncontroversial topics as charity. He never permitted the *Star* to become a mouthpiece of his own opinions, even if he was uninterested in contrary opinions. His conservatism probably helped keep his paper from being so loudly in favour of the federal Liberals as, say, the Toronto *Star*. Nevertheless, the ongoing tug-of-war between McConnell, on one side, and John and Ferguson on the other, with regard to coverage of divergent opinions went on until 1953, when John took over almost completely. McConnell found himself frequently having to dissociate himself from the editorial opinions expressed thereafter. As we have seen, he did summon Ferguson in 1956 to complain about the *Star*'s coverage of the Suez crisis, but in general he held his tongue and remained on cordial terms with him.

In May 1949 John, general manager H.G. Brewer, and production manager D.R. Parker sent a memorandum to McConnell detailing options for consolidating the operations of the *Star*, the *Herald*, the *Family Herald*, and the *Standard*, each of which had separate facilities in different buildings. One was to renovate completely the facilities on St James Street; another was to occupy a completely new building. They canvassed the options carefully, noting the financial problems of the *Family Herald* among other issues, but events dating back to Lord Atholstan's agreement with the British American Publishing Company in 1931 rapidly overtook them.[40] The tax issues that arose as a result are fairly technical, even in the simplified form in which they are here summarized. But, for McConnell, this was to a large extent what his business was about, and so it is necessary to allude to them to see why the family of newspapers that he had inherited from Atholstan shrank under his ownership.

The *Herald* was not a profitable paper even when the *Star* was. Because of the 1931 agreement and previous arrangements, the deficits of the *Herald* and of the Herald Publishing Company served as business losses deductible from the profits of the *Star* from 1927 onwards. The 1931 agreement said that the *Star* would "make good any financial deficits" of British American revealed by the audited accounts of British American, which had to include provision for depreciation. In 1949 the Department of National Revenue changed its policy and declined to permit the MSCL to deduct as of that year its losses from the *Herald*. The MSCL appealed, and in the process the question of the losses of the *Standard* unavoidably arose, since, like the *Herald* (run through British American), it was a subsidiary of the MSCL.

In 1939 the *Standard*'s losses amounted to almost $114,000, but they were amortized by the MSCL over 1940, 1941, and 1942, resulting in a total tax benefit to the profitable *Star* of almost $92,000, as opposed to the $75,000 profit that it would have gained had it deducted all these losses in 1939 alone. Unlike the situation with the *Herald*, however, no written agreement existed to justify deducting these losses from the profits of the *Star*. The *Star* reached a complicated settlement in respect of the special losses of the *Herald* for 1940–43 and for the *Standard* in 1942. But it then filed an appeal objecting to the failure of the Department to allow the deduction of about $10,000 in sales-promotion losses incurred by the *Herald*.

Towards the end of 1951, the losses of the *Herald* were growing alarmingly. In 1949, they had been about $10,500, and in the first ten months of 1951 they were $116,234. By contrast, the *Star*, over the same ten months, had earned $1,758,520. The consequences of the *Herald*'s continued deterioration could be disastrous for the MSCL if the *Herald*'s losses could not be deducted from the *Star*'s income. McConnell concluded that the *Herald* could not continue to bleed the company if a favourable tax ruling on deducting its losses did not result.

McConnell maintained that he had taken over only a "shell" of a plant for the *Star* in 1938 and had had immediately to expend $600,000 on new presses, which by 1951 were obsolete.[41] During the past fourteen years, the MSCL had not earned enough after taxes to finance a new building and plant such as McConnell had been planning for the site on Sherbrooke and Metcalfe streets. McConnell himself had not taken any profits from the business, or interest on the investment since 1938. Even the preferred dividend of 7 per cent, amounting to $105,000 a year, had not been paid since then. From 1940 to 1950, the MSCL paid over $5 million in income and excess-profits taxes plus interest of about $30,000, and in 1951 it was estimating its taxes as over $745,000, which averaged out to about $500,000 a year. From 1931 to 1951, the combined net losses of the Herald Publishing Company and the Herald Press had amounted to $1,730,009. Even if this total amount were deductible, the MSCL was not, in McConnell's view, profitable enough to replace ageing plant and equipment out of its revenues.

Further, although Altholstan had bought the *Herald* to pre-empt any other Liberal paper, McConnell was using it as a way of capturing some of the market (otherwise held by the *Gazette*) for a morning paper in Montreal. Without the *Herald*, the *Star* would have to invest new money in an opposition paper, "employing methods spurned by the Star, such as sensationalism, sex, gossip, etc., which would undoubtedly win circulation and be harmful to the Star's revenues." The *Star* had only two alternatives, either to publish morning editions to replace the *Herald* or to keep the *Herald* "as an economical tabloid production with strong consumer acceptance restricted mostly to the late morning and noon hours."

The uncertainty persisted until October 1952, when the Department of National Revenue rejected the MSCL's deduction of British American losses for 1949, 1950, and 1951. The MSCL had already sold the Herald Press the previous May, and in November 1952 it took over the assets of Herald Publishing. No public announcement was made of this change, and the *Herald* continued to appear until October 1957, when, after a history of more than 150 years, it ceased publication (though a morning edition of the briefly renamed *Montreal Star and Herald* began to appear in its place).[42]

Of course, for McConnell as for others, then and since, there was more to news-paper publishing than the money involved. Though he kept his distance from the *Star*'s editorial operations, McConnell took great pride in his role as a newspaper owner and cultivated the friendship of several of the so-called English press lords of his time. These were not merely social connections, for he learned a good deal from some of the most able newspaper owners in what in retrospect was a golden age for newspapers. All were extremely successful businessmen, mostly self-made like him, and well versed in all aspects of newspapers. They were stupendously rich, but they maintained a high ideal of their role as one being above party politics, although they, like McConnell, were personally very conservative. McConnell tried to model himself as a newspaper owner on them. He was closest to lords Iliffe (Edward Iliffe), Camrose (William Berry), and Kemsley (Gomer Berry), who were for thirteen years, until 1937, the joint owners of the *Daily Telegraph*, the *Financial Times*, and the *Sunday Times*. By 1940, he was also was close to John Astor (later Lord Astor of Hever) of *The Times* and others, such as lords Beaverbrook (Max Aitken) of the *Daily Express* and South-wood (Julius Saltwood Elias) of the Odhams Press and the *Illustrated London News*.

Little is known about how McConnell came to meet these men, but he probably developed an interest in the press through his friend Sir Campbell Stuart, whom he had recruited to help him in the Victory Loans campaign of 1917. In the same year, Stuart became military secretary to Lord Northcliffe, a co-proprietor of *The Times* and chairman of the British War Mission in Washington. Stuart was managing editor of that paper in 1920–22 and then became a director of it for life. It is also possible that McConnell's first connection was through the Chamberlain family of Birmingham. McConnell had first met Joseph and Neville Chamberlain in 1904, and they were almost neighbours of Iliffe. At any rate, McConnell's friendship with Iliffe was estab-lished by the 1920s and it lasted for the lives of the two men. Indeed, it seems to have been a closer friendship than the one Iliffe enjoyed with his own business partners, the Berrys. Iliffe ended his business relationship with Camrose and Kemsley while holidaying with McConnell in 1938, but he continued to take holidays with McCon-nell until at least 1956. Charlotte, his wife, was particularly close to Lil, and the two couples seem to have travelled together on several occasions.[43]

In contrast to other wealthy newspaper owners, including Iliffe and his own brother Camrose, Kemsley became extremely reactionary.[44] Invariably formally attired and requiring stiff collars among his employees, he was among the most rigid and unre-pentant of Tories, and he made the *Sunday Times* virtually into an organ of the Con-servative Party. But he was also was a master of advertising, and from 1938 he owned the largest newspaper group in Great Britain, including the *Sunday Times*, the *Daily Sketch* (later the *Daily Graphic*), the *Empire News*, and the *Sunday Chronicle*. Kems-ley was horrified by the *Daily Mirror*, which had begun in 1903 for women of breed-ing but soon developed a reputation for sensationalism. McConnell shared some of

In front: Kit, Lady Kemsley (seated), and Lil; in back, from left: unknown lady,
Lord Kemsley, McConnell, Pamela Berry (later Marchioness of Huntly), John,
Miss Ghislaine Dresselhuys (daughter of Lady Kemsley), and Douglas Berry.
Pine Avenue, c.1939. Private collection.

Kemsley's prudery, and he was determined that the *Star* should in no way resemble
the *Daily Mirror*. In 1938 Kemsley launched in his *Daily Sketch* a "Clean and Clever"
campaign, to contrast its chaste pictures with the salacious ones published by the
Daily Mirror. At the *Star*, McConnell, too, censored photographs that he deemed
indecent.[45]

During the Imperial Press Conference – a periodic gathering of journalists from
all over the empire – held in Canada in 1950, McConnell presided over the opening
dinner at the Ritz-Carlton in Montreal. This was the culmination of his newspaper
career, for three years later he would pass control of the Montreal *Star* group to his
son John. As he surveyed the vast assemblage, he could take satisfaction from the
fact that Canadian journalists were now part of a profession encompassing emerging
democracies of the British Commonwealth, such as India, Pakistan, and Ceylon, all
of which sent delegates to the conference, as did such venerable colonies as Gibraltar,
Bermuda, and the Bahamas and the four white dominions as well as the United Kingdom. At the head table with him were his old friends Colonel John Astor of *The Times*
and his wife, Lady Violet, a daughter of Lord Minto, the former governor general.

E.J. Robertson of the *Daily Express*, Major-General Lord Burnham (managing director of the *Daily Telegraph*), and McConnell, at the Imperial Press Conference in Montreal in 1950. Private collection.

Rupert Murdoch (left), Senator Rupert Davies (third) of the Kingston *Whig-Standard*, Victor Drury, and an unknown man (far right) at Ashburton, in conjunction with the Imperial Press Conference of 1950.

McConnell was unusually jovial in delivering his speech, and he joked about the modesty of the Montreal newspapers. The *Gazette*, he noted, claimed to be the oldest newspaper in the country; *La Presse,* the most popular; and the *Star*, simply the greatest. After the official proceedings concluded, the McConnells invited many of the delegates to Dorval for a garden party, one of the last big events that they were to preside over. The guests constituted a roll call of the press elite of the twentieth century – in Great Britain, Canada, and the Commonwealth generally. Lord Burnham, whose family had owned the *Daily Telegraph* before the Berrys and Iliffe, and whose father had presided over a previous Imperial Press Conference in Montreal, which McConnell had also attended, came. So did Sir Keith Murdoch of Australia and his son Rupert, himself to become one of the most prominent media moguls of the second half of the century and into the next.[46]

On a more serious note, in newspaper matters as in much else, McConnell has long been attacked for his close relationship with Maurice Duplessis, and one critic in particular, Gérard Boismenu, has made specific allegations of government favouritism towards the *Star* in the area of newsprint prices. Boismenu claims:

Le premier Duplessis entretient des rapports étroits avec les diverses composantes de la bourgeoisie, notamment avec les grands financiers canadiens-anglais dont McConnell … Ces dirigeants de journaux ont à lutter contre le contrôle à la hausse des prix du papier journal par les companies dans la branche et contre les difficultés d'approvisionnement, compte tenu de l'augmentation de leur besoins.

En 1950, Bassett et McConnell "suggèrent" à Duplessis d'intervenir auprès des producteurs de papier journal afin d'introduire un système de double prix, l'un pour la consommation au Québec et l'autre pour l'exportation. Le Premier ministre s'exécute et, comme en 1947, sert un avertissement au président de la *Saint Lawrence Paper Mills* dans des termes péremptoires et contradictoires. Quelques mois plus tard (en 1951), McConnell demande à Duplessis d'intervenir auprès des compagnies de papier journal afin que le *Star* puisse se procurer "la quantité nécessaire plus deux mille tonnes de papier journal pour terminer l'année." Le Premier ministre, en moins de quarante-huit heures, contraint les compagnies, sous peine de diminuer ou d'annuler leurs concessions forestières et d'augmenter les redevances ou d'annuler les permis d'essouchement, à procurer le volume de papier journal pour discuter, à huis clos, du niveau des prix et tenter d'empêcher la hausse des prix en les menaçant de la création d'une régie du papier journal.

Le conflit intermonopoliste s'accentue, les difficultés d'approvisionnement continuent et les prix sont considérés trop élevés par les propriétaires des journaux. A la fin d'octobre 1955, les producteurs monopolistes de papier haussent leurs prix. Duplessis fait une mise en garde et leur demande de réétudier la situation. Les compagnies maintienent leurs prix et le principal fournisseur du Québec, la *Consolidated Paper*, élève son prix de 4 $ la tonne. A ce moment Duplessis annonce le dépôt d'une loi touchant la production, le contrôle des prix et la distribution du papier journal fabriqué au Québec.

La loi de 2 février 1956 assure, sous l'autorité de la Régie du papier journal, l'approvisionnement des journaux du Québec et le maintien des prix à un niveau inférieur à celui prévalant dans le reste du Canada et aux Etats-Unis. Cette loi ne trouvera pas sa pareille au cours de la période du gouvernemnt de l'Union nationale de 1944 à 1960.[47]

Boismenu does not cite any sources for these claims, and evidence of the alleged arrangements between McConnell and Duplessis in 1950–52 is absent from the McConnell Papers. But Boismenu is correct when he goes on to suggest that these arrangements were hardly practical as a long-term policy. In 1948 the *Star* had made a contract with Northeastern Paper Products to supply newspaper for ten years, and in 1949 it had contracted with Consolidated Paper to supply newsprint from 1951 to 1955. If the newspaper did benefit from the actions of Duplessis in 1951, these contracts would have been affected, at a time when McConnell himself was a shareholder of Consolidated Paper. The *Star* itself was probably a shareholder in this company at this time, for in 1963 it sold 40,000 shares in it to raise $1.5 million.[48]

What Boismenu does not say of the 1956 arrangement, moreover, is that both John G. McConnell, on behalf of the *Star* papers, and Charles Peters, on behalf of the *Gazette*, immediately declined to accept any benefit from Duplessis's order-in-council,[49] in the belief that any other course would fatally compromise the credibility of their newspapers.[50] Peters, on behalf of the White family, was to recall forcing Bassett to resign as president of the *Gazette* over this matter. It is possible that McConnell at the *Star* and Bassett at the *Gazette* had lobbied Duplessis for price concessions, but by 1956 John McConnell was definitively in charge of the *Star*, and even if his father had obtained temporary concessions, it is clear that the newspaper rejected Duplessis's offer. On 13 February a *Star* editorial announced that the newspaper would "continue with its [existing] contracts," since it had enjoyed "normal relationships with it suppliers" for eighty-six years and hoped to maintain them "unimpaired." It wanted "no cloud, not even the suspicion of a cloud, upon its liberty."

Three years before this decision by John, on 16 February 1953, J.W. McConnell had resigned as president and director of the MSCL. Since his takeover in 1938, the *Star*'s circulation had increased from 130,135 to 150,846, the *Herald*'s from 22,481 to 37,599, and the *Standard*'s from 75,365 to 97,086.[51] Though John replaced him as president, he did not become publisher of the *Star* until 1959. John also replaced H.G. Brewer, who retired as general manager at the same time. Brewer had worked for McConnell for fifteen years and for Atholstan for thirty years before McConnell. Wilson and David McConnell also joined the board. A.J. West remained editorial director under Ferguson as editor, but Walter O'Hearn replaced Samuel Morgan-Powell in 1954 as literary and drama editor.

A reading of the *Star*, through both the Atholstan and the McConnell eras, suggests that McConnell tried consciously to be as little like Atholstan as possible, at least with regard to political partisanship. In contrast to Atholstan's extravagant campaigns to shame government into action, McConnell seems to have shaped an opaque, even inscrutable, paper ideologically. His conservative views on the empire certainly come through, but they were far more sober than Atholstan's (then Graham's) jingoism in the debates leading to Canadian participation in the Boer War. Similarly, McConnell immediately withdrew the automatic support of the *Star* for the Conservative Party in Ottawa, and he was cautious about overt support for the Liberal government that was in power throughout his presidency of the MSCL.

Notwithstanding the distinction of George Ferguson, it seems fair to conclude that, editorially and otherwise, the *Star* was a prissy paper under McConnell, certainly in comparison to the paper of the Atholstan era. Although aggressive in promoting its business, McConnell would not have countenanced any reporting in the least sensational. Was he a great newspaperman, like William Randolph Hearst or Lord Beaverbrook or the Sulzbergers? Certainly not, but he never aspired to be one. And he may still have been an extremely good if not a great publisher.

In McConnell's time, the evolution of the publisher into an entrepreneur led to concentration of the industry into fewer and fewer hands, a process that itself was fuelled by money from the burgeoning business of advertising.[52] McConnell's eventual stable of newspapers – the *Star*, the *Herald*, and the *Standard* – was modest in comparison with the empires of the Southams and of his friends among the English presslords, Camrose, Kemsley, and Iliffe in particular. Nonetheless, he did play a distinct role in this trend towards concentration of opinion as well as of ownership. What differentiated McConnell from other successful publishers, including his predecessor as owner of the *Star*, Lord Atholstan, however, was that he had not made his fortune from publishing. This fact ensured him a certain freedom from dependence on the sensationalism that was keeping other newspapers prosperous and that he so despised. Yet steady profits he did make, which, given his record in business, was only to have been expected.

Some financial data survive to indicate the financial performance of the *Star in* the period from 1926 to 1961.[53] In these years, interest on *Star* bonds amounted to $1,132,000, and other interest to $387,000, for a total of $1,519,000. Presumably all this interest accrued to Atholstan at least to the end of 1937. We do not know precisely who all the shareholders were in this period, in particular how many shares Atholstan and McConnell owned. At any rate, between 1926 and 1961, dividends on preferred shares amounted to $1,295,000 and on common shares to $3,774,000, for a total of $5,069,000. In addition, $2,500,000 of bonds and related notes were redeemed, making the total return on investment $9,088,000.

If, as we have concluded, the purchase price of the newspaper in 1925 was $2,500,000, this was also its book value at the time McConnell bought it. The book value of the *Star* at the end of 1961 was $19,239,000, which suggests that McConnell had invested an additional $16,739,000 into the company after purchasing it. At the same time, the market value over book of the portfolio of shares of other companies held by the *Star* was $5,539,000, making the total assets of the newspaper $24,778,000, which was almost ten times, in constant dollars, of what McConnell had bought it for. Taking into account the inflation of 1925–61, McConnell had increased the value of the MSCL by about 1.71 times.

This increase does not take into account the fact that he was making donations from the *Star* to his Foundation, as was doubtless his intention even before taking over complete control in 1938. It is important to keep a proportionate view of these donations to the Foundation, and to appreciate that they were of shares in its investment portfolio rather than out of its net profits, in contrast to McConnell's use of the profits of St Lawrence. In 1961 *Time* magazine accused McConnell of looting the *Star* in order to endow the Foundation, which was then about to give $4.5 million to McGill. The McConnells were outraged by this accusation, since it attacked the arm's-length relationship that they had been trying to maintain between the newspaper and the Foundation. John declared: "The newspaper's profits are not used to finance any program of charities or gifts to education. At present, the earnings of THE STAR are rather fully employed in the building of the most modern newspaper plant in North America." He continued: "Stories which have appeared over the last five years in Time Magazine have a weird consistency. The thesis, demonstrably false, is that under its present management, THE STAR is being starved in order to serve the benefactions of the McConnell Foundation. In fact, THE STAR employs more full-time correspondents at home and abroad than any other Canadian newspaper, and has one of the largest local staffs in the country, as well as the fullest complement of news and photo services."[54]

McConnell, it is safe to conclude, was reinvesting his profits into the *Star* itself, and this was the source of his financial success with it. Through this success, furthermore, he was able to remain faithful to his principle that the newspaper was a public trust. Generally, he oversaw editorial policy so that it reflected his own moderate and essentially non-partisan political views, contrary to rumours that he used the *Star* for the promotion of his other business interests. Upholding the public trust explicitly excluded such conflict of interest. At the same time, however, he lacked the necessary journalistic flair – and Canada, Quebec, and Montreal lacked the necessary level of interest in public affairs – for him to transform the *Star* into an equivalent of *The*

Times of London, as he had wanted. Yet he did build on Atholstan's work by making the newspaper a thriving business.

The *Star*, which closed down in 1979, after it had passed from the ownership of the McConnell family, is now a purely historical memory, like the *Herald* and the *Witness* and so many other Montreal papers. For over a century, it both reflected and shaped the life of English Montreal at its height, and, eagerly read even in rarefied circles in London, it represented Canada to the empire more widely. It called itself "Canada's Greatest Newspaper," just as Montreal considered itself Canada's greatest city. As McConnell himself knew, his paper was certainly not the greatest in circulation or advertising revenues or intellectual distinction. But it had been a great institution when he bought it from Atholstan, and McConnell had made it greater still.

CHAPTER SEVENTEEN

Grandescunt Aucta Labore: Building McGill University for the Future, 1920–63

In some special sense we were a partnership in the development of McGill. I hope that some future historian of the University will realise that – for me personally – his death marks the end of an epoch and leaves me with a realisation that the world is emptier.

Retired Principal F. Cyril James to Lily McConnell,
29 November 1963

McGill University, as the next chapter will show, was the chief object of McConnell's benefactions through his Foundation. But his contribution went beyond this. As a member of the McGill's Board of Governors from 1928 to 1958 – and as a governor emeritus and a life governor thereafter – he devoted considerable time and effort to promoting the university's interests in the face of unprecedented social and political change in Montreal, in Quebec, and in Canada. He naturally perceived the issues relating to McGill as a financier. Many have accused him of having a hidden political agenda for the university, but the evidence for this agenda is at best slender. What evidence we have in abundance, however, includes his opinions about, and actions in response to, some of the chief challenges facing McGill in his time. There we can glimpse how his fellow governors saw him, and how fundamentally uninterested he was in taking personal credit for his work or in receiving public attention more generally.

McConnell's support for the university continued after his death, as it continues to this day, in the form of the McConnell Scholarships, which he had endowed, and the grants made by his foundation. More than James McGill himself, the founder, or perhaps even Sir William Macdonald, its greatest benefactor before him, McConnell lavished on the university his time as well as gifts. Through his fundraising as well as his own donations, he saved McGill from financial crisis more than once and indeed he did much to put it on a firm financial and administrative footing for the future. As Stanley Frost, an official historian of the university, has concluded: "John Wilson McConnell was a complex person, shrewd in business, forthright in his loyalties, kindly in personal relationships, and socially motivated to immense generosities. As a benefactor of the university, he ranks with Strathcona and Macdonald. Yet no man sought to interfere less with the institution he so richly endowed."[1]

McConnell's success in raising money for the YMCA in 1909 led directly to his long involvement with McGill University, not only as a fundraiser and benefactor in his own right but also as a member of its Board of Governors. At this point, we need to survey his early fundraising efforts on the university's behalf, starting in 1911 and culminating with the McGill Centennial Endowment Campaign of 1920. It was these efforts – combined with others in support of McGill's affiliated hospitals – that led the public to see McConnell as a McGill "governor-in-waiting."

McGill had never been strong financially, and, in the years just before the First World War, it had been running growing deficits.[2] When Sir William Peterson, the principal, approached the owner of the Montreal *Star*, Sir Hugh Graham, for aid, Graham did not contribute as hoped but told Peterson to "pick some one person in whom your friends have entire confidence – someone whose experience justifies you in believing he would be likely to succeed. Let him formulate his own plan. Give him a free hand in the choice of his assistant. Promise him any support he may call for."[3] Graham's advice correctly underlined that McGill could no longer depend over-whelmingly, as it had been doing, on contributions from its rich governors. A new plan was necessary to widen the university's revenue sources.

In 1910 the McGill Board of Governors asked W.M. Birks, vice-president of his father Henry Birks's jewellery firm, and a businessman with a reputation for both toughness and effectiveness, to nominate a slate of four to six younger men to their ranks. The average age of a McGill governor was then seventy-six. Birks nominated the accountant J.W. Ross, the iron merchant George E. Drummond, the textile manu-facturer C.B. Gordon, the paper manufacturer F. Howard Wilson, and the "Copper King of America," Dr James Douglas of New York.

The new board, inspired by the YMCA campaign in which many of its members had been intimately involved, decided to mount a McGill fundraising campaign with-out delay. The 1911 McGill University Endowment Fund Campaign, as it was formally called, was in almost every respect modelled on the 1909 YMCA campaign, especially its competing teams of fundraisers. McConnell's role in that campaign had drawn the attention both of Birks and of J.W. Ross, and he was made a team captain. The goal was $1 million, later raised to $1.5 million.

The teams battled furiously in the McGill campaign. All of them contained social and business leaders of Montreal with whom McConnell was to be associated, in some cases for decades. McConnell's own team, no. 6, included Lorne Webster, importer and agent for Nova Scotia Steel and Coal; Nathaniel Curry, president of Canadian Car and Foundry; E.-A. Robert of Canadian Light and Power and Montreal Tram-ways; and F. Howard Wilson, president of Tram-Power.

By the end of the campaign, $1,526,965 was raised – $25,000 from McConnell himself. In contributing such a large amount, McConnell was placing himself in the same league as Sir Hugh Graham. For someone whose salary had been only $3,500 six years before, his contribution was nothing short of astounding. Moreover, McConnell's team had raised almost one-third of the total, and at the close of the campaign he "was most loudly acclaimed as the most successful worker and as a future governor of McGill."[4] From the lists of subscribers, it is not possible to determine which of them were actually successfully canvassed by McConnell himself. He was, however, by this time part a group of investors, Imperial Trust, which included H.A. Lovett, G.B. Allison (Hudson's brother), and C.H. Cahan, all of whom made significant contributions.

In 1912 McConnell headed another remarkably successful fundraising campaign, this time for the Wesleyan Theological College, which was loosely affiliated with McGill and whose board McConnell had recently joined. The goal was to erect a new building for the college on University and Milton streets, and, again, it was achieved. McConnell himself was to lay the foundation stone of the building on 15 September 1914, in place of Chester Massey, who was ill. On 3 October a ceremony held in the new school was addressed by a group of dignitaries including McConnell, Johnston, W.M. Birks, and the Reverend S.D. Chown, general superintendent of the Methodist Church. McConnell remained indispensable to the board until his resignation in 1918, when he was called to work in Ottawa, but he later resumed his place on it until the college was merged into the United Theological College in 1928.[5]

The next fundraising campaign for McGill as a whole began in November 1920, prompted by a challenge grant from the Rockefeller Foundation. This grant was for a $1-million endowment for the Faculty of Medicine, on condition that a matching amount was raised for new buildings for various medical departments.[6] The McGill Centennial Endowment Campaign of 1920, as the effort was named, had other goals as well. These included: (a) endowment funds for the library, staff salaries, equipment and laboratory apparatus, the lighting, heating, and maintenance of buildings, and the new School of Commerce; and (b) a capital fund for new buildings and rooms.

Like the McGill campaign of 1911, this new one adopted the methods of the YMCA campaign of 1909. Operationally, it also drew upon the methods employed by the Canadian Patriotic Fund in 1914–16, to the extent of using its canvassing lists. In personnel, it bore a remarkable resemblance also to the Victory Loan campaigns of 1917–20, the principals including J.W. Ross the accountant, Sir Vincent Meredith of the Bank of Montreal, Edward Beatty of the CPR, Sir Charles Gordon of Dominion Textile, W.M. Birks the jeweller, Percy Cowans the stockbroker, H.R. Drummond the sugar refiner, A.D. Anderson, and D.A. Budge of the YMCA. Perhaps because 1920 was a difficult year for McConnell and his sugar business, he served merely as an honorary vice-chairman of the citizens' committee, composed of non-graduates.

But, since most of the canvassers were like him businessmen who had not graduated from McGill, by now he was embodying a vital as well as an established tradition of support for the university.

The total collected by the 1920 campaign was in excess of $6,321,511 ($63,553,732 in 2008), including the $1 million initially promised by the Rockefeller Foundation. It also included $250,000 each from the Royal Bank, the Bank of Montreal, and the CPR. McConnell himself – despite the insolvency of his sugar company – gave the substantial sum of $100,000 ($1,005,357 in 2008), which was more than all Protestant educational institutions in Quebec combined had received from the province in 1914–15.[7]

Foreshadowing the opposition that McConnell was to face as chairman of the Joint Hospital Campaign of 1927, not everyone was overwhelmed by such generosity. At least one correspondent wrote to Principal Sir Arthur Currie that the amounts raised had been taken from high service charges to the public, dividends due to shareholders, and excess-profit tax due to the government. "It is useless," he noted, "to talk as the Government and banks pull together in the interests of Big Business; the masses pay the piper and dance to any tune that the *Big* interests see fit to put on."[8]

The list of firm subscriptions to the 1920 campaign, dated 18 December 1929,[9] makes it plain that McGill had entered a period of strong dominance by what was roughly and not very accurately called St James Street. The subscriptions by McGill governors totalled $861,000. Of this sum, subscriptions of $10,000 or more made up $840,000 or 97.5 per cent. Further, of the total of $6,321,511 collected by the fund, the $840,000 from the "big business" governors constituted 13 per cent. McConnell's election as governor in 1928, after he had contributed $100,000, or 15.8 per cent of the total collected in 1920, merely solidified this trend towards a board dominated by rich businessmen.[10]

After the deaths of Lord Strathcona in 1914 and Sir William Macdonald in 1917, and the endowment campaign of 1920, which actually carried on for most of the decade, there remained no spectacularly generous university governors, except for McConnell himself and Walter Stewart, who represented the Macdonald estate. Until then, the McGill board had consisted of men of either inherited or self-made wealth or both. McConnell's fortune was not at all inherited but that of a self-made entrepreneur. Yet he escaped the traditional mould in being also a salaried executive of various companies, and thus he embodied a fundamental shift in the complexion of the board, as it became almost exclusively a group of salaried corporate executives. McConnell did more than symbolize this transition. What made him exceptional among his colleagues even in 1928 was his record as a fundraiser, his success as an investor, and his generosity as a benefactor. What made him unique among them over the following thirty years was his ability to mobilize support for McGill from the new corporate wealth, while continuing to give as a rich individual in the Macdonald tradition. All this he achieved in an environment of unprecedented internal and external strain for the university.

By the end of the 1920s, McGill, a distinguished but privately run institution, not substantially supported by taxes and catering overwhelmingly to the relatively prosperous English-speaking and Protestant minority that had established it, was facing also two crises of identity. Internally, the English Protestant stranglehold over McGill was under threat, not linguistically but religiously and culturally, with Jews competing for limited places at McGill as notional Protestants, defined legally in the system of public schools as those who were not Roman Catholic. With the costs of equipment and buildings rising, educational institutions were demanding unprecedented funding.

Outside the university, there were growing demands by the French-speaking and Roman Catholic majority for higher education. These posed the second challenge faced by McGill, one largely beyond its control. French, Roman Catholic Quebecers were divided among themselves on how to finance their universities and on to what extent to secularize them. McGill was by definition excluded from their struggle over secularization since, although historically and culturally Protestant, it was not denominational, and it did not teach dogma. But the question of how to finance the French-speaking universities was relevant to it. McGill was linguistically less isolated from the rest of the province than often depicted, but the majority of voters in Quebec were French-speaking, and so any project of public funding for universities was unlikely to favour it.

Nevertheless, McGill was quietly influential in producing leaders, French- as well as English-speaking, for the industrializing society of the province in which it found itself. Although discreet, McConnell, McGill, and most English-speaking Protestants favoured those French Canadians who wanted to secularize, industrialize, and otherwise modernize their society. They had nothing in common with, say, Canon Lionel Groulx or with other advocates of a return to an agricultural past. They could, however, speak the same language, often literally as well as figuratively, as the businessmen, the politicians, and the scientists who were reshaping French Canadian society, even though these could also be nationalists.

Superimposed on these two issues of internal expansion and external funding were the broader financial crises caused by the Great Depression and the Second World War. Within McGill, there were, moreover, years of disrupted administrative leadership, with three different principals in office in 1935, 1936, and 1937 alone, and then a fourth in 1939. Conflicting political ideologies affected both their appointments and certain academic ones for even longer. Despite them, McConnell personally rose to the various financial challenges confronting McGill, to the extent at times of paying for teachers out of his own pocket. He was less deft in confronting the political and ideological issues that were bedevilling the university. For this perceived want, he was maligned, even by contemporaries.

Because, too, he was unwilling to defend himself, his often anonymous generosity has been unrecognized or grossly underestimated or even associated with vaguely defined wrongdoing in business, probably dating back to the tramways episode of his life. Such is the background to the question of why McConnell, unlike Macdonald and many other businessmen, failed to become the chancellor of McGill, its symbolic head as well as chairman of its governors. This particular issue did not surface until 1943, but it casts harsh light on other aspects of McGill, to which we now turn before what happened in that year and its aftermath.

Why, it may be asked, was McGill special to McConnell and to Canada as a whole? Most obviously, the McGill governors consisted essentially of corporate directors, so that it was the pre-eminent board of boards, in Montreal and by extension arguably in all of Canada. Beginning in 1928, McConnell sat on the Royal Victoria Hospital board as well as on that of McGill, the Bank of Montreal, the Sun Life Assurance Company, and the Canadian Pacific Railway. Together, these five boards held an undisputed sway over most of social and economic life in Montreal, chiefly because their memberships largely overlapped. There were in Montreal, however, other boards of almost equal distinction, such as that of the Montreal General Hospital or Canadian Industries Limited, and they also had representatives on the McGill board.

An executive committee of the McGill board, on which McConnell and the principal also sat, provided the university's administrative leadership. Though this little knot of McGill governors, however distinguished, did not always operate with one mind, it imposed upon its members the burden of maintaining the university as the foremost educational institution in Montreal and Quebec, if not in all of Canada, and the best known both at home and abroad. Its function was therefore decidedly not to be exclusive and parochial but to reach out to a wider community, radiating from English Montreal to Quebec, and then to Canada, North America, the British Empire, and beyond. Because the corporate and cultural interests, as well as experience, of its members were often international, McGill saw itself as a window on the world for Montreal.

Even locally, despite its role as the only university, apart from Bishop's, run by the English-speaking Protestant minority in Quebec, McGill tried hard not to be isolated from the province. Engagement with much of Quebec was not easy to achieve, since the French-speaking Roman Catholic majority, as a matter of principle, kept its institutions self-sufficient from governments as well as insulated from English-speaking Protestant influences. It was in business and government, not in education, that the majority and the minority tended to intersect. In McConnell's time, two premiers, Sir Lomer Gouin and L.-A. Taschereau, were directors of both Sun Life and the Bank of Montreal. Gouin, who had received an honorary degree from McGill as early as 1911, was also a director of Shawinigan Water and Power, International Paper and Power, and Lake of the Woods Milling, among other concerns. Taschereau, through his family, was even more closely tied with Shawinigan and through it to Montreal

Power via United Securities. Although the two premiers were not also on the McGill Board of Governors, Sir Arthur Currie, the principal of McGill, was on the Sun Life and Bank of Montreal boards with them, as were McConnell and other McGill governors, although their terms were not necessarily identical. Gouin and Taschereau, with the aid of English-speaking capital, laid the basis for the industrialization of Quebec in the first half of the twentieth century, followed by Premier Duplessis. Premier Godbout, who expropriated Montreal Power, was more of a modernizer than all the others. Through its governors, McGill saw it in its own interest to ally itself with these essentially business-oriented leaders, and it viewed their increasing efforts to create a French-speaking middle class, educated in business and technology, not as a threat but as complementary to its own role for English-speaking Quebecers.

Nevertheless, McGill was definitely not provincial. Its chief rival, the University of Toronto, was – in wealth, influence, research, and teaching – rapidly catching up to, if not outstripping, it. But Toronto was designated as "the provincial university" of Ontario, funded by and dedicated to the taxpayers of its province; and, unlike McGill, it had little incentive to attract promising students and teaching staff from other provinces and countries. The government of Ontario appointed the University of Toronto board, whereas, relatively speaking, the head and the governors of McGill were not in the least beholden to provincial politics or preoccupations. In fact, McGill thought of itself as the "national" university, since students in engineering or applied science at five other Canadian universities would move to McGill for their fourth year; and students from Alberta would transfer there for their fourth year. Moreover, McGill students might move on to the universities of Oxford, Cambridge, or Dublin to complete their education.[11] Also, McGill habitually searched for internationally known businessmen or retired politicians to serve as its chancellor – its chairman of the board and effectively its chief executive, as distinct from its principal, its chief administrative officer.

As the university became increasingly funded by corporations, the chancellor came to head a board composed of largely of other chairmen, whose own boards were some of the most important in Canada. In casting his vote, the chancellor wielded no more influence than his fellow governors; but, as their first among equals, he presented their public face, and by extension that of the university. The first two chancellors of the twentieth century were Lord Strathcona, a builder of the CPR, and Sir William Macdonald, the builder of a tobacco fortune – both self-made men. Then McGill appointed the former prime minister, Sir Robert Borden, but he served for less than a year. After Borden had resigned through ill health, its chancellor from 1920 to 1943 was Edward (from 1935 Sir Edward) Beatty, the president and the chairman of the CPR, the largest employer in the country. He had spent his career in the CPR as a lawyer before becoming its president, and he exemplified the triumph on the board of the corporate mentality. Decisive, authoritarian, and tirelessly devoted to McGill,

Sir Edward Beatty, chancellor of McGill University, reviews a guard of honour
of the Canadian Grenadier Guards, n.d. Montreal *Gazette* Archives.

he brought to his position power as well as distinction, and he served as its de facto
principal as well as chancellor during the two interregnums of the 1930s. He was succeeded first by Morris Wilson and then by B.C. Gardner.

While all the presidents of the University of Toronto were from Ontario, McGill
also emphasized its determination to build its reputation internationally in its choice of
principal. In McConnell's time as governor, two Englishmen (A.E. Morgan and Cyril
James), one American of Canadian origins (Lewis Douglas), and only one native-
born Canadian (Sir Arthur Currie) occupied this position. None was from Quebec
much less from English Montreal. The choice of principal was a sensitive one, since
the desire for an internationally distinguished man could not outweigh local interests
and concerns. Sir William Peterson, whose term ended with his death in 1921, had
been thoroughly British in orientation and not universally popular. McConnell's first
principal, Currie, was a Canadian general of imperial and even global renown, and
hardworking, imaginative, and generally popular as principal, but it proved impossible to find a Canadian to replace him on his death in 1935. His successor, Morgan,
was very English and never at home in Canada and sacked after a year. He had never
enjoyed an international reputation in any case. In contrast, his American successor,
Douglas, had been a member of the cabinet of President Roosevelt as director of the
budget. After less than two controversial years at McGill, Douglas was to return to the
United States, respected but not remembered for his interest in Canada.

James, although English by birth and very English in manner, had obtained his
doctorate from, and taught at, the University of Pennsylvania, and he was already

Lil with Principal Lewis Douglas, 4 February 1939.
Montreal *Gazette* Archives.

a professor at McGill at the time of his appointment. James proved to be the most successful principal while McConnell was a governor, not least because the two men reinvigorated the international reorientation of the university while adding lustre to its identity as a Canadian institution.

In the McGill of McConnell's time, businessmen with degrees of any kind were rare, and the graduates among them had usually been born of rich families with interests beyond business. Neither were professionals typically graduates. Accountants, engineers, and even many lawyers were often without university degrees and they obtained their designations through apprenticeships. McConnell himself was not a graduate, and he used his own lack of an earned degree as an excuse consistently to decline an honorary degree. For long the only systematic business studies in the province were pursued at the École des Hautes Études Commerciales (HEC), founded in 1905–07 as a special cause of Sir Lomer Gouin, then premier, who correctly saw it as productive of a new, French-speaking managerial class for Quebec.[12] In 1907 McGill did begin a two-year diploma course in commerce, in the Department of Economics and Political Science; in 1911 it formed a School of Commerce within the department, and in 1918 it approved a three-year program leading to the degree of bachelor of commerce, but one designed to be as practical as possible, with even courses on how to write business letters. Evening classes for actuaries, accountants, and bank employees began after the First World War, but a School of Commerce distinct from the Department of Economics and Political Science did not begin until after the Second, and even then, unlike the HEC, it depended on private funding.[13]

McGill was justifiably much better known for its faculties of engineering and science than for its commerce studies, but even here it faced provincially funded competition to its privately funded efforts. These were the École Polytechnique (founded in 1876 and affiliated first with Université Laval and then, from 1918, with the Université de Montréal), and an engineering school at Laval that was established in 1938. Both received substantial support from the provincial government, while McGill did not. For it, therefore, private funding was crucial.

The greatest benefactor to McGill before McConnell had been William McDonald who, upon receiving a knighthood in 1898, changed his name to Macdonald. Although with almost no formal education himself, since 1861 he had built up hugely profitable business in tobacco and set up scholarships for McGill students in 1870. Firmly against religious influences, he continued to endow the university with gifts for practical, secular education. He revolutionized the notion of higher education, until then largely dominated by the classics, and he firmly established McGill in the same league as the Carnegie Institute of Technology, the Massachusetts Institute of Technology, and other hothouses of American innovation. In 1891 he gave more than $10 million for the faculties of engineering and science, including buildings specifically for physics, chemistry, mining, and engineering, together costing over $1 million, with a further endowment of $400,000 for professors of physics, electrical and mining engineering, architecture, and chemistry.

In the following decade, in 1906–07, Macdonald established a college bearing his name in suburban Sainte-Anne-de-Bellevue to teach agriculture and pedagogy. He was generous to the McGill Faculty of Law and endowed a chair of history, in addition to supporting the salaries of teaching staff and meeting deficits. The scale and the imagination of his projects confirmed McGill as the foremost secular and practical institution of higher education in Quebec, and probably in Canada. His influence stretched to the Ontario College of Agriculture in Guelph, where he established an institute of domestic science for women, and to the McGill University College of British Columbia, later the University of British Columbia. Although they disagreed on the importance of religious education, McConnell was later to walk in Macdonald's shadow and to enlarge Macdonald's legacy. The McConnell Engineering Building, for example, stands beside the Macdonald Engineering Building.

With Macdonald's endowment, McGill became famous around the world for its graduates in engineering and science. In 1913 almost 45 per cent were from Quebec, 40 per cent from elsewhere in Canada, almost 15 per cent from Great Britain, and 6 per cent from the United States. It had produced twice as many Quebec-born engineers as the Polytechnique, and not all of these were native English-speakers. The McGill Faculty of Engineering produced about 37 French-speaking students between 1871 and 1911, out of a total of 1,115.[14]

The professional school of McGill most clearly connected to French Quebec, however, was its Faculty of Law. Because its graduates were expected to function in the Quebec legal system, dominated by French-speaking judges and juries, with a Civil Code largely derived from France, the McGill law school was inevitably far from a bastion of Anglo-Saxon isolation. Charles Dewey Day, judge of the Court of Queen's Bench and of the Superior Court of Lower Canada, a member and president of the McGill Board of Governors, temporary principal and chancellor, and founder of its Faculty of Law, was one of the three commissioners charged with drafting the Civil Code of Lower Canada, which was and remains the central document of the distinct legal system of Quebec.[15] Within the profession at large, there were judicial positions traditionally reserved for English-speaking Quebecers on the provincial Court of Appeal and on the Superior Court that sat in Montreal, and both of these inevitably included graduates of McGill. With their education in English as well as French law, these graduates played a key role in the administration of justice. The criminal law of all of Canada, including Quebec, derived from English common law and was bound by common law jurisprudence, all in the English language; and appeal from the courts of Quebec, even in civil matters, went to the Supreme Court in Ottawa, and then possibly to the Privy Council in London. In effect, all successful Quebec lawyers had to be bilingual, in English and French, in order to master the relevant case law and legal theory, and they also shared a common knowledge of Latin. McGill law graduates often exhibited a breadth and a depth of culture alien to most English Montreal businessmen.

In McConnell's time, there were in practice federal senatorships, provincial legislative councillorships, and seats in both the federal and provincial parliaments and cabinets reserved for English-speaking Quebecers. Thus, for example, until the era of Duplessis, the provincial treasurer (minister of finance) was always from English Quebec and almost inevitably a graduate of McGill – a practice that Duplessis saw as symbolic of the power of St James Street, even though English-speaking treasurers had always been more than mere mouthpieces of the Street.

In any event, the McGill Faculty of Law embodied these traditions and deepened them. Sir John Abbott, professor of criminal and commercial law at McGill, dean of the faculty, and governor, twice turned down the position of chief justice of Quebec but also became a member of the Legislative Assembly and three times a Member of Parliament, before serving first as solicitor general and later as prime minister. Sir Wilfrid Laurier, a McGill law graduate in 1864, was the first French Canadian prime minister. Gérard Fauteaux, the first French Canadian dean, grandson of Premier Honoré Mercier, nephew of Premier Sir Lomer Gouin, and brother of Lieutenant Governor Gaspard Fauteux, became a chief justice of Canada. Aimé Geoffrion, grandson of Sir Antoine-Aimé Dorion, chief justice of Quebec, was professor of civil law at McGill and one of the greatest litigators of his time. Of similar international reputation was Eugène Lafleur.

Many of these were known to McConnell, but he was particularly close to R.A.E. Greenshields, for eight years acting dean and dean of the McGill Faculty of Law, and a chief justice of the Superior Court of Quebec, as well as with his brother J.N. Greenshields, whose first client was the leader of the North-West Rebellion, Louis Riel. He was even closer to F.E. Meredith, son of Chief Justice Sir William Meredith of Ontario and cousin of Sir Vincent Meredith of the Bank of Montreal and some-time dean of the McGill Faculty of Law and *bâtonnier* of the Montreal bar, educated at Laval and in France as well as at Bishop's University in Lennoxville (of which he became chancellor).

Since McGill's governors were its principal source of funding, the university of the 1920s urgently required both new leadership and new drive. McConnell supplied both. After his success in raising money for McGill in 1911, McConnell became known, particularly from 1920 onwards, as a governor-in-waiting. Then, in 1928, when he joined Principal Currie and Chancellor Beatty to form a virtual triumvirate responsible for running and financing McGill, the university found itself governed by three Ontarians, born and bred. Despite Beatty's education at Upper Canada College, officially a non-sectarian but culturally an Anglican institution, these three men were essentially all products of Egerton Ryerson's strictly non-denominational system of education. They therefore had no qualms in advancing Macdonald's vision of a modernizing, secular McGill open to students of all religions or of none.

There are many myths surrounding McConnell's tenure on the McGill Board of Governors, and one of the longest-lasting portrays him as a determined foe of academic freedom. In the 1930s McGill was convulsed by controversies involving the right claimed by certain of its academics to promote their political views outside the classroom. One of these academics was Leonard Marsh, director of the university's Social Science Research Project. Marsh, who joined the CCF-linked League for Social Reconstruction in 1932 and served as its president from 1937 to 1939, and who collaborated with Frank Scott in publishing *Social Planning for Canada*, a critique of capitalism, attracted the ire of Principal Douglas and Chancellor Beatty for his extra-curricular political activity. The university's response to this activity – first criticism of Marsh's conduct and then the termination of his contract in 1940[16] – angered many leading figures among the country's intellectual elite, including not only Frank Scott but also McGill's Stephen Leacock, the University of Toronto's Frank Underhill, and B.K. Sandwell of *Saturday Night*.

In all of this controversy, however, there is absolutely no evidence that McConnell took any part whatsoever. Neither is there any evidence that he had a hand, even behind the scenes, in the firing of two other McGill academics for much the same reasons, the economist Eugene Forsey and the religious studies professor King Gordon.[17] On the contrary, there is evidence that he was far from wholly unsympathetic with state planning, whatever he may have thought of these men. His friend Arthur Purvis, the president of CIL and one of the leading governors of McGill, conducted an inquiry which led to the passing of the first Unemployment Insurance Act for Canada in 1940. And McConnell almost undoubtedly met Sir William Beveridge, the teacher of Leonard Marsh, when he came to Montreal in 1943. McConnell owned a copy of Beveridge's famous report, *Social Insurance and Allied Services*, published the year before, which dealt largely with state pensions, and he even praised it to Wendell Willkie, Roosevelt's chief adversary. McConnell was deeply supportive of pensions generally, as is evidenced by his work in 1941–42, with W.M. Birks, to establish pensions for United Church ministers. McConnell's work by himself to establish pensions for the Victorian Order of Nurses (1944–46) and for the nurses of the Royal Victoria Hospital speaks likewise.[18]

The portrait of McConnell as an enemy of academic freedom, however, focuses principally not on the Marsh, Forsey, or Gordon cases but on that of Frank Scott. It is said that McConnell did all he could to prevent Scott, Marsh's comrade-in-arms and a professor in the McGill Faculty of Law, from becoming dean of law, to the extent of reaching deep into the practising bar to find Bill Meredith, the son of his old friend Fred Meredith, for the position. Yet the truth is that there is only the scantiest evidence of how McConnell felt about academic freedom in general or that of Scott in particular. This fact alone suggests that, contrary to rumour, McConnell is highly unlikely to have been a leader in forming opinion at McGill on these matters.

Others were far more influential and vocal in this area, most notably Beatty. McConnell almost never spoke in public at McGill, partly because he was not an orator but also because he wrongly felt himself to be ill equipped intellectually to address academics. His own family made no attempt to disabuse him of this notion, and his son John was terrified on one occasion that his father might make a grammatical error when he was absolutely obliged to speak at a McGill meeting. In fact, McConnell had no difficulty in speaking frankly to fellow governors, who were businessmen like him. And it seems that he was more bemused and even awed by academics than inclined to interfere in academic policy. In nearly all the voluminous correspondence pertaining to McConnell and McGill, virtually the only topic addressed was that of funding.

Scott himself charged that McConnell was the person responsible for blocking his promotion to the deanship of the Faculty of Law on four separate occasions. This may have happened, or not, but there seems to be no hard evidence What is incontrovertible, however, is that even before McConnell's death, and despite his alleged efforts, Scott's career did advance. Long before 1958, he had been acting dean and held the Greenshields professorship of law, both appointments requiring the approval of the board, which then included McConnell, although whether or how he voted on these appointments is not known. Moreover, before McConnell's death in 1963, Scott had become dean – as well as a Queen's Counsel and the recipient of both honorary degrees and almost universal praise from distinguished academics, jurists, St James Street lawyers, politicians, and the general public.

Undeniable, too, is that McConnell and Scott disliked each other intensely. Certainly, they could not have been more different. Scott had tried to enlist to fight in the Great War five times and he then became a pacifist. McConnell had not tried to enlist even once and yet remained a firm supporter of conscription through both world wars. Scott, a son of an Anglo-Catholic priest and poet and a brother of another priest and theologian, had found his religion in the mystic St Thomas à Kempis and the professor of Hebrew and ritualist Edward Bouverie Pusey. McConnell, a son of a failed and barely literate farmer, had found his religion in the hymns of the Wesleys and in the Epworth League. Scott, a Rhodes Scholar, a poet, a dreamer, and an aesthete, had hardly ever seen the floor of a factory or met, much less hired or himself been, a factory worker; and yet he was to emerge as one of the most ardent self-appointed defenders of the working class. McConnell, largely self-educated, a bookkeeper and uninterested in the arts, had for years worked in manufacturing and yet become a firm opponent of trade unions and the employer of hundreds of workers in various enterprises from a department store to a sugar refinery.

The two men epitomized more than their different backgrounds. They represented conflicting visions of the past, the present, and the future of Canada. Scott became a staunch opponent of the empire and possibly a republican, while McConnell remained to the end fiercely loyal to the empire and to the throne. Scott savaged and trounced Duplessis in the courts over the premier's suppression of freedom of speech and religion and due process. McConnell was a firm and public friend of Duplessis and he (although not the *Star*, as we have seen) endorsed Duplessis's Padlock Law ostensibly for its value in combating communism. In the 1960s Scott was to sit on the Royal Commission on Bilingualism and Biculturalism and be a godfather of the Charter of Rights and Freedoms attached to the "patriated" British North America Act of 1982. McConnell, though not opposed to bilingualism, had no interest in constitutional law or human rights and was a symbol of an essentially unilingual English dominance over Quebec.

Although generally and rightly noted for his tolerance and his fairness, from early in his life Frank Scott harboured an abiding animus against big business, and he felt sure that big business was out to destroy him. His was the contempt for, and the incomprehension of, business characteristic of many people exclusively educated in the humanities, and unmodified by further education in the law. As an undergraduate at McGill, he ridiculed Principal Currie as a big businessman in the pocket of such other big businessmen as McConnell, although Currie's only business experience, as a real estate agent, had been disastrous. Upon his return from Oxford, Scott was shocked and dismayed by how "commercial" Montreal seemed. He found the CPR particularly offensive, though its president, Sir Edward Beatty, had sent him and at least one other declared socialist to Oxford on Rhodes Scholarships.

By the end of the Second World War, most of Scott's LSR colleagues at McGill had gone – some claim expelled by McConnell and Beatty – and so Scott naturally saw himself as somewhat beleaguered. In the post-war period he slowly emerged as the grand old man not of socialism but of a new form of liberal social democracy. There was virtual unanimity that he had been wronged by McConnell, and that McConnell had, perhaps single-handed, denied him the acclaim that he had long richly deserved, first by banning mention of him and the CCF in the *Star* and secondly by engineering his exclusion as dean of law from 1947 onwards. It is reasonable to assume that such warm admirers of Scott as Bora Laskin and Pierre Trudeau shared this opinion, as did even Peter Laing, McConnell's son-in-law, and George Ferguson, the editor of the *Star*.

The fact that Scott became perhaps the most lethal of Duplessis's enemies merely reinforced his reputation as a dragon slayer, the dragons in his case being Duplessis himself and by extension McConnell and others that he saw as Duplessis toadies, as well as what he thought that they stood for. Scott, moreover, was to outlive Duplessis and McConnell by almost a quarter-century, and in that period nearly everything that he represented, apart from doctrinaire socialism, became part of the orthodoxy of the vast bulk of thinking people in the country.

They were more than polar opposites as individuals: they embodied different generations of an English Montreal that was revealing new fissures after the war. The prevailing post-war, nationalist conception of Canada in this community was an English-speaking, centralizing one. Scott saw it as a socialist one as well whereas, as we shall see, McConnell's position implicitly and curiously endorsed the bold view of Quebec autonomy held by Duplessis. Like McConnell's support for Duplessis more generally, this view commanded little assent at McGill outside, and even inside, the board and in English Montreal at large.

The accusations against McConnell in connection with Frank Scott are often linked with his alleged role in another matter, the refusal of the McGill Board of Governors to admit Samuel Bronfman, one of the most famous distillers in the world and probably the only man in Canada comparable to McConnell in wealth, into its ranks. In this case, though, the charge has nothing to do with politics and everything to do with race and religion – Bronfman was a Jew – and, furthermore, is tied to the larger issue of the role of alleged anti-Semitism in imposing a quota on the admission of Jewish students to McGill.

The issue is a complicated one. From McGill's earliest days, Jews were never excluded as either students or teachers. On the contrary, McGill was known as "the favored university of Canadian Jews,"[19] a status reflected in the appointment of Rabbi

Abraham De Sola as professor of Hebrew and Oriental languages in 1849, as well as in the fact that in 1905 Israel Isidore Rubinowitz became the first Jewish Rhodes Scholar to proceed from McGill to Oxford. In the 1930s Beatty personally intervened to send another Jew, David Lewis, to Oxford as a Rhodes Scholar, even after Lewis, a socialist and a future leader of the socialist New Democratic Party, had told Beatty that he wanted to nationalize the CPR.

A quota on Jewish students at McGill does seem to have been introduced in the 1920s and to have lasted into the 1950s, but the documentary evidence for it – what it involved and why it was imposed in the first place – is slight. In general, it appears to have been motivated not by race or religion but by financial considerations – it was an effort to bring the proportion of Jewish students into line with the financial contribution of the Jewish community to the university. What is more, far from exciting any controversy at the time, the quota was openly discussed and even negotiated with representatives of the Jewish community. In the 1920s, it seems that the quota was in the range of 9–10 per cent of the student body, but by the early 1940s it had risen to 14–17 per cent. This number was considerably higher than the proportion of Jewish students at either Queen's University in Kingston (9.2 per cent) or the University of Toronto (10 per cent). The quota, however, does not seem to have been applied uniformly across the university – it was lower in medicine than in any other faculties – and it must be remembered that in the 1920s the proportion of Jews in the McGill student body was much higher than the proportion of Jews in the Canadian population as a whole (1.5 per cent).

Ira MacKay, dean of arts in the 1930s, is generally cited as the most prominent anti-Semite to leave a record at McGill. At the start of the open German persecution of the Jews in 1933, MacKay wrote to Principal Currie objecting to the admission to Canada Jewish refugees as university professors, schoolteachers, and judges.[20] Jews were of "no use" to Canada, he stated, and their favoured occupations of merchandising, money-lending, medicine, and law were already full of "our own [Protestant] people." McGill, MacKay concluded, owed a duty to the French and English people of Canada. It "would not for a single moment entertain over three hundred of our own French fellow-countrymen unless they contributed accordingly to the maintenance of this University, and I see no reason why we should treat Jews with any greater sympathy."[21] Yet, even for MacKay, it is clear that the issue of Jewish admissions was largely one of availability of space at McGill generally, combined with the perceived lack of Jewish support for the university, and not anti-Semitism in a purely racist sense.[22]

What did McConnell think about McGill's Jewish quota? Again, there seems to be no written evidence on which to make any judgments. However, contrary to his reputation as an anti-Semite, there is evidence that he was deeply concerned about the isolation of the Jewish students at McGill and that he wanted them to work harder to fit into McGill in the interest both of themselves and of the university. Evidence for this is in the form of the draft of a speech to Jewish students that dates probably from 1940–43. In places, the draft is illegible, but it demonstrates unequivocally that McConnell's approach to Jewish students was inclusive:

> To the Jewish students – you above all should *work* for co-operation for ... a vital part in making McGill greater & more influential than she has ever been in the past and feel keenly that you have only a short time in which to do it ... You must do, you must give. Your principal and VC [James] is a young man ... Get behind your principal, get behind your teachers. Strive in every way possible to encourage them. Take with you *a glow of pride* [in] this university ... If you would *learn* you must *teach* – help others as you go on your way. I'll throw out a challenge. I'll suggest a job in which you may all take part ... You must pay the price. Nothing worth while is cheap. You should have a goal which is co-operation – pride in your self, pride in your work, and in your university.[23]

This returns us to the question of Bronfman. There is an oral tradition in which McConnell is widely rumoured to have used his power to block the appointment of Samuel Bronfman as a governor of McGill, indeed, to have pledged to block it over "my dead body." But how likely is this? From the point of view of McGill funding alone, the story is extraordinary, for Bronfman – whose burgeoning liquor distilling, sales, and export business grew into an international empire after his relocation from Winnipeg to Montreal in the 1920s – was a major contributor to McGill long before he joined the board, and it was not characteristic of McConnell to discourage charitable donations from any source. It is true that Bronfman did not become a governor until 1964, a year after McConnell's death. Yet, if McConnell was opposed to Bronfman's appointment, his opposition was probably not decisive, because, long before the appointment, McConnell had retired from the board (formally in 1958 but practically in about 1955). His status as honorary governor conferred on him no vote. Also, decisions on appointments required more than one vote, McConnell's or any other. There is no evidence – influential as he was – that McConnell exercised overwhelming power over the votes of his fellow governors before his retirement, much less after it. The contrary is proved both by Scott's promotion to the deanship of law in McConnell's time and by the opposition on the board to McConnell's own appointment as chancellor in 1942–43. The conclusion that he was omnipotent on the board simply because he was its greatest donor cannot stand.

There is the complementary claim that not merely McConnell but the board in general were anti-Semitic, and that Bronfman was merely a victim of their prejudice. It is true that the governors elected no Jew as governor in McConnell's time. And it would have insulated the university from much criticism if they had accepted at least a token Jew among them. It also would have probably have brought shrewd counsel, financial and other. Why no Jew was appointed to the board until after McConnell's death is an open question, but this fact does not really prove that any or all of the board were necessarily anti-Semitic, and still less does it prove that keeping Bronfman out was based on this. There may well have been other reasons for not electing him.

Bronfman, who lobbied for an appointment to the Senate probably even more vigorously than for one to the McGill board, never received that either, although his Jewish lieutenant, Lazarus Phillips, who was a great admirer of McConnell, did. As Maxwell Henderson, a financial adviser to Bronfman from 1945 to 1956, and later auditor general of Canada, was to recall, the appointment by St Laurent of David Croll as the first Jewish senator, in 1955, left Bronfman "inarticulate with anger" and Bronfman "virtually ignored Laz Phillips's existence" from Phillips's appointment in 1968 until Bronfman's death in 1971. Henderson's understanding was that "the Bronfman reputation from the old days" would make a senatorship for him out of the question.[24] Henderson's reference seems to be to Bronfman's alleged links to organized crime in the United States. Seen in this light, Bronfman's appointment to the McGill board was bold even in 1964.

Two reasons are given for McConnell's alleged opposition to Bronfman. One is that Bronfman was a manufacturer of liquor and the other is that Bronfman was a Jew. Although it is true that McConnell was a teetotaller, through his entire career he both worked with and befriended people involved in the purveying of alcohol. From Markland Molson, Herbert Molson, and Senator Marcelin Wilson (then a mentor of Bronfman's) in the early days to various members of the Dawes family over several decades, he was publicly and privately associated with manufacturers and distributors of beer and spirits. He sat with two generations of Molsons, both presidents of Molsons brewery, Herbert and then Hartland, on the McGill board, and it has never been alleged that he objected to Hartland Molson's appointment to either the Senate or the McGill board.

McConnell was associated, it is true, with fewer Jews than brewers and distillers, but as early as about 1910 he had hired a scion of one of the most famous Jewish families in Quebec, Henry Joseph, as his agent for Montreal-London Securities in London, and his assistance to Rabbi Harry Stern, who received an honorary degree from McGill in 1938, and to Stern's Temple Emmanu-El in Westmount represented a pioneer effort at strengthening understanding between Christians and Jews in Montreal.

Further, in contrast to the widespread anti-Semitism of French-speaking Quebec in this era, even his harshest critics have never accused McConnell of sympathy towards fascism. In fact, he was publicly on record as wanting both English and French Canadians to be conscripted for military service. He also seems, if *Star* editorials are any indication, to have been a harsh critic of the Vichy regime, again unlike many representatives of the province's French-speaking elite. Probably all his friends, and nearly everyone else of prominence in English Quebec except Frank Scott, agreed with him. It is no exaggeration to say that the war definitively turned English Quebec generally against anti-Semitism, and that the community saw its support of conscription as necessary to the defence of civilization and of human decency.

Yet what did McConnell think of Bronfman and Jews as individuals? The answer is important because it is central to his view of funding for McGill and similar causes. In truth, if in his life McConnell held any documented attitude towards Jews, it was one of admiration. Through his years in the poorest Jewish district of Toronto, he had seen first hand the misery of Jewish immigrants, who formed the bulk of his neighbours. Later, early in his career as a fundraiser, McConnell warmly praised the organizational ability of Jewish businessmen, from the Victory Loan campaign of 1917 through the Joint Hospital Campaign of 1927 (for which the Jew Mark Workman raised $110,000) and onwards.

With the rise of the Nazis in Germany from 1933, the position of the Canadian Jews actually came to be more prominent and secure, at least in English-speaking Montreal, which was almost unanimously horrified by Nazism. The opening of the Jewish General Hospital by Lord Bessborough in 1934 culminated a fundraising campaign led by Allan Bronfman that had won the support of English Protestants. It was in striking contrast to the strike in June of that year by French-speaking Roman Catholic doctors in five Montreal hospitals protesting the appointment of Sam Rabinovitch as the senior intern at the Notre-Dame Hospital, a strike that led to Rabinovitch's resignation. It would take about sixty years for the Jewish General to come to bear the name of Sir Mortimer Davis, the Jew who had earned his knighthood at least in part for contributions to the Victory Loan Campaign of 1917. But this renaming, like the hospital itself, recalled McConnell's efforts – with Davis as well as with the Bronfmans and other Jews – to raise money for the founding of the hospital. Indeed, in a period in which there was little social contact between Gentiles and Jews, philanthropy was a unique field for their cooperation, as Bronfman's son Edgar has noted, and no Gentile was more active in this field than McConnell.

McConnell followed with particular attention the work of the Federation of Jewish Philanthropies, founded during the Victory Loan campaign of 1917. In November 1938 he was the guest of honour at a dinner hosted by Bronfman for two hundred Jewish businessmen at the Montefiore Club on Guy Street. The purpose of this dinner was to launch the federation's campaign for $290,000. McConnell took the opportunity to praise Jewish communal efforts over the previous twenty-one years. He was aware of the wide range of these efforts. In addition to the Jewish General, he singled out the Mount Sinai Sanatorium. Beyond medical establishments, he praised Jewish work in immigrant and family welfare, the Jewish arbitration court, the Jewish Employment Bureau, the Jewish Summer Home, the Jewish Old People's and Sheltering Home, the Jewish Neighbourhood House, and the Jewish Free Loan Association. He congratulated the "thorough manner" in which the Jewish community helped those in distress.

In his own speech that followed, Bronfman reviewed how charity had evolved through benevolence and philanthropy into welfare, and he described McConnell as "possibly the greatest leader" in good works in Canada: "He has, truly, an understanding heart," Bronfman concluded. McConnell in turn praised Bronfman for reaching outside the Jewish community by giving $10,000 to Bishop's University, which was run by the Church of England.[25] In one of the few public expressions of his credo, and doubtless of his self-understanding, that have survived, McConnell disclosed to this Jewish meeting his belief that "the innermost character of a man was revealed by his charitable acts." It mattered not whether this character was Jewish or Christian or other, for

> the greatest need in all the world today is a leader of a charitable nature, … one who is ready to suffer long and be kind. There is about charity neither false pride nor vanity because charity worketh always in the interests and for the cause of the poor and needy, the sick and the helpless.
>
> Therefore when one sees banded together a group of men prepared to engage in a noble charitable effort, one is at once conscious of the presence of a special type of men marked out very definitely as leaders in the community, who are willing to put self interest aside for the general good, men who in any emergency may be counted upon to do the right thing, and above all modest men. To predict for your campaign anything short of complete success would be uncomplimentary to the Jewish people with their widely known and unbroken record of success in charitable work.[26]

What McConnell had found in the Victory Loan and other campaigns was what many other Gentiles found, namely, that Jews often made better fundraisers and more generous donors than Gentiles. There is no hint in surviving evidence that he ever made such bitter remarks about the meanness of Jews as he often made of Scots Canadians! In any event, he was too familiar with Jews not to realize that they would probably contribute more to education generally, and to medical education in particular, than others, including Protestants. And so he gladly accepted Bronfman's help with the McConnell Wing of the Montreal Neurological Institute, and he did nothing to resist Bronfman's funding for the School of Commerce, which was housed in Purvis Hall, built by Sir Mortimer Davis and given by McConnell himself to McGill in 1942. It was this funding by Bronfman that stimulated McConnell to seek assurances from the Department of National Revenue that corporate contributions to charity were deductible from taxes. And it was these assurances that were the key to the success of his personal campaign to raise $7 million for the university in the following year.

It is unnecessary here to judge whether Bronfman and McConnell were truly friends. They seem never to have met except at fundraising events for charity. But it is fair to conclude that the two businessmen did cooperate in ways generally not remembered, and that their cooperation was of enormous importance. It was important not merely to McGill but to charitable causes generally, and it marked the definitive entry of Jews in addition to the corporations that McConnell cultivated as major if not pre-eminent contributors. The cooperation between Bronfman and McConnell integrated Jewish Montrealers into the McGill mainstream, so that in the following century the university would have a Jewish principal and a Jewish chairman of the Board of Governors, with the issue of contributions proportionate to admissions long forgotten. As for McConnell himself, his entire philanthropic career both envisioned and exemplified unity and diversity in philanthropic efforts, which is why even in his will he left money to various charities – Jewish, Roman Catholic, English, and French – and to every individual Protestant, Roman Catholic, and indeed Jewish hospital in Montreal.

Allegations that McConnell somehow sided with other Protestant members of the Board of Governors against outsiders – especially Jews – also fail to recognize that some of McConnell's Protestant colleagues on the board despised him. This became apparent when his name surfaced as a possible candidate to succeed Beatty as chancellor, a prospect that immediately encountered stiff opposition from several of his fellow governors. Their reasons are fairly but not completely clear, and they in any case evolved over time. In the end, two or three of his enemies in particular prevailed probably to render his candidacy untenable, at least in the eyes of McConnell himself.

Although there was undoubtedly personal animosity involved, his enemies couched their opposition in terms of their desire for reform of the office of the chancellor after what they perceived as the highhandedness of Beatty, although they had themselves apparently backed Beatty in his brutal ouster of A.E. Morgan as principal. Their other call was for an "academic" to be chancellor while some relatively younger man, probably a businessman, would chair the board. Their primary candidate to succeed Beatty was Charles W. Colby, a minor historian with a PhD who had been pursuing a distinctly non-academic career selling Remington "noiseless" typewriters and whose suitability for the chancellorship was seen by Principal James and others as risible. He was seventy-seven, plagued by indifferent health, uninterested in the position, and, above all, both a supporter and a great friend of McConnell's and virtually unknown to the public.

The ringleaders among McConnell's opponents on the board were George C. McDonald and George Currie, cousins and partners in the accounting firm named after them, McDonald, Currie. Both were at least as much part of St James Street as McConnell, and to all appearances men of the highest sense of public duty. McDonald's speeches reveal him to have been the soberest of men, incisive and possessed of

The McGill board with honorary graduates:
Back: J.W. Ross, A.B. Wood, H.R. Drummond, W.M. Birks, McConnell,
C.W. Colby, W.W. Chipman. Front: F.C. James, E.A. Graham, T. Rinfret,
G.F. Towers, E.M. Cameron, M.W. Wilson, May 1944. MUA, PRO14113.

vigorous and broad sympathies. But he seems also to have been unusually obstrep-
erous and even violently quarrelsome, and it very much appears that his clash with
McConnell was an issue of personality rather than of principle. In essence, his dislike
of McConnell seems to have been rooted in his resentment of what he saw as McConnell's ostentation, and he was not above taking as allies others less than enamoured of
McConnell's wealth and social presumption.

The saga began at the end of March 1942, when, with Beatty's health rapidly
failing, James approached McConnell about the chancellorship, saying that Beatty
agreed with him that McConnell was "the only appropriate person for the job."
McConnell said that he did not like making speeches, but James responded that
Beatty had made few speeches and Sir William Macdonald none. Though McConnell
was non-committal, James felt "reasonably certain that he would accept."[27]

James then went to McDonald, who told him that he (McDonald) and a number
of other governors would oppose McConnell. According to McDonald, McConnell
was "too overbearing" and McGill "definitely did not want another Chancellor who
mixed himself up with administration." James denied that Beatty had ever done this
"when there was anybody there to do it for him," but McDonald insisted that an "academic man" of "outstanding eminence" was needed, and he proposed Colby. When
James insisted that McGill needed someone who was a household name in Canada,
the United States, and Great Britain, not a virtual unknown like Colby, McDonald
retorted that all the chancellor should do was preside over convocation and leave the
chairmanship of the governors to a junior businessman, as at Queen's.[28]

James was convinced that McDonald himself wanted to be both principal and chairman of the board. Another board member, Dr W.W. Chipman, concluded that ten governors, of the total of twenty-six, would support McConnell and seven would support McDonald. Morris Wilson, however, calculated the board as evenly split about McConnell, with only four or five governors "violently opposed" to him. If there were great enthusiasm for an academic chancellor, Wilson would propose suggesting Chipman or Alfred Bazin to split the Colby vote. The next day, McConnell himself told James that he had decided to decline the chancellorship. James entreated him to reconsider, noting that he, James, was "very eager" to have him and all the members of the executive committee, apart from McDonald, wanted him too. He suggested seeing first whether the board preferred an academic chancellor and then whether it contained a substantial recalcitrant minority. McConnell insisted that "he did not want anybody to think that he was standing round waiting for it" but also that he "would be very glad to have me keep his refusal up my sleeve to use as I wished to." If the university really needed him, he would take the position, "although his wife and family were strongly against it and he himself was by no means eager to take on further responsibilities."[29]

Then the executive and finance committees voted to add Fred Southam, Walter Molson, and Alfred Bazin to its number to consider the chancellorship. James pointed out to McDonald that Lewis Douglas and McDonald himself had approved altering the statutes to make the chancellor position in no sense academic. In a private conversation after the meeting, McDonald emphasized that "he had no quarrel at all" with James but that the old guard on the board, particularly McConnell's friend William Massey Birks, had done nothing for years. Paul Sise told James that he, Southam, and Molson felt that Colby would be the best chancellor for the next two or three years, following which they would accept McConnell. He further noted that active campaigning by Birks and McDonald, respectively for and against McConnell, had "very nearly produced bitter dissension" on the board. James replied that McConnell as chancellor had the potential to "bring the university money enough to enable us to achieve our ideals" whereas Colby might be thought a "joke."[30]

By June of the following year, 1943, Beatty having finally died in March, the question of the chancellorship was both more urgent than ever and still awaiting solution. Colby himself told James that he felt himself too old for the position and that he supported McConnell, while adding that G.W. Spinney would be a good candidate if the opposition to McConnell proved too great. But then McConnell declared that he had, upon reconsideration, decided definitely not to accept and that he would prefer instead the presidency of the Royal Victoria Hospital, which would be less onerous. James reminded McConnell that Beatty had been holding both this particular presidency and the chancellorship simultaneously, and he also pointed out to him that McConnell's own preference for the chancellorship, Morris Wilson, was not yet ready.[31]

On 30 June 1943 the fourth meeting of the special committee on the chancellorship was held at the Mount Royal Club. The written nominations were counted. Colby was the first choice of five, and suggested by two others, for a total of seven. McConnell was the first choice of twelve and suggested by three others, for a total of fifteen. Wilson was the first choice of one, and suggested by eight others, for a total of nine. Spinney was suggested by four. Colby wrote to support McConnell or, failing him, Huntly Drummond, Wilson, or Spinney. The committee – Bazin, Birks, Chipman, Southam, and Spinney, with James in the chair, and all of them friends of McConnell – unanimously decided on McConnell. McDonald, who was away on a fishing trip, later complained bitterly that they had changed the rules for making a decision. Nevertheless, the committee still found that, of the other governors, six (including McDonald) remained opposed to McConnell. Given McConnell's expressed reluctance, the committee felt strongly that unanimity, or near unanimity, was necessary before approaching him again.

Through July, James lobbied for McConnell's candidacy and in the end he found only McDonald and Senator Adrian Knatchbull-Hugessen absolutely opposed. The latter declared that he thought that McGill would be making "a serious mistake, that it was selling its birthright for a mess of pottage" in considering McConnell. Walter Molson, hitherto in league with McDonald, said that he was willing to vote for McConnell after the withdrawal of Colby.[32] On the morning of 13 July, the crisis came to a head with two meetings of the special committee and the visit of a delegation to McConnell. McConnell reiterated his refusal, but James still felt that he would accept a formal invitation from the majority of the governors. McDonald, James found, was "damnably eager to postpone the whole business for three months," and Southam was willing to agree. McDonald offered to resign from the special committee if the others insisted on unanimity but he was urged to reconsider.

W.M. Birks had obtained McConnell's agreement to accept the chancellorship only six weeks before, in a private conversation. His letter to James on 13 July captures his indignation over recent events:

> I cannot but feel that your Committee in striving to please an over-critical small minority (some of whom won't play unless they get their way) has been unwise and with tragic results.
>
> *Academic snobbery* has lost to McGill the best man in Canada, and somebody bears a heavy responsibility; for his genuine interest (direct and indirect) would have meant many millions.
>
> They quote Sir William Mulock as Chancellor at Toronto, but Varsity is supported by the Ontario Government. If McGill could live on the Quebec Government, appoint my friend, Chief Justice Bond, and confine the Governors to academicians and "let George [McDonald?] thumb his nose at 'St. James Street.'"

Charlie Dunning, Chancellor of Queen's, never even saw the inside of a high school!

From James McGill, Redpath, Molson, Strathcona and Macdonald onwards, McGill must depend on financial Montreal, – first our fur traders and railway kings, then our bankers and merchant princes of the English-speaking minority, and none of them graduates.

...

There has been steady pressure ever since to appoint graduates, but I did not think that I would live to hear two members say openly, "only academicians" and scorn "St. James St."

The Board is rapidly shaping so that no mere financial man would feel comfortable upon it, in which case we have damned McGill.[33]

The next day, the governors continued to do battle. Wilson wanted to send another delegation to McConnell, but Chipman and A.B. Wood declared that he would not change his mind. Knatchbull-Hugessen and McDonald repeated their adamant opposition, and McDonald added that he would rather have Samuel Bronfman as chancellor for ten years than McConnell for five. Southam and Wilson proposed a delay of three months, which was carried. James felt bitter that he had failed to tackle McDonald and "got rid" of him "for good," but also that McConnell's continued expressions of refusal had undermined him. In a letter to James, Birks commented on the disdain that three of McConnell's opponents felt for his money:

Colonel Magee (whom I so admire) wishes to appoint such a figure [as a Lord Rector] as Chancellor, but would not object to McConnell doing the work, give or secure the cash, but deny him the honour, – very nice, but it won't work!

Senator Hugesson also wishes a big academic figure as in England and Toronto, where the Government finances the Universities. McGill is not in England or Ontario.

McDonald insists on calling the tune – also with condescension will permit McConnell to pay the piper – nice, but it won't work![34]

In conclusion, it is unclear precisely why McConnell declined or was denied the chancellorship. It seems most likely that he genuinely did not want the position very much, if at all, apparently because he regarded it as too burdensome. Southam, a close friend, said that McConnell was "not a strong man," presumably physically, at that stage. Under pressure from Lil, who was concerned about his health, he had already declined the offer of a seat in the federal cabinet in 1940. With regard to his opponents, it seems that McDonald's animosity dated back to the battle over the tramways franchise, when he may have concluded that McConnell was dishonest. There appears to be no record that this was McDonald's accusation. But he had spoken against Tram-Power in 1910 and what he thought of the Montreal Power monopoly may be gauged by the fact that he was one of the first government-appointed commissioners of the Quebec Hydro-Electric Commission when it took Montreal Power over in 1944, shortly after the struggle over the chancellorship had concluded. There is also the hint by James, already described, that McDonald may have been hoping to succeed James as principal, or at least as chairman of the Board of Governors, and in either position he could not have circumvented McConnell.

McConnell, for his part, once he realized that he could not, would not, or should not be chancellor, recommended Morris Wilson for the position, and the board accepted this recommendation. Subsequently, he was to be the kingmaker of the next two, or perhaps even more, chancellors, and the power behind their throne.[35] The fact that McConnell was able to name three or more successive chancellors suggests that he had not "lost" the chancellorship except through genuinely not wanting it. The fact that he offered the chancellorship in 1946 to Prime Minister Mackenzie King, as described in chapter 15, underscores his continuing preponderant influence on the board. It also suggests that he did not think it necessary or perhaps even proper for a benefactor, such as himself, to be chancellor. Although Strathcona and Macdonald had been rich benefactors, Borden and Beatty had not been, and neither were Morris Wilson, B.C. Gardner, Associate Chief Justice Tyndale, or others whose appointments as chancellor he was to support.

His power derived from his continued generosity to the university, which actually increased after his rejection for the chancellorship. Named the board's first "Senior Governor," McConnell found that his influence was greater than ever, not because he commanded the undivided allegiance of the board, but because he generally commanded the undivided allegiance of James. Theirs was a curious alliance, since there is no real warmth in the extensive surviving correspondence between the two men. They were, however, complementary in their skills and united by their devotion to the university. James, though a hard and conscientious worker and a professor of finance, and perhaps a great principal, had no gift for fundraising. McConnell, of course, had this gift in abundance, but within the academic community he was no consensus builder, which James was. They also possessed a shared vision for the university, as an internationally known centre particularly for the sciences and medicine, as it had developed through the benefactions of Peter Redpath, J.H.R. Molson, Sir William Macdonald, and Lord Strathcona, among others.

For a while, even after the installation of Wilson as chancellor, a threat remained on McGill's Board of Governors. Frustrated in his efforts to reduce the role of the chancellor, McDonald then openly turned against Principal James and lobbied the governors for James's ouster. When he found little support, he resigned from the board in bitterness. Then, it appears, Macdonald's cousin and partner George Currie took up the campaign against James. McConnell supported James throughout Currie's campaign against him, to the point of supplementing James's salary when it appeared that the principal might be leaving for the presidency of the University of Pennsylvania. It seems fair to conclude that he did not want to work with any other principal, and, as usual, his will prevailed. Together, James and McConnell boxed in Currie, who, like McDonald, resigned.

McConnell himself alluded to the resignations of McDonald and Currie in a letter to James many years later:

> I shall not soon forget the merry fight in a certain quarter with respect to the election of the late Morris Wilson as Chancellor [instead of McConnell], and the most disagreeable and spiteful speech delivered against you, resulting in a resignation [by G.C. McDonald]. Nor the event later on where an inside man [G.S. Currie] made the unbelievable declaration that 50% of the Governors would like to see you go.
>
>   At your request, and upon your withdrawal from the meeting, I took the Chair and poled [sic] the Board one by one so that each member would express his views on the subject without persuasion, which resulted in 100% vote of confidence for you. I have no reason to believe that any of them have since changed their minds.[36]

In an apparent reference to Currie, McConnell also remarked in a footnote: "This resulted in another resignation, though a bit slow in coming. Loyalty cannot be bought at a price – but where it exists, it is well worth rewarding."

McConnell let no hard feelings over the issue of his candidacy for the chancellorship detract from his commitment to McGill, even for a day. During the many months through which the governors were debating his candidacy, he continued to work closely with James on acquiring new properties for the university and on preparing them for new uses. James described him as resembling a little boy, as McConnell scrambled through a new principal's house that he had bought for him. Then, after the question of the chancellorship had been settled, he maintained the same pace. In a few months, he would begin a new project for McGill that would erase any doubts that even his harshest critics might have had about his devotion to McGill.

By 1943, the financial situation at McGill was so dire that McConnell undertook to raise, single-handed, an endowment of $7 million, chiefly from corporations, and in preparation he wrote to C. Fraser Elliott, deputy minister (taxation) at the Department of National Revenue, for assurance that the 5 per cent of taxable corporate profits that was deductible for charitable purposes applied to donations to educational institutions. This was, in McConnell's view, another crucial step in the process of tapping new sources of wealth for good causes. The process had begun with the YMCA fundraising campaign of 1909 and continued through the McGill campaigns of 1911 and 1920 and the Joint Hospital campaign of 1927. The last of these had given rise to the Bank of Montreal case of 1928, in which it was established by the courts that a corporate contribution to charity was generally allowed if agreed to by the board of the company.

Elliott replied unequivocally in terms that guaranteed the inducement of a tax deduction for prospective corporate donors to McGill:

> In advising you that such donations, made to an educational institution, will be allowed as a deduction from income, perhaps it would be well to state that the government is conscious of the fact that gentlemen of substantial incomes in Canada who are required by law to transfer, under the new tax rates, substantial portions of their income to the Exchequer, will find it difficult to maintain their heretofore generosity. The University might therefore suffer some diminution from such sources.
>
> ...
>
> It therefore follows that corporations, particularly those favoured with an upswing in profits in the war period, or even those which have maintained their usual quantum of income, should, by their officers, realize that they might reasonably be expected to do better than they have heretofore, splendid as they may have been, and thus fill the gap, to some degree, left by individuals who, by reason of the increased bracketed rates of tax, find they cannot.[37]

Armed with this letter, McConnell launched a fundraising campaign unprecedented in its success, even for him. He became the one-man University Financial Exploration Committee, with a view to raising $7 million to be invested in Victory Bonds that would yield an annual income of $210,000. Although he never called it the McConnell Campaign, almost everyone else did, even in official documents, which was extraordinary since no other McGill fundraising effort had ever been named after an individual before, and none has been since. His famous and sometimes intimidating skills of persuasion over the telephone and otherwise did not fail.

A draft of McConnell's "pitch" to corporations has survived. It is remarkable evidence of the power of his salesmanship. To his corporate targets, McConnell cited first "the constantly increasing demand on the resources, buildings, and equipment of the University due to war, and the consequent need for greater scientific development & research, and for medical treatment and care of wounded servicemen." He proceeded to discuss the heavy tax burden on individuals and the inadequacy of the 10 per cent limit on charitable deductions from their incomes to meet these needs. Then he observed:

> Industry now at production capacity due to war demands is earning high gr [gross] profits, viz. before normal tax and excess profit tax, fixed chgs

[charges] and dvid [dividends]. From these gr profits the Fed Gov permits deduction donations to [the] extent of 5% to [a] defined list of charitable works, hospital, educational and certain works of scientific research. Out of this Govt allowance of 5% all vital educational needs, Hospital Expansion and equipment and other charitable works might be largely provided. The Govt has given private Industry this rare opportunity while yet it may … It need hardly be recalled that critical opposition to private Industry [is] now definitely on the rise on this continent, and perhaps most particularly just now, in Canada. The signs are emblazoned in red on the rising sun for all to see who wish to take heed. Well the point is that from many angles private Industry must awake before it is too late. Private Ind [industry] [must] broaden out, must become more generous, must break the bonds that bind it to old fashioned ideas, one … of these] narrow-minded ideas being that Corporations have no right to give away their shareholders money … [This idea] is not only stupid, it is very bad business for the shareholders, it is a sign of a warped and narrow outlook [… one that] if applied to all executive viewpoints may hasten the day of CCF power & the actual control of Ind which is now openly threatened.

[Now that] the oppty [opportunity] of Generous Gifts to charity is now made so easy that I cannot for the life of me see why the privilege is not exercised. What pray is the matter with our Ind super men with super intellects, when they fail to see their great opportunity in availing themselves of this special Govt provision in the interest of Charity and Education …[38]

The survival of a stack of dozens of file cards shows how methodical McConnell, working apparently alone with his secretary, was in his campaign and by extension probably other campaigns. They reveal not merely telephone calls but also appeals in person before boards of directors and repeat visits to the reluctant. On each card, he typed the name, address, and telephone number of the company or individual to be approached, together with the company's taxable profits for 1942 and its tax provision, all of which he had probably personally researched. On each card there are pencilled remarks with McConnell's initials, usually naming the person approached and any further leads. Even for one of his own companies, Ogilvie Flour Mills, he wrote: "Saw CDD [Charles Dunning] request 100000." Ogilvie had had taxable profits in 1942 of $1,135,384 and a tax provision of $456,172. He was not to be put off. For Bell Telephone, he wrote: "Interviewed CFS [Sise] 3 times. Delivered written appeal personally. Approved at Board meeting 11.30, 24th. $250,000 paid." He meticulously made out a card for himself, complete with his name, address, and telephone number, and on it he scrawled simply: "$250,000 First one obtained JWM."[39] When Sun Life offered a cheque that he deemed inadequate, he immediately tore it up. McConnell collected $4,750,000 in cash (as opposed to pledges) from others.

McConnell addresses the McGill Graduates Society, c.1944. Private collection.

On the conclusion of McConnell's campaign, the Godbout government gave a further $1 million as a capital grant to McGill in 1944, in explicit connection with the McConnell effort. McGill also began to receive further steady though modest grants from the province, amounting to $120,000 annually.[40] The previous Duplessis government of 1936–39 had proposed provincial funding of the universities in proportion to the languages of their students, either English or French. After the defeat of Duplessis, the new Godbout government implemented the same pledge, simultaneously giving $375,000 annually to the Université de Montréal, on the continued assumption that it was exclusively French while McGill was exclusively English.

Despite the meagreness of its provincial grants, McGill was able, to the end of the war, to remain largely self-sufficient, and therefore private and independent, as it wanted and was indeed obliged to be. Contributions from the governors personally amounting to $424,551 in addition to McConnell's campaign – which had raised $7,113,978 – balanced the budget.[41] McConnell personally contributed $250,000, the largest single contribution though equalled by those of St Lawrence Sugar, Molson's Brewery, the Distillers' Corporation, the Canadian Pacific Railway, and the Bank of Montreal. If the contribution of St Lawrence is deemed to be that of McConnell himself, his total contribution was $500,000. In 2008 terms, in 1943 he gave $6,397,727 out of the total of $91,026,582 that he had raised for the university.

Despite its success, the 1943 campaign made it clear to McConnell that even corporate donors could no longer supply the needs of a growing university, any more than individual private donors could after the First World War. Two years later, however, a new source of funds emerged. With the end of the Second World War, the federal government began to concern itself with education, initially that of the returning soldiers but soon more generally. In such efforts, Ottawa was intruding into a field that belonged in principle to the provinces – that of funding education – a field that Quebec in particular had in recent years begun to "occupy" more generously.

Under the British North America Act of 1867, health and education were both under exclusively provincial jurisdiction, and Premier Duplessis was determined to protect what he saw as Quebec's rights in this area. As a stopgap measure, McConnell could help by giving to the university and its affiliated hospitals through his Foundation, but his Foundation could not by itself bail them out indefinitely. In calculating how McGill might be funded in the future, McConnell was essentially pragmatic. He had no real interest in constitutional divisions of power, and so he did not object in principle to the funding of education by the federal government. Yet, in the end, he agreed with Duplessis and opposed federal funding in favour of provincial funding. Almost no one at McGill agreed with him, from Principal James to the governors, the teachers, and the students. Almost no one even understood his rationale, and there were whispers, not stilled over fifty years later, to the effect that he was undermining McGill either for private gain or out of some irrational pique. It was his last big fight at and for McGill, and it dragged on for almost a decade. Its outcome was to shape the character of the university and its relationship with Quebec long after he had retired from its board, as well as the relationship of English Montreal more generally with Quebec.

Before 1950, there had been three major and a few minor provincial grants to McGill. The first major capital grant was for $1 million from the Taschereau government in 1920, which matched the Rockefeller Foundation grant for medical studies of that year. McGill also received a less specific grant, apparently renewable annually, in 1921–22, amounting to $42,000. In 2008 terms, the $2 million from the Rockefellers and the Taschereau government translates into $20,107,142.[42] Later, after the market crash of 1929, Currie and Beatty felt that a comprehensive policy towards provincial grants to universities was necessary.

In 1933, as Beatty observed to Athanase David, the provincial secretary, the following grants were allocated for 1934–35: the École Polytechnique, $175,000; the Directeur de l'Instruction Technique, $25,000; the École des Hautes Études Commerciales, $165,000; and the École des Beaux Arts, $80,000. At McGill, the School of Commerce was to receive $7,000 but the Faculty of Engineering and the School of Architecture nil. Beatty took pains to emphasize that he was not asking for grants to McGill equal to those to the French-speaking institutions. Nor did he insist on grants proportionate to the number of students at McGill within the student population of the province as a whole. Indeed, he insisted, he was grateful to the Taschereau government for its grant in 1920 and for a grant to the Neurological Institute in 1931–33. But, under the impact of the Depression, even McGill was suffering funding problems, and Beatty was hinting that more provincial aid would not be unwelcome. McGill ran up several deficits in 1933–34; its total deficits for that year amounted to $316,735, and its accumulated deficit was $2,800,000, or $43,189,141 in 2008 terms.[43]

By 1936, Beatty was coming to see merit in dividing the provincial university grants roughly in proportion to the native languages of the students attending the universities of Quebec. He was willing to accept that the total annual provincial and civic grants to universities should be divided as follows: Université de Montréal, $800,000 or 66.7 per cent; McGill, $272,000 or 22.2 per cent; and Laval, $137,500 or 11.1 per cent.[44] Nothing came of this suggestion. But the Second World War then changed the domestic political landscape by conferring unprecedented power on the federal government. In January 1945 McGill received grants from the Department of Veterans' Affairs to educate returned servicemen, and these helped both them and the university enormously. In 1946, aided by federal government assistance, 35,000 veterans registered as university students, whereas the entire full-time undergraduate registration in Canadian universities and colleges in 1939 had only been 35,164. In 1950 McGill ranked third in federal grants to student veterans, with $1,916,141, or 11.5 per cent of the total.

To Quebec nationalists of every stripe, this federal incursion into provincial authority over education was alarming if not illegal. In 1945, possibly to redress the balance, the Duplessis government tried to cut the already authorized McGill grant from $120,000 to $100,000, while the Université de Montréal was to receive from the province $800,000 a year for at least two years. Although the cut of $20,000 from the McGill allocation was restored, as it had to be legally, by the end of 1947 James was reporting to Duplessis that McGill had still incurred a deficit of $94,786 in the previous academic session.[45] Duplessis was not altogether unsympathetic, and he promised McGill $334,700 in provincial grants for the following year. The only other provincial grant for McGill for 1947 was the ongoing grant of $30,000 a year that had been arranged in 1942.

James asked various influential English Montrealers to lobby for more. McConnell was rather distant, but he wrote to James that a *Star* editorial had approved of aid by the Labour government in Britain to universities. He suggested asking the city for $750,000 and the province for double this amount.[46] In November 1948 James asked Duplessis for $4 million. In connection with the McGill Fund campaign of 1948, which had a goal of $9,075,000, Duplessis had already promised $1.5 million for the following year.[47]

Then a new ingredient was added to the mix: with a view to expanding federal influence over culture, Prime Minister St Laurent appointed a Royal Commission on National Development in the Arts, Letters and Sciences under the chairmanship of Vincent Massey.[48] Among the members was Father Georges-Henri Lévesque, the dean of social sciences at the Université Laval, who had earned Duplessis's enmity by supporting the strikers during the bitter Asbestos Strike of that summer. Duplessis wrote to Massey in September, refusing to cooperate with the commission on constitutional grounds.

St Laurent was acutely aware of Duplessis's opposition to federal intrusion into provincial jurisdiction. The commission's terms of reference therefore both stipulated excluding from its scrutiny the financial problems of universities and enjoined its respect for provincial jurisdiction over education. They permitted, however, the commission to investigate grants for scholarships through federal agencies. The National Research Council was already adequately funded to help science students, and so Massey tried to confine discussions among the commissioners to setting up a scholarship plan for students in the humanities and the social sciences. Then the National Conference of Canadian Universities (NCCU) recommended grants for technical and professional education, with no limitations on the provincial administration of them. The Chambre de Commerce of Quebec protested that Ottawa should return tax monies allocated to education to the province for distribution, but other French Canadian organizations were sympathetic to the NCCU proposal.

In June 1950 James, as president of the NCCU, pressed the Massey Commission to consider federal aid to universities more comprehensively, and, by October, St Laurent had committed Ottawa's support for greater intervention along those lines. Lévesque feared an explosion in Quebec, but he declined to accept Massey's offer of the right to veto any recommendation by the commission in this regard. Adding to the controversy, Lévesque proceeded to accuse Duplessis of working for his dismissal from Laval by threatening to cut half of the $4 million that the Quebec government had promised to the university, and of threatening the funding of the Université de Montreal as well. Eventually, Lévesque came round to favouring increased federal funding. Massey, however, wisely adhered to his terms of reference.

Although the Massey Commission's 1951 report carefully recommended only federal scholarships for undergraduates and post-graduates, and scholarships, bursaries, and loans for vocational training, its tenor was clear to Duplessis, who prepared to do battle on constitutional grounds.[49] In themselves, the Massey recommendations of increased federal funding for universities were not sufficient reason for a constitutional crisis. But, in the context of the apparently centralist recommendations of the report of the Rowell-Sirois Royal Commission on Dominion-Provincial Relations of 1944, they constituted a new threat to what Duplessis called provincial "autonomy."[50]

In June 1951, with the program of grants to veterans' education about to expire, St Laurent asked for parliamentary approval of $7,100,000 for Canadian universities, as a supplement to provincial grants and to maintain quality rather than to increase existing facilities. To McGill, he offered $449,000 for 1951–52, which would cover the deficit expected in that year but still not provide for any reasonable increase of salaries, which were below those at the University of Toronto and uncompetitive with those in business and industry. Duplessis accepted the federal grant for 1951–52, but he refused to accept it as a precedent and was to accept no more.

On 12 February 1952 Duplessis set up his own Royal Commission of Inquiry on Constitutional Problems – with a focus on taxation powers – under the chairmanship of his long-time friend and political ally, Chief Judge Thomas Tremblay of the Court of Sessions of Montreal. Tremblay was a close friend of Duplessis and had been a judge since 1938, and chairman of the Rural Electrification Board from 1945 to 1950. In 1945 he became chairman of the arbitration tribunal charged with evaluating the assets of Montreal Power and Montreal Island Power, expropriated by the Godbout government in the previous year. Despite Tremblay's acceptance of the argument, at this arbitration, that McConnell (though unnamed) had watered the "securities" of Montreal Tramways and Power in 1911–12, McConnell was actually on very cordial terms with him.

On 19 February, the executive and finance committee of the McGill governors expressed its "deep concern" about the Tremblay Commission. It noted the policy of the university to educate returning veterans, even if deficits were incurred, as indeed they were, amounting as of May 1951 to $1,370,765. The *Star* and the *Gazette* were, however, at best lukewarm about asking Ottawa for more. On the 21st, James went to see Prime Minister St Laurent, whom he described as disappointed that McConnell and Bassett (of the *Gazette*) were taking the side of Duplessis, who was posing as "St. George protecting Quebec for the English-speaking dragon."

On 27 February 1953 James met members of the teaching staff at McGill. He explained that there was now no practical way by which McGill could accept the federal grant of $615,000 annually, and this fact would mean higher deficits for the university. The elections expected in the next twelve to fifteen months had already made the grants a political issue, on which it was inadvisable for McGill to take a stand, and there was no prospect of joint action by all the Quebec universities either. Even with a federal grant, there would be nothing in it for an increase in salaries. The governors had previously agreed to raise $585,000 for salary increases in 1954, but the unfeasibility of accepting a federal grant had now ended the plans of the governors for 1954 and a new budget was needed to address the growing deficit.

McConnell himself was unusually well informed on the depth of opposition in Quebec to federal funding of universities. With an eye on the financial survival of McGill in the long term, he concluded that St Laurent's position, also held by James, was politically untenable in Quebec. This was to become all the more evident to him as pressure grew on McGill to accept federal grants in defiance of Duplessis. He was probably unsure of whether Duplessis would not try to match the federal grant or whether he would try in some way to "punish" McGill by withdrawing provincial support. In the latter event, he believed, McGill stood to lose more from Quebec than

Principal F. Cyril James, McConnell, and Premier Maurice
Duplessis at McGill, November 1954. MUA, PR019528.

it stood to gain from Ottawa. Moreover, sensitive as he was to the vagaries of political
opinion, he could not have taken comfort in any promised largesse from Ottawa, particularly since he still saw it as the role of private contributors, whether individuals,
corporations, or foundations, to smooth out these vagaries and not be lulled into the
total funding of universities by the state, at whatever level. His tough pragmatism on
university funding would soon become clearer.

In 1956 the Tremblay Commission released its report, which eviscerated the
Massey Commission's centralist bias on education and concluded: "The duty of
the federal government in this field [education] ... is not to intervene directly but to
ensure, through its general and fiscal policy, that the provinces be able to discharge
their functions fully by themselves. These are the real demands of the common good,
responsible government and true federalism."[51] Later that year, on 7 November,
the McGill governors held a crucial meeting on university funding. St Laurent had
announced that Ottawa was intending to double the grants to be distributed through

the NCCU throughout Canada on a per-capita student basis. Duplessis had refused these grants, and there was indignation building among the governors against the threat to the "integrity and independence of Universities." James asked them for advice on what stand he should take at a meeting of the NCCU in a few days. The minutes of the meeting reported tersely that McConnell "would rather depend on generosity of Mr. Duplessis. If both Federal & Quebec grants are accepted private streams will dry up. French Universities want McGill to help them."[52]

When James returned from the NCCU meeting, he reported to the governors that the rectors of the Université de Montréal and Laval wanted him to sign a joint statement. On a resolution proposed by Knatchbull-Hugesson and R.T. Powell, the majority of the governors gave him the necessary authorization, McConnell himself again being among those present. It is possible that he was against, but his dissent is not recorded. The statement read in part:

> … the governing bodies of the universities of the Province of Quebec cannot incur the responsibility of refusing grants and gifts from any source, providing that they in no way affect their independence. They feel that a refusal would impede their normal development and would be detrimental to the professors, the students, the parents – in a word – to the province and the whole country as well.
>
> Respectful of the opinion of the sister institutions of Canada with whom they have always closely collaborated and above all, desirous of causing them no prejudice of any kind whatsoever, the universities of the Province of Quebec wish to join them in thanking the Prime Minister of Canada for increasing the grants to universities and for entrusting their impartial distribution to an organization so independent of political parties as the National Conference of Canadian Universities.[53]

The following year, at a meeting of the governors on 13 February, B.C. Gardner, the chancellor, reported that the executive and finance committee had met representatives of the McGill Senate on the 8th. They had agreed to wait until either a cheque arrived from Ottawa or Quebec asked for a declaration from the university before paying the provincial grants. Gardner suggested seeking a legal opinion on whether there was any legal bar to accepting the federal grant.

On 21 June, the governors announced that they had decided two days before to return to the NCCU a cheque for $1,184,693. This was McGill's share of the grant of $16 million made by Ottawa to the universities of Canada during the previous academic session.[54] Its rationale for this action was far from clear, but it appears that McConnell's opinion was decisive. To his diary, James confided that he had expressed to the governors his "strong personal feeling" that McGill should accept the grants. As a result, he had "lost something of the confidence of McConnell (who is angry) and of some of the other senior members." He had also lost the confidence of the academic staff, in not siding openly with them against the board. He felt that he no longer had his old "energy, patience and skill" and contemplated resigning as principal.[55]

McConnell then wrote James a curious letter, thanking him for his letter of 6 July, no copy of which seems to have survived, "telling me for the first time that you actually sponsored the Federal Grants, and had been urging them at Ottawa for several years past." He continued:

> The Governors of McGill, I think, ought to have been told that, frankly, at the outset, which would have lessened the long arguments and debates, because I feel sure this was known to few, if any of the Governors.
>
> It would have been more easily explained to the Committee at Ottawa, how impossible it was for the McGill Board to accept the Grants at once, because of Quebec's stand on the subject …
>
> The present Federal Prime Minister [the newly elected John Diefenbaker] may find a way to work out something with Quebec, which will include Federal Grants to Universities, as well as Tax settlements, whereas the late P.M. [St Laurent] said (according to the Press) that whilst he and Mr. D. in Quebec were very cordial, they could not manage to co-operate. With the newly elected P.M. another way may be found by negotiation. Meanwhile, Quebec Grants might well be increased by degrees, until they exceed the Federal's $1,188,000.00 per annum.
>
> Let us hope that we may never again be found on opposite sides of the fence.[56]

The official historian of McGill, and a former vice-principal of the university, Stanley Brice Frost, records the crisis from the principal's point of view thus:

> James had never been in such a difficult situation. On the one hand, the academic leaders on campus were looking to him to continue the logic of his previous arguments and activities by coming out boldly for acceptance of the federal funds; on the other hand, the majority of the members of the board favoured observance of the premier's prohibition. The strength of James' position at McGill had always been that he was the loyal servant of the Board of Governors and had carried out their policies – even if most of the time it was he who conceived and formulated those policies. But this time the board members, knowing their business interests were at stake, would not leave him to determine the course of action. This was particularly true of James' protector, benefactor, and

friend, John Wilson McConnell who was more vulnerable than most on the Board to vindictive retaliation.[57]

Coming as it does from someone who is as well informed as Frost, who was closely associated with James, this appears to be a weighty judgment. Effectively, it charges that the majority of the governors, led by McConnell, breached their fiduciary duty to act in the best interest of the university by favouring their private interests instead. It charges further that the greatest benefactor of the university in its history – more generous than Sir William Macdonald, Lord Strathcona, and James McGill himself – betrayed the university out of fear of what Duplessis might do to his economic interests, and that, of all the McGill governors, McConnell had the most to lose as a result of the federal-provincial clash.

What is the evidence for this? First, the companies represented on the McGill board by three or more directors were Royal Trust and/or Bank of Montreal, the Royal Bank, Sun Life, Dominion Bridge, Dominion Engineering, and Montreal, London & General Investors – that is, two major banks and a trust company attached to one of these, an insurance company, two construction companies (with the same three governors as directors of each), and an investment company. How Duplessis could have threatened the banks, the trust company, the insurance company – given their federal charters – and the investment company (also possibly federally chartered) is unclear. It is possible that, as suggested by Frost, he threatened the governors with punitive taxes. But, although legally possible, provincial income taxes were not first levied until later.

Secondly, how did the governors vote so as to hamstring James? If we return to the minutes of the meeting of the governors of 7 November 1956, we see a considerable diversity of opinion reported, with nobody agreeing completely with McConnell.[58] There seems to have been nothing like a consensus, and the meeting adjourned without a decision. Nothing at all in these minutes suggests that there was much agreement between McConnell and the other governors.

It is still possible, of course, that various governors felt their business interests threatened, and that these interests covered more than one company. Indeed, this is numerically necessary if we are to believe that the governors were divided equally with regard to federal funding, and if we assume that those opposed were those threatened. The Bank of Montreal boasted among its directors the highest number of McGill governors, ten, less than half the potential twenty-two votes on the McGill board, (excluding those of Gardner and James). The four governors on the Sun Life board were among these same ten. The Royal Bank had as directors four other governors, but they too were less than eleven. If all the governors who were bank directors voted against federal funding, they would total fourteen, which would be a majority, not half of the votes possible. Yet in this case why would they be led by McConnell, who was not a director of any of these companies? And, as the banks were only federally chartered and regulated, why in any case would the governors who were bank directors feel threatened by a provincial premier?

With regard to McConnell as an individual, why was he "more vulnerable than most" to Duplessis's "vindictive retaliation"? In 1956 he was a director only of the *Star*, St Lawrence Sugar, and Canadian Liquid Air. None of his colleagues on the McGill board was a director of any of these companies. It is therefore impossible to see how he could have induced others to rally round him in defence of his own businesses, if we assume that they would have acted at least to some extent out of their own interests as well as at his behest, which is what Frost implies. It is, of course, possible to speculate that directorships are not so clear a measure of economic interests as, say, shareholdings. But, as we have seen in the case of Brazilian Traction, in which McConnell was apparently the largest single individual shareholder at least in the 1930s, shareholdings do not of themselves entail overwhelming influence, and all the more in the absence of a directorship.

The extant correspondence between McConnell and Duplessis seems complete for 1946, at least, and it makes clear that the two men were most concerned and in accord about the threat of strikes by communist-inspired trade unions, and certainly not about any threats by Duplessis himself to business, whether owned by McConnell or others. Indeed, in not one surviving letter between the two, until Duplessis's death in 1959, is there the slightest hint of a threat to McConnell's interests. To be sure, McConnell had a rational basis for fearing communist subversion, as did Duplessis, and communists were wreaking havoc with one of McConnell's economic interests, CSL. But Duplessis had no power to deal with either Fred Rose or the communist union that was laying siege to CSL.

Consequently, it is simply a distortion to suggest, for example, that Duplessis would discipline the seamen if McConnell acquiesced in his position on university grants. Then there is the matter of preferential prices on newsprint, which, as recounted earlier, Duplessis had first offered in 1951 and then renewed by order-in-council in 1956. In this case, far from threatening McConnell's most obvious economic interests, Duplessis had finally, a few months before McGill was to deposit its grants with the NCCU rather than accept them, conferred on McConnell a tangible benefit. While it is possible to surmise that McConnell's stance against federal funding was the quid pro quo for the order-in-council, the newsprint offer was, as we saw in the previous chapter, an unsolicited and deeply embarrassing favour to the *Star* and the *Gazette* by Duplessis. By then, John G. McConnell had taken the *Star* over from his father, and neither it nor the *Gazette* was to accept the benefit conferred by the new order-in-council.

Apart from the *Star*, McConnell's other major interest remained St Lawrence Sugar. Almost three-quarters of the cost of production for the refinery was raw sugar, the price of which was essentially determined by the world market and Canadian tariff policy, which was a federal, not provincial, responsibility. It is therefore hard to see how Duplessis could have threatened St Lawrence in any serious way. Furthermore, it is unlikely that he should have wanted to, since St Lawrence was a major employer in Montreal, and, in any case, threatening McConnell's interests would not have generated the alleged warm support given to Duplessis by McConnell.

To accept Frost's interpretation, we must accept that McConnell was willing, at the age of eighty, and as probably the richest man in the country, to enrich himself to the point of imperilling McGill. We must accept that he had suddenly, and radically, changed his priorities since the time he had first energetically campaigned for the university more than forty-five years before. We must accept that he was lining his pockets while coincidentally and systematically giving millions of dollars away, principally to McGill and generally in complete anonymity. We must accept that he was acting inconsistently in having given, for example, $2.2 million in 1953 alone to McGill, essentially to help it pay salaries and wages, and all anonymously if not secretly, while the proposed federal grant to McGill in 1956 amounted to a mere million. In 2008 terms, McConnell had given $17,821,582 to McGill versus the proposed federal grant of $8,100,719. This, we must further accept, was because of intolerable pressure brought to bear upon his economic interests by Duplessis, none of which have been specified.

It also should be noted that Duplessis's stand against federal funding was endorsed by no less than Pierre Trudeau, his bitter critic during the Asbestos Strike of 1949 and afterwards, who was then teaching constitutional law at the Université de Montréal.[59] The desire of other academics, chiefly through the McGill Association of University Teachers, to obtain federal funding was understandable enough. But it was at the time not politic, and it has proved subsequently to have been unsupportable in constitutional law. McConnell was not so fastidious about legal niceties. But he was experienced in the politics of funding, and it cannot be doubted that, like Trudeau, he fully understood Duplessis's stand on provincial jurisdiction and its practical implications, not least as expounded by Tremblay's Royal Commission and as endorsed by counsel retained by the university and probably by constitutional authorities generally. McConnell's securing of provincial aid for McGill may be criticized on the ground of thenceforth exposing the university to political pressure. But at the time, and indeed in the decades following, there was no serious alternative to accepting this aid.[60]

McConnell himself was doubtless worried about the effect of a blood feud between the university and the premier, but, in contrast to his attack on Duplessis in 1939, he appears to have decided to use his subsequent cultivation of the premier to his advan-

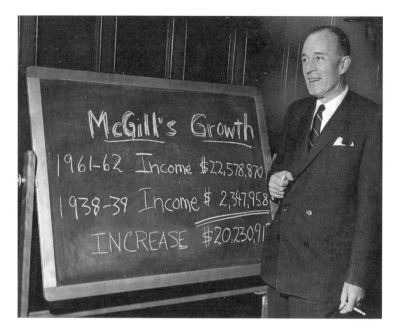

Principal F. Cyril James summarizes the growth in income of McGill,
1938 to 1962, 4 December 1962, Montreal *Star* photograph by
Adrian Lunny. Montreal *Gazette* Archives.

tage. The *Star*, which was now controlled by John McConnell and George Ferguson,
might declaim against the premier, but McConnell would again deliver the necessary money. If this analysis is correct, then McConnell's position on provincial grants
must go to the heart of McConnell's essential role as a fixer, not as a person driven by
ideology or self-interest or prejudice.

Apart from his arranging of provincial funding, McConnell had been behind most
of the fundraising for McGill in the two decades after the war, as well as in the two
decades before it. In 1960 James drew McConnell's attention to a summary of money
raised by public campaigns during the previous twenty years for all Canadian universities. This showed that McGill had received $25,694,738, more than a quarter of
the total amount of $94,930,245. It also showed that, of the four regions of the coun-
try surveyed (western Canada, Ontario, Quebec, and the Maritimes), Quebec was
the only one in which campaigns were oversubscribed. Indeed, within Quebec, the
McGill campaigns were the only ones that were oversubscribed, although it unclear
to what extent this was because of a "topping up" of the subscriptions by McConnell
himself, which had been McConnell's habit for decades.[61] Just before McConnell's
death, James summed up how the yearly income of the university had increased ten-
fold since 1938 (as pictured above).

It is sometimes implied that McConnell targeted his donations to McGill so as to favour the study of business against the social sciences and the humanities, which tended to be "left-wing." Yet a close study of McConnell's contributions to the university in the post-war period demonstrates no interest whatever in any field outside medicine and helping financially needy students. He did not, for example, withhold money from the reform-minded Faculty of Social Work and give it instead to the School of Commerce. In fact, he did not believe in business education, and he even declined to support the School of Commerce, which was largely underwritten by Sam Bronfman, although he did not oppose Bronfman's use of Purvis Hall (which McConnell had bought for the university) for this school.

Over forty years after McConnell's death, McGill is still largely shaped by him. Yet his real contributions to the university remain largely unknown. His securing of provincial funding and thus his transformation of the university into a public, largely tax-funded, and politically vulnerable institution is at best a mixed blessing. But provincial rather than federal funding of universities is now taken for granted across Canada, as it had not been in 1945–56. The McConnell Scholarships at McGill remain the chief source of private aid to needy students, and many live in McConnell Hall, play in the McConnell Arena, take classes in the McConnell Engineering Building, and benefit from ongoing projects by the McConnell Foundation. Jews, as McConnell probably foresaw and desired, are a considerable financial mainstay of the university, and as already noted McGill has had a Jewish principal. And, despite setbacks and crises, McGill is more open to the poor, to immigrants, and certainly to the academically qualified than ever before, as McConnell had intended in setting up his scholarship program which, unlike many scholarships in 1945, was open to all Canadians without discrimination on religious, racial, or other grounds.

It would be wrong to suggest that the McGill of today is overwhelmingly, much less solely, a product of McConnell's work. Thousands of others have contributed, and he would have been delighted to see the generous benefactors who have followed him. But it is hard to imagine that McGill would have been the same without him. Without him, it might have gone effectively bankrupt and taken years to emerge from bankruptcy. Without him, a vision of financial solvency, dependent on corporations and governments as well as individuals, might well have taken longer to evolve. For someone who dropped out of school at the age of fifteen, he displayed remarkable prescience as well as determination in caring for generations of McGill graduates whom he modestly declined to join, even with an honorary degree.

For this legendary investor, McGill may well have been the greatest of his investments. For this legendary promoter, the McGill for the future that he was building was probably the greatest of his promotions, as he attracted to it the firm support not merely of the rich individuals whom he had long cultivated but also of the new corporate sponsors who replaced them, and even of the province that had so long

J.W. McConnell
Montreal

In dedicating to me the 1952 issue, the Managing Board of "Old McGill" have done me a great honour. To all members of the graduating class I send warm greetings.

All McGill graduates now entering the wide field of human endeavour will have two objectives in view; to achieve success — and to find happiness.

I venture to suggest the essential ingredients in the formula for a successful life. Hard work, enthusiasm, unceasing determination; and to mellow and enrich the whole there must be an agreeable disposition, a cheerful countenance, a spirit of co-operation and infinite patience. One who is willing to adopt this formula will find a pleasurable path to a successful career, however great the obstacles may be.

Cultivate the habit of sound thinking, without which there can be no safe action; for there is nothing either good or bad; but thinking makes it so. It has been said by one of great wisdom — "As a man thinketh in his heart, so is he."

The second and all important objective is a happy life. Without this, all other gains are as dross. I suggest, therefore, that you examine the way of the Good Samaritan, for in all that is implied in that Parable you will find the path that leads to happiness. The unselfish life; the desire to do the thing really worth while. To give aid and comfort to those in trouble; and to lend a helping hand to the needy. In brief — happiness derives from anything one can do to make others happy.

To all graduates embarking upon the great adventure of life, I can offer no better advice than that given by our late beloved Sovereign, King George VI, in his first Christmas broadcast;

The Neurological Institute

"I said to a man who stood at the gate of the year,
Give me a light that I may tread safely into the
unknown - and he replied - Go out into the darkness
and put your hand into the hand of God. That shall
be to you, better than light and safer than the known
way."

To all McGill students I send sincere wishes for a happy and successful life.

J.W. McConnell

McGill University Archives, 1952, Old McGill Yearbook, 9.

given it so little, and of the Jews so long discriminated against. He helped, in short, to ensure a central role for McGill in a society in constant flux. In 1952 he offered probably his only credo to McGill graduates, reproduced here. Less than a decade later, he left new students his last gift, McConnell Hall, a residence opened by the Duke of Edinburgh. Almost fifty years later, it is clear that he left to Canada almost a reborn university, and one still in the first rank.

CHAPTER EIGHTEEN

We Give Thee but Thine Own: The Making of the McConnell Foundation, 1928–63

He's buying his way into heaven … That's a widespread opinion on his huge gifts to charity. But so far he has refused to make any attempt to explode the stories, whether they are legends or not.

"Sugar Baron," *New Liberty*, March 1949, 22

Apart from his work for war efforts, McConnell's preoccupations with medicine, education, and the young were at the root of his activities as a fundraiser and a benefactor over the course of his entire adult life. They received their most enduring support through the Foundation that he established in 1937 and that continues in existence today.

McConnell's first provisions had been for his family, both immediate and extended. By 1928, he was fifty-one years old, but he remained attached to his siblings and their descendants long after most of them had gone in 1901–05 to California. As early as 1905, he had made his first trip from Montreal to California to visit his aunt Lena and to attend a wedding. He returned in 1923 and 1927 to see dying sisters and to meet the spouses of relatives who had married since his last visit. In June 1928 he set up a private trust for his relatives in California, with C.H. McLean, his lieutenant at St Lawrence Sugar, as trustee. The trust capital was $195,000 and consisted of bonds of Sterling Coal, Royal Montreal Golf Club, Kingston Elevator, Montreal Light, Heat and Power, and Gatineau Power. This trust was still in force at the end of the century.

In 1935 McConnell, like John D. Rockefeller, Jr, began setting up trusts for all his children. Parliament had already imposed a gift tax under the Income War Tax Act of 1917 (later redrafted as the Income Tax Act of 1949), although it was not to legislate a federal succession duty until 1941. This gift tax was directed at the rich, to discourage them from transferring income-earning property, such as stocks and bonds, to less wealthy persons. It was not designed to discourage charitable giving, and so gifts to anyone worth $1,000 or less, as well as gifts to recognized charities and to governments, were exempt.[1] In addition, in Quebec, the Succession Duty Act had imposed a duty on all property, moveable or immoveable, transmitted as a result of death. It taxed, as part of the estate, gifts made to individuals within five years of death, but not charitable gifts. Both the federal income tax and the provincial succession duty compelled McConnell to begin serious estate planning. Also encouraging him to move in this direction was the fact that his children were beginning to marry and none of his sons was showing signs of his intense interest in making and managing money.

McConnell's first concern was how to value the preferred shares of St Lawrence for the federal transfer tax on their conversion into trust property. These shares were not listed on any stock exchange, no transactions involving them had taken place in the years since the implementation of the tax in 1917, and no preferred dividends had been paid on them for ten years. With a view to valuation, he had to look to other preferred but actively traded shares in sound Canadian and American companies. In due course, he settled on $74 as the valuation of each St Lawrence preferred share. And once this valuation had been accepted, he paid the federal transfer tax of $3 per share on the 40,000 shares that had been transferred to C.H. McLean in trust on 11 October 1932.[2] The amount then in trust was therefore $2,960,000 less $120,000 in tax, or $2,840,000.

Apart from the transfer tax, however, there was the question of the dividends attaching to the shares that had been so far unpaid and the income tax that they would attract if they were paid. On these matters, McConnell obtained a ruling from his friend C. Fraser Elliott, commissioner of income tax at the Department of National Revenue. This was to the effect that McConnell might, without attracting income tax, redeem the 40,000 preferred shares of St Lawrence Sugar then outstanding, without premium or bonus, as long as there was no payment of dividends, in whole or in part.[3] These unpaid dividends amounted to $3,291,750, and McConnell's children, who were to benefit from the trust holding the preferred shares, waived any claim for dividends or premium, and so neither they nor McConnell paid income tax on this amount. At about the same time, McConnell granted to C.H. McLean, as trustee under the 1935 marriage contract of Wilson and Marjorie McConnell, the option to purchase all the common stock of the Montreal Star Company for $800,000 and all of the stock of the Standard Publishing Company for $200,000.[4]

At this stage, we need to digress, not only to explain how trusts operate, but also to review their complex history and how trusts have come to differ from foundations. The creator of a trust sets aside property, usually but not always money, for the benefit of someone else. The essence of a trust is the trustee, a person other than the creator of the trust or the beneficiary of the trust, who administers trust property on behalf of the beneficiary. The "fiduciary" duties of the trustee prohibit him or her from receiving personal benefit from the property held in trust, apart from specified administrative fees. In McConnell's time as today, "private" trusts, which are for the benefit of named individuals or classes of individuals (such as members of a family in one or more generations), were subject to the legal rule against perpetuities, which obliged the trust to "vest" – close down – within a period consisting of a "life in being," at the time of the settlement (or the establishment) of the trust, plus twenty-one years. The "life in being" chosen by McConnell for his family trusts was that of his last-surviving child. Twenty-one years following the death of this child, his family trusts were bound to expire.

Another category of trusts emerged in the medieval period, when hospitals, schools, convents, and other institutions could be called "foundations." People gave them gifts subject to conditions, such as what particular objects might to be served by their gifts. But there was no external oversight to ensure that the conditions imposed by the donors were observed, particularly as generations passed. Crucially, these foundations did not incorporate the English idea of a trust as a legal instrument, one that permitted the courts to examine and to intervene in the administration of a gift by a trustee. Over time, unfettered by fear of court enforcement of the fiduciary duties imposed by trust law, such foundations often developed a reputation for corruption, the most notable example being the monastic foundations operated by the Roman Catholic Church in the Middle Ages.

The grafting of fiduciary or trust duties onto the medieval idea of a foundation produced the invigorated hybrid of the charitable or public trust. Unlike the private trust, the charitable trust is exempt from the operation of the rule against perpetuities, but it ceases operation when the object or the purpose of it disappears or when its endowment runs out, which is likely to happen eventually since its endowment is typically fixed. The next stage in the evolution of the modern foundation, incorporation, gave the charitable trust distinct advantages. Strictly speaking, a charitable trust cannot be a corporation, since trusts and corporations require legal instruments to create them that are distinct both in concept and in effect, but the modern foundation resembles a charitable trust in intention while it is a corporation in form. When incorporated, the foundation enjoys indefinite life until it is formally wound up. Unlike a trust, it may continue to exist even after its capital is depleted, and it can be endowed with fresh funds. Modern foundations are not the same as charitable trusts, however, but rather evolved out of them. They were still not, even in the 1930s, readily distinguishable from them, except by lawyers, for whom foundations differed by not being exclusively dedicated to specific public causes such as hospitals and schools.

The incorporation of charitable trusts began in the eighteenth century, with Thomas Coram's creation of the London Foundling Hospital. A charitable corporation still resembled a charitable trust in that it was subject to public oversight and focused on a specific cause, but it differed in that people other than its founder could donate to it. It was a long time, however, before incorporation became the norm for charities and charitable causes. In Canada, only a few charitable trusts were incorporated before the twentieth century, notably the Montreal General Hospital, founded in 1821 and incorporated two years later.

Confusion between charitable trusts and modern foundations, and between medieval and twentieth-century foundations, has led to much misunderstanding about such creations as McConnell's.[5] Critics have accused them of being essentially tax shelters, designed to shield the earnings of their founders. Alternatively, critics have claimed that foundations are tax-exempt vehicles for promoting peculiar political or other agendas of dubious benefit to the public. There have been more critics than defenders of modern foundations in part because the critics have often been correct, but also because some have not grasped what makes most foundations conceptually distinct.

Even by McConnell's time, most modern foundations were operating in areas and in ways unknown to traditional charitable trusts, whether these trusts were incorporated or not. Such foundations had received their endowments from one person or one family, and not necessarily all at the same time. Their operations by definition were more general than those of charitable trusts, which were sometimes called "purpose" trusts. One twentieth-century development in corporate law permitted the expansion of the operations of foundations. This was the loosening, or even the abandonment, of the practice of defining corporate objects. Corporate objects had originally been a necessary element of company charters, but the increasingly standard practice of making them so general as to be meaningless, or dropping them altogether, broadened the legitimate activities of modern foundations well beyond traditional definitions of charity.

By the 1930s, most modern foundations lacked specific religious purposes. They dedicated themselves to general causes, such as medical research or universities, rather than to more specific ones, like a particular institution. Endowed with perpetual legal life, they were outliving many of their original projects and thus inclined to develop new ones. This practice reflected a spirit wholly different from that of private or even public trusts. Yet, insofar as they tried to reflect the preferences of their founders, they remained distinct from one another while collectively they were expanding their scope to include all of humanity. In other words, they were becoming more philanthropic and less charitable despite the specificity of the causes that they were aiding.

To call the new large foundations "charitable" rather than philanthropic is to recall their origins in charitable or public trusts. But it obscured how far they had developed from these origins. Modern foundations are not charitable, in the Elizabethan sense of being established exclusively for the relief of poverty. It took centuries for this disjunction between foundations and charity to take place. In 1891 charitable purposes for public trusts were expanded by the judgment of the House of Lords in the *Pemsel* case.[6] The *Pemsel* judgment, construed with the Statute of Charitable Uses, was to govern the view taken by Canadian courts of charitable purposes for some time.[7] These purposes included the relief of poverty, the advancement of education and religion, and almost any other object of "public utility." The courts, in considering the validity of bequests resulting in the creation of *public charitable trusts* for specific purposes, have generally tried not to disallow them.

Moreover, while even today non-discretionary *private* trusts always fail in the courts, when their objects are not ascertained or ascertainable, the courts have been able to step in to supply specific purposes to *public* trusts explicitly and solely set up for charitable purposes generally. In practice, this issue has seldom been litigated, since the *Pemsel* judgment seems to cover a wide variety of charitable activities and trustees possess a certain inherent discretion to decide on what these activities are to be. By extension, the courts have been reluctant to pass judgment on the activities of incorporated foundations that might go beyond those of public trusts. Thus, in McConnell's time, no donation to his Foundation was challenged in the courts as non-charitable. Then and since, more important than court judgments has been the position of the Department of National Revenue on the tax exemptions available to foundations. In effect, for incorporated foundations, the stretching of the meaning of a charitable use, beyond *Pemsel*, can take the form of a specialized mission that may or may not fall under the definitions in that case.

By the time McConnell was planning his Foundation, there remained, in the United States at least, some doubt about what a foundation was, and for several reasons. In addition to all the confusion about private and public trusts, and medieval and modern foundations, there was no widespread acceptance that philanthropy was the same as charity, even as defined by the *Pemsel* case, which in any event did not bind American courts. The word "philanthropy" derives from the Greek phrase for "love for mankind," and it seemed especially appropriate for foundations incorporated with few or no specific objects. Especially since the very concept of charity had been exploded by *Pemsel* to include any object of "public utility," foundations now seemed more properly described as "philanthropic" than as charitable in the old trust sense.

With all this doubt, it was time to try to identify what organizations were actually calling themselves foundations, and to ascertain what they were in fact doing. In 1928 Evans Clark, executive director of the Twentieth Century Fund, itself despite its name a foundation, began compiling a list of American foundations. It was published as *American Foundations and their Fields*, but, even by its fifth edition in 1942, this book conceded that it could not purport to be "a central register for philanthropic funds." Clark complained that even a commercial organization that sold toothpaste might describe itself as a "foundation" or a "fund." Self-styled foundations might also still be set up for limited purposes, such as the erection of a statue, or they might have no assets.

As a solution to this muddle, Clark proposed four criteria for recognizing a "charitable trust" as a "foundation." First, it had to be a separate body with its own board of trustees or directors, and not part of some other institution such as a university, library, museum, or hospital. Secondly, it must be established not to make money but to distribute it. Thirdly, it must distribute its income not exclusively in operating its own activities but at least in part through grants to outside beneficiaries. And, finally, it must possess at least the nucleus of an endowment fund.[8] These criteria possessed no legal force, but they were a major step in the clarification of how to define foundations as a distinct form of charity.

By the 1930s, there was already a tradition of setting up private foundations, especially in the United States, but it had not been a very long one, at least in the American sense of using the large fortune (or part of it) of one man, or one family, as the entire endowment. In the first half of the nineteenth century, the tendency in the United States was for major charitable bequests to be merged with other endowments and administered by governments or government-related trustees, the most famous example being the Smithsonian Institution, created by the bequest of James Smithson in 1829. Such "community" foundations also arose in Canada, though considerably later, one of the first being the Winnipeg Foundation, established by W.F. Alloway in 1921.[9] Beyond community foundations, the idea of regular cooperative solicitations for public purposes also caught on. In Canada, Community Chests, the United Way, Red Feather, and like organizations differed from ad hoc campaigns in maintaining full-time staff and in making their appeals annually. They differed from community foundations in being fundraising activities rather than trusts in the fixed sense recognized by law. Even if, in the opinion of some, they were in some sense "foundations" rather than mere collecting agents for operating charities, they lacked both the capital and the focus of the large privately endowed funds that most people still regard as defining characteristics of foundations.

George Peabody established the first major independent charity that did not become a community foundation. This was the Peabody Education Fund, which operated from 1867 to 1915 and had as its goal the advancement of education in the American south, particularly for ex-slaves and poor whites. Because it was, in contrast to the Smithsonian, unrelated to government, and because it was unrelated to a larger community effort, the Peabody Education Fund was probably the first private large foundation in the United States. Other such foundations in the first half of the twentieth century varied as much as the individuals or families who had established them, and in subsequent generations they often foundered or radically changed course. The most energetic pioneer of these early efforts and the inspirer of all of the others was Andrew Carnegie, who started his philanthropic career in the late nineteenth century as a builder of libraries across the United States.

Subsequent privately established foundations appeared in waves, some in response to changes in tax law. The US Revenue Act of 1913 exempted from income tax those organizations that operated exclusively for religious, charitable, scientific, or educational purposes. The two most important new foundations before the First World War, however, were exceptions. Since the Carnegie Corporation had been set up in 1911, it clearly was not established in response to this provision. Neither was the Rockefeller Foundation, which was incorporated in 1913 but only after previous unsuccessful efforts.[10] The second wave of new foundations occurred in the 1930s, with an amendment in 1935 to the American income-tax law to permit corporations to deduct their charitable contributions up to the equivalent of 5 per cent of their taxable income – a development that McConnell himself was not to secure for Canadian corporations until 1943. Among the new foundations that now emerged were the Nemours Foundation and the Ford Foundation, both created in 1936, and the Lilly, Longwood, Houston, and Irvine foundations, all created in 1937, the same year as the McConnell Foundation. There followed in the United States a remarkable third wave of growth in the number of foundations after the Second World War, among them the Pew Memorial Trust (1948), the Andrew W. Mellon Foundation (consolidating previous foundations, 1969), and the Henry J. Kaiser Family Foundation (1948). By 1968, there were 25,000 foundations in the United States, big and small.

In Canada, foundations remained almost unknown when McConnell's incorporated his in 1937. Apart from community foundations, charitable trusts were still the favoured instrument of philanthropy.[11] The Massey Foundation was probably the only Canadian one to have much influence on McConnell because other efforts had been very limited.[12]

In 1896, having already distributed over $300,000 to good works in his lifetime, Hart Massey directed in his will that the residue of his property not required for the payment of legacies, bequests, expenses, and disbursements should be administered by his executors for further, undefined charitable purposes. He further gave his executors the discretion to hold his shares in Massey-Harris and other companies – which formed the bulk of the residue – for at least twenty years, and to use them as they saw fit.[13] At the time of Massey's death, the residue amounted to about $1 million, out of a total estate of $2.2 million, which the executors were to use to assist religious and educational institutions and other objects that they thought would be in accordance with Massey's views.

The twenty years following Massey's death proved unexpectedly profitable for the Massey-Harris company, and its shares appreciated considerably in market value. It therefore seemed natural to the trustees to think of some mechanism beyond the estate for administering the family's philanthropy. The immediate cause of the establishment of the Massey Foundation was the Income War Tax Act of 1917, which raised

Vincent Massey with his grandfather Hart Massey, n.d.
University of Toronto Archives, B87–0082121(09).

the issue of whether income from the estate of Hart Massey, even if used for charitable purposes, was subject to income tax. There was in addition the question of the
taxation of the income used for the charitable disbursements of the estate. An incorporated foundation, which would take the form of a public trust of indefinite duration, would not see its income so taxed, and so it could increase its endowment to the
extent of the tax saved through its charitable status.

The Massey Foundation was created in 1918,[14] and, from the start, Chester's son
Vincent – Chester himself having died in 1926, after years of illness – made it his
personal cause. He had been inspired by George E. Vincent, the half-brother of his
mother and the second president of the Rockefeller Foundation from 1916 onwards,
in succession to John D. Rockefeller, Jr, who had incorporated it in 1913. George E.
Vincent's father, the Methodist bishop John H. Vincent, had been a co-founder of the
Chautauqua summer retreats, in New York State, in the 1870s, where the Vincents
and the Masseys first became acquainted.

When Vincent Massey's long friendship with McConnell began is unknown, but
it was no later than about 1913. McConnell may have first encountered the Masseys
in Toronto as early the 1890s, through the Fred Victor Mission, endowed by Hart,

or through the Young Men's Bible League, founded by Walter (the third son of Hart) in 1891 at the Central Methodist Church on Bloor Street. He may also have met them through his employers, the Gouldings, who were related to the Masseys by marriage. At any rate, by 1914, McConnell's prominence in Methodist affairs was such that – as recounted in chapter 17 – he presided (in the absence of Chester Massey, who was indisposed) at the opening of the new building of the Wesleyan Theological College in Montreal, a venture supported by the Massey family and financed in part by a successful fundraising campaign conducted for it by McConnell in the previous year. By 1918, McConnell had also almost undoubtedly met Vincent Massey, when the latter was working in the secretariat of the war cabinet in Ottawa and McConnell was director of licences for the War Trade Commission there.

The Massey Foundation's capital provided an annual income of almost $119,000 in 1919. Hart House, a lavish neo-Gothic centre for male students at the University of Toronto, built between 1911 and 1918, was the first beneficiary of funds from the Foundation. Another of its early ventures, in May 1919, was to appoint a commission on all the secondary schools and colleges operated by the Methodist Church. Although these institutions did not include the Wesleyan Theological College, one of the commissioners was its principal, the Reverend James Smyth, and so it seems reasonable to assume that McConnell became aware of the Massey Foundation through the work of its commission. By 1937, the Massey Foundation was focused on cultural and educational activities that were of only tangential interest to McConnell. Nevertheless, he was closer to Vincent Massey than ever, and, as recounted earlier, he did cooperate with the Massey Foundation in funding at the least one of the Massey causes in England during the Second World War, the Beaver Club.

The Rockefeller Foundation, founded in 1913, and the Carnegie Corporation, founded in 1911, were only the two best-known of several foundations founded by the Rockefeller family and Andrew Carnegie. Carnegie, who was a friend of Sir William Macdonald's, personally gave McGill $100,000 for general purposes in 1909. The Rockefellers began their association with McGill with their challenge grant of 1920, discussed in chapter 17. John D. Rockefeller, Jr had come to Montreal in 1918 at the invitation of William Massey Birks, McConnell's close ally in fundraising for the YMCA in 1909, McGill in 1911, and the war effort in 1914–18, and from this time the connection between the university and the Rockefellers was established, especially since Birks had been a governor of McGill since 1910. Birks himself was to set up a foundation of his own in 1929, but most of its money went to the building of Divinity Hall on University Street. It merged in 1961 with foundations established by his brothers.

In 1918, Rockefeller stayed in Montreal with his friend from when they had been children in Cleveland, Mrs Arthur Drummond, a sister-in-law of Huntly Drummond, another friend of McConnell's. He went on from Montreal to stay with his best friend of all, Mackenzie King, the minister of labour, who had been his adviser during the riots in Ludlow in Colorado. King had already refused the presidency of the Carnegie Corporation, but he always remained very interested in philanthropy, and by the 1940s he was describing McConnell as his closest friend along with John D. Rockefeller, Jr.

Since there would probably be similar challenge grants to that of 1920, through the Rockefeller Foundation or its affiliates, in the future, a trustworthy local source of funds – such as McConnell – was required. McConnell could never hope to equal the Rockefellers in the endowments that he made, but he was the richest and the most generous man in Montreal, and thus an obvious person to complement the work of the Rockefellers.

Another influence on McConnell was foundations established by the Milbank family of New York. Elizabeth Anderson, the daughter of Jeremiah Milbank, a banker and the founder of the Borden Company, had established the Milbank Memorial Association (later renamed the Milbank Memorial Fund) in 1905. It specialized in public health and social welfare, and especially psychiatry, encouraging government support by providing private funding first. Anderson's nephew, Albert G. Milbank, the founder of the law firm Milbank, Tweed and the chairman of the Borden Company, expanded its endowment through shrewd investment. McConnell's vast investment in and directorship of the Borden company led him to a close friendship also with Jeremiah Milbank's grandson, who carried the same name and was the president. During the First World War, the younger Jeremiah Milbank donated $50,000 to the Red Cross to set up an institute for the rehabilitation of disabled veterans. By 1930, he had given this institute $700,000, and in 1930–32 he undertook to cover its entire costs, amounting to $1.4 million.

Milbank was temperamentally opposed to the committees that had taken over the Rockefeller efforts, and he wanted his own children to carry on his philanthropic work, and so in 1924 he established the JM Foundation with a handful of employees. Its purpose was to aid in the rehabilitation of people with disabilities, to assist disadvantaged youth and their families, and to "support projects which strengthen values essential to the preservation of a free society."[15] Milbank had a profound influence on McConnell, especially in his creation of Boys' Clubs and in his promotion of medical research and rehabilitation, and the two families remained close to the end, with Jack and Lil visiting the Milbank winter home in South Carolina, Turkey Hill, in the 1950s.

The J.W. McConnell Family Foundation, as it came to be called after McConnell's death, was established in stages. In January 1935 a "charitable organization" called the Belvedere Foundation was incorporated under the Quebec Companies Act. Two years later, in April 1937, McConnell became president and director of the Belvedere Foundation, Wilson McConnell vice-president and director, and C.H. McLean secretary-treasurer and director. Later in the same month, and under the same act, the Belvedere Foundation became the J.W. McConnell Foundation, confirmed by supplementary letters patent in May. The precise reason for the change of name is now unknown, but the basis for the endowment of the McConnell Foundation – the name by which it is most commonly known – is clear.[16]

The McConnell Foundation was empowered by its by-laws only "to operate exclusively as and to perform any or all of the functions of a charitable organization."[17] By now, the Department of National Revenue had already confirmed for McConnell the understanding of the courts of England that "a charitable organization is one of the widest terms that can be used so that monies distributed by a charitable organization for educational purposes would still be included as a charitable donation," and, as already mentioned, the department had ruled that all income of "charitable institutions" that did not accrue "to the personal profit of or is paid or payable to any proprietor thereof or shareholder therein" was exempt from tax.

In 1937 the department's "main concern" was "to make certain that the donor has irrevocably parted with any personal interest which he may have in the capital." Neither must the donor "be able to so control the income of the corporation that he can personally benefit from receiving any of the corporation's income for his personal use, except possibly future appropriate isolated drawings to maintain the usual living standards of himself and his family in case of need therefore." There was no objection to McConnell's serving as one of the trustees or directors of the Foundation, "so that he can personally direct the charitable donations of the company [Foundation] into such channels as he may choose." Moreover, as long as the by-laws did "not contravene the main purpose of the Foundation to distribute all of its income for charitable purposes, there would not appear to be any objection to whatever By-laws you might ultimately adopt."[18] In effect, the McConnell Foundation could now operate in almost any way McConnell desired, as long as it used its income for charitable purposes, which were "defined in the widest terms."

Once the charitable intention of the Foundation had been accepted by the Department of National Revenue, McConnell and the other trustees were free either to conserve or to dispose of the trust property or endowment of the Foundation as they pleased, as long as none of it reverted to him or to them. Charitable trusts, and by extension foundations, were not subject to the rule against inalienability which, like the rule against perpetuities, had been designed to prevent tying up property, chiefly land, indefinitely.[19] Thus, at that stage they could hold their capital indefinitely. Conversely, they were not forced to expend their income or their capital at a certain rate.

With its establishment in 1937, the McConnell Foundation became one of the pioneers among the big private foundations in North America, as well as probably only the second chronologically in Canada, after the Massey Foundation. From the beginning, McConnell ran the operation virtually single-handed. He had made the money for its endowment, and he decided how and to what extent it was to be endowed. There were minor changes of personnel, but all involved either trusted employees or members of the family. After the death of C.H. McLean in July 1941, John G. McConnell became a director of the Foundation and Mary F. Clarke, McConnell's personal secretary, became also the Foundation's secretary. In 1952 Peter M. McEntyre replaced Clarke and became secretary-treasurer, and on the last day of that year David McConnell became a director. Lil was one of the first directors, but she resigned in 1959 and was replaced by McEntyre. In April 1963 Kit McConnell's husband, Peter M. Laing, became a director, followed by Kit herself in June of the same year. Insofar as the McConnell Foundation was the creation of one man, who also shaped its policies, it was the antithesis of, say, the Carnegie Corporation and the Rockefeller Foundation. Even by 1937, these were in the hands of investment and policy professionals rather than of their founders or of their descendants.

At its start, the McConnell Foundation had a portfolio of investments as its endowment. There were two deeds of donation, one to the Belvedere Foundation in March and the other from it to the J.W. McConnell Foundation in April. It is probable that the initial portfolio consisted of certain securities merely transferred from the portfolio that McConnell held in the name of St Lawrence Sugar, in addition to cash for new purchases. The transfer procedure was all part of a larger strategy of tax planning. Inter-corporate dividends were not taxable, and so the dividend income received by St Lawrence was free of tax, and then the transfer of the assets producing dividends ensured the continuation of their tax-free status in the hands of the charitable Foundation and their full application to charitable purposes. With time, the endowment came overwhelmingly to comprise securities previously owned by St Lawrence.

After such securities had formed part of the Foundation's endowment, McConnell would trade them as though as he would have done had they been in any other portfolio. Thus, as early as 16 July 1937, he was selling $225,000 of Consolidated Paper Bonds, $195,000 of Beauharnois Light and Power bonds, $10,000 of Radio Corporation of American common shares, $2,500 of Canada Dry Ginger Ale common shares, $1,000 of People's Gas, Light and Coke common shares, and $575 of United States Rubber preferred shares.[20] He replaced these with 5,000 of Brazilian Traction common shares, 1,360 of Canada Cement preferred, and 1,975 of St Regis preferred, since all of the latter were, unlike the securities sold, producing investment income.

At the end of its first calendar year, 1937, the Foundation held $37,704 in cash and $1,972,533 in securities, for a total portfolio of $2,010,237. It had received $80,403 in income and disbursed $27,500, including $1,000 (out of a total of $5,000 pledged) to the Cancer Research Fund of Dr Edward Archibald's Cancer Research Fund, $1,000 to the Art Association of Montreal, $500 to the Boys' Farm at Shawbridge, and $25,000 to McGill University. The fact that the largest of these contributions went to McGill reflected the university's status as McConnell's principal philanthropic interest, a status that it would retain until his death.

From 1937 until 1942, the amount held in the Foundation's portfolio remained fairly static, as did the amounts disbursed. In 1938 Bishop's University received $5,000; the Boy Scouts, $1,000; the National Committee on Mental Hygiene, $2,000; Loyal College, $500; the Montreal Convalescent Hospital, $5,000; the Salvation Army, $1,500. But there were also large grants, to McGill of $25,000 and to the United Church of $15,000, making the total grants $57,750. The year 1939 saw a larger grant to McGill of $58,333, as well as $1,000 to the Old Brewery Mission, $2,500 to the Salvation Army, and $250 to the School for Graduate Nurses at McGill, making the total $62,083. The grant to the School for Graduate Nurses was very small, but it reflected his ongoing interest in the welfare of the nurses of the Royal Victoria Hospital in particular, which can be traced to his friendship with the future Mrs Frank Knox there. In 1938 Mabel Hersey, who had been superintendent of the school since 1908, and had promoted the bill for the provincial registration of nurses in 1920, retired. This grant of $250 probably went towards the commissioning of a portrait of her. Through McConnell's ongoing chairmanship, into the 1940s, of the Royal Victoria Hospital Charity Ball, he continued his interest in the nurses at the "Vic" and even set up a separate pension fund for them outside the Foundation.

In 1941 there was considerably less given: $500 to the Federation of Catholic Charities, $15,367 to McGill, and $1,000 for YMCA foreign work, for a total of $16,867. In 1941 McConnell subscribed $100,000 to the Canadian Sanatorium Association, which was developing a hospital at Lorne McGibbon's old house in Sainte-Agathe. In addition, the Foundation distributed $6,000 among the Gideons, the Montreal Children's Library, the Boy Scouts, the National Council of Education, YMCA foreign work, the School of Graduate Nurses, the Canadian National Committee for Mental Hygiene, and the Boys' Farm and Training School at Shawbridge. In 1942 the Foundation made $42,925 in grants, but details of these are unavailable.

Over the first two full years of the war, McConnell had begun to give some of the net profits of St Lawrence to his Foundation. In 1940 St Lawrence's net profit was $633,000 and the company transferred $300,000 of it to the Foundation.[21] In 1941 St Lawrence had $540,000 in net profit, and it transferred to the Foundation $479,000 of it, including, for reasons unclear, $300,000 to Lord Beaverbrook's Spitfire Fund in 1940. Then, following a pledge by McConnell to Prime Minister King in 1942, all of St Lawrence's net profit was annually to be transferred to the Foundation's endowment until the end of the war. This was defined as all of its income, net of dividends and other expenses, from 1942 to 1945. More specifically, the profit figures were determined after the levying of federal tax – on gross income and on excess profits, at the effective rate of 30 per cent – and British and foreign (essentially US) tax, for the remaining years of the war, as declared in income-tax returns for the year specified.[22] In fact, St Lawrence's annual contribution was considerably more than its net profit: from 1942 to 1945, the company's net profit was just over $2 million but its contributions to the Foundation totalled almost $16 million.

J. Arthur Mathewson (provincial treasurer), F. Munroe (superintendent of
nurses, Royal Victoria Hospital), Dr W.W. Chipman (president of the Royal
Victoria Hospital), Lady Allan, Sir Montagu Allan, McConnell, and
Morris W. Wilson (chancellor of McGill University), at the opening
of the Allan Memorial Institute, 12 July 1944. Private collection.

In 1943 the Foundation supported almost fifty causes, with contributions ranging
from $25 (Lachine General Hospital) to $250,000 (the Montreal Neurological Institute), with the overall total being $515,430. One of the largest grants that year was
$40,000 for what became known as the Allan Memorial Institute. This sum financed
the renovation of the interior of Ravenscrag to serve as a psychiatric institute for
McGill. Ravenscrag, just to the west of the Royal Victoria Hospital, had for long been
the largest house in Montreal, the seat of the Allans, commanding the city's proudest
vista. Built by Sir Hugh Allan in 1862, it was modelled on a house of Lord Lorne in
Ayrshire and had been the scene for many of the most glittering receptions in Montreal for almost eighty years. With the tragic loss of three of their children in the Great
War, in battle and on the *Lusitania*, and finally the death of their daughter Martha,
Sir Montagu and Lady Allan decided in 1939 to donate their vast house to McGill.
McConnell had probably met Sir Montagu as early as 1901, when he sold him shares
of Standard Chemical, and then through war and peace they had worked together, in
fundraising, on boards, and in commercial ventures.

The story leading to the conversion of Ravenscrag dates back to 1919, with the
establishment of a psychiatric clinic that ran half a day a week at the Royal Victoria

Hospital, sponsored by the Montreal branch of the National Committee for Mental Hygiene, itself set up only in 1918 and after 1950 known as the Canadian Mental Health Association. In 1929 the Montreal branch incorporated itself as the Montreal Mental Hygiene Institute, closely associated with McGill. The Faculty of Medicine had appointed a clinical professor of psychiatry the year before, but, unable to find hospital beds for psychiatric patients, he left for the University of Chicago in 1936. This experience underlined the fact that psychiatrists could find training only at the Institute or at the Verdun Protestant Hospital, known from 1881 to 1925 as the Protestant Hospital for the Insane.[23] McConnell was well aware of the difficulties posed by the distance between Verdun and the Institute downtown, since he had been a member of the board of management at the hospital since 1925. Rotating interns were working in Verdun from the Royal Victoria and Montreal General Hospitals, which they continued to do until 1957, but a hospital closer to McGill would do much to advance psychiatric training and care.

It was only through the aid of the Rockefeller Foundation and the Quebec government that the university was able to set up a department of psychiatry in 1943, with the Montreal Mental Hygiene Institute becoming part of the department. The new Allan Memorial Institute was financed from several sources. In addition to the McConnell Foundation grant of $40,000, McConnell personally and anonymously gave $75,000 for the cost of the "clinical department." The province pledged $30,000 annually for twenty years to maintain the new fifty-bed public and private clinic. The Rockefeller Foundation also contributed. The Allan complemented the Verdun Protestant Hospital by being "open," in the sense of permitting its patients to come and go as they pleased, whereas the Verdun hospital confined its patients. By 1946, five major psychiatric laboratories were operating at the Allan, working in conjunction with the department in the training of psychiatrists.[24] Among those present at the institute's opening was the new director, Dr D. Ewen Cameron, whose "brainwashing" work at the Allan for the American Central Intelligence Agency in the 1950s was to bring a degree of notoriety that none at the opening could have expected in their worst nightmares.[25]

In 1944 the Foundation gave only $353,091 to various causes, $150,000 of which was to the Victorian Order of Nurses Pension Fund Campaign. The VON, as the order was colloquially known, was one of the causes dearest to McConnell's heart. Founded in the 1890s as a result of the efforts of Lady Aberdeen, wife of the governor general, and with branches in Quebec, Ontario, and the Maritimes, it was funded by a combination of periodic campaigns conducted by the wives of successive governors general, contracts with insurance companies, and grants from provincial and municipal authorities. McConnell was familiar with the work of the Milbank Memorial Fund, in New York and elsewhere, in instituting home care by travelling nurses and, from his years in Toronto, with the work of the Methodist deaconesses associated with the Fred Victor Mission. His involvement with the VON likely had a source closer to home, however – the Montreal Maternity Hospital.

In June 1926 the governor general, Lord Byng, and Lady Byng came to open the new maternity wing of the Royal Victoria Hospital, after McConnell had helped to arrange that hospital's absorption of the Montreal Maternity. The wife of the governor general was by tradition patroness both of the VON and of the Royal Victoria Hospital ball (chiefly to benefit the maternity wing), of which McConnell long served as chairman. In 1926 the order incurred a deficit of about $4,000, and its nurses' benefit fund was only $5,175.

If, as seems likely, it was Lady Byng who acquainted McConnell with the VON, it was in Lady Willingdon's time, in 1931, that he became a governor of the organization. Under the Princess Alice, wife of Governor General Lord Athlone and patroness from 1943 to 1946, McConnell served as president of the VON. Aware of his aid to the nurses of the Royal Victoria Hospital, Princess Alice solicited his aid in establishing a VON pension fund. By 1944, the organization was forty-seven years old, which meant that its oldest members were about ready for retirement, and so some plan was necessary for their support. Having been unusually successful in raising $7 million for McGill in 1943, McConnell undertook to raise $500,000 for the VON pension fund. The campaign ran from May 1944 to February 1946, and ultimately the Foundation gave $83,950 to bring it to a successful conclusion, once McConnell realized that the goal of $500,000 would be inadequate as an endowment for the pensions. He personally gave $333,950, or 27.2 per cent of the total of $1,224,300 contributed – an amount that was almost two hundred times larger than what the pension fund had been at the end of 1936.[26] In 2008 terms, he personally gave $4,155,185 out of the $14,984,367 total contributions. Pleading the pressure of other work, McConnell soon retired as VON president, gratified that not only the pension fund was firmly established but also the general funds were increased.[27]

Apart from its grant to the VON in 1944, the Foundation allocated grants to "annual subscriptions due for renewal," such as the Welfare Federation, the Canadian Red Cross, YMCA foreign work, the United Church, the Jewish General Hospital, the Boy Scouts ("final payment"), and the Mackay Institute. It seemed now established practice for it to make pledges extending over a few years, and to make various grants in instalments. But there were new grantees in 1944, such as the Religious Education Council, the Gideons, Polish relief, an Air Cadet Squadron, war charities of Mrs Vincent Massey, and Alma College (in St Thomas, Ontario, where McConnell's in-laws were living).

The Foundation also gave a grant of $3,750 for the endowment of scholarships at McGill to commemorate the McGill men and women who had died in war service,[28] which it was about to expand a year later with a grant of $300,000, the total endowment by 1945 being $3,758,489 in 2008 terms. These scholarships, known initially as

Conclusion of the Red Cross campaign for $1 million: Samuel Bronfman, Huntly Drummond, R.N. Watt (seated), Henri Groulx, McConnell, T. Bouchard, Jackson Dodds, Mrs L. de Gaspé Beaubien, Wilfrid Gagnon, Allan M. Mitchell, and R.F. Haldeney congratulate Watt, co-chairman. *Montreal Daily Star* photograph, 3 October 1940. Watt had been an early colleague of McConnell's in fundraising during the Great War, and this was one of the last campaigns in which they both participated.

the War Memorial Scholarships and later as the McConnell Scholarships, were still a major source of funding for students at the university over fifty years later. Designed to be sufficient to cover the full fees of twelve students selected from across Canada and Newfoundland, as well as their residence at Douglas Hall or Royal Victoria College, it provided for the funding of up to four years for students in arts and science and engineering.[29]

By the end of 1945, the Foundation's income was the highest ever, $989,191, in addition to which McConnell had made further contributions of $759,003. In this year he was especially concerned with the international deficit of the YMCA and with the deficit account of the Montreal Boys' Association. The Foundation decided to give the YMCA $10,000 and the Boys' Association, which served "all creeds and nationalities," $2,200 a month indefinitely. In the final quarter of 1945, the Foundation contributed $40,000 to the Red Cross, $14,000 to the McGill War Memorial, and $16,500 to the Welfare Federation.

In 1946 McConnell went to the Bahamas for an extended vacation, which led to Foundation contributions to the charitable work of his friend Mrs H.L. (Tootie) Beardmore and to the Nassau Red Cross. Among the other new causes were Brandon College, the Canadian Legion War Memorial, the Canadian Youth Commission, the Oxford Group, Rosedale United Church, Bishop's College School, the Kerby Memorial Fund, Belgian war relief, the Save the Children Fund, Selwyn House School, the Knox United Church in Port Arthur, the Salvation Army in Fort William, St Michael's Hospital in Toronto, the Windsor Tornado Relief Fund, and a carillon for the Church of All Hallows by the Tower in London. Aid was also given to several causes that had been helped in earlier years: $25,000 to the Art Association for its Sustentation Fund, $11,426 to the Old Brewery Mission for a new kitchen and dining room at its Lake Chapleau camp, and $40,000 to the Royal Victoria Hospital for a new elevator to transport patients to the operating theatre and other floors in the Ross Pavilion. In addition, McGill received $10,000 as the first of five instalments for the Neurological Institute, $10,000 for a Morris Wilson Memorial Fund, and $5,000 in memory of Dr Edward Archibald, who had died the previous year.[30]

Also in 1946, the Boys' Farm and Training School at Shawbridge, a reformatory for boys in the Laurentians and a favourite cause of Montreal businessmen, received $12,500 from the Foundation for its special building campaign.[31] This institution, which had been established in 1909 as an offshoot of the Boys' Home in Montreal, was based on the premise that juvenile delinquents were not criminals but misguided children, and accordingly it taught its young residents such skills as tending crops and caring for animals, housework, mechanical drawing, and gardening. Financial problems had surfaced from the start, despite provincial government assistance that was increased substantially under Premier Taschereau. In 1919 the farm was separated from the Boys' Home in Montreal, and two years later Edward Beatty took over its presidency, a post he held until 1942. The Beatty years were the farm's most successful period, in which McConnell played a significant part. Named a director of the farm in 1927, McConnell promptly wrote a cheque for $15,000, to meet general expenses. This donation inspired Beatty to contribute the cost of a new gymnasium, amounting to more than $30,000. Beatty opened the gymnasium, which was named after him, but he gave most of the credit to McConnell, who had apparently contributed to this project as well but was then visiting his dying sister in California.[32] McConnell himself was the farm's honorary president at his death in 1963.

One of the largest Foundation grants in 1946 – out of a total amount dispensed of $574,176 – was $100,000 for the Chancellor Dunning Trust at Queen's University. Made anonymously, this grant left it to the endowment's trustees at Queen's to decide how best to use the income from the trust "to promote understanding and appreciation of the dignity, freedom and responsibility of the individual person in human society," and eventually Queen's would establish the Chancellor Dunning Lectures with the income.

The largest grant of 1946, however, was $200,000 for the United Church of Canada Pension Capital Fund, made in June. This was in response to the sort of emergency situation that McConnell saw as the Foundation's chief responsibility. At the Erskine and American Church in April, W.M. Birks had launched an appeal for $3.5 million to augment the existing Ministers' Pension Fund. Calling the existing pensions for ministers a "scandal," Birks pledged $1 million from Quebec alone. He had discussed the endowment with J.S. McLean and John David Eaton in Toronto and obtained a pledge from McConnell for $200,000, or $2,447,826 in 2008 terms, to "set the pace."[33] McConnell and his son John were on the national committee.

In 1947 McConnell was particularly concerned by the failure of the Welfare Federation to meet its fundraising goals, and he raised the Foundation's pledge to the organization to $25,000, $8,500 over the previous year. Among the new beneficiaries of Foundation grants that year were the Iona Fund, Canadian aid to China, the Nassau Leper Colony, the Canadian Association for Adult Education, McMaster University, Dalhousie University, and Greek war relief.

In 1948 there was a major grant of $35,000 to McGill University to buy the old J.K.L. Ross house, formerly the house of his father James Ross and later owned by the federal government, for the Faculty of Law. The purchase of the Ross house involved more than $35,000 but also an exchange of another property for it. McConnell had first bought the property of the Royal Edward Institute on Saint-Urbain Street for $88,000, apparently not through the Foundation. Then McGill transferred this property in exchange for the Ross house. After the Ross house had been converted into offices and classrooms, at a further cost to him of $25,000, McConnell agreed initially that it should be called McConnell Hall. But he never liked having anything named after him except as a rare encouragement to others to contribute. McConnell therefore later proposed that it should be called Tyndale Hall, in honour of Associate Chief Justice O.S. Tyndale, the chancellor. Tyndale declined, but he agreed to sit with McConnell and Principal Cyril James on a committee to find a new name for the building, which was eventually, in 1950, named Chancellor Day Hall, after a previous chancellor and judge.

Also in 1948, in addition to paying for the Ross house, the Foundation gave $250,000 to McGill University generally. This grant was in connection with the McGill campaign to raise $9,075,000 in September of that year. The corresponding figures in 2008 would be $2,469,298 and $89,635,526. Blair Gordon, son of the late Sir Charles Gordon and his successor as president of Dominion Textile, was the chairman. McConnell served as one of the four general, or working, vice-chairmen.

In 1948 as well, the Foundation contributed $25,000 to the Royal Victoria Hospital's deficit fund, the Neurological Institute received $10,000, and a small grant of $7,500 was made to help endow the first professorship in a new faculty of divinity – a project to which McConnell, at the urging of W.M. Birks, had earlier contributed $400,000. Dr James S. Thomson became the J.W. McConnell Professor of Philosophy of Religion and the dean of the new faculty.

The following year, 1949, was marked by a substantial gift to one of McConnell's favourite causes – the East End Boys' Club in the Montreal district of Maisonneuve,

Lord Alexander speaks at the opening of the East End Boys' Club, with
Lady Alexander and McConnell behind him, 1951. Private collection.

where the St Lawrence sugar refinery was located. The first Boys' Club had been
established in New York by E.H. Harriman, financier and president of the Union
Pacific. McConnell probably became familiar with it through Albert Milbank, chairman of the Borden Company. In any event, Boys' Clubs soon spread throughout
North America, and the first club in Montreal was probably the one founded by the
printer Fred Southam in Griffintown, east of Point St Charles, in 1908. Subsequently,
the McConnell Foundation supported the Montreal Boys' Association, which was
dedicated to keeping boys out of mischief by keeping them constructively occupied,
but its facilities were inadequate.

Particularly with the removal of the Montreal Boys' Home to Shawbridge, McConnell wanted to ensure that work among boys in the city should remain complementary
to that at Shawbridge, and indeed to discourage the very need for Shawbridge, which
was a reformatory. This led to a major Foundation grant to a new East End Boys'
Club. Mayor Camillien Houde laid the foundation stone in 1949, and the building
was opened by Lord Alexander, the governor general, in 1951. Within its first three
months of operation, the club was to be used by 1,600 young people, girls as well
as boys. Located at the corner of Hochelaga Street and Bennett Avenue in Maisonneuve, it contained a games room with three billiard tables, a workshop with power

lathes and other machinery, a swimming pool, and a boxing ring. McConnell estimated the total cost as $425,000, including landscaping, seeding, and planting by W. Ormiston Roy.

As early as March 1949, McConnell could foresee unprecedented demands upon his Foundation in the following year, including $500,000 for the new Joint Hospital Campaign and at least $1 million for the Neurological Institute. He offered this guidance to the Foundation's future trustees:

> While careful investment of available funds is vitally important, the prudent distribution of revenue among the most worthy and the most needy charitable causes is equally so; that during lean years when income is lower, charitable contributions ought not necessarily [to] be lessened. During periods of reduced revenue, charitable contributions should be maintained, even to the point of encroaching upon Capital Assets as provided by the Foundation's Charter. For, during such years, charitable institutions are always in far greater need, because contributions from business concerns and private sources may be – and doubtless will be – reduced … Hence, the necessity of charitable foundations conserving resources during prosperous times, and in turn, giving more liberally during bad times – *thus helping to fill the gap, so that work may not suffer in aid of which this Foundation was established.*[34]

This warning was as close as McConnell ever came to setting out a mission statement for the Foundation. He returned to the same theme two years later, when, referring to the possibility of a third world war, he declared that "inasmuch as the Foundation has conserved a goodly portion of its revenue during good times, it ought with like judgment and consideration, give generously if overtaken by bad times." He explained that "it would be wise to conserve during times of unusual prosperity against less prosperous years which might come about by conditions presently unforeseeable." It was necessary, he continued more explicitly, for the Foundation to "maintain contributions at average prosperity level by drawing upon revenue reserves."[35]

By the time of this statement, McConnell had already won a significant battle on behalf of his Foundation. The battle had begun with new federal legislation in 1950 designed to force foundations to spend 90 per cent of their revenue in a given financial year. McConnell lobbied the Department of National Revenue until he received a uniquely favourable ruling in 1951. Its effect was to exempt the McConnell Foundation from the new requirement, on the ground that it had been incorporated before 1940.

Towards the end of 1951, the Foundation gave $200,000 (later $500,000, which would be $4,201,493 in 2008) to the new Joint Hospital Campaign in Montreal, the first such campaign since the one chaired by McConnell himself in 1927. Hartland

Molson was the chairman of this new effort, McConnell himself being too old to head further fundraising campaigns.

Nevertheless, he was actively involved in its planning, and a preliminary report by two consultants was submitted to the new Joint Hospital Committee on which he sat. Addressing the state of McGill's teaching hospitals, this report noted that the teaching hospitals had "an unfortunate and unfounded suspicion of the motives of the Medical School and the University in any attempt to develop a closer relationship" with them, and it also offered an incisive analysis of the financial pressures that the hospitals were then experiencing. Among other things, the report recommended the reconstruction of the Children's Memorial Hospital and the Royal Victoria Hospital on their present sites, and the construction of a new Montreal General between Cedar and Pine avenues. The Joint Hospitals Committee accepted these recommendations and they were duly carried out following the 1951 campaign.

The Children's Memorial Hospital had long been one of McConnell's special interests, especially since he had raised $1,175,000 for it in a fundraising campaign in 1939, or $17,448,553 in 2008 terms. Established in 1902 on Guy Street, the Memorial had moved in 1909 to Cedar Avenue, just to the north and the east of McConnell's future house on Pine Avenue. Though a favourite cause of Sir Hugh Graham and his newspaper, the *Star*, it had accumulated a deficit of $4,000 by 1911. The following year, the Quebec legislature voted it an annual grant of $300, and the city of Montreal offered a one-time grant of $500, in two instalments. Clearly, private support was to remain essential to the survival of the institution. James Carruthers gave $100,000 for a new wing in 1919. Five years later, Lord Beaverbrook, whose brother Allan lived across the road from it, gave £200. But there was no endowment fund, and, under the Public Charities Act, the province provided only a third of the costs of an indigent inpatient, the other two-thirds coming from the city of Montreal and the hospital itself, with no help at all for outpatients.

Despite its financial problems, the Children's Memorial developed a good reputation. In 1932 the Montreal Foundling and Baby Hospital, founded in 1892, and latterly on Saint-Urbain Street, amalgamated with it, expanding the facilities of the Memorial until 1943, when the building on Saint-Urbain Street was closed. When the Montreal Children's (or Vipond) Hospital, founded in 1920, on Saint-Antoine Street, also joined the Memorial, in 1940, the physical facilities again grew significantly, but there was still an urgent need to expand the building on Cedar Avenue. In 1948 the Memorial decided to extend westwards along the north side of Cedar Avenue, at the same time as the Montreal General had purchased property on the south side. Discussions, however, soon led to the decision to move all the services of the General to Cedar Avenue, and to sell the western division of the General, in Cabot Square, to the Memorial as the site (along with certain properties on Essex Street) for a completely new building. This was to replace the old facilities on Cedar Avenue and

The laying of the cornerstone of the Montreal Neurological Institute,
6 October 1933. McConnell is behind Principal Sir Arthur Currie (holding
mortarboard), the Right Reverend John C. Farthing (lord bishop of Montreal)
is speaking, and His Excellency the Earl of Bessborough, governor general of
Canada, is to the right of the bishop. Private collection.

Saint-Antoine Street. The removal of the Memorial to Cabot Square, just north of
Tupper Street, where the McConnells had lived very early in their marriage, in 1956
was in part to be the result of the 1951 Joint Hospitals Campaign. With this move, the
Memorial took the name of its affiliate since 1940, becoming known as the Montreal
Children's Hospital.[36]

By then, McConnell was hard at work on another hospital project, the expansion
of the Montreal Neurological Institute. His role in this project demonstrates how a
major grant from his Foundation typically involved a large commitment of his time
and attention. It also shows well his method of fundraising, including such elements as
keeping track of the changing financial situation of various key donors, studying their
habits, and using his own money to leverage money from others. It serves almost as a
study in how he built his reputation as one of the indispensable fixers of his time.[37]

The opening of the Neurological Institute in 1933 had been the culmination of over
a decade in the growth of the hospitals affiliated with McGill.[38] In 1924 the Royal
Victoria had inaugurated a neurosurgery division, under the direction of Dr Wilder
Penfield, for a probationary period of five years, and the success of this experiment

led McGill and the Royal Victoria to make a strong proposal to the Rockefeller Foundation for a new grant to create a new institute for a permanent neurosurgery department. How McConnell first became involved with the project is unknown, but probably it was through Dr Edward Archibald, surgeon-in-chief at the Royal Victoria since 1928 and the doctor who, as recounted earlier, would accompany the McConnells on their round-the-world trip in 1936. Archibald and Dr Jonathan Meakins of the Royal Victoria University Clinic were strongly in favour of making the neurosurgery division permanent, and they persuaded Penfield that he should head it. McConnell's respect for Meakins, Penfield, and Archibald virtually ensured that he would be a mainstay of the new project, which, with a $1-million endowment grant from the Rockefeller Foundation,[39] supplemented by $115,367 from McConnell himself and $100,000 from Sir Herbert Holt, was opened by Lord Bessborough in 1933.[40] McConnell's and Holt's contributions were so significant – $1,709,253 and $1,324,706 respectively, in 2008 terms – that Penfield, the director, proposed naming the second floor and third floors after them.[41]

Once the Institute had begun its work, McConnell maintained a deep personal interest in it. In 1938 he donated a further $3,000, and the following year he and Holt each gave $5,000 towards a new electro-encephalography laboratory. He was a frequent visitor to the patients' wards, where he would appear, unannounced and sometimes unrecognized, carrying flowers from his own garden. No detail escaped his eye, and he was full of suggestions for practical improvements to the fabric of the building – suggestions that took on special urgency at the end of the Second World War. By then, the Institute was seriously short of both space and money and unable to continue its work. Whereas its total costs to 1944 had been less than $1 million, by about 1947 it needed $1,400,000 for new construction and equipment and a further $1 million for a "stabilizing endowment." The income from the $1-million Rockefeller endowment had been falling steadily, so that it was now only $37,500 annually. Furthermore, the annual income from supplemental gifts was totalling only $2,500, so that the annual research budget was $40,000, whereas really it should be $60,000 a year over the next ten years.[42]

In September 1946 McConnell had invited Penfield, Cyril James, W.W. Chipman, and Jonathan Meakins to the Mount Royal Club to discuss these needs. They considered whether more could be charged for private rooms or whether more private patients could be found. James said that, if general income from patients could be increased by 10 per cent ($25,000), and a further $15,000 could be obtained from the province, the annual deficit of $40,000 would be covered. McConnell said that the Institute's scientists should seek research funding from the province.[43] Over the next year, with a view to both research and operating grants, Penfield approached George Marler, then on the Montreal city council; Albini Paquette, the provincial minister of health; Prime Minister Mackenzie King; Paul Martin, the federal minister of health;

and John Bassett. Not receiving a satisfactory response, he asked McConnell to print the Institute's annual report in the *Star* to influence Paul Martin. He wanted Martin and Premier Duplessis together to create a fund for scientific development, and he observed that only McConnell's recent gift of $10,000 had temporarily saved the Institute's scientific budget.[44] McConnell replied that he hoped that a research grant from the federal government would become annual, and that he had already spoken to Prime Minister King about it.

Penfield was not familiar with the politics of fundraising. In particular, he took long to appreciate how jealously Parliament guarded its oversight over finances. Over the next several years, he was to continue to lobby unsuccessfully prime ministers St Laurent and Diefenbaker for an endowment of $2 million from which the Institute's research expenses could be covered. The Rockefeller Foundation had said that the Institute should now depend on local, that is Canadian, support, but this strategy became increasingly problematic as Quebec and Ottawa quarrelled over their respective areas of constitutional responsibility. It was not altogether clear, for example, whether research might fall under provincial competence for education, and the Institute as a hospital seemed to fall within provincial competence for health.

It is not that anyone doubted the Institute's importance. Both King and Duplessis received Penfield courteously in 1947, and they respectively granted $40,000 and $50,000 thousand for the following year, the provincial grant renewable for at least the following three years.[45] By the time of his meeting with Duplessis in May 1947, Penfield had realized that perhaps a new wing, catering largely to private patients, was part of the solution to paying the deficit incurred through caring for non-paying, public patients. He asked the premier for $1.25 million for such a wing as well as $1 million as a research endowment.[46] But he really could not wait indefinitely for a decision on these requests.

In 1949–50, with its accumulated debt on operating or "clinical" expenses about $200,000 and rising, the Institute mounted its first fundraising campaign since its foundation. Just before the start of the campaign, Penfield and Henry W. Morgan hired George A. Brakeley, Jr, vice-president of the John Price Jones company of New York, which had assisted in the McGill fundraising campaign of 1948, to evaluate all potential donors, including McConnell. Brakeley's advice revealed how the tactics of challenge grants, of which McConnell had proved himself so masterful, was now standard practice. "In approaching him [McConnell] for any amount," Brakeley said,

> I suggest that you subtly stress the need for some sort of yard-stick gift, even if on conditional terms. In other words, would he set the pace with $250,000 on the understanding that it is to be matched by a few similar gifts and some lesser ones. This might give you an entre[é] and an amount to talk over with Killam, Bronfman and others.

Certainly Mr. McConnell should be consulted on the use of the presentation [to potential donors] and, if he is attracted to it, he might get the ball rolling for an informal special gifts campaign for whatever he can't make up himself. He is more apt to be influenced if he thinks a Provincial grant is possible for $1,250,000 to $1,500,000. It might be that he would be interested in helping you raise the remainder towards a 2½ or 3 million dollar goal. It is well to remember in dealing with the Premier [Duplessis], however, that Mr. McConnell's papers are antagonistic towards the present Provincial administration, and he is reportedly not at all in favour in Quebec City.[47]

This judgment on McConnell's relations with Duplessis was far from what would later be accepted as fact. In any case, McConnell was busily cultivating Duplessis at the time. He was not a formal chairman of the Institute's campaign, but he was instrumental in raising the biggest contributions, including $100,000 from Olive Hosmer, $50,000 from Canada Cement, $25,000 from Henry Birks and Sons, and $25,000 from the J.H. Birks Foundation. He also gave Penfield much practical advice on how to approach others himself.

With regard to Penfield's projected meeting with Harry Bronfman, for example, McConnell noted that Gerald Bronfman, Harry's son, had already asked how much McConnell would like him to give: "Now it strikes me that question would not have been asked by the son had he not been quite sure that the father was willing to give, what might be called, a substantial personal contribution – perhaps a total of $100,000 in two payments. It would be preferable to have that amount sure – than the uncertainty with which you are now faced, for you may be sure the $18,000,000 Hospital Campaign about which much has been said in the Press, has not escaped their attention."[48] As for Samuel McLaughlin of General Motors, McConnell advised Penfield to ask Ross McMaster and Charles Dunning to call on him while they were all on holiday in Bermuda. With respect to I.W. Killam, whom McConnell had unsuccessfully approached for aid three times already, McConnell observed that Killam had just sold his interest in a large company in British Columbia. And so "a note to Nassau [where Killam was wintering] where he must be free from business cares, might be an appropriate moment to suggest the use of a portion of his idle money."[49]

In the meantime, McConnell secured an immediate grant from the federal Department of Health of $173,535 for equipment. He also obtained a pledge of $40,000 from J.O. Asselin, the chairman of the Executive Committee of the city of Montreal, to be appealed for annually. And he agreed to approach William H. Donner, of the Donner Foundation, whose wife was being treated at the Institute, who eventually agreed to raise his contribution to $20,000 annually, in perpetuity. McConnell remarked, "This constitutes a very fine gift since it is equal to 4% in $500,000.00 capital – and that is a slight shade better than McGill is averaging on its entire portfolio."[50]

As he came to realize that the goal of $2,400,000 would not be soon realized, McConnell had to decide on his own contribution. In November 1949 he brought Penfield to a crucial meeting with Duplessis. As Penfield recorded:

> He [McConnell] then explained that if the clinical deficits of the Neurological Institute could be taken care of by the province in a sufficiently permanent manner, that he could guarantee that funds would be forthcoming for the building of the wing that was needed to replace the present temporary annex. There followed a considerable discussion of the danger of communism. Mr. Duplessis pointed out that McGill was somewhat negligent of control of communists within the university. Mr. McConnell described the difficulties raised by the formation of a guild among the personnel in publishing offices. This seemed to interest Mr. Duplessis very much. Mr. Duplessis said finally that he would do what he could, and turning to Mr. McConnell he said "If we do that will you take care of the building?"[51]

This memorandum shows how McConnell extracted almost a doubling of the provincial grant to the Institute, to $90,000 a year. To what extent it demonstrates a quid-pro-quo arrangement between McConnell and Duplessis is unclear. One extreme interpretation is that McConnell agreed to repress communists at McGill in return for the increased grant, but Penfield does not make this explicit. After writing his memorandum, Penfield noted that McConnell and Duplessis had asked him to leave the room in the course of the meeting, so that even Penfield did not know exactly what passed between them.[52] But clearly communism was an issue.

McConnell was generally frustrated with the failure of the public to support Penfield. Hearing that his old enemy, the anglophobic Chicago publisher Robert McCormick, who had described McConnell as an imperialist toady, might be willing to help, he wrote to Penfield at the end of 1950: "If some quite independent person, like Mr. Edward Farley, who believes in your Institution, were willing to suggest to Colonel McCormick that he should send a voluntary contribution, I think that it would be foolish to refuse his money. For my part, I would be willing to accept money from his Satanic Majesty if it were to be devoted to the excellent work you are doing at the Neurological."[53]

By March 1951, McConnell had begun to provide himself most of the funds for a new wing, $1,500,000 or $12,604,478 in 2008 terms. Penfield confessed himself to be "somewhat awed by your generosity and by the simple and understanding way in which you give your help." "It makes one," he continued, "feel humble and makes me turn to examine whether we who are on the staff deserve this confidence."[54] To this $1,500,000 McConnell added $10,000 ($84,030 in 2008) to complete the "artistic roof" of the wing.[55]

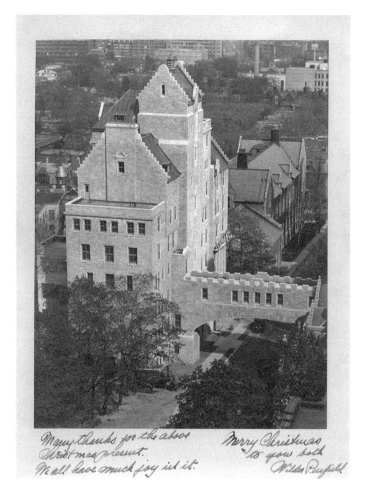

The McConnell Wing of the Montreal Neurological Institute,
c. 1953, with an inscription to McConnell from Dr Wilder Penfield.
Private collection.

The project involved the building of a new north wing to the building that had been opened by Lord Bessborough in 1933 and also an extension to the south. It was to include a disaster-casualty ward to be used in case Montreal was subject to atomic attack.[56] The result would be a doubling of the Institute's space and a tripling of its bed capacity. With the McConnell grant, half the construction was completed by December 1952, entitling the Institute to $222,880 from the province, half of the construction grant that it had promised, and there was $415,674 from other sources as well as $468,449 pledged by Ottawa.

Meanwhile, three years after McConnell had first approached J.O. Asselin of the Executive Committee of Montreal, there was still no grant secured from the city.

Asselin had fallen ill, and his position of chairman had been temporarily taken by Conrad Saint-Amant, the director of the city's social services. Penfield approached Gordon McLeod Pitts, the vice-chairman, and incidentally the McGill representative on the city council, to see if he could secure a favourable response to the Institute's request for $67,000 a year. McConnell, however, was sure that only Asselin could pass the measure: "This nonsense about the Councillors being tough on such an important matter as this makes me sick. Surely the vital work of this Institution is for the benefit of all citizens including the 'famous' 99 Councillors. Do they not realize that this is the finest Institute of its kind in the world, and that it happens to be in the French Canadian city of Montreal, which they are supposed, with great wisdom, to guide and administer?"[57]

By the 1950s, even some of McConnell's fiercest critics or their relatives had benefited from the Institute, such as Stanley Knowles, a CCF MP; the wife of the CCF leader, M.J. Coldwell; and Judge Thomas Tremblay, of the Court of Sessions of the Peace in Montreal, the same judge who had, in his 1949 valuation of the assets of Montreal Tramways, found McConnell's alleged stockwatering of almost forty years previously so unconscionable, and who later went on to lead the provincial commission on Quebec-Ottawa relations. Tremblay in particular became a link between Penfield and Premier Duplessis.

He and Penfield had hoped that the Duke of Edinburgh would come to open the new McConnell Wing.[58] But a tour of the empire with the queen kept him away, and instead Vincent Massey, the governor general, performed the ceremony on 20 November 1953. McConnell himself, not wishing to receive more congratulations and cause a fuss, did not attend, but Lil and their son John received the guests on his behalf.

Duplessis was now firmly a friend of English-language hospitals, and he laid the cornerstone for a new Montreal General Hospital in the previous May. Several months later, McConnell arrived with the premier for the unveiling of a mural paying tribute to him and other founders of the Institute, and to examine the new equipment.

At about the same time, McConnell was helping the Institute in another way. When Penfield's efforts to set up an endowment fund for scientific research proved fruitless, McConnell stepped in. For some time, the Foundation had held shares of Beauharnois Light, Heat and Power, part of the Montreal Power empire. The provincially run Quebec Hydro-Electric Commission had decided to appropriate Beauharnois, and McConnell was actively involved in calling for a fair valuation of the shares that the Foundation was holding in it. Arbitration hearings ensued. In April 1953 McConnell, believing that Beauharnois shares would soon advance beyond $30 each, their present price, accepted his colleague Peter McEntyre's recommendation that the Foundation buy more of the company's shares "outside the market" at $30, and in considerable numbers, as a short-term investment. The Foundation swiftly bought 38,201 shares at $30. The profit made on their forced sale to Hydro in May yielded roughly the $1 mil-

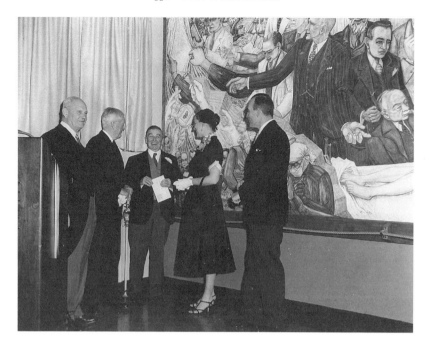

Chancellor B.C. Gardner, McConnell, Premier Maurice Duplessis, Miss Filer,
and Dr F. Cyril James at the unveiling of a mural depicting them at the
Montreal Neurological Institute, 16 November 1954, Private collection.

lion required for the Institute's research endowment, although the actual endowment
took the form of a transfer of securities from the Foundation. This was a challenge
grant, completed only when the city of Montreal had also agreed to make an annual
grant to the Institute, which it eventually did.

Through these years, the Foundation's other work was continuing. One extraordinary grant was in November 1951 to Princess Elizabeth of $29,337, for distribution
in her name to charities that she had chosen. In making such a grant, the Foundation
was following a tradition established, and then maintained over several years, with
Mrs Winston Churchill in 1944, for contributions through her to her favourite charities. The total amount disbursed by the Foundation in 1951 was $1,542,023.

A new project in 1952 was another Boys' and Girls' Club in Point St Charles, which
McConnell estimated would cost $900,000. He also offered challenge grants to a pro-
jected Boys' Club in Ottawa and to the Montreal Association for the Blind. A major
grant in this year was $500,000 for the Royal Victoria Hospital Building Fund. In
1952, gravely ill with pneumonia, McConnell was unable to attend the opening dinner of the Royal Victoria Hospital fundraising campaign, but, as John Bassett put it,
he was certainly present in spirit.

McConnell and children at the opening of the Point St Charles
Boys' and Girls' Club, 1953. Private collection.

In the early 1950s, the Foundation was also a key supporter of cancer research. That cause had become a national preoccupation in 1931, when the Canadian Medical Association set up a study committee on it. In 1935 the governor general, Lord Bessborough, appealed by radio for Canadian support of the King George V Jubilee Cancer Fund, which had been set up to mark the silver anniversary of the king's coronation. The king himself was to die of cancer the following January. McConnell was a major contributor to the fund, which raised $500,000 in Canada, and later, in 1937, his new Foundation's very first grant went to Dr Edward Archibald for his own research into cancer.

Then, however, the Cancer Fund became inactive, prompting McConnell to dispatch an indignant protest to Brooke Claxton, minister of health, in 1947. A draft of his letter survives in his papers. Characteristically trenchant, it is entitled "Re Half million KG [King George] memorial cancer fund" and reads as follows:

It seems to me that something is strangely amis[s]. Have the trustees ceased
to function or have they lost all sense of responsibility with respect to the
fund, which has lain virtually dormant for 12 years. The fund was subscribed

by thousands of Canadians from coast to coast, who were deeply interested in discover[ing] the cause, and finding a cure, for cancer. They were led to believe by the then G/G. L.B. [Governor General Lord Bessborough] and the then PM R.B. Bennett that the fund for which they both made ardent appeals to the people by radio would be put to work immediately in the fight against the cancer scourge. But what has happened? Nothing worthy of mention. Nothing in the way of research. Nothing to the credit of those whose responsibility it is to set this fund to work actively & efficiently. You ask me for a suggestion as to what might be done. To my mind only one thing can be done with the hope [of] favorable results. Use up the fund completely within 5 yrs, allocating it on even bases between the only two centres equipped to deal with the matter, namely Toronto University & McGill. At these 2 institutions competent research scientists are available, and very quickly an organization can be set up to work efficiently and even frantically, in the greatest effort ever made in Canada to get at the cause & find a cure for this dread disease. Over 12 years, whilst the principal sum of this fund has been wholly idle, cancer has consistently ravaged, and taken its terrible toll, which is on good authority said to be one in every 9 of the population. At this very moment, men, women and children are dying in every hospital in Can[ada], while in their home [illegible] cancer victims suffer the torture of that dread disease. Let us, I beg of you, suffer no longer delay but get this entire fund to work. Otherwise most of the subscribers stand betrayed.[59]

In response, Claxton set up the National Cancer Institute as the research partner of the Canadian Cancer Society.[60] McConnell then leaped to benefit cancer treatment with a new Canadian discovery. Shortly after the end of the Second World War, the National Research Council of Canada had determined that the cobalt-60 radioactive isotope was suitable for treating cancer, and in 1947 the Atomic Energy Commission of Canada opened its heavy-water production facility, at Chalk River, Ontario, which produced the necessary cobalt. This was cheaper, safer, and more powerful than the radium used in conventional X-rays. Projects to produce it for therapeutic use began in 1949, and prototypes were ready by 1951. The cobalt bombs that resulted were called Mark II Cobalt 60 Beam Therapy Units. They were used to treat deep-seated tumours, and they were to raise the cure rate for cervical cancer from 25 per cent to 75 per cent. Although largely superseded by new technology by 1965, cobalt bombs were the forerunner of all other radiation-therapy units used in treating cancer, at least until the end of the century.

McConnell must have been one the first purchasers of them, in the very year that they were approved for medical use. The Foundation provided them to the Royal Victoria and the Montreal General hospitals – later joined in 1954 by the Notre-Dame and Hôtel-Dieu hospitals and in 1955 by St Mary's and the Jewish General – all in

Montreal – and the Hôtel-Dieu in Quebec City. Each cost about $65,000, or $519,078 in 2008 terms. Through the new federal minister of health, Paul Martin, McConnell also provided a cobalt unit to the British Empire Cancer Campaign for installation in England. This cost the Foundation $70,000 and was paid to the Atomic Energy Commission of Canada.

At the end of 1952, McConnell announced the transfer of $3,995,626 in securities to the Foundation from the portfolio of St Lawrence Sugar. There was a gift of $70,000 to the YMCA to replace its endowment fund, which had been used to complete its new building on Stanley Street in Montreal, behind and attached to the building that McConnell had helped to raise the funds to build in 1909. At McGill, he set up a Fund for Special Aid and endowed it with about $300,000 in securities, yielding an income of approximately $15,000 a year. The Foundation also pledged $250,000 to the building fund of Sir George Williams College (later Concordia University), with the possibility of $50,000 more if necessary.

By the close of 1953, McConnell could look back with satisfaction at the opening of the Point St Charles Boys' and Girls' Club, which had cost $910,000, only $10,000 over budget. The Foundation allocated $520,000 for a Winter Auditorium (later called the McConnell Arena) for McGill, to serve as an indoor skating rink, located in Fletcher's Field between the Sir Arthur Currie Memorial Gymnasium-Armoury and the monument to Sir George-Étienne Cartier. Other major grants included £5,000 for the restoration of the bombed Coventry Cathedral in England, $75,000 for the Jeanne d'Arc Hospital, and $100,000 for Westminster Abbey, as well as $25,000 each for St Francis Xavier College and the YMCA of Saint John, New Brunswick.

In 1953 McConnell created the Gardner-James Special Fund, later called the McGill Fund, with an endowment of $260,000, or $2,106,167 in 2008. Its purpose was to provide for special needs of the staff, such as emergency medical expenses, to be distributed at the discretion of the principal. In the same year came the J.W. McConnell Fund of over $1 million for salaries and wages, and the Lily Griffith McConnell Fund of $1 million for research into neurology and neurosurgery, the total being $16,201,439 in 2008 terms. McConnell supplemented the Gardner-James Fund in January 1956 with a further $366,000, so that the endowment was now worth $803,000, yielding a dividend of $38,450. Another grant to Gardner-James in September 1956, of Socony Mobil Oil and Standard Oil of Ohio shares, brought the endowment to over $1 million.

There were in 1954 grants of $25,000 each to the Salvation Army Eventide Home building fund and to the Montreal Museum of Fine Arts, as the Art Association had been renamed, in addition to $10,000 for the capital campaign of the Canadian National Institute for the Blind. There was $16,500 for the Knob Lake Sub-Arctic Research Laboratory, run by McGill, to be followed in 1958 with a further $10,000 for a building extension to it. There were grants also for the Collège Sainte-Anne de

Pocatière, the Summerlea United Church, the St George Cathedral Choir in Kingston, the Loisirs du Sacré-Coeur, the Hôpital de la Miséricorde, the Hôpital Général de Québec, the Canadian Institute for International Affairs, the Halifax YMCA, and the Boys' Club in Trois-Rivières.

In 1956 a new sort of grantee emerged. Two years before, at the Hélène de Champlain Restaurant on St Helen's Island, the newly elected mayor Jean Drapeau had convened a meeting of twenty-four lawyers and businessmen to convince them of the necessity of a concert hall for the city.[61] McConnell was probably among them. In any case, by 1956, he was to serve as the liaison between the mayor and Premier Duplessis, an old enemy of Drapeau's, on the issue. McConnell himself probably held no warm memories of Drapeau, who had been involved in anti-conscription agitation with André Laurendeau and who had been closely associated with the nationalist Abbé Lionel Groulx. McConnell also had no personal interest whatever in the public performance of music, and he displayed only a nominal interest in the theatre. Nevertheless, he still adhered to his practice of cultivating cordial relations with almost all sitting politicians, and Drapeau was to be no exception.

Duplessis was himself in favour of a new concert hall, and his support was essential, particularly since the charter of the city did not permit Montreal to act in this matter. The architect Hazen Sise, veteran of the Republican cause in the Spanish Civil War, friend of Norman Bethune, grandson of the founder of Bell Telephone, and son of the president of Northern Electric, had been devoting much of his life to the cause. Jean Michaud, another architect and the winner of the competition to design the Queen Elizabeth Hall in Vancouver, joined him. Local opinion was broadly propitious, and the question was where to locate the new hall.

By 1956, three proposals for a site had emerged: first, the south side of Dominion Square (later Place du Canada), the site of the future Château Champlain Hotel; secondly, Maisonneuve Park in the east; and thirdly, a site between the other two, bounded by St Catherine, Ontario (later President Kennedy), Jeanne-Mance, and Saint-Urbain streets. The first site was the traditional centre of English Montreal. The second was in the almost exclusively French-speaking east end. And the third was between two streets commonly seen as the border between English and French Montreal, Bleury Street to the west of Jeanne-Mance and St Lawrence (or Saint-Laurent) Boulevard to the east of Saint-Urbain, with Ontario Avenue as the northern boundary.

Drapeau and McConnell toured the sites together, and the mayor urged McConnell to choose the third proposal if McConnell wanted to see a concert hall in his lifetime. "You are probably right, Mr. Mayor," McConnell replied, and he presumably forwarded the choice to Duplessis.[62] In 1958 Duplessis had the necessary letters patent issued, naming the corporation responsible for the building after Sir George-Étienne Cartier. It was perhaps the last monument to the Cartier compromise between French and English Montrealers, and as such, in the politically volatile atmosphere of the times, it was doomed.

McConnell always referred to the project as the Cartier Concert Hall, but it later became better known as the La Place des Arts, without an English translation of its name. The transition of the hall from a symbol of civic pride to a battleground of Quebec nationalism sums up much of the deterioration of community relations that poisoned McConnell's last years. He personally donated $250,000 ($1,827,922 in 2008) to the second subscription for the construction of the hall in 1960, and he was the largest individual supporter of the project, so that after McConnell's death Maurice Germain, the general manager, wrote to Lil: "No one has contributed more to the very existence of this corporation than Mr. McConnell and his name will forever be attached to La Place des Arts."[63] Apart from this cheque, McConnell probably had little personally to do with the actual construction, but he knew all the principals involved, and Peter Laing, his son-in-law, became treasurer of the Sir Georges-Etienne Cartier Center (using the French spelling of "George" and the American spelling of "Center"), as it was initially known.[64]

Also in 1956, McGill University received seven grants each of $5,000 and others of $64,700, $366,000 (in securities, for the Gardner-James Fund, bringing its endowment up to $1 million), and $1,500,035 and $300,000 (for the building fund). The McGill Winter Auditorium received $200,000; Université Laval, $20,000; Stanstead College, $100,000; Lower Canada College, $670; and both the Christian Leadership Training School and the University of Western Ontario, $10,000 each. Various hospitals received grants, and a further cobalt bomb, worth $56,180, went to the Jewish General Hospital.

As his eightieth birthday was approaching in 1957, McConnell endowed a separate foundation, named after his parents and described in chapter 1, for the needy of Muskoka with $500,000 ($3,856,164 in 2008). As president he appointed County Court Judge Douglas Thomas, whose wife, Arla, was the daughter of his teacher Bessie Killen. Universities apart from McGill received attention in this year. The University of New Brunswick received Consolidated Paper shares worth about $100,750, to be applied to the building of a men's dormitory. Bishop's University received $250,000, King's College in Halifax $10,000, and Carleton College in Ottawa $25,000.

Towards the end of his life, McConnell did not flag in his generosity. But nearly all the causes were ones that he had already supported, with a few exceptions. In 1958 he gave to McGill $2 million to assist students in science and engineering and $2.5 million to cover the cost of constructing a new engineering building, which was later named after him, the total being $33,556,291 in 2008 terms. Attached to the engineering building named after Sir William Macdonald, his greatest predecessor as a benefactor to McGill, this McConnell Engineering Building was a major contribution to maintaining the university's high reputation. McConnell did not attend its opening

The opening of the McConnell Engineering Building. From left: Dean Donald
Mordell, Chancellor R.E. Powell, His Excellency Major-General Georges
Vanier (visitor of McGill), Madame Vanier, Principal F. Cyril James, Lil, Air
Vice Marshal Adélard Raymond, and John G. McConnell, November 1959.
Montreal *Star* photograph, Montreal *Gazette* Archives.

by the governor general, Georges Vanier, but he must have recalled that almost fifty
years before, in 1914, he himself had laid the foundation of the Wesleyan Theological
College, which his new building was now facing. Also in 1958, he gave $50,000 to
liquidate the $26,000 deficit of the Neurological Institute, the balance to be applied
to a fund for aid to students and members of staff "in need of help from time to time,
owing to sickness or otherwise." With an eye to the expansion of attendance at sporting events, he gave $200,000 for 4,600 new seats for Molson Stadium, which he hoped
would bring "substantially more revenue to McGill."[65]

   In 1959 the trend to helping French-language institutions became more evident,
with Foundation grants of $50,000 each to the universities of Montreal and Sher-
brooke and the Collège de Joliette, $100,000 to the Hôpital Saint-Valier in Chicou-
timi, $75,000 to the Association Athlétique Nationale de la Jeunesse, $50,000 to the
Jean-Talon Hospital, and $10,000 to Université Laval. So great were the demands
upon the Foundation that, in its financial year ending in April 1959, it had spent

over $955,000 in excess of its income of about $3.5 million. Nevertheless, McConnell pledged in June $1 million for an old peoples' home to be run by the United Church of Canada, and $1.3 million for a new men's residence at McGill.

In 1960, although he had been retired as a university governor for two years, McConnell's gifts to McGill continued to flow. There was the McConnell Engineering Building to support, and then $600,000 to buy the Protestant School Board building and Presbyterian College, both on McTavish Avenue, for the university. Principal James was happy to report that the provincial government seemed likely to contribute to the cost of the latter project.[66] He confessed to McConnell: "I still miss you at the meetings of the Board of Governors, but your spirit is always close and tangible in every part of the University."[67]

In McConnell's lifetime, he was effectively one and the same as his Foundation. His sons John and Wilson – and on rare occasions Lil until 1959 – attended meetings of the trustees with him,[68] but it was McConnell himself who had accumulated the endowment and who increased and disbursed its income. Seen as a whole, the Foundation's many gifts appear to encapsulate much of McConnell's personality. He enormously enjoyed giving money to good causes and a new major project almost every year. Moreover, his efforts to give anonymously make it clear that his giving was not an expression of sheer vanity. Like many rich men, he tried hard to avoid appearing like what the historian Robert Rumilly called him, a *mécène*, a Maecenas or rich patron. This is one reason at least why he did not attend the openings of the McConnell Wing of the Neurological Institute and the McConnell Engineering Building. Had he had his own way, there would have been no building or scholarship or other gift named after him.

Ever aware of the transience of life, he saw his fortune as to be both held and used largely for others. It must not lie idle, as the YMCA had taught him, but rather had to be usefully employed, just as he had to remain usefully employed to the end. The role that McConnell truly enjoyed was that of a trustee – for his family as well as for the public.

A trustee is typically distinct from the creator of the trust, the donor of the endowment. McConnell's double role made him unique. His view that his Foundation should answer emergency calls made its role also unique, at least inasmuch as these calls were made on him personally. As Peter Laing wrote in a memorandum in 1978, the Foundation "was used by him solely as a channel for his numerous benefactions; no decisions were made by the Board of Directors; the grants went where Mr. McConnell said they were to go." On McConnell's death in 1963, Laing said, "everyone was pretty much at a loss to know what should be done":

Rightly or wrongly, the Foundation was then viewed as part of Mr. J.W. McConnell's patrimony. His sons who took over the direct of the Foundation

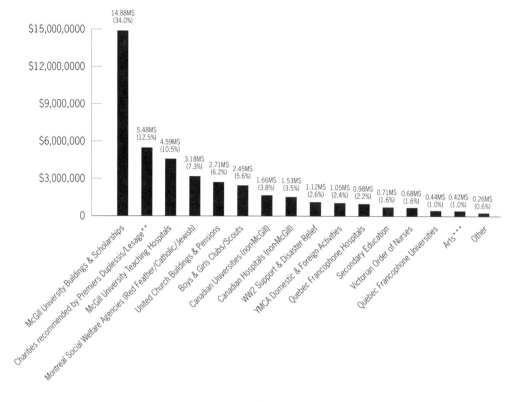

J.W. McConnell Foundation
Summary of Charitable Donations, 1937–1963, Total: $43.7 million*

* $328.1 million adjusted annually and cumulatively for 2002 dollars
** For Quebec-based religious, educational, health and charitable organizations
*** For Montreal's Place des Arts, and the Montreal Museum of Fine Arts

had not received any instructions from Mr. McConnell as to how the Foundation was to be run and nothing useful could be gathered from reading the charter as to what its real purposes were.

It was, therefore, decided that we should try and carry on supporting those charitable endeavours which Mr. McConnell had or would have, in the Board's opinion, supported. This, of course, involved a certain amount of clairvoyance but there were certain obvious recipients of the Foundation's bounty which we could still continue to benefit: McGill, the hospitals, boys' clubs, old people's homes, Y.M.C.A. and Red Feather [now Centraide] were obvious prime beneficiaries but the fact remains that no coherent policy of donations was worked out. Wilson and John McConnell were obviously perplexed and did not appear to be inclined to develop any new policies and as the Foundation was viewed as patrimonial property, it would, I think, be fair to say that while they did not feel inclined to initiate any policies themselves, they rather resented any outsider seeking to do so ... The obvious solution, I suggest, is that the Board should entrust the task of a comprehensive review of the Foundation to a committee which will undertake the necessary studies with the help of paid professionals, if necessary, and bring in its recommendations for the Board's approval or disapproval.[69]

As a result of Laing's recommendation, the Foundation set upon a very different course from McConnell's. But its endowment remained essentially his creation. The McConnell Foundation had never been as glamorous or as innovative as, say, the Ford and the Rockefeller foundations. But it was never so controversial or troubled either, and through it his descendants were, most unusually, to remain personally involved in practising the philanthropy that is his most enduring legacy.

CHAPTER NINETEEN

Keep Right on to the End of the Road, 1945–63

What a pity the warmth of kindly feeling displayed at this Season could not endure through-out the whole year – and year by year. If we are unhappy and discontented with things as they are; the fault lies not in our friends or our neighbours, but in ourselves – for we get out of this good old world only what we put into it; nothing more and nothing less.

J.W. McConnell to Mr and Mrs Francis Wasserboehr, 17 December 1946[1]

I'd like to say we've got no lesson on that score to take from the McConnells – from anyone that has been dominating Quebec like a bunch of Rhodesians – the white group! If we had coloureds here you'd feel it, and that is something we will not stand for any more, this pater-nalistic WASP – and it is that typically – the WASP arrogance of the ones who have been lead-ing our government, and, through the slush funds they contribute to, leading both of our hack parties by the nose for too long.

René Lévesque in *The Champions*, a film directed by Donald Brittain and produced by the National Film Board of Canada, 1978 and 1986

The end of the Second World War almost coincided with the weddings of the McConnells' two youngest children. Four days after V-E Day, Kit married Peter Marshall Laing, a lawyer educated at Oxford and from a family long in business in Montreal and later in London. The wedding took place at the Erskine and American United Church, where the Laings had also been prominent. Since Wilson had been married at the house of his bride and John outside Canada, this was the first time that the McConnells had an opportunity to hold a church wedding in Montreal. The cook, Mrs Rendall, who had trained as a pastry chef but had seldom had a chance to display pastry skills, at last found her opportunity to produce a wedding cake of many tiers. Among the guests were Ray Atherton, the American ambassador; Malcolm MacDonald, the British high commissioner; Baron Silvercruys, the Belgian ambas-sador in Washington; and Herbert and Angela Bruce (the former lieutenant governor of Ontario and his wife) of Toronto.[2]

The wedding of Kit and Peter Laing, May 1945.
McCord Museum, M2003.8.6.8.58.

In the following October, David, the youngest McConnell son, married Cynthia Gordon at the Anglican Church of St James the Apostle. Cynthia's father, Dr Keith Gordon, had been the medical officer of Sun Life Assurance, and one of her sisters married the money manager Hartland Molson MacDougall, a relative of the Hartland St Clair MacDougall who had built Ashburton.

By 1945, McConnell was sixty-eight years of age, tired and increasingly beset with illness. In 1951 he suffered a bout of pneumonia that laid him up for months. In the years following, he frequently suffered from bronchial problems and influenza. Rheumatism developed and eventually chronic lymphocytic leukaemia. Generally, however, until 1957, when he turned eighty, he was fairly mobile and only most reluctantly did he give up swimming, canoeing, golf, and tennis. There were golf trips with Lil to Georgia and winter escapes to Florida, Arizona, the Bahamas,[3] and elsewhere, and, contrary to the old Methodist prohibition, he took up bridge.

The last eighteen years of McConnell's life, indeed, were as full as he could make them. His address books and Lil's for this period are filled with new acquaintances, in Canada, the United States, Britain, and the Commonwealth. In England alone, these ranged from Field Marshal Lord Montgomery of Alamein and Air Chief Marshal Sir Arthur Harris to Clement Attlee, the Labour prime minister, as well as Barbara Ward, the environmentalist, and her husband, Sir Robert Jackson, of the Gold Coast Development Commission. After the war, he kept up with old friends serving in the evolving Commonwealth, such as Malcolm MacDonald, governor general of both Malaya and Singapore and later Kenya, and Sir Firozhkhan Noon, whom he called "Sir Ferocious," prime minister of Pakistan. His son-in-law introduced him to the future Sir David Steel, one of the leaders of British industry until almost the end of the twentieth century.

Although his great hope for the American presidency, Wendell Willkie, had died in 1944, some of his other and younger American friends were still developing their careers and shaping what they saw as the "American Century." Lewis Douglas, for example, after leaving McGill, served as American ambassador to London in 1948–50 and was closely involved in the formulation of the Marshall Plan, the establishment of NATO, and the reconstruction of West Germany. Douglas's brother-in-law, John J. McCloy, was another friend. After serving as US under-secretary of state for war under Harold L. Stimson from 1940 to 1945, McCloy became president of the World Bank (1946–47); high commissioner to Germany (1948–51); chairman of the Chase Bank and later the Chase-Manhattan Bank (1954–60); chairman of the Ford Foundation (1958–66); and adviser to every US president from Harry Truman to Ronald Reagan.[4] McConnell's friends were as much men of substance as ever, and through them he remained well informed about contemporary affairs. There were also grandchildren and great-grandchildren to fill his spare moments, and hundreds of new individuals and causes to help. His curiosity never diminished, and he was as interested in rubber in Malaya as in a new subway for Montreal.

When they were able, he and Lil returned to England, to visit old friends whom in most cases they had known for decades. In 1949, for example, they spent from 2 September to 18 October there, renewing their links with the Amerys, the Edens, the Barings, the Bessboroughs, the Ashley Coopers, the Iliffes, and many others. On 26 September, they lunched with Prime Minister Attlee and dined with Lord Beaverbrook. They met Lord Ivor Churchill and Sir Oswald Birley, the portrait painter, and there were special receptions for Jack at Canada House and at the Bank of England.

The restoration of continuity was very comforting. They closely followed the marriages and the children of old friends. Many in England had Montreal connections, such as Sir Sacheverell Sitwell, the writer, who was married to a daughter of Arthur Doble, Aitken's colleague in the Canada Cement merger and McConnell's in the Wings for Britain. They saw more of Sonia Cubitt, a daughter of Mrs George Keppel, mistress of King Edward VII, who she hinted was her real father. Well into the 1950s they continued to mix with such Edwardian stalwarts as Sir Harold and Lady Zia Wernher and Maggie Grenville.

With time, however, Lil also became somewhat disabled and subject to illness, and so travelling, never a great pleasure for him, became more difficult for both of them. Yet, although some, such as Sir Patrick Ashley Cooper, noticed that McConnell was becoming more garrulous, he never became senile. As noted earlier, he did not quit the McGill board until 1958, thirty years after joining it, and even then he was made the first honorary governor in the history of the university. A few weeks before he died, he presided over his last meeting of the board of the McConnell Foundation. He was an active trader in the stock market and on the watch for bargains almost to the end. Heward Stikeman, then a young lawyer, recalled unsuccessful post-war trips with McConnell to Ottawa to find cheap war-surplus materiel, and to Winnipeg to corner the market in folding chairs.[5] Derek Price, since 1954 one of his grandsons-in-law, was asked by him to place orders on the New York Stock Exchange on one Saint Jean-Baptiste Day, when the Montreal exchange was closed. Every morning until he was bedridden, he would groom himself fastidiously, combing his hair first one way and then the other, as though about to go out to make a sale. With his faithful Walter caring for his clothes, he was always immaculately attired.

All the while, the world in which McConnell had prospered was rapidly changing, in many ways disintegrating. For him and many other observers, new and disquieting economic and strategic realities were emerging in the Cold War between communist and capitalist states. This began in 1945 and was not to end until 1989. For Canadians particularly, it involved also the rise of American hegemony and the progressive erosion of the economic, military, and cultural order embodied in the British Empire. Probably nobody in McConnell's lifetime could have imagined how many profitable links, stretching back to the Hudson's Bay Company in the seventeenth century through the CPR in the nineteenth, would be severed in less than a decade after his death. Intimate ties between the British and Canadian economies had been intertwined with his own associations with the Hudson's Bay Company, Standard Chemical, Sherwin-Williams, International Nickel, Ogilvie Flour Mills, St Lawrence Sugar, and even the Montreal *Star*. And it was the same ties that underpinned his close surviving post-war friendships with such men as Lord McGowan of ICI, Sir Edward Peacock of Barings and the Bank of England, and Sir Anthony Eden, the British prime minister in succession to Churchill. McConnell's view of the empire was rooted only slightly in pure sentiment, and not at all in nostalgia, but profoundly in the trade, the friendships, and the strategic strengths and weaknesses of a global economic bloc.

McConnell probably understood, although he did not share, the desire for the decolonization of Canada promoted by King and St Laurent. But there is no indica-

The inauguration of McConnell's electrified carillon at St George's,
Dominion Square, 3 December 1958. Montreal *Gazette* Archives.

tion that he ever saw them as treacherous in selling Canada off to the United States, or indeed that he was particularly relieved to find Diefenbaker fighting to revive Anglo-Canadian links. Equipped as he was with a sharp understanding of questions of currency, he grasped the wider context.[6] Still, as the empire continued to unravel, he could only mourn. Widely perceived and described as the leading citizen of Montreal, if not of Canada, he continued to meet, almost ex officio, distinguished British visitors at luncheons at the Mount Royal Club, as young as the future Prime Minister Harold Wilson. But his perspective remained rooted in the past. He realized that the empire that he cherished was probably doomed, particularly with the Suez debacle, but, for him, the only alternative seemed to be communism. He took increasing comfort in the familiar.

Among the familiar things that made up his material world, few were as precious to McConnell as church bells and carillons, though now mechanized. He paid for the installation or the renovation of them at St George's Church in Dominion Square, St James Church on St Catherine Street (in honour of the coronation of Elizabeth II), and elsewhere, such as his Point St Charles Boys' Club. He also paid for the reconstruction of the steeple of Christ Church Cathedral in Montreal in aluminium, after its predecessor had collapsed through overweight.[7]

Overseas, among McConnell's many post-war contributions was £5,000 for eighteen bells for the Church of All Hallows Barking-by-the-Tower in London in 1949.

Sir Ion and Lady Hamilton Benn, the McConnells,
and the Reverend P.B. Clayton at All Hallows' Church,
Barking, n.d. Private collection.

His friend from before 1914, the broker Sir Ion Hamilton Benn, was churchwarden there. The vicar of All Hallows, Philip Byard Clayton, also arranged in 1949 for McConnell to contribute $5,000 to send a group of ten young Canadians to the devastated East End of London to help with the rebuilding there.[8] Hard information on McConnell's other contributions to reconstruction in Europe is fragmentary, but he also made donations to the rebuilding of Westminster Abbey and of the cathedrals in Coventry and Malta.

By the end of the Second World War, few of the comforts of McConnell's pre-1914 world were standing or, if standing, seemed sound. The one exception was the royal family. In the eyes of most of the public, it had transformed itself after the abdication of King Edward VIII into the very embodiment of a happy family life, of simple decency and of hope in the future, and later, in the war, it had acquired an exemplary reputation for courage and leadership. In McConnell's case, the pomp attendant upon royalty on state occasions meant almost nothing to him. Even the grandeur of England and of its empire was more part of his subconscious assumptions than an object of fascination. But, once he concluded that they were under threat, he came to cherish them. In his last years, he grew closer and closer to royal circles, not out of pretentiousness, but because they symbolized order, again the reassuringly familiar.

All his life, McConnell loved England and was very fond of English people. Imbued with the novels of Dickens and Scott, he felt that "British" culture was his own, as did most Canadians of his generation and for long afterwards. Beyond the British Isles, in his eyes, the empire was an international extension of Canada, as well as of Britain. This was more than a conventional piety. Sherwin-Williams of Canada and Sun Life of Canada were known all over the empire, as were Massey-Harris and International Nickel. The cultural and even moral ideals of Britain, such as fair play, democracy, and the rule of law, remained not merely alive for him but fundamental to his view of the world, which he broadcast through the *Star*. Because for him to be Canadian was to be British, it is wrong to see his loyalty as anglophilia. Much as he admired England, he never felt the need to adopt particularly English clothes or mannerisms or speech in order to feel himself at home there. He saw himself not merely as British but as Scots-Irish, and, more specifically, an Ulsterman.

Neither was he a social climber. He understood a good deal about English society, and he mixed with the grandest of the kingdom, but he saw people as individuals and had little inclination or talent for performing class roles. The day of a Sir Henry Pellatt, with his preoccupation with soldiers and castles and titles and honours, had largely though not completely passed with the end of the Great War. Such an alleged Canadian nationalist as Mackenzie King was far more obsessed with royalty and rank than McConnell ever was. In 1945, when asked whether his son John would, for his work with the Queen's Canadian Fund during the war, accept the honour of Companion of the Order of the British Empire (CBE), he snorted "Certainly not!" – although John did in fact accept the honour with pleasure.

McConnell was also modest without being humble, having gone much farther than he could ever have dreamt. By at least 1910, when he was thirty-three, he already had little to prove, and he genuinely felt that his philanthropy was no more than the duty of any decent citizen. Yet, although egalitarian in manner, he always accorded full and informed respect to rank, and he seems to have had not the slightest reservation about imperial titles and honours for Canadians other than himself. There is the unconfirmable legend that he declined the Order of Merit, which is confined at any time to twenty-four members. It is almost certain that he was happy to see Mackenzie King and Wilder Penfield join it. He was no less happy to see Lord Alexander, Albert Schweitzer, Malcolm MacDonald, and various other acquaintances do likewise. He almost undoubtedly worked to have honorary McGill degrees conferred on such people as Princess Marina (wife of Prince George, Duke of Kent, the fourth son of

Anthony Eden (with Dr F. Cyril James and McConnell) arrives at Dorval
Airport for the special convocation at McGill University at which he will receive
the honorary doctor of laws, November 1950. Private collection.

George V and Queen Mary), Sir Anthony Eden, and Lord Montgomery, while again
firmly declining them for himself. The frustration of his close friends Herbert Bruce
and William Massey Birks over not receiving knighthoods was wholly alien to him.

Particularly in the post-war period, the basis of McConnell's view of the English,
including the royal family and the aristocracy as well as the bombed-out poor of the
East End, was compassion. By 1945, Britain was utterly exhausted and bankrupt, its
people having been on rations for years and still subject to exchange controls. And,
if anyone could see need in any station of life, it was McConnell. From his point of
view, people such as Queen Mary, Princess Marina, Sir Anthony Eden, and Lady
Churchill were neighbours. They may not have considered themselves as such, but,
sometimes reluctantly and eventually always gratefully, they accepted his solicitude
and even material support. Since the 1920s, when they came to know the Willingdons, he and Lil had been cheerfully dispensing hospitality and assistance, without
expecting anything in return, particularly to their English friends.

Princess Alice, having relied on McConnell's aid to the Victorian Order of Nurses,
later sought his assistance for a new chapel at the University College of the West
Indies, in Jamaica, of which she was chancellor. McConnell gave it £40,000 in 1955,

Lil with the Vincent Massey, probably at an exhibition of Dutch pictures
at the Montreal Museum of Fine Arts, 1944. Private collection.

and Lil and their son John attended its dedication in 1960, promising more for a chapel portico. A year later, following McConnell's advice to put the contract out to tender, Princess Alice was delighted to see the estimate reduced. She wrote to tell him that, "as usual, your master mind has carried the day."[9]

The restoration of peace made it possible for McConnell to renew his acquaintance with Viscount Alexander, whom he had first met in New Delhi in 1936 and who had subsequently become a field marshal, noted especially for his role in commanding the final rearguard action at Dunkirk in 1940, for his victory at the Battle of Tunis in May 1943, and for leading the invasion of Italy that same year. Alexander became governor general of Canada in 1946, in succession to Athlone. At the Quebec Conference of 1944, there were rumours that Prime Minister Mackenzie King was hoping to appoint McConnell as the eventual successor to Athlone, but McConnell would never have accepted.

Peace also brought home McConnell's old friend Vincent Massey, who had been the Canadian high commissioner in London during the war and who was to succeed Alexander as governor general. Finally, peace brought a new friend to McConnell in the person of another of the great commanders of the war, Viscount Montgomery of Alamein, who visited Canada several times in his capacity as chief of the Imperial General Staff. Montgomery and Alexander were very different men – Montgomery

Field Marshal Viscount Montgomery of Alamein, with McConnell and R.E. Powell (chancellor of McGill), probably 28 August 1946, on the occasion of the award of the degree of doctor of laws to him at McGill University. Private collection.

being "prickly, antisocial, graceless," capable of "appalling brutality" towards close associates,[10] while Alexander was courteous, modest, and urbane – and the fact that both warmed to McConnell suggests the latter's ability to get along with military officers, and even to forge close bonds with them – an ability seen earlier in his warm friendships with Sir Arthur Currie and Air Marshal Billy Bishop. He even managed to induce Montgomery to do little favours for him, such as presenting $100,000 to the Westminster Abbey Restoration Fund on his behalf as an anonymous donor.

With Alexander, there was naturally much more time to spend, at all three of McConnell's houses as well as at Government House. The two men were famously at ease with each other, which Alexander's elder son attributes to the fact that both had long enjoyed careers of notable success and that, in consequence, neither had anything to prove to, or to ask of, the other.[11] McConnell himself would say to another Ulsterman, his friend John Bassett of the *Gazette*, that their sort of Anglo-Irishman combined Irish intelligence and humour with Scots logic and industry.

The Alexanders, with two young sons and an appetite for winter sports, captured some of the post-war informality and energy of Canada. Alexander painted Canadian landscapes, and even did some pictures together with Lil. Official duties also joined the two families, with McConnell himself in almost constant attendance, especially

The Alexanders with Lil (to the right) at St Mary's Ball, Mount Royal Hotel,
November 1951. Private collection.

at charity balls. In November 1950, for example, Alexander arrived in Montreal in his capacities of visitor of McGill, commander-in-chief of Canada, and a much-admired field marshal. He first opened the regimental museum of the Canadian Grenadier Guards, closely connected to the university and of which he was honorary colonel. On the following day, 1,200 watched him open the bronze doors of the Memorial Hall of the Sir Arthur Currie Gymnasium-Armoury, its stone from Monte Cassino and its marble from Normandy, where so many Canadian soldiers had recently fallen. A few minutes from it, east along Pine Avenue, at the armoury of the Fusiliers Mont-Royal, built by Sir Rodolphe Forget, he unveiled another memorial. Two days later, the Alexanders joined the McConnells for the opening of the new East End Boys' Club, which McConnell had built.

In February 1951 Alexander accepted an invitation from R.E. Powell, the senior vice-president of Alcan and chancellor of McGill, to spend two days visiting the aluminium works in the Saguenay region. McConnell joined him for a dinner given by Lieutenant Governor Gaspard Fauteux for Premier Duplessis at Bois de Coulonges, the former Spencer Wood or Government House in Quebec City, recently given its French name by Duplessis. There the governor general invested the premier with the Order of St John of Jerusalem. Then, in temperatures that hovered near 26 below zero Fahrenheit and in the midst of a terrible blizzard, McConnell accompanied Alex-

Dinner at Bois de Coulonge, Quebec, 7 February 1951, tendered by Dr Gaspard
Fauteux, lieutenant governor of Quebec, to His Excellency Viscount Alexander,
governor general of Canada. Front row from left: McConnell, Fauteux, Alexander,
Premier Maurice Duplessis, R.E. Powell. Second row, from left: Maurice Samson,
Mayor Lucien Borne, Paul Beaulieu, Onésime Gagnon, Antoine Rivard, Lt.-Col. D.B.
Papineau, and Major A.C. Price. Back row, from left: Major J.P. Martin and Major
Mark Milbank (comptroller of the household). Private collection.

ander on an inspection of the Alcan installations, probably the last of his energetic
tours of new industrial plants extending back over half a century.

Alexander's posting in Ottawa came to an end rather abruptly early in 1952, when
Prime Minister Churchill, on a visit to Ottawa, invited him to become minister of
war. Alexander accepted, and, barely a week after the death of King George VI on 6
February, he and Lady Alexander left for England. Rose, Alexander's daughter, who
was just entering McGill, stayed on in Canada, and when her brothers Shane and
Brian also entered McGill, McConnell set up scholarships to finance their education.
Alexander's subsequent acceptance of a directorship of the Aluminium Company of
Canada enabled him to keep up his links with Canada. When Rose married Captain
Humphrey Crossman in 1956, a delighted McConnell wired her funds to buy any car
she wanted. The Alexanders returned to Canada in 1957 and 1958, when Lord Alexander had a heart attack in Ottawa. He recovered and was able to visit Montreal, for
the last time, for Expo '67.

In 1952, when Alexander had returned to England, there was much discussion about appointing a Canadian as his successor. Lord Hardinge, a friend of the McConnell's since his time as an aide-de-camp to Lord Willingdon, had hopes, since he had long been a resident of Canada and was married to a granddaughter of Sir Sandford Fleming. *Le Soleil*, the newspaper in Quebec City, proposed McConnell himself. McConnell's *Star* called for the appointment of another Briton. Prime Minister Louis St Laurent decided to appoint Vincent Massey.

McConnell was dropping out of public life. He was not even present when Massey opened the McConnell Wing of the Neurological Institute. But both were very close to the British prime minister from 1953 to 1957, Sir Anthony Eden, and Massey would come to know even McConnell's grandchildren, Murdoch and David Laing, when they were at Trinity College School, near Massey's house outside Port Hope. In cultural and even philanthropic interests, in manner and in self-image, McConnell and Massey superficially had little in common. More fundamentally, however, they had everything in common. McConnell had even replaced Massey's father at the opening of the Wesleyan Theological College, and both continued to share a supremely Methodist and unwavering sense of public duty as well as a profound loyalty to the crown.

Although on occasion sentimental, McConnell was not nostalgic. But his fondness for the royal family never dimmed. For him, the royal family and the empire were comforting constants through world war, depression, and social revolution. Hence his response to a particular appeal made after the war by Queen Mary, the widow of George V. In November 1949 Queen Mary decided to make a needlework carpet out of pieces of wool tapestry and to sell it to raise foreign exchange for the British treasury. After considering various bids, in June 1950 a committee decided to accept an offer from the Canadian branch of the Imperial Order Daughters of the Empire (IODE), of which Lil was a member. According to this offer, $100,000 would be paid for the carpet, and the IODE would sponsor a national fund for Canadians to contribute. The carpet would tour the country and any proceeds above the original $100,000 would be added to the purchase price. Ultimately, the IODE would present the carpet to the National Gallery of Canada for permanent exhibition.

McConnell, however, was worried that the campaign might not reach its target. Desperately ill with pneumonia, he wrote to his son John a letter to be opened only in the event of his death, to the effect that the McConnell Foundation must cover any shortfall from the $100,000. On 24 June he also wrote to Mrs John G. Chipman, the national president of the IODE, that he would cover any shortfall. In July the campaign concluded, with McConnell secretly making up the deficit. Queen Mary wrote to thank him for his "great help," expressing the hope that the carpet might by degrees "be the means of bringing in more dollars for our impoverished country."[12] McConnell replied that her letter had given him "a wonderful thrill" and that the carpet had "stirred the hearts of countless thousands" and "created a feeling of goodwill and admiration beyond expression." He concluded:

Your Majesty's example, unparelled [sic] through all the trials & tribulations of the last half century, is something that the whole civilized world may look upon with admiration & *reverence*.

The gift of Your Majesty's carpet, representing an immense piece of personal work, stands out as a shining example of unselfish devotion in a dark and troubled world.

May Gods [sic] richest blessing rest upon His devoted Servant for many happy years to come.[13]

Queen Mary later invited Jack and Lil to tea at her London home, Marlborough House. One story says that, as the visit dragged on, the queen rose to remind the McConnells that they must have many other things to do. She certainly saw them to the door, which was a high honour rather than an insult, particularly in view of her growing infirmity. On her visit to Ottawa in the autumn of 1951, Princess Elizabeth, a granddaughter of Queen Mary, unveiled the carpet in the Parliament Buildings, to mark its presentation to the National Gallery.

This 1951 visit by Princess Elizabeth and her husband, Prince Philip, the Duke of Edinburgh, was one of the proudest moments of McConnell's life, particularly since, in the course of their tour of the country, which covered all of Canada from Quebec to Vancouver Island, the royal couple stayed for a weekend at Saran Chai. The tour began at Dorval Airport in October, when Lord Alexander and Prime Minister St Laurent and about 25,000 others were waiting to welcome the princess and the duke. The couple then went on to Quebec City before returning to Montreal, where McConnell, despite being stricken with phlebitis a few days earlier, was among those to welcome them at the airport. With a rare Gallic flourish, the *Star* described Montreal as "En Fete" for the visitors, and indeed every building along the routes followed by them seemed festooned with Union flags and bunting. St James Street was almost unrecognizable under its layers of red, white, and blue decorations.

The Windsor Hotel, where they were staying, was similarly swathed in the imperial colours, as was the city hall. Twenty events occupied the visitors over two days in Montreal, beginning with a hockey game in the Forum on the evening of their arrival and continuing the next day with a royal salute outside the Windsor Hotel. After the salute, a Cadillac lent by McConnell, and bearing the princess and the duke, proceeded up Peel Street to St Catherine and then University before turning onto Sherbrooke and through the Roddick Gates. At a ceremony in the McGill Arts Building, Jack and Lil were among the few presented to the couple, who then moved on to receptions at Molson and Delormier stadiums, where they were greeted first by Protestant and then by Catholic schoolchildren, and at the Canadian Vickers shipyard. Afterwards, they were the guests of honour at a luncheon at the Chalet on Mount Royal (attended by Kit and Peter Laing), the Université de Montréal, and city hall. It all culminated with a gala dinner at the Windsor Hotel, also attended by about 1,350

The McConnells greet Princess Elizabeth and the Duke of Edinburgh at the Arts Building of McGill University, William Massey Birks to McConnell's left and F. Cyril James to his right, 1951. McCord Museum, M2003.8.6.4.51.

Princess Elizabeth, Jack, the Duke of Edinburgh, and Lil at Saran Chai, 2 November 1951. Private collection.

other guests, with the McConnells at the head table. The next day the royal party, after a brief visit to the Queen Mary Veterans' Hospital on Queen Mary Road, was off to Dorval Airport and Washington. Upon their return from Washington, the princess and the duke spent the weekend of 3 and 4 November at the McConnells' house at Saran Chai, amidst mountains that were – early for the time of year – deep in snow.

Princess Elizabeth and Prince Philip seem genuinely to have enjoyed their visit, for they used a picture of Saran Chai on their Christmas card for 1951, and the princess had seemed especially captivated by the snow, out of which they had made a snowman.[14] Only about eight weeks after their royal visit, Saran Chai burned to the ground with all its contents. The furnace had blown up and all was reduced to cinders within hours. The loss was a terrible blow to the family and their friends. People from the secretary to the new queen, who had succeeded to the throne on 6 February 1952, to the staff of the *Star* and close personal friends wrote letters of condolence. Walter Molson urged them to build again, and indeed McConnell drew up plans for an exact replica, but these were never executed. While Lil built a little cottage for herself in Saint-Sauveur, Jack never visited it, and not until their son John rebuilt near the site once occupied by Saran Chai did any of the McConnells return to a house in the Laurentians faintly comparable to it.

In October 1951 McConnell bought a regal portrait of the princess, as she still was, from Margaret Lindsay Williams, its painter, to present to McGill, where it was to hang in Redpath Hall. This was one of the best-known portraits of the queen after her accession, reproduced by the thousands for schools, post offices, and other institutions. So ubiquitous did it become that it was virtually *the* definitive portrait of the queen in Canada until the 1960s, when a portrait by Piero Annigoni began to replace it in official settings.

Now known to the new queen, the McConnells obtained an invitation to her coronation in Westminster Abbey in June 1953. Although they had been attending royal events for decades, this invitation was still an exceptional mark of favour. By now, McConnell was rather frail but not in failing health, and he and Lil left for England on 15 May for the occasion. He kept a little and incomplete diary of his stay in England, which extended to 7 July, and it captures well the uncomplicated, almost unreflective patriotism that marked him to the end. It also affords some insight into his wide circle of acquaintances in England, which had broadened steadily over the preceding half-century.

Jack and Lil, sailing on the *Empress of Scotland*, arrived in London on 22 May. Over the next seven weeks, they attended innumerable lunches and dinners – with, among others, the Alexanders, the Amerys, the Ashley Coopers, the Bessboroughs, Baron Silvercruys, Princess Alice and Lord Athlone, High Commissioner Norman Robertson, and Prime Minister St Laurent and his wife – two plays (*The Young Elizabeth* and *Dear Charles*), and one opera (Benjamin Brittain's *Gloriana*), they were formally pre-

McConnell with binoculars, Viscount Camrose (standing), the Countess
of Birkenhead and Col. John Astor aboard Camrose's yacht, coronation
review of the fleet, Spithead, 1953. McCord Museum, M2003.8.6.5015.

sented to the Queen Mother and Princess Margaret, and they had a private audience
with the new Queen Elizabeth II and Prince Philip. The highlight, of course, was 2
June, coronation day. Lil accepted an invitation to Westminster Abbey for the event,
but Jack, feeling the worse for wear, decided to watch it on television at their hotel.

Though day was cold and wet, McConnell recorded that the throngs of people on
the procession route, many of whom had started lining up twenty-four hours earlier,
were "very good looking and good natured" and "seemed out for fun rain or shine but
for one purpose – to see the Young Queen on her 'Great Day.'" Lil had to be at the
Abbey by 7 a.m., and she was sitting to the right of the royal box as the queen "floated
down the long aisle, her dress too beautiful, and her trainbearers moving in perfect
unison." On returning from the abbey, she joined Jack for dinner with Lady Moyra
Browne (the daughter of the Bessboroughs) and together they watched the coronation
fireworks on television in the evening. One special occasion was a voyage on Lord

Jack, the Countess of Airlie, Lil, and the Earl of Airlie, 26 April 1954.
McCord Museum, M2003.8.6.7.52.

Camrose's yacht to observe the coronation review of the fleet at Spithead. In April of the following year, Lord and Lady Airlie visited Pine Avenue, followed by their son Angus Ogilvy, who was to marry Princess Alexandra of Kent in 1963.

Princess Alexandra herself came to Montreal with her mother the Duchess of Kent (Princess Marina) in September 1954. McConnell had long admired the duchess. The McConnells had probably first met the Duke of Kent on his visit to Canada in 1942. His death in an air crash shortly afterwards left the duchess, now a young widow with three children, in straitened circumstances. She did not benefit from the Civil List that supported other members of the royal family, and the king – fearing disclosure that Queen Mary was receiving £70,000 a year tax-free – refused to let Parliament grant her an allowance. The duke had received an allowance of £25,000 a year, but, after his death and the payment of duties on his estate, the duchess was left with an annual income of £1,000 a year and she resorted to selling family possessions and wearing cast-off clothing.[15] Her plight attracted the sympathy of McConnell and others.

It was at least in part through McConnell's urging that the duchess came to Montreal in 1954, on her way to Toronto to open the Canadian National Exhibition. She and her daughter arrived at Central Station on the 8th, to be met by a band of the RCMP and a guard of honour, and, after resting at the Windsor, they were driven to

Princess Alexandra of Kent, B.C. Gardner (chancellor of McGill), the Duchess of Kent (Princess Marina), Dr F. Cyril James (principal), and McConnell, at McGill University, 14 September 1954.

Ashburton for luncheon with the McConnells. The fact that Princess Marina broke her tooth there probably endeared her even more to McConnell, and he arranged for her to be seen by his dentist before her reception at city hall. They seem to have joined her later at the Windsor Hotel for a private dinner and then at a concert at the Chalet on Mount Royal. The following day, Lil went to a Junior League luncheon for Princess Alexandra at the Ritz-Carlton, and Princess Marina visited the Montreal Neurological Institute, followed by a private dinner, again with the McConnells, at the Forest and Stream Club. After spending the weekend with Hartland Molson at his house in the Laurentians, the duchess and princess attended a dinner given by the city at the Windsor Hotel for six hundred guests, among them the McConnells. Then, on Tuesday the 14th, McConnell attended a special McGill convocation to award the duchess an honorary degree, following which he attended another luncheon in her honour.

After visiting Montreal, scarcely had Princesses Marina and Alexandra reached New York than McConnell wrote a letter offering the duchess some substantial present. Her private secretary consulted the keeper of the privy purse and then wrote that she could not accept his "most generous gift for her personal use." But she was willing to accept in trust a gift for charitable purposes, such as the RAF Benevolent Fund. McConnell was delighted with the suggestion, and he recommended "some sound equity shares" on the London Exchange to be bought in consultation with

Last visit of the Earl and Countess of Bessborough to the McConnells,
Dorval, September 1955. McCord Museum, M 2003.8.6.2.51.

Sir Edward Peacock, to serve as the capital for a trust fund. By 1956, the duchess
was using the proceeds from the trust to help the Lord Mayor's Fund for Hungarian
Refugees.

The Kents were to invite the McConnells to the weddings of both Princess Alexandra and of her brother Prince Edward (in 1961) to Katharine Worsley. They were
unable to attend, but Katherine Worsley's brother John married Carolyn, a daughter
of their friends Lord and Lady Hardinge in 1954. It was a poignant occasion, with
John G. McConnell's adopted son Royden serving as a page, just as David McConnell had served as a page to Carolyn's parents, at their wedding in 1928. But other old
friends were also passing. Camrose died only a few months after the coronation. In
1955 the Bessboroughs came to Dorval for a final visit, only a few months before the
death of the former governor general.

The fiftieth anniversary of the wedding of Jack and Lil, on 5 October 1955, was
one of the last great family occasions. It was also an occasion for congratulations from

Golden wedding anniversary luncheon at Kit's, 5 October 1955.
Jack and Lil seated; in back from left: John, Peggy, Wilson, Marjorie,
Kit, Peter (Laing), Cynthia, and David. Private collection.

all over the world, including a telegram from the Queen and Prince Philip. Editorials appeared in the Toronto *Telegram*, *La Patrie*, and *La Presse*. The governors of
McGill expressed their "abiding and admiring friendship," wishing the couple many
more anniversaries in health and happiness.[16] With all their four children married,
Jack and Lil could now with look back, with some satisfaction, on a most extraordinary saga begun in the Douglas Church in 1905. There was a family luncheon at Kit's
on Redpath Crescent and then a dinner at Pine Avenue, before which they surprised
everyone by descending the stairs dressed in costumes first worn at Percy Cowans's
ball in 1924.

With Christmas approaching, Jack and Lil were watching their favourite television
program, *Life Worth Living*, hosted by the Roman Catholic bishop Fulton J. Sheen,
which regularly attracted twenty-five million viewers. Lil proposed sending something to the bishop to help the needy, and Jack characteristically replied, "If you will
give $100.00, I will give $1,000.00."[17] On the following day, McConnell was present at
McGill for the conferring of an honorary degree on the Princess Royal, the daughter

The McConnells in 1955 wearing their costumes made for Percy
Cowans's ball in 1924. McCord Museum, M2003.8.6.8.97.

of King George V and Queen Mary. She had already presided over the opening of
the first Red Feather Campaign and attended a civil luncheon and then dinner at the
Mount Royal Club. Subsequently, after opening the new Montreal General Hospital
on Cedar Avenue, she attended receptions given by the Royal Canadian Corps of
Signals in Westmount and the Royal Canadian Regiment, followed by visits to the
Université de Montréal, Sainte-Justine's Hospital, the Botanical Gardens, and the
Comédie Française.

The Queen and the Duke of Edinburgh toured Canada again in 1957, and McConnell followed their progress with close attention. As he wrote to her, "never in history
has a Monarch been so justly acclaimed with such inexpressible admiration. Your
Majesty, with all modesty, intelligent interest, integrity, and gracious loveliness, won
all hearts." He praised her "earnest sincerity" and the "easy grace of delivery" of her
"classic" public addresses, and he thanked her for her gracious reference to her earlier stay at Saran Chai.[18]

The McConnells with the Wilder Penfields waiting to board the Royal
Yacht *Britannia*, docked at Montreal, for dinner with Queen Elizabeth
and the Duke of Edinburgh, 24 June 1959. Private collection.

The highlight of the next royal visit, in 1959, was the queen's opening of the St Lawrence Seaway with President Eisenhower. As recounted in chapter 9, the McConnells
met the queen and the duke at dinner aboard the Royal Yacht *Britannia*, docked at
Montreal, on 24 June, the day before the opening. It was a small affair, with everyone
else present in an official capacity and only the McConnells described as being "personal acquaintances" of the queen and the duke.

Lil kept up her social life through the fifties, retaining her zest at balls at the Museum of Fine Arts in particular. But for both her and Jack, the first three years of the
1960s were cruel. For some time crippled with arthritis, McConnell began walking with a cane and then was gradually reduced to sitting propped up with pillows.
Sometimes he would sit by himself on the terrace at Dorval or on the little porch
on Pine Avenue, bundled in blankets. Lil herself was often ill and in hospital, but all
the children came when they could. He told Kit that he had had a good life and was
ready to go.

The McConnells at Ashburton, c.1962. Private collection.

His last public appearance was an appropriate summing-up of much of his life. The occasion was the opening and dedication ceremony in 1961 of the Griffith-McConnell Home for Elderly People, to be run by the United Church of Canada.[19] The United Church was already operating sixteen such homes, housing nine hundred residents, from Vancouver to St John's. For elderly women, it operated the Dunedin Home in Montreal West, itself built by McConnell, and another home on Pine Avenue in Montreal. McConnell had wanted to build yet another for the elderly, both men and women, for some time, but it was only in 1959 that he was able to find the land and an architect, Francis J. Nobbs, the son of Percy Nobbs, formerly professor of architecture at McGill. As in the case of most of his later projects, McConnell took a personal interest in the smallest detail, specifying that double syringas must be planted on the property rather than single-bloom ones.

He wanted to keep his contribution, initially for $1 million, anonymous. His total contribution to the project amounted to $3,480,000 ($25,779,474 in 2008 terms), approved by him personally, in addition to a further $3.3 million given by his foundation from 1965 to 1988. Only two or three days before his death, he had given his final instalment of $1.7 million to the home, for what was to become known as the McConnell Memorial Wing. In doing so, he commented, "We'd better see some of these people to the end of the road."

On opening day, 15 May 1961, Jack and Lil, both leaning heavily on canes, came to Kildare Avenue in Côte Saint-Luc. They watched Premier Jean Lesage cut the ribbon and the Reverend J.R. Mutchmor, moderator of the United Church, unveil a memo-

Premier Jean Lesage opens the Griffith-McConnell Home,
Côte Saint-Luc, 1961. Private collection.

rial plaque.[20] One of the first residents was H.C. Patterson, who wrote to McConnell
about first hearing of McConnell's charitable gifts in 1909, when – at the age of twenty-
four and fresh from Collingwood, Ontario – Patterson became assistant director of
the Central YMCA. In time, the home would house many others unable to look after
themselves, including McConnell's own secretary, Mary Clarke, who died there.

Just as he was providing for the very old in his own old age, McConnell also made
a last provision for the very young, which some of his own children and grandchildren were to continue in years to come. Maeda Primavesi was an Austrian who came
one day to Kit's house on Redpath Crescent, selling Christmas cards. She told Kit
of her dream of setting up a refuge for abused children, and McConnell soon bought
her a house, a few doors to the east of his own on Pine Avenue, formerly occupied
by Murray Ballantyne, a son of Senator C.C. Ballantyne. He paid $90,000 for it and
it became known as the Children's Mountain Cottage. John G. McConnell, among
others, raised money for the not-for-profit corporation that was to run it, and it was
later to expand to a farm in West Brome.

In May 1962 the Duke of Edinburgh opened a complex of men's residences for
McGill, just north of the Neurological Institute on University Street. This complex
included Molson Hall, given by Hartland and Tom Molson; Gardner Hall, named
after the chancellor from 1952 to 1957, Bertie Gardner; and McConnell Hall, given

by McConnell. Bishop Mountain Hall, named after the first Church of England bishop of Quebec and principal of McGill, was to serve the others as the common dining hall. The duke was in Montreal to preside over the Second Commonwealth Studies conference, whose three hundred delegates were to be the first lodgers in the complex.

Most of McConnell's closest friends were to die before him. Ross McMaster of Stelco, an uncle of Peter Laing, whose career had paralleled McConnell's from 1910 onward, died in January 1962. They had sat on various boards together, but it was a common view of the world that they shared. Throughout his business career – in addition to Stelco, he had been a director of the Bank of Montreal, the CPR, Sun Life, Ogilvie Flour, and the Royal Victoria Hospital – McMaster waged war on waste and inefficiency, thereby appealing to Jack's sterner side.[21] Victor Drury, president of E.B. Eddy, Canadian Car and Foundry, and Canadian Hydro-Electric, and a director of Sherwin-Williams, who died in July 1962, was close to McConnell for much the same reasons. Cleveland Morgan, who died in October 1962, was a different sort of friend. He had been, to be sure, a businessman, as a director of Henry Morgan and Company, Morgan Realities, and the Morgan Trust Company, but since 1916 he had been the chief inspiration of the Art Association of Montreal, later the Montreal Museum of Fine Arts, to which he gave six hundred items from his own collection. He had been president of the museum from 1947 to 1956 and then honorary president. He and his wife were fixtures in the social life of the McConnells.

But, of all of McConnell's close friends, perhaps none was more distinguished than Sir Edward Peacock, vice-president of Brazilian Traction, director of Barings and the Bank of England, and financial adviser to kings George V and Edward VIII. After the war, in 1952, he was involved in the setting up of Harris and Partners, a joint venture in Toronto between Barings and Morgan Grenfell. In the same year, he devised the Commonwealth Development Finance Company, of which he was a director until 1959. This was a vehicle to provide aid to developing countries in the Commonwealth. Peacock died in November 1962, fifty or possibly even sixty years after he and McConnell had first met. He had been extremely close to both Jack and Lil, writing in 1950: "I love and admire both of the McConnells. If a world of good wishes from thousands of people have [sic] any influence their happiness is secure."[22]

No loss was crueller, however, than that of McConnell's own son David. On St Patrick's Day, in 1963, David McConnell, who had been working for St Lawrence Sugar, learning about investing from his father, and had been elected to the board of the Bank of Montreal, shot himself at his house in Dorval, which was beside Ashburton. McConnell's reaction was one of deep grief mingled with resignation, as he kept repeating, "The Lord giveth, and the Lord taketh away."

The two other McConnell sons, Wilson and John, also died prematurely. Wilson died of problems relating to medication on 12 January 1966, three years after his father. He had been largely a recluse from his friends since the end of the war in 1945, although he lived at home with his family. John, who had done such fine work at the *Standard* and the *Star*, also suffered a tragic fate. In 1961, after several difficult years of marriage, he obtained a divorce in Mexico from his wife, Peggy, and married his secretary at the *Standard* since 1959, Elspeth Bagg, in Nevada. Their marriage was not recognized in Canada, however, since their divorce in Mexico was not valid under Canadian law. John was therefore a bigamist. He and Elspeth went to inform McConnell of the problem, and the old man, by now very mellow in the face of the vagaries of life, joked: "Bigamy? She doesn't look big to me!"

It was necessary to obtain a divorce through a resolution of the Senate of Canada, and this went through in 1964. In 1970 John and Elspeth married again in the Erskine and American United Church. But the next years were painful. Long afflicted with a bipolar disorder – which had forced him to give up his jobs as publisher and president of the *Star* – John took his own life on 12 July 1974, at his home in Val David. He had been highly respected for his work and was also a major patron of the arts, both as a supporter of the Montreal Museum of Fine Arts and as a collector.

The early deaths of the three sons have raised questions about McConnell's role as their father. It is not, of course, possible to be definite about a matter that is by its nature very private. But there is evidence that deserves consideration. Hundreds of family letters suggest that both Jack and Lil were probably overly protective of all their children, whom they loved very much and encouraged and nurtured in every way. They were indeed also very indulgent, particularly Lil. David showed an interest in flying and so was given his own seaplane. Wilson was very interested in mechanics and was given the means to assemble a collection of rare vintage cars. John was interested in journalism, and it was probably for him that his father bought the *Star* and the *Standard*. In the end, wealth and privilege proved stifling to the next generation, all of whom were unusually sensitive by nature and uninterested in maintaining the way of life of their parents. Nevertheless, the sons showed considerable devotion to their parents. John, in particular, had a high respect for his father's wisdom and business acumen, and consulted him constantly, and Wilson was especially devoted to his mother. All three sons, unfortunately, suffered from alcoholism, which had always been Jack's greatest horror. Alcoholism had probably destroyed his own father, or at least limited him, and now it had returned.

The father and his sons were clearly very different people. Even John, for all his talent as a publisher, was not a gifted businessman. It would have been extraordinary if even one of them had inherited their father's genius. It would have been equally remarkable if they had not felt inhibited by their father's success. The lives of sons of self-made men generally are rarely easy. The sons of McConnell's friends Sir Herbert Holt and Milton Hersey were similarly troubled. For someone such as McConnell, who had devoted much of his life to providing for his family in order to save his children from the poverty of his own youth, it was almost impossible to understand how young men did not share the burning desire that he had known to pursue a useful career. Yet his own very prominence, and his ability to give his sons jobs in his own companies, precluded this possibility, unless the sons had moved outside Canada, which they never did.

It is hard, at least for an outsider, to know what more McConnell could have done, much less what he should have done. If he had not provided his sons with the advantages and houses that he did, or the employment, he would have been accused of a lack of generosity, which was certainly not part of his personality. Wilson and David thought that he did not give them responsibility to match their positions at St Lawrence Sugar, but it is not really clear that they were qualified to assume such responsibility, or even that they were interested in the sugar business or in business generally. John, who loved newspapers, was given not only responsibility but also an endless flow of advice and support from his father. The problem seems to be that McConnell did not realize that wealth itself could be a burden. Having begun with none, he found the making of it very satisfying and the giving of it to good causes even more satisfying. In giving he demonstrated not control, as some thought, but love and care. For someone so shy and sensitive, it was the easiest way to express emotion. And so he gave Lil share certificates on her birthday. And so he showered coins on his sons at Christmas, letting them fall out of a hole in his pocket for them to pick up.

McConnell's private world began to collapse with David's death, while his public world began to deteriorate in the face of the increasing political violence in Quebec. On the night of 20 April 1963 the Front de Libération du Québec killed its first victim, a war veteran, with a bomb planted behind the Army recruiting centre in Strathcona Hall, the former McGill YMCA headquarters on Sherbrooke Street. On the night of 9 May, it dynamited a wall of the Black Watch armoury on Bleury Street. Early on the morning of 17 May, five out of ten bombs planted in mailboxes, which at that time were painted in Imperial red and bore the Canadian coat of arms, exploded in Westmount. The Army spread through Westmount, inspecting all mailboxes. On McConnell's last Victoria Day, 20 May, the FLQ set off seventy-five sticks of dynamite at another armoury, and in July Prime Minister Pearson announced the creation of a Royal Commission on Bilingualism and Biculturalism, chaired by McConnell's former protégé Davidson Dunton and the anti-conscriptionist nationalist André Laurendeau. During the summer the Armée de liberation du Québec was born. On 13 July it used dynamite to topple the monument to Queen Victoria in Quebec City. It set fires at the armoury of the Fusiliers de Mont-Royal at Pine Avenue, which had been largely funded by Sir Rodolphe Forget, the armoury of the Régiment de Maisonneuve on Craig Street, and the Royal Canadian Legion Building in Laval West; it also robbed a branch of the Royal Bank of Canada in Outremont. The revolt that had begun was professedly socialist and anarchist as well as separatist, and against almost everything that McConnell had ever stood for.[23]

McConnell as lucid and decisive as ever, continued to give. Almost on his last day, he instructed Peter McEntyre to donate $125,000 to make up the actuarial deficit of the pension fund of the Victorian Order of Nurses that he had set up in 1944–46.[24] His very last cheque seems to have been for $25,000 to pay for a new wing to the Catherine Booth Hospital run by the Salvation Army. As Commissioner W. Wycliffe Booth was to write to Lil, "my heart is moved as I think of his generous gift coming so shortly before his Home Call."[25]

McConnell spent eight days in October at the Ross Pavilion of the Royal Victoria Hospital and then went home, only to return to hospital on 6 November 1963, after pneumonia had set in. Lil was herself very ill at home. At about 2 o'clock in the afternoon he died at the Royal Vic, almost alone, his hand held by a nurse.

The Reverend Norman Slaughter conducted his funeral two days later at the Erskine and American United Church. There was no eulogy, and at the request of the family there were no official representatives, and no press coverage. McConnell was buried in a plot in the Mount Royal Cemetery that he had chosen the previous April. It occupied once of the highest points in the cemetery, roughly analogous to the position of his house on Pine Avenue in relation to the Square Mile, with even Sir Herbert Holt a little lower, as his house on Stanley Street had been.

McConnell's death provoked genuine regret among friends and critics alike, bringing together English and French Quebec in particular. Hundreds of tributes to McConnell poured in, from individuals such as the Queen and Prince Philip to the institutions and the needy that he had helped. Princess Alice, Princess Marina, and Sir Anthony Eden wrote. Present and former governors general – Vanier, Massey, and Alexander – paid tribute, as did Lady Tweedsmuir, present and former prime ministers Pearson, Diefenbaker, and St Laurent, and one future one, John Turner. C.M. Drury (son of Victor) was one of the federal cabinet ministers who wrote to the family. So did Tommy Douglas, leader of the NDP; Réal Caouette, leader of the Créditistes; and Robert Thompson, leader of the Social Credit Party. The two chairmen of the Royal Commission on Bilingualism and Biculturalism, Davidson Dunton (John McConnell's colleague at the *Standard*) and André Laurendeau, remembered him. Premiers Leslie Frost of Ontario and Louis Robichaud of New Brunswick, did likewise. In Quebec, Premier Jean Lesage seemed particularly moved and said: "How many persons fervently pray for him every day without even knowing the name of the anonymous philanthropist who helped them in their distress." One ungracious note was struck by Daniel Johnson, Duplessis's heir as leader of the Union Nationale and ultimately premier, who grumbled to the press that McConnell had been involved in the price fixing of sugar.

Few remembered McConnell from his early days, but Mary Goodfellow Doane, married to a chairman of International Paper, recalled her father's stories about being in a rooming house in Montreal with him when they had first arrived in the city in 1901. The Masonic Royal Victoria Lodge, founded in 1876, remembered that McConnell had been a brother mason since 1904. Charles Johnston, a son of George F. Johnston, recalled McConnell's partnership with his father and Hudson Allison. From England, Sir Shuldham Redfern, formerly private secretary to Lords Tweedsmuir and Athlone at Government House in Ottawa, remembered him from 1935 onwards as "always young in spirit, gay and active" and noted that even in old age "his mind was razor sharp, his gaiety unruffled and his kindliness unlimited." He was, Redfern concluded, "a great Canadian, one of the greatest men of the age."[26] Thérèse Casgrain recalled him from the days of her father, Sir Rodolphe Forget. The Greek ambassador recalled McConnell's aid to Greece during the Second World War.

From the United States, Justice Tom C. Clark of the Supreme Court and Jeremiah Milbank communicated their condolences. J.D. McKeown, the son of a prominent governor of the Wesleyan Theological College, recalled a visit of Jack and Lil to Knowlton, in which Jack climbed the trees near the house of his parents.[27] Jewish admirers seemed unusually moved. Lazarus Phillips, lawyer to the Bronfman family and later a senator, wrote in a letter to John:

> Canada has not produced a son to equal him nor is it likely that such will ever be the case.
>
> He was indeed endowed by the Creator with such qualities of heart and mind as to make him a compelling personality.
>
> Many men in our country have been philanthropists and many have been successful in business – none however put the fruits of success in business to such humanitarian and worthy purposes as did your Father.
>
> He was a beacon of light and inspiration certainly to men of my generation. In the too few instances where I had the opportunity of being with him he radiated towards me an intense warmth of friendship which gladdened my heart. There is no man in this country whom I respected or admired more. His loss to Canada and indeed to the world is irreparable.[28]

Allan Bronfman wrote to Lil that it had been "my personal privilege to know your husband and to appreciate his great qualities of heart and mind." McConnell's had been "a rare and exemplary life." Sam Bronfman wrote, Sam and Helen Steinberg sent a basket of fruit, and Philip Garfinkle, of the Jewish General Hospital, described McConnell as one of its "close friends and amongst its most generous contributors." "His broad concepts of philanthropy knew no bounds of race and creed, and his benefactions were bestowed out of his love of humanity."[29] Rabbi Harry J. Stern wrote a eulogy for the newsletter of his synagogue, the Temple Emmanu-El. The Jewish National Fund of Canada informed Lil that some anonymous old man had made a contribution to plant five trees in Israel in honour of McConnell. McConnell had indeed been a supporter of Israel, but he was very aware of the humanitarian problem that had accompanied the state's creation in 1948. M.S. Massoud, president of the Canadian Arab Friendship League, said: "In the loss of Mr. McConnell, the down-trodden refugees lost a very ardent friend and supporter."

The rector and vice-rector of the Université Laval, the only institution that managed to confer on McConnell an honorary degree, and still probably without his approval, wrote in condolence, and so did the governors of the Université de Montréal.[30] Sister Thérèse Trottier, superior of the l'Hôtel-Dieu et les Réligieuses Hospitalières, wrote to assure John of their prayers for the repose of "la chère âme que vous pleurez." The Hôpital Sainte-Justine recalled him as "such a devoted friend of the sick children" and among its most generous benefactors." It assured Lil, "Our young patients will pray to God to give him heavenly rest and peace." The Chambre de Commerce de District de Montréal, the Sisters of St Joseph's Hospital in Trois-Rivières, the Hôpital Notre-Dame of Montreal, the Hôtel-Dieu of Quebec, and the Collège Jean de Brébeuf all recorded their gratitude. Among businessmen, Sévère Godin, the long-time secretary of Sir Herbert Holt and later sometime vice-president of Montreal Power, recalled that McConnell "was always so sympathetic to me every time I had occasion to see him from the time of my boyhood," and Colin Webster, son of Lorne, said the same.[31]

Elsewhere from the business world, Consolidated Paper, Anglo-Canadian Pulp and Paper, Trans-Canada Airlines, the Borden Company, Penman's, Canadian Liquid Air, Ogilvie Flour, International Nickel, Montreal Trust, the Robert Simpson Company, Loblaw's Groceterias, the Canadian Bank of Commerce, and the Bank of Montreal wrote to John, but few individuals seemed left who had done business with his father. The owners, publishers, and editors of newspapers offered particular recognition, in part because of John's own career at the *Star*. Lord Beaverbrook, Lord Astor of Hever, and Lord Thomson of Fleet and his son Ken Thomson remembered McConnell from England. Beaverbrook wrote, presumably with reference to his own foundation: "I recall over the years so much that I have gained from his inspiration & example. For he showed me the way of public duty and in a very small measure I have followed his example."[32] The Toronto *Star* and the Winnipeg *Free Press* – neither friendly to McConnell in life – published tributes. So did smaller journals such as the Sarnia *Observer*, the Fredericton *Gleaner*, the Fort-Williams *Times Journal*, and the Windsor *Star*.

Perhaps the tributes that would have pleased McConnell most were those from old staff members of the *Star*. A.J. West recalled "the fifteen years of our close association" as "the most rewarding of my life, and serving him a rare privilege indeed."

L.W. Glover, a typographer for over thirty years, remembered that "his unequalled spirit of generosity was exemplified by the manner in which he revised and reorganized the pension scheme as existed under the Presidency of the late Lord Atholstan. For this alone he earned the ultimate gratitude of we pensioners." George A. Plummer, secretary-treasurer of the Montreal Typographical Union, No. 176, recalled from meetings McConnell's "foresight and keen interest in the welfare of his fellow man."[33] Even *Star* delivery boys and members of the elevator staff wrote.

Numerous hospitals and charities sent their condolences, such as the Allan Memorial Institute, the Canadian Cancer Society, the Montreal Council of Social Agencies, the Salvation Army, the Ottawa Boys' Club, the Boy Scouts of Canada (of which McConnell had been honorary president), the Welfare Federation, the Montreal Council of Social Agencies, the Royal Edward Laurentian Hospital, the Montreal General Hospital, the Queen Elizabeth Hospital, the Montreal Neurological Institute, the Montreal Children's Hospital, the Royal Victoria Hospital, the Occupational Therapy and Rehabilitation Centre (for which he had bought its building on Ottawa Street in Montreal), the Griffith-McConnell Home for Elderly People, the Sherbrooke Hospital, the YMCA, the Canadian Red Cross, the Hellenic Red Cross, the Priory of Canada of the Most Venerable Order of St John of Jerusalem, St Mary's Hospital, the Reddy Memorial Hospital, the Lachine General Hospital, the Barrie Memorial Hospital in Ormstown, the Girls' Cottage School in St Bruno, the Fresh Air Fund in Chambly, and the Dieppe Home for Epileptics in Saint-Hilaire.

On behalf of the East End Boys' Club, Stuart Molson recalled the new skating rink that McConnell had given. Major-General Edouard de Bellefeuille Panet wrote both personally and on behalf of the Canadian Paraplegic Association. The Montreal Association for the Blind, which had had McConnell as patron, in addition to Lord Alexander and Lord Beaverbrook, recorded its loss. From the arts, Zubin Mehta, the conductor of the Montreal Symphony Orchestra, wrote, as did Alan Jarvis, the sculptor and director of the National Gallery of Canada, and Pierre Béique of the Place des Arts.

The University of New Brunswick, Bishop's University, and other educational institutions did not forget him. From McGill, the Department of Electrical Engineering remembered his role in providing its new building. Both the McGill Association of University Teachers and the McGill Students' Society paid tribute. From McConnell Hall, and from the governors and the Senate of the university, came flowers. Lewis Douglas, the former principal, recalled from Arizona that McConnell had been "one of my main anchors in Montreal," and Dr H. Rocke Robertson, the current principal, recalled how he had "saved the University time and again."

Cyril James, now retired as principal, confided to his diary that McConnell "could be ruthless – witness George McDonald and the Chancellorship fight! I should not have liked him as an enemy. But I remember him as the staunchest of friends, without whose aid I could not have lasted 23 years at McGill let alone accomplished all the things that we were able to do together. I feel a bitter lost [sic] that he is no longer within reach of the telephone."[34] James wrote to Lil that "nobody could have been a truer and more loyal friend" to him during his years as principal: "Entirely apart from his great and generous financial aid to the University, I treasure the memory of his personal interest. There was no major problem – no crisis – that I did not share with him, from the time of the controversy with George McDonald after Beatty's death, and in every case the solution was as much his as mine. I do not think that we ever differed on the final solution of any problem – although we argued often before that situation was reached – and in the latter years he was the only member of the Board of Governors who had been on that Board when I took office in 1939."[35]

We may leave the last word to one of McConnell's younger friends, Malcolm Mac-Donald. Writing to Lil from Government House in Nairobi, where he was the last colonial governor and about to become the first governor general of Kenya, he stated:

> One of the shining lights in my life has been extinguished. I admired him without limit for all his great and glorious qualities, and I felt an affection for him which will be for ever abiding. He was a wonderful person, with an ability, understanding, wisdom, generosity, public spirit, and goodness, all of which collectively were unsurpassed in any other individual I have known. His services to Canada, and to many fine international as well as national causes, were titanic. Yet he performed them all with a modesty, and even a self effacement, which had an almost saintly touch. No-one – thank goodness! – would have called Jack a saint; he was splendidly human. And yet there was a rare quality of unselfishness about him that was in some ways superhuman.
>
> It was his human qualities which were most appealing – his friendliness, his complete lack of "side" in spite of his great distinction, his spontaneous readiness to treat everyone (however exalted or lowly) with respect as fundamental equals, his gaiety, his bubbling sense of humour, his sincerity, and all sorts of other virtues. They shone in him, and were of course enhanced by that superbly handsome physical presence, which still stayed with him even when he was a semi-invalid in his late 80's propped up against the pillows in his bed.

He continued: "What a wonderful partnership you made, what a great life you led together, and what superb pleasures and happiness you have given to everyone who had the privilege of staying, however briefly, under your roof!" These memories would abide with him "fresh and evergreen, as long as I remain on this Earth." In her grief, he hoped that Lil would not forget how much she meant to Jack and what "a joyous, creative contribution" the two of them had made "to many other people's lives, and to the life of Canada itself."[36]

By the time of his death, McConnell had outlived nearly all his contemporaries, and was now generally remembered only as a philanthropist and a former newspaper owner. The businessmen Sir William Mackenzie, Arthur Peuchen, Sir Rodolphe Forget, Sir Herbert Holt, Lord Strathcona, E.-A. Robert, Sir Joseph Flavelle, Senator Lorne Webster, and so many others were already distant memories. McConnell's friends among politicians, such as Sir Lomer Gouin, Maurice Duplessis, and Mackenzie King, were all gone. Among his fellow newspaper proprietors, Lords Iliffe, Camrose, and Kemsley were likewise, and Beaverbrook would be dead within weeks. Within months, too, Churchill would finally expire, the last great leader of the empire.

Although Lil was to live on to 1972, the big house in Dorval, Ashburton, burned down suddenly, with all its contents, just as Saran Chai had in 1952. Soon, the *Star*, St Lawrence Sugar, and Ogilvie Flour had all passed from family hands and disappeared or lost their identities. With the empire gone, Canada was to abandon the Union flag and the Canadian Red Ensign, and Britain was to join the European Common Market. St James Street had already yielded its financial role to Dorchester Boulevard (eventually to be renamed Boulevard René-Lévesque after the separatist premier) and Place Victoria, and Montreal its financial pre-eminence to Toronto. Separatists were to gain power in Quebec, rename Pine Avenue as Avenue des Pins and St James Street as rue Saint-Jacques, and effectively lead to the exile and dispossession of hundreds of thousands of Montrealers.

These exiles were mainly English-speaking, and many of them personally were pillars of, or descended from pillars of, the economic success of Montreal. With them fled much of the city's wealth and corporate head offices, at least two centuries of its tradition, and much of its collective memory. In particular, Sun Life, the CPR, and even the Bank of Montreal, as well as all the other major banks and the trust companies and many of the companies that McConnell had known and served, either fled or became simply regional offices.

McConnell had signed the last version of his will at Dorval in August 1961. Apart from personal bequests, he gave the house on Pine Avenue to his Foundation, to be held in trust for Lil for life. His final charitable bequests in his will showed the lifelong consistency of his interests. The YMCA, the YWCA, and the United Church each received $25,000, the church's share "to form part of the pension fund for aged and infirm ministers." The Salvation Army, the Victorian Order of Nurses, and the Old Brewery Mission received $25,000. The British and Foreign Bible Society, the Welcome Hall Mission, and Frontier College each received $10,000. The most important beneficiaries, however, were hospitals, boys' clubs, and universities. McGill was given $200,000, and $100,000 went to the Royal Victoria Hospital, the Université de Montréal, the Université Laval, Sainte-Justine Hospital, Notre-Dame Hospital, and the Montreal General Hospital. The Montreal Children's Hospital received $50,000, as did the Montreal Boys' Association (for emergency requirements of the East End Boys' Club and the Point St Charles Boys' Club). The Grace Dart Home Hospital, the Jewish General Hospital, the Montreal Association for the Blind, the Queen Elizabeth Hospital, the Julius Richardson Convalescent Hospital, St Mary's Hospital, the Reddy Memorial Hospital, and the Montreal Convalescent Hospital all received $25,000.

None of McConnell's companies now exist. Atlantic Sugar took over its old and bitter rival, St Lawrence, after his death and subsequently became part of BC Sugar, so that all the Canadian sugar companies are now one huge monopoly, with the exception of Redpath, which is now owned by Tate and Lyle of the United Kingdom. The *Star* closed down in 1979 and John's building (dating from 1961) was subsequently occupied by its rival, the *Gazette*; it is now due to become condominium apartments. Ogilvie Flour, once the largest miller in Canada, the British Empire, and indeed the world, is part of the American firm ADM (Archer Daniel Midland). Montreal Securities exists in name only, owned by the Webster family, and Montreal-London Securities, Mount Royal Bonds, and nearly every other company with which McConnell was associated has changed its name or disappeared. One exception is Imperial Trust, still operated by the Websters. Other exceptions are such big companies as INCO, but even Brazilian Traction has become Brookfield Holdings, and the once-mighty ICI and Courtaulds are virtually gone. CIL remains a minor paint company. The Bank of Montreal, Royal Trust (now vestigially part of the Royal Bank), and Sun Life have long been headquartered in Toronto, leaving their former head offices in Montreal as ghostly shells. The CPR survives, with its headquarters in Calgary, its Windsor Station used for charity events and up for sale. The Windsor Hotel, much truncated, has been turned into offices.

The Royal Victoria, the Montreal General, and all the other English-speaking hospitals of Montreal seem destined for abandonment and reconstitution under the prosaic name of the McGill University Health Centre. Morgan's, Eaton's, and Simpson's are gone. St James Street, now called the rue Saint-Jacques, is now used primarily as a movie set, and Sir Rodolphe Forget's Stock Exchange is now the Centaur Theatre. For many years, McConnell's house on Pine Avenue was a monastery and a meditation centre, much used as a movie set depicting the ultimate robber baron's mansion, until it was purchased and extensively renovated by another family.

The brokerage houses and the banks and the stock exchange that financed much of Canada from Montreal are relocated or gone. The names once engraved on their buildings have nearly all been sandblasted away and replaced by nothing or by unmemorable acronyms. The Power and the Tramways Buildings, respectively the headquarters of Sir Herbert Holt and E.-A. Robert, on Craig Street are gone, and Craig Street itself has become rue Saint-Antoine, although, curiously, the old Street Railway Chambers hangs on – long, dusty, vacant, and nameless but about to be converted into condominiums. The Erskine and American Church has merged with the St Andrew's-Dominion-Douglas United Church to form the Mountainside Church, and its building on Sherbrooke Street is now part of the Museum of Fine Arts. But the St James United Church survives, its front at last shorn of the stores that McConnell had urged to be built to earn it revenue. The Mount Royal Cemetery, where Jack and Lil and other McConnells are buried, remains undisturbed. So does the Mount Pleasant Cemetery in Toronto, where his parents and his sister Sue are buried.

Yet, if we look again at the extant physical vestiges of McConnell's Montreal, we see that the desolation is far from complete. It is true that the Square Mile has been almost totally and wantonly destroyed, but McConnell's house survives on Pine Avenue, almost unique in the retention of most of its interior as well as most of its exterior. At the time of writing, its survival seems more secure than ever since McConnell's death, with both its exterior and interior protected as of historical interest. The Dominion Express Building, though bereft of its name, stands as proud as ever beside the Bank of Montreal, completely refurbished, with the elegant offices of an agency of the Quebec government occupying McConnell's eighth floor. At McGill, McConnell Hall, the McConnell Engineering Building, the McConnell Wing of the Neurological Institute, McConnell Scholarships, Purvis Hall, Chancellor Day Hall, the Allan Memorial Institute, Molson Stadium, the McConnell Arena, the Faculty of Religious Studies, and much else still serve the needs that McConnell envisioned for them. Concordia University boasts a huge J.W. McConnell Building that McConnell could never have dreamt of.

The Foundation remained until beyond 2000 as by far the best-endowed in the country. Now the Fondation Lucie et André Chagnon, established by a French Canadian who barely survived the hunger of the Great Depression, has almost six times the McConnell endowment. In the United States, the foundation established by Bill Gates, dedicated to the relief of poverty and the eradication of disease, dwarfs the Rockefeller, Ford, and other foundations of McConnell's era. As Sir Richard Branson and others have declared, money exists to be put to productive use. As described in chapter 2, this principle had been the essence of the capitalism taught at the Toronto YMCA in McConnell's youth. Moreover, the endowments of most foundations are now invested in common stock, the reviled "water" that so tainted such men as McConnell among many of their contemporaries. Philanthropy is a greater force globally than ever, and it is hard to think that McConnell, who established once of the first major philanthropic foundations anywhere, would not have been delighted to see it so.

The central YMCA in Montreal opened new facilities in 2001, while retaining a little of the building that McConnell helped to fund in 1909. It continues to use even massive "thermometers" modelled on the one used in that fundraising campaign. Dominion Square, its northern part now called Dorchester Square, is still surrounded by the Dominion Square Building, the Sun Life Building, and part of the former Windsor

Hotel. It also still contains the statue of Laurier, to the erection of which McConnell contributed; and in what is now Place du Canada, formerly the southern part of Dominion Square, there remains the memorial to Sir John Macdonald, beheaded in the 1990s but now bearing a new head provided by the McConnell Foundation.

Montreal will remain no doubt, as it has been for so long, a contested space. The past will continue to be at war with the present and the future, French will supplant English and vice versa, and new industries, businesses, and residences will rise over the rubble of the old. None of this would have surprised or dismayed McConnell. Indeed, he would probably be surprised to know that probably more of his Montreal survives than, say, the Toronto of Goulding and Peuchen and Flavelle. Indeed, in addition to the revitalization of the Lachine Canal, the Old Port area of Montreal now houses carefully restored commercial buildings from even earlier generations of Montrealers than McConnell's, such as the Allans, with their names still boldly emblazoned on them.

McConnell did not particularly want his own name emblazoned anywhere, but through his many gifts, and through his Foundation, he continues to give, and his giving is his monument. As Cyril James wrote, McConnell deserved the epitaph on the tomb of Sir Christopher Wren in St. Paul's Cathedral, translated as: "If you seek a monument, look around you." Even better perhaps as an epitaph is a quotation saved by McConnell himself. It is from Addison's essay on Westminster Abbey:

> When I look upon the Tombs of the Great, every Emotion of Envy dies in me; when I meet with the Grief of Parents upon a Tombstone, my Heart melts with Compassion; when I see the Tomb of the Parents themselves, I consider the Vanity of grieving for those whom we must quickly follow: When I see Kings lying by those that deposed them, when I consider rival Wits placed Side by Side, or the Holy Men that divided the World with their Contests and Disputes, I reflect with Sorrow and Astonishment on the little Competitions, Factions and Debates of Mankind. When I read the several Dates of the Tombs, of some that dy'd Yesterday, and some six hundred Years ago, I consider that great Day when we shall all of us be Contemporaries, and make our Appearance together.

J.W. McConnell's Investment Holdings:
An Overview, 1921–51

Nicolas McConnell

While records of McConnell's early career as a promoter are fragmentary, more exists on his investment holdings for the period after 1918, beginning with a "Statement of Assets & Liabilities" of 1921. The profits from his pre-war promotions had now been consolidated into publicly traded securities, many unrelated to his earlier investments. As close to a complete inventory of McConnell's assets, it reveals,[1] for example, no fewer than six real estate development companies.[2] The Montreal Securities Corporation, essentially a financial vehicle, and Dominion Manufacturers, an early amalgamation of casket makers, were holdovers from the past.

St Lawrence Sugar Refineries (purchased by McConnell in increments from 1912 to 1924) was new, and it became his privately owned company for holding shares as well as for manufacture. His salary as president, company dividends, and operating profits all fuelled his purchase of stocks and bonds over time.[3] He kept a portfolio of private investments in it from about 1924 onwards. After he had gained control of the Montreal Star Publishing Company in 1938, he kept another portfolio in it. Calculating present-day valuations for the privately held holdings listed in the 1921 Statement is difficult. The fate of the real estate companies remains obscure, while McConnell's commercial and personal real estate holdings were either disposed of without a trace or gifted to family members.[4] Further, a valuation for Montreal Securities Corporation[5] remains elusive, and Dominion Manufacturers was ceded, or sold in an unrecorded transaction, to a business associate in the 1950s.

McConnell's only other early financial record is "St Lawrence Sugar Refineries Limited, Memorandum of Investments, Sept. 23rd, 1929."[6] This records 120 publicly traded companies with a market value of over $45 million His listing of $2.5 million in Montreal *Star* bonds and shares confirms McConnell's purchase price for the *Star* group in 1925. There were tax efficiencies in holding his securities within his privately owned corporation. Between 1924 and 1930, dividends and interest posted to the investment account of St Lawrence doubled to just over $1 million annually.[7]

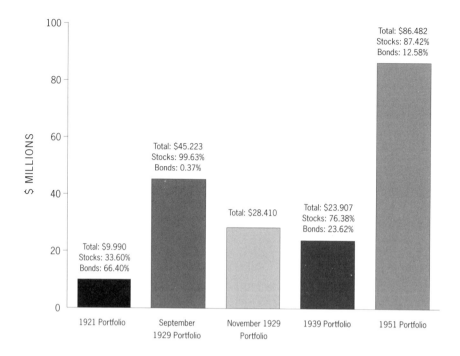

Chart 1   Estimated Total Stock and Bond Portfolios, 1921–1951

In the mid-1930s, McConnell began to purchase, for accounts outside St Lawrence, the J.W. McConnell Foundation (1937), the Montreal Star Publishing Company (1938), and newly created family trusts. He often allocated identical amounts in new acquisitions among these accounts. Evidence of these has largely survived, in ledger-books (sometimes incomplete), company tax returns, or typed audited financial statements. These records reveal an overwhelming emphasis on common shares.

Incomplete evidence suggests that he kept bonds in his "personal" accounts. A ledger marked "J.W. McConnell Personal" survives only for the 1950s. In his 1921 statement of assets personally held, there were significant amounts of bonds, two-thirds of all the investments. About 25 per cent of the $4 million in his personal account, thirty years later, was also in bonds. Between these dates we know nothing about his personal holdings. In 1939, however, $2 million of Dominion of Canada bonds went into the J.W. McConnell Family Trust,[8] probably from a personal account that has not survived.[9] The personal ledgers missing for 1922–50 must have recorded assets beyond those in the 1929 memorandum and the trust record for 1939 that has survived.[10]

A 1964 audited statement for McConnell's Commercial Trust Company can be used to calculate the value of his portfolios at the time of his death in 1963. The total

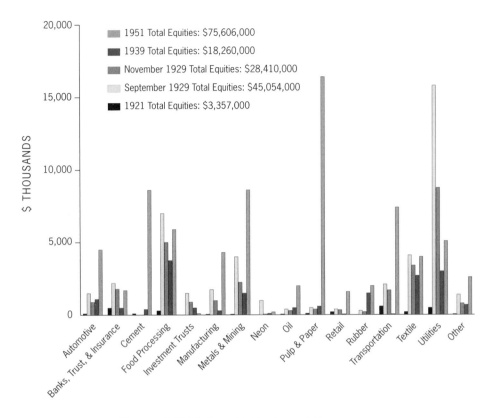

Chart 2   J.W. McConnell: Stock portfolios, 1921–1951,
estimated dollar values by sector

of $192 million[11] – or $1,351,200,000 in year 2008 dollars – excludes contemporary market valuations for St Lawrence Sugar Refineries, the Montreal Star Publishing Company, and Commercial Trust, all wholly owned by him, as well as any real estate holdings, and of course all that he had given away during his lifetime.

The accompanying charts[12] illustrating J.W. McConnell's investment holdings in publicly traded securities over four decades were generated from data for company holdings for 1921–51. Chart 1, Estimated total stock and bond portfolios, 1921–51, illustrates the estimated total value of McConnell's securities portfolios for these years. Chart 2, Stock portfolios, 1921–51, showing dollar values by sector, illustrates McConnell's *stock holdings* for the same period, broken down into sixteen representative sectors of investment. Chart 3, comprising four graphs, illustrates McConnell's top stock holdings measured as a percentage of the dollar value of his equity portfolios. Chart 4, comprising four graphs, illustrates McConnell's top holdings measured as a percentage of a held company's outstanding common shares.

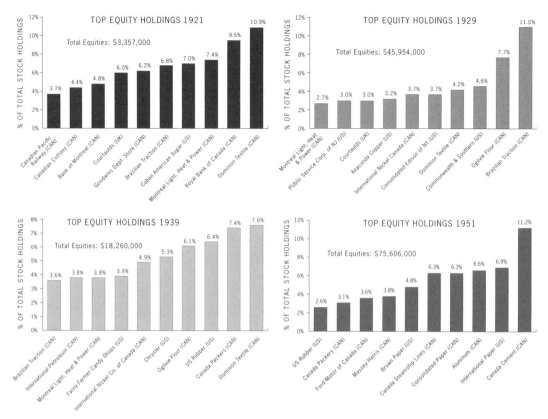

Chart 3 Estimated stock portfolios, 1921–1951, top holdings
as percentage of total dollar value of stock portfolios

The charts illustrate McConnell's investment in publicly traded securities only. The contemporary market values assigned these securities have been derived in one of two ways. In the case of the 1921 and 1929 portfolios, share valuations have been taken directly from these stand-alone documents, though verified independently in Moody's Directories to ensure accuracy. For the later two "combined" portfolios for 1939 and 1951, share valuations have been taken directly from investment ledgers, audited financial statements, and surviving company tax returns found among McConnell's papers. In the case of tax returns, reported company dividends have been used to generate the number of shares McConnell held. The share price, in turn, has been quoted as the average of a share's "high/low range" reported in Moody's Directories for the year in question.

The figures for the 1939 and 1951 combined portfolios derive, in part, from the St Lawrence Sugar Refineries investment ledger books. These appear to be missing individual page entries for certain companies McConnell was known to have invested

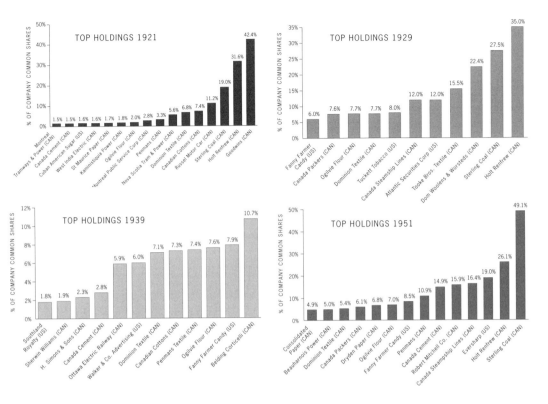

Chart 4   Stock portfolios, 1921–1951, top holdings as
percentage of company's outstanding common shares

in. This obtains for the 1951 investment ledger entries marked "J.W. McConnell Personal" as well.[13] All missing entries are listed below in the relevant sections.

As already stated, excluded from all illustrated portfolios are figures for McConnell's privately held St Lawrence Sugar Refineries, Dominion Manufacturers, and the Montreal Star Publishing Company, as well as other closely held corporate or real estate vehicles. Holdings under $1,000 have also been excluded, while all figures have been rounded to the nearest thousand dollars (000) to simplify the presentation of the accompanying charts and tables.

Background summaries to the portfolios illustrated in the accompanying charts can be found in separate sections that follow. Each summary has been broken down into short explanatory sections – "valuation," "reconciliation," "composition," and "exposition."

1921 PORTFOLIO

The data for the 1921 portfolio derive from the surviving "Statement of Assets & Liabilities of J.W. McConnell as at December 31st, 1921." McConnell prepared this statement as collateral for a loan he secured from the Bank of Montreal for St Lawrence Sugar Refineries during the 1921 sugar crisis.

Valuation

The 1921 Statement values J.W. McConnell's assets at $10,859,977.11 ($116,460,324 in 2008).

Since 1921 predates McConnell's use of St Lawrence Sugar Refineries as a privately held investment vehicle, his acquisition of the Montreal Star Publishing Company, and the establishment of the J.W. McConnell Foundation and other family trusts, we have assumed that this Statement values all McConnell's holdings for that year.

Reconciliation

For the purpose of generating a portfolio of McConnell's publicly traded securities, we have taken the $10,859,977.11 total from the 1921 Statement and subtracted the following holdings:

- real estate/golf clubs ($542,040.35/$10,400.00);
- real estate companies ($101,450.00); and
- cash/accounts receivable ($125,343.82)

Also excluded is McConnell's interest in privately held or closely associated

- Dominion Manufacturers ($41,251);
- Imperial Trust ($50,000);
- St Lawrence Sugar Refineries ($1); and
- Montreal Securities Corporation ($1)

The total of publicly traded securities amounts to $9,989,492.94. Rounded to ($000), the total is $9,990(000).

Composition

The portfolio of publicly traded securities extracted from the 1921 Statement breaks down as follows:

1921 J.W. MCCONNELL

ASSET ALLOCATION	$ 000	% OF TOTAL
Company Stocks	3357	33.60

ASSET ALLOCATION	$ 000	% OF TOTAL
Company Bonds	427	4.27
Government Bonds	6206	62.12
Portfolio Total	9990	100.00

EQUITIES ALLOCATION	$ 000	% OF TOTAL
Canadian	2672	79.59
US	523	15.58
Foreign	162	4.83
Equities Total	3357	100.00

EQUITIES ALLOCATION BY SECTOR	$ 000	% OF TOTAL
Automotive	40	1.19
Banks, Trust, and Insurance	560	16.68
Cement	155	4.62
Food Processing	459	13.67
Investment Trusts		
Manufacturing	40	1.19
Metals and Mining	46	1.37
Neon and Advertising Signage	–	–
Oil	51	1.52
Pulp and Paper	150	4.47
Retail	256	7.63
Rubber	–	–
Textiles	250	7.45
Transport	727	21.66
Utilities	592	17.63
Other	31	0.92
Sector Totals	3357	100.00

Exposition

The asset allocation for 1921 is perhaps most striking for a man whose early career depended largely (and profited hugely) from common shares. Fully two-thirds of the portfolio is made up of Dominion of Canada 5.5 per cent bonds. Were contemporary valuations provided for McConnell's privately held companies – St Lawrence Sugar Refineries in particular – the proportion of bonds to McConnell's total holdings listed in the 1921 Statement would, of course, be significantly reduced.

Eighty per cent of the equities listed in the portfolio are Canadian. This is hardly surprising, since optimism in the country's prospects was the trademark of the promoter's outlook. The kinds of companies represented in the portfolio are varied

– pianos, airplanes, and automobiles, to name but a few. At the same time, a number of sectors that would define McConnell's investing over time are discernible. These sectors are retail,[14] utilities,[15] textiles,[16] and food processing.[17]

The retail sector in 1921 largely comprises Goodwin's, a publicly traded company launched by McConnell (1911), and Holt Renfrew, reorganized in 1919. At just over 2 per cent of the 1921 total, Goodwin's was a rare survival from his pre-war promotions. Other such survivals include Montreal Tramways at 1.25 per cent and Sterling Coal at 0.34 per cent.

Larger holdings in Canadian utilities companies such as Brazilian Traction (2.28 per cent) and Montreal, Light, Heat and Power (3.20 per cent) hark back to McConnell's earliest promotion of Canada Light and Power. Held without interruption through the 1940s and later, they foreshadowed greater enthusiasm for this new and volatile sector.

In the case of the British textile company Courtaulds (held in both 1921 and 1951), McConnell's investor loyalty proved disadvantageous, on account of sterling depreciation during the Second World War, but its dividends were very rich and secure. Textiles generally, and notably Dominion Textile, provided him with the most consistent and stable of returns.

Providing equal steadiness was the food-processing sector. The 1921 Statement records a decided preference for sugar companies, largely American. This was natural enough for a refiner. Yet, perhaps owing to the 1921 sugar crisis, it was not a pattern of investment that he would maintain. His 2 per cent stake in Ogilvie Flour Mills in 1921 foreshadows diversification *out* of sugar into milling by the late 1920s.

McConnell's significant later holding in Canada Cement (see the 1951 table), rumoured to date from its 1910 merger, does not appear to date from 1921. While shares in Canada Cement represent 1.10 per cent of his 1921 portfolio, entries for the company disappear from the record after 1921. He purchased large stakes of Canada Cement for his St Lawrence Sugar Refineries investment account from 1939 on – but not before.

It is interesting to note that, while the financial sector did not in fact attract much of McConnell's investment interest over time, his 1921 holding of 1,000 Bank of Montreal shares made him one of the larger shareholders of the bank.[18] There are no Dow components among McConnell's 1921 holdings.

While it is impossible to provide contemporary valuations for the real estate development companies listed,[19] approximately 6 per cent of McConnell's total listed holdings in 1921 are made up of real estate.[20] These include 700 shares in the "McGill Building" ($50,000), an undisclosed number of shares in Montreal Industrial Land ($50,000), and 50 shares in Montreal West Realties ($1,450). Also included are McConnell's commercial/residential holdings ($279,253.80)[21] and personal properties ($267,786.19).[22]

McConnell's interests in golf clubs were essentially real estate ventures too. In addition to an investment in the Royal Montreal Golf Club ($10,000), included also are two shares in the Beaconsfield Golf Club ($400), fifteen shares in the Mount Bruno Golf Club ($1), and ten shares in the Winter (skating) Club ($1).

1929 PORTFOLIO (PRE-CRASH)

The data here derive from "St Lawrence Sugar Refineries Limited, Memorandum of Investments, Sept 23rd, 1929." This important document – consisting of typed lists of company stocks and bonds held in the investment account of the sugar company one month prior to the October 1929 Crash – is not among the surviving corporate records of St Lawrence Sugar Refineries but was found quite by chance among unrelated personal papers.

Valuation

The 1929 Memorandum values the total investments held by St Lawrence at $48,520,990 ($593,397,727 in 2008). Given that September 1929 predates McConnell's formal takeover (though not purchase) of the Montreal Star Publishing Company and the establishment of the J.W. McConnell Foundation and various family trusts, we can assume that this document values all his corporate but not his personal holdings.

Reconciliation

For the purpose of generating McConnell's investment holdings in publicly traded securities, we have taken the $48,520,990 total from the 1929 Memorandum and subtracted the book value of the following:

· $1,000,000 Montreal Star Publishing Company bonds;
· $1,500,000 Montreal Star Publishing Company shares;
· $92,000 Dominion Manufacturers total shares; and
· $34,000 St Lawrence Sugar Refineries bonds

We have also subtracted the value of the following real estate or charitable holdings:

· McGill Building ($50,000); and
· Study School ($5,000)

Excluded, too, are various obscure non-publicly traded holdings.[23]

We have further had to adjust for a footnoting error in the original 1929 Memorandum which overstated the value of the St Lawrence Sugar Refineries portfolio by some $616,000.[24] Thus, we have subtracted $616,000.

The total value of publicly traded securities amounts to $45,222,990. Rounded to $000, the total value for publicly traded securities in the 1929 Memorandum Pre-Crash is $45,223(000).

Composition

The portfolio of publicly traded securities (pre-Crash) extracted from the 1929 Memorandum breaks down as follows:

1929 PRE-CRASH

ASSET ALLOCATION	$ 000	% OF TOTAL
Company Stocks	45054	99.63
Company Bonds	169	0.37
Government Bonds	n/a	n/a
Portfolio Total	45223	100.00

EQUITIES ALLOCATION	$ 000	% OF TOTAL
Canadian	20216	44.87
US	23018	51.09
Foreign	1820	4.04
Equities Total	45054	100.00

EQUITIES ALLOCATION BY SECTOR	$ 000	% OF TOTAL
Automotive	1518	3.37
Banks, Trust, and Insurance	2264	5.03
Cement	–	–
Food Processing	7194	15.97
Investment Trusts	1492	3.31
Manufacturing	1770	3.93
Metals and Mining	3954	8.78
Neon and Advertising Signage	1163	2.58
Oil	497	1.10
Pulp and Paper	644	1.43
Retail	546	1.21
Rubber	375	0.83
Textiles	4363	9.68

EQUITIES ALLOCATION BY SECTOR	$ 000	% OF TOTAL
Transport	2142	4.75
Utilities	15751	34.96
Other	1381	3.07
Sector Totals	45054	100.00

Exposition

The date of the 23 September 1929 Memorandum is noteworthy, recording as this document does valuations for holdings of McConnell's largest investment vehicle one month prior to the Crash of October 1929 and just three weeks after the market (as measured by the Dow Jones Industrial Average [DJIA]) had peaked on 3 September 1929.[25]

As if to underscore the degree to which McConnell's investments for his sugar company are representative of the time, we note that the portfolio is heavily invested in utilities holding companies. Fully 35 per cent of McConnell's portfolio is concentrated in a sector (22 per cent US; 13 per cent Canadian) identified as much with the speculative excesses of the 1920s as telecom companies would be in the 1990s.

Notable, too, is McConnell's stake in US investment trusts (3 per cent), themselves highly invested in utilities. Even his $1 million investment in Sun Life (2.3 per cent) could be viewed as a proxy for investment in utilities companies of the period. Thus, the total exposure to utilities comes to just over 40 per cent.

The interest in the neon signage – with positions in ten related companies or subsidiaries of Claude Neon Lights (N.Y.) – is of interest. Also significant are holdings in cinema and tobacco and a recent, sizeable purchase of Imperial Chemical Industries shares. As in 1921, holdings in the food processing, textiles, and utilities sectors were considerable in 1929, but McConnell's sale of Goodwins Department Store in 1926 accounts for the decrease in the retail sector.

A large position in International Nickel highlights not only a company long associated with McConnell personally but also a new sector (metals and mining) which would increasingly become an investment mainstay of his from the late 1930s on.

There are five Dow components in McConnell's September 1929 refinery investment holdings – Chrysler, International Nickel, National Cash Register, Union Carbide, and US Steel.

1929 PORTFOLIO (POST CRASH)

The data for the 1929 post-Crash table derive, in part, from the same 1929 Memorandum already cited, on which C.H. McLean, refinery vice-president, pencilled in a column of stock values for 26 November 1929 (he wrote "Nov 26/29"), one month after the 24–30 October Crash.

These valuations have been compared to those published in Moody's Directories[26] to verify their contemporary accuracy. They have, in turn, been cross-referenced with surviving tax returns for St Lawrence Sugar Refineries to confirm independently that McConnell actually held these positions at the time indicated by the Memorandum.

Valuation

According to the annotations entered on the 1929 Memorandum, on 26 November 1929, the refinery's investment account of publicly traded company stocks is valued at $28,410(000) ($347,713,695 in 2008).

From the 23 September 1929 peak valuation of $45,054(000) recorded in the previous section to the valuation of $28, 410(000) for 26 November 1929, we note a decline of $16,644(000),($203,708,086 in 2008) or some 37 per cent. This was how much he lost in the Crash.

Composition

The trajectory of the peak September portfolio – downward – is highlighted by the decline in individual sectors of publicly traded securities after the 24–30 October 1929 Crash:

SECTORS	23 SEPT. 1929 $ 000	26 NOV. 1929 $ 000	DECLINE %
Advertising and Signage[27]	1163	60	-94.84
Automotive	1518	787	-48.16
Banks, Trust, and Insurance	2264	1755	-22.48
Cement	–	–	–
Investment Trusts	1492	833	-44.17
Manufacturing	1770	1106	-37.51
Metals and Mining	3954	2242	-43.30
Food Processing	7194	5170	-28.13
Oil	497	371	-25.35
Pulp and Paper	644	510	-20.81
Retail	546	459	-15.93
Rubber	375	250	-33.33
Transport	2142	1536	-28.29
Textiles	4363	3544	-18.77

SECTORS	23 SEPT. 1929	26 NOV. 1929	DECLINE
	$ 000	$ 000	%
Utilities	15751	8856	-43.77
Other	1381	931	-32.59
Portfolio Total	45054	28410	-36.94

The decline of approximately 37 per cent for the total St Lawrence Sugar Refineries investment portfolio between September and November 1929 is somewhat worse than that recorded by the DJIA for the week of the October Crash.[28]

Exposition

The above losses are striking – all the more in light of interviews and published sources indicating that McConnell anticipated the 1929 Crash and had withdrawn all his investments from the market.[29]

It is likely that McLean's pencilled valuations for "Nov 26/29" were entered onto the 1929 Memorandum at a later date. Since valuations have also been entered in an almost identical script for a less complete column marked "July 17/36," it is more than probable that both sets of valuations were entered as late as 1936,[30] possibly for McConnell's trust, estate, and charitable planning. For the sake of argument, however, it is conceivable that the valuations were made to indulge a curiosity as to what *might* have happened to the St Lawrence Sugar Refineries portfolio had it retained the holdings listed for 23 September 1929. Assigning authority to the valuations prima facie is thus problematic. It would mean estimating contemporary valuations for McConnell's holdings based on pencilled notations likely made after the fact.

Fortunately, tax returns for St Lawrence Sugar Refineries have survived.[31] These returns record not only the company's income from its investment portfolio; they also list the companies held and the dividends generated by these same companies. By correlating the companies listed in the 23 September 1929 Memorandum with those listed on the 1930 St Lawrence Sugar Refineries tax return, we can discount McLean's pencilled values as our only evidence for the condition of the portfolio post-Crash and assess the composition of McConnell's refinery portfolio for this period with much greater confidence.

Of the 120 publicly traded companies listed in the 23 September 1929 Memorandum with a value over $1000,[32] fully 75 or 62.50 per cent are listed on the 1930 tax return as having generated dividends for the refinery in 1930. More telling is the fact that these same 75 companies account for 85.57 per cent ($38,616[000]) of the *value* of the $45,054(000) 23 September 1929 Memorandum portfolio.

This 85 per cent correlation between the holdings listed in the 23 September 1929 Memorandum and those extrapolated via St Lawrence's 1930 tax return is sufficient to posit a high degree of continuity in the refinery's investment holdings for 1929–30, indicating no wholesale shift in the investment holdings of the company during this critical time.[33]

It is also important to note that many companies held in the September 1929 St Lawrence portfolio would not have reported dividends for the year 1930. Fifteen companies[34] listed in the 1929 Memorandum passed on their 1930 dividends and could not have been included on the St Lawrence 1930 tax return. Thus, the number of companies likely held beyond 23 September 1929 and through the October crash increases to 90 (or 75 per cent) of those listed in the 1929 Memorandum, accounting for 89.10 per cent or $40,145(000) of the $45,054(000) value of the 23 September 1929 Memorandum.

Consideration of the US investment trusts and the neon-related companies listed in the 1929 Memorandum further underscores the continuity between the years 1929 and 1930. Out of the twelve investment trusts McConnell held in 1929 in St Lawrence, eleven were US-based[35] – many connected with the US financier Louis Seagrave.[36] By definition, the general performance of these trusts was dismal though some actually generated small dividends for St Lawrence.[37]

Over the course of the 1930s, Moody's Directories record that Seagrave consolidated many of his investment trusts under one vehicle, American and General. Hatch similarly reorganized his trusts around the Atlas Corporation. Interestingly, the surviving St Lawrence Sugar Refineries tax returns indicate that both of these companies generated dividends for the refinery's account late into the 1930s and early 1940s.[38] Since the refinery held an interest in these successor entities, we can confidently assume that McConnell had not disposed of the Seagrave trusts in the short period between the date of the 23 September Memorandum and the week of the October 1929 Crash.

We can thus add an additional four companies to our list.[39] This brings our total to ninety-four companies or 78.33 per cent of the companies listed in the 1929 Memorandum likely to have been carried over, accounting for $40,992(000) or 90.98 per cent of its $45,054(000) value.

Of the ten neon-related companies listed in the 1929 Memorandum, only three generated dividends for St Lawrence in 1930 and were thus undoubtedly held through the 1929 October Crash. Yet the most important of these, Claude Neon Lights of New York, described by Moody's as "a holding company owning substantial minority stock in licensed companies," paid no dividends for 1930 and would not have appeared on the refinery's 1930 tax return. One of its subsidiaries, Walker and Company, did generate a 1930 dividend for St Lawrence and remained a McConnell holding (albeit transferred to the Foundation) well into the 1950s. The fate of most of the other neon subsidiaries during the 1930s remains terribly obscure, with neither a Moody's Directory listing nor contemporary newspaper listings. As in the case of the investment trusts, however, one or two subsidiaries reported dividends for St Lawrence into the late 1930s.[40]

Were we to consider that McConnell held on to the majority of these subsidiary holdings, at least until 1930, it would increase the number of companies from the 1929 Memorandum likely held over through the Crash of October and into 1930 to 101, or 84.16 per cent of the Memorandum total, accounting for $41,772(000) or 92.71 per cent of the $45,054(000) value of the 23 September 1929 Memorandum.[41]

Fourteen companies listed in the 1929 Memorandum and recorded as having paid dividends in 1930 by Moody's Directories fail to appear on the St Lawrence 1930 tax return. Ten may well have been disposed of between late 1929 and 1930.[42] But four – Sun Life, Montreal Trust, Aluminium, and Air Liquide – are known to have been held among McConnell's investment holdings after 1930. These four additional companies would bring our total to 111 companies or 88 per cent of the original 120 companies listed in the original 1929 Memorandum as having been likely carried over and held by St Lawrence during the October 1929 Crash.[43]

THE 1930S: AFTERMATH

If we compare the 1929 Memorandum with surviving St Lawrence tax returns for the later 1930s, the pattern of continuity previously confirmed still obtains to a significant degree. While the refinery's 1937 tax returns correlate with the 120 holdings listed in the 1929 Memorandum at a much lower level numerically (only 40), in terms of the more important *value* indicator, we still find continuity of $24,642(000) or 54.69 pr cent. The 1939 tax return correlates at roughly the same rate numerically (34), but at a lower value level of $19,128(000), or 42.45 per cent.

The tax returns support the conclusion that McConnell held on substantially to his original 1929 position in securities. At the same time, it is clear that, by the mid-1930s, many of the important holdings, particularly US utilities, began to be disposed of – undoubtedly at a loss. This pattern of holding/disposal is consistent with losses recorded in the minute-books of St Lawrence Sugar Refineries. We read of "substantial" "investment losses" for 1929 and, for the following years, we read as follows:[44]

SLSR INVESTMENTS	LOSSES
1929	"substantial"
1930	$1,653,612
1931	$1,756,465
1932	$1,092,513

SLSR INVESTMENTS	LOSSES
1933	$1,491,442
1934	$1,488,455
1937	$1,719,000
1938	$1,143,000
1940	$1,077,000
Total Losses	$10,921,486

Since the 1930s pre-date capital gains taxes, these losses do not appear on the St Lawrence tax returns and were recorded for private purposes. Yet, realized or not, the *record* of investment losses is very real.

After the autumn 1929 crash, markets recovered in early 1930 – only to hit real bottom in mid-1932.[45] McConnell clearly held on through 1930. Yet, since the above list indicates a record of losses throughout the 1930s, it is clear McConnell consolidated losses in certain more volatile holdings while remaining loyal to other securities.

Many company names listed in the September 1929 Memorandum simply disappear after 1930. It may well be that the rumours about McConnell getting out of the market refer to the second, less precipitous but more devastating (90 per cent) crash of 1930–32. Curiously, our run of surviving tax returns for St Lawrence omits the critical years 1931–36, so there is no evidence of whether McConnell's stock disposals occurred before severe declines hit again.

The July 1936 valuations pencilled in by C.H. McLean on the 1929 Memorandum, however, do offer some clues about the condition of the St Lawrence Refineries portfolio in the mid-1930s.[46] According to these valuations, the July 1936 St Lawrence portfolio totalled $16,516(000), or $251,311,027 in 2008 terms. It had thus declined by 63.34 per cent (or $28.5 million) from its peak valuation in September 1929.

Moreover, this represented a further 41.86 per cent decline from the portfolio's post-Crash valuation of 29 November 1929. If we add the holdings that McLean's notations had omitted[47] but that we know McConnell was holding in July 1936, our estimate of 1930s decline changes only somewhat.[48] Accordingly, the St Lawrence portfolio totalled $17,611(000) in July 1936. It had thus declined a little less – 60.91 per cent (or $27.4 million) – from the peak valuation of September 1929. Moreover, this represented a 38.01 per cent decline from the 29 November 1929 post-Crash valuation. Clearly, McConnell's St Lawrence holdings had diminished in both name and number by 1936.

In assessing the trajectory of McConnell's 1929 company portfolio through the 1930s, it is clear that it was precisely *because* its performance in the 1920s had been so spectacular that it sustained such losses for the decade after October 1929. The allocation of stocks in the 1929 portfolio, overweight in speculative utilities and investment trusts, was hardly conventional. Moreover, with only five Dow components, McConnell's portfolio did not necessarily behave in quite the same way as certain investment measures positing market recovery by 1936.[49]

We can see just how in keeping McConnell's heavy losses were to his particular asset allocation by first tracking the percentage declines of his holdings by sector as follows:

SECTOR	% DECLINE SEPT TO NOV 1929	% DECLINE SEPT 1929 TO JULY 1936	% DECLINE SEPT 1929 TO DEC 1939
Automotive	-48	-38	-61
Banks, Trust, and Insurance	-22	-67	-67
Food Processing	-28	-36	-51
Investment Trusts	-44	-94	-98
Metals and Mining	-43	-48	-41
Oil	-25	-42	-77
Retail	-16	-87	-83
Textiles	-19	-37	-49
Transportation	-28	-82	-77
Utilities	-44	-76	-84

The above chart indicates that the losses McConnell sustained were real by the only measure that counts: that of his own portfolio. No sector was immune, with utilities, retail, investment trusts, and insurance especially exposed. The sectors that held their value relatively well from the admittedly stratospheric September 1929 valuations were food processing, textiles, and metals and mining.

By also tracking the share price of the top ten holdings listed in the peak 23 September 1929 Memorandum, we can see how the trajectory of decline recorded above for the more general sector allocation obtains for specific company share holdings:

TOP TEN HOLDINGS ON 23 SEPT. 1929	SHARE PRICE SEP 1929	SHARE PRICE JUL 1936	SHARE PRICE DEC 1939
Ogilvie Flour (CAN)	600	210	(Adjusted)[50] 272
Anaconda Copper (US)	123	39	30
International Nickel of Canada (CAN)	55	50	47
Courtaulds (UK)	16	13	6
Dominion Textile (CAN)	92	68	89

TOP TEN HOLDINGS ON 23 SEPT. 1929	SHARE PRICE SEP 1929	SHARE PRICE JUL 1936	SHARE PRICE DEC 1939
Brazilian Traction (CAN)	68	13	8
Montreal Light, Heat and Power (CAN)	150	33	89
Public Service Corp. of New Jersey (US)	135	44	46
Commonwealth & Southern (US)	23	4	2
Consolidated Gas/Edison of New York (US)	167	37	31

Interesting, too, was the performance of certain other holdings long associated with McConnell. His Sun Life holding went from $3500/share in 1929 to $500/share in 1936 and $340/share in 1939. His holding in Canada Steamships went from $84/share in 1929 to $7/share in 1936 and $5/share in 1939. Massey Harris went from $55/share in 1929 to $5/share in 1936 and $5/share in 1939. Holt Renfrew common went from $125/share in 1929 to $7/share in 1936 and $15/share in 1939.

Aside from stocks in textiles (Dominion Textile held its value, going from $92/share in 1929 to $68/share in 1936 and $89/share in 1939), food processing (Canada Packers held at $100/share in 1929, $89/share in 1936. and $102/share in 1939), banks (Bank of Montreal went from $348/share in 1929 to $192/share in 1936 and $210/share in 1939), McConnell's smaller holdings in tobacco stocks suffered roughly 15 per cent declines over the decade.

There is very little evidence, then, of a mid-1930s market recovery (as measured by more abstract formulas) affecting McConnell's *real* stock holdings.

Summary

The confusion over McConnell's record during the Crash no doubt arises from a certain degree of myth making. Over time, the distinction between his anticipating the Crash and his weathering the Crash appears to have simply blurred.

The research indicates that, at least as regard his most important investment vehicle (St Lawrence Sugar Refineries), he was in 1929 most certainly not out of the market. Yet it is equally clear that he weathered the Crash and ensuing market crisis handily. He maintained his lifestyle, continued making sizeable charitable donations, and, as indicated by the listing for reorganized MacDougall and Cowans on the 1937 St Lawrence tax return, helped colleagues who fell on hard times.[51]

A more compelling explanation for McConnell's experience during the 1930s may also obtain. With a personal investment portfolio, with operating revenue from both his newspaper and sugar businesses, and with a still sizeable company portfolio, McConnell could afford to hold on.

1939 PORTFOLIO

The data for the 1939 table derive in part from 1939 entries for the St Lawrence Sugar Refineries investment ledger. In addition, since the late 1930s were marked by McConnell's preoccupation with succession and formal estate planning – he was now in his fifties – as well as his formal takeover of the Montreal *Star*, there are other investment portfolios to consider. Thus, we have also drawn on surviving investment records from 1939 for the J.W. McConnell Foundation (established 1937), the J.W. McConnell Family Trust (established 1938) and the Kathleen G./David G. Trusts,[52] and those belonging to the Montreal Star Publishing Company (formally taken over in 1938).

In the case of the Foundation, the sources relied on consist of the Foundation's full set of audited financial statements. For the family and children's trusts, the sources relied on consist of audited statements prepared by the Commercial Trust Company. In the case of the Montreal Star Publishing Company, the sources relied on consist of a full run of company tax returns.

Valuation

The value of publicly traded securities held in the combined McConnell portfolios in 1939 is estimated to have been $23,907(000) ($354,201,078 in 2008).

Reconciliation

As in the case of the 1929 table, a personal investment ledger for McConnell's own account is missing from the 1939 table.

The $23,907(000) combined portfolio consists of:

1939 INVESTMENT ACCOUNTS	CO. SHARES $ 000	CO. BONDS $ 000	GOV. BONDS $ 000	TOTALS $ 000
St Lawrence Sugar Refineries	16573	2132		18705
Trusts			3328	3328
J.W. McConnell Foundation	1687	30		1717
Montreal *Star*			157	157
				23907

Composition

The portfolios combined to represent McConnell's holdings in publicly traded securities in 1939 break down as follows:

1939

ASSET ALLOCATION	$ 000	% OF TOTAL
Company Stocks	18260	76.38
Company Bonds	2162	9.04
Government Bonds	3485	14.58
Portfolio Total	23907	100.00

EQUITIES ALLOCATION	$ 000	% OF TOTAL
Canadian	11632	63.70
US	6173	33.81
Foreign	455	2.49
Equities Total	23907	100.00

SECTOR ALLOCATION	$ 000	% OF TOTAL
Automotive	1080	5.91
Banks, Trust, and Insurance	537	2.94
Cement	490	2.68
Food Processing	3817	20.90
Investment Trusts	385	2.11
Manufacturing	292	1.60
Metals and Mining	1466	8.03
Neon and Advertising Signage	130	0.71
Oil	904	4.95
Pulp and Paper	772	4.23
Retail	75	0.41
Rubber	1163	6.37
Textiles	2739	15.00
Transport	67	0.37
Utilities	3483	19.07
Other	860	4.71
Portfolio Total	18260	100.00

Exposition

The decline in post-Crash valuations, continuing through the 1930s, is confirmed a decade later by McConnell's combined 1939 portfolio. Here, the speculative froth of the 1929 company portfolio has disappeared completely. Most striking is the shift of US assets generally, accounting for only a third in the combined 1939 portfolio as compared to just over 50 per cent in the 1929 company portfolio. Consolidation has occurred in the sector of US utilities especially. Half a dozen US utilities have disappeared, notably Wendell Willkie's Commonwealth and Southern and Floyd Carlisle's Niagara Hudson.

Notable, however, is the consistency of two McConnell mainstays – food processing and textiles. Both sectors were relatively immune from the 1930s distress. Looking forward, however, one detects an emerging sector: cement. The St Lawrence Sugar Refineries investment ledger entries begins to record McConnell's purchases of Canada Cement in 1938–39, an accumulation that would result in the very large 1950s holding in cement.

Examination of investment accounts other than St Lawrence for 1939 reflect the US-Canadian shift. The Foundation's 1939 portfolio is almost completely US in composition (85 per cent US stocks). In 1937, when McConnell transferred these stocks to the Foundation from the St Lawrence Sugar Refineries account, the composition was much the same. Interestingly, these transfers were all recorded at lower than book value, a further indication of McConnell's actual 1930s losses. This is also in marked contrast to the creation of most modern foundations, typically endowed with appreciated stock with an eye to tax advantage.

The source of the $2 million in bonds contributing to the creation of the J.W. McConnell Trust cannot be accounted for. Undoubtedly, these bonds were transferred from another account (personal) that has not survived.[53] The creation of this trust, additional to the California relatives' and children's trusts, reflects McConnell's preoccupation with estate planning in the later 1930s.

In 1939 the investment portfolio of the Montreal *Star* is negligible since McConnell took formal control of the newspaper company only in 1938. There are three Dow components in McConnell's 1939 combined portfolios: Chrysler, International Nickel, and Dupont.[54]

1951 PORTFOLIO

The data for the 1951 table derive from 1951 entries for the St Lawrence Sugar Refineries investment ledger; from 1951 tax returns for the Montreal *Star* investment portfolio; from 1951 entries for the sole surviving J.W. McConnell Personal Investment ledger; from 1951 audited statements for the J.W. McConnell Foundation; and from 1951 audited statements prepared by Commercial Trust for the J.W. McConnell Trust, the California (Relatives') Trust, and the Wilson G./John G./Kathleen G./David G. McConnell Trusts.

Valuation

The value of publicly traded securities held in the combined McConnell portfolios in 1951 is estimated to have been $86,482(000) ($726,706,955 in 2008).

Reconciliation

Unlike the 1921 and 1929 tables, derived from lone documents surviving out of the context of formal records, the data for the combined 1951 portfolios are taken from audited statements and intact investment ledgers with quoted market valuations formally recorded.

The $86,482(000) combined portfolio consists of

1951 INVESTMENT ACCOUNTS	CO. SHARES $ 000	CO. BONDS $ 000	GOV. BONDS $ 000	TOTALS $ 000
J.W. McConnell Foundation	40385	2177	1963	4140
St Lawrence Sugar Refineries	23230	625	1235	25090
Montreal *Star*	4538	170	2643	7351
J.W. McConnell (Personal)	4000	314	837	5151
Trusts	3453	147	765	4365
Totals	75606	3433	7443	86482

Composition

The portfolios combined to represent McConnell's investment holdings in publicly traded securities in 1951 break down as follows:

1951

ASSET ALLOCATION	$ 000	%
Company Stocks	75606	92.05
Company Bonds	3433	4.18
Government Bonds	3098	3.77
Portfolio Total	82137	100.00

EQUITIES ALLOCATION	$ 000	%
Canadian	53358	70.57
US	21875	28.93
Foreign	373	49.00
Equities Total	75606	100.00

SECTOR ALLOCATION	$ 000	%
Automotive	4453	5.89
Banks, Trust, and Insurance	1614	2.13

SECTOR ALLOCATION	$ 000	%
Cement	8453	11.18
Food Processing	5990	7.92
Investment Trusts	106	0.14
Manufacturing	4437	5.87
Metals and Mining	8547	11.30
Neon and Advertising Signage	206	0.27
Oil	1985	2.63
Pulp and Paper	16643	22.01
Retail	1265	1.67
Rubber	2011	2.66
Textile	4084	5.40
Transport	7752	10.25
Utilities	5325	7.04
Other	2735	3.62
Sector Totals	75606	100.00

Exposition

The combined 1951 portfolios illustrate the second wind that buoyed McConnell's investments from the start of the Second World War. Had he died prior to 1939, his legacy would have been materially quite different – especially as regards the funds made available to his charitable foundation.

The story of the 1951 combined portfolios is that of the boom in made-in-Canada materials and resources that coincided with the post-war period. McConnell's 15 per cent holding of Canada Cement dates to purchases begun in the late 1930s, not to the days of its initial merger in 1910. The boom in construction/housing after the Second World War made this an especially good investment. The same profile holds for metals and mining. If the 1930s story had been International Nickel, the post-1939 story is really the one of McConnell's aluminum investments. But, if metals are part of McConnell's investment profile, mining is not. Only Noranda, in small amounts, appears in McConnell's mid-1950s personal portfolio.

The other story of the combined 1951 portfolio is obviously pulp and paper. An investment that began in the late 1920s finally appears profitable. In the same way that the bar graph extends for utilities in 1929, here it is for pulp and paper – at 22 per cent of the value of the combined 1951 portfolio. The increase in pulp and paper holdings is traced largely in the investment portfolio of the Montreal *Star* from the late 1930s on. After a period of industry depression in the 1930s, pulp and paper stocks rebounded.

The bar graph indicates that the *value* of Canada Steamship Lines grew in this post-1939 period. A big loser in the 1929–36 portfolio, McConnell's increased 1930s holding (likely secured during the company's financial distress) participated in the company's post-war renaissance. Notable, too, is the wave of accumulation in candy in the 1940s: over 10 per cent of Fanny Farmer Candy Shops, with significant positions in Laura Secord and Lowneys.

There are only two Dow components in McConnell's 1951 combined portfolios – Chrysler and International Nickel.[55]

A Glimpse of the Interconnectedness
of McConnell's Circle

Note: McConnell's life was largely shaped by individuals associated by blood or business or both. This appendix is not meant to be a who's who or a comprehensive account of all the individuals in his story: it merely supplements the main text with emphasis on the connections of a selection of people with one another as well as with McConnell. In most groups, the names of the most important individuals are in bold type, especially if they knew McConnell. The connections here try to capture some of the variety of the life in that period, but they are only a small selection and could be expanded virtually infinitely. The abbreviations "qv" and "qqv" invite the reader to explore cross-references.

Aikins Family. James Eakins (sic) arrived in Upper Canada in 1820, from Ireland, via Philadelphia; his family converted from Presbyterianism to Methodism. One of his sons was William T. Aikins (1827–1897), the first dean of medicine at the University of Toronto, whose wife was a founder of the predecessor to the Fred Victor Mission, established by Hart Massey (qv). His other son was James Cox Aikins (1823–1904), a temperance advocate, supporter of the Dominion Church in Montreal, senator and minister in the Macdonald Government, and lieutenant-governor of Manitoba (1882–88). He set up the Manitoba and North West Loan Company to provide mortgages on properties evaluated and conveyed by his two sons. These were **(1) John Somerset Aikins**, of the realty firm of Aikins and Pepler in Winnipeg, who was closely associated with Johnston, McConnell & Allison in 1907. In 1879 he began his real-estate business and became a politician. He married a daughter of Charles C. Colby, another minister under Macdonald and a founder of the Stanstead Wesleyan College. He was a brother-in-law of Dr Charles William Colby, professor of history and a fellow governor and warm supporter of McConnell's at McGill. **(2) Sir James Albert Manning Aikins,** KC (1851–1929), knighted in 1914, counsel for the CPR in western Canada, 1881–1911. He drafted the Manitoba Prohibition Bill of 1900, was MP for Brandon in 1911–15, and then became Conservative leader in Manitoba. Also married to a Colby, he was a director and chairman (1888–1907) of Wesley College in Winnipeg and president of the Winnipeg YMCA (1879–82), having been first president of the University of Toronto YMCA in 1873. He was founder and first president of the Manitoba Bar Association and of the Canadian Bar Association. He was elected as an anti-Reciprocity MP in 1911, leader of the provincial Conservatives in 1915–16, and appointed lieutenant-governor of Manitoba, serving 1916–26. He was a leading supporter of the United Church and on the board of the Wesleyan Theological College in Montreal with McConnell.

Airlie, David Ogilvy, seventh Earl of, KT, GCVO, MC (1893–1968), lieutenant-colonel in the Scots Guards, Lord Chamberlain to Queen Elizabeth the Queen Mother in 1937–65, married to Lady Bridget Coke, daughter of the third Earl of Leicester. The Airlies became friends of the McConnells and visited Pine Avenue in 1954, as later did their second son Angus (Sir Angus Ogilvy, KCVO, PC), who in 1963 married Princess Alexandra of Kent (qv).

Alexander Family. (1) **Field Marshal Harold Alexander, first Earl of Alexander of Tunis** (1946), KG, PC, GCB, OM, GCMG, CSI, DSO, MC, first knighted in 1942 (1891–1969). A son of the fifth earl of Caledon, he became one of the great commanders of the Second World War. During Alexander's posting as governor general of Canada (1946–52), the Alexanders and the McConnells became close friends. After leaving Canada, he became minister of Defence under Churchill, and later a director of Alcan. (2) **Ghislaine Dresselhuys Alexander** (1922–2001), actress and broadcaster, daughter of Cornelius Dresselhuys by Edith du Plessis, who became the second wife of the first Viscount Kemsley (qv) and was an aunt of Renée Merandon du Plessis, wife of the second Baron Iliffe (qv). She married first Denis Alexander, brother of (1) and later sixth Earl of Caledon; second, Henry Cubitt (later fourth Baron Ashcombe), of Sonia Cubitt (qv); and third, the eighth Baron Foley.

Allan and Meredith Families. (1) **Sir Hugh Allan** (1810–1882) began business in Montreal and in 1872 tried unsuccessfully to win the contract to build the Canadian Pacific Railway. He was a director of the Richelieu and Ontario Navigation Company in 1874–76, and president of the Merchants' Bank, 1877–82, when it was the second-largest in Canada. His brother Andrew Allan (1822–1901) established a shipping firm with him in 1846–54, which became the Allan Line Steamship Company Limited in 1897. He was also president of Montreal Rolling Mills and Montreal Telegraph and Citizens' Gas, and his daughter Isabel Brenda married Henry Vincent Meredith (qv). (2) **Sir Montagu Allan**, CVO (1860–1951), son of (1), was a close friend of McConnell's for almost half a century. He was the receiver for his uncle Andrew's failed Manitoba

North Western Railway in 1894, which he amalgamated with the CPR in 1900. He was chairman of the Allan Line in 1909–12 and president of the Merchants' Bank in 1909–22. By 1912 he was president of the Acadia Coal Company, the Canadian Rubber Company, the Canadian Paper Company, the Carlton Hotel Company, and Royal Securities. He was a director of the Montreal Rolling Mills Company, the Montreal Street Railway Company, the Montreal Light, Heat and Power Company, the Ogilvie Flour Mills Company, and other companies associated with McConnell. The donor of the Allan Cup for amateur hockey, he was also a master of the Montreal Hunt, president of the Montreal Jockey Club, vice-president of the Montreal Racquet Club, a leader in the Charity Organization Society, on the management board of the Montreal General Hospital and the Society for the Prevention of Cruelty to Animals. In 1893, he married **(3) Marguerite Ethel MacKenzie**, daughter of Hector MacKenzie, head of J.G. MacKenzie & Co., drygoods merchants. She was a particularly good friend of the McConnells.

Amery and Greenwood Families. (1) Leo Amery (1873–1955), PC, CH, born in India of English and Hungarian-Jewish parentage, Fellow of All Souls, and correspondent for *The Times*, for which he wrote *The Times History of South Africa* (1900–09), and from 1911–45 an MP. His career reflected the development of Imperial thinking after the First World War, as summed up in his memoirs. In 1919, he became under secretary of State for the Colonies; in 1921, parliamentary and financial secretary of the Admiralty; in 1922, first lord of the Admiralty. He became colonial secretary in 1924 and set up the Empire Marketing Board. In 1925, he also became the first dominions secretary. In 1927–28, he toured the Dominions, and in 1929 he made a long visit to Canada. Churchill appointed him secretary of state for India and Burma in 1940–42. He married a Canadian, Florence Louise Hamar Greenwood, CI, CStJ, in 1910, sister of **(2) Hamar Greenwood** (1870–1948), first Viscount Greenwood (first baron 1929, baronet 1915, KC 1919, PC 1920), of Whitby, Ontario. His career epitomized how easily a Canadian might move into Imperial politics. He began as a Liberal MP in York County, Ontario, 1906–10; in England he became a Conservative MP for Sunderland 1910–12, and for East Walthamstow 1924–29. In 1933–38, he was treasurer of the Conservative Party and then for a year president of the British Iron and Steel Association. In the cabinet, he was under secretary of state for home affairs 1919; secretary for overseas trade 1919–20; and chief secretary for Ireland 1920–22. **(3) Captain the Hon. Simon Rodney** (1895–1966), Grenadier Guards, married Gladys Cecil Hamar Greenwood (Sadie), another sister of (2), a particularly close friend of Lil's, in 1922. He was descended from the first governor of Newfoundland, and his parents were the seventh Baron Rodney and Corisande Evelyn Vere Guest, daughter of the first Baron Wimborne (qv).

Astor of Hever, John Jacob Astor, first Baron (1956) (1886–1971). Known for most of his life as Col. John Astor, he was a descendant of the New York Astors and a younger son of the first Viscount Astor. As the chief proprietor of *The Times* newspaper (1922–66), he, with the Montrealer Sir Campbell Stuart (qv), was an important influence on McConnell's work as a newspaper proprietor. Astor's wife was Lady Violet Mary Elliott-Murray-Kynynmound (1889–1965), only daughter of the fourth Earl of Minto, governor general of Canada. She was the sister of the fifth earl, who was an aide-de-camp to the Duke of Devonshire, when the duke was governor general in Ottawa (1918–19). The fifth earl married Marion Cook (died 1976), a daughter of G.W. Cook, McConnell's early landlord in Westmount and an aunt of Mark Farrell (qv). The younger Mintos, Larry and Marion, maintained a property north of Montreal near Saran Chai. The Astors were especially warm friends of the McConnells and often in Canada; Astor received an honorary degree from McGill in 1950.

Ballantyne and Cottingham Families. (1) The Hon. Charles Colquhoun Ballantyne (1867–1950), president of Sherwin-Williams Company of Canada after its organization by McConnell in 1912, was McConnell's next-door neighbour in Dorval and one of his closest friends. The parent Sherwin-Williams Company was American and based in Cleveland; Ballantyne was its managing director in Canada from 1898 to 1911, opening offices in Toronto, Winnipeg, and Vancouver. He broke with Sir Wilfrid Laurier over Reciprocity in 1911 and became a minister under Sir Robert Borden and later a senator. In 1910, Max Aitken (qv under Beaverbrook) appointed him vice-president of the newly formed Canada Cement Company. In the same year, Ballantyne became a director of Canadian Explosives Limited (CXL), a merger of several companies in Montreal put together by Harry McGowan of Nobel's Explosives of England. CXL was the forerunner of Canadian Industries Limited (CIL). Ballantyne's wife, Ethel Maude Trenholme, was related to Mary Clarke, who worked as McConnell's secretary for decades. The Trenholmes had established Elmhurst Dairy in Montreal. **(2) Charles Trenholme Ballantyne** (1902–1966), first son of (1), practised law from 1926 with F.E. and William Meredith (qqv) in Meredith, Holden, Heward & Holden. During World War II, he served as secretary of the Anglo-French Purchasing Commission in 1940 and then of the British Supply Council until 1943. He returned to practise law with David Ross McMaster, son of Ross H. McMaster (qv), and with Theodore Meighen, son of the Rt Hon. Arthur Meighen in what became McMaster, Meighen. **(3) James Ross Ballantyne**, the second son of (1), was a stockbroker with the firm of Craig, Ballantyne, later part of MacDougall, MacDougall, McTier (qv under MacDougall). His second wife was Hazel, daughter of the second Baron Shaughnessy. **(4) Murray Gordon Ballantyne**, the third son of (1), worked briefly for CIL and taught history at Loyola College. He married Frances, daughter of George

Washington Stephens II, and became a socialist and a Roman Catholic. **(5) Walter Cottingham** (1866–1930) became sales agent for the American Sherwin-Williams and managing director of its "Canadian department" in 1897, when (1) became his sales manager. Cottingham became president of the US parent in 1909.

Beaverbrook, Maxwell Aitken, first baron (1917), first baronet (1916), and knight (1916) (1879–1964). One of the ablest and most controversial businessmen and politicians of his time, he was both a rival and an ally of McConnell's in 1909–11. After several extremely successful industrial promotions in Canada, he moved to England to become an M P (1910–16) and then a member of the House of Lords. Although always retaining close ties to Canada, in England he became minister of Information in 1918. His first wife was **Gladys Drury**, whose brother was Victor Drury, a lifelong friend of McConnell's, and his second wife was the widow of Sir James Dunn, another friend, in later life, of McConnell's. As the owner of the *Daily Express*, Beaverbrook tried unsuccessfully to hire John G. McConnell as a journalist in the 1930s. The senior McConnell did not cooperate with Beaverbrook until the latter became the British minister for aircraft production in 1940–41, when McConnell gave him $1 million to spend on Spitfires. In their later years, McConnell advised him on foundations and aided him in establishing his cultural gifts to New Brunswick, including the Beaverbrook Art Gallery.

Berry Family. (1) Camrose, William Berry, first viscount (1941), first baron (1929), first baronet (1921) (1879–1954). Editor-in-chief of the *Sunday Times* (1915–36) and the *Daily Telegraph* (1928–54). Of humble Welsh beginnings, he became chairman of Amalgamated Press Ltd and was one of the great newspaper proprietors of his time, like his brother Gomer (qv below). With their partner in the ownership of the *Daily Telegraph* and the *Financial Times*, the first Baron Iliffe (qv), they were both very close friends of McConnell's and advised him on newspaper ownership and politics. **(2) Kemsley, Gomer Berry, first viscount** (1945), first baronet (1928), and first baron (1936), G B E, (1883–1968). Chairman, Kemsley Newspapers Ltd and editor-in-chief of the *Sunday Times* (1937–59), stepfather of Ghislaine Alexander (qv). He sold his newspapers to Roy Thomson, later first Baron Thomson of Fleet. **(3) William Nicholas Berry** (1911–2006), **Baron Hartwell** (1968) and third viscount and Baron Camrose (these peerages disclaimed by him in 1995**)**, second son of (1) and chairman of the *Daily Telegraph* until its sale in 1985 to Conrad Black, later Baron Black of Crossharbour. He married Lady Pamela Smith, daughter of the first Earl of Birkenhead, lord chancellor. Sheila Berry, second daughter of (1) married the second Earl of Birkenhead, and thus two generations of the intertwined Smith and Berry families, like the Astor and Iliffe families, were well known to the McConnells.

Birks, Drummond, and Savage Families. **(1) Henry Birks** (1840–1928) joined the firm of Savage, Lyman and Co. in 1857 (see (8) below) and then founded his own firm, Henry Birks and Co., in 1879, which was incorporated in 1905. In 1895, it became Henry Birks and Sons, the largest firm of jewellers in the Dominion. **(2) William Massey Birks,** CBE (1868–1950), first son of (1), vice-president from 1904 and president from 1928 of the family firm. He was a director of Sun Life, a governor of McGill, and chairman of the joint board of theological colleges affiliated to McGill. He was also chairman of the Canadian Patriotic Fund, Red Cross, and military YMCA financial campaigns. By 1912, he had expanded his firm from Montreal to Ottawa, Winnipeg, Toronto, and Vancouver. He was one of McConnell's closest friends and allies. **(3) John Henry Birks,** second son of (1) (1870–1949), known as Harry, became vice-president of the firm in 1928. **(4) Col. Gerald Walker Birks**, OBE (1872–1950), third son of (1), became treasurer of the firm in 1892 and went to France as general supervisor of the YMCA in 1915. He married Phyllis, daughter of John W. Ross (qv). **(5) J. Earl Birks** (1876–1948), a nephew of (1), married Salina Torrance Savage. Their son, Lt.-Col. Arthur H. Birks, DSO, worked with Ryrie-Birks in Toronto, 1928–29, and became managing director of Birks in London, Ontario, in 1948. **(6) Lois Birks**, the youngest daughter of (2), married Charles Herbert (Bert) McLean (qv), manager of the St Lawrence Sugar Refinery. **(7) George Edward Drummond** (born 1858, unrelated to the family of Sir George Drummond) and his brother Thomas set up the Canadian Iron Corporation in 1908 and the Lake Superior Corporation in 1909, as well as the Drummond, McCall Co. (with J.T. McCall). One of Drummond's daughters, Lilian, married (2), and their first son was named George Edward Drummond Birks. Another Drummond daughter, Kathleen, married first Harold Pease, son of E.L. Pease, general manager of the Royal Bank of Canada, and second C. Gordon Cockshutt, chairman of Cockshutt Farm Equipment Ltd., the firm associated with Col. Henry Cockshutt, lieutenant-governor of Ontario and a director of the Bank of Montreal with McConnell. **(8) Savage Family**. From 1855 to 1860, in the firm of Lyman(s), Savage, Alfred Savage worked with the brothers Benjamin and Henry Lyman in a drug business founded in 1800. The firm later became known as Lyman, Knox, with J.W. Knox (qv) as its principal. This was the same Savage family associated with (1) and (5). The connections between McConnell and the Savages are obscure, although a Savage was his best man and John G. Savage had a farm just northwest of McConnell's first house in Dorval. One of Savage's daughters married the Liberal politician Brooke Claxton. A granddaughter married the second J.W. Knox, son of Frank Knox, McConnell's lieutenant and grandson of the first J.W. Knox (qqv).

Bourne, Dr Wesley (1886–1965) was an anaestheologist and professor at McGill, whose work was actively supported by McConnell and who attended McConnell during surgery on his hand in Chicago. In 1915, he became assistant anaesthetist at

The Royal Victoria Hospital and in 1926 he joined the staff at the Women's Pavilion. In 1945, he founded the McGill department of anesthesia and in 1954 he was made emeritus professor of anesthesia. His son **Lt.-Col. John Bourne**, CVO, married Joan, daughter of Sidney Dawes (qv). Bourne succeeded Dawes as president of Atlas Construction Co. Ltd. and was also the commanding officer of the Black Watch (The Royal Highland Regiment) of Canada.

Brand and Ford Families. (1) Robert Henry Brand (1878–1963), first Baron Brand (created in 1946), fourth son of the second Viscount Hampden and thus a relation of Lord Willingdon, was a Fellow of All Souls, long-time managing director of Lazard Brothers, a member under Joseph Flavelle of the Imperial Munitions Board of Canada, 1916–18; head of the British Food Mission in Washington, 1941–44, representative of His Majesty's Treasury in Washington, 1944–46, and chairman of the British Supply Council in Washington, 1945–46. He married Phyllis, one of the famous Langhorne sisters of Virginia, another of whom, Nancy, married the Anglo-American Waldorf Astor, second Viscount Astor (and was thus the sister-in-law of Lord Astor of Hever (qv)). Brand's daughter Virginia's second husband was **(2) Sir Edward William Spencer Ford**, GCVO, KCB, ERD, OStJ (1901–2006). He tutored the son of Alan Lascelles, private secretary to Lord Bessborough in Ottawa, and then King Farouk of Egypt. In London, he served as deputy private secretary to King George VI under Lascelles in 1946–52, and then in the same position under Queen Elizabeth II, the first two private secretaries following Lascelles being Sir Michael (later Lord) Adeane, a former aide-de-camp in Ottawa to the Lord Bessborough (qv) and then to Lord Tweedsmuir (qv), and Sir Martin (later Lord) Charteris, all three private secretaries being friends of the McConnells.

Burton Family. (1) Charles Luther Burton (born 1876) worked as an office boy in a law office and then as an inventory clerk for H.H. Fudger, a fancy-goods merchant. In 1882, a Scottish draper, Robert Simpson, had founded his own store in Toronto, but he died suddenly in 1897, and after his death Joseph Flavelle, A.E. Ames, and Fudger, all members of the Sherbourne Street Methodist Church, bought his chattels and stock in trade. Fudger reorganized his own wholesale fancy-goods business and made Burton a partner. In 1911, Fudger (now president of Simpson's) hired Burton as assistant general manager of Simpson's, under James Wood. Wood was the link among Simpson's, Goodwins, and Eaton's. He became a director of Goodwins in 1912 and negotiated the sale of it to Eaton's in 1925, after having become the secretary of the latter. Burton came to know McConnell in about 1912, when he became, in addition to his duties at Simpson's, acting general manager of Murphy's in Montreal. By this time, Senator G.A. Cox had taken over his son-in-law Ames's interest in Simpson's and greatly expanded the store, in addition to buying Murphy's. Burton was active in the Canadian Patriotic Fund campaigns during the Great War, and in the YMCA for much of his life. In 1920 Flavelle sold his meatpacking company, which was taken over by McConnell's friend J.S. MacLean, and took over most of the management of Simpson's, although Fudger remained president. Burton did not get along with Flavelle, and in 1925 and 1929, with the aid of J.H. Gundy (qv under Holt), he finally took control of Simpson's from Flavelle and the Cox heirs. McConnell greatly admired Burton's memoirs, *A Sense of Urgency* (Toronto: Clarke, Irwin & Company Limited, 1952).

Cavendish, Edward Simon Myles (1928–1947) was the only son of Lady Gweneth Frida Cavendish, a sister of Lord Bessborough (qv), and her second husband, Col. Henry Voltelin Cavendish, CBE, MVO, DL. Lady Gweneth had been married previously to the Hon. Windham Baring, managing director of Baring Brothers, who had died in 1922, and they had three sons – Robin (particularly close to the McConnells), Mark, and Patrick Baring. Patrick's death in action in May 1940 provoked Lady Gweneth to send her youngest son to the McConnells to live with George Ponsonby (qv), James Ashley Cooper, Lord March, and Lord Nicholas Gordon Lennox. (qqv).

Colby, Charles W., PhD, DCL, LLD, born in 1867 and educated at Stanstead College, McGill, and Harvard, was a director of the Canadian Bank of Commerce, Moore Corporation Limited, the Dominion Wire Rope and Cable Co., the F.N. Burt Co., the American Sales Book Co., and the Pacific Manifolding Co., and vice-president of Asbestos Corporation Ltd. and the Goulds Pump Co., as well as chairman of the Remington Rand Co. With strong Methodist antecedents, he also became briefly the first fulltime professor of history at McGill. He refused the offer of the chancellorship of McGill and favoured McConnell for the position. Two members of his family married into the Aikins family (qv).

Cowans and Paterson Families. (1) Percy Cowans (1878–1954), one of McConnell's closest friends, was the son of Robert Cowans by his second wife Elizabeth Parsons, whose father, E.H. Parsons, became editor of the *Daily Telegraph* of Montreal, the short-lived paper that briefly absorbed the *Herald* in 1912. By his first marriage, Robert had had a son, John, who was managing director of the Cumberland Coal and Railway Co. from 1889. Robert's cousin, the broker Edgar Mill McDougall, son of the iron-founder John McDougall and his wife Mary Cowans (apparently the sister of Robert Cowans), was vice-president of Cumberland in addition to being president of the John McDougall Iron Works Co. (later the Canada Iron Corporation). Col. F.C. Henshaw (qv), McConnell's first mentor in Montreal in 1901, was married to a daughter of John McDougall and thus related to both Robert Cowans and Edgar Mill McDougall. Percy Cowans became a director of Cumberland Coal in 1908 and a governor of the Montreal Stock Exchange in the following year. In 1893 Cumberland became associated with the Dominion Coal Co. of Cape Breton, owned by a syndicate led by the Boston financier Henry M. Whitney (the developer of electric tramways in Boston), with James Ross (of the CPR syndicate) succeeding Whitney as president in 1901 and F.L. Wanklyn becoming vice-president in 1903. The Rosses and the Wanklyns were connected to McConnell over two generations, socially and in business. Between themselves, the Cowanses and the McDougalls were also connected for two generations. Purves, son of Edgar Mill McDougall (as late as 1912 still a vice-president of Cumberland Coal and president of the John McDougall Caledonian Iron Works Co. Ltd.), joined Percy Cowans in forming the brokerage firm of McDougall and Cowans, of which McConnell was a major client for his entire life. Percy Cowans had attended the High School of Montreal and then gone out to Alberta, where he worked as a cowboy and developed his horsemanship. In addition to his half-brother John Cowans, Percy had one sister and three full brothers. His sister Amy married George Lighthall Cains, a partner of the wholesalers Greenshields Limited. Amy was a fundraiser for the Montreal Maternity Hospital. One of the two Cains daughters, Elizabeth, married Captain Herbert Paton Holt, son of Sir Herbert Holt and Lady Holt (who had been born Jessie Paton, daughter of Andrew Paton, the textile-manufacturer of Sherbrooke). The other, Olsa, married Group Captain Richard Dawes (brother of Sidney Dawes, qqv), who joined McDougall, Cowans. One of Percy's brothers, Russell, was married to Doris Allan (daughter of Andrew Alexander Allan, son of Andrew Allan and nephew of Sir Hugh Allan, qqv). After nine years at the brokerage firm of Greenshields, he joined Percy, managing the Winnipeg office of McDougall & Cowans in 1910–12. McDougall and Cowans, established in 1900, became the biggest brokerage house in Canada, with offices from Halifax to Vancouver. Among its brokers over two generations were Purves McDougall and Purves McDougall, Jr, Russell Cowans and Russell Cowans, Jr, John Cowans (son of Percy), and Richard Dawes (qv). The senior Percy Cowans had married Mabel Cassils (1880–1937), whose brother Charles was representative in Canada of Carnegie Steel, and was connected to the McIntyre family of the CPR and Canadian Light and Power. Percy and Mabel Cowans had two daughters, Ruth (married to Allan Mackay, a cowboy from Lethbridge, son of Senator Robert Mackay), and Anna (Mrs Alex Paterson). They also had three sons – Percy and John the stockbrokers and Fred, a dealer in china. Among Percy's grandchildren, Ruth Cowans Mackay's daughter married the lawyer David MacKenzie, of the same family as Lady (Montagu) Allan (qv). Anna Cowans Paterson's son James married Rosalie, daughter of Senator C.C. Ballantyne (qv). **(2) Alex Paterson** (Alexander Thomas Paterson (III)). With his brother Hartland MacDougall Paterson, Alex ran the brokerage firm of Paterson & Co. Their grandfather, Alexander Thomas Paterson (I) (1850–1909), was a director of the Bank of Montreal and a founder of the Royal Victoria Hospital, married to Geraldine MacDougall, sister of Hartland St Clair MacDougall (qv). Alexander Thomas Paterson (II) (1861–1931) married Isobel Serafina Mackenzie, whose cousin Marguerite Mackenzie married Sir Montagu Allan (qv). The daughter of Alexander Thomas Paterson II, Grace Elspeth, married Sidney Dawes, brother of Richard Dawes (qqv).

Cubitt, Sonia, OBE, DStJ (1900–1986). Daughter of the Hon. George Keppel, her mother was a mistress of King Edward VII. In 1930 she married, and in 1947 divorced, Ronald Cubitt, later third Baron Ashcombe. Their son, Henry, the fourth Baron Ashcombe, married Ghislaine Dresselhuys Alexander (qv). Their daughter, Rosemary Cubitt, married Major Bruce Shand and became the mother of Camilla (Mrs Andrew) Parker-Bowles, who later married Charles Prince of Wales, adopting the style of Duchess of Cornwall. Sonia Cubitt was connected to the McConnells through Lord Kemsley (qv) and Eric Harrington (qv), a partner of her husband's, and she lived briefly in Montreal.

Dawes, Hastings, and Harrington Families. (1) Norman James Dawes (1874–1967) was president and managing director of National Breweries Ltd. and a director of the Royal Trust Co., Dominion Bridge Co. Ltd., Dominion engineering Co. Ltd., B.J. Coghlin Ltd., Atlas Construction Co. Ltd., Consolidated Paper Corporation Ltd., Wabasso Cotton Co., Dominion Rubber Co., Shawinigan Water and Power Co., Ice Manufacturing Co. Ltd., Canadian Arena Co., Canadian Investment Fund Ltd., and Dominion Scottish Investment Ltd. He was president of the Montreal Board of Trade and chairman of the Financial Federation. His house on Pine Avenue was next to the McConnells' and he was a close friend of both. His daughter Elizabeth married Ernest LeMesurier, the cartoonist; his daughter Patricia married Robert Wakeham Pilot, the painter; his son Ormiston married Jean, daughter of Charles W. Cassils, which made Ormiston a son-in-law of Percy Cowans. **(2) Sidney Dawes**, MC (1888–1968) married Grace Elspeth, daughter of Alexander Thomas Paterson II. He was the president of Atlas Construction, and his daughter Joan married John Bourne (qv). **(3) Richard Dawes**, DFC (1897–1962), of Macdougall and Cowans, married Edyth Lighthall Cains and his daughter Jane married R.D. Peter Yuile. The four Yuile sisters were closely connected to the McConnells. Gail married Algernon Lucas, founder of Selwyn House School; Marguerite married Jack Watson, probably McConnell's closest social friend; Jane married an American diplomat, Philip Brown, and was associated with the decoration of the Pine Avenue house; and Helen married Charles Hodgson (qv). **(4) Hazel Hastings,** a close friend of Kit McConnell's, was the daughter of John Ogilvie Hastings, who was closely associated with the broker A.J. Nesbitt (qv) and then with the firm of Ryan, Grier and Hastings, following which he became a director of Hanson Brothers. He was married to a daughter of H.A. Ekers, former mayor of Montreal. Ekers Brewery was one of the companies amalgamated by

Norman Dawes to form National Breweries. In 1939, Hazel Hastings married **(5) Eric Harrington**, president of Anglin Norcross Corporation Ltd. and a director of Holland & Hannen and of Cubitts Ltd. of London (see Cubitt, Sonia). Her sister, Joan, married the brother of Eric Harrington, Conrad, who became president of the Royal Trust Co. and chancellor of McGill University. Eric and Conrad were sons of Bernard J. Harrington, a geologist and son-in-law of Sir William Dawson, principal of McGill.

de la Rozière, Lieutenant-Colonel Comte Richard (1902–1970) had been a pilot in France before the war, and came to Montreal in 1940. He was a descendant of the Marquis Carlet de la Rozière, a maréchal-de-camp ennobled by King Louis XV. He was a regular guest of the McConnells during the Second World War, when he was flying aircraft out of Dorval. After the war, he trained pilots for Air France in Reading, Pennsylvania, and he piloted the first direct commercial flight between New York and Paris. In 1951, he married and moved to Mexico City for the remainder of his life. His wife, Ginette, had a daughter by another marriage who married the Hon. Nicholas Berry, second son of Lord Hartwell (Michael Berry. qv), himself the second son of McConnell's friend the first Viscount Camrose (William Berry, qv).

Endicott Family. The Rev. James Endicott (1865–1954) served with the Methodist Home Mission in western Canada. Under the inspiration of John Mott of the YMCA, he worked with the West China Mission in 1907–10. He was general secretary for foreign missions for the Methodist Church and then the United Church (1913–25), and he was moderator of the United Church, 1926–28. One of his daughters married H.P. Gundy, brother of the broker J.H. Gundy (qv). His elder son, the Rev. James Gareth Endicott (1898–1993), sponsored by the Timothy Eaton Memorial Sunday School, joined the West China Mission with the Rev. R.O. Jolliffe. Like Jolliffe, J.G. Endicott was inspired by the founding of the CCF by J.S. Woodsworth, and he won the Stalin Peace Prize in 1952. To McConnell's horror, E.B. Jolliffe, the leader of the CCF and apparently a relation of R.O. Jolliffe, came within a few seats of forming the government of Ontario in the general elections of 1943. This event provoked McConnell's highly controversial cultivation of Premier Maurice Duplessis of Quebec, after he had been repudiated by both McConnell and the electorate as a whole in the provincial elections of 1939, and Duplessis's re-election in 1944.

Farrell Family. (1) Gerald Farrell, stockbroker from Halifax briefly with Royal Securities in Montreal, married to Eileen O'Meara, died in 1919. **(2) Desmond Farrell**, son of (1), married Raymonde Chevalier, a granddaughter of Senator L.-J. Forget (qv). **(3) Charles Farrell**, son of (1), married Lady Katharine Paget, twin sister of the Marquess of Anglesey. **(4) Mark Farrell** (1913–2005), son of (1). Educated at Ampleforth, he obtained his Bachelor of Commerce degree from McGill. He articled for Macdonald Currie, became a socialist and managing editor of the *Canadian Forum* in Toronto, and in 1946 joined J.G. McConnell and Davidson Dunton as sales manager for the *Standard* in Montreal and worked to new obtain new printing presses for *Weekend Magazine*. Among his cousins were the four daughters of George W. Cook, McConnell's early landlord in Westmount. One became Countess of Haddington, a friend of McConnell's, and another became Countess of Minto (qv under Astor).

Finley Family. William Copeland Finley, son of Samuel Finley, born in Montreal in 1865, was head of Finley Smith & Co. Ltd., wholesalers of woollens and tailors' trimmings from its establishment in 1895. He was vice-president of Montreal Tramways (under E.A. Robert) and a director of Montreal Cottons, Canadian Light and Power, Arena Garage Ltd, and the Montreal Industrial Law Company, and president of the Boy Scouts' Association of Quebec. His brother was Dr. Frederick Gault Finley, CB (1861–1940), professor of clinical medicine and honorary librarian at McGill University and principal physician at the Montreal General Hospital with Dr. Henri-Amédée Lafleur. Dr Finley was a close friend of McConnell's from 1913 onwards.

Fleming Family. **(1) James Fleming**, McConnell's first employer, at the Fleming Estate in 1892, was a seedsman and florist. From 1877, he pursued a career as alderman for St John's Ward. Especially given the small size of Toronto at this time, it is possible that James Fleming was related to **(2) Robert John Fleming** (1854–1925), a Methodist who became president of the Dominion Prohibitory Alliance in 1895. Robert was elected in 1884 as alderman (1886–90) and then as mayor of Toronto in the annual election of 1891 (taking office in 1892), re-elected the following year on a strong temperance platform, and then again in 1896. In 1904, he joined the Toronto Railway Company, soon becoming general manager of it and other utility companies associated with William Mackenzie and Henry Pellatt. One of his nephews was McConnell's friend Sir Thomas White, who became general manager of National Trust in 1901 and served as the dominion minister of Finance from 1911 to 1919.

Forget Family. **(1) Senator Louis-Joseph Forget,** owner of the Montreal Street Railway. Forget's daughter Marguerite married the broker Armand Chevalier. The Chevaliers had three children. Paul, a physician serving in Canadian diplomatic missions overseas, married Marie-Claire, daughter of Kenneth Rea, McConnell's architect. Raymonde, presented at Court with Kit, was married first to the broker Desmond Farrell (brother of the journalist Mark Farrell, qv). **(2) The Hon. Lt.-Col. Sir Rodolphe Forget**, MP (knighted in 1911), born in Terrebonne in 1861, joined the Montreal Stock Exchange in 1890 and was chairman from 1908 to 1911. Until 1907, he worked with his uncle (1). By 1912 he was president of the Richelieu and Ontario Navigation Company, the Quebec and Saguenay Railway, the Canadian Car and Foundry Company, the Quebec Railway, Light, Heat and Power Company, and the Eastern Canada Steel and Iron Works Limited.

Gordon Lennox Family. (1) Elizabeth Grace Hudson, wife of Charles Henry Gordon Lennox, the ninth Duke of Richmond, was a niece of Lady Willingdon (qv). The Duchess met the McConnells in New Delhi in 1936, and her sister and two sons stayed with the McConnells in Montreal in 1940. **(2) Charles Henry Gordon Lennox, Earl of March and Kinrara**, born in 1929 and educated at Eton and at William Temple College, Rugby, later served as a second lieutenant in the King's Royal Rifle Corps and became a chartered accountant and active in education and church affairs. In 1992 he succeeded his father as tenth Duke of Richmond and fourth Duke of Gordon, as the Duc d'Aubigny in the peerage of France. He was a chartered accountant and chancellor of the University of Sussex and lord lieutenant of West Sussex. **(3) Lord Nicholas Charles Gordon Lennox**, KCMG, KCVO (1931–2004), educated at Eton and Worcester College, Oxford, also served in the King's Royal Rifles Corps and joined HM Diplomatic Service. He served in Washington, Santiago, and Paris and ultimately as Her Britannic Majesty's ambassador at Madrid. He was a governor of the BBC and a director of Southeby's

Greenshields Family. (1) Edward Black Greenshields (1850–1917) was head of the family firm of Greenshields Limited. Founded in 1833 as S. Greenshields and Son, this drygoods firm was absorbed in 1933 into the firm of Hodgson, Sumner. E.B. Greenshields, a grandson of the founder, had joined it in 1869 and was its sole owner by 1893. He had incorporated Greenshields Limited in 1903 and ran it until his death. His brother **(2) James Naismith Greenshields,** QC, was chief counsel for Louis Riel in 1885 and closely involved with McConnell as president of the Montreal-London Securities Corporation. Another brother, **(3) Robert Alfred Ernest Greenshields,** became chief justice of the Superior Court of Quebec and also closely associated with McConnell.

Griffith Family. The Rev. Thomas Griffith (1844–1912), McConnell's father-in-law, was born in Harrowsmith, near Kingston, Ontario. He married Agnes Edmondson of Etobicoke. Ordained in Hamilton in 1868, he was a Primitive Methodist until 1883, after which he was a minister of the new Methodist Church of Canada. His charges included Euclid Avenue and Carlton Street in Toronto, Orangeville, Brampton, Broadway Church in Toronto, Brockville, Quebec City, Douglas Church in Montreal, and First Church in St. Thomas. He obtained his MA and PhD degrees by correspondence from the Wesleyan University in Bloomington, Indiana. While pastor at the Wesleyan Chapel in Quebec City, 1899–1902, he made the acquaintance of Lorne Webster, and through him began the long association of the McConnells with the Websters. Lorne Webster moved to Montreal in 1911 but remained a supporter of the Wesleyan Chapel until its 1931 union with the Chalmers Church to form the Chalmers-Wesley United Church. In 1941, the former Wesleyan Chapel was restored by Webster and became the Institut Canadien. At the Douglas in 1902–05, Griffith was president of the Montreal Conference, with Salem Bland as his vice-president.

Hardinge Family. (1) Caryl Nicholas Charles Hardinge, fourth Viscount Hardinge (1905–1979), seventh Hussars, educated at Sandhurst, had succeeded to his peerage in 1924 on the death of his father. Hardinge's sister Ruby was married to Captain Beaumont-Nesbitt, brother of Mrs. R.B. Osborne, secretary to Lady Willingdon. As an aide-de-camp to Willingdon, Hardinge met his wife **(2) Margaret (Margot) Fleming**, a granddaughter of Sir Sandford Fleming. Their son **(3) Nicholas Hardinge, fifth Viscount Hardinge** (1929–1984), married Zoe Molson, only child of Senator Hartland de M. Molson. Their daughter **(4) Gaye Hardinge** married Pierre Raymond, son of Air Vice Marshal Adélard Raymond (qv). Their daughter **(5) Caroline Hardinge** married John Worsley, brother of Katharine Worsley, later Duchess of Kent (qv).The Hardinges were friends and neighbours of the McConnells over many decades. David McConnell, the youngest son of Jack and Lil, was a page at the wedding of (1) and (2) and Royden McConnell, the adopted son of John G. McConnell, was a page at the wedding of (5).

Henshaw Family. (1) F.W. Henshaw married Maria, daughter of John Scott of London and sister of Dr W.E. Scott, professor of anatomy at McGill and father of the army padre Canon (later Archdeacon) F.G. Scott and thus grandfather of the law professor Frank Scott. **(2) Col. Frederick C. Henshaw** (1851–1907), McConnell's mentor in the sale of Standard Chemical stock in 1901, was vice-consul of Uruguay and Argentina, commanding officer of the Victoria Rifles, and above all a great sportsman. Most notably, Henshaw was connected with the stockbrokers Senator L-.J. Forget and Forget's nephew Rodolphe (qqv). When his sister Mary married Forbes Angus, the eldest son of R.B. Angus, president of the CPR and the Bank of Montreal, Henshaw became connected to Mary's siblings, all of whom became part of the McConnell's circle. Among these were Edith, married to the railway engineer F.L. Wanklyn (of the Toronto and Montreal transit systems), Maud, married to Dr. W.W. Chipman, Elspeth, married to the broker Charles Meredith, and Margaret, married to Dr C.F. Martin, dean of medicine at McGill.

Hodgson Family. The five Hodgson brothers, sons of Jonathan (1827–1914) and Margaret Cassils Hodgson (sister of Jane Allan Cassils, who married Duncan McIntyre, first vice-president of the CPR, under the presidency of George Stephen, first Baron Mount Stephen) were Charles Jonathan, John Cassils, Archibald Arthur, William Cassils, and Thomas Emerson. C.J. Hodgson had first worked for the family dry-goods firm of Hodgson, Sumner, and then with his brother John in J. & C. Hodgson as manufacturers of wrought-iron pipe, later absorbed into Montreal Rolling Mills and the Steel Company of Canada. From 1902 to 1912, he worked as a stockbroker with George R. Marler in Marler & Hodgson. In 1913, he established the brokerage house of C.J. Hodgson & Co. (later Deacon, Hodgson, when his business merged with that of McConnell's first stockbroker in Toronto). A.A. Hodgson, who scored the winning goal of the first Stanley Cup hockey final, married his cousin Mary, daughter of Duncan McIntyre. Their son Duncan McIntyre Hodgson married Hylda, daughter of J.K.L. Ross and granddaughter of the railway promoter James Ross (who had been an early partner of Herbert Holt), whose house McConnell was to buy for the faculty of law at McGill. The James Ross house (later known as Chancellor Day Hall) was to the south of the Duncan McIntyre house, known as Craguie, which was given by McIntyre descendants to McGill in 1947 and became the site of the McIntyre Medical Building. Mrs A.A. Hodgson's sister, Jean McIntyre, married Dr L.L. Reford, brother of Robert Reford (who was married to Elsie Meighen, niece of Lord Mount Stephen). Dr and Mrs L.L. Reford, Mrs Hartland Brydges MacDougall (qv), and Mrs W.H. Clark-Kennedy all joined Mrs A.A. Hodgson as the chief benefactors, with McConnell and Sir Herbert Holt, of the Montreal Neurological Institute in 1931. W.C. Hodgson, a lacrosse champion, was vice-president of Hodgson, Sumner & Co. Ltd. and later director of the merger of Greenshields, Hodgson & Racine Ltd. (1933). The investment dealer George Ritchie Hodgson (of Hodgson, Roberton & Laing, founded in 1928), a son of T.E. Hodgson, was the first Canadian to win two gold medals at the Olympic Games (for swimming, in Stockholm in 1912). Also of the younger generation, David Yuile Hodgson, whose mother was one of four sisters close to the McConnells, was at McGill with David McConnell, the youngest son of J.W. McConnell.

Holland, Charles Cushing. Charles Cushing Holland succeeded as manager of his father's paper company in 1882. Holland began an additional career as a real-estate developer and became a director of the Linton Apartments, a 1912 development on Sherbrooke Street, where two of the Ross brothers were to live. He was a governor of the Montreal General Hospital, vice-president of the YMCA and the Metropolitan Council of the Methodist Church, recording steward of the Dominion Methodist Church, director of the Old Brewery Mission and the French Institute, and member of the Laymen's Methodist Dominion Council. Later he was a member of the Dominion-Douglas Church. His daughter married John W. Ross (qv).

Holt and Gundy Families. (1) Sir Herbert Samuel Holt, by the time of his death in 1941 at the age of eighty-five, had been partially retired for eleven years but was still chairman of Montreal Light, Heat and Power Consolidated and of the Royal Bank of Canada and president of Montreal Trust, London Canadian Investment Corporation, Hampstead Land & Construction Co.; chairman and vice-president of Montreal Cottons Ltd.; chairman of Andian National Corporation, Beauharnois Power Corporation, Dominion Textile Co. Ltd.; vice-president, member of the executive committee and director, Consolidated Mining & Smelting Co. of Canada Ltd., and member of the executive committee and director, Canadian Pacific Railway Co. In addition, he was director of Anglo-Canadian Pulp & Paper Mills Ltd., British Columbia Power Corporation, Canada Cement Co. Ltd., Canadian Airways Ltd., Canadian Bronze Co. Ltd., Canadian General Electric Co. Ltd., Cedars Rapids Manufacturing & Power Co., Charles Walmsley & Co. (Canada), Consolidated Bakeries of Canada Ltd., Dominion Bridge Co. Ltd., Dominion Coal Co. Ltd., Dominion Engineering Works Ltd., Dominion Steel & Coal Corporation Ltd., Dominion Tar & Chemical Co. Ltd., Gillette Safety Razor Co., Holt, Renfrew & Co., Howard Smith Paper Mills Ltd., Hydro-Electric Bond & Share Corporation, Minneapolis, St. Paul & Sault Ste. Marie Railway Co., Montreal Island Power Co., Ogilvie Flour Mills Co. Ltd., Ogilvie Grain Co. Ltd., Paton Manufacturing Co. Ltd., Provincial Light, Heat & Power Co., Quebec-New England Hydro-Electric Corporation, Ritz-Carlton Hotel Co., Shawinigan Water & Power Co., Simpson's Ltd., The Robert Simpson Co. Ltd., Sun Life Assurance Co., Tuckett Tobacco Co. Ltd., and West Kootenay Power & Light Co. Ltd. Even by 1928, Holt had been not only president of the Royal Bank, the St Maurice Valley Corporation , Montreal Light, Heat and Power, the Belgo-Canadian Paper Company and Montreal Trust, but was also vice-president of the Dominion Textile Company and the Montreal Cotton Company; chairman of the Port Alfred Pulp & Paper Company; and a director of the CPR, the Canada Paper Company, the Pennsylvania Water & Power Company, the Canadian General Electric Company Limited, the Imperial Life Assurance Company of Canada, the British Empire Steel Corporation, the Monterey Railway, Light & Power Company, Ogilvie Flour Mills Company Limited, Price Brothers & Company Limited, the Shawinigan Water & Power Company, the Sun Life Assurance Company of Canada, the St. Maurice Power Company, the Paton Mills Manufacturing Company, the Ritz-Carlton Hotel Company Limited, and the International Power Securities Corporation. He seems to have been unrelated to John H. Holt, the founder of Holt Renfrew. **(2) J.H. Gundy** joined (1) in about 1928 to form Holt, Gundy. In February 1928, it acquired the insolvent British Empire Steel Corporation, the successor to the Dominion Iron and Steel Corporation. In March, Holt, Gundy, George Montgomery, and C.B. McNaught (qv) incorporated the Dominion Steel and Coal Corporation to take over all the securities of various predecessor companies, largely associated with McDougall and Cowans: Dominion

Coal, Dominion Iron and Steel, Dominion Public Utilities, Cumberland Railway and Coal, Nova Scotia Steel and Coal, British Empire Steel, and many others. **(3) Major Andrew Paton Holt**, a son of (1) and closely associated with McConnell in Brazilian Traction, was a partner in Andrew Holt and Company in London and Montreal and a director of the Anglo-Canadian Bond and Share Corporation, the Investment Corporation of Canada Limited (chairman), the British Columbia Power Corporation Limited, Canadian and Foreign Investment Trust Limited, Hydro-Electric Bond and Share Corporation, Investment Securities Limited, the Mexican Light and Power Company Limited, the Power Investment Corporation, and the Dominion Tar and Chemical Company Limited, Famous Players Canadian Corporation Limited, the Montreal Trust Company, Scottish Grain Distilling Co. Ltd., British Lion Film Corporation Ltd., London Express Newspaper Ltd., and Seager Evans and Co. Ltd. He served in the Great War as captain and adjutant in the 14th Canadian Battalion, Royal Montreal Regiment, and was later attached to General Headquarters, British Expeditionary Force Intelligence. He wore a monocle and lived in London for much of his life. Lord Beaverbrook tried unsuccessfully to obtain a knighthood for him.

Iliffe, Edward Mauger Iliffe, first Baron (1933), GBE (1877–1960). MP 1923–29, president of the Birmingham Post and Mail Ltd, sometime owner with William and Gomer Berry (qqv) of the *Daily Telegraph*, the *Sunday Times,* and the *Financial Times.* He and his wife, Charlotte, were among the McConnells' closest friends and they often holidayed together. His son Langton, the second baron, married Renée Merandon du Plessis, a niece of Lady Kemsley, and they spent part of their honeymoon at Dorval.

Kent Family. (1) HRH The Prince Edward, Duke of Kent, fourth son of King George V, married **(2) HRH Princess Marina, Duchess of Kent. (3) HRH Princess Alexandra of Kent** married Angus Ogilvy, a younger son of the Earl and Countess of Airlie (qv). **(4) HRH Prince Edward of Kent** (succeeded (1) as duke) married Katharine Worsley, daughter of Sir William Worsley, Bt, and her brother John Worsley married the Hon. Carolyn Hardinge (qv).

Knox Family. (1) James Wilson Knox was the son of a John Knox who was possibly from County Armagh in Ireland. J.W. Knox entered the employ of Lyman, Clare (sometimes erroneously written as "Claire") and Co. at the age of eighteen and became a partner in this pharmaceutical firm, which was reorganized into Lyman, Savage in 1860, Lyman and Sons in 1879, Lymans Ltd. in 1908, and finally the National Drug and Chemical Co. Ltd. It appears that Lyman and Sons may have become Lyman, Knox when Knox became its financial officer in 1880, but the sources are unclear. From about 1878 to 1898, he was superintendent of the Methodist Sunday school in Point St. Charles. The Knoxes owned much of what became the City of Verdun, and they are still commemorated by a street there. He spent the following twenty years as superintendent of the Sunday school at the Douglas Methodist church. He was a regular lay delegate to both the Montreal and the general Methodist conferences, a director of the YMCA, and a governor of the Wesleyan Theological College and of the Bible Society of Montreal. His wife, Frances Hannah Hadley (1849–1939), was a life member of the Women's Missionary Society and also taught at the Douglas Sunday School. **(2) Frank J. Knox** (1878–1951), son of (1), began his career with the Lyman Knox Company and then with Montreal Securities; with C.H. McLean he ran much of the day-to-day affairs of McConnell's businesses from about 1909 until his retirement due to illness in the 1940s. He married Molly Jones, a sister of Caroline Elizabeth Jones, who married George C. Goodfellow (qv). His sister, Gertrude Knox, married Charles Herbert McLean (qv). **(3) Col. J.W. Knox**, MBE, ED (1915–98), a son of (2) and partner of Knox, Vickers, McLean, as well as commanding officer of the Black Watch. He was married to Georgina Winifred Grier, who, through her mother (Winifred Savage Grier), was a granddaughter of John George Savage and a niece of J. Earl Birks (qv) and of Brooke Claxton (minister of National Health and Welfare and of National Defence). Through her father (George Wardrope Grier), Mrs. J.W. Knox was a niece of Dr Henri Lafleur of McGill University and of Kenneth B. Thornton, general manager of the Montreal Tramways from 1930, all people well known to McConnell. G.W. Grier was son of George Arthur Grier, a lumberman in the Ottawa Valley and founder of G.A. Grier and Sons. (Charles) Brockville Grier, G.W. Grier's brother, was vice-president of this company and in 1919 he became a partner in Ryan, Grier & Hastings, a firm of stockbrokers in Montreal. John Ogilvie Hastings, another partner, was the father of Hazel Hastings Harrington. In 1950, Sir Ion Hamilton Benn, Bt., one of McConnell's oldest friends, married as his second wife Katharine Winifred Grier, daughter of C. Brockville Grier. Allan Savage was best man at McConnell's wedding in 1905, but it is unclear how he was related to other Savages.

Laing Family. (1) Peter and James Neil Laing (1864–1952) were brothers. Peter had two children, Campbell and Ruth, who married, respectively, Hazel Marshall of Calgary and Ross H. McMaster (qv). **(2) Peter Marshall Laing**, QC, married Kathleen (Kit) McConnell, only daughter of J.W. McConnell. James had a son, Murdoch (or Murdock) McLeod Laing (1894–1916), who married Florence Cruger Birks (1871–1960), a niece of Henry Birks and cousin of W.M. Birks (qqv). The elder son of Peter Marshall and Kit Laing is named after him.

McDougall Family I. These stockbroking McDougalls were associated with the Cowans family, beginning with the marriage of John McDougall (c. 1825–1892), the iron-founder, to Mary Cowans. The association continued through the partnership of their son, Edgar Mill McDougall, with Robert Cowans in the formation of the Canada Iron Corporation. It culminated in the firm of McDougall and Cowans, made up of Purves McDougall, Senior, and Percy Parsons Cowans (the son of Robert Cowans. qqv), which was the most important brokerage house in Montreal in the 1920s. When Percy and his brother Russell Cowans retired together, Purves McDougall, junior, joined Alec Christmas to form the firm of McDougall & Christmas. Another Cowans brother, Douglas (born in 1886) was an insurance broker and a partner of the E.A. Whitehead Co. John R. McDougall (born 1898 and a son of Edgar Mill McDougall) was another stockbroker, with Hanson Brothers, then Jencks Gwynne in New York, and finally with R. Moat in Montreal.

McDougall Family II. The stockbroking McDougalls are not to be confused with these political and legal McDougalls, who include the Hon. William McDougall, QC, (1822–1905), his son Mr. Justice J.M. McDougall, and his grandson, Errol Malcolm McDougall, KC (born in 1881), who worked first with McGibbon, Casgrain, Ryan and Mitchell, and then with Casgrain and McDougall.

MacDougall Family I. (1) Robert W. MacDougall (born 1848), a director of Gault Brothers. **(2) Gordon Walters MacDougall,** KC (1872–1946), son of (1), bâtonnier of the Bar of Montreal 1921–22, professor of private international law at McGill. His law partners included Eugene Lafleur, Lawrence Macfarlane, Gregor Barclay, William B. Scott, the Hon. Adrian Knatchbull-Hugesson, and J. Arthur Mathewson, of whom Barclay and Mathewson were particularly close to McConnell. The firm later became MacDougall, MacFarlane, Scott and Hugesson. Gordon was the vice-president of Shawinigan Water and Power and director of the Royal Bank of Canada. He married a daughter of William de Montmollin Marler (qv), notary and legal scholar. **(3) Robert Ernest MacDougall** (1877–1950) founded MacDougall & MacDougall with Hartland Brydges MacDougall (qv) in 1920. He married Hilda Marler, sister of Sir Herbert Marler (qv). He was the father of Barbara Helen, Gordon Howard, Elizabeth, Josephine Emma, and Diana. Barbara Helen married Senator George Buchanan Foster (Bunny), KC, MLA, a director of the Bank of Commerce and of the firm of Foster, Hannen, Watt, Leggat & Colby. **(4) Elizabeth MacDougall** (1913–2000), daughter of (3), known as Toppy and later as Topsy, had been promised $500 for not smoking until she was twenty-one. With this money she went to Asia from November 1935 to May 1936, where she met the McConnells.

MacDougall Family II. (1) Hartland St Clair MacDougall (d.1917) was a founder of the Montreal Stock Exchange. His house in Dorval, Ashburton, passed from him to his son, **(2) Hartland Leonard St Clair MacDougall**, who sold it to McConnell in 1919. The lawyer for the sale was Gordon Walters MacDougall (qv), who was both the son of the stockbroker Robert MacDougall and a brother of Robert Ernest Mac-Dougall (qv) a business partner of **(3) Hartland Brydges MacDougall**, a nephew of (1). There is some dispute about the name of the first MacDougall stockbroking firm in Montreal. There seems to have been Prentice & MacDougall but also MacDougall Bros., consisting of D. Lorn(e) and (1), which may have operated as early as 1849–50. **(4) Dugald or Douglas Lorn(e) MacDougall** (1811–1885) is said to have opened the first stockbroker's office in Montreal with John Glass in 1840. **(5) George Campbell MacDougall** joined his brothers (1) and (4) to incorporate the Montreal Stock Exchange in 1874. (4) was chairman of the Exchange in 1874–83, and (1) was chairman in 1894–95 and 1897–99. (3), born in 1876, a son of (5), married Edith, a daughter of Robert Reford MacDougall. He was chairman of the Exchange 1914–15 and in 1929 and then founded MacDougall & MacDougall with Robert E. MacDougall (qv), later MacDougall, MacDougall and MacTier. He had three sons: **(6) Hartland Campbell MacDougall**, Robert Reford, and Peter Lewis MacDougall. (6) married Dorothy Molson, eldest daughter of Col. Herbert Molson, MC. Their son, **(7) Hartland Molson MacDougall**, CVO, president of Royal Trust and vice-chairman of the Bank of Montreal, married Eve, a sister of Cynthia, Mrs David G. McConnell. Dorothy Molson MacDougall's brother, Senator Hartland de Montarville Molson, OC, OBE, was named after Hartland Brydges MacDougall. (4) also had two daughters: Grace, who married Ward Pitfield, and Lorna, who married Brigadier John H. Price, OBE, MC, ED, son of Sir William Price. Derek Price is a son of the Brigadier and married Jill McConnell, daughter of Wilson McConnell, the first son of J.W. McConnell.

Marler Family. (1) William de Montmollin Marler (1849–1929), McConnell's notary and neighbour in Dorval, professor of notarial and civil law at McGill, and father of **(2) Sir Herbert Meredith Marler**, KCMG (1935) (1876–1940), who married **(3) Beatrice Isabel Allan** (1880–1968), granddaughter of the elder Andrew Allan (qv), one of the founders of the Andrew Royal Mail Line, and of Mathew Hamilton Gault, a founder of the Sun Life Assurance Company. **(4) George Carlyle Marler**, was a half-brother of (2) and a Montreal and provincial politician.

Massey Family. (1) Hart Almerrin Massey (1823–1896) was one of the foremost manufacturers of agricultural implements in the world and a model for McConnell in giving. Massey merged his company with Harris to form the Massey-Harris Co. Ltd. in 1891, which had a monopoly on the manufacture of farm machinery in Canada. Massey was a harsh employer but a generous supporter of Methodist education and churches. He built the Massey Music Hall in 1892–93 and endowed and rebuilt the renamed Fred Victor Mission in 1892–94 in memory of his sons Charles and Fred. **(2) The Rt Hon. (Charles) Vincent Massey**, CC, CH, grandson of (1) of Chester, was

Canadian high commissioner in London and governor general of Canada and a very good friend of McConnell's, probably from about 1912.

McGill, Air Vice Marshal Frank S., RCAF, secretary of the Dominion Oilcloth and Linoleum Co. Ltd., born in Montreal in 1894. His father, **John J. McGill**, was the "golf professional" of the Royal Montreal Golf Club depicted with McConnell, Lloyd George, and Sir Arthur Currie in this book. McGill's son, Air Vice-Marshal Frank McGill, CB, ADC, born in 1894, was an accomplished athlete in his own right and also a good friend of McConnell's and vice-president (sales) of Dominion Oilcloth & Linoleum Co. Ltd.

McKim Family. (1) John Nelson McKim was the brother of Anson McKim, Sr (1855–1917), and they were partners with W.B. Somerset and Henry Edward Stephenson in the A. McKim Advertising Agency Limited. Founded in 1889, this company was the first advertising agency in Canada. At the beginning of the twentieth century it was the foremost of the nineteen advertising agencies in Montreal, with 150 large corporate clients, such as the Bank of Montreal, Henry Birks and Sons, the T. Eaton Company, and Henry Morgan and Company. Anson McKim was to help McConnell in the Victory Loan Campaign of 1917. **(2) Anson McKim, Jr**, OBE (born in 1905), son of Anson McKim, Sr, succeeded to the advertising agency and married Joan, daughter of Ross McMaster (qv). He worked for the accountants P.S. Ross & Sons (1925–26), and for CIL (1929–40). In 1940–42, he was an assistant to Arthur Purvis, director general of the British Purchasing Commission in Washington, and then was deputy British representative in the Canadian Department of Munitions and Supply (1942–45). After the war, he became Canadian representative to the International Civil Aviation Organization in Montreal and chairman of the executive of the Boys' Farm and Training School at Shawbridge. He was a director of Consolidated Paper and National Trust, vice-president (traffic) for Trans-Canada Air Lines (1945–51), and vice-president and manager and then president of Merck & Co. Ltd. (1945–60).

McLean Family. William McLean (1847–1919) married Sarah Jennings (1851–1938) and they lived in Port Hope, Ontario. They had ten children, including **(1) (Charles) Herbert (Bert) McLean** (1881–1941), McConnell's lieutenant at Montreal Securities, who married Mary Gertrude Knox (1884–1942), a daughter of J.W. Knox (qv), formerly courted by McConnell. **(2) (James) Stanley McLean** (1876–1954), brother of (1), was president of Canada Packers and married to Edith Lillian Flavelle, a niece of Sir Joseph Flavelle (qv). He had courted Lily Griffith (later McConnell). **(3) (William) Ernest McLean** (1877–1961), another brother, the father of Eric McLean, music critic for the *Star*, was the son of (3). **(4) Herbert Knox McLean** (1911–1999) was the first son of (1) and manager of the St Lawrence Sugar Refinery. He married Lois Signoury Birks (qv).

McMaster Family. (1) William McMaster of Mount Royal Rolling Mills **(2) Ross H. McMaster,** son of (1) was one of McConnell's closest friends and the president of the Steel Company of Canada. He married Ruth Laing, daughter of Campbell Laing, and was therefore an uncle of Peter Marshall Laing (qv). **(3) Joan McMaster**, daughter of (2), married the younger Anson McKim (qv). **(4) Sherrill**, daughter of (2), married (Arthur) Deane Nesbitt, the younger brother of Brigadier (James) Aird Nesbitt of Ogilvy's department store, which had been bought in 1927 by their father, A.J. Nesbitt (qv). **(5) D. Ross McMaster**, son of (2) was a partner of Theodore Meighen in the law firm of McMaster Meighen.

McNaught Family. (1) William Kirkpatrick McNaught, president of the American Watch Co., an Ontario Conservative MPP, and promoter of radial railway lines and closely associated with Sir Adam Beck in the expropriation of private electrical companies. He was a commissioner of the Hydro-Electric Commission of Ontario, president of the Canadian Manufacturers' Association and the Canadian National Exhibition, and a Baptist temperance advocate. **(2) Charles Boyd McNaught**, son of (1), was an insurance broker with Reed, Shaw, McNaught, and a contemporary of McConnell's on the boards of Canada Steamship Lines and Sun Life Assurance. He was president of British Empire Steel Corporation, Conger-Lehigh Coal and Sterling Coal, and Canada Paper, and associated with Sir Herbert Holt and J.H. Gundy in St Maurice Paper, Canada Paper and Power Corporation, the Royal Bank of Canada, and Montreal Trust, among his other business interests. He was a member of the War Trade Board, under the chairmanship of McConnell. His sister Edna married Hilton Tudhope (of the Orillia carriage-manufacturing family), president of the brokers A.E. Ames, where he had sold Victory Loans in the First World War. **(3) Carlton McNaught**, son of (1), was a reporter and then a copywriter for J.J. Gibbons and Anson McKim (qv). In 1938, he gave $1,000 to the *Canadian Forum*, which enabled the University League for Social Reconstruction to take over the journal and make it a voice for the CCF and writers such as McConnell's *bête noire*, Frank Scott. **(4) Kenneth McNaught**, son of (3), became a prominent socialist and professor of history at the University of Toronto.

Meredith Family. (1) Frederick Edmund Meredith, KC (1862–1941), corporate lawyer of the firm of Meredith, Holden, Heward & Holden, director of the Bank of Montreal and the CPR, and chancellor of Bishop's University (1926–32), son of Sir William Collis Meredith (1812–1894), chief justice of the Superior Court of Quebec. He was married and divorced from Anna van Koughnet, a chancellor of Upper

Canada and formerly the wife of Wolferston Thomas, and he was one of McConnell's closest friends. **(2) Sir (Henry) Vincent Meredith**, first and last baronet, created 1916 (1850–1929), president of the Bank of Montreal (1913–27), brother of Sir William Ralph Meredith (1840–1923), chief justice of Ontario and leader of the Ontario Conservative Party, and of Richard Martin Meredith, chief justice of common pleas and president of the high court division of Ontario, and of the broker Charles Meredith (qv), and married to Isabella Brenda Allan, daughter of Andrew Allan, the brother of Sir Montagu Allan (qv). Sir Vincent was a cousin once removed of (1), a director of Dominion Textile, the CPR, the Laurentide Company, and the president of the Royal Victoria Hospital; his wife was a prominent fundraiser. **(3) William Campbell James Meredith** (1904–1960), son of (1) and dean of law at McGill (1950–60) and said to have been appointed at the instigation of McConnell. **(4) Charles Meredith** (1854–1928), president of the Montreal Stock Exchange in 1902–05 and founder of C. Meredith & Co., brother of (2), married to Elspeth Hudson Angus, daughter of R.B. Angus. **(5) Sir William Ralph Meredith** (1840–1923, knighted in 1896), brother of (2), leader of the opposition in 1878, chief justice of the common pleas in 1894, and chancellor of the University of Toronto in 1900, serving on the Royal Commission on the University in 1905.

Molson Family. (1) Henry (Harry) Markland Molson (1856–1912), grandson of the Hon. John Molson, pioneer of steam navigation on the St Lawrence, and the son of William Molson, one of the founders of Molsons Bank. By the time of his death on the *Titanic* in 1912, he was the proprietor of Molson's Warehouses, Wine Vaults and Frost-Proof Storage, and a director of the National Trust Company, Molsons Bank, the Richelieu & Ontario Navigation Company, the Montreal City & District Savings Bank, the Canadian Paper Company, the Crown Life Insurance Company, the Canadian Transfer Company, the Standard Chemical Company, the Blaugas Company, and the Canadian Rubber Company. He was vice-president of the Montreal Cotton Company and president of the Montreal SPCA. He had been alderman of the West Ward of Montreal in 1906. **(2) Walter Molson**, born in 1883, son of John Thomas Molson, established Molson, Lobley & Co. Ltd., real-estate, insurance, and financial agents in 1911, and was a director of the Montreal District and Savings Bank, the Dominion Oilcloth and Linoleum Co. Ltd., Remington Rand Ltd. (Canada), the National Trust Company, the Lake of the Woods Milling Co. Ltd., the Dominion Glass Co. Ltd., the Reliance Insurance Company of Canada, Goulds Pump Inc., the Standard Life Assurance Company, and other companies.

Morgan Family. (1) (Frederick) Cleveland Morgan (1881–1962), born to James Morgan II and Anna Lyman, worked at Morgan's department store from 1904 to 1952. He was vice-president from 1940 until 1952. More interested in science and art than in business, he was chairman of the museum committee of the Art Association of Montreal from 1916 and continued in the position after the association was renamed the Montreal Museum of Fine Arts in 1948. He was the first president of the museum, in 1948–52, and chairman and then honorary chairman until his death. He was also in charge of the antiques department at Morgan's, which lent the store a unique cachet. His brother **(2) Harold Morgan** (1882–1940) was general manager of the store from 1911 and in 1923 he expanded the area of the store threefold. He was president of Morgan's from 1932 to 1940. His son **(3) Bartlett Morgan** was associated with Peter M. Laing (qv) in the building of the Place des Arts.

Nesbitt Family. (1) Arthur James Nesbitt (1880–1954). He was a principal of Nesbitt, Thomson, formed in Montreal in 1912. Nesbitt was one of McConnell's closest friends and is chiefly remembered for promoting Power Corporation, with which he was associated from 1925 to 1951. This firm, which specialized in the securities of electrical utilities, became Nesbitt Thomson Bongard, and in 1986 merged with F.H. Deacon, Hodgson Inc., a successor firm to one of McConnell's early stockbrokers in Toronto, F.H. Deacon, to form Nesbitt Thomson Deacon. **(2) Brigadier (James) Aird Nesbitt** (1908–1984). Although, thanks to his father (1), already the owner, he began as assistant to the general manager of Ogilvy's department store in 1929 and became vice-president and general manager in the following year, and then president. James A. Ogilvy, Senior (1841–1911) had migrated to Montreal in 1863 and started in the drygoods business with James Morrison, on St Antoine Street, making Ogilvy's the oldest retail drygoods business in Canada. His distinguished war career with the Black Watch led to his command of the West Nova Scotia Regiment in Italy and Holland, and to the rank of brigadier. After the Second World War, he was equerry to Princess Elizabeth during the Royal Tour of 1951, honorary aide-de-camp to the governor general (Vincent Massey), and commanding officer of the Tenth Militia (Quebec). He married Honor Graham Mathewson, whose sister Sheila married Sir John Child, second baronet, aide-de-camp to Lord Bessborough as governor general of Canada, 1931–3. Nesbitt was a governor of the Dominion Drama Festival and a director of the Prisoners' Aid and Welfare Association. He financed and in part wrote a society magazine called the *Passing Show*, 1926–33, which was modelled on the *Tatler* of London and later evolved into the *Montrealer* magazine, which was modelled on the *New Yorker*.

Ponsonby Family. (1) The Hon. George St. Lawrence Neuflize Ponsonby (1931–1951) died early in a car accident, while serving with the 9th Lancers. His death was a profound grief to the Bessboroughs, who had lost their son Desmond in a riding accident in 1925. At his baptism in Ottawa, Sir Robert Borden stood proxy for the king, George's godfather. The Duchess of Richmond attended his funeral with her two sons, Charles and Nicholas. **(2) Eric Ponsonby, Viscount Duncannon, later tenth Earl of Bessborough,** was brother of (1). He fought for twenty-four hours at Dunkirk, and then was stranded on the beach for two and one half days before being rescued. He briefly became an aide-de-camp to the Canadian General Andrew Macnaughton. In May of 1941, he became secretly engaged to Mary Churchill, daughter of the prime minister. Their marriage did not take place, and Mary Churchill married instead the diplomat Christopher Soames, later Baron Soames and the last governor of (Southern) Rhodesia. **(3) Roberte Neuflize, Countess of Bessborough** worked chiefly for the St John Ambulance and the Red Cross and as organizer of emergency services at the County Hall in Chichester. Her daughter Moyra began her long nursing career in Chichester and Lord Bessborough worked for French relief in London. The Bessborough family frequently visited wounded Canadians in military hospitals in England and entertained hundreds of Canadian and Free French soldiers. Their house became a centre for visitors from Canada bearing letters from the McConnells, particularly Lord Halifax, Malcolm MacDonald, Count Dick De la Rozière, and John G. McConnell. Her best friends were Lil McConnell and Mrs Lionel de Rothschild. **(4) Lady Moyra Blanche Madeleine Ponsonby** (born 1918) was the only daughter of the Bessboroughs and inherited her mother's interest in nursing and the St John's Ambulance Brigade, of which she became superintendent-in-chief in 1970. In 1945, she married an Australian surgeon, Sir Denis John Wolko Browne, KCVO, FRCS, who died in 1967. Both Lady Moyra and one of her daughters, Rosemary (Countess Franco Aleramo Lanza), were to remain close friends of Kathleen McConnell.

Raymond Brothers. **(1) Air Vice Marshal Adélard Raymond** (1883–1961), pilot with the Royal Flying Corps in World War I, vice-president and general manager of the Queen's Hotel in Montreal, delivered clandestine US aircraft to France in 1940, ADC to the governor general (Vanier), director of Canadair. His son married the Hon. Gaye Hardinge (qv). **(2) Senator Donat Raymond** (1880–1962), Liberal senator 1926–62, implicated in the Beauharnois scandal, president of the Canadian Arena Co. and developer of the Montreal Forum with McConnell. Like (1), he was a friend of McConnell's, unlike **(3) Maxime Raymond** (1883–1861), Liberal MP for Beauharnois 1926–40, leader of the Bloc Populaire Canadien, and opponent of conscription.

Ross Family. John W. Ross, LLD, was born in Montreal in 1870 and worked with James Walker and Co., a hardware merchant, before joining his father's accountancy firm, P.S. Ross and Sons, in 1892. He married a daughter of C.C. Holland (qv). He was vice-president of the Ross Realty Co. and a director of Sun Life Assurance, Canadian Tube and Steel Products (organized by McConnell), and Crown Trust and Dominion Equity Securities. Much of Ross's life was devoted to charitable causes, and he was a governor of the Protestant House of Industry and Refuge, the Protestant

Hospital for the Insane, the Montreal General Hospital, the Lachine Hospital, the Art Association of Montreal, and the United Theological College. The YMCA was his special cause, and he was director of the Montreal association and a member of the National Council and of the International Committee. Until the 1950s, he maintained an active interest in Roman Catholic and Jewish as well as Protestant charities and the Red Cross. Howard Ross, his son, eventually became chancellor of McGill University. Howard's son, Gerald, was dean of management at McGill at the beginning of the twenty-first century.

Sims Family. (George) Ross (Haig) Sims (1885–1960), was son of the shirt-manufacturer Major (Anthony) Haig Sims (1853–1924), director of the Richelieu and Ontario Navigation Co. (in succession to Col. F.C. Henshaw) and Victoria Life Insurance Co., and mayor of Dorval in 1907. Ross Sims was married to Caro Kingman, sister of Abner Kingman, investor and governor of McGill. Among the other Kingman sisters were Mary, who was married to Walter Molson, realtor and another governor of McGill; and Eva, who married as her fourth husband Henry Morgan (IV), cousin of Cleveland Morgan (qv). Mary Kingman (Mrs. Walter) Molson had a daughter, Caro, who married William Angus, son of D. Forbes Angus (qv) and grandson of R.B. Angus. Ross Sims had three daughters. Libby married the stockbroker Herbert Bogert; Peggy married C.F. (Bill) Carsley, president of Canada Vinegar and a grandson of the drygoods merchant Samuel Carsley; and Mary married Alan Gordon, president of Royal Securities after I.W. Killam.

Thornton and Williams-Taylor Families. Sir Henry Thornton, a next door neighbour of the McConnells on Pine Avenue, a portly and high-living American with a knighthood earned for his services to English railways, married, as his second wife, Martha Waitriss, whose parents had also been divorced. Lady Thornton's mother had then married Charles Wetmore, the architect of Grand Central Station in New York, and his father had married a daughter of Sir Frederick Williams-Taylor, general manager of the Bank of Montreal and a close acquaintance of the McConnells. Williams-Taylor, married to Jane Henshaw (qv), lived across the street from the Thorntons and the McConnells at 605 Pine Avenue. Sir Henry's marriage to Miss Waitriss made Sir Frederick his stepfather. The minister of Railways responsible for the CNR in 1928–29, when the decision to lease the house to the Thorntons was made by the CNR directors, was Charles Dunning, and Lady Williams-Taylor became his close companion. Dunning, previously premier of Saskatchewan and later dominion minister of finance, was to succeed McConnell as president of Ogilvie Flour Mills in 1941. The new Lady Thornton furnished the house lavishly with antiques and it became famed for champagne parties lasting well into early morning. They prolonged the roaring twenties into the abyss of the Depression, and few forgot that they were

American. The raucous partying of the Thorntons did not last long: in 1932 a Royal Commission on the future of the Canadian railways, chaired by Sir Lyman Duff, heard that Thornton had rented the house nominally from George H. Séguin, a clerk in the office of E.R. Décary, a director of the CNR, who had bought the house and then rented it to the CNR with a kickback for arranging the transaction. Although Thornton derived no benefit except the use of the house for less than two years, this scandal, among other grave criticisms, led to his resignation as president of the CNR in July 1932 and to his sudden death eight months later.

Wernher, The Hon. Major-General Sir Harold, KCVO (later third baronet), GCVO, TD, (1893–1973), was chairman of Associated Theatre Properties (London) Ltd., Electrolux Ltd., and Ericsson Telephones Ltd., and director of the Anglo-Spanish Construction Co. Sir Harold was a son of Sir Julius Wernher, first baronet, of the developers of South Africa, and Lady Zia was of the Russian Imperial family. Her brother, Grand Duke Mikhail Mikhailovitch of Russia, gave McConnell a book that he had written on spirituality. The Wernhers were to become closer to the McConnells particularly after 1945, when the McConnells went to stay at their house, Luton Hoo, in Bedfordshire

Wimborne, **Ivor Churchill Guest** (1873–1939), second baron and later first Viscount Wimborne. A relative of Lord Bessborough, he had been lord lieutenant of Ireland during the Troubles of 1915–18 and married to a daughter of the second Baron Ebury, whose cousin Susan Grosvenor married John Buchan, later first Baron Tweedsmuir, Bessborough's successor as governor general. Lionel Guest, the brother of the first Viscount Wimborne (both being uncles of Joan Lascelles) had been the first chairman of the Ritz-Carlton Hotel in Montreal, which opened in 1912. Lionel Guest was associated in the venture with Montrealers Herbert Holt, C.R. Hosmer, Sir Montagu Allan, Charles Blair Gordon, T.J. Drummond, and William Massey Birks, and with Harry Higgins, the solicitor of the Ritz Hotel in London. The mother of the ninth Earl of Bessborough, was Blanche Vere Guest, daughter of Sir John Guest, MP, first baronet, making her an aunt of the first Viscount Wimborne and of Lionel Guest, who were therefore cousins of Lord Bessborough, the governor general.

Notes

CHAPTER ONE

1 Much of this chapter is based on memories and information provided by Mrs Dora Kerr, Mrs M.A. Kienholz, Mrs P.M. Laing, Dr Murdoch Laing, Mr and Mrs William McConnell, Terence McConnell, Harold Rawson, Marian Press, Mrs Mary Redmond, Walker Riley, Cynthia Smith, and Judge and Mrs D.C. Thomas.

2 York Township as a territorial division dated from 1791, the western end of a line of eleven townships on the north side of Lake Ontario. Scarborough bounded it on the east, Etobicoke on the west, and Vaughan and Markham on the north.

3 Fraser, *History of Muskoka*, 4.

4 Cited by Lower, *The North American Assault on the Canadian Forest*, 177.

5 Hall, "The Social and Economic Development," 60–1.

6 Fraser, *History of Muskoka*, 146.

7 Its provisions are summarized in *Guidebook and Atlas of Muskoka & Parry Sound Districts*, 41–2.

8 McMurray, *The Free Grant Land of Canada*, 17 and 19.

9 Peterson, "The Development of Farming in Muskoka," 69 and 71.

10 "An Emigrant Lady," *Letters from Muskoka*, 39.

11 See Thomas, "The Beginning of Navigation and the Tourist Industry in Muskoka," 101–5.

12 Wolfe, "The Summer Resorts of Ontario."

13 *Guidebook and Atlas of Muskoka & Parry Sound Districts*, 10–12.

14 Adam, *Muskoka Illustrated*, 12.

15 Ahlbrandt, *Beaumaris*, 9 and 10.

16 Peterson, "The Development of Farming in Muskoka," 72.

17 Cited by Fraser, *History of Muskoka*, 130–5.

18 Mrs Keith Gordon, interview with Nicolas McConnell, 2002.

19 Cook, "'Continued and Persevering Combat,'" 348–9.

20 Cookson, *Tattle Tales of Muskoka*, 108–9.

21 Parvin, *Authorization of Textbooks for the Schools of Ontario*, appendix A3, 149.

22 Stamp, *The Schools of Ontario*, 10.

23 Houston and Prentice, *Schooling and Scholars*, 243.

24 Quoted in ibid., 244.

25 Whately, *Easy Lessons*, 12.

26 Stamp, *The Schools of Ontario*, 45.

27 Interview with Nicolas McConnell, 1985.

28 Houston and Prentice, *Schooling and Scholars*, 215 and 217.

29 *Report of the Minister of Education (Ontario) for the Year 1896*.

30 Boyer, *Memories of Bracebridge*, 4.

31 To this capital sum he added $100,000 in 1960.

CHAPTER TWO

1 *Census of Canada 1901*, 1: 8, 9.

2 Carter-Edwards, "Toronto in the 1890's," 15.

3 Kluckner, *Toronto: The Way It Was*, 134.

4 Palmer, *Working Class Experience*, 119.

5 Gerald Tulchinsky, "Hidden among the Smokestacks: Toronto's Clothing Industry, 1871–1901," in Keane and Read, eds, *Old Ontario*, 279.

6 Census of Canada, cited by Kealey, *Toronto Workers Respond to Industrial Capitalism*, 307.

7 Burr, *Spreading the Light*, 158.

8 Speisman, *The Jews of Toronto*, 73.

9 King's letters are cited in Burr, *Spreading the Light*, 152.

10 Forrester, *Out of Character*, 86–7.

11 After the great fire of Toronto in 1904, the firm moved round the corner to 55 Wellington Street.

12 This was Ruth Goulding, who became Mrs Lentz and who, in admiration and gratitude, named her son John after McConnell. Other Gouldings who sent Christmas cards to McConnell even decades later were Jeanne (who may have been a daughter-in-law) and Robert.

13 Rodgers, *Think: A Biography of the Watsons and IBM*, 16.

14 McConnell Papers, T.D.D. Lloyd to J.W. McConnell, 15 September 1904.

15 Coombs, "The Emergence of a White Collar Work Force in Toronto 1895–1911," 83.

16 By the end of the twentieth century, both buildings had long disappeared and been replaced by a new YMCA on Grosvenor Street, still only a few minutes' walk from the site of the McConnell house on Gerrard Street.

17 Ross, *The Y.M.C.A.*, 77.

18 Ibid., 72.

19 Cited in ibid., 71.

20 Ibid., 88.

21 Cleveland and Powell, *Railroad Finance*, 35–8.

22 Marx, *Capital*, 249.

23 Ibid., vol. 1, pt 2, ch.4

24 Poovey, *A History of the Modern Fact*, 30.

25 The reworking of the data in the original book of entry, the inventory, involved the translation of monetary values into a single currency, the money of account; the placement of data to

highlight certain critical relations between words and numbers by linking narrative information to monetary values, and by creating conditions for an index, and by shortening the narrative to its verbal essence (adapted from ibid., 43).

26 Johnson, *A Merchant Prince*, 112.

27 See the "Souvenir Programme" of the 1897 convention (Toronto: Methodist Book and Publishing House 1897).

28 *Methodist Discipline 1906*, s.351. All other quotations regarding the League are from this section.

29 Armstrong and Nelles, *The Revenge of the Methodist Bicycle Company*, 156.

30 Ibid., 157.

31 Sabbatarianism was doomed in any case. In 1903 the Privy Council was to rule that the province of Ontario lacked the jurisdiction to pass Sabbatarian legislation, such as *An Act to Prevent the Profanation of the Lord's Day,* since it was within the exclusive competence of the Dominion Parliament to legislate on matters of criminal law. The so-called Lord's Day Act is found in the *Revised Statutes* of Ontario 1897, c.246; the ruling of the Privy Council is in [1903] AC 524.

CHAPTER THREE

1 McConnell Papers.

2 A modern biography of Sir William Mackenzie is Fleming, *The Railway King of Canada*.

3 All this and other company information is from the board minutes provided by Domtar Inc. in Montreal. Acetone was one of several new products being tried to modify the amplification of the wave set off when ammunition was detonated in big guns, or artillery. Each detonation within a big gun eroded its chamber and reduced its life. The erosion occurred as incandescent gases rushed through the driving ring of the projectile. Acetone acted as a gelatinizing agent to incorporate gun cotton in the chamber into nitroglycerine. The effect of this incorporation was similar to that of the detonation of the dynamite originally invented by Alfred Nobel for use in construction. Cordite, which was the combination of acetone, nitroglycerine, and gun cotton, was called "smokeless powder." It was so called because, unlike the black powder that had been standard, it did not foul the gun barrel. Standard's acetone was expensive, requiring eighty to one hundred tons of birch, beech, or maple "waste" to produce a ton of it, but its production method was not to be improved upon until the First World War, when bacteria replaced yeast in the fermentation of the wood scrap – an innovation discovered in the production of hydrocarbon compounds used in synthetic rubber, another subject of great interest to McConnell.

4 It is unclear now precisely where this was. One atlas shows 800 St James Street as just west of Atwater Avenue, the boundary between St Henry Ward to the west and Saint-Antoine Ward to the east, but the street addresses of Montreal later changed in number, over a period of years.

5 On Henshaw, see *The Storied Province of Quebec*, 3: 122.

6 McConnell Papers, J.W. McConnell to Lily Griffith, 7 July 1904.

7 Ibid., J.W. McConnell to Lily Griffith, 28 July 1904.

8 Ibid., apparently 19 July 1904.

9 Maxim's life, particularly his inventions, is detailed in Mottelay, *The Life and Work of Sir Hiram Maxim*.

10 See Marsh, *Joseph Chamberlain*.

11 McConnell Papers, J.W. McConnell to Lily Griffith, 31 August 1904.

12 The day before their marriage, the couple entered into a marriage contract before the notary Robert B. Hutcheson. This was customary among English-speaking Quebecers, in order to avoid the equal division of assets upon any dissolution of the marriage (including death), prescribed by the Civil Code of Lower Canada in its provision for community of property between spouses.

13 *Gazette*, 5 May 1905. Their daughter Kit was to wear this tiara at her wedding in 1945.

14 Cooper, Edmonds, and Hedley, *Official Souvenir*, 25–6.

15 McConnell Papers, Lily McConnell to Agnes Griffith, 22 June 1905.

16 In 1911 they moved to 400 Elm Street, at the corner of Sherbrooke Street, in Westmount.

17 McConnell Papers, 6 March 1905.

18 In February 1907, while he was based in the west, McConnell would sell this house for $7,500. Ibid., red "My Vacation" book.

19 McConnell Papers, Thomas Griffith to J.W. and Lily McConnell, November 1905.

20 Ibid., J.W. McConnell to Lily Griffith, 13 February 1905.

21 Ibid., 6 March 1905.

22 In 1905 it seems that his father and his brother Walter started a grocery and postal outlet near their house, a venture for which McConnell lent them $1,000.

23 Johnston would become a business partner of McConnell in 1907–12, and his son Morgan was to be manager of McConnell's St Lawrence Sugar Refinery, succeeded in this post by a son of McConnell's long-time associate Bert (Herbert Knox) McLean; James Wilson Knox's son Frank (known as "Sport") – McConnell's closest associate until the 1940s – was to manage McConnell's Montreal Securities company and was to create out of it the insurance-brokerage firm of Knox, Vickers, McLean; Frank Knox's son, also named James Wilson, was to deal at this firm with McConnell's insurance matters.

24 McConnell Papers, "D.E. Ledger," 183–6, contains McConnell's list of subscribers and their pledges in the fundraising campaign that began in February 1907.

25 Brown, "Dominion-Douglas United Church," 5.

CHAPTER FOUR

1 Kuntz, ed., *The Titanic Disaster Hearings*, 192–3.

2 McConnell placed check marks beside all the lines except the last two.

3 "Financial agents" charged various fees – typically from 2½ per cent for merely placing securities to 10 per cent for guaranteeing sales. Sometimes they owned the securities they were selling, and in these cases they were functioning as underwriters and thus putting themselves at risk to the extent that they had committed themselves to sell what they had thus purchased.

4 McConnell Papers, J.W McConnell to Lily, 12 January 1907.

5 Dirks, "Getting a Grip."

6 Johnston, "History of the Norman and Madge Johnston Family" (c.1996).

7 Johnston, in particular, managed to recruit Sir William Van Horne as an investor.

8 McConnell Papers, G.F. Johnston to J.W. McConnell, 30 January 1912.

9 Ibid., J.W McConnell to Lily, 8 January 1907.

10 Ibid., J.W. McConnell to Lily, 29 August 1906.

11 "Boosterism and the Development of Prairie Cities," in Artibise, ed., *Town and City*, 211.

12 Ibid., 213.

13 Ibid., 218.

14 His brother, J.N. Greenshields, was a lawyer and a director of the Montreal-London Securities Corporation, for which, as explained below, McConnell acted as salesman.

15 Almost no evidence seems to have survived on his company for this venture, Canadian Western Development, and in any case it appears to have stalled before his departure from Winnipeg. It is possible that he was trying to compete with the Alberta Railway and Irrigation Company in Lethbridge, incorporated in 1904 by Elliott Galt (son of Sir Alexander Galt, who had been a Montreal pioneer in developing the west). See den Otter, *Civilizing the West*, 232.

16 See Foran, "The CPR and the Urban West," chapter 5 of Dempsey, ed., *The CPR West*.

17 McConnell Papers, J.W. McConnell to Lily, 5 April 1907.

18 He was to continue making payments on these properties at least until April 1909.

19 McConnell Papers, J.W. McConnell to Lily, 14 April 1907. James Brown Pepler, born in England, had come to Canada in 1868 and worked with Canada Landed and National Investment and a family wholesale leather business in Toronto before establishing J.B. Pepler and Company, real-estate and insurance brokers, in Winnipeg in 1882.

20 Two Winnipeg residents served as directors – William Harvey of D.W. Harvey, a firm of land agents, and W.J. Tupper, who was practising law with his brother J. Stewart Tupper, their father being the former prime minister Sir Charles Tupper.

21 McConnell Papers, Personal Ledger, 1906–12, 37 and 35.

22 McConnell Papers, J.W. McConnell to Lily, 3 August 1907.

23 The recession in Winnipeg is described in Bellan, *Winnipeg's First Century*, chapter 6.

24 Of the eight Patrick children, Lester (1883–1960) and Frank (1885–1960) were to become two of Canada's most famous hockey players.

25 *A Life in the Woods*, 41–2.

26 Mrs Shawn Lamb, of the Nelson Museum, has provided invaluable help for this section on Patrick Lumber, which is also based on Whitehead, *The Patricks*; Feed, ed., *Nelson: A History in Pictures*; *The Silvery Slocan*; and Chapman, "A History of Logging in the West Kootenays." The late Martin Lynch of Kaslo was particularly helpful in providing historical context.

27 Whitehead, *The Patricks*, 45. The house was still standing at the end of the century.

28 McConnell Papers, J.W. McConnell to Lily, 19 September 1907.

29 Ibid., J.W. McConnell to Lily, 22 September 1907.

30 Ibid., J.W. McConnell to Lily, 10 October 1907.

31 British Columbia Lumber lasted only four years. Harry William Birks put it into bankruptcy, ruining Johnston almost completely but not McConnell. The partnership proper did not involve itself in Patrick Lumber except in 1910–11, Johnston's interest afterwards being personal, as McConnell's involvement in 1907 had been.

The organization of Patrick Lumber suggests how McConnell, with relatively little capital, may have begun investing in the myriad of companies that were to preoccupy him for the following five years and beyond. The authorized capital was $200,000, of which Joseph Patrick subscribed $80,000; McConnell $25,000; Markland Molson, William C. McIntyre, and G.F. Johnston $20,000 each; William Molson Macpherson, F.J. Knox, and David Mitchell (a Quebec City lumberman) $10,000 each; and Isaac Patrick $5,000. The subscribers had to pay up half at the start. McConnell almost immediately sold $5,000 of his shares to Joseph Patrick, and so he paid up $10,000 by January 1907, and his balance of $10,000 in instalments from September 1908 to May 1909, by which time he owned a tenth of the company. It is not clear whether McConnell kept these shares until the sale of the company in 1911. But if he did, and if the sale price was $440,000, McConnell's profit was $68,000 or 380 per cent.

32 Johnston lived at 56 Bellevue Avenue; Hudson at 1308 Belmont Road; and G.B. Allison, Hudson's brother, at 572 Roslyn Avenue.

33 There a new McConnell house did arise, to be occupied by Wilson's family and finally his widow until 2000.

34 The Cooks were also to be neighbours of the McConnells in Val David, in the Laurentians north of Montreal.

35 McConnell bought a portion of a syndicate share for $6,300 and 5 per cent bonds for $3,150, along with common stock worth $15,000. This was probably in 1909 and it marked the start of one of his most important ventures, the takeover of the Montreal Street Railway.

36 He underwrote $20,000 at $85, for a net expenditure of $17,000.

37 He bought 2,000 5 per cent first mortgage bonds at $88 for $1,760.

38 He bought his Manitoba Land securities from Frank Patch of Hartley, Iowa, and later sold them to Sir Trevor Dawson of Vickers.

39 Cleveland and Power, *Railroad Promotion*, 133.

40 See Marchildon, "'Hands Across the Water,'" particularly 70–3, for an overview of promotion.

41 Common shares offer dividends that vary according to the shares' market value, itself a reflection of the market's assessment of a given company's fortunes. They entitle their holders to votes in determining the composition of a company's board of directors, and so "control" of a company falls into the hands of those who own a majority of the common shares.

42 Preferred shares offer dividends that are declared by the company's board at its discretion but at a fixed rate and before the payment of dividends on common shares.

43 Montreal *Herald*, 28 April 1909.

44 Henry Labouchere (1831–1912) had founded *Truth* in 1877. His newspaper was so controversial that Queen Victoria prevailed upon W.E. Gladstone to exclude him from the government formed in 1892 (Thorold, *The Life of Henry Labouchere*, chapter 15). The weekly survived until 1957.

45 *Truth*, 1 October 1913.

46 There was a mile of railway for every 250 inhabitants of Canada, as compared to 400 people in the United States, 2,000 in Great Britain, and 4,000 in Russia.

47 Stevens, *Canadian National Railways*, vol. 2, chapter 17, describes the last days of the Grand Trunk Railway and of the Grand Trunk Pacific Railway.

48 Born in Ingersoll, Ontario, and educated at Victoria College in Toronto, Deacon taught school before founding his firm in 1905, the same year in which he married the daughter of Henry R. Emmerson, who had retired as premier of New Brunswick in 1900 and then served as the minister of railways and canals under Sir Wilfrid Laurier from 1903 to 1908. Ames, the son of a Methodist minister in Lambeth, Ontario, and the son-in-law of George Augustus Cox, started out in banking before establishing his own stockbrokerage and then becoming president of the Toronto Stock Exchange. In 1908 his firm purchased the first issues of municipal bonds by public tender, and it was probably the first Canadian investment house to conduct successfully a stockbrokerage and bond-investment business under the same roof. From 1909 to 1913, it offered sixteen issues of bonds and shares of thirteen companies. See the A.E. Ames and Company brochure published in January 1969 and found in the F.H. Deacon Papers, Archives of Ontario.

49 His Sterling holdings in 1921 were valued at $34,000.

50 Marchildon, "The Role of Lawyers in Corporate Promotion," 196–7.

51 Halifax *Morning Chronicle*, 15 April 1910.

52 Most of the information on this proxy fight comes from a scrapbook on the subject in the papers of R.E. Harris in Nova Scotia Archives and Records Management, Halifax.

53 Epp, "Cooperation among Capitalists," 312–13.

54 *Star*, 25 June 1915.

55 Montreal *Herald*, 18 April 1911; Montreal *Gazette*, 19 April 1911.

56 This entire account is derived from Epp, "Cooperation among Capitalists," chapter 4, with additional information from the McConnell Papers.

57 Ballantyne became a close friend and next-door neighbour of McConnell in Dorval. He would be appointed minister of fisheries in Robert Borden's Unionist cabinet in 1917, and, though defeated in 1921, he would later be named to the Senate, on McConnell's recommendation (McConnell had first been offered the seat but had turned it down). In 1931 Sherwin-Williams of the United States secured complete control of its Canadian division.

58 McConnell Papers, G.F. Johnston to McConnell, 30 January 1912.

59 Ibid.

60 In later years, it was rumoured that the McConnells had been booked on this same voyage but then cancelled their reservations at the last minute. There is no evidence for this. Alan Hustak, the author of *Titanic: The Canadian Story*, has kindly provided many of the details on Allison and the *Titanic*.

61 Duncan, *Not a One-Way Street*, 120.

62 McConnell never owned this company outright, but one of the nasty rumours about him was that he held a monopoly on all coffins manufactured in Ontario and Quebec and raised the prices of them during the influenza epidemic of 1918.

63 The lawyer (and later Chief Justice) R.A.E. Greenshields kept a scrapbook of press cuttings on the boom, available at the McCord Museum Archives (MMA) as MG 2066, c. 1.

64 Montreal *Herald*, 20 December 1911, statement by P. Collins, assistant city accountant.

65 Montreal *Herald*, 12 September 1912.

66 A measure of McConnell's conservative accounting methods is that in 1913 he reported a loss (net income minus expenses) of $22,000. This analysis does not include unrealized profits on investments.

67 This general account is adapted from Marchildon, *Profits and Politics*, 7–12.

68 In 1900, of the $1.2 billion external investment in Canada, 85 per cent was British; in 1910, of the $2.5 billion external investment, 77 per cent was from Britain.

69 Based on calculations done by Gerald Wareham on sources that may not be complete.

CHAPTER FIVE

1 Many former employees of St Lawrence (SLS) have assisted in the research for this chapter, including the late David Wanklyn and Bruce Foster (director and plant manager, 1950–86).

2 From 1912 to 1930, SLS sometimes produced more sugar annually than its nearest rival, Canada Sugar. But then in 1930 Canada Sugar merged with Dominion Sugar to form Canada and Dominion Sugar (C&D) and to become the largest producer of sugar in the country. The SLS refinery in Montreal probably continued to produce more than the C&D refinery in Montreal, but the beet factories in western Ontario of C&D (formerly belonging to Dominion) raised the combined production of C&D to exceed that of SLS. SLS never operated from more than one refinery, although McConnell much expanded it.

3 The text of the agreement is found in the McConnell Papers and quotations are from this original executed copy. There are minor discrepancies between this and the agreement described by Feltoe in *Redpath*, 179.

4 Another story is to the effect that McConnell simply stole the company from Baumgarten after Baumgarten had toasted the German kaiser at a dinner at Sainte-Agathe. The date of this dinner is unclear. If, as is alleged by one source, the toast took place before the outbreak of war in 1914, it is hard to see anything in principle exceptionable about it. The kaiser was a nephew of King Edward VII, and King Edward had paid a state visit to Germany shortly before the war. The apparent propriety of such a toast in July notwithstanding, this story goes on to say that Baumgarten's friends cut him off as soon as war broke out shortly afterwards, in August 1914. This may have happened, as is suggested by the fact that some time after August 1914 Baumgarten ceased attending meetings of the board of the Bank of Montreal. But, by then, McConnell was already established as president of SLS, having succeeded Baumgarten in the previous February. There was therefore no need for him to steal something he already had.

    A competing story is that Baumgarten delivered his notorious toast in May 1915, after Germany's sinking of the *Lusitania*. This would have been a provocative act indeed, so much so that it seems highly unlikely. Furthermore, far from parading his German allegiance after August 1914, Baumgarten was ostentatiously patriotically British from the outbreak of the war onwards, and he lavishly contributed to the Canadian Patriotic Fund campaigns headed by McConnell in 1914 and 1915. Then there is the possibility that reports of Baumgarten's toast were part of an orchestrated campaign to destroy him. But a reading of the *Star*, the *Gazette*, the *Financial Times*, and the *Monetary Times* for May 1915 does not reveal one reference to Baumgarten's German identity, much less to his alleged toast.

5 A copy of the will is in the possession of Kennan Gault of New York.

6 McConnell Papers.

7 SLS Minutes, 13 May 1915. All the minutes books of St Lawrence Sugar are in the J.W. McConnell Fonds at the McGill University Archives.

8 It is not clear where this was published, but several copies of the announcement are in the McConnell Papers.

9 Redpath Sugar Museum Archives (RSMA), Huntly Drummond to Sir George Foster, 12 September 1914.

10 RSMA, "Dominion of Canada Imports of Sugar for Fiscal Years Ending 31 March, 1908 to 1917."

11 RSMA, Drummond to Bruce, 18 February 1918.

12 RSMA, Bruce to Drummond, 24 July 1918.

13 RSMA, Drummond to Lloyd Harris, 8 October 1918.

14 RSMA, Drummond to Samuel Lee and Sir George Foster, 26 September 1918, and Lloyd Harris, 8 October 1918.

15 This account is taken from a "General Sugar Memorandum," 27 August 1919, apparently prepared for the Board of Commerce on the basis of information from the Canada Food Board.

16 McConnell Papers, J.W. McConnell to Lil, 28 April, 16 May 1919.

17 Order no. 2, 28 August 1919.

18 Order no. 3, 2 September 1919.

19 Montreal *Star*, 4 September 1919.

20 Order no. 70, 26 February 1920.

21 Order no. 82, 18 June 1920.

22 LAC, MG 30, E79, vol. 6, St Lawrence and Sugar Investments file; and the typed transcript in the McConnell Papers of the "Examination before Trial" of J.W. McConnell, 7 June 1922, before Morgan J. O'Brien, referee, in the Supreme Court, New York County, in the case of *Muller-Fox Brokerage Co. v. St. Lawrence Sugar Refineries, Ltd.*

23 Fairbairn seems to have been a friend of McConnell's from "our Muskoka." McConnell Papers, Rhys Fairbairn to J.W. McConnell, 5 February 1938.

24 LAC, St Lawrence and Sugar Investment file, J.W. McConnell to W.F. O'Connor, 9 April 1923.

25 There was extensive coverage of the refiners' position in the press, as in the *Financial Times* for 23 October 1920, which blamed the Board of Commerce and the Canadian Trade Board totally for the crisis in the industry.

26 Toronto *Mail and Empire*, 26 October 1920.

27 SLS Minutes, 2 November 1920 and 26 January 1925.

28 SLS Minutes, 20 January 1926.

29 Ibid., 3 May 1928.

30 Ibid., 17 January 1930.

31 SLS Minutes, 19 July 1933.

32 Ibid., 13 December 1933.

33 University of New Brunswick, Harriet Irving Library, R.B. Bennett Papers, box 949, T.A.V. Gordon to J.W. McConnell, 28 February 1934, J.W. McConnell to T.A.V. Gordon, 1 March 1934, and J.W. McConnell to R.B. Bennett, 3 March 1934.

34 SLS Minutes, 19 December 1934.

35 Ibid., 13 November 1935.

36 Ibid., 16 December 1936.

37 Ibid., 13 November 1935, special by-law no. 59, approved by a special meeting of shareholders on 4 December 1936.

38 Ibid., 23 December 1937, enacted by by-law no. 43(a).

39 Ibid., 30 July 1941.

40 To this end, McConnell came to rely heavily on James Russell Crawford. The Scottish-born Crawford joined St Lawrence Sugar as a clerk, probably in 1915, and worked there for fifty-one years. Even before the death of Bert McLean in June 1941, he was running the day-to-day business of the company. On McLean's death, he became vice-president, and eventually he would become also executive vice-president of Commercial Trust, the company that was to administer, among other things, the distribution of the dividends of St Lawrence among the McConnell family.

41 The funnelling of these profits into the foundation raises an issue that was to receive much public attention, particularly in the United States in the 1960s and 1970s: the use of charitable foundations either as holding companies to avoid hostile takeovers or as vehicles for avoiding the payment of corporate taxes. In the case of the McConnell Foundation, however, it never owned anything remotely like a controlling interest in any of McConnell's companies, including St Lawrence, and so it was not able to act as a holding company for them. It also appears that, apart from whatever St Lawrence shares McConnell gave to the foundation, he owned all the others himself, and so there was never any question of losing control to hostile bidders. It is not clear whether St Lawrence had ever been listed on a stock exchange, but, in any case, by the time it was giving to the foundation it had long been a privately owned corporation. Generally speaking, the assets transferred to the foundation by St Lawrence consisted either of cash or of the securities of corporations, often American, held by St Lawrence as a passive investor. With regard to tax avoidance, this would have been of use to McConnell personally only if he had illegally turned the income earned by his foundation to his personal use. But the evidence is that all this income was either given to legitimate charities, at arm's length from any of McConnell's economic interests, or reinvested to expand the endowment.

42 It is also unclear whether there was a secret session of the Commons to debate SLS profits. Baron Robert Silvercruys sent Lily a strange undated editorial from the *Globe and Mail*, discussing "the torpedoing in the St. Lawrence," which seems to refer to Coldwell's call for a hearing on St Lawrence Sugar. Apparently King had first refused a secret session and then agreed to it, citing the unlikely John Bassett, one of McConnell's closest friends, as his authority for a change of mind. (McConnell Papers, Baron Silvercruys to Lily McConnell, 14 April 1942.)

43 House of Commons *Debates*, 19 March 1944, 1385–7.

44 Much of this account is taken from Canada, Department of Justice, Restrictive Trade Practices Commission, *Report concerning the Sugar Industry in Eastern Canada*.

45 SLS Minutes, 26 November 1941.

46 Interviews with R.E. Miller, 2003 and 2004. Miller would go on to become vice-president (1969–72) and then president (1972–75) of SLS.

47 SLS Minutes, 26 November 1947.

48 Ibid., 29 December 1949.

49 A long ton was 2,240 lbs; a short ton was the equivalent in pounds of a regular ton, i.e., 2,000 lbs.

50 SLS Minutes, 26 April 1950.

51 Ibid., 13 December 1950.

52 Ibid., copies of three letters inserted between 25 April and 13 June 1951, C.D. Howe to Wilson McConnell, 4 May, W.G. McConnell to C.D. Howe (in response, undated), and C.D. Howe to L.J. Seidensticker, 17 May 1951.

53 These figures were reported by the Restrictive Trade Practices Commission, but the SLS Minutes themselves record five reductions of its price of refined sugar in 1953 alone (21 April 1954).

54 Ibid., 24 December 1952.

55 *Report concerning the Sugar Industry*, 148.

56 Ibid., 4.

57 Ibid., 240.

58 Montreal *Star*, 7 May 1963.

59 Quebec Superior Court (Criminal Division), case no. 01–5094–73, judgment rendered on 19 December 1975, affirmed by the Quebec Court of Appeal on 14 March 1978 and by the Supreme Court of Canada on 18 July 1980.

60 Montreal *Star*, 20 December 1975.

61 Montreal *Gazette*, 23 December 1975.

62 *Finance Capital*.

63 See Wells, *Antitrust and the Formation of the Postwar World*.

64 "Historical Sketch of the St. Lawrence Sugar Refining Company 1879–1932," 38.

CHAPTER SIX

1 MMA, Canadian Patriotic Fund Fonds, P17.

2 This account of the YMCA campaign is taken from Cross, *One Hundred Years of Service with Youth*, 224–5.

3 Ross had probably known McConnell from McConnell's arrival in Montreal in 1901, since he was married to the daughter of C.C. Holland, a real-estate developer and the president of G.A. Holland and Son, dealers in wallpaper, furniture, and sporting and fancy goods, who was well known to Lil's family, the Griffiths, being the recording steward of the Dominion Square Methodist Church as well as vice-president of the Montreal YMCA, a director of the Old Brewery Mission, and a governor of the Montreal General Hospital. The Hollands were good friends of the McConnells by 1905, accompanying them on their trip to England after their marriage that year.

4 Montreal *Herald*, 27 March 1911, "Prominent Business Men Give Maxims of Success to Young Montrealers."

5 Cross, *One Hundred Years of Service with Youth*, 228–34.

6 MUA, J.W. Ross Papers, P217-c/10, 6 and 8 November 1912.

7 Ibid., 19 November 1912.

8 Nearly all this information on the Montreal branch is from ibid.

9 Unless otherwise indicated, all dollar amounts cited in this chapter are approximations.

10 19 January 1917.

11 The grants were not large. Childless wives received $5 a month and women with regular work received nothing. The average grant per family, until the beginning of 1917, was $16.45 a month.

12 *McGill News*, vol. 1, no. 1 (December 1919): 7, 8, and 55, contains a brief description of the work by women for the Canadian Patriotic Fund.

13 *The Canadian Patriotic Fund*, 244.

14 The general account of wartime finance is largely adopted from White, *The Story of Canada's War Finance*.

15 Ibid., 24.

16 Ibid., 53.

17 LAC, RG 19 E–5(C), vol. 4013, A.E. Ames, typescript report on the 1917 Victory Loan campaign to Sir Thomas White.

18 Most of the following details on the first Victory Loan campaign come from *Canada's Victory Loan Montreal 1917*, a privately printed report for Lord Shaughnessy and Sir Thomas White found in the McConnell Papers.

19 *Gazette*, 23 October 1918.

20 Ibid.

21 LAC, HJ 5909 K55, 1918 fol.

22 Killam to Borden, 12 September 1918, "The Case Against Tax-Exempt Bonds," 4.

23 Unidentifiable newspaper, 28 October 1918, in the McConnell Papers.

24 Montreal *Gazette*, 2 November 1918.

25 McConnell had his own reasons to reflect on Ypres. With Sir Herbert Holt, J.R. Booth, Sir Clifford Sifton, Sir John Craig Eaton, and "Klondike Joe" Boyle, he had underwritten the 1st Canadian Motor Machine Gun Brigade, which he credited with closing a gap in the British line at the second Battle of Ypres and thereby saving the whole British front. In command of the brigade had been Brigadier-General Raymond Brutinel, who had been the first to use the machine-gun not as simply a rapid-firing rifle but as a weapon of artillery.

26 McConnell Papers, J.W. McConnell to Lil, 21 May 1919.

27 White, *The Story of Canada's War Finance*, 61.

28 McConnell Papers, J.W. McConnell to Lil, 20 May 1919.

29 At the very end of his life, in 1963, McConnell would give $900,000 to the YMCA-Sir George Williams campaign. After his death, two boys' and girls' clubs that he had built became YMCAs, in the east end of Montreal.

CHAPTER SEVEN

1 The story of the tramways in Boston is of considerable interest and has been carefully studied. See Hager, *History of the West End Street Railway*, and Mason, *The Street Railway in Massachusetts*.

2 McDowall, *The Light*, provides much of the information on which this account is based. See also St Clair Hall, "Electrical Utilities in Ontario," 203–4.

3 Centre d'Archives de l'Hydro-Québec, Montreal, F9/3443, file 2924.

4 Rumilly, *Histoire de la Province de Québec*, 13: 22.

5 Heaton, *The Trust Company Idea*, 11.

6 Imperial Trust's minute-books are in the offices of the RHW Foundation in Montreal. Through the kindness of the late Eric Webster and Norman Webster, copies of the minutes from 1910 to 1925 are archived as part of the McConnell Papers.

7 *Montreal Daily Star*, 3 August 1910.

8 Jacqueline Francoeur, the secretary to Senator L-J. Forget for thirty years, claimed that the money came from J.K.L. Ross, son of Forget's partner James Ross. See *Trente ans rue St-Francois-Xavier et ailleurs* (Montreal: Éditions Édouard Garand, 1928).

9 26 October 1910.

10 5 November 1910.

11 15 November and 2 November 1910.

12 Boards of Control were an innovation of this era's urban-reform movement, which believed that administrative bodies made up of businessmen, rather than politicians, with the power to oversee the operations of city councils, would bring an end to corruption and introduce efficiency to municipal politics.

13 Montreal *Star*, 22 February 1911.

14 Ibid., 25 February 1911.

15 Montreal *Star* and Montreal *Herald*, 22 February 1911.

16 Montreal *Witness*, 27 February 1911.

17 Ibid., 21 February 1911.

18 Ibid., 25 February 1911.

19 Montreal *Gazette* and Montreal *Herald*, 27 February 1911.

20 Montreal *Star*, 27 February 1911.

21 Montreal *Herald*, 27 February 1911.

22 Ibid., 2 March 1911.

23 Montreal *Gazette*, 9 March 1911.

24 Montreal *Herald*, 9 March 1911.

25 Ibid., 10 March 1911.

26 Montreal *Gazette*, 13 March 1910.

27 Charter of the Montreal Tramways Company, 2 Geo. V, c.77.

28 Montreal *Herald*, 23 February 1912.

29 Montreal *Gazette*, 18 December 1912.

30 Bellavance, *Shawinigan Water and Power*, 56–9.

31 Cited by Veilleux, "La motorisation," 104.

32 Montreal *Gazette*, 18 October 1913.

33 Montreal *Witness and Telegraph*, 14 November 1913.

34 Montreal *Herald*, 15 November 1913.

35 Ibid., 17 November 1913.

36 Ibid., 18 November 1913.

37 Montreal *Daily Mail*, 12 November 1914.

38 Montreal *Gazette*, 20 November 1914.

39 One board member who urged speedy acceptance of the new franchise was McConnell's close friend C.C. Ballantyne of Sherwin-Williams.

40 Montreal *Daily Mail*, 2 December 1914.

41 Ibid., 11 December 1914.

42 Beck is probably not a trustworthy reporter, since he was convicted of defamation in 1915.

43 Veilleux, "La motorisation," 107n.55, gives a more detailed account of the litigation.

44 City of Montreal Archives, City Council, 2nd Series, Reports and Files, no. 2873, Canadian Autobus Company file, is the basis for this account.

45 Montreal *Evening News*, 30 June 1915.

46 Montreal *Daily Mail*, 1 July 1915.

47 Made and executed on 28 January 1918 under Act 7, Geo.V, c.60, s.28, and Act 1, Geo.V, 2d Session, c.77; ratified in virtue of Act 8, Geo.V, c.84, s.75; sanctioned 8 February 1918.

48 Montreal *Gazette*, 25 September 1922.

49 Massell, *Amassing Power* 175–6.

50 Belfield, "The Niagara Frontier," 416–7.

51 Ibid., chapter VIII, footnotes 24, 25 and 26 and pages 426–61.

52 This account is essentially that of Armstrong and Nelles, "Getting Your Way in Nova Scotia," 105, from which the figures presented here are derived.

53 Nova Scotia Archives and Records Management, Borden Papers, MG 2/173/F1 and F2, Borden to Robert, 28 February 1910, and Robert to Borden, 1 March 1910.

54 Ibid., MG 2 /181/16035/F2, C.H. McLean to Borden, 15 March 1912. Borden arranged to sell these shares less than a month later: ibid., MG 2/181/16179/F4, McConnell to Borden, 11 April 1912. The lumber shares were bought from G.F. Johnston: MG 2/182/16622/F7, Johnston to Borden, 19 September 1912. Borden seems to have paid only $2,500 initially towards his subscription, and then a further $2,500 in January 1913, by which time the company was heading towards insolvency: MG 2/184/16913/F1 and MG 2/184/16954A/F1, Johnston to Borden, 6 and 15 January 1913.

55 See March, *Red Line*, 113–14.

56 Halifax *Daily Recorder*, [8?] May 1914.

57 Nova Scotia Archives and Records Management, NSPUC ruling, 17 December 1915.

58 Ibid., 14 February 1916, 27.

59 Ibid., 19 September 1916.

60 Interview with Bruce Kippen, 2002.

CHAPTER EIGHT

1 Veilleux, "La motorisation," 109–10.

2 By 1939, McConnell had bought shares in the many remnants of the old Insull empire, including Commonwealth Edison ($200,000); People's Gas, Light and Coke ($53,000); and North American Light and Power ($335,000).

3 Dillon, *Wendell Willkie*, 83.

4 On the ideology of the TVA, see Selznick, *TVA and the Grass Roots*; Hargrove, *Prisoners of Myth*; and Colignon, *Power Plays*.

5 This discussion generally follows Regehr, "Entrepreneurs and the Canadian Newsprint Industry, 1923–1931." On the Ontario ban on exports of unfinished pulp and paper, see Oliver, *G. Howard Ferguson*, 210.

6   This discussion of International Paper largely follows Heinrich, "Product Diversification in the US Pulp and Paper Industry."

7   Montreal *Gazette*, 27 October 1928.

8   This account of the power industry in New England is adapted from Landry and Cruikshank, *From the Rivers*.

9   Montreal *Gazette*, 12 October 1929.

10 Ibid., 1 December 1928.

11 Ibid., 25 March 1929.

12 Ibid., 3 November 1928.

13 Ibid., 24 December 1928 and 10 April 1929.

14 McConnell may have been instrumental in Gatineau's takeover that year of Ottawa and Hull Power, acquired by an old associate, A.J. Nesbitt (of Nesbitt, Thomson), in 1923.

15 Oliver in *G. Howard Ferguson*, 295, says that both the Carillon and the Georgian Bay leases with Ottawa "expired" on 1 May 1927, and that they were not renewed because of pressure from Taschereau and Ferguson. This may have been technically true, but at least in respect of Carillon uncertainty remained that led in 1930 to the formation of General Securities, by IP and Shawinigan (United Securities) to hold the shares of National Hydro Electric until the resolution of the constitutional questions that the two Premiers had raised.

16 See Oliver, *G. Howard Ferguson*, 186–7, in which Meighen's communication with Sir Henry Drayton on the matter is compared to that from Sir John A. Macdonald to Sir Hugh Allan in the Pacific Scandal, "Must Have Another $10,000."

17 *Gazette*, 14 and 30 August 1928.

18 The US Public Utility Holding Company Act of 1935 forced the separation of International Power form International Paper, so that the holding company IP&P was dissolved. But the separated companies did well nonetheless.

19 Queen's University Archives, Gerald S. Graham Fonds, Adds.A. Arch. 2169 and 2170, Sir Edward Peacock's memoir, file 16. Unless otherwise noted, all the information here is from the Graham Fonds, the *Dictionary of Business Biography* (London, 1984), and the *Dictionary of National Biography*.

20 The account that follows is from LAC, MG 18, Brascan Papers, series III 112, vol. 136, file 310.11 (pt. 2).

21 Ibid., pt. 1, Mackenzie to Lash for transmission to Loewenstein, 16 November 1926.

22 Ibid., pt. 6, E.R. Peacock to Miller Lash, 21 March 1928.

23 Ibid., letter to shareholders of International Holding and Investment, 22 March 1928.

24 Thompson, *The Odyssey of the Gentlemen Adventurers*.

25 McConnell Papers, J.W. McConnell to Lil, 13 and 24 September 1928.

26 For a general account of the reorganizations of this period, see Dales, *Hydroelectricity and Industrial Development*; and Bolduc and Larouche, *Québec: un siècle d'électricité*.

27 This allegation remains to be confirmed by closer study. With respect to 1898–1940, Dales found that "'the price of industrial electricity,' far from being a simple figure, is a complex thing of many dimensions, a concept more suitable as a weapon in the public-versus-private-power controversy than as a tool of economic analysis" (*Hydroelectricity and Industrial Development*, 8).

28 See Hogue, Bolduc and Larouche, *Québec: un siècle d'électricité*, chapter 6, and Regehr, *The Beauharnois Scandal: A Story of Canadian Entrepreneurship and Politics*.

29 The Roberts entered into an agreement with Narcisse Cantin in 1921 to develop the water rights that they still owned. Cantin failed to exercise his option to develop, and to make his required full payment, for part interest in the site, by October 1922. He had hired R.O. Sweezey, however, as his chief engineer. Sweezey offered himself to the Roberts as the developer of their site through their Beauharnois Light, Heat and Power Company (Beauharnois Power for short), originally incorporated in 1902. This company had laid cables in central Montreal in 1906, as discussed in chapter 7.

Sweezey paid the Roberts $100,000 in 1926 or 1927, and set up a syndicate of investors with shares for the Roberts, his own firm of Newman, Sweezey, and Dominion Securities. Another investor was McConnell's close friend, Frank P. Jones, who had worked with L.J. Forget in Dominion Steel and then with Sweezey under Max Aitken. Jones had just sold Canada Cement, of which he had been general manager from 1908 and then president, to Holt and J.H. Gundy, for a personal profit of $47 million.

Jones became president of Beauharnois Power. Senator Donat Raymond, another friend of McConnell's, was an investor, and he acted as the lobbyist for Beauharnois Power with Prime Minister King and Premier Taschereau. Sweezey had his plan to build a new canal from Lake St Francis to Lake St Louis passed through the Quebec Legislature in 1928. It was at this stage that McConnell, after he had become a director of the MLHPC, became at least tangentially involved with Beauharnois Power, as the MLHPC had been opposed to the syndicate led by Sweezey because his project seemed to threaten its markets. McConnell, as thus essentially opposed to Sweezey, was not involved in the bribery scandal arising form the Beauharnois project. Prime Minister Mackenzie King accepted favours, including a holiday in Bermuda, and Premier Howard Ferguson of Ontario probably accepted a bribe of $200,000, from the syndicate, in addition to the bribe of $125,000 accepted by John Aird, Jr, on behalf of the Ontario Conservative Party. See Regehr, *The Beauharnois Scandal: A Story of Canadian Entrepreneurship and Politics*, chapters 1 and 2, and his "'High-powered Lawyers, Veteran Lobbyists, Cunning Propagandists': Canadian Lawyers and the Beauharnois Scandal," chapter 13 of Wilton, ed., *Essays in the History of Canadian Law*, vol. IV, *Beyond the Law: Lawyers and Business in Canada, 1830 to 1930*. Ferguson's principal biographer concludes that the evidence for his bribe did not exist (Oliver, *G. Howard Ferguson: Ontario Tory* 199), but Sweezey himself admitted to the bribe or at least payment to Aird.

30 The new board of Beauharnois Light, Heat and Power in 1937 included J.S. Norris as president, who had succeeded Holt as president of Montreal power, along with C.S. Bagg and Sévère Godin, Jr., vice-presidents of the Montreal Power. The other directors included George Montgomery (vice-president); Norman Dawes, president of National Breweries; Aimé Geoffrion; J.H. Gundy of Wood, Gundy; T.A. Russell, formerly of Russell Motor Car and now president of Massey-Harris; A.F. White vice-president of the Bank of Commerce; M.W. Wilson, vice-president and general manager of the Royal Bank of Canada; and the Hon. Lucien Morand, KC.

31 Fleury, *Les porteurs de lumières*, 27.

32 Bergeron, *The History of Quebec*, 171–3.

33 There is no hard evidence that McConnell indulged in this lobbying, but, in light of his decision to reconcile with Duplessis just after the Duplessis's defeat of Godbout in the elections of 1944, and also of his cultivation of Judge Thomas Tremblay, who was evaluating the assets of the MLHPC with a view to compensating the shareholders, it seems likely that he did.

34 Young, "Dimensions of a Law Practice: Brokerage and Ideology in the Career of George-Etienne Cartier," chapter 3 of Wilton, ed., *Essays in the History of Canadian Law*, vol. IV, *Beyond the Law: Lawyers and Business in Canada, 1830 to 1930*, 92. See also his *George-Etienne Cartier* and *The Politics of Codification*.

35 This information from the Quebec press is taken from Roby, *Les Québécois et les investissements américains*, chapter 3.

36 Dales, *Hydroelectricity and Industrial Development*, 120–3.

37 *Report on the Electricity Commission of the Province of Quebec to the Prime Minister of the Province* (Quebec: 21 January 1935).

38 This is not to suggest that coal was unimportant, as it still was the standard fuel for domestic use before the introduction of oil and electricity.

CHAPTER NINE

1 The cultural innovation of department stores, as a channel of distribution, becomes clearer from the fact that the Montreal dry-goods stores, with the exception of Morgan's, did not transform themselves into department stores. Department stores were the product of a new concept of retailing, and the money made from the established dry-goods stores tended to be invested elsewhere as the department stores were opening, a good example being Greenshields.

2 Miller, *The Bon Marché: Bourgeois Culture and the Department Store*, cited by Saisselin, *Bricobracomania*, 33.

3 The chief sources for this account of Eaton's is Eaton, *Memory's Wall*.

4 Montreal *Gazette*, 18 March 1911.

5 In June and July, McConnell appears to have bought a further $10,000. The preferred shares of the company in 1915 seem to have totalled $1,679,000, with McConnell by far the principal shareholder. AO, F2290127, the T. Eaton Co. Papers, vol. 65, Goodwin's [sic] Limited Private Ledger, 1909–15.

6 It is not clear how this translated into floor space, of which Macy's in New York at least had 47,000 square feet. Hower, *History of Macy's*, 323.

7 Saisselin, *Bricobracomania*, 39–40.

8 Montreal *Gazette*, 17 May 1913.

9 Ibid., 1 January 1925.

10 *Financial Times* and *Financial Post*, 27 March 1925.

11 AO, T. Eaton Co. Papers, vol. 290 (suppliers' ledger, 1919), relating to Goodwins. There were also suppliers in Boston, Buffalo, New Haven, Jersey City, Newark, and other American towns.

12 LAC, MG 26, Meighen Papers, I, reel C3223, vol. 24, 13701, document 013707, Meighen to McConnell, 12 December 1921.

13 These and similar data are from McConnell's ledgers and *Financial Post* records. The two sources are not always in accord. For example, the *Financial Post* records that common shares of Holt Renfrew in 1944 sold at between $10 and $8, while McConnell in his private ledger recorded his shares at $1, which is perhaps a reflection of his extreme conservatism in accounting.

14 Black, *Duplessis*, 604.

15 Salmon, "This 'Remarkable Growth.'" The author has kindly provided a copy of this paper and is working on a history of CSL. Most of the account here is adapted from Salmon's. The manuscript collection of CSL at the Marine Museum of the Great Lakes in Kingston, Ontario, reveals little about McConnell's role in the company.

16 Unfortunately, Kilbourn, *The Elements Combined*, does not address the relationship with CSL.

17 There is this curious reference in Collard, *Passage*, with reference to a report of Mr Justice Norris, chair of an inquiry into inland shipping, which said of CSL in 1963 that it did "nothing but gave support to [Hal] Banks, the law breaker." Collard remarks: "The report had been a 'bombshell,' and 'the press was full of news and critical editorials,' with the Montreal *Star* publishing one of the most vicious. The *Star*'s proprietor, J.W. McConnell, was one of CSL's largest shareholders. McConnell was away when the editorial appeared, but when he saw it he 'was most upset' and convened a meeting of the editorial staff, together with McLagen and CSL's Captain Baxter" (320). While it may be that McConnell was upset, it is most unlikely that he convened a meeting of the editorial staff. He had severed his position as publisher of the newspaper almost a decade before, and in July 1963 he was barely mobile and indeed on the verge of death.

18 Bank of Montreal, report of the Annual General Meeting, 1 December 1930.

19 University of Manitoba Archives, Ogilvie Flour Mills Papers, MSS 120, box 1147d 2, 21 November 1935.

20 Warrington and Nicholls, *A History of Chemistry in Canada*, 343–4 and 56. See also *Liquid Air in Canada* and Jemain, *Les conquérants de l'invisible*.

21 McConnell became a director of Dominion Bridge on 18 February 1929. Montreal *Gazette*, 19 February 1929.

22 Canada, *Report of the Royal Commission on the Textile Industry*, 136–8.

23 McConnell's portfolio indicates that his dividend in 1929 was 15 rather than 12.5 per cent, but the figures used here are from Coleman, *Courtaulds*, 2:315, Table 67. He had owned 24,000 common or ordinary shares in Courtaulds as early as 1921, which he valued at $162,000.

24 Less stylishly, rayon became incorporated into towels, tablecloths, and car tires. In 1937 rayon constituted only 0.3 per cent of American tire fabric, but by 1950 its share had increased to 70 per cent. McConnell's investment of $375,000 in 1929 in US Rubber was effectively in these tires.

25 Canada, *Report of the Royal Commission on the Textile Industry*, 25–8.

26 Ibid., 126–7.

27 Markham, *Competition in the Rayon Industry*, 2.

28 "International" here refers to the scope of marketing or production operations, or both, and not necessarily to the source of control, which could still be essentially, say, German, British, or American.

29 Taylor, "Management Relations in a Multinational Enterprise," reprinted in Traves, ed., *Essays in Canadian Business History*, chapter 7. Between 1927 and 1951, the parent companies did hold between 46 and 48 per cent of all voting shares of CIL and between 92 and 94 per cent of all the shares of all classes of it.

30 This account is adapted from Howard-White *Nickel*; Stanley, *Nickel*; Thompson and Beasley, *For the Years to Come*; Swift and the Development Education Centre, *The Big Nickel*; Main, *The Canadian Nickel Industry*; Cohen, *The Life of Ludwig Mond*; Boldt, Jr, *The Winning of Nickel*; and Bolitho, *Alfred Mond*.

31 The basic facts of the BANCO story are to be found McDowall, *Steel at the Sault*, 114–17, and Colussi, "The Rise and Fall of the British America Nickel Corporation."

32 This was the reasoning behind the reorganization of Alcoa in 1928, which resulted in the formation of Aluminium Ltd as a separate Canadian corporation.

33 To admit that Americans controlled INCO after 1928 as well as before is not to say that the Canadianization of the company in 1918–19 was a total sham. In 1915 almost all the shareholders of INCO had been American. By 1934, Canadians owned 21 per cent of the shares, British residents 33 per cent, and US residents 42 per cent.

34 These figures are from the *Financial Post* and Main, *The Canadian Nickel Industry*, 105.

35 Although exports of nickel to Germany were suspended with the entry of the United States into the war at the end of 1941, IG Farben continued to flourish in other fields during and indeed after the war. During the war, it established, for example, a chemical works at the Auschwitz concentration camp near Krakow, and it manufactured the Zyklon-B gas used to exterminate inmates there and elsewhere in German-occupied Europe.

36 This account of the Canadian company is based on an unpublished typescript history, written in 1967 and supplied by Nicholas R. Iammartino of Borden, Inc. of Columbus, Ohio.

37 The same newspaper, it must be admitted, qualified this claim three months later, in describing the INCO reorganization alone: "The benefits have not been confined solely to Canada, and it is perhaps appreciated better in Wall Street than in Canada that Montreal has a constructive financial genius who is qualified to rank among the first of America, which means the first as far as these things go." Montreal *Gazette*, 28 December 1928, editorial, "Nickel Again Leader."

CHAPTER TEN

1 Hudson's Bay Company Archives, Winnipeg, E125/13, Patrick Ashley Cooper, Diary, 15 July 1939, 109.

2 Montreal *Star*, 11 November 1931; Montreal *Herald*, 3 and 22 February 1932. It is said that the loan was interest-free and that Cowans repaid it only shortly before his death. Some of this information comes from interviews with John Cowans in 1999 and 2001.

3 A more detailed analysis of McConnell's assets can be found in the appendix to this book by Nicolas McConnell.

4 It should be noted that the largest industry group in his 1921 portfolio is Canadian textile companies, which comprised 7.1 per cent of the total. There were extremely high tariffs protecting the products of these companies, for the maintenance of which it is possible that McConnell lobbied, just as he was lobbying for continued sugar protection.

5 LAC, MG 26-J, Mackenzie King Diary, 26 March 1943.

6 British Library, Oriental and India Office Collections, Willingdon Papers, MSS Eur-37/8, Willingdon to Inigo Freeman-Thomas, 20 February 1928.

7 Ibid., 16 September 1928.

8 Ibid., MSS F237/8, 23 September 1928.

9 Ibid., F237/9, 31 August 1929.

10 Ibid., 16 November 1929.

11 Ibid., F237/10, 6 January 1930.

12 Ibid., 8 August 1930.

13 Black, *Duplessis*, 604.

14 McConnell Papers.

15 The chief source for the Morgan holding companies is Chernow, *The House of Morgan*, especially chapter 16. See also Lamont, *The Ambassador from Wall Street*.

16 Until a projected new history of the company is published, the chief works on it are Harris, *The President's Book*; and Schull, *The Century of the Sun*.

17 Between 1899 and 1914, the stock and bond components of Canadian insurance-company investments rose from 24 to 50 per cent, with a corresponding decline in the traditional, more conservative mortgage component of their investments.

18 Schull, *The Century of the Sun*, 63.

19 Among his papers, information on his early policies survives. As of November 1910, for example, he had insured his life with the Travellers Life Assurance Company of Canada for $50,000; with New York Life for $17,000; with Mutual of Canada for $10,000; with Aetna Life for $10,000; with Canada Life for $2,000; and with United States Life for $2,000. He continued to buy, of course, other insurance on his life as well as on property, such as $92,477 worth from Lloyds for Lil's jewellery in 1921.

20 He held his 300 shares up to the end of 1949, and in October 1950 he sold 25 of them for $1,000 each. In 1951 there was a ten-for-one stock split, and his remaining 275 shares became 2,750. In 1958 the company was mutualized, and he was obliged to surrender his shares at a value of $325 each. It is not clear whether he still owned 2,750 shares at this time, but if he did, they yielded him $893,750. This figure, combined with the $25,000 generated through the sale of 25 shares in 1950, totals $918,750. If we subtract his adjusted cost base of $75,000 (in 1929 dollars), we see that he had made a total profit of $843,750.

21 The file of the Court of King's Bench in *The King v. Harpell*, was originally numbered 10-000084-32, but can now be found in the ANQ as nos. 500-01-9932-32 (trial) and 500-10-81-32 (appeal).

22 McConnell Papers, "The Borden Co. Limited" diary, entry for 1936.

23 These portfolios are estimates only, based on slightly incomplete data from what is known about his personal share and bond holdings and from those in the names of the family trusts, St Lawrence Sugar, and the Montreal *Star*. Moreover, the assumption is made here that all his shares were common rather than preference, while he probably had some preference shares at every stage.

24 Sloan's *Everyman and his Common Stocks: A Study of Long Term Investment Policy* appeared in 1931.

25 ANQ, Archives de Séminaire de Trois-Rivières, Fonds Maurice-Duplessis, FN–0019.C.09. 0568, J.W. McConnell to Maurice Duplessis, 27 May 1952.

CHAPTER ELEVEN

1 Appendix 16 of Burrough, ed., *Hemingway: The Toronto Years.*

2 For a discussion of "high society" at this time, see Homberger, *Mrs. Astor's New York.*

3 This account is essentially based on the McConnell Papers, on notarial documents found by Dr Mary Anne Poutanen, and on research by Stephen Otto, Robert Hill, and Robert Little.

4 Robert Little has written a book, not yet published, on the McConnell houses and their interiors.

5 Most of the information on the history of Dorval is from Duval, *Dorval.*

6 LAC, MG 26-J, Mackenzie King Diary, 19 October 1946.

7 More on the Forget and MacDougall-McConnell houses can be found in Gagnon Pratte, *Country Houses for Montrealers,* 70–81 and 96–8.

8 Laurin, *Histoire des Laurentides,* provides a much broader account of the region. There are several other books on the Laurentians, such as Neil and Catharine McKenty, *Skiing Legends.*

9 The documents of title are bound in one volume entitled "Report on Title on Properties at Ste-Agathe des Monts belonging to J.W. McConnell Esq.," in the McConnell Papers.

10 Queen's University Archives, Tweedsmuir Papers, box 9, Lady Tweedsmuir to Caroline Grosvenor, 15 March 1938.

11 This information is derived from Marks, *Rackets in Canada.* The club has sometimes been described as the "Racquets Club," but this official history calls it the Montreal Racket Club, and the petition for incorporation in 1889, reproduced on p. 121 of Marks's book, does the same.

12 Much of the information here is adapted from Cooper, *The History of the Montreal Hunt.*

13 It was not demolished until 2000.

14 Most of this information comes from *The Royal Canadian Yacht Club 1888–1988.*

15 The Forest and Stream Club and the Dorval Historical Society have provided the information on which this account is based. The membership roll for 1888–1947 was the most useful document.

16 Montreal *Gazette,* 9 October 1923.

17 There is a considerable literature on hockey, of which Brown, *The Montreal Maroons,* is particularly helpful on the Canadian Arena Company and the Forum.

CHAPTER TWELVE

1 Delivered to the Quebec Canadian Club. Amery, *The Empire in a New Era.*

2 Consider, for example, his support of Laurier in the election of 1911, which implies support both of the Liberal policy of reciprocity with the United States and of an independent, albeit small, Canadian navy.

3 In Canada, there were by 1914 an estimated thirty-five Round Table groups, with three hundred members. Rose, *The Cliveden Set,* 88.

4 Louis, *In the Name of God, Go!* 28.

5 "Government House" is the official term for the residence of the governor general, and of the sovereign when in Canada, in Ottawa. "Rideau Hall" is an informal name and was objected to by Queen Victoria, who wanted all her governors and governors general to live each in his own Government House.

6 Canada, *Royal Commission on the Textile Industry*, 47–8.

7 Bank of Montreal, report of the Annual General Meeting, 1 December 1930, 7.

8 Ibid., 7 December 1931, 8.

9 Memorandum, 5 August 1932, reproduced in appendix II of Drummond, *Imperial Economic Policy*, 296–9.

10 Churchill College, Cambridge, Lascelles Papers, Alan Lascelles to Joan Lascelles, 15 August 1932.

11 Bank of Montreal, report of the Annual General Meeting, 5 December 1932, 6.

12 It would be an arduous but an interesting task to trace how McConnell's economic interests fared in the midst of changing imperial trade relationships between the wars and after 1945. See, for example, McKenzie, *Redefining the Bonds of Commonwealth*.

13 The Prince of Wales to Mrs Freda Dudley Ward, in Godfrey, ed., *Letters from a Prince*, 176–7.

14 Frankland, *Witness of a Century*, 272.

15 The University Lying-in Hospital began in 1843. It changed its name to the University Maternity Hospital in 1884 and to the Montreal Maternity Hospital in 1887. In 1924 the Montreal Maternity merged with the Royal Victoria Hospital, and it moved into its new building, on the grounds of the Royal Victoria, in 1926. McConnell was president of the Montreal Maternity during its amalgamation with the Royal Victoria Hospital, and he presided over the Royal Victoria Hospital Ball, which was essentially for the benefit of the maternity wing, from then to the 1950s. See Munroe, *The Training School for Nurses*, 90–3, and "Charity Ball 1913," an anonymous typescript in the scrapbook kept by the Montreal Maternity Hospital (MUA, RG 95, container 396).

16 Interview with Mrs David Hankinson (Lavinia), a daughter of Sir Alan Lascelles, 1998.

17 Lascelles's daughter Lavinia (Mrs David Hankinson) has given permission to consult Sir Alan's papers at Churchill College, Cambridge, and Rupert Hart-Davis, the editor of two volumes of Lascelles's diaries and letters, has provided helpful advice on this period, as have David Hankinson and the late John Grigg.

18 Churchill College, Cambridge, Lascelles Papers, LALS II 1/1, Alan Lascelles to Joan Lascelles, 29 March 1933.

19 Much of this account of the trip is derived from diaries kept by McConnell, Lil, Kit, David, and Dr Edward Archibald.

20 Edward Archibald was chief surgeon at the Royal Victoria Hospital in Montreal. See Entin, *Edward Archibald*, and chapter 18.

21 McGill University, Osler Library, E.W. Archibald, "Bed Side Notes: Notes of Trip to India," Acc. 545/3, 7–10 January 1936.

22 Some hint of what the McConnells in consequence missed is to be found in the memoir of Baron Jean Pellenc, who had visited the Willingdons in India only a few months before and

reported in detail the state ball that he had attended. See Bence-Jones, *Palaces of the Raj*, 202–3.

23 MUA, Currie Papers, RG 2 , C47, 2207B 476, McC 1921–1939, 11 May 1931.

24 Knox, *Robert Byron*, 217.

25 Cited in Davies, *Splendours of the Raj*, 227 and 229.

26 See Hussey, *The Life of Sir Edwin Lutyens*.

27 British Library, Oriental and India Office Collections, London, Willingdon Papers, MSS Eur F-237, F/37/16, Willingdon to Lord and Lady Ratendone, 1 March 1936.

28 Archibald, "Bed Side Notes," 9 March 1936.

29 Hillyer, ed., *From the Orient with Love*, 16 April 1936.

30 Montreal *Star* and Montreal *Gazette*, 24 May 1936.

31 Indiana University, Lilly Library, Manuscripts Department, Willkie Papers, McConnell to Willkie, 5 November 1942.

32 McConnell Papers, J.W. McConnell to Kit McConnell, 3 December 1936.

33 McConnell Papers, Eric Mackenzie to Lil McConnell, 25 December 1936.

34 Montreal *Star*, 22 January 1937.

35 Ibid., "Brilliancy and Beauty at State Drawing Room," 29 January 1938.

36 Queen's University Archives, Tweedsmuir Papers, box 9, Lady Tweedsmuir to Caroline Grosvenor, 15 March 1938.

37 Interview with Betty Reitman, 2002.

CHAPTER THIRTEEN

1 McConnell Papers. Mrs Wasserboehr, born as Muriel Edith LeBarr, was a daughter of McConnell's sister Margaret Anna, who had married William Franklyn LeBarr, and she and her husband lived in California.

2 McConnell Papers.

3 Austin, *Saving China*.

4 Ibid., 47, citing the *Canadian Methodist* (December 1885), 561.

5 In the 1950s, Floyd Chalmers, a great philanthropist in his own right, wrote to McConnell asking for aid for the Stratford Festival. McConnell replied: "I regard the theater as secondary in priority to all the needs of a human character." But he added a footnote saying that he had just read the letter to his son, John, "who disagrees with me entirely and thinks my argument is crazy and fallacious. I have instructed my secretary to send you a check for $25,000." Grace Lydiatt Shaw, *Stratford under Cover*, quoted in *Reader's Digest*, April 1979.

6 Interview with Mrs Mary Redmond, daughter of Tim Curtis, a neighbour of McConnell's in Dorval, 1996.

7 McConnell may have had little talent for theology, but he certainly appreciated its importance. When in 1942 the McGill Senate set up a Faculty of Divinity for the university, McConnell endowed one of the new chairs.

8 The statement comes from John 11: 25 and 26, but McConnell added to it.

9 McConnell Papers, "The Business Year Book 1939," entry for 1941.

10 McConnell knew two doctors at the General: F.J. Tees, the hospital's medical superintendent, a physician who worked closely with McConnell on the YMCA campaign of 1909; and Frederick Gault Finley ("Fin"), brother of the businessman W.C. Finley, who was associated with McConnell in the Montreal Street Railway takeover in 1910.

11 According to MacDermot, *A History of The Montreal General Hospital*, 59, the annual report for 1872 recorded the registered patients – apparently from the opening of the hospital to date – as: 28,473 Roman Catholics, 24,947 Protestants, 9 Jews, and 1 atheist.

12 This account is derived from Lewis, *Royal Victoria Hospital 1887–1947*.

13 Michael M. Davis and Anna C. Phillips, American Hospital Association Service Bureau on Dispensaries and Community Relations of Hospitals, "Summary of Survey of Hospital Situation in Montreal Canada" (5 January 1922). A copy of this is in the McConnell Papers, with a covering letter from Herbert Molson, 17 August 1923.

14 MUA, RG 2, C0068, American Hospital Association, "Survey of the Hospital Situation in Montreal, Canada" (unpublished reported dated 5 January 1922), 7.

15 Montreal *Star*, 6 June 1922.

16 This appeared to be an extension of Sir William Osler's appeal to Dean H.S. Birkett of McGill and John D. Rockefeller, Jr in 1919 for coordination of the clinical training of medical students in hospitals with their academic training at the Faculty of Medicine at McGill. The value of such coordination had become particularly clear during the war, when the No. 3 Canadian General Hospital (McGill), which included doctors from different hospitals back home, gained wide recognition for its important services on the front lines.

17 McConnell had personally written to Sir Joseph Flavelle for the Ontario figures. See Queen's University Archives, Flavelle Papers, box 14, nos. 9215–23, correspondence with McConnell in January and February 1926.

18 Montreal *Star*, 4 February 1926.

19 The Chambre even said that municipalities should be responsible for all the actual expenses of caring for indigents. As the situation stood, a hospital was expected to pay a third of the $2 that was assumed to be the actual cost of indigent patients. In fact, some argued that this cost was $3, so that these proposals would still, after the increased provincial grant, leave the hospital to cover a third of the actual cost. The rise of combined municipal and provincial grants to $2 would thus effectively reduce but not limit the deficits. This would change, however, if a proposal to cover all the actual costs of indigents were adopted.

20 Montreal *Star*, 10 February 1926.

21 McConnell to the editor of the Montreal *Star*, 9 February 1926.

22 Montreal *Star*, 20 March 1926.

23 Montreal *Gazette*, 20 March 1926. In 1941 its scope was to be extended to include dining cars and most other establishments. The rate was 5 per cent on the price of each meal costing 60 cents served, including the price of beer, wine, and other beverages. All revenues from the duty were paid into the Public Charities Fund, from which grants were made for the support of hospitals, and the municipalities were empowered to impose a similar tax under the same legislation. See Perry, *Taxation in Canada*, 210.

24 Montreal *Star*, 26 April 1927.

25 Ibid., 28 April 1927.

26 Ibid., 27 April 1927.

27 May 1927.

28 Montreal *Star*, 28 May 1929.

29 Charitable donations under the 1917 Income War Tax legislation were deductible by individuals, if made to the Red Cross or patriotic funds. But this deduction was removed in 1919 and not restored until the 1930s. The circumstances of the restoration of charitable deductions by individuals are unclear, although it appears that Herbert Marler was behind it. See Perry, *Taxes, Tariffs & Subsidies*, 1: 216.

30 Neither did he hold the suit against the Jeffery Hale Hospital: in October 1950, through Premier Duplessis, he gave it $50,000.

31 McConnell gave $25,000 to the Governors Fund in 1936–37, the same amount as Sir Herbert Holt. His total contributions towards reducing annual deficits, from 1936 to 1939, were $54,166. In 1938 the governors set up an all-powerful executive and finance committee, on which he joined Beatty and Lewis Douglas, among others. He also became chairman of the Financial Appeal Committee, and by May 1939 he had secured for McGill subscriptions totalling $30,000 to $40,000 a year, for four years.

32 Taschereau's biographers ignore his role in this funding. See Vigod, *Quebec before Duplessis*; Dupont, *Taschereau* and *Les relations entre l'Église et l'État sous Louis-Alexandre Taschereau*. The aftermath of funding policies for hospitals is well covered, however, in chapter 4 of Vaillancourt, *L'Évolution des politiques sociales au Québec*.

33 This was not McConnell's first involvement with the cause of "settlements": as early as 1909, he supported the McGill University Settlement in Montreal, a special cause of his friend the Unitarian scientist Milton Hersey. The cause of children's health was particularly dear to McConnell. One of Montreal's smaller hospital was the Alexandra, for children with tuberculosis, founded by R.B. Angus and Senator George Drummond in 1906. The board contained representatives of the General and the Royal Victoria, and in 1940 McConnell was made one of its four governors on the board, representing the Royal Vic. Later, in 1946, McConnell and John Molson set up two research fellowships, in medicine and in surgery, for the expanded Montreal Children's Hospital, each with an annual value of $1,000.

34 McConnell also became a member of the advisory committee of the Financial Federation – organized in 1922 to run the fundraising campaigns of the Montreal Council of Social Agencies – in 1928. In 1937 the Montreal Council became the Federated Charities, which in turn became the Welfare Federation of Montreal in 1943, and McConnell was made its honorary president in 1945. It changed its name again to United Red Feather Services in 1960, before becoming part of the provincially sponsored Centraide in 1966.

35 Printed address to fundraising workers, undated but probably 1926, in the McConnell Papers.

36 These quotations are from an undated cutting in the McConnell Papers, probably from February 1926, reporting on a meeting of the trustees of St James.

37 Kit later moved to St George's Anglican Church in Dominion Square after her marriage to Peter Laing in 1945.

38 Archives Nationales du Québec, P603, S2, SS39, J.H. Birks to W.M. Birks, 7 March 1938.

39 A stimulating study of the architecture of the Erskine Church (later the Erskine-American) is Zubalik, "'Advancing the Material Interests of the Redeemer's Kingdom,'" which is also a useful guide to the history of Presbyterianism in Montreal. Zubalik cites Birks's description of the Erskine as "not a church at all, but an auditorium … a specimen of one of the worst periods of American architecture" (79).

CHAPTER FOURTEEN

1   McConnell sent copies of this editorial and the one shown below it to J.J. Astor, Lord Beaverbrook, Viscount Camrose, Anthony Eden, Viscount Kemsley, Sir Walter Layton, Vincent Massey, Viscount Southwood, and Sir Campbell Stuart.

2   McConnell Papers, McConnell to Mr and Mrs Francis Wasserboehr, 15 December 1942.

3   LAC, Mackenzie King Papers, MG 26-J1, vol. 309, nos. 260956-9.

4   Ibid., MG 26-J, Mackenzie King Diary, 16 August 1940.

5   McConnell Papers, Angela Bruce to Lily McConnell, 27 June 1940.

6   Ibid., J.W. McConnell to Lil, 4 July 1940.

7   The term "aeroplane" rather than "airplane" is used here, although even at this time the latter was probably more widely used in Canada, because it was the standard British term and this discussion is of aircraft used by the Royal Air Force. Lord Beaverbrook, both before and during his tenure as minister for aircraft production, tried to force his newspapers to use the term more current in America and Canada, but without success.

8   Cartland, *The Years of Opportunity*, 87.

9   The story of King George II is told in Vickers, *Alice: Princess Andrew of Greece*.

10 House of Lords, London, Beaverbrook Papers. All citations from communications between McConnell and Beaverbrook in this period are from this collection.

11 LAC, Arthur Meighen Papers, MG 26, vol. 176, reel C-3567, no.154022, Carman to McConnell, 12 July 1938.

12 Ibid., no. 154023, McConnell to Meighen, 13 July 1938.

13 Adapted from an unpublished manuscript by Air Chief Marshal L.D. Dalzell McKean, "History of the UK ALM – Canada," 30 March 1945 (British National Archives [BNA], AVIA 38/1246). Hall, in *North American Supply* (22), says that the plan trained 137,739 pilots.

14 UTA, Massey Papers, J.W. McConnell to Vincent Massey, 15 August 1940.

15 UNBA, Beaverbrook Papers, Case 76, file 1a no. 11, letters from Lord Beaverbrook to John G. McConnell, and from George Thomson to Lord Beaverbrook, n.d.

16 McConnell Papers. McConnell kept a black binder in which were pasted this copy of his letter to Churchill and the original letters and telegrams that he himself received after the announcement of his gift.

17 Of all the legendary aeroplanes from the Second World War, the Spitfires remain perhaps the most widely remembered. Over their twelve years of production beginning in 1937, more than 22,000 were built. At the end of its development life, the Spitfire carried an engine giving more than twice the power and weighing about three-quarters more than the original; its rate of climb had almost doubled; and its firepower had increased by five times. It was the pride of

the RAF, and it also served thirty other air forces on six continents; about a thousand Spitfires went to each of the Soviet and the American air forces.

18 Taylor, *Beaverbrook*, 550.

19 Barnett, *The Audit of War*, 144.

20 BNA, AVIA, 38/72, Captain Balfour on his interview with Secretary Morgenthau, 1 September 1940, and letter from C.D. Howe to Arthur Purvis, 26 September 1940; and AVIA 38/3, correspondence between Arthur Purvis and M.W. Wilson, copy of a memorandum by Purvis to Sir Arthur Salter, 2 October 1940, and of Beaverbrook's reply, 3 October 1940.

21 Among the books consulted for this account of Ferry Command were Bennett, *Pathfinder*; McVicar, *Ferry Command*; and Powell, *Ferryman*.

22 Margaret Purvis, his widow, remained a close friend of the McConnells. McConnell bought the Purvis house to give to McGill as the home of the School of Commerce.

23 Adapted from BNA, AVIA, 38.

24 UNBA, Beaverbrook Papers, Case 64a, file 1a no. 1, Lord Beaverbrook to John G. McConnell, 29 September 1954.

25 A basic account of ATFERO and of its successors is by Powell, *"Per Ardua ad Astra."*

26 McConnell Papers, Lord Knollys to Lily McConnell, 21 October 1944.

27 LAC, Mackenzie King Diary, 1 and 3 February 1941. There seems to have been no love lost between McConnell and Ralston, perhaps dating back to the days of McConnell's takeover, with E.A. Robert, of the Halifax transit system, when Ralston was a lawyer for the opposite side. On 18 September 1939 George Ferguson had reported to J.W. Dafoe that John Bassett had been demanding that McConnell should be appointed Canadian minister in Washington but "was dealt with in short order by Ralston." Provincial Archives of Manitoba, J.W. Dafoe Papers, MSS 3, box 2, file 7.

28 The legal and other documents and accounts by Price Waterhouse, as well as a book of press cuttings, are in the McConnell Papers.

29 Bishop, *The Canadian Y.M.C.A. in the Great War.*

30 UTA, Massey Papers, J.W. McConnell to Vincent Massey, 15 August 1940, enclosing a copy of a letter from Major J.W. Beaton, which confirmed the delivery of McConnell's cheque.

31 In 1941 McConnell himself had been considered for the Canadian Legation in Washington, in succession to Loring Christie, who had died suddenly. The reasons for his rejection are unclear, although they seem to relate to opposition by Minister of Defence J.L. Ralston. McConnell was in fact qualified by neither experience nor personality to be a diplomat, although he would probably have made a greater impression than the man who was appointed in his place, the lawyer Leighton McCarthy.

32 Borthwick Institute (York, UK), Halifax Papers, A 7 8.9, diary for 19 August 1941.

33 Letter to the author from Lord Chatfield, who had accompanied them, 4 December 1996.

34 University of Durham, MacDonald Papers, 132/1/86.

35 Ibid., MacDonald to Dorothy Hyson, 29 April 1941.

36 See, for example, McConnell Papers, MacDonald to Lily McConnell, 11 March 1942.

37 MacDonald Papers, 132/1/142, MacDonald to Dorothy Hyson, 29–30 October 1941.

38 Ibid., MacDonald to Dorothy Hyson, 31 October 1941.

39 McConnell Papers, MacDonald to Lily McConnell, 11 November 1963.

40 Sanger, *Malcolm MacDonald*, 323.

41 This biographical account is adapted from the introduction to Hooker, ed., *The Moffat Papers*. The references in this text are to volumes of the unpublished Moffat manuscripts at the Houghton Library of Harvard University, Ms Am 1407.

42 McConnell Papers, Baron Silvercruys to Lily McConnell, 9 August 1939.

43 This is confirmed by the Mackenzie King Diary, 4 April 1941.

44 Hooker, ed., *The Moffat Papers*, vol. 46, 28–29 April 1941. Beaverbrook continued to cultivate McConnell and visited him in September 1941.

45 Indiana University, Willkie Papers, Willkie to McConnell, 14 November 1942; McConnell to Willkie, 21 November 1942 and 9 December 1942.

46 Ibid., McConnell to Willkie, 9 December 1942.

47 Ibid., McConnell to Willkie, 17 August 1943; Montreal *Star* editorial, 17 August 1943.

48 Willkie Papers, McConnell to Helen M. Tucker, Willkie's secretary, 22 September 1944.

49 LAC, Mackenzie King Papers, MG 26, J-1, vol. 309, no. 260948.

50 Moffat Papers, vol. 47, 24 January 1942.

51 Ibid.

52 If such were the views of McConnell's circle, they were not universally shared even in English Montreal, to say nothing of French Montreal. After the plebiscite, Frank Scott continued to lead the small English-speaking opposition in Montreal to conscription, and indeed to Canadian participation in the war. His views brought him into conflict not only with businessmen such as J.M. Macdonnell but also with his fellow socialist Eugene Forsey.

53 Another version of the story is that McConnell called Prime Minister King. In any case, his call was almost immediately effective.

54 He raised this £2,000 to £5,000, for the YMCA to provide huts, canteens, and leave clubs for women serving with the armed forces. *The Times*, 5 October 1944.

55 Soames, *Clementine Churchill*, 322. This reference is omitted in the second edition of the biography.

CHAPTER FIFTEEN

1 Montreal North: VLB Editeur 1978 (165–6). Translation: "You have heard the howlings on St. James Street, you have read the articles in newspapers, 'Duplessis chases away capital.' 'Duplessis harms investments.' Have you noticed that as soon as a government of Quebec lifts its head and then asks to be respected, funds leave, investments flee? There are those who wanted us to live on our knees, to put ourselves on our knees before the Liberal Party, on our knees before Ottawa, on our knees before the Imperialists, on our knees before Bassett, McConnell. Now I say this, that the Union Nationale has just one master, and this master is not on St. James Street, he is not in Ottawa, he is not in London, he is here this evening and this master is the people of the province of Quebec. This is the only master that we have ever had and the only master that we shall ever have!' From the context, this speech is set in 1939.

2 LAC, Arthur Meighen Papers, MG 26, vol. 76, reel O-3445.

3 LAC, MG 26-G, Laurier Papers, vol. 690, reel C-906, nos. 188925–33, McConnell to Sir Wilfrid Laurier, 14 August 1911.

4 This was at least claimed by the Toronto *Star*, 4 July 1940, discussing the possible appoint-ment of McConnell to a national government under Mackenzie King.

5 In 1940 Senator Raoul Dandurand pressed Prime Minister Mackenzie King for a knight-hood for McConnell, arguing that McConnell "had really been responsible for the results of a previous campaign." King recalled that "it was the one against Sir Wilfrid in 1917" and he "declined absolutely to consider the matter at all." LAC, MG 26-J, Mackenzie King Diary, 25 January 1940.

6 LAC, MG 26-I, Meighen Papers, vol. 233, reel C-3223, 13018–9, docs. 013018–9.

7 In 1926 McConnell was apparently still hoping that White would come out of retirement. He asked Meighen to confirm gossip about "Sir T.W. coming out, *at your request*, and coupled with his name that of a prominent French Canadian, to lead Quebec out of darkness into light." LAC, Meighen Papers, vol. 114, reel e-3463, no. 7188, McConnell to Arthur Meighen, 23 February 1926.

8 Cited by Gray, "Our First Century – A Lot of It Was Fun," 9 and 10, apparently relying on Graham, *Arthur Meighen: And Fortune Fled*, 150.

9 Graham, *Meighen: And Fortune Fled*, 150–1.

10 Ibid., 2:149–50.

11 LAC, Meighen Papers, vol. 81, reel C-3447, no. 041139, Murray Williams to Arthur Meighen, 28 September 1925.

12 Ibid., no. 041137, Arthur Meighen to Murray Williams, 11 October 1925.

13 Michaud, *L'Enigme du sphinx*, 117.

14 Imperial Trust, controlled by Webster in 1925, had been supporting *La Patrie* with loans for over ten years.

15 LAC, Meighen Papers, no. 046389, McConnell to Arthur Meighen, 7 December 1925.

16 Ibid., no. 049596, McConnell to Arthur Meighen, 6 November 1925; and no. 049633, Arthur Meighen to McConnell, 11 November 1925.

17 Ibid., no. 046389, McConnell to Arthur Meighen, 7 December 1925.

18 Ibid., nos.148510–1, Arthur Meighen to Roger Graham, 12 February 1952.

19 Despite Patenaude's conduct, Prime Minister Bennett was later to reward him with the lieutenant-governorship of Quebec, in time for the visit to Canada of King George VI and Queen Elizabeth in 1939.

20 Glassford, *Reaction and Reform*, 87–8.

21 Ibid.

22 LAC, MG 26-K, R.B. Bennett Papers, vol. 949, reel M3/76, nos. 0599888–9, McConnell to Bennett, 28 November 1932.

23 The list of guests is in the McConnell Papers.

24 LAC, Bennett Papers, nos. 0599900–1, McConnell to Bennett, 18 January 1935.

25 A former cabinet minister in the Bennett government, H.H. Stevens, running under the ban-ner of his own Reconstruction Party, accounted for the loss of 75 to 100 seats to the Liberals. Given that 90 per cent of Stevens's supporters were Conservatives, these seats would other-wise have been won by the Conservative Party.

26 LAC, Mackenzie King Diary, 15 November and 12 December 1925.

27 LAC, MG 26, J-1, Mackenzie King Papers, vol. 271, nos. 189273, 229530, and 229633; vol. 236, nos. 203234–5.

28 LAC, Mackenzie King Diary, 28 April 1937.

29 Ibid., 30 April 1937.

30 Ibid., 9 October 1937.

31 Ibid., 10 October 1937.

32 Montreal *Star*, 11 August 1938, cited by Granatstein, *The Politics of Survival*, 18.

33 LAC, Mackenzie King Diary, 5 and 19 January and 28 September 1939.

34 McConnell seems to have been edging towards support of King two years before. LAC, Mackenzie King Diary, 5 January 1939.

35 Ibid., 14 March 1938.

36 Montreal *Star*, 5 October 1939.

37 UTA, Massey Papers, McConnell to Alice and Vincent Massey, 14 October 1939, enclosing a copy of the *Star* editorial of 5 October 1939. See also Herbert Bruce to Lord Beaverbrook, 27 February 1939, cited in Granatstein, *The Politics of Survival*, 24.

38 J.L. Granatstein, "Financing the Liberal Party, 1935–45," in Cross and Bothwell, eds, *Policy by Other Means*, 189, citing the diary of Norman Lambert.

39 McConnell Papers, J.M. Macdonnell to Lil McConnell, 7 November 1963: "I went to him for assistance many times over the years beginning with the Conservative Party and never came away empty-handed." Only a few weeks before his death, McConnell had given Macdonnell a "magnificently generous" contribution to Davie Fulton, formerly minister of justice and attorney general in the Diefenbaker government.

40 Montreal *Star*, 1 September 1939.

41 The term "national government" was used in England, and to some extent in Canada, but the idea of a "coalition" government is perhaps clearer in this context since "national" governments in Canada have been identified with federal governments.

42 Arthur Meighen to G.B. Jones, 26 February 1940, cited in Granatstein, *The Politics of Survival*, 50.

43 McConnell Papers, J.W. McConnell to Mr and Mrs Francis Wasserboehr, 20 December 1943.

44 LAC, Mackenzie King Papers, vol. 408, 36808.

45 LAC, Mackenzie King Diary, 13 June 1948. In the same entry, King records: "Spoke strongly of my belief that I know is fundamentally shared very strongly by Mr. McConnell as to survival of personality, of things working together for good."

46 McConnell Papers, J.W. McConnell to Lil, 28 July 1950.

47 Black, *Duplessis*, 212, 268, 272, 354, 394, 478, and 602–11. See also Gérard, *Le Duplessisme*, 143–5; and Dion, *Québec 1945–2000*, 2: 41, 90–1, 101, and 119.

48 Barrette, *Mémoires*, 186. Barrette regretted that McConnell's charitable gifts were so often anonymous and suggested that Duplessis himself had wanted to publicize McConnell's good works better (ibid., 187).

49 ANQ, Fond Maurice Duplessis, J.W. McConnell to Duplessis, 6 June 1946.

50 Ibid., Maurice Duplessis to J.W. McConnell, 18 June 1946.

51 Ibid., J.W. McConnell to Maurice Duplessis, 17 August 1946.

52 It is sometimes suggested – and implied by Black – that even McConnell's fundraising for relief work after the fires in Rimouski and Cabano, in May 1950, was designed to support Duplessis. In both cases, sparks from a lumber-mill fire blew onto the housetops of towns, causing millions of dollars in damage. Nearly 50 per cent of Cabano's houses were destroyed, only 20 per cent of them insured. Financial aid poured in from all over the world, and even Pope Pius XII sent $10,000. Apart from his own contribution, McConnell lined up $10,000 from Alcan, $10,000 from Dominion Textile, and $6,000 from North Shore Paper. If Duplessis himself was to benefit from these contributions, however, it is not clear how.

53 Montreal *Star*, 30 May 1953. Mayor Camillien Houde had given the deed to the land for the new club to the Montreal Boys' Association in March of the previous year. The club cost $1 million to build, and the provincial government contributed $50,000 towards operating costs. McConnell's contribution was $375,000. Montreal *Gazette*, 14 March 1952.

54 Montreal *Herald*, 12 February 1954.

55 Black, *Duplessis*, 606.

56 Dion, *Québec 1945–2000*, 2:118–19.

57 Black, *Duplessis*, 607.

58 Ibid., 606. Black cites Auréa Cloutier, Duplessis's secretary, as authority for this statement.

59 Angell, *Provincial Party Financing in Quebec*, 19.

60 See ibid., 21, where Angell implies that McConnell represented big corporate donors.

61 As Angell puts it: "Stories abound of capitalists like J.W. McConnell of THE (Montreal) STAR walking into Duplessis' office with a briefcase packed with banknotes 'for Le Chef's good works.'" Ibid., 104n.79.

62 The first request is recorded in minute-book no. 3 of the J.W. McConnell Foundation, 30 March 1960; another is recorded in the minutes for 29 March 1963.

63 There is a vast literature on the Suez Crisis. See, for example, Finer, *Dulles over Suez*; Neff, *Warriors at Suez*; and Kyle, *Suez*.

64 For a dispassionate account, see Eayrs, *The Commonwealth and Suez*.

65 University of Birmingham, Eden/Avon Papers, AP24/45/3, McConnell to Anthony Eden, 5 July 1957.

66 Ibid., AP24/45/57, J.W. McConnell to Anthony Eden, 22 July 1957.

67 Ibid., AP24/45/58, J.W. McConnell to Anthony Eden, 25 August 1957.

68 Ibid., AP24/45/59, J.W. McConnell to Lady Eden, 11 September 1957.

69 Ibid., AP24/45/16A, J.W. McConnell to Anthony Eden, 11 December 1957. By January 1959, Eden had reached an agreement with *The Times* about serial rights in England.

70 Ibid., AP24/45/20, Anthony Eden to J.W. McConnell, 5 January 1958.

71 Ibid., AP24/45/24, Anthony Eden to J.W. McConnell, 17 February 1958.

72 Ibid., AP24/45/26A, J.W. McConnell to Anthony Eden, 18 April 1958.

73 Ibid., AP24/45/26B, Anthony Eden to J.W. McConnell, 4 June 1958.

74 Ibid., AP24/45/29, J.W. McConnell to Anthony Eden, 10 June 1958.

75 Ibid., AP24/45/31, J.W. McConnell to Anthony Eden, 6 August 1958.

76 Ibid., AP24/45/29, J.W. McConnell to Anthony Eden, 10 June 1958.

77 Ibid., AP24/45/26B, Anthony Eden to J.W. McConnell, 4 June 1958.

78 Ibid., AP24/45/39, J.W. McConnell to Anthony Eden, 19 October 1959.

79 Ibid., AP24/45/46, J.W. McConnell to Anthony Eden, 30 July 1963.

80 Quebec Provincial Division of the Canadian Red Cross Society, *Annual Report 1956*, report of Commissioner G.P. Hedges, 31.

81 McConnell Papers, J.W. Knox to Lily McConnell, 19 November 1963.

82 There was at least one grant, as well, to the Lord Mayor's Fund for Hungarian Refugees in London.

CHAPTER SIXTEEN

1 *Fair Dinkum*, 112. Numerous former employees of the *Star*, the *Herald*, and the *Standard* have been interviewed in the research for this chapter, including the late Edward Whittaker.

2 Over time, the paper operated under various names: *Evening Star*, 1869–77; Montreal *Daily Star*, 1877–1957; Montreal *Star and Herald*, 1957–58; Montreal *Star*, 1958–79. In this book, the newspaper is referred to simply as the *Star*.

3 Green and West, "Headlining a Century," circa 1869, was commissioned by John G. McConnell but never published. J.W. McConnell refused to cooperate by offering information, and the narrative is generally vague and completely without footnotes. John McConnell apparently rejected it as unpublishable. It is also often wrong in its judgments. Nevertheless, since Green was the editor of the *Family Herald* and West was an editor of the *Star*, it is an important source. Copies of this typescript are available at the library of Loyola College at Concordia University and with the McConnell Papers at McGill University.

4 Ibid., 582–5.

5 In December 1947 a dividend of $17.22 per share on 25,000 common shares of MSCL was declared, amounting to $430,730. Together with the $105,000 of dividends on preferred shares received by St Lawrence at the same time, these dividends equalled the undistributed income on hand at the end of 1939 less corporation tax paid. MSCL Minutes, 23 December 1947.

6 Montreal *Star*, Minutes, 31 July 1931. The minutes are part of the McConnell Fonds at the MUA.

7 Ibid., 15 April 1932.

8 Ibid., 19 September 1934.

9 Ibid.

10 McConnell Papers, 13 October 1933.

11 Montreal *Star*, 9 May 1935.

12 This letter, and Atholstan's reply of 8 October 1935, are in the *Star* Minutes of 9 October 1935.

13 Montreal *Star*, Minutes, 31 May 1938.

14 McConnell Papers, 2 February 1938.

15 LAC, MG 26-I, Arthur Meighen Papers, vol. 232, reel C-360, no.154011, Meighen to McConnell, 6 February 1938, and no. 154013, McConnell to Meighen, 10 February 1938.

16 Ibid., no. 154012, McConnell to Flavelle, 7 February 1938.

17 The author found this book, with McConnell's bookplate, in the McConnell house in Montreal.

18 Quoted by Heintzman, "The Struggle for Life," 3.

19 This was the full name of the *Family Herald*, which did not drop *"Weekly Star"* from its mast-head until 1956.

20 It appears that the employees of St Lawrence Sugar received essentially the same benefits as those of the *Star* during the Second World War.

21 The lot on Sherbrooke Street was to become the site of the Scotiabank Tower in about 2000, when the McConnell Foundation moved to it.

22 The *Star* entered into contracts with unions between August and October 1950. These unions included the Montreal Brotherhood of Bookbinders Union Local 91, the Montreal Newspaper printing Pressmen's Union No. 41, the Montreal Typographical Union No. 176, and the Montreal Stereotypers' and Electrotypers' Union Local 33. MSCL Minutes, 30 July 1931.

23 As M.G. Dunham, manager and chief negotiator of the Montreal Newspaper Guild, is reported as saying, "au Montreal Star, les conditions de travail étaient bonnes et il y régnait une atmosphère familiale; les journalistes étaient heureux d'y travailler et ne cherchaient pas à se syndiquer de moins lorsque John McConnell était le propriétaire. A sa mort, son fils a pris la relève et l'atmosphère a beaucoup changé. John McConnell Jr. mettait beaucoup plus de pression sur employés et les journalistes ont alors senti le besoin de se syndiquer" (Déom, *40 ans de syndicalisme chez les journalists québécois*, 31–2). It was not until May 1972 that the Newspaper Guild was accredited at the *Star*, as local 111 of the Canadian Labour Congress affiliated with the AFL-CIO, and not until 1977 that it was accredited at the *Gazette*. In contrast, the Fédération de l'Imprimerie (founded in 1925) was accredited at *La Presse* in 1944, at *Le Devoir* in 1945, and at *Le Soleil* in 1950, under the provisions of the provincial Labour Relations Act of 1944. In 1963 there were difficult negotiations between the *Star* and the American Newspaper Guild. MSCL Minutes, 20 November 1963.

24 McConnell Papers, undated memorandum but probably about 8 August 1940, from John G. McConnell to J.W. McConnell.

25 Pat Pearce, "Memories of an Old Friend," Montreal *Star*, 4 June 1962.

26 McConnell Papers, memorandum from J.G. McConnell to J.W. McConnell, 14 December 1945.

27 The story of *Weekend Magazine* is briefly told in Sutherland, *Monthly Epic*, 188–90, and in Carroll, *The Life and Times of Greg Clark*, chapter 35. Mark Farrell, in his unpublished memoirs, gives a much more detailed account.

28 University of New Brunswick Archives, Beaverbrook Papers, J.G. McConnell to Lord Beaverbrook, 2 October 1961, 57871.

29 McConnell Papers, J.G. McConnell to J.W. McConnell, 29 March 1944 ("1944 Memorandum").

30 Kierans, *Remembering*, 47.

31 Forsey, *A Life on the Fringe*, 58.

32 A copy of the pamphlet is in the McConnell Papers.

33 This reply takes the form of a memorandum, dated 28 March 1944, typed but almost undoubtedly written by McConnell himself, found in his papers at his house, and published as an editorial in the *Star* on 16 May 1944. McConnell immediately sent a copy to Louis St Laurent, the minister of justice, who agreed with him: "It is encouraging to note that responsible

papers are not disposed to allow the influence they have acquired to be used, even in their advertising columns, for propaganda which obviously runs counter to right thinking on matters of genuine public concern." (McConnell Papers, Louis St Laurent to J.W. McConnell, 18 May 1944.) J.W. McConnell's memorandum bears the same date as his son's memorandum to him, which refers to a conversation between the two of the day before.

34 Djwa, *The Politics of the Imagination*, 221–2; the authority for this account is given as an interview with Scott in January 1983.

35 Donnelly, *Dafoe of the Free Press*, describes this incident at 175–6. On McConnell as propagandist, see the University of Manitoba Archives and Special Collections, J.W. Dafoe Papers, MSS 3, file 6, George Ferguson to J.W. Dafoe, 30 January 1938.

36 Ferguson and Underhill, *Press and Party in Canada*, 21.

37 Brennan, *Reporting the Nation's Business*, 161, citing a letter from Ferguson to MacDermot, 12 July 1953.

38 Ferguson and Underhill, *Press and Party in Canada*, 15.

39 Sarra-Bournet, *L'Affaire Roncarelli*, 116–17.

40 McConnell Papers, J.G. McConnell, H.G. Brewer, and D.R. Parker to J.W. McConnell, 19 May 1949.

41 A hint of how bad the facilities had remained under Atholstan is found in two letters cited in the Minutes for 25 September 1928. Albert R. Carman, the editor-in-chief, complained that in the financial department he had "four men working in a two-by-nothing room which would be uncomfortably crowded by two." He concluded: "It is no wonder that mistakes are made in figures when these men must handle them at rush speed with so much confusion about them," and of course there was no room for another ticker or more men. Indeed the "whole floor" was so crowded that "we are losing much of the value of our people's work, and the sporting and proof rooms were particularly inadequate." J.M. Letham, the composing-room superintendent, complained along the same lines.

42 There was a settlement of outstanding issues between the MSCL and the department. In the McConnell Papers, there is a memorandum from McConnell to Brewer, dated 24 October 1952, saying that "no assessment will be made against the Herald Publishing Company from the end of December 1951, in consideration of our agreeing that losses in dispute on the former years 1950–1951 would not be chargeable against STAR profits." The MSCL dropped further tax appeals in respect of this issue.

43 Interviews with Renée Lady Iliffe and with the 3rd Lord Iliffe.

44 See, for example, the unflattering portrait of him by his personal secretary and later the editor of the *Sunday Times* – Denis Hamilton – in *Editor-in-Chief*, chapters 9–12.

45 See Cudlipp, *Publish and Be Damned!* chapter 16.

46 McConnell actually took the young Rupert Murdoch under his wing, and Rupert was later to regret that he did not keep up the connection. (Letter from Rupert Murdoch to the author, 1999.)

47 *Le Duplessisme*, 143–5 (footnotes omitted), Translation: "Prime Minster Duplessis maintained close links with diverse components of the bourgeoisie, notably with the great English Canadian financiers of whom McConnell [was one] … These directors of newspapers set out to battle against the control of the increase in the price of newsprint by dominant producers and against the difficulties of supply, taking into account the growth of their needs.

"In 1955, Bassett and McConnell 'suggested' to Duplessis that he intervene with the producers of newsprint in order to introduce a system of double prices, one for consumption in Quebec and the other for export. The Prime Minister brought himself to do this and, as in 1947, served a warning on the president of St Lawrence Paper Mills in peremptory and contradictory terms. A few months later (in 1951), McConnell asked Duplessis to intervene with newsprint companies so that the *Star* could procure for itself 'the necessary quantity, more than 2,000 tons, of newsprint, to finish the year.' The prime minister, in less than 48 hours, constrained the companies, under the threat of diminishing or cancelling their forest concessions and increasing the fees or cancelling the permits for the removal of tree-stumps, to procure the volume of newsprint needed by the *Star*. At the end of the year 1952, Duplessis met 11 representatives of the newsprint-producing companies to discuss, behind closed doors, the level of prices and to try to prevent the rise in prices, and he threatened them with the creation of a newsprint regulatory agency.

"The conflict among the monopolists intensified, supply difficulties continued, and the prices were considered much too high by the newspaper proprietors. At the end of October 1955, the monopolistic paper producers raised their prices. Duplessis put them on notice and asked them to reconsider the situation. The companies maintained their prices, and their principal producer in Quebec, Consolidated Paper, raised its price to $4 a ton. Duplessis then announced the tabling of a bill on the production, the control of prices and the distribution of newsprint produced in Quebec.

"The law of February 2, 1956 ensured under the supervision of the Newsprint Bureau the provision of newsprint to newspapers in Quebec at a price lower than that prevailing in the rest of Canada and in the United States. This law had no parallel during the National Union administration from 1944 to 1960."

48 MSCL Minutes, 20 November 1963.
49 Bassett had been in favour of accepting the subsidy, but Peters felt so strongly about this that he had Bassett removed as president of the *Gazette*. Peters, previously executive vice-president, became president and managing director. (Interview with Charles Peters, 1997; Montreal *Star*, 21 March 1956.)
50 Interview with Charles Peters, 1997.
51 *Newspaper and Magazines*, 1953, with the figures for 1938 from the *Canadian Newspaper and Magazine Directory*.
52 Sotiron, *From Politics to Profit*.
53 This section is based on an analysis of *Star* ledgers and other material by Gerald Wareham.
54 Montreal *Star*, 17 October 1958.

CHAPTER SEVENTEEN

1 Frost, *McGill University*, 2: 424.
2 MUA, William Peterson Papers, Acc. no. 641/83, ref. 4. The following account of the McGill campaign is derived in part from LAC, MG 30, Henry Birks and Sons Family Papers, A92, vol. 4, A. Robert George, "A Man of Affairs: William Massey Birks, C.B.E., LL.D., 1868–1950" (typescript).

3 MUA, Peterson Papers, 641–83/33, 19 December 1910.

4 MUA, W.M. Birks Papers, 641–82/41.

5 All this is taken from United Church Archives, Montreal, Wesleyan Theological College, Board of Governors, Minute-Book.

In the same year as this fundraising campaign, Wesleyan Theological College became the first administrative home of the theological colleges affiliated with McGill, a development that McConnell strongly supported. The constituent colleges retained their separate denominational identities but cooperated on matters that were not strictly denominational. Subsequently, in 1926, the Second General Council of the United Church united the Methodist, Presbyterian and Congregational colleges into the United Theological College (UTC), which received its charter in 1928. McConnell sat on the board of the UTC as well.

Wesleyan Theological College housed a diminishing number of students of the UTC until 1941, when the RCAF requisitioned the building, and in 1945 the federal government bought it outright. The UTC retained the use of the northern third of the building, which was renamed Sir Edward Beatty Memorial Hall. In 1965 McGill took over the entire building for its Department of Social Work and Graduate School of Nursing, renaming it Morris W. Wilson Hall.

6 The Rockfeller Foundation diversified its donations geographically, among McGill, the University of Toronto, and Dalhousie University, and originally each was intended to receive $1 million, although later the total grant was $5 million.

7 LAC, MG 27-IIIB4, Lomer Gouin Papers, vol. 13, Principal William Peterson of McGill to Premier Sir Lomer Gouin, 4 March 1914.

8 MUA, A.J. Stanley Hopkins to Sir Arthur Currie, 11 December 1920.

9 MUA, RG 2, Principals' Office Papers, C57, 853.

10 By 1929, of the more than $6,400,000 pledged in the 1920 campaign, less than $200,000 remained unpaid, of which $100,000 was the balance of J.K.L. Ross's subscription. A pencilled addition to the list of firm subscriptions by the governors, dated 18 December 1929, indicates that McConnell paid this balance. If we are to believe the memoirs of the secretary to Louis-Joseph Forget, this discharge of Ross's debt by McConnell, if it occurred, may have been in return for the secret financing for the takeover of the Montreal Street Railway by McConnell and E.-A. Robert in 1910–11, but there will probably be never any definitive proof of this (see chapter 7).

11 See Fedunkiw, *Rockefeller Foundation Funding*, 85.

12 See Harvey, *Histoire de l'École des Hautes Etudes Commerciales de Montréal*.

13 See Boothman, "Culture of Utility: The Development of Business Education in Canada," chapter 1 of Austin, *Capitalizing Knowledge*.

14 Gagnon, *Polytechnique*, 101.

15 See Young, *The Politics of Codification*.

16 Marsh went on to Ottawa, where he became research director for the federal Advisory Committee on Post-War Reconstruction, which led to his 1943 *Report on Social Security for Canada*. This report was a key document in the designing of social security in Canada after the war, comparable to Beveridge's *Report on Social Insurance and Allied Services* published in the previous year.

17 It is charged, too, that McConnell's opposition to the establishment of an institute for Soviet studies led to the creation of an institute of Islamic studies instead. Here, again, evidence is lacking.

18 See Finkel, *Business and Social Reform in the Thirties*, for an interesting discussion of that ultimate businessman turned politician, C.D. Howe.

19 Brown, *Jew or Juif?* 189.

20 W.M. Birks was at this time proposing to the board that special efforts should be made to admit German Jewish scholars to teach at McGill.

21 MUA, RG 2, C46, "Jewish Affairs," Ira MacKay to Sir Arthur Currie, 21 July 1933.

22 The above discussion of the issue of the Jewish quota is based on research in the Principal Papers at MUA.

23 McConnell Papers, "The Business Year Book 1939," pages at the end titled "Cash Accounts," February to June.

24 Henderson, *Plain Talk*, 130.

25 Montreal *Gazette*, 11 November 1938.

26 Montreal *Star*, 11 November 1938.

27 MUA, MG 1017, C49, James Diary files, 30 March 1942.

28 Ibid., 2 April 1942.

29 Ibid., 11 May 1942.

30 Ibid., 14 May 1942.

31 Ibid., 7, 17, and 22 June 1943.

32 Ibid., 9 July 1943.

33 LAC, Henry Birks and Sons Family Papers, A92, vol. 4, W.M. Birks to F. Cyril James, 13 July 1943.

34 Ibid., W.M. Birks to F. Cyril James, 15 July 1943.

35 As he wrote in 1956 to a daughter of his teacher in Muskoka, Mrs D.C. Thomas: "I have been Senior Governor on the McGill Board for more than six years; and for a much longer time, Chairman of the Nominating Committee. During that time I have nominated and secured three Chancellors, including the present Chancellor, Mr. B.C. Gardner, ex-President and Chairman of the Bank of Montreal." McConnell Papers, 25 October 1956.

36 MUA, MG 1017, C75, James Diary Files, 10 July 1957.

37 McConnell Papers, C. Fraser Elliott to J.W. McConnell, 2 November 1943, in response to McConnell's letter to him of 28 October 1943.

38 McConnell Papers, "The Business Year Book 1939," draft written on the pages for 18 December to the end of the book.

39 The cards are in the McConnell Papers.

40 There were other specific grants, bringing the total provincial aid to McGill to $1,061,481 in 1943, but this was not much more than the one-time grant of $1 million in 1920.

41 MUA, RG 2, C129, Cyril James to Duplessis, 6 November 1948.

42 Ibid., James to Dr W.W. Chipman, 5 June 1949.

43 Ibid., Edward Beatty to Athanase David, 30 November 1934.

44 Ibid., Owen Stredder to A.E. Morgan, 9 March 1936.

45 Ibid., Cyril James to Premier Duplessis, 17 December 1947.

46 Ibid., J.W. McConnell to Cyril James, 19 December 1947.

47 Ibid., Cyril James to Premier Duplessis, 6 November 1948, and acknowledging Duplessis's gift, 14 December 1948.

48 Litt, *The Muse, the Masses, and the Massey Commission*, especially chapter 7; and Finlay, *The Force of Culture*, especially chapter 6.

49 *Report: Royal Commission on National Development in the Arts, Letters and Sciences 1949–1951*, chapters 12 and 22.

50 *Report of the Royal Commission on Dominion-Provincial Relations*. See also Ferguson and Wardhaugh, "'Impossible Conditions of Equality."

51 *Report of the Royal Commission of Inquiry on Constitutional Problems*, vol. 2, pt. 3, 249.

52 MUA, Minutes of the Board of Governors, 7 November 1956.

53 Ibid., 21 November 1956.

54 MUA, MG 1017, C75, James Diary files, press release, "Federal Grants to Universities," 21 June 1957.

55 Ibid., James Diary, 23 June 1957.

56 Ibid., 10 July 1957.

57 Frost, *The Man in the Ivory Tower*, 2: 226.

58 MUA, Minutes of the Board of Governors, 7 November 1957.

59 *Cité Libre*, February 1957, reprinted in Trudeau, *Federalism and the French Canadians*, 90.

60 McConnell's support of Duplessis in this dispute appears to have led to tension not only between him and James but also between him and his son John. In the McConnell Papers, there is an undated memorandum from John to his father. It reads in part: "There is a rapidly-growing feeling that the English Press does not dare say anything in opposition to the Prime Minister. Of course this is true. The Prime Minister is really over-sensitive to criticism. He is in the business of politics, and frequently says rash things. The reputation of The Star would be greatly improved if it occasionally spoke out when the Prime Minister goes too far." McConnell Papers, undated memorandum found in material relating to J.G. McConnell.

61 MUA, RG 2, C250, Cyril James to J.W. McConnell, 9 May 1960.

CHAPTER EIGHTEEN

1 A gift of $1 million to an individual, however, attracted a gift tax of 28 per cent. Perry, *Taxation in Canada*, 115–17.

2 McConnell Papers, pencilled memo by McConnell, undated.

3 Ibid., C.F. Elliott to McConnell, 20 December 1935.

4 Ibid., McConnell to C.H. McLean, 27 December 1935.

5 See, for example, Stewart, *The Charity Game*, which describes McConnell thus: "He made his millions by cornering the sugar market with St. Lawrence Sugar Refineries and then multiplied them with investments in publishing – he owned four Montreal newspapers and wouldn't allow any of them to print his name or photograph – as well as banking, transportation and insurance. Today the Foundation controls nearly $400 million in assets and during 1993 distributed sixty-three grants that amounted to $16,072,800; it declines to say exactly

where the money went, except that it is interested in 'social development, arts and culture'"
(136). Stewart concludes that "philanthropic foundations are not charities at all, in the real
sense of helping the poor. A poor person who turned up on the premises of the Ford Foundation or the J.W. McConnell Foundation would be bounced back out onto the street. These
institutions exist to protect the money of the elite so that it can be spent as the elite wants it
spent, and the rationale is provided by the fourth head of charity – benefit to the community"
(142). This comment may be applicable to the charitable trust, but, as will be seen presently,
it confuses the charitable trust with the modern foundation.

6 *Commissioners of Income Tax v. Pemsel* [1891] AC 531. In this case, Lord Macnaghton defined
   public purposes for charitable trusts as: "(1) the relief of the indigent through money, provisions, education, medical assistance etc.; (2) the advancement of learning; (3) the advancement of religion; and (4) the advancement of "objects of general public utility."

7 For a study of the Canadian jurisprudence, see Waters, *Law of Trusts in Canada*, 550–603.

8 Seybold, ed., *American foundations and Their Fields*, 4 and 5.

9 By 2001, Canada had 114 community foundations with $1.4 billion in assets, distributing
   about $70 million annually.

10 By the end of 1944, McConnell had transferred about $5.2 million to his Foundation, which
    made it roughly equal in endowment to the Alfred P. Sloan Foundation in 1940, the thirty-
    fourth largest American foundation in that year (Seybold, *American foundations and Their
    Fields*, table III, 26). The current status of the McConnell Foundation as the second major
    private foundation in Canada depends on whether the Birks Foundation is to be regarded as
    major, but details on the endowment of this foundation are unavailable.

11 The community trusts in Canada tend to be well supported. In 1998 the Vancouver Founda-
    tion, established in 1943, had assets of $562,646,570, making it the best-endowed foundation
    of all. The McConnell Foundation in that year was second, with $496,153,478, but third was
    another community trust, the Hospital for Sick Children Foundation (largely supported by
    the McLaughlin Foundation), worth $323,859,000.

12 The others that followed included ones created by J.S. Atkinson (1942), the family of the
    late Joseph Flavelle (1945), J.S. McLean (1945), Richard Ivey (1947), J.P. Bickell (1951), R.S.
    McLaughlin (1951), Samuel and Saidye Bronfman (1952), Marjorie and Gerald Bronfman
    (1955), Sir James Dunn (1957), the Molson family (1958), Lord Beaverbrook (1960), R. Howard
    Webster (1967), David Stewart for the Macdonald estate (1967), and the estate of W. Garfield
    Weston (1987).

13 UTA, Vincent Massey Papers, B 87–0082, 95 (1), will of Hart Massey, paragraphs 30 and 32.

14 The idea of a foundation also came almost naturally to the minds of the Masseys, not least
    because of pressure from Vincent Massey's favourite uncle, George Vincent, president of the
    Rockefeller Foundation since 1916.

15 *The JM Foundation: 1995 Annual Report*, 4. In 1995 the Milbank Foundation for Rehabilita-
    tion was created in connection with the International Center for the Disabled and the New
    York Hospital–Cornell Medical Center Network, to complement the work of the JM Founda-
    tion. Jeremiah Milbank II and Chris K. Olander, executive director of the JM Foundation,
    have kindly provided this and other material on the Milbank family and its philanthropy, as
    has Joseph Milbank of Charlottesville, Va. The chief source on Jeremiah Milbank is Briggs's

privately printed memoir, *The Face of the Family*. Another source is de Kay's unpublished typescript, "Biography: Jeremiah Milbank, Sr."

16 The Foundation's evolution was even more complicated than this short account suggests. The Belvedere Foundation was incorporated by letters patent in Quebec on 4 January 1935. On 28 April 1937 its name was the J.W. McConnell Foundation by supplementary Quebec letters patent. In 1975 it also acquired the French name of "La Fondation J.W. McConnell." In 1966 the Griffith Foundation, named in honour of Mrs J.W. McConnell, was incorporated under federal charter. With political uncertainties in Quebec, the J.W. McConnell Foundation transferred its assets in 1977 to the Griffith Foundation. The Griffith Foundation distributed its income to the J.W. McConnell Foundation for grant-making purposes. In 1987 the Griffith Foundation changed its name to the J.W. McConnell Family Foundation. In 1988 the J.W. McConnell Foundation surrendered its Quebec charter and dissolved, transferring its remaining assets to the J.W. McConnell Family Foundation. For the sake of simplicity, all of these foundations are referred to in this book as the "McConnell Foundation."

17 Special By-law "A" and Supplementary Letters Patent, 27 April 1937, article 2 on "objects."

18 McConnell Foundation Archives (MFA), C.F. Elliott to J.W. McConnell, 17 April 1937.

19 Waters, *Law of Trusts in Canada*, 516–20.

20 All internal data presented in this chapter on the Foundation are from its Minutes.

21 All these figures are from the records of the company, principally income-tax returns. In addition to the $300,000 transfer to the Foundation, St Lawrence gave $300,000 in 1940 to the Spitfire Fund.

22 In 1942–43 McConnell successfully applied for the Foundation's exemption from the 15 per cent US withholding tax, to which charitable and religious corporations were entitled. In 1945 the Foundation received $376,135 in dividends and interest on its American portfolio, and the exemption obtained saved it about $56,000 in withholding tax.

23 Sir Hugh Allan, father of Sir Montagu, had been one of the incorporators in 1881. Later it was named the Douglas Hospital after Dr James and Dr James S. Douglas, respectively the grandfather and the father of Principal Lewis Douglas of McGill University. See Cahn, *Douglas Hospital*.

24 Cameron and Silverman, "Tale of Two Institutes."

25 See Collins, *In the Sleep Room*, and Gilmor, *I Swear by Apollo*.

26 His children anonymously contributed a further $10,000.

27 McConnell Papers, draft of his retirement speech to the VON in "Dominion Textile Company Co. Ltd. Daily Reminder, Year Book 1942," on the pages for 12 to 16 July.

28 Montreal *Star*, 30 September 1944.

29 They were not available initially to students in dentistry, law, agriculture, medicine, or music, or in graduate studies, and they were forfeited if their holders lost first-class standing.

30 The Foundation grant in honour of Archibald was independent of a personal contribution by McConnell and his wife of $6,000 to help to establish the Edward Archibald Surgical Research Fund. For several years from 1947 onwards, the McConnells made further annual instalments of $6,000 to the fund. In 1946 McConnell had also personally promised a further $50,000 for teaching under Dr Wilder Penfield, in five annual instalments.

31 The basic account is Dawson, *My Story of the Boys' Farm at Shawbridge*.

32   Montreal *Gazette*, 27 June 1927.

33   Only $197,010 of this $200,000 pledge proved necessary by 1947 in order for the campaign to reach its goal.

34   MFA, Minutes, 6 April 1949. Emphasis added.

35   Ibid., 31 December 1951, reproducing a letter from H.W. Edwardson, chief assessor, corporation assessments, Department of National Revenue, 3 November 1951. This ruling exempted the McConnell Foundation from the operation of section 57(1)(e)(b) of the Income Tax Act. The rationale for this ruling is obscure and not contained in section 57(1)(e) (b)(iii), cited by Edwardson. It appears that the ruling was made exclusively to accommodate the McConnell Foundation. (Nicolas McConnell's interview with Art Bond, CA, 16 October 2001.) As the minister of national revenue, Douglas Abbott, admitted, "the change is to cover a particular case that was brought to my attention in connection with the wording." (House of Commons *Debates*, 13 June 1951, 4063.) It was ratified by *Statutes of Canada*, 1951, chapter 51, section 20(1)(iii), which, through the amendment of section 57(1)(e)(b)(iii) of the Income Tax Act, deleted the application of the 90 per cent disbursement rule to "a corporation that was, before the first day of January, 1940, constituted exclusively for charitable purposes." The 1950 and 1951 amendments to the Income Tax Act did not apply to the disbursement of capital gains, the taxation of which was not introduced until 1972. Also in 1972, John Turner, minister of finance, convened a Charity Study Group under Arthur Drache, which resulted in legislation in 1975 requiring the disbursement by foundations of 5 per cent of the market value of their investment portfolios as determined in the previous financial year. In 1981 the federal budget proposed the additional requirement of disbursing 90 per cent of capital gains accumulated by foundation endowments in a taxation year but, under pressure from various foundations, the government abandoned this proposal and even reduced the required disbursement of 5 per cent to 4.5 per cent of the market value of the investment portfolio as determined in the previous financial year. For further discussion, see Waters, *Law of Trusts*, 531–48.

36   Scriver, *The Montreal Children's Hospital*, is the principal source for this account. With John H. Molson, McConnell had established for this hospital, after the Second World War, research fellowships in medicine and surgery (ibid., 128–9).

37   See, for example, Penfield, *No Man Alone*.

38   The official history is being written by Dr William Feindel, a former director.

39   By 1937, the Rockefeller Foundation had given a total of $2,879,588 for medical research at McGill, along with a grant of $2,500 for research in pharmacology, $57,500 for the study of "child life," and $160,000 for research in the social sciences, spread over nine years, between 1930 and 1939.

40   Archibald then retired as surgeon-in-chief to pursue research into cancer, another favourite cause of McConnell's. During the Second World War, he was to enlist as the oldest medical man in active service, and he died in 1945. See Entin, "Dr. Edward W. Archibald."

41   Holt accepted this offer but it is not clear that McConnell did. The total financing of the original Montreal Neurological Institute in 1932–34 was as follows: Rockefeller Foundation, $232,652; private subscriptions (including McConnell's and Holt's), $250,000; provincial government, $24,744; Penfield research fund (given by Mrs Ottman, the mother of an American patient), $22,279. The total cost was $529,676. In 1937 the operating room was air-

conditioned at a cost of $6,767; in 1939 the electro-encephalography laboratory, funded by McConnell, Holt, and G.H. Duggan of Dominion Bridge), cost $21,360; in 1940 a bridge between the Institute and the Royal Victoria Hospital was built by the Bronfman family at a cost of $10,557; and in 1944 the X-ray and operating suites were enlarged at a cost of $80,000 to McGill and $91,059 to the Maple Leaf Division of British War Relief. Finally, a military annex to the south (at the corner with Pine Avenue) was built by the federal government in 1944, at a cost of $138,100, making a total of $363,211 in additions since 1934. In 1944, therefore, the Institute's book value was $892,887, exclusive of the Rockefeller Foundation's $1-million endowment. (McGill University, Osler Library, Penfield Papers, A/N 14–1/2 and 16–5.)

42 Ibid., A/N 14/1–1, Wilder Penfield to W.L.M. King, 3 February 1947.

43 Ibid., A/N 16–2, memorandum by Wilder Penfield, 11 September 1946.

44 Ibid., A/N 16–5, 13 May 1947; McConnell replied on 10 May 1947. The McConnell Research Fund gave $10,000 to the Institute annually for five years, 1946 to 1951.

45 The federal grant was in fact to be renewed annually, and by 1959 it had risen to $48,500, paid as a "consolidated grant" through the National Research Council, which was more likely to be renewed than an ordinary annual grant but still tied to an individual, in this case probably Penfield.

46 Penfield Papers, A/N 14–1/1, Wilder Penfield to W.L.M. King, 28 May 1947.

47 Ibid., A/N 16.3.

48 Ibid., A/N 15, J.W. McConnell to Wilder Penfield, 26 January 1950.

49 Ibid., 21 December 1949. In May 1950 Killam gave $50 thousand anonymously to the new wing, and he also arranged for anonymous donations of $5,000 each from International Power, Ottawa Valley Power, Calgary Power, British Columbia Pulp and Paper, and the Mersey Company. (Ibid., A/N 15/3.)

50 Ibid., Penfield Papers, 28 December 1950. McConnell approached Donner probably as early as July of the same year. By October 1951, Donner's gift had been increased to $20,400 annually for the experimental neurochemistry laboratory, so long as its research was carried out or the Donner Foundation was wound up, in which case there would be a cash settlement. Penfield Papers, Wilder Penfield to J.W. McConnell, 17 October 1951.

51 Ibid., A/N 14/2–3, memorandum of a meeting on 19 November 1947 at Montreal's New Courthouse.

52 Ibid., A/N 32/1–1, Wilder Penfield to Judge Thomas Tremblay, 19 February 1971.

53 Ibid., A/N 15, J.W. McConnell to Wilder Penfield, 5 December 1950.

54 Ibid., Wilder Penfield to J.W. McConnell, 13 March 1951.

55 Ibid., J.W. McConnell to Wilder Penfield, 21 January 1952. In October 1952 McConnell also anonymously contributed a cobalt bomb to the Institute (ibid., Wilder Penfield to J.W. McConnell, 30 October 1952).

56 Ibid., A/N 8/3 press release, 1951.

57 Ibid., A/N 15, J.W. McConnell to Wilder Penfield, 22 January 1953. Asselin, back as chairman, secured the $67,000 grant, annually over twenty years, by May (ibid., Wilder Penfield to J.W. McConnell, 12 May 1953).

58 Ibid., C/G 9–1, Wilder Penfield to Sir Alan Lascelles, February 1953.

59 McConnell Papers, "Dominion Textile Ltd. Diary Reminder, Yearbook 1942," pages marked 16 June to 6 July.

60 McConnell Papers, Paul Martin to James A. Oastler, 8 April 1957.

61 This account is largely derived from Duval, *L'Etonnant dossier de la Place des Arts*.

62 Ibid., 30.

63 McConnell Papers, Maurice Germain to Lil McConnell, 12 November 1963.

64 Those interested some in the political consequences of McConnell's large gift may read Illien, *La Place des Art et la Révolution tranquille*.

65 MUA, RG 2, C38, J.W. McConnell Personal and Donations, McConnell to James, 7 May 1958.

66 After their purchase, the Protestant School Board building became known as Peterson Hall and the Presbyterian College was largely pulled down, its surviving part being called Morrice Hall.

67 McConnell Papers, Cyril James to J.W. McConnell, 20 December 1960.

68 David McConnell also attended occasionally from 1958 onward.

69 MFA, "P.M.L.'s Comments," 28 April 1978, delivered to the annual general meeting of 2 May 1978 and reproduced in extended form as appendix A of a commissioned "Report to the Directors of the J.W. McConnell Foundation Inc."

CHAPTER NINETEEN

1 McConnell Papers.

2 Montreal *Star*, 14 May 1945.

3 The McConnells' first trip to the Bahamas was in 1911, and they felt so at home there in subsequent years that McConnell even obtained a Bahamian passport.

4 On Douglas and McCloy, see Bowder and Smith, *Independent: A Biography of Lewis W. Douglas*; and Bird, *The Chairman: John J. McCloy*.

5 Interview in 1998 with Heward Stikeman.

6 This context is succinctly presented in Muirhead, "Trials and Tribulations," 50. See also his PhD thesis, "Canadian Trade Policy, 1949–57."

7 The new steeple for Christ Church Cathedral was an anonymous donation. Its erection occurred in 1930–40 at a cost to McConnell of $100,000. See Adams, *A History of Christ Church Cathedral*, 87.

8 These Canadians were called Osler fellows, after Sir William Osler, the Canadian physician and McGill graduate who eventually became professor of medicine at Oxford.

9 McConnell Papers, Princess Alice to J.W. McConnell, 4 April 1961.

10 Chalfont, *Montgomery of Alamein*, 2.

11 Interview with the 2nd Earl Alexander of Tunis, 1996.

12 Ibid., Queen Mary to J.W. McConnell, 13 July 1950.

13 Royal Archives, Windsor Castle, RA GV CC47/2483, J.W. McConnell to Queen Mary, 5 August 1950.

14 McConnell Papers, Princess Elizabeth to Lil McConnell, 4 November 1951.

15 "Why the Palace Thwarted Churchill's Attempt to Lift Duchess out of 'Poverty,'" *Daily Telegraph*, 17 May 2005.

16 MUA, RG 4, C16, Minutes of the Board of Governors, vol. 12, 11 May 1955.

17 McConnell Papers, J.W. McConnell to Bishop Fulton J. Sheen (copy), 19 December 1955.

18 Ibid., J.W. McConnell to the queen, 18 October 1957 (copy).

19 The main building was opened in May. A new wing, also paid for by McConnell, was opened in November 1961. A further wing, with an infirmary and an auditorium, was built in 1963. In 1965 Dr H. Rocke Robertson, the principal of McGill, opened a new fourteen-storey J.W. McConnell Memorial Wing, another addition. By 1965, the Griffith-McConnell Home housed 150; the Dun-Edin (as it was then called) Home housed 23; the Griffith-McConnell Infirmary accommodated 35; and the J.W. McConnell Memorial Wing housed 150. The McConnell Foundation gave a further $2 million to the home in 1987, and it was thus saved from relying on government aid. It had a policy of not turning away residents because of inability to pay, and the Good Samaritan Fund – also supported by the Foundation – helped to pay its deficits.

20 Premier Lesage, in February 1963, also opened the Otolaryngological Institute at the Royal Victoria Hospital, endowed by McConnell and the late Mrs Ross McMaster, as well as by the federal and provincial governments.

21 Montreal *Star*, 2 January 1962.

22 McConnell Papers, Sir Edward Peacock to Lil McConnell, 21 December 1950.

23 Fournier, *FLQ: Histoire d'un mouvement clandestine*, chapter 3.

24 McConnell Papers, Senator Wallace McCutcheon to Lil McConnell, 7 November 1963.

25 Ibid., Commissioner W. Wycliffe Booth to Lil McConnell, 8 November 1963.

26 Ibid., Sir Shuldham Redfern to J.G. McConnell, 7 November 1963.

27 Ibid., J.D. McKeown to Lil McConnell, 20 November 1963.

28 Ibid., Lazarus Phillips to J.G. McConnell, 7 November 1963.

29 Ibid., Philip Garfinkle to Lil McConnell, 8 November 1963.

30 Ibid., Léon Lortie to J.G. McConnell, 19 November 1963.

31 Ibid., Sévère Godin to J.G. McConnell, 6 November 1963.

32 Ibid., Lord Beaverbrook to Lil McConnell, 10 November 1963.

33 Ibid., A.J. Watts to J.G. McConnell, 7 November 1963, L.W. Glover to J.G. McConnell, 7 November 1963, and George A. Plummer to J.G. McConnell, 11 November 1963.

34 MUA, RG 220A, MG 107, C75, Cyril James Diary, 9 November 1963.

35 McConnell Papers, F. Cyril James to Lil McConnell, 29 November 1963.

36 Ibid., Malcolm MacDonald to Lil McConnell, 11 November 1963.

APPENDIX

1 Prepared for the purposes of securing a loan for St Lawrence Sugar Refineries from the Bank of Montreal, the 1921 Statement is recorded in the St Lawrence minute-book as representing a "pledge of all [McConnell's] assets." This is the reason that St Lawrence itself is listed in the 1921 Statement as having value $1.

2 At least one of the real estate companies listed in the 1921 Statement – Interboro Realties – was active well after the Second World War. We find another – Montreal Industrial Land Company – among McConnell's 1951 holdings.

3 Funded in large measure by McConnell's transfer of the 1921 Statement holdings into the company in about 1924, the St Lawrence Sugar Refineries investment portfolio reached a peak value of $45.2 million in publicly traded securities in 1929. The portfolio was valued at $24.8 million at the time of McConnell's death in 1963. The value of the Montreal Star Pub-

lishing Company investment portfolio increased from $78,715 in 1938 (the year McConnell took formal control of it) to just under $11.6 million in 1961. Between 1943 and 1963, these two companies contributed $37.4 million to the J.W. McConnell Foundation either in the form of operating profits or from direct transfer of stocks from the company's investment account.

4 One of the real estate holdings listed in the 1921 Statement – Holt/Gordon Lots (later Sunnyside Avenue, Westmount) – was given to McConnell's eldest son, Wilson, at the time of the latter's marriage in 1935.

5 Montreal Securities found its way into the insurance business associated with both the Knox and McLean families. Ultimately, the name came into the possession of the financier Lorne Webster.

6 It was in the mid-1920s that McConnell purchased all outstanding shares of St Lawrence Sugar Refineries, exercising an option granted him in return for his earlier pledge of personal assets to secure a loan for the refinery during the sugar crisis of the early 1920s.

7 In 1924 St Lawrence Sugar Refineries dividend income from publicly traded companies was $511,761.61, with an additional $4,185 flowing from wholly controlled Dominion Manufacturers. In 1930 St Lawrence recorded dividend income from publicly traded companies of $1,003,382.60, with an additional $548,537 flowing from the wholly owned Montreal *Star* and $4,270 from Dominion Manufacturers.

8 $1,675,000 of Dominion of Canada 4.5 per cent 1948/58 and $325,000 of Dominion of Canada 4.5 per cent 1949/59 are listed as one of two holdings of the J.W. McConnell Trust in 1939. The other comprises 27,000 shares of St Lawrence Sugar Refineries valued at $2,000,000. (Commercial Trust Company, Financial Statements, 31 December 1939.)

9 McConnell transferred securities among his various accounts. An example is those in the Sun Life Assurance Company. In the 1929 St Lawrence Sugar Refineries investment portfolio, 300 common shares are listed. This holding disappears completely from St Lawrence Sugar Refineries tax returns, even for years in the 1930s when dividends were known to have been paid and when McConnell was still a director of the company. Sun Life, however, reappears in the 1951 J.W. McConnell Personal investment ledger comparable to the holding of 1929 (adjusted for splits).

10 This is also the case, though perhaps less significantly so, for the illustrated value of the 1939 portfolios.

11 This figure breaks down as follows: J.W. McConnell Foundation Investment Portfolio: $121.2 million; St Lawrence Sugar Refineries Investment Portfolio: $24.8 million; (Personal) Estate Portfolio: $17 million; Montreal Star Publishing Company Investment Portfolio: $11.6 million; Children's Trust Portfolio: $10.8 million; Grandchildren's Trust Portfolio: $4 million; California Relatives' Trust Portfolio: $1.6 million; Commercial Trust Investment Portfolio: $1 million.

12 Acknowledgment must be made of the contributions of several people in the preparation of these tables. Most especially: William Fong; Gerry Wareham (CA), George McCammon (CA), and Claude David (CA). Also: Pam Main, Jean-Rene Bouchard, Newton Siao, John Salib, Carl Otto, and all the support staff of the J.W. McConnell Family Foundation.

13 The heavy, old-fashioned company investment ledger for St Lawrence Sugar Refineries is organized alphabetically. At the starts of each letter entry, there is a table of contents listing the name of the companies held. Some of these have been crossed out and are assumed not to

be relevant to an assessment of McConnell's holdings. Where a company is listed but a page entry is missing for that company, it is assumed to be missing.

14 Goodwin's; Holt Renfrew.

15 Montreal, Light, Heat and Power; Brazilian Traction.

16 Dominion Textile, Courtaulds, Penmans, Canadian Cottons.

17 Ogilvie Flour, McCormick Manufacturing, Cuban Cane Sugar Corporation, Cuban American Sugar Company, and Dominion Sugar.

18 McConnell appears to have purchased his shares some time after 1915, since he is not listed as one of the shareholders for that year. Shareholders with over 1,000 shares, in 1921, were: Baroness Strathcona and Mt Royal (3,014); Walter M. Stewart (3,038); T. Howard (3,400); Charles Hosmer (1,650); Baumgarten Estate (1,619); R.B. Angus (1,485); William Barrett (1728); McGill College (1,100); William Murray Estate (2,000); Royal Trust Special Acct #1 (3,207). Other prominent shareholders: Sir Charles Gordon (800); Huntly Drummond (690); Lady Drummond (523); Maurice Drummond Estate (464); Vincent Meredith (705).

19 These include fifty-four in Laurier Park Land and Development Company and undisclosed interests in Interboro Realties, Montreal Development and Land Company, and Commercial Properties ($1).

20 As with all values extracted from the 1921 Statement, this figure would be reduced were contemporary values assignable for the listed private companies.

21 These include Montreal properties on Craig Street, St Catherine Street/McGill College Avenue, St James/Inspector streets, and St Catherine Street ($219,580.79); and lots in Montreal West and Notre Dame de Grace ($6,723.74), Sortin Junction Farm ($52,946.78), and (one) Saskatoon ($2.49).

22 These include McConnell's Dorval estate, Ashburton ($188,912.45); other Dorval lots (Carsley and Doble lots, $17,064.74); and the Holt/Gordon lots in Westmount ($61,809).

23 These unvalued listings include Montreal Securities Corporation, Godfrey Realty Company, Beaconsfield Golf Club, Mount Bruno Golf Club, and Winter Club.

24 Acknowledgment is made to Newton Siao, formerly of Deloitte, Touche, for pointing out this error.

25 According to the Markets Measure (Dow Jones, 1999), 61: "Stock Prices peaked on September 3, when the Dow Jones Industrial Average hit 381.17 on September 3, up 27% since the end of 1928."

26 These include Moody's Industrials, banks and finance, utilities, and railroads.

27 The values and percentage in this section refer only to losses sustained by Foster and Kleiser and Photo Engravers and are therefore overstated, given that the 1929 Memorandum lists no less than ten such neon signage companies. Moody's has no listings for these in its 1930 Annual. Those companies held by St Lawrence in 1929 but missing accurate post-Crash valuation are: Claude Neon Lights (N.Y.), Claude Neon Lights of Canada, Claude Neon of Maryland; Claude Neon of Australasia, Claude Neon Strauss, Elliott-Claude Neon, Neon Products of Western Canada, New Jersey Claude Neon, and Walker and Company. The St Lawrence 1930 tax return does, however, record dividend income from two related neon companies for that year: Anuncios KP Luz Neon and Alpha Claude Neon Corporation. Additionally, a related neon company, Claude Neon Southern, not listed in the 1929 Memorandum, is listed

as generating dividends on the St Lawrence 1930 tax return. In a St Lawrence 1937 tax return, one related neon company, Claude Neon Electric Products, is listed as generating a dividend for that year. In a St Lawrence 1939 tax return, one related neon company, Electrical Products, is listed as generating a dividend for that year. The exception to this pattern is Walker and Company, a related neon company, which is reported in the St Lawrence 1930 tax return and which McConnell holds on at least to 1951.

28 Karen Blumenthal, *Six Days in October: The Stock Market Crash of 1920* (New York: Atheneum Books for Young Readers 2002), 118: "In just six days [24–29 October 1929] the Dow Jones Industrial Average had fallen by a third. More than $25 billion in individual wealth had been lost."

29 "McConnell … had foreseen the [Great Depression] and had largely withdrawn from the market in the summer of 1929, awaiting the debacle with tens of millions of dollars in cash" (Conrad Black, *Duplessis*, 604). Mrs John Kirwan-Taylor (J.W. McConnell's daughter-in-law) has also suggested that McConnell had avoided the Crash.

30 This date, interestingly, coincides with the first year that the Dow had returned to November 1929 levels. It also coincides with the time of McConnell's transfer of sizeable US holdings into his newly created Foundation.

31 Dominion of Canada tax returns for St Lawrence Sugar Refineries have survived for 1924–28, 1930, and 1937–46. Unfortunately, no returns exist for critical year 1929 or for the Depression years 1931–36.

32 Excluded from the 120 with their respective 23 September 1929 Memorandum value are: Montreal Cottons ($375), Dominion Coal ($355), Neon Products of Western Canada ($500), Ford (France) ($128), and Union Tobacco ($0).

33 One possible scenario – McConnell sold his entire holdings after 23 September and repurchased them in time for the 1930 tax year – is unlikely given the volume and consistency of the holdings held over the fifteen-month period under study. The fact that McConnell was away from Montreal in October 1929 would tend to undermine the notion that such drastic action was taken in such a short time period.

34 These companies, with their 23 September 1929 pre-Crash value of $1,529,205, are: US Rubber ($375,000); Northern Aerial Mining Exploration ($25,000); Claude, Paz and Silva ($30,395); Duluth Superior ($54,840); Pantepec Oil ($20,000); Tobacco Products ($76,700); Ottawa Traction ($25,000), Dominion Woolens and Worsted ($224,000); Fox Theatres ($432,000); Kolster Radio ($84,000); Sterling Coal ($34,410); Aluminium ($96,000); Kirkland Lake Mining ($15,000); Canada Power and Paper ($30,000); and Wabasso Cotton ($6,850). McConnell held on/added to the Aluminium, Wabasso Cotton, Sterling Coal, US Rubber, and Canada Power (Consolidated Paper) into the post-Second World War period.

35 The exception was Canadian and Foreign Investment, listed at $30,000 in the 1929 Memorandum. The US-based non-Seagrave-related investment trusts with their 1929 Memorandum values are: Prudential Investors ($144,000); Alleghany ($11,600); the 1930 dividend-yielding United States and International ($100,000), organized by US financier C. Douglas Dillon; and Select Investments ($35,000), dissolved in 1931.

36 The Seagrave trusts held in the St Lawrence Sugar Refineries investment portfolio with their 1929 Memorandum values were: American Founders ($63,955); American and General Secu-

rities ($7,200); American and Continental ($144,000); Second International ($20,000), and United Founders ($740,000). Other related trusts were Atlantic Securities ($116,400) and Shenandoah ($130,000).

37 These have already figured in our calculations of correlations between the 1929 Memorandum and the 1930 tax returns.

38 The 1937 tax return reported $1,860 from American and General and $1,189.60 from Atlas. The 1938 tax return reported $1,860 from American and General and $371.75 from Atlas. The 1939 tax return reported $1,860 from American and General and $1,124.25 from Atlas. The 1940 tax returns reported $1,860 from American and General and $746 from Atlas. The 1941 tax return reported $2,175.75 from American and General and $746 from Atlas. Tax returns after 1941 do not itemize US company dividend income.

39 These companies, with their 23 September 1929 pre-Crash value of $847,200, are: Seagrave's American and General ($7,200); Second International ($20,000); United Founders ($740,000); and Hatch's Shenandoah ($130,000).

40 We find Claude Neon Electric Products generating a small dividend for the St Lawrence Sugar Refineries account in 1937.

41 These companies, with their 23 September 1929 pre-Crash value of $850,000, are: Claude Neon Lights of New York ($750,000), Claude Neon Lights of Canada ($12,500), Claude Neon of Maryland ($24,000), Claude Neon of Australasia ($1,750), Claude Neon Strauss ($12,500), Elliott-Claude Neon ($37,500), and New Jersey Claude Neon ($11,250). Since the three additional neon-related companies (Walker and Company, Alpha Claude Neon, and Anuncios K.P. Luz Neon) paid dividends in 1930 and are reported on the 1930 St Lawrence Sugar Refineries tax return, they were included in the first correlation calculation.

42 These companies are: Royal Trust, Central Public Service, Baltimore and Ohio Railway, National Cash Register, National Enamel, US Steel, United Shoe Machinery Ltd., General Baking, ICI, Carreras, and American Commonwealth Power.

43 Of the companies listed in the original 1929 Memorandum, the following do not appear as generating dividend income on the 1930 St Lawrence tax return: American Commonwealth Power (assets taken over 1934); Central Public Service Corp (dividends paid quarterly to 15 June 1931); Royal Trust (Moody's reports dividend for 1930); Montreal Trust (Moody's reports dividend for 1930); Sun Life (Moody's reports dividend for 1930); Baltimore and Ohio Railway (Moody's reports dividend for 1930); American and General (absorbs American Founders, American and Continental, Second International Securities, and United Founders during 1930s); Alleghany; Prudential Investors; Shenandoah (absorbed, with Atlantic Securities, into Atlas Corporation during the 1930s); Select Investments; United Founders (Moody's reports only stock dividend for 1930); National Cash Register (Moody's reports dividend for 1930); National Enamel (Moody's reports dividend for 1930); US Steel (Moody's reports dividend for 1930); United Shoe Machinery (St Lawrence reported "sold"; Moody's reports dividend for 1930); US Rubber (Moody's reports no dividend for 1930); Pantepec Oil (Moody's has no listing); Carreras (Moody's reports dividend for 1930); Tobacco Products (Moody's reports no dividend for 1930; dissolved 1938); Ottawa Traction (Moody's reports no dividend for 1930; assumed by Ottawa Electric Railway in 1939); Aluminium (Moody's reports no dividend for 1930); Dominion Woollens and Worsteds (Moody's reports no divi-

dend for 1930); Fox Theatres (Moody's reports no dividend for 1930); ICI (Moody's reports dividend for 1930); Kolster Radio (Moody's reports company sold in 1930); Canada Power and Paper (Moody's reports no dividend for 1930; assumed by Consolidated Paper in 1931); Sterling Coal (Moody's reports no dividend for 1930); Select Investments (Moody's reports company dissolved 1931); Wabasso Cotton (Moody's reports no dividend for 1930); Air Liquide (Moody's reports dividend for 1930); General Baking (Moody's reports a dividend for 1930); Duluth Superior (Moody's reports no dividend for 1930); Paz and Silva (Moody's has no listing); Northern Aerial Mining Exploration (Moody's reports no dividend for 1930); Claude Neon Lights of New York (Moody's reports no dividend for 1930); Claude Neon Lights of Canada (Moody's reports no dividend for 1930); and Claude Neon of Maryland, Claude Neon of Australasia, Claude Neon Strauss, Elliott-Claude Neon, Neon Products of Western Canada, and New Jersey Claude Neon (all of which have no listing in Moody's).

44 Acknowledgement is made to George McCammon, CA, for pointing out these figures and sharing his expertise on this and other research matters.

45 *The Markets Measure*, Dow Jones and Company (1999), 64: "From 230 [in late October 1929], the [Dow] industrial average zigzagged, heading south to 199 in November, then north to nearly 300 the next spring. But then it began a long, sickening slide that saw it bottom at just 41 on July 8, 1932. A bargain-hunter who bought on November 30, 1929, and did not sell in the 1930 rally, had to wait until July 1936 to show a profit, according to Ned Davis Research Inc. in Venice, Fla. And that's assuming all stock dividends were reinvested. Looking at stock price alone, an investor who bought in 1929 had to wait until 1954 to see the Dow industrials claw their way back to their October 1929 highs."

46 McLean's valuations accord with McConnell long-term holdings to anyone with a familiarity with McConnell's investments through 1951. The share prices McLean pencilled in his column are also accurate when compared with Moody's Directory. To ensure accuracy, we also cross-referenced McLean's valuations with McConnell's 1937 tax return and, as in the case of the 1929 pencilled valuations, found a high degree of consistency. Those companies with no valuation entered are generally ones that McConnell had clearly disposed of by 1936. Indeed, in many cases, he would have had no choice – many had been dissolved, reorganized, or (in the case of utilities holding companies) legally disbanded.

47 The companies for which McLean provided no pencilled valuation for July 1936 but which McConnell held include such McConnell mainstays as Wabasso Cotton, Imperial Tobacco of Great Britain and Ireland, Tubize Artificial Silk, Bank of Montreal, Royal Bank of Canada, Royal Trust Company, Sterling Coal, Belding Corticelli, Montreal Trust, and Canada Liquid Air.

48 The estimate for these combined holdings in 1936 is just under $1.1 million.

49 See, for instance, Ibbotson, *Stocks, Bonds, Bills, and Inflation* (2001 Yearbook), 94. In these Indices for Large Stocks, we can see 1928 value of 2.018 falling to 1.516 in 1930 and to .789 in 1932, only to recover to 2.367 in 1936. Acknowledgment to investment counsellor Carl Otto for supplying this information.

50 In 1938 Ogilvie Flour split 8:1 and the 1939 price is thus recorded in Moody's Directories as 34. Here it is adjusted simply for ease of comparison with the 1936 share price.

51 This brokerage, operated by McConnell's very close associate Percy Cowans, went bankrupt in the early 1930s. McConnell reportedly helped bail Cowans out personally. The 1937 tax return listing is evidence that, at the very least, he actively participated in the brokerage reorganization.

52 Those for Wilson G./John G. do not survive for 1939. Including these – as well as the California (Relatives') Trust, the 1939 records of which have not survived – would probably add roughly $1 million to the total value of the illustrated portfolio for 1939.

53 Gerald Wareham has pointed out that the large Dominion of Canada bond holdings listed in the 1921 Statement were sold, no doubt to finance purchases of stock in the 1920s. The source of these trust bonds cannot be traced.

54 The surviving St Lawrence Sugar Refineries investment ledger from which data for the representative 1939 and 1951 portfolios were taken had individual page entries for any company whose stocks or bonds McConnell purchased for his sugar company's investment portfolio. This particular ledger's first entries are for 1939; the last usable entries are for 1951. Ledger pages for the following companies listed in the index but found missing are as follows: Abasand Oil, Abitibi Power and Pulp, Brazilian Traction, Brompton Pulp and Paper, Boston and Maine Railway, Canada Foreign Investment, Canadian Power and Paper Investments, Canadian Fur Auction Sales, Dominion of Canada, Dye and Chemical, Holt Renfrew (common), International Petroleum, Imperial Oil of Canada, Lamaque Gold Mines, Laura Secord Candy Shops, and Montreal Light, Heat and Power.

55 Missing pages for the investment ledger marked "Personal" from which data for the representative 1951 portfolio was extracted are as follows: Abitibi Pulp and Paper, American Gas and Electric, American Light and Traction, Baltimore and Ohio Railway, Commonwealth and Southern Railway, Canada Dry Ginger Ale, Chrysler, Consolidated Mining and Smelting, Consolidated Edison, Commonwealth Edison, General Motors, Illinois Light Heat and Power, Montreal Light Heat and Power, Niagara Hudson Power, Mohawk Power, Madison Gas and Electric, Montreal Locomotive, Southland Royalty, Southern California Edison, Standard Radio, Twin City Rapid, US Rubber, and United Light and Railway.

Bibliography

ARCHIVAL MATERIAL

ARCHIVES NATIONALES DU QUÉBEC
Archives de Séminaire de Trois-Rivières, Fond Maurice-Duplessis

ARCHIVES OF ONTARIO, TORONTO
F.H. Deacon Papers
T. Eaton Co. Papers

BORTHWICK INSTITUTE YORK
Halifax Papers

BRITISH LIBRARY, ORIENTAL AND INDIA OFFICE COLLECTIONS, LONDON
Willingdon Papers

BRITISH NATIONAL ARCHIVES, KEW
AVIA

CHURCHILL COLLEGE, CAMBRIDGE
Lascelles Papers

HOUSE OF LORDS RECORD OFFICE, LONDON
Beaverbrook Papers

HUDSON'S BAY COMPANY ARCHIVES, WINNIPEG
Patrick Ashley Cooper, Diary

INDIANA UNIVERSITY, LILLY LIBRARY, MANUSCRIPTS DEPARTMENT
Wendell Willkie Papers

LIBRARY AND ARCHIVES CANADA (LAC)
R.B. Bennett Papers
Henry Birks and Sons Family Papers
Brascan Papers
Lomer Gouin Papers
W.L.M. King Papers
Wilfrid Laurier Papers
Arthur Meighen Papers
Willis-O'Connor Papers

MCCORD MUSEUM ARCHIVES, MONTREAL
Canadian Patriotic Fonds
R.A.E. Greenshields Papers

MCGILL UNIVERSITY, OSLER LIBRARY, MONTREAL
Penfield Papers

MCGILL UNIVERSITY ARCHIVES (MUA), MONTREAL
W.M. Birks Papers
Arthur Currie Papers
Cyril James Diary
McConnell Papers
William Peterson Papers
J.W. Ross Papers

NOVA SCOTIA ARCHIVES AND RECORDS MANAGEMENT, HALIFAX
Robert L. Borden Papers
R.E. Harris Papers

QUEEN'S UNIVERSITY ARCHIVES, KINGSTON
Joseph Flavelle Papers
Gerald S. Graham Fonds
Tweedsmuir Papers

ROYAL ARCHIVES, WINDSOR
George V Papers

UNITED CHURCH ARCHIVES, MONTREAL (now at the Archives nationales de Québec)
Wesleyan Theological College, Board of Governors, Minute-Book

UNIVERSITY OF BIRMINGHAM
Eden/Avon Papers

UNIVERSITY OF DURHAM
Malcolm MacDonald Papers

UNIVERSITY OF MANITOBA ARCHIVES AND SPECIAL COLLECTIONS, WINNIPEG
J.W. Dafoe Papers
Ogilvie Flour Mills Papers

UNIVERSITY OF NEW BRUNSWICK, HARRIET IRVING LIBRARY, FREDERICTON
R.B. Bennett Papers
Beaverbrook Papers

UNIVERSITY OF TORONTO ARCHIVES
Massey Papers

NEWSPAPERS

Daily Telegraph
Family Herald and Weekly Star
Financial Post
Financial Times
Globe and Mail
Halifax *Daily Recorder*
Halifax *Morning Chronicle*
Monetary Times
Montreal *Daily Mail*
Montreal *Evening News*
Montreal *Gazette*
Montreal *Herald*
Montreal *Star*
Montreal *Witness and Telegraph*
Toronto *Mail and Empire*

PRINTED MATERIAL

Acheson, Thomas William. "The Social Origins of Canadian Industrialism: A Study in the Structure of Entrepreneurship." PhD thesis, University of Toronto 1971.
Adam, G. Mercer. *Muskoka Illustrated*. Toronto: William Bryce 1888.
Adams, Frank Dawson. *A History of Christ Church Cathedral Montreal*. Montreal: Burton's Limited 1941.
Ahlbrandt, Patricia Walbridge. *Beaumaris*. Erin, Ont.: Boston Mills Press 1989.
Airhart, Phyllis D. *Serving the Present Age: Revivalism, Progressivism and the Methodist Tradition in Canada*. Montreal, Kingston: McGill-Queen's University Press 1992.

Akenson, Donald Harman. *Small Differences: Irish Catholics and Irish Protestants, 1815–1922: An International Perspective.* Kingston, Montreal: McGill-Queen's University Press 1991.

Allen, L.Dean. *Rise Up, O Men of God: The Men and Religion Forward Movement and the Promise Keepers.* Macon, George: Mercer University Press 2002.

Amery, L.S. *My Political Life,* vol. 3. London: Hutchison 1955.

– *The Empire in a New Era: Speeches Delivered during an Empire Tour, 1927–1928.* London: Edward Arnold 1928.

Anctil, Pierre. *Le rendez-vous manqué: Les juifs de Montréal face au Québec de l'entre-deux-guerres.* Quebec: Institut québécois de recherché sur la culture 1988.

Angell, Harold M. *Provincial Party Financing in Quebec.* Lanham, Md.: University Press of America 1996.

Arcand, Denys. *Duplessis.* Montreal North: VLB Éditeur 1978.

Armstrong, Christopher. *Blue Skies and Boiler Rooms: Buying and Selling Securities in Canada. 1870–1940.* Toronto: University of Toronto Press 1997.

– and H.V. Nelles. "Getting Your Way in Nova Scotia: 'Tweaking' Halifax, 1900–1917." *Acadiensis* 5, no. 2 (spring 1976), 105.

– and H.V. Nelles. *Monopoly's Moment: The Organization and Regulation of Canadian Utilities 1830–1930.* Philadelphia: Temple University Press 1986.

– and H.V. Nelles. *Southern Exposure: Canadian Promoters in Latin America and the Caribbean 1896–1930.* Toronto: University of Toronto Press 1988.

– and H.V. Nelles. *The Revenge of the Methodist Bicycle Company.* Toronto: M Peter Martin Associates Ltd 1977.

Artibise, Alan F.J. "Boosterism and the Development of Prairie Cities, 1871–1913." In Artibise, ed., *Town and City.* Regina: Canadian Plains Research Centre 1981.

– *Winnipeg: A Social History of Urban Growth 1874–1914,* Montreal, Kingston: McGill-Queen's University Press 1975.

Aslet, Clive. *Enchanted Forest: The Story of Stansted in Sussex.* London: Weidenfeld & Nicolson 1984.

Audet, Louis-Philippe. *Histoire du Conseil de l'instruction publique de la province de Québec 1856–1964.* Montreal: Editions Leméac 1964.

– *Le Système Scolaire de la Province de Québec.* Quebec: Les Presses de l'Université Laval 1952.

Austin, Alvyn J. *Saving China: Canadian Missionaries in the Middle Kingdom, 1888–1959.* Toronto: University of Toronto Press 1986.

Ayala, César J. *American Sugar Kingdom: The Plantation Economy of the Spanish Caribbean, 1898–1934.* Chapel Hill: The University of North Carolina Press 1999.

Ayer, Shirley. *A Great Church in Action: A History of Timothy Eaton Memorial Church Toronto Canada 1909–1977.* Whitby, Ontario: Plum Hollow Books 1978.

Bales, R.F. "The 'Fixation Factor' in Alcoholic Addiction: A Hypothesis Derived from a Comparative Study of Irish and Jewish Social Norms." PhD thesis, Harvard University 1944.

Bardof, C.F. "Historical Sketch of the St. Lawrence Sugar Refining Company: 1879–1932." Typescript, McConnell Papers.

Barnett, Corelli. *The Audit of War*. London: Macmillan 1986.

Barrette, Antonio. *Mémoires*. Montreal: Librairie Beauchemin Limitée 1966.

Baskerville, Peter and Eric W. Sanger. *Unwilling Idlers: The Urban Unemployed and Their Families in Late Victorian Canada*. Toronto: University of Toronto Press 1998.

Baudhuin, Fernand. *Histoire économique de la Belgique 1914–1939*. Bruxelles: Etablissements Emile Bruylant, 2nd ed. 1946.

Bauer, P.T. *The Rubber Industry: A Study in Competition and Monopoly*. Cambridge, Massachusetts: Harvard University Press 1948.

Beaverbrook, Lord. *Courage*. Fredericton: Brunswick Press 1961.

– *Friends*. London: Kingswood House, Heinemann 1959.

Bedford, A.G. *The University of Winnipeg: A History of the Founding Colleges*. Toronto: University of Toronto Press 1976.

Belfield, Robert Blake. "The Niagara Frontier: The Evolution of Electric Power Systems in New York and Ontario, 1880–1935." PhD thesis, University of Pennsylvania 1981.

Bellan, Ruben. *Winnipeg's First Century: An Economic History*. Winnipeg: Queenston House Publishing 1978.

Bellavance, Claude. *Shawinigan Water and Power, 1898–1963: Formation et déclin d'un groupe industriel au Québec*. Montreal: Les Éditions de Boréal 1994.

Bence-Jones, Mark. *Palaces of the Raj: Magnificence and Misery of the Lord Sahibs*. London: Allen and Unwin 1973.

Bennett, D.C.T. *Pathfinder*. London: 1983.

Benson, George F. *Historical Record of the Edwardsburg and Canada Starch Companies*. Privately printed c.1959.

Berger, Carl. *The Sense of Power: Studies in the Ideas of Canadian Imperialism 1867–1914*. Toronto: University of Toronto Press 1970.

Bergeron, Léandre. *The History of Quebec: A Patriote's Handbook*. Toronto: NC Press 1975.

Best, Henry M. *Margaret and Charley: The Personal Story of Dr. Charles Best, the Co-Discoverer of Insulin*. Toronto: The Dundurn Group 2003.

Bevan, Joan C. and Maria A. Pacelli. *Wesley Bourne: The Quintessential Canadian Anaesthetist: A Retrospective on the Foundations of McGill Anesthesia*. Montreal: McGill University Libraries 1996.

Beveridge, William, Sir. *Social Insurance and Allied Services*. London: His Majesty's Stationery Office 1942.

Bird, Kai. *The Chairman: John J. McCloy: The Making of the American Establishment*. New York: Simon and Schuster 1992.

Birks, W.M. *The Chancel Before and After*. Toronto: The United Church Publishing House 1947.

Bishop, Charles W. *The Canadian Y.M.C.A. in the Great War*. National Council of Young Men's Christian Associations in Canada 1924.

Bissell, Claude. *The Imperial Canadian: Vincent Massey in Office*. Toronto: University of Toronto Press 1986.

– *The Young Vincent Massey.* Toronto: University of Toronto Press 1981.

Black, Conrad. *Duplessis.* Toronto: McClelland and Stewart 1977.

Blake, Herbert W. *The Era of Streetcars in Winnipeg 1881 to 1955.* Winnipeg: privately printed 1971.

Bliss, Michael. *A Canadian Millionaire: The Life and Business Times of Sir Joseph Flavelle, Bart, 1858–1939.* Toronto: Macmillan of Canada 1978.

– *William Osler: A Life in Medicine.* Toronto: University of Toronto Press 1999.

Bland, Samuel Goldsworth. *James Henderson, D.D.* Toronto: McClelland and Stewart Ltd. 1926.

Blum, John Morton, ed. *Public Philosopher: Selected Letters of Walter Lippman.* New York: Ticknor & Fields 1985.

Boismenu, Gérard. *Le Duplessisme.* Montreal: Les Presses de l'Université de Montréal 1981.

Boldt, Jr, Joseph R. *The Winning of Nickel.* Toronto: Longmans Canada 1967.

Bolitho, Hector. *Alfred Mond First Lord Melchett.* London: Martin Secker 1933.

Bonbright, James C. and Gardiner C. Means. *The Holding Company: Its Public Significance and Its Regulation.* New York: McGraw-Hill 1932.

Boothman, Barry E.C. "Culture of Utility: The Development of Business Education in Canada." In Barbara Austin, ed., *Capitalizing Knowledge: Essays in the History of Business Education in Canada.* Toronto: University of Toronto Press 2000.

Borden Milk Company. Typescript history supplied by Nicholas R. Iammartino.

Bothwell, Robert and William Kilbourn. *C.D. Howe: A Biography.* Toronto: McClelland and Stewart 1979.

Borthwick, J. Douglas, Rev. *Historical and Biographical Gazeteer of Montreal to the Year 1892.* Montreal: John Lovell & Sons 1892.

Bowder, Robert Paul, and Thomas G. Smith. *Independent: A Biography of Lewis W. Douglas.* New York: Alfred A. Knopf 1986.

Boyer, E. Victoria. *Memories of Bracebridge.* Bracebridge, Ont.: Herald-Gazette Press 1975.

Boyer, R.J. "Tourism – How It Came and Its Impact." *Heritage Muskoka*, 34–54.

Bradbury, Bettina. *Working Families: Age, Gender and Daily Survival in Industrial Montreal.* Don Mills: Oxford University Press 1993.

Brady, W.T. *"Corn Products Refining": A Half Century of Progress and Leadership (1906–1958.* New York: The Newcomen Society in North America 1958.

Bray, Matt and Angus Gilbert. "The INCO-Mond Merger of 1929: A Case Study in Entrepreneurial Failure." *Canadian Historical Review* 82, no. 1 (March 1995), 19.

Brennan, Patrick H. *Reporting the Nation's Business: Press-Government Relations during the Liberal Years, 1935–1957.* Toronto: University of Toronto Press 1994.

Briggs, John. *The Face of the Family.* Greenwich, Conn., 1992. Privately printed.

Bronfman, Edgar M. *The Making of a Jew.* New York: G.P. Putnam's Sons 1996.

Brown, Martha. "Dominion-Douglas United Church, Westmount: Historical Sketch 1865 1876 1944." Typescript, 1944.

Brown, Michael. *Jew or Juif?* Philadelphia: Jewish Publication Society 1987.

Brown, William. *The Montreal Maroons.* Montreal: Véhicule Press 1999.

Buckley, K.A.H. *Capital Formation in Canada.* Toronto: University of Toronto Press 1958.

Burns, Robin B. "The Montreal Irish and the Great War". CCHA *Historical Studies* 52 (1985), 67.

Burr, Christina A. *Spreading the Light: Work and Labour Reform in Late-Nineteenth-Century Toronto.* Toronto: University of Toronto Press 1999.

Burrough, William, ed. *Hemingway: The Toronto Years.* Toronto: Doubleday 1995.

Burton, C.L. *A Sense of Urgency.* Toronto: Clarke, Unwin 1952.

Cahn, Charles H. *Douglas Hospital: 100 Years of History and Progress.* Privately printed, 1981.

Cameron, D. Ewen, and Baruch Silverman. "Tale of Two Institutes." *American Journal of Psychiatry* 122, no. 2 (August 1965), 189.

Campbell, Duncan. *Global Mission: The Story of Alcan,* vol. 1. Privately published.

Campbell, Robert, Rev. *A History of the Scotch Presbyterian Church St. Gabriel Street, Montreal.* Montreal: W. Drysdale 1887.

Canada. Department of Justice, Restrictive Trade Practices Commission. *Report Concerning the Sugar Industry in Eastern Canada.* Ottawa: Queen's Printer and Controller of Stationery 1960.

– Department of Justice, Combines Investigation Act, Report of Commissioner. *Flour-Milling Industry: Investigation into an Alleged Combine in the Manufacture, Distribution and Sale of Flour and Other Grain-Mill Products.* Ottawa: King's Printer 1948.

– Department of Justice (T.D. Macdonald, Commissioner under the Combines Investigation Act). *Rubber Products.* Ottawa: King's Printer 1952.

– *Report of the Royal Commission on Dominion-Provincial Relations.* Ottawa: King's Printer 1940.

– *Report of the Royal Commission on Insurance.* Ottawa: King's Printer 1907.

– *Report of the Royal Commission on National Development in the Arts, Letters and Sciences 1949–1951.* Ottawa: King's Printer 1951.

– *Report of the Royal Commission on the Textile Industry.* Ottawa: King's Printer 1938.

Canada's Victory Loan Montreal 1917 (privately printed report for Lord Shaughnessy and Sir Thomas White, McConnell Papers).

Canadian Manufacturers' Association. *Official Souvenir: Visit of the Canadian Manufacturers to Great Britain.* Toronto: R.G. McLean, c.1906.

Canadian Newspaper and Magazine Directory

Canadian Red Cross Society (Quebec Provincial Division). *Annual Report 1956.*

Cannadine, David. *Ornamentalism: How the British Saw their Empire.* London: Allen Lane, The Penguin Press 2001.

Careless, J.M.S. *Toronto to 1918.* Toronto: James Lorimer and The National Museum of Man 1984

Carnegie, Andrew. *The Gospel of Wealth and Other Timely Essays.* Edward C. Kirkland. ed. Cambridge, Massachusetts: Harvard University Press 1962.

Carroll, Jock. *The Life and Times of Greg Clark: Canada's Favorite Storyteller.* Toronto: Doubleday Canada 1961.

Carter-Edwards, Dennis Russell. "Toronto in the 1890's: A Decade of Challenge and Response." MA thesis, University of British Columbia, 1973.

Cartland, Barbara. *The Years of Opportunity, 1939–1945*. London: Hutchison, n.d.

Census of Canada 1901, vol. 1

The Centenary Book of the Parish of St. John the Evangelist Montreal 1861–1961. Montreal: privately printed 1961.

Chafetz, Morris E. and Harold W. Demone, Jr. *Alcoholism and Society*. New York: Oxford University Press 1962.

Chalfont, Alun. *Montgomery of Alamein*. London: Weidenfeld and Nicolson 1976.

Chandler, Alfred D. and Stephen Salisbury. *Pierre S. Dupont and the Making of the Modern Corporation*. New York: Harper and Row 1971.

Chapman, Carol A.G. "A History of Logging in the West Kootenays." BSc essay, University of British Columbia 1988.

Chernow, Ron. *The House of Morgan: An American Banking Dynasty and the Rise of American Finance*. New York: Atlantic Monthly Press 1990.

Christie, Nancy and Michael Gauvreau, *A Full-Orbed Christianity: The Protestant Churches and Social Welfare in Canada, 1900–1940*. Montreal, Kingston: McGill-Queen's University Press 1996.

Chisholm, Anne and Michael Davie, *Beaverbrook: A Life*. London: Hutchison 1992.

The Church of St. John the Evangelist: A Historical Record in Commemoration of the Jubilee of the Parish Church (1878-1928). Montreal: privately printed 1928.

Cleveland, Frederick A., and Fred Wilbur Powell, *Railroad Finance*. New York and London: D. Appleton 1912.

Cleveland, Frederick A., and Fred Wilbur Powell. *Railroad Promotion and Capitalization in the United States*. New York: Longmans, Green 1909.

Cleveland, Harold B., Thomas F. Huertas, et al. *Citibank 1812–1970*. Cambridge, Massachusetts: Harvard University Press 1985.

Cohen, J.M. *The Life of Ludwig Mond*. London: Methuen 1956.

Coleman, D.C. *Courtaulds: An Economic and Social History*, vol. 2. Oxford: Clarendon Press 1969.

Colignon, Richard A. *Power Plays: Critical Events in the Institutionalization of the Tennessee Valley Authority*. Albany: State University of New York Press 1997.

Collard, Edgar Andrew. *First in North America, One Hundred Years in the Life of the Ordre des Comptables Agréés de Québec*. Privately printed 1980.

– *Montreal's Unitarians 1832–2000*. Montreal: The Unitarian Church of Montreal 2001.

– *Passage to the Sea: The Story of Canada Steamship Lines*. Toronto: Doubleday Canada 1991.

– *The Royal Montreal Golf Club 1873–1973: The Centennial of Golf in North America*. Montreal: privately printed 1973.

Colley, Linda. *Britons: Forging a Nation 1707–1837*. New Haven: Yale University Press 1992.

Collins, Anne. *In the Sleep Room: The Story of the CIA Brainwashing Experiments in Canada*. Toronto: Key Porter Books 1988, 1997.

Colussi, James. "The Rise and Fall of the British America Nickel Corporation, 1913–1924." MA essay, Laurentian University n.d.

Cook, Ann. "'Continued and Persevering Combat': The Ontario Women's Christian Temperance Union, Evangelicalism and Social Reform, 1874–1916." PhD thesis, Carleton University 1990.

Cook, Ramsay. *The Politics of John W. Dafoe and the Free Press.* Toronto: University of Toronto Press 1963.

– *The Regenerators: Social Criticism in Late Victorian Canada.* Toronto: University of Toronto Press 1985.

Cook, Sharon Ann. *"Through Sunshine and Shadow": The Woman's Christian Temperance Union, Evangelicalism and Religion in Ontario, 1874–1930.* Montreal, Kingston: McGill-Queen's University Press 1995.

Cookson, Joe. *Tattle Tales of Muskoka.* Bracebridge, Ont.: Herald-Gazette Press 1976.

Coombs, David G. "The Emergence of a White Collar Work Force in Toronto, 1895–1911." PhD thesis, York University 1978.

Cooper, John Irwin. *The History of the Montreal Hunt.* Montreal: Montreal Hunt 1953.

Cooper, Edmonds and Hedley, Messrs. *Official Souvenir: Visit of the Canadian Manufacturers to Great Britain.* Toronto: R.G. McLean c.1906.

Copp, Terry. *The Anatomy of Poverty: The Conditions of the Working Class in Montreal, 1897–1929.* Toronto: McClelland and Stewart 1994.

Corbett, E.A. *Henry Marshall Tory.* Toronto: The Ryerson Press 1954.

Crail, W.A. *A History of Canadian Journalism,* vol. 2. Toronto: The Ontario Publishing Company 1959.

Crook, J. Mordaunt. *The Rise of the Nouveaux Riches.* London: John Murray 1999.

Cross, Harold C. *One Hundred Years of Service with Youth: The Story of the Montreal YMCA.* Montreal: privately printed 1951.

Cross, Michael, and Robert Bothwell, eds. *Policy by Other Means: Essays in Honour of C.P. Stacey.* Toronto: Clarke, Irwin 1972.

Cruikshank, Jeffrey L. *From the Rivers: The Origins and Growth of the New England Electric System* (New England Electric System 1996).

Cruikshank, Ken. "Taking the Bitter with the Sweet: Sugar Refiners and the Canadian Regulatory State, 1904–20". *Canadian Historical Review* 74, no. 3 (1993), 384.

Cudlipp, Hugh. *Publish and Be Damned!: The Astonishing Story of the Daily Mirror.* London: Andrew Dakers 1953.

Dafoe, John W. *Clifford Sifton in Relation to His Times.* Toronto: Macmillan 1931.

Dales, John H. *Hydroelectricity and Industrial Development: Quebec 1898–1940.* Cambridge, Mass.: Harvard University Press 1957.

Davies, Philip. *Splendours of the Raj.* London: John Murray 1985.

Dawson, Owen. *My Story of the Boys' Farm at Shawbridge, also Angels I Have Met.* Privately printed, 1952.

Dean, Arthur H. *William Nelson Cromwell 1854–1948: An American Pioneer in Corporation, Comparative and International Law.* Privately published 1957.

Decarie, Malcolm Graeme. "The Prohibition Movement in Ontario: 1894–1916." PhD thesis, Queen's University, Kingston 1972.

de Forest, Lynda. *Proud Heritage: A History of the Royal Victoria Hospital Training School for Nurses, 1894–1972.* Montreal: The Alumnae Association of the Royal Victoria Hospital Training School for Nurses. 1994.

den Otter, A.A. "Bondage of Steam: The CPR and Western Canadian Coal." In Harold A. Dempsey, ed., *The CPR West.* Vancouver: Douglas & McIntyre 1984.

– *Civilizing the West: The Galts and the Development of Western Canada.* Edmonton: University of Alberta Press 1982.

Denison, Merrill. *The People's Power: The History of Ontario Hydro.* Toronto: McClelland and Stewart 1960.

Déom, Esther. *40 ans de syndicalisme chez les journalistes québécois.* Montreal: PME, 1989.

Desjardins, Marc, et al. *Histoire de la Gaspésie.* Quebec: Institut québécois de recherche sur la culture 1999.

"The Development of Farming in Muskoka." *Heritage Muskoka.* Parry Sound: Algonquin Regional Library System 1976.

Dewart, E.H., DD. *Brief Outlines of Christian Doctrine.* Toronto: William Briggs 1898.

Dictionary of National Biography. Oxford: Oxford University Press.

Dillon, Mary Earhart. *Wendell Willkie, 1892–1944.* New York: J.B. Lippincott 1952.

Dion, Léon. *Québec 1945–2000: Les Intellectuels et le temps de Duplessis*, vol. 2. Sainte-Foy, Que.: Les Presses de l'Université Laval 1993.

Dirks, Patricia. "'Getting a Grip on Harry': Canada's Methodists Respond to the 'Big Boy' Problem, 1900–1925." In Neil Semple, ed., *Canadian Methodist Historical Society Papers*, vol. 7. Toronto 1990

– "Serving Church and Nation: Methodist Sunday Schools in Canada's Century." In Neil Semple, ed., *Canadian Methodist Historical Society Papers*, vol. 10. Toronto, 1995.

Djwa, Sandra. *The Politics of the Imagination: A Life of F.R. Scott.* Vancouver: Douglas and McIntyre 1989.

Donnelly, Murray. *Dafoe of the Free Press.* Toronto: Macmillan of Canada 1968.

Dow, Alexander. "Finance and Foreign Control of Canadian Base Metal Mining, 1918–55." *Economic History Review* 37 (1984), 58.

Doyle, Richard J. *Hurly-Burly: A Time at the Globe.* Toronto: Macmillan of Canada 1990.

Drummond, Ian M. *Imperial Economic Policy, 1917–1939: Studies in Expansion and Protection.* London: George Allen and Unwin 1974.

Du Boff, Richard B. and Edwaard S. Herman. "The Promotional-Financial Dynamic of Merger Movements: A Historical Perspective." *Journal of Economic Issues* 23, no. 1 (March 1989), 107.

Duncan, James S. *Not a One-Way Street.* Toronto: Clarke, Irwin 1971.

Dupont, Antonin. *Les relations entre l'Eglise et l'Etat sous Louis-Alexandre Taschereau 1920–1936.* Montreal: Guérin 1972.

– *Taschereau.* Montreal: Guérin 1997.

Duval, André. *Dorval: Three Hundred Years of History.* Privately printed, 1989.

Duval, Laurent. *L'Étonnant dossier de la Place des Arts 1956–1967.* Montreal: Louise Courteau, éditrice, 1988.

Eagle, John A, *The Canadian Pacific Railway and the Development of Western Canada, 1896–1914*. Kingston, Montreal, Kingston: McGill-Queen's University Press 1989.

Easy Lessons as Elements of Political Economy or How Individuals and a Country Become Rich. Toronto: Copp Clark 1877.

Eaton, Flora McCrea. *Memory's Wall*. Toronto: Clarke, Irwin 1956.

Eayrs, James. *The Commonwealth and Suez*. London: Oxford University Press 1964.

– "The Round Table Movement in Canada, 1901–1920," *Canadian Historical Review* 38, no. 1 (March 1957), 1

Edey, H.C. "Company Accounting in the Nineteenth and Twentieth Centuries". In Michael Chatfield, ed., *Contemporary Studies in the Evolution of Accounting Thought*. Belmont, California: Dickenson Publishing 1968.

Eichner, Alfred S. *The Emergency of Oligopoly: Sugar Refining as a Case Study*. Baltimore: The Johns Hopkins Press 1969.

Elliott, G.A. *Tariff Procedures and Trade Barriers: A Study of Indirect Protection in Canada and the United States*. Toronto: University of Toronto Press 1955.

"An Emigrant Lady," *Letters from Muskoka*. London: Richard Bentley and Son 1878.

Encyclopedia Titanica. www.encyclopedia-titanica.org.

Entin, Martin A. *Edward Archibald: Surgeon of the Royal Vic*. Montreal, Kingston: McGill University Libraries 2004.

Epp, Abram Ernest. "Cooperation among Capitalists: The Canadian Merger Movement, 1909–13." PhD thesis, John Hopkins University 1973.

Fagan, Cary, *The Fred Victor Mission Story*. Winfield, BC: Wood Lake Books 1993.

Farrell, Mark. "Stammering Through: My Adventures in Print." Typescript, prepared with Tim Creery, 1993.

Fedunkiw, Marianne P. *Rockefeller Foundation Funding and Medical Education in Toronto, Montreal and Halifax*. Montreal, Kingston: McGill-Queen's University Press 2005.

Feed, Colin, ed. *Nelson: A History in Pictures*. Nelson, B.C.: Niche Publications, n.d.

Feltoe, Richard. *Redpath: The History of a Sugar House*. Toronto: Natural Heritage/Natural History 1991.

Ferguson, Barry, and Robert Wardhaugh. "'Impossible Conditions of Equality': John W. Dafoe, the Rowell-Sirois Royal Commission, and the Interpretation of Canadian Federalism." *Canadian Historical Review* 84, no. 4 (2003).

Ferguson, G.V., and F.H. Underhill. *Press and Party in Canada*. Toronto: Ryerson Press 1955.

Finer, Herman. *Dulles over Suez*. London: Heinemann 1964.

Finkel, Alvin. *Business and Social Reform in the Thirties*. Toronto: Lorimer 1979.

Finlay, Karen A. *The Force of Culture: Vincent Massey and Canadian Sovereignty*. Toronto: University of Toronto Press 2004.

Fleming, R.B. *The Railway King of Canada: Sir William Mackenzie 1849–1923*. Vancouver: University of British Columbia Press 1991.

Fleury, Jean-Louis. *Les porteurs de lumières: L'histoire de la distribution de l'électricite au Québec*. Sainte-Foy, Que.: Éditions MultiMondes 2004.

Foran, Max. "The CPR and the Urban West, 1881–1930." In Hugh A. Dempsey, ed., *The CPR West: The Iron Road and the Making of a Nation.* Vancouver and Toronto: Douglas and McIntyre 1984.

Forrester, Maureen. *Out of Character.* Toronto: McClelland and Stewart 1986.

Forsey, Eugene. *A Life on the Fringe: The Memoirs of Eugene Forsey.* Toronto: Oxford University Press 1990.

Forster, Ben. *A Conjunction of Interests: Business, Politics and Tariffs 1825–1879.* Toronto: University of Toronto Press 1986.

Fortin, Jean-Charles and Antonio Lachausseur. *Histoire du Bas-Saint-Laurent.* Quebec: Institut québécois sur la culture 1995.

Fosdick, Raymond B. *The Story of the Rockefeller Foundation.* New York: Harper & Brothers 1952.

Fournier, Louis. *FLQ: Histoire d'un mouvement clandestine.* Rev. ed. Montreal: Lanctôt Editeur 1998.

Francoeur, Madame [Jacqueline]. *Trente ans rue St-François-Xavier et ailleurs.* Montreal: Éditions Édouard Garand 1928.

Frank, David. "The Cape Breton Coal Industry and the Rise and Fall of the British Empire Steel Corporation." *Acadiensis* 7, no. 1 (Autumn 1977), 3.

Frankland, Noble. *Witness of a Century.* London: Shepheard-Walwyn 1993.

Frantz, Joe B. *Gail Borden: Dairyman to a Nation.* Norman: University of Oklahoma Press 1951.

Fraser, Alexander. *A History of Ontario.* Toronto and Montreal: The Canada History Company 1907.

Fraser, L.R. *History of Muskoka.* Bracebridge [1946].

Freeman, Neil B. *The Politics of Power: Ontario Hydro and its Government, 1906–1995.* Toronto: University of Toronto Press 1996.

French, Goldwin. *Parsons and Politics: The role of the Wesleyan Methodists in Upper Canada and the Maritimes from 1780 to 1855.* Toronto: The Ryerson Press 1962.

Frost, James D. *Merchant Princes: Halifax's First Family of Finance, Ships and Steel.* Toronto: James Lorimer. c. 2003.

Frost, Stanley Brice. *The Man in the Ivory Tower: F. Cyril James of McGill.* Montreal, Kingston: McGill-Queen's University Press 1991.

– *McGill University: For the Advancement of Learning.* Montreal, Kingston: McGill-Queen's University Press 1984.

Gagnon, Alain-G. *Les Spécialistes des sciences sociales et la politique au Canada: entre l'ordre des clercs et l'avant-garde.* Montreal: Les Editions du Boréal 1994.

Gagnon, Robert. *Histoire de la Commission des écoles catholiques de Montréal.* Montreal: Les Editions de Boréal 1996.

– *Histoire de l'Ecole Polytechnique de Montréal 1873–1990: La montée des ingénieurs francophones.* Montreal: Les Éditions du Boréal 1991.

Gray, James H. *Trouble-maker.* Toronto: Macmillan of Canada 1978.

Gauvin, Michael. "The Municipal Reform Movement in Montreal, 1886–1914." MA thesis, University of Ottawa 1972.

General Conference of the Methodist Church of Canada and Newfoundland. *The Doctrine and Discipline of the Methodist Church 1906* [also known and cited as *Methodist Discipline 1906*]. Toronto: William Briggs 1907.

Gibson, Frederick W. *Queen's University,* vol. 2. Montreal, Kingston: McGill-Queen's University Press 1993.

Gillen, Mollie, *The Masseys.* Toronto: Ryerson 1965.

Gilmor, Don. *I Swear by Apollo: Dr. Ewen Cameron and the CIA-Brainwashing Experiments.* Montreal: Eden Press 1987.

Girard, Camil. *Un pays fragil: Le Times de Londres et l'image du Canada (1908–1922).* Chicoutimi: Les Editions JCL 1994.

Glassford, Larry. *Reaction and Reform: The Politics of the Conservative Party under R.B. Bennett, 1927–1938.* Toronto: University of Toronto Press 1992.

Godfrey, Rupert, ed. *Letters from a Prince.* London: Little, Brown 1999.

Graham, Benjamin and Donald Le Fevre Dodd. *Securities.* New York: McGraw-Hill 1940 (Titled *Securities Analysis* in subsequent editions)

Graham, Roger. *Arthur Meighen: And Fortune Fled.* Toronto and Vancouver: Clarke, Irwin 1963.

Granatstein, J.L. "Financing the Liberal Party, 1935–45." In Michael Cross and Robert Bothwell, eds., *Policy by Oother Means: Essays in honour of C.P. Stacey.* Toronto: Clarke, Irwin 1972.

– *The Politics of Survival: The Conservative Party of Canada, 1939–1945.* Toronto: University of Toronto Press 1967.

Gray, James H. *R.B. Bennett: The Calgary Years.* Toronto: University of Toronto Press 1991.

Gray, John. "Our First Century – A Lot of It Was Fun." Special supplement, "The Montreal Star: One Hundred Years of Growth, Turmoil and Change 1869–1969," Montreal *Star,* 16 January 1969.

Green, H. Gordon, and A.J. West. "Headlining a Century." Typescript, McConnell Papers.

Guest, Dennis. *The Emergence of Social Security in Canada.* Vancouver: UBC Press 1997.

Guidebook and Atlas of Muskoka & Parry Sound Districts in 1879. Toronto: H.R. Page 1879. Repr. Erin Mills, Ont.: Boston Mills Press 2000.

Guillet, Edwin C. *The Pioneer Farmer and the Backwoodsman.* Toronto: Ontario Publishing 1963.

Haber, L.F. *The Chemical Industry 1900–1930.* Oxford: Clarendon Press 1971.

Hager, Louis P. *History of the West End Street Railway.* Boston: privately printed, 1892.

Hake, Eric R. "Financial Innovation as a Facilitator of Merger Activity." *Journal of Economic Issues* 32, no. 1 (March 1998), 145.

– "The Stock Watering Debate: More Light, Less Heat." *Journal of Economic Issues* 35, no. 2 (June 2001), 423.

Hall, Carl Ansel St Clair. "Electrical Utilities in Ontario under Private Ownership 1890–1914." PhD thesis, University of Toronto 1968.

Hall, H. Duncan. *North American Supply.* London: Her Majesty's Stationery Office 1955.

Hamilton, Denis. *Editor-in-Chief: The Fleet Street Memories of Sir Denis Hamilton.* London: Hamish Hamilton 1989.

Hanaway, Joseph and Richard Cruess. *McGill Medicine: Volume I, The First Half Century 1829–1885.* Montreal, Kingston: McGill-Queen's University Press 1996.

Hargrove, Erwin C. *Prisoners of Myth: The Leadership of the Tennessee Valley Authority, 1933–1990.* Princeton: Princeton University Press 1994.

Harkness, Ross. *J.E. Atkinson of the Star.* Toronto: University of Toronto Press 1963.

Harris, Brian F. *Shared Monopoly and the Cereal Industry: An Empirical Investigation of the Effects of the FTC's Antitrust Proposals.* East Lansing: Michigan State University 1979.

Harr, John Ensor and Peter J. Johnson. *The Rockefeller Conscience: An American Family in Public and in Private.* New York: Charles Scribner's Sons 1991.

Harris, George H. *The President's Book: The Story of the Sun Life Assurance Company of Canada.* Montreal: privately printed, 1928.

Harrison, Brian. *Drink and the Victorians.* London: Faber and Faber 1971.

Hart-Davis, Duff, ed. *In Royal Service: Letters & Journals of Sir Alan Lascelles from 1920 to 1936.* London: Hamish Hamilton 1989.

Harvey, Pierre. *Histoire de l'École des Hautes Etudes Commerciales de Montréal.* 2 vols. Montreal: Les Éditions Québec-Amérique 1994.

Hawkins, W.E. *Electrifying Calgary: A Century of Public and Private Power.* Calgary: University of Calgary Press 1987.

Heaton, Ernest. *The Trust Company Idea and Its Development.* Toronto: Hunter Rose 1904.

Heinrich, Thomas. "Product Diversification in the U.S. Pulp and Paper Industry: The Case of International Paper [sic], 1898–1941." *Business History Review* 75, no. 3 (autumn 2001), 465–505.

Heintzman, Ralph Ripley. "The Struggle for Life: The French Daily Press of Montreal and the Problems of Economic Growth in the Age of Laurier 1896–1911." PhD thesis, York University 1977.

Henderson, Maxwell. *Plain Talk: Memoirs of an Auditor General.* Toronto: McClelland and Stewart 1984.

Heron, Craig. *Booze: A Distilled History.* Toronto: Between the Lines 2003.

Hilferding, Rudolf. *Das Finanzkapital: Eine Studie über die jüngste Entwicklung des Kapitalismus* (Vienna, 1910). Translated as *Finance Capital: A Study of the Latest Phase of Capitalist Development* (Tom Bottomore, ed.). London: Routledge and Kegan Paul 1981.

Hillyer, Mrs Peter Norman, ed. *From the Orient with Love: Letters from Sir Herbert Marler K.C.M.G. and Lady Marler to Their Daughter Mrs. Cecil Jackson North.* Jupiter, Fla.: Privately published 1982.

The History of The Times: The 150th Anniversary and Beyond 1912–1948. London: privately printed 1952, pt. I.

History of Toronto and the County of York Ontario. Toronto: C. Blackett Robinson 1885.

Hogue, Clarence, André Bolduc, and Daniel Larouche. *Québec: un siècle d'électricité.* Montreal: Éditions Libre Expression 1979.

Holli, Melvin G. *Reform in Detroit: Hazen S. Pingree and Urban Politics.* New York: Oxford University Press 1969.

Holman, Worthington C. *Ginger Talks.* Libertyville, Illinois: Sheldon University Press 1910.

Homberger, Eric. *Mrs. Astor's New York: Money and Social Power in a Gilded Age.* New Haven: Yale University Press 2002.

Hooker, Mancy Harvison, ed. *The Moffat Papers.* Cambridge, Mass.: Harvard University Press 1956.

Hopper, Mrs R.P. *Old-Time Primitive Methodism in Canada.* Toronto: William Briggs 1914.

Houston, Susan A., and Alison Prentice. *Schooling and Scholars in Nineteenth-Century Ontario.* Toronto: University of Toronto Press 1988.

Howard, Oswald. *The Montreal Diocesan Theological College: A History from 1873 to 1963.* Montreal: McGill University Press 1963.

Howard-White, F.B. *Nickel: An Historical Review.* Toronto: Longmans Canada 1963.

Howell, David, and Peter Lindsay. "Social Gospel and the Young Boy Problem 1895–1925." *Canadian Journal of the History of Sport* 18, no. 2 (December 1987), 26.

Hower, Ralph M. *History of Macy's of New York, 1858–1919.* Cambridge, Mass.: Harvard University Press 1946.

Hughes, Thomas P. *Networks of Power: Electrification in Western Society, 1800–1930.* Baltimore and London: The Johns Hopkins University Press 1983.

Humphries, Charles W. *"Honest Enough to be Bold": The Life and Times of Sir James Pliny Whitney.* Toronto: University of Toronto Press 1985.

Hurst, Allan M. *The Canadian Y.M.C.A. in World War II.* National War Services Committee of the National Council of Young Men's Christian Associations of Canada. Np, nd.

Hussey, Christopher. *The Life of Sir Edwin Lutyens.* London: Antique Collectors' Club 1984; originally published by *Country Life* in 1950.

Hustak, Alan. *Titanic: The Canadian Story.* Montreal: Véhicule Press 1998.

Hyatt, A.M.J. *General Sir Arthur Currie: A Military Biography.* Toronto: University of Toronto Press 1987.

Illien, Gilas. *La Place des Art et la Révolution tranquille: Les fonctions politiques d'un centre culturel.* Sillery, Que.: Les Éditions de l'IQRC and Les Presses de l'Université Laval 1999.

Innis, Harold A. *Settlement and the Mining Frontier.* In W.A. Mackintosh and W.L.G. Joerg, eds, *Canadian Frontiers of Settlement,* vol. 9. Toronto: Macmillan of Canada 1936.

Irving, Allan. "Leonard Marsh and the McGill Social Science Research Project," *Journal of Canadian Studies.* 21, no. 2 (Summer 1986), 6.

The J.M. Foundation: 1995 Annual Report. New York: privately printed 1996.

J.P. Bickell Foundation Report No. 23. Toronto: National Trust Company 1998.

Jameson, Sheilagh S. *Chautauqua in Canada.* Calgary: Glenbow-Alberta Institute 1979.

Jasen, Patricia. *Wild Things: Nature, Culture, and Tourism in Ontario, 1790–1914.* Toronto: University of Toronto Press 1995.

Jemain, Alain. *Les conquérants de l'invisible: Air Liquide 100 ans d'histoire.* Paris: Fayard 2002.

Jeremy, D.J. *Dictionary of Business Biography.* London: Buttorwoths 1984.

Johnson, Hugh. *A Merchant Prince: Life of Hon. Senator John Macdonald.* Toronto: William Briggs 1893.

Johnston, Charles. "History of the Norman and Madge Johnston Family." Typescript, c.1996.

Johnston, Russell. *Selling Themselves: The Emergence of Canadian Advertising.* Toronto: University of Toronto Press 2001.

Kaplan, William. *Everything that Floats: Pat Sullivan, Hal Banks, and the Seamen's Unions of Canada.* Toronto: University of Toronto Press 1987.

Kendle, John. *The Round Table Movement and Imperial Union.* Toronto: University of Toronto Press 1975.

Kennan, George. *E.H. Harriman.* Boston: Houghton, Mifflin 1922.

Kilbourn, Willliam. *The Elements Combined: A History of The Steel Company of Canada.* Toronto, Vancouver: Clarke, Irwin 1960.

Kay, Ormonde de. "Biography: Jeremiah Milbank, Sr." Typescript.

Kealey, Gregory S. *Toronto Workers Respond to Industrial Capitalism.* Toronto: University of Toronto Press 1980.

Kesterton, W.H. *A History of Journalism in Canada.* Toronto: McClelland and Stewart 1967.

Kierans, Eric. *Remembering.* Toronto: Stoddart 2001.

Kilbourn, William. *The Elements Combined: A History of the Steel Company of Canada.* Toronto, Vancouver: Clarke, Irwin 1960.

Kluckner, Michael. *Toronto: The Way It Was.* Toronto: Whitecap Books 1988.

Knowles, Valerie. *From Telegraph to Titan: The Life of William C. Van Horne.* Toronto: The Dundurn Group 2004.

Knox, James. *Robert Byron.* London: John Murray 2003.

Koss, Stephen. *The Rise and Fall of the Political Press in Britain,* vol. 2. London: Hamish Hamilton 1984.

Kunz, Diane B. *The Economic Diplomacy of the Suez Crisis.* Chapel Hill: The University of North Carolina Press 1991.

Kuntz Tom (ed.). *The Titanic Disaster Hearings: The Official Transcripts of the 1912 Senate Investigation,* New York: Pocket Books 1998.

Kwavnick, David, ed. *The Tremblay Report: Report of the Royal Commission of Inquiry on Constitutional Problems.* Toronto: McClelland and Stewart 1973.

Kyle, Keith. *Suez.* New York: St Martin's Press 1991.

Lambert, Angela. *1939: The Last Season of Peace.* London: Weidenfeld & Nicolson 1989.

Lamont, Edward M. *The Ambassador from Wall Street: The Story of Thomas W. Lamont, J.P. Morgan's Chief Executive.* Lanham, Md.: Madison Books 1994.

Lamont, Thomas W. *My Boyhood in a Parsonage.* New York: Harper & Brothers 1946.

Landry, John T. and Jeffrey L. Cruikshank. *From the Rivers: The Origins and Growth of the New England Electric System.* New England Electric System 1996.

Lank, H.H. and E.L. Williams. *The Dupont Canada History.* Privately printed 1982.

Laurin, Serge. *Histoire des Laurentides.* Quebec: Institut québécois de recherche sur la culture 1995.

Lavertu, Yves. *L'affaire Bernonville: Le Québec face à Pétain et à la Colloboration (1948–1951).* Montreal: VLB Editeur 1994.

Leach, Campbell W. *Coopers & Lybrand in Canada: A Chronicle of the McDonald, Currie Years 1910–1973.* Montreal: privately printed 1976.

Leff, Mark H. "Strange Bedfellows: The Utility Magnate as Politician" In James H. Madison, ed., *Wendell Willkie: Hoosier Internationalist.* Bloomington: Indiana University Press 1992.

Legate, David M. *Fair Dinkum.* New York: Doubleday 1969.

Lewis, Jefferson. *Something Hidden: A Biography of Wilder Penfield.* Toronto: Doubleday Canada 1981.

Lewis, Robert. *Manufacturing Montreal: The Making of an Industrial Landscape, 1850 to 1930.* Baltimore: The Johns Hopkins Press 2000.

Leyburn, James G. *The Scotch-Irish: A Social History.* Chapel Hill: University of North Carolina Press 1962.

A Life in the Woods. Nelson, B.C.: Kootenay Museum and Historical Society 1994

Linteau, Paul-André. *Maisonneuve: comment des promoteurs fabriqent une ville 1883–1918.* Montreal: Boréal Express 1981.

Liquid Air in Canada. Privately printed, 1986.

Lisagot, Nacy and Frank Lipsius. *A Law unto Itself: The Untold Story of the Law Firm Sullivan & Cromwell.* New York: William Morrow and Company 1988.

Litt, Paul. *The Muse, the Masses, and the Massey Commission.* Toronto: University of Toronto Press 1992.

Louis, Wm Roger. *In the Name of God, Go!: Leo Amery and the British Empire in the Age of Churchill.* New York: W.W. Norton 1992.

Lower, Arthur R.M. *Great Britain's Woodyard: British America and the Timber Trade, 1763–1867.* Montreal, Kingston: McGill-Queen's University Press 1973.

- *The North American Assault on the Canadian Forest: A History of the Lumber Trade between Canada and the United States.* Toronto: Ryerson Press 1938

- *Settlement and the Forest Frontier in Eastern Canada.* In W.A. Mackintosh and W.L.G. Joerg, eds, *Canadian Frontiers of Settlement,* vol 9. Toronto: Macmillan of Canada 1936.

Lownie, Andrew. *John Buchan: The Presbyterian Cavalier.* London: Constable 1995.

Marshall, David B. *Secularizing the Faith: Canadian Protestant Clergy and the Crisis of Belief, 1850–1940.* Toronto: University of Toronto Press 1992.

MacDermott, H.R, MD, FRCP. *A History of The Montreal General Hospital.* Montreal: Montreal General Hospital 1950.

- *History of the School of Nursing of the Montreal General Hospital.* Montreal: The Alumnae Association 1940.

Macdonald, Florence. *For Greece a Tear.* Fredericton: Brunswick Press 1954.

MacDonald, Joan. *The Stanstead College Story.* Stanstead: The Board of Trustees of Stanstead College 1977.

Mackenzie, Norman Hall. "The Economic and Social Development of Muskoka 1855–1888. MA thesis University of Toronto 1943.

MacLennan, Anne. *Red Feather in Montreal.* Montreal: Red Feather Foundation 1996.

MacLeod, Kenneth O. *The First Century: The Story of a Canadian Company: Henry Birks & Sons 1879–1979.* Montreal: Henry Birks & Sons 1979.

Main, O.W. *The Canadian Nickel Industry: A Study in Market Control and Public Policy.* Toronto: University of Toronto Press 1955.

Mair, Nathan H. *The United Theological College 1927–1977.* Montreal: privately printed 1977.

Mangan, J.A. *The Games Ethic and Imperialism: Aspects of the Diffusion of an Ideal.* Harmondsworth: Viking 1986.

March, William. *Red Line: The Chronicle-Herald and The Mail-Star 1875–1954.* Halifax: Chebucto Agencies 1986.

Marcil, Eileen Reid. *Tall Ships and Tankers: The History of the Davie Shipbuilders.* Toronto: McClelland and Stewart 1997.

Marchildon, Gregory P. "'Hands Across the Water': Canadian Industrial Financiers in the City of London, 1905–20." *Business History* 34, no. 3 (July 1992).

– *Profits and Politics: Beaverbrook and the Gilded Age of Canadian Finance.* Toronto: University of Toronto Press 1996.

– "The Role of Lawyers in Corporate Promotion and Management." Typescript.

Markham, Jesse W. *Competition in the Rayon Industry.* Cambridge, Mass.: Harvard University Press 1952.

Marks, Christopher G. *Rackets in Canada and the Montreal Racket Club.* Montreal: Price-Patterson 1990.

Marks, Lynne, *Revivals and Roller Rinks: Religion, Leisure and Identity in Late Nineteenth-Century Small-Town Ontario.* Toronto: University of Toronto Press 1996.

Marler, Howard. *Marler: Four Generations of a Quebec Family.* Montreal: Price-Patterson Limited 1987.

Marrus, Michael R. *Mr. Sam: The Life and Times of Samuel Bronfman.* Toronto: Viking 1991.

Marsh, D'Arcy. *The Tragedy of Henry Thornton.* Toronto: Macmillan of Canada Limited 1935.

Marsh, Peter T. *Joseph Chamberlain: Entrepreneur in Politics.* New Haven: Yale University Press 1994.

Marx, Karl. *Capital: A Critique of Political Economy*, vol. 1, trans. Ben Fowkes. Harmondsworth: Penguin, 1976 [orig. 1867]

Mason, Edward. *The Street Railway in Massachusetts: The Rise and Decline of an Industry.* Cambridge, Mass.: Harvard University Press 1932.

Massell, David. *Amassing Power: J.B. Duke and the Saguenay River, 1897–1927.* Montreal, Kingston: McGill-Queen's University Press, 2000

Massey, Vincent. *What's Past is Prologue.* Toronto: Macmillan of Canada 1963.

Masters, D.C. *Bishop's University: The First Hundred Years.* Toronto: Clarke, Irwin 1950.

– *The Rise of Toronto, 1850–1890.* Toronto: University of Toronto Press 1947.

Mavor, James. *My Window on the Street of the World.* London: J.M. Dent and Sons Limited 1923.

– *Niagara in Politics: A Critical Account of the Ontario Hydro-Electric Commission.* New York: E.P. Dutton 1925.

McCraw, Thomas K., ed. *Creating Modern Capitalism.* Cambridge, Mass.: Harvard University Press 1997.

McCurdy, J.F., ed. *Life and Work of D.J. Macdonnell Minister of St. Andrew's Church, Toronto.* Toronto: William Briggs 1897.

McDonald, Forrest. *Insull.* Chicago: University of Chicago Press 1962.

McDowall, Duncan. *Quick to the Frontier: Canada's Royal Bank.* Toronto: McClelland and Stewart 1983.

– *Steel at the Sault: Francis H. Clergue, Sir James Dunn, and the Algoma Steel Corporation 1901–1956.* Toronto: University of Toronto Press 1984.

– *The Light: Brazilian Traction, Light and Power Company Limited 1899–1945.* Toronto: University of Toronto Press 1988.

McIntosh, Robert. *Different Drummers: Banking and Politics in Canada.* Toronto: Macmillan Canada 1991.

McKay, John P. *Tramways and Trolleys: The Rise of Urban Mass Transit in Europe.* Princeton: Princeton University Press 1976.

McKay, Paul. *Electric Empire: The Inside Story of Ontario Hydro.* Toronto: Between the Lines 1983.

McKenty, Neil and Catharine. *Skiing Legends and the Laurentian Lodge Club.* Montreal: Price-Patterson 2000.

McKenzie, Francine. *Redefining the Bonds of Commonwealth, 1939–1948.* Basingstoke, UK: Palgrave Macmillan 2002.

McMurray, Thomas. *The Free Grant Land of Canada, from Practical Experience of Bush Farming in the Free Grant Districts of Muskoka and Parry Sound.* Bracebridge, Ont.: Office of the "Northern Advocate" 1871.

McNally, H.B. *Bruno 1918–1993.* St Bruno: Mount St Bruno Country Club 1993.

McNaught, Kenneth. *Conscience and History: A Memoir.* Toronto: University of Toronto Press 1999.

– *A Prophet in Politics: A Biography of J.S. Woodsworth.* Toronto: University of Toronto Press 1959.

McVicar, Don. *Ferry Command.* Shrewsbury, UK: Airlife Publishing 1981.

Meighen, Arthur. *Unrevised and Unrepented: Debating Speeches and Others.* Toronto: Clarke, Irwin 1949.

Michaud, Nelson. *L'Enigme du sphinx: Regards sur la vie politique d'un nationaliste (1910–1926).* Quebec: Les Presses de l'Universite Laval 1998.

Michie, Ranald. "Dunn, Fischer & Co. in the City of London, 1906–14." *Business History* 30, no. 2 (April 1988), 193.

Middleton, Jesse Edgar. *The Municipality of Metropolitan Toronto: A History.* New York and Toronto 1923.

The Milbank Memorial Fund: A Meeting Commemorating the Twenty-fifth Anniversary. New York: privately printed 1930.

Miller, Carman. *Painting the Map Red: Canada and the South African War 1899–1902.* Montreal, Kingston: Canadian War Museum and McGill-Queen's University Press 1993.

Miller, Michael B. *The Bon Marché: Bourgeois Culture and the Department Store.* Cited in Rémy G. Saisselin, *Bricobracomania: The Bourgeois and the Bibelot.* London: Thames and Hudson 1985.

Miller-Barstow, D.R. *Beatty and the C.P.R.* Toronto: McClelland and Stewart 1951.

Milligan, Frank. *Eugene A. Forsey: An Intellectual Biography*. Calgary: University of Calgary Press 2004.

Mills, Allen. *Fool for Christ: The Political Thought of J.S. Woodsworth*. Toronto: University of Toronto Press 1991.

Moen, Jon and Ellis W. Talman. "The Bank Panic of 1907: The Role of Trust Companies." *The Journal of Economic History* 52, no. 3 (September 1992), 611.

Moodey, Edgar C. and Robert A. Speirs. *Veritas: A History of Selwyn House School Montreal 1908–1978*. Westmount: Selwyn House Association 1978.

Morgan, David. *The Morgans of Montreal*. Privately published 1992.

Moritz, Albert and Theresa Moritz. *Stephen Leacock: His Remarkable Life*. Markham, Ontario: Fitzhenry & Whiteside 2002.

Morris, Philip H., ed. *Canadian Patriotic Fund* (published privately by the fund's executive committee in Ottawa, 1919).

Morrison, Theodore. *Chautauqua: A Center for Education, Religion and the Arts in America*. Chicago: The University of Chicago Press 1974.

Morrow, Don. *Sporting Evolution: The Montreal Amateur Athletic Association 1881–1981*. Montreal: privately printed 1981.

Morton, Desmond. *Fight or Pay: Soldiers' Families in the Great War*. Vancouver: UBC Press 2004.

– and Glenn Wright. *Winning the Second Battle: Canadian Veterans and the Return to Civilian Life 1915–1930*. Toronto: University of Toronto Press 1987.

Mottelay, P. Fleury. *The Life and Work of Sir Hiram Maxim*. London: John Lane, Bodley Head 1920.

Muirhead, Bruce. "Canadian Trade Policy, 1949–57: The Failure of the Anglo-American Option." PhD thesis, York University, 1986.

– "Trials and Tribulations: The Decline of Anglo-Canadian Trade, 1945–50." *Journal of Canadian Studies* 24, no. 1 (spring 1989).

Munroe, Marjorie Dobie. *The Training School for Nurses, Royal Victoria Hospital, 1894–1943*. Montreal: Royal Victoria Hospital 1943.

Neal, Larry. "Trust Companies and Financial Innovation, 1897–1914." *Business History Review* 45 (1971), 35.

Neary, Peter. "Canadian Universities and Canadian Veterans of World War II." In Peter Neary and J.L. Granatstein, eds., *The Veterans' Charter and Post-World War II Canada*. Montreal, Kingston: McGill-Queen's University Press 1998.

Neatby, Hilda. *Queen's University*, vol. 1. Montreal, Kingston: McGill-Queen's University Press 1978.

Naylor, James. *The New Democracy: Challenging the Social Order in Industrial Ontario 1914–25*. Toronto: University of Toronto Press 1991.

Neff, Donald. *Warriors at Suez*. New York: Linden Press/Simon and Shuster 1981.

Nevins, Allan. *John D. Rockefeller: The Heroic Age of American Enterprise*, vol. 2. New York: Charles Scribner's Sons 1940.

Newspapers and Magazines, 1953.

Nicholl, Christopher. *Bishop's University 1843–1970*. Montreal, Kingston: McGill-Queen's University Press 1994.

Nicholson, G.W.L., Col., CD. *The Gunners of Canada: The History of the Royal Regiment of Canadian Artillery*. Toronto: McClelland and Stewart Limited 1967, vol. 1.

Nimocks, Walter. *Milner's Young Men: The "Kindergarten" in Edwardian Imperial Affairs*. Durham, North Carolina: Duke University Press 1968.

Noel, Jan. *Canada Dry: Temperance Crusades before Confederation*. Toronto: University of Toronto Press 1995.

Noppen, Luc and Lucie K. Morriset. *Art et architecture des églises à Québec*. Quebec: Les Publications du Québec 1996.

Norcliffe, Glen. *The Ride to Modernity: The Bicycle in Canada, 1869–1900*. Toronto: University of Toronto Press 2001.

Norris, William. *The Man Who Fell From the Sky*. New York: Viking 1987.

O'Geran, Graeme. *A History of the Detroit Street Railways*. Detroit: Conover Press 1931.

Ontario. *Report of the Royal Ontario Nickel Commission*. Toronto: The King's Printer 1917.

Oliver, Peter. *G. Howard Ferguson: Ontario Tory*. Toronto: University of Toronto Press 1977.

100 Years of Inspiration: The Air Liquide Adventure. Paris: Les Éditions Textuel 2002.

Oreskovich, Carlie. *Sir Henry Pellatt: The King of Casa Loma*. Privately published 1996.

Oswald, Howard. *The Montreal Diocesan Theological College: A History from 1873 to 1963*. Montreal: McGill University Press 1963.

Palmer, Bryan D. *Working Class Experience*. Toronto: McClelland and Stewart 1992.

Parvin, Viola Elizabeth. *Authorization of Textbooks for the Schools of Ontario, 1846–1950*. Toronto: University of Toronto Press 1965.

Passer, Harold C. *The Electric Manufacturers 1875–1900: A Study in Competition, Entrepreneurship, Technical Change and Economic Growth*. Cambridge, Mass.: Harvard University Press 1953.

Peckham, Brian W., Dr. "The First Hundred Years of Corn Refining in the United States." *Corn Annual 2000*. Corn Refiners Association, Inc. 2002.

Pecora, Ferdinand. *Wall Street under Oath: The Story of Our Modern Money Changers*. New York: Simon and Schuster 1939.

Penfield, Wilder. *No Man Alone: A Neurosurgeon's Life*. Boston and Toronto: Little, Brown 1977.

Penton, D. Stephen. *Non Nobis Solum: The History of Lower Canada College and its predecessor St. John's School*. Montreal: The Corporation of Lower Canada College 1972.

Perry, J. Harvey. *Taxation in Canada*. Toronto: University of Toronto Press 1951.

– *Taxes, Tariffs & Subsidies*. Toronto: University of Toronto Press 1955.

Pharand, Jacques. *Les tramways de Québec*. Beauport, Quebec: MNH Inc. 1998.

Pilarczyk, Ian. *"A Noble Roster": One Hundred and Fifty Years of Law at McGill*. Montreal: McGill University Faculty of Law 1999.

Piva, Michael J. *The Condition of the Working Class in Toronto, 1900–1921*. Ottawa: University of Ottawa Press 1979.

Platt, D.C.M. *Business Imperialism 1840–1930: An Inquiry based on the British Experience in Latin America.* Oxford: Clarendon Press 1977.

Poovey, Mary. *A History of the Modern Fact.* Chicago: University of Chicago Press 1998.

Porter, Theodore M. *Trust in Numbers: The Pursuit of Objectivity in Science and Public Life.* Princeton: Princeton University Press 1995.

Pound, Richard W. *Stikeman Elliott: The First Fifty Years.* Montreal, Kingston: McGill-Queen's University Press 2002.

Powell, Griffith. *"Per Ardua ad Astra": A Story of the Atlantic Air Ferry.* Montreal: Herald Press 1945.

– *Ferryman.* Shrewsbury, UK: Airlife Publishing 1982.

Prang, Margaret. *N.W. Rowell: Canadian Nationalist.* Toronto: University of Toronto Press 1975.

Pratte, France Gagnon. *Country Houses for Montrealers 1892–1924.* Montreal: Meredien Press 1987.

Preston, W.T.R. *My Generation of Politics and Politicians.* Toronto: D.A. Rose 1927.

Pugh, Emerson W. *Building IBM: Shaping an Industry and its Technology.* Cambridge, Mass.: MIT Press 1995.

Putnam, J. Harold. *Egerton Ryerson and Education in Upper Canada.* Toronto: William Briggs 1912.

Quebec. *Report of the Royal Commission of Inquiry on Constitutional Problems.* Province of Quebec 1956.

Quigley, Carroll. "The Round Table Groups in Canada, 1908–38." *Canadian Historical Review* 43, no. 3 (September 1962), 204.

The R. Samuel McLaughlin Foundation: 40 Years of Philanthropy. Privately published 1991.

Rawlyk, G.A. *The Canada Fire: Radical Evangelicalism and British North America 1775–1812.* Montreal, Kingston: McGill-Queen's University Press 1994.

Reader, W.J. *Imperial Chemical Industries: A History.* London: Oxford University Press 1970.

Reader's Digest. April 1979.

Redmond Thomas. "The Beginnings of Navigation and the Tourist Industry in Muskoka." *Ontario History*, 42, no. 2 (1950).

Regehr, T.D. "Entrepreneurs and the Canadian Newsprint Industry, 1923–1931." Paper presented to the Canadian Business History Conference, Trent University, Peterborough, 25–27 May 1984.

– "'High-powered Lawyers, Veteran Lobbyists, Cunning Propagandists': Canadian Lawyers and the Beauharnois Scandal." In Carol Wilton, ed., *Essays in the History of Canadian Law*, vol. 4, *Beyond the Law: Lawyers and Business in Canada, 1830 to 1930*, ch. 13. Toronto: The Osgoode Society, 1990.

– *The Beauharnois Scandal: A Story of Canadian Entrepreneurship and Politics.* Toronto: University of Toronto Press 1990.

– "The Irish childhood and youth of a Canadian capitalist." In Patrick O'Sullivan, ed., *Patterns of Migration,* vol. 1, ch. 7. The Irish World Wide Heritage series, Leicester: Leicester University Press 1992.

Report of the Minister of Education (Ontario) for the Year 1896.

Report of the Royal Commission on Dominion-Provincial Relations. Ottawa: King's Printer 1940.

Report of the Royal Commission of Inquiry on Constitutional Problems. Vol. 2, part 3. Province of Quebec 1956.

Report: Royal Commission on National Development in the Arts, Letters and Sciences 1949–1951. Chapters 12 and 22. Ottawa: King's Printer 1951.

Remillard, François. *Mansions of the Golden Square Mile 1850–1930.* Montreal: Meridien Press 1987.

Reynolds, Lloyd G. *The Control of Competition in Canada.* Cambridge, Mass.: Harvard University Press 1940.

Rexford, E.I. and I. Gammell and A.R. Bain, *The History of the High School of Montreal.* Montreal: privately printed c.1950.

Ritchie, Charles. *The Siren Years.* Toronto: Macmillan 1979.

Roberts, Andrew. *Eminent Churchillians.* London: Weidenfeld & Nicolson 1994.

– *The Holy Fox.* London: Weidenfeld & Nicolson 1991.

Roby, Yves. *Les Québécois et les investissements américains (1918–1929).* Quebec: Les Presses de l'Université Laval 1976.

Rodgers, William. *Think: A Biography of the Watsons and IBM.* New York: Stein and Day 1969.

Rose, Norman. *The Cliveden Set: Portrait of an Exclusive Fraternity.* London: Jonathan Cape 2000.

Rose, Samuel P., DD. *Our College: A Backward and Forward Glance.* Montreal: printed for private circulation by H.B. Grant 1930.

Rosenbluth, G. and H.G. Thorburn. *Canadian Anti-Combines Administration 1952–1960.* Toronto: University of Toronto Press 1963.

Ross, Murray G. *The Y.M.C.A. in Canada.* Toronto: Ryerson Press 1951

Roy, Patricia. "The Fine Art of Lobbying and Persuading: The Case of the B.C. Electric Railway, 1897–1917." In David S. Macmillan, ed., *Canadian Business History: Selected Studies, 1497–1971.* Toronto: McClelland and Stewart Limited 1972, 239.

The Royal St. Lawrence Yacht Club, 1888–1988. Privately printed, 1988.

Rumilly, Robert. *Histoire de la Province de Québec.* Vol. 13. Montreal: Éditions Bernard Valiquette.

Russell, Daniel J. "H.B. Ames as Municipal Reformer." MA thesis, McGill University 1971.

Salmon, M. Stephen. "This 'Remarkable Growth': Investment in Canadian Great Lakes Shipping, 1900–1959." Working draft of a paper presented to the 4th International Congress of Maritime History, Corfu, Greece, June 2004.

Sanderson, J.E. *The First Century of Methodism in Canada.* Toronto: William Briggs 1910.

Sanger, Clyde. *Malcolm MacDonald: Bringing an End to Empire.* Montreal, Kingston: McGill-Queen's University Press 1995.

Sarra-Bournet, Michel. *L'Affaire Roncarelli: Duplessis contre les Témoins de Jéhovah.* Quebec: Institut québécois de recherche sur la culture 1986.

Saywell, John T. "F.H. Deacon & Co., Investment Dealers: A Case Study of the Securities Industry 1897–1945." *Ontario History* 85, no. 2 (June 1993), 167.

– *"Just call me Mitch": The Life of Mitchell F. Hepburn.* Toronto: University of Toronto Press 1991.

Sclater, D. Lewis. *Royal Victoria Hospital, 1887–1947.* Montreal: McGill-Queen's University Press 1969.

Schull, Joseph. *The Century of the Sun: The First Hundred Years of Sun Life Assurance Company of Canada.* 2 vols. Toronto: Macmillan of Canada.

Scriver, Jessie Boyd. *The Montreal Children's Hospital: Years of Growth.* Montreal, Kingston: McGill-Queen's University Press 1979.

Selznick, Philip. *TVA and the Grass Roots: A Study in the Sociology of Formal Organization.* Berkeley and Los Angeles: University of California Press 1949.

Seybold, Geneva, ed. *American Foundations and Their Fields.* 5th ed. New York: Raymond Rich Associates 1942.

Shore, Marlene. *The Science of Social Redemption: McGill, the Chicago School, and the Origins of Social Research in Canada.* Toronto: University of Toronto Press 1987.

The Silvery Slocan. Prepared for the West Kootenay Touring Society, 1992.

Skeoch, L.A. *Restrictive Trade Practices in Canada: Selected Readings.* Toronto: McClelland and Stewart Limited 1966.

Sloan, Lawrence H. *Everyman and His Common Stocks: A Study of Long Term Investment Policy.* New York: McGraw-Hill 1931.

Smart, Reginald G., and Alan C.V. Ogborne. *Northern Spirits: A social history of alcohol in Canada.* Toronto: Addiction Research Foundation 1996.

Smith, Allan. "The Myth of the Self-made Man in English Canada, 1850–1914." *Canadian Historical Review* 59, no. 2 (1978), 189.

Smith, George David. *From Monopoly to Competition: The Transformation of Alcoa, 1888–1986.* Cambridge: Cambridge University Press 1988.

Sneath, Allen Winn. *Brewed in Canada: The Untold Story of Canada's 350-Year-Old Brewing Industry.* Toronto: The Dundurn Group 2001.

Soames, Mary. *Clementine Churchill.* London: Cassell 1979.

Sotiron, Minko. *From Politics to Profit.* Montreal, Kingston: McGill-Queen's University Press 1997.

"Souvenir Programme" (Epworth League, 1897 Convention). Toronto: Methodist Book and Publishing House 1897.

Speisman, Stephen A. *The Jews of Toronto.* Toronto: McClelland and Stewart 1979.

Spender, J.A. *Weetman Pearson First Viscount Cowdray 1856–1927.* London: Cassell 1930.

Stacey, C.P. *A Very Double Life: The Private World of Mackenzie King.* Toronto: Macmillan of Canada 1976.

Stamp, Robert M. *The Schools of Ontario, 1876–1976.* Toronto: University of Toronto Press 1982.

Stanley, Robert C. *Nickel: Past and Present.* Toronto: International Nickel Company of Canada 1934.

Stark, Rodney. *The Victory of Reason: How Christianity Led to Freedom, Capitalism and Western Success*. New York: Random House 2005.

Stephens, George Washington. *The St. Lawrence Waterway Project*. Montreal: Louis Carrier 1930.

Stephenson, H.R. and Carlton McNaught. *The Story of Advertising in Canada: A Chronicle of Fifty Years*. Toronto: Ryerson Press 1940.

Stevens, G.R. *Canadian National Railways*. Vol. 2. Toronto and Vancouver: Clarke, Irwin 1962.

Stewart, Walter. *The Charity Game: Greed, Waste and Fraud in Canada's $86-Billion-a-Year Compassion Industry*. Vancouver and Toronto: Douglas and McIntyre 1996.

Stivers, Richard. *A Hair of the Dog: Irish Drinking and American Stereotype*. University Park: The Pennsylvania University Press 1976.

The Storied Province of Quebec. Vol. 3. Toronto: Dominion Publishing 1931

Strange, Carolyn. *Toronto's Girl Problem: The Perils and Pleasures of the City, 1880–1930*. Toronto: University of Toronto Press 1995.

Stuart, Campbell, Sir. *Opportunity Knocks Once*. London: Collins 1952.

Sutherland, Fraser. *The Monthly Epic: A History of Canadian Magazines 1789–1989*. Markham, Ont.: Fitzhenry and Woodside 1989.

Sutton-Smith, Brian. "Games, the Socialization of Conflict." *Canadian Journal of History of Sport and Physical Education* 4, no. 1 (May 1973), 1.

Swift, Jamie, and Development Education Centre. *The Big Nickel: INCO at Home and Abroad*. Kitchener, Ont.: Between the Lines 1977.

Taggart, Norman, Rev. "The Irish Factor in World Methodism in the Eighteenth and Nineteenth Centuries." PhD thesis, Queen's University, Belfast 1981.

– "The Irish in Canadian Methodism" in Neil Semple, ed., *Canadian Methodist Historical Society Papers*. 3 (Toronto 1983).

Taylor, A.J.P. *Beaverbrook*. London: Hamish Hamilton 1972.

Taylor, Graham D. "Management Relations in a Multinational Enterprise: The Case of Canadian Industries Limited, 1928–1948." *Business History Review* 55, no. 3 (autumn 1981). Repr. in Tom Traves, ed., *Essays in Canadian Business History*. Toronto: McClelland and Stewart 1984.

Thomas, John. "The Master's Vineyard: The Origins, Work and Growth of the Fred Victor Mission, 1886–1911." PhD research paper in the United Church Archives, Toronto.

Thompson, Andrew. *The Odyssey of the Gentlemen Adventurers Travelling into the Brazils*. Ottawa: privately printed, 1928.

Thompson, Austin Seton. *Jarvis Street*. Toronto: Personal Library Publishers 1980.

Thompson, John F., and Norman Beasley. *For the Years to Come: A Story of International Nickel of Canada*. New York: G.P. Putnam's Sons, and Toronto: Longmans, Green 1960.

Thorold, Algar Labouchere. *The Life of Henry Labouchere*. New York: G.P. Putnam's Sons 1913.

Thorpe, D.R. *The Life and Times of Anthony Eden, First Earl of Avon, 1897–1977*. London: Chatto & Windus 2003.

Traves, Tom. *The State and Enterprise: Canadian Manufacturers and the Federal Government, 1917–1931.* Toronto: University of Toronto Press 1979.

Trudeau, Pierre Elliott. *Federalism and the French Canadians.* New York: St Martin's Press 1968.

Tucker, William Jewitt. "The Gospel of Wealth." *Andover Review* 15 (June 1891), 637.

Tulchinsky, Gerald. "Hidden among the Smokestacks: Toronto's Clothing Industry, 1871–1901." In David Keane and Colin Read, eds, *Old Ontario: Essays in Honour of J.M.S. Careless.* Toronto: Dundurn Press 1990.

– *The River Barons.* Toronto: University of Toronto Press 1977.

Tunis, Barbara Logan, BN. *In Caps and Gowns: The Story of the School for Graduate Nurses at McGill University 1920–1964.* Montreal: McGill University Press 1966.

United States. Congress. Senate. *Stock Exchange Practices: Report of the Committee on Banking and Currency pursuant to S. Res. 84.* Washington: United States Government Printing Office 1934.

Vaillancourt, Yves. *L'Évolution des politiques sociales au Québec, 1940–1960.* Montreal: Les Presses de l'Université de Montréal 1988.

Valverde, Mariana. *The Age of Light, Soap and Water: Moral Reform in English Canada, 1885–1925.* Toronto: McClelland and Stewart 1991.

van der Pijl, Kees. *The Making of the Atlantic Ruling Class.* London: Verso 1984.

Vaughan, Walter. *The Life and Work of Sir William Van Horne.* New York: The Century Company 1920.

Veilleux, Denis. "La motorisation ou 'la rançon du progrès': tramways, véhicules-moteurs et circulation (Montréal, 1900–1930)." PhD thesis, McGill University 1998.

Vickers, Hugo. *Alice: Princess Andrew of Greece.* London: Hamish Hamilton 2000.

Vigod, Bernard L. *Quebec before Duplessis: The Political Career of Louis-Alexandre Taschereau.* Montreal, Kingston: McGill-Queen's University Press 1986.

Voight, Paul L. *The Sugar Refining Industry in the United States.* Phildelphia: University of Philadelphia 1908.

Wall, Joseph C. *Andrew Carnegie.* Pittsburgh: University of Pittsburgh Press 1989.

Warner, Sam B. *Streetcar Suburbs: The Process of Growth in Boston (1870–1900).* Cambridge, Mass.: Harvard University Press 1978.

Warrington, C.J.S., and R.V.V. Nicholls. *A History of Chemistry in Canada.* Toronto: Sir Isaac Pitman and Sons 1949.

Warsh, Cheryl Krasnick, ed. *Drink in Canada: Historical Essays.* Montreal, Kingston: McGill-Queen's University Press 1993.

Waters, D.W.M. *Law of Trusts in Canada.* 2nd ed. Toronto: Carswell 1984.

Watson, Thomas J., Jr. *Father Son & Co., My Life and IBM and Beyond.* New York: Bantam Books 1990.

Way, Ronald L. *Ontario's Niagara Parks: A History.* Niagara Parks Commission 1946.

Weaver, John C. "Elitism and the Corporate Ideal: Businessmen and Boosters in Canadian Civic Reform, 1890–1920." In Michael S. Cross and Gregory S. Kealey, eds, *The Consolidation of Capitalism, 1898–1929,* 143. Toronto: McClelland and Stewart 1983.

Weizmann, Chaim. *Trial and Error.* New York: Harper & Brothers 1949.

Wells, Wyatt. *Antitrust and the Formation of the Postwar World*. New York: Columbia University Press 2002.

Westley, Margaret A. *Remembrance of Grandeur: The Anglo-Protestant Elite of Montreal, 1900–1950*. Montreal: Editions Libre Expression 1990.

Wheeler-Bennett, John, Sir. *Special Relationships: America in Peace and War*. London: Macmillan 1975.

Whitaker, Reg and Gary Marcuse. *Cold War Canada: The Making of a National Insecurity State 1945–1957*. Toronto: University of Toronto Press 1994.

White, Ronald C., Jr, and C. Howard Hopkins. *The Social Gospel: Religion and Reform in Changing America*. Philadelphia: Temple University Press 1976.

White, Thomas. *The Story of Canada's War Finance*. Montreal, 1921.

Whitehead, Eric. *The Patricks: Hockey's Royal Family*. Halifax: Formac Publishing Company 1993.

Wigmore, Barrie A. *The Crash and Its Aftermath: A History of Securities Markets in the United States 1929–1933*. Westport, Conn.: Greenwood Press 1985.

Wilcox-Magill, Dennis William, and Richard C. Helmes-Hayes. "Leonard Charles Marsh: A Canadian Social Reformer." *Journal of Canadian Studies* 21, no. 2 (Summer 1986), 49.

Williams, Jeffrey. *First in the Field*. St Catherines, Ontario: Vanwell Publishing 1995.

Winter, Thomas. *Making Men, Making Class: The YMCA and Workingmen, 1877–1920*. Chicago: University of Chicago Press 2002.

Wolfe, Roy I. "The Summer Resorts of Ontario in the Nineteenth Century." *Ontario History*. 54, no. 3 (1962).

Wood, Charles Rowell, Rev. "The Historical Development of the Temperance Movement in Methodism in Canada." BD thesis, Emmanuel College, Victoria University, Toronto 1958.

Wright, Robert. *A World Mission: Canadian Protestantism and the Quest for a New International Order, 1918–1939*. Montreal, Kingston: McGill-Queen's University Press 1991.

Young, Brian. "Dimensions of a Law Practice: Brokerage and Ideology in the Career of George-Etienne Cartier." In Carol Wilton, ed., *Essays in the History of Canadian Law*, vol. 4, *Beyond the Law: Lawyers and Business in Canada, 1830 to 1930*, ch. 3. Toronto: The Osgoode Society, 1990.

– *George-Etienne Cartier: Montreal Bourgeois*. Montreal, Kingston: McGill-Queen's University Press 1981.

– *The Politics of Codification: The Lower Canadian Civil Code of 1866*. Montreal, Kingston: McGill-Queen's University Press 1994.

– *Respectable Burial: Montreal's Mount Royal Cemetery*. Montreal, Kingston: McGill-Queen's University Press 2003.

Zeff, Stephen A. *Forging Accounting Principles in Five Countries: A History and an Analysis of Trends*. Champaign, Illinois: Stipes 1972.

Zubalik, Janis R. "'Advancing the Material Interests of the Redeemer's Kingdom': The Erskine Presbyterian Church, Montreal, 1894." MA thesis, Concordia University 1996.

Index